The Hidden Genius of Emotion

This thoughtful and beautifully written book demonstrates compellingly that emotions are central to individual personality development across the lifespan. Emotions are key also to understanding how the patterns of personality replicate in subsystems of the whole person and constantly provide information to support identity. Carol Magai and Jeannette Haviland-Jones draw on a wealth of contextual and film material to forge an original empirical and theoretical analysis of stability, complexity, and chaos that bridges the domains of attachment, thought, and behavior. Their unit of analysis is the individual. The search for abundant, matched case materials led them to the mid-twentieth century psychologists Carl Rogers, Albert Ellis, and Fritz Perls. These lives focus the lens on lifespan transformations – of themselves and then on those whom they would transform, their clients. *The Hidden Genius of Emotion* presents a new approach to personology, autobiography, biography, narrative studies, psychotherapy, and theory of emotions and will itself be a dynamic for new directions in the twenty-first century.

Carol Magai is Professor of Psychology and Founding Director of the Center for Studies of Ethnicity and Human Development at Long Island University. She has authored more than one hundred publications and is a charter member of the International Society for Research on Emotions and a Fellow of the American Psychological Association.

Jeannette Haviland-Jones is Professor of Psychology at Rutgers University and Director of the Human Emotions Laboratory. She is coauthor of *Contemporary Adolescence* and coeditor of the first and second editions of *The Handbook of Emotion,* which received the Critics Choice Award. Professor Haviland-Jones is also a charter member of the International Society for Research on Emotions.

STUDIES IN EMOTION AND SOCIAL INTERACTION
Second Series

Series Editors

Keith Oatley
University of Toronto

Antony S. R. Manstead
University of Cambridge

This series is jointly published by the Cambridge University Press and the Editions de la Maison des Sciences de l'Homme, as part of the joint publishing agreement established in 1977 between the Foundation de la Maison des Sciences de l'Homme and the Syndics of the Cambridge University Press.

Cette publications est publiée co-édition par Cambridge University Press et les Editions de la Maison des Sciences de l'Homme. Elle s'intègre dans le programme de co-édition établi en 1977 par la Foundation de la Maison des Sciences de l'Homme et les Syndics de Cambridge University Press.

Titles published in the Second Series:

The Psychology of Facial Expression
James A. Russell and José Miguel Fernández-Dols
Emotion, the Social Bond, and Human Reality: Part/Whole Analysis
Thomas J. Scheff
Intersubjective Communication and Emotion in Early Ontogeny
Stein Bråten
The Social Context of Nonverbal Behavior
Pierre Philippot, Robert S. Feldman, and Erik J. Coats
Communicating Emotion: Social, Moral, and Cultural Processes
Sally Planalp
Emotions across Languages and Cultures: Diversity and Universals
Anna Wierzbicka
Gender and Emotion: Social Psychological Perspectives
Agneta H. Fischer

(continued on page following the Index)

The Hidden Genius of Emotion

Lifespan Transformations of Personality

Carol Magai
Long Island University

Jeannette Haviland-Jones
Rutgers, The State University of New Jersey

CAMBRIDGE
UNIVERSITY PRESS

& Editions de la Maison des Sciences de l'Homme
Paris

PUBLISHED BY THE PRESS SYNDICATE OF THE UNIVERSITY OF CAMBRIDGE
The Pitt Building, Trumpington Street, Cambridge, United Kingdom

CAMBRIDGE UNIVERSITY PRESS
The Edinburgh Building, Cambridge CB2 2RU, UK
40 West 20th Street, New York, NY 10011-4211, USA
477 Williamstown Road, Port Melbourne, VIC 3207, Australia
Ruiz de Alarcón 13, 28014 Madrid, Spain
Dock House, The Waterfront, Cape Town 8001, South Africa

http://www.cambridge.org

First published 2002

Printed in the United Kingdom at the University Press, Cambridge

Typeface Palatino 10/13 pt.   *System* LATEX 2_ε [TB]

A catalog record for this book is available from the British Library.

Library of Congress Cataloging in Publication Data

Magai, Carol.
    The hidden genius of emotion : lifespan transformations of personality /
    Carol Magai; Jeannette Haviland-Jones.
        p.   cm. – (Studies in emotion and social interaction. Second series)
    Includes bibliographical references (p.) and index.
    ISBN 0-521-64094-6
    1. Personality and emotions.   2. Personality development.   I. Haviland-Jones,
    Jeannette M.   II. Title.   III. Series.
BF698.9.E45 M33   2002
152.4 – dc21
                                                            2002019255

ISBN 0 521 64094 6 hardback

To the memory of my mother
The mother and daughter reunion is only emotion away

CM

To Terry
The genius who transformed this life

JMH-J

Contents

Preface

In this book we use concepts from emotions theory, dynamic systems theory, complementarity, and attachment theory to model the complex process of personality development and change. Like other accounts of complex systems from the time of Freud and Allport, through Skinner, Erikson, and Block, we use the individual as the unit of discovery and understanding. In the introductory chapter, we examine the thesis that affect is the central organizing force in individual personality and the integrative link between domains of psychological functioning. In doing so, we briefly present the historical context of research on emotion.

Even though the field of psychology has seen many recent and significant advances in emotions theory over the last two decades, much of the contemporary work on human development, clinical work, and personality development is still fragmented. In this book, we take advantage of the new understandings from emotion theory and research to forge a more integrated view of human development. Additionally, there are lessons to be learned from the hermeneutic, the postmodern, and dynamic systems approaches to knowledge that have arisen in recent times to challenge Cartesian methods of thought and analysis. Years ago, John Bowlby dared to integrate the seemingly disparate theoretical paradigms of psychoanalysis, ethology, and general systems theory in building a model of how and why humans form attachments. It has proven to be a richly generative theory that has grown beyond its own beginnings. Similarly, psychology might well profit from perspectives from today's newer epistemological and scientific models. We bring these perspectives to bear in the present project.

We view the emotion system as providing the linchpin for a more integrated science of human development. Eminent emotions scholars – most notably Silvan Tomkins, Carroll Izard, Paul Ekman, and Robert

Plutchik – have written persuasively about the centrality of emotion in personality functioning, and Izard, especially, has written widely on the developmental aspects of the topic. We draw inspiration from these germinal writings. We explore not only the idea that affect is a central organizing force in personality development but also the idea that affect may not always behave in logical or linear ways; thus, applications from the newer epistemologies are brought to bear. To further the analysis of affect as an integrative factor across domains of personality functioning and across time, we take a lifespan perspective, applying our theoretical lens and research methods to *lives* rather than to isolated psychological processes or isolated moments in time.

Three lives are the focus of our investigation – Carl Rogers, Albert Ellis, and Fritz Perls. The rationale for these particular individuals is provided in the opening chapter. The availability of extensive data on each individual – including autobiographies, biographies, vast holdings of written work, and the vivid film records of all three men in brief therapy with the same client – were important considerations. In this context, we had personality data that cut across domains of relationships, cognition, and behavior and that would be essential to document how affect organizes various modes of psychological functioning. Moreover, many of these materials were available across a long stretch of time, allowing us to track the course of development across the lifespan.

We also note the irony that although Rogers's, Ellis's, and Perls's theories are in many ways about emotion, they themselves were not aware of how affect-specific aspects of their own behavior played an important role in their theories and the ways in which they conducted therapy. Thus, the book has relevance for clinical practice as well as for personality theory. We place the work of these three clinical psychologists within the historical context of their own time as well as relate it to contemporary theory and practice.

In the second chapter of Part I, we look at the place of affect in earlier accounts of human development, most notably attachment theory and discrete emotions theory. At this point, we also introduce certain concepts from dynamic systems theory, which will serve as a basis for analyses that follow in the remaining sections of the book.

Part II is designed to illustrate the relationship between early and late developmental experiences and the way that later experiences produce and modify the architecture of emotional lives. Here, Magai (principally) uses the biographical and autobiographical materials available on each man to present their socioemotional development from the perspective of contemporary developmental theory. In the first chapter, which focuses on Rogers, personality is viewed from the perspective of attachment theory and research as well as from the perspective of discrete emotions theory. We trace the development of shame and interest, as linked to attachment goals, and their incorporation as ideoaffective structures over time. We show how attachment theory is enriched within the context of a lifespan view of development and how affect and attachment are integrally related but also distinct in their influence on choice points in the lifespan.

In the second chapter, which focuses on Ellis, the attachment theoretical approach to personality and socioemotional development is expanded to include the theory called self-organization, which is related to dynamic systems theory. Once again, the advantage of integrating personality research with emotional process is highlighted. The final chapter concerns the affective system of Perls; his particular therapeutic techniques, including his confrontational style, are seen as closely associated with cumulative developmental experiences, an atypical attachment pattern, and the dominance, and instability, of certain affects.

Part III deals with the link between emotion and cognition; it begins with an introduction to the system of analysis used in this part and the theoretical framework in which uses of emotional terms are shown to be related to the favoring of particular logical systems. Haviland-Jones (principally) uses this system to analyze the theoretical work of Rogers, Ellis, and Perls across their lifetimes. Emotion is shown to be the bridge between personality and theory construction. For example, Rogers is shown to have made a false start with his work on diagnosis. This early work was lacking in both passion and any focused form of logic. As Rogers elaborated specific areas with emotional content, he became capable of analyzing them with increasingly sophisticated logical systems. Inhibition of a particular emotion, in his case anger, was found to be associated with inhibition of thoughtful process. Even though Rogers had an identifiable ideoaffective system, it developed and changed across his lifespan within his work. On the other hand, Ellis's affective system is circular; that is, emotions lead to other emotions rather than to ideas, people, or content. This circularity sets up what we call an addictive ideoaffective system. The addictive system is resistant to change but becomes more elaborated by continuously amassing new data. Perls's system departs from most known models; it is both the most disorganized and most creative system of the three, swinging between extremes.

These chapters are all directed at a deep examination of the relationship of the individual to his or her philosophical or logical systems. The relativisms of postmodern approaches are partially resolved by linking each system to affective biases within the individual. In that sense, each system is subjective, but the distinction between subjective and objective will be seen as requiring new definition as boundaries fade.

Part IV examines emotion as the integrative link between personality and therapeutic behavior. Here we focus on the "affective postures" of each therapist, that is, the embodiment of or the physical representation of the affective structure of personality, as revealed by facial expressions and body language. The affective postures are shown to be closely aligned to the value structure of each theory and to the therapeutic goals as articulated in Client-centered, Rational Emotive, and Gestalt theories. Here, the link between emotion as the integrative link in therapeutic behavior is graphically illustrated. Not only are the words and implications set out in an introductory segment in the film, but the interactive sessions with the client Gloria also bring the personalities of the three therapists alive in the immediacy of visual and audio images. The previous analyses of words and thoughts are shown to extend to and to be captured by posture and nonverbal behavior. A microanalytic exposition of sections of each session shows how the nonverbal and verbal uses of emotion influence the behavior of the client on a moment-to-moment basis and how she in turn affects each therapist. This affective interaction is the very substance of what psychoanalysts refer to as transference and countertransference but here the emotion-specific aspects of this process become observable. Ultimately, each therapeutic system, like each man, presents a particular emotional focus for the client. When offered the choice of therapist for continuing contact, the client, Gloria, chooses the one most closely aligned with her current emotional conflicts.

In Part V, we draw together the various observations that emerged in the course of this study and integrate them with existing knowledge about emotion processes and dynamic systems. We also address the issue of the progress of lives over time, a process that is particularly difficult to study in the laboratory but that is rendered uniquely feasible by the analysis of personal documents such as theoretical writings produced over a forty-year period of time and aided by biographical material. Our three clinicians provide exemplars of both stability and change, and particular emotions are shown to be linked to particular kinds of change or lack of change.

This final section reintegrates the work in this book with prior work on the systems of emotion in pathology, healthy personality, and creative work. In the end, we return to the point that Rogers, Ellis, and Perls use their own emotion biases – *not* their "techniques" per se, but their biases – to clinical advantage; as such they were emotional savants of a sort, albeit they were opaque to their own processes.

PART I

Introduction

1 Challenging the Prevailing View

The Affective Connection

Knowledge of emotional processes can give a person a sense of second sight or even magic. Years ago a young man was being introduced to his new professional colleagues in the department of psychology; among them was Silvan Tomkins. As the young man elaborated on his many interests, views, and intellectual dilemmas, he quite exceeded the time that other speakers had taken. Silvan turned to a colleague, lowered his voice, and said, "That young man lost his beloved mother at an early age." In fact, he had. But when Silvan was queried about his acquaintanceship with the young man, he replied, strangely enough, that he had never even met him.

This story is emblematic of the Silvan mystery. Tomkins seemed endowed with a supernatural knowledge of the human mind and its longings. He always seemed to know more about people than was discernable from the observable facts. Indeed, at the memorial service held for Silvan in 1991, not only did renowned psychiatrists single out his uncanny ability to fathom the essential elements of people in a way that few could, but even his garbage man described him as a "yoda" – a wise man.

Sometimes Silvan would explain his inductive process, and one could follow it, but it took a long time to absorb and understand just what was taking place. If one studied with him a while, it became apparent that he more or less had a system for putting together emotions and thoughts, a system he called the ideoaffective system. He could work with the system himself, but he never really made it accessible to others, although a few notable attempts to break the code have been made. He was a marvelous teacher, but only for those willing to endure his idiosyncratic style of thinking and discovery and personal eccentricities. One felt that it was important to remain close to Silvan, for it appeared that he possessed or was closing in on the holy grail of personality; emotion was the code or the process that brought together the many varied aspects of personality, and, somehow, Silvan knew how it was encrypted.

Tomkins' intuitions have led the present authors to consider emotion to be the missing link in modern approaches to personality development. Over the years, we have learned to decode some of the enigmas ourselves, but the process is an ongoing effort – exciting, perplexing, and ever surprising. We have come to appreciate the chaotic, unbounded character of the emotion system, as Silvan must have early on, before the mathematicians and physicists had a name for such nonlinear systems. Dynamical systems, as even developmentalists are now understanding (Emde, 1994; Lewis, 1995; Thelen, 1990), are not to be apprehended in the kind of straight-line, logico-deductive method that so infuses scientific thinking of our time and our Cartesian science. There is an emerging awareness that entrenched paradigms and patterns of thinking must be broken. It is our feeling that the time is particularly ripe for this. One has but to examine the typical psychology colloquium offerings around our college campuses to be impressed with the immediacy of the need; a recent sampling from one campus follows:

"Using event related potentials to investigate priming in schizo-phrenic and normal populations"
"Evolution of the human brain through runaway sexual selection"
"Modality effects on syntactic parsing"
"SHT and disorders of cognition"

Here we see a few bits and pieces of the world of psychology as it is currently practiced. The field has grown enormously technical, relying on years of study for each new addition to gain acceptance or to just become another piece of flotsam in the widening sea of knowledge. The "massive"ness of the field – massive numbers of subjects, massive numbers of observations, massive numbers of researchers, massive amounts of information – seems to cry out for some form of meaningful organization. Yet there has been little attempt to bridge the fragmentation. No attempt is made for one seminar topic to speak to another. The shards of information that are produced en mass are allowed to stand without challenge or comment. There is little collaboration across even closely allied topical areas, one of the results of a mechanistic and linear approach to science. It has led to a search for "elements" of the human psyche, which in turn has led to a fragmentary science of human functioning. There is little emphasis on the relative nature of those elements and even less emphasis on the dynamic whole.

But even more notable is the fact that no individuals are ever mentioned. The individual intellect, individual presence, or individual case example seems to have been obliterated in this vast sea of disconnected pieces. This phenomenon – the depersonalization of psychology in the interest of finding elementary building blocks – is remarkable when one considers that among the social sciences, psychology was, at one time, unique for its focus on the individual. Fragmentation has occurred, despite the fact that ultimately everyone appreciates psychology when it fits the bits and pieces together in the context of singular persons such as Little Hans (Freud), Martin Luther (Erikson), the man who mistook his wife for a hat (Sachs), Lorens (Piaget), and Little Albert (Watson).

In the present volume, we take a lesson from the individualizing tradition and at the same time integrate it with other systems. In this instance, our aim is not to target clinical disorders as in other case studies but to bring the individual fragments of the subject matter of psychology back into perspective. It is our hope that in crossing the boundaries of the specialty areas of the analytic, cognitive, and affective, a new view of psychological processes will emerge. Emotions are at its core and are, in our terms, the missing links to an integrated psychology of the human being.

We chose to personalize and individualize this integrative approach through the lives and work of individuals who are already well known to many readers; they are three innovative psychologists of mid-20th century – Carl Rogers, Fritz Perls, and Albert Ellis. We bring an ideoaffective analysis of personality to bear on our treatment of the material at hand. The term "ideoaffective organization" was introduced by Silvan Tomkins (1962) and was originally used as a shorthand to describe the way in which emotions are integrally related to the structure and dynamics of personality. According to Tomkins, ideoaffective organizations – or emotional/cognitive schema – which are unique to each individual, emerge from recurrent or particularly salient affective "scenes" over the course of development; these organizations then become dynamically active agents affecting an array of cognitive, behavioral, and interpersonal processes. This phenomenon is richly in evidence in the present work. Indeed, an ideoaffective analysis of the lives of Rogers, Perls, and Ellis provides a compelling illustration of the centrality of affect and its interrelation with thought, behavior, ideology, and practice. This is not to say that the clinical techniques they introduced in and of themselves do this. Rather, it is the relation between each theory's development and each man's unique personality or ideoaffectology.

The choice of our subjects was both fortuitous and deliberate. Originally, it was not dictated by the fact that Rogers, Perls, and Ellis were therapists, nor was it essential that they be particularly emotionally gifted – though in some ways they were. We could have in fact chosen any three individuals – ordinary or otherwise. However, there were two especially compelling reasons to select these particular individuals.

The fortuitous aspect of the choice is related to the rediscovery of a film that was originally produced in 1963 and that had been widely shown in introductory psychology classes: *Three Approaches to Psychotherapy* (Shostrom, 1966). In the film, each therapist – Ellis, Rogers, and Perls – conducts a half-hour interview with a client, Gloria; it was intended to illustrate what psychotherapy is like, and that there are several modalities of psychotherapy practice. It had been a good twenty-five years since either of us had seen the film, certainly way before our professional immersion in emotions theory and our various works on the centrality and idiosyncracy of affect. This time, we were startled as we watched each man in action. What leapt out at us at once were the gross differences in the three clinical psychologists' affective communication patterns – not their particular techniques, but the specific qualities of emotion embedded within them. In spite of our expectation that there would be commonality to individuals in the same profession, we immediately saw that Perls had a style thoroughly saturated with contempt, whereas Rogers's style was replete with shame, distress, and joy. Ellis seemed angry much of the time. Yet these three men with their contempt, shame, and anger were legitimately renowned for their clinical skills and innovative discoveries. In this volume, we focus on the fact that each individual therapist illustrated a particular combination of wisdom and passion. This observation violates the common belief that "good" people have largely "positive" emotions, and it violates the belief that highly successful men are "unemotional." None of the three men were unemotional; neither were they wholly full of enjoyment. In this volume, we intend to document how Perls, Ellis, and Rogers deployed their own emotion biases toward theoretically creative ends. At the same time, we show that each had limited appreciation and awareness of themselves as having particular emotional biases and that these were at the basis of their particular therapeutic skills.

Although the fact that the individuals in this project are clinical psychologists was not important to us at first, the study of the emotional aspects of their personalities had ramifications for clinical theory and practices. That these men's theories are about psychological experience and the functioning of personality, but nonetheless lack a place for such influences, adds a particularly ironic twist. Of course, individual personality influences on therapeutic practice have long been an issue in psychoanalytic and psychodynamic circles, but we wanted to know how well they have been studied and why the studies are limited. We are not the first to raise this point. People's ideoaffective systems and dynamics are ordinarily invisible to others, and they necessarily pose problems for psychological theories rooted in Cartesian ontology. The choice of Rogers, Ellis, and Perls and their work is related both to the issue of personality influence on therapeutic practice and of personality influence on the conduct of science. Once again, we believe that emotion is the missing link in comprehending the relationship.

In this volume, we develop the thesis that human lives are profoundly shaped and structured by emotional experiences and that affect or emotion itself is the creative and organizing force behind all mental life. This new view takes emotion out of the realm of the epiphenomenal and gives it a central role in the development of life histories and in the growth of intellectual and behavioral skills. Our position is admittedly radical for a discipline of psychology in which a century's worth of work has either ignored the emotions, treated them as residuals, "sinful . . . , or, . . . a nuisance" (Jersild, 1946, p. 834).

For much of the 20th century, few areas of psychology had had much use for the emotions. Max Meyer, writing in 1933, set the tone for academics in experimental psychology. He championed a "hardheaded" science of psychology and dismissed the entire concept of emotion as superfluous and artifactual, claiming that the concept of emotion was the modern-day equivalent of phlogiston – the early chemists' hypothetical material at the heart of combustion. Moreover, he predicted that the term "emotion" would no longer be in use by the 1950s. Meyer's prediction was fulfilled, in part. The term had indeed largely dropped out of usage by 1950, but it was very much at work again in scientific research by the 1980s.

In clinical practice, Freud understood the central role that "strangulated emotion" played in neurosis but failed to appreciate fully the significance of emotion in either the phenomenon of abreaction or normal psychological functioning. In addition, the emphasis in Freud's mature works on "remembering rather than repeating, and on remembering instead of acting" (Lewis, 1981, p. 210) meant that emotions were often subordinated to intellect.

Freud originally coined the term *Uebertragung* (transference) to describe the phenomenon in which feelings experienced by a patient toward his or her parents transferred or were generalized to other significant relationships including the psychotherapeutic encounter. The issue of transference in the patient as well as in the therapist (countertransference) has been and continues to be of central theoretical and practical import in the clinical literature (Orange, Atwood & Stolorow, 1997; Stolorow & Atwood, 1992; Tansey, 1989). However, an explicit examination of the role of affect in the process and course of psychotherapy has not been systematically undertaken. Freud himself, who in his earlier writings understood intuitively that affects played a powerful role in neurosis and that it was important to attend to them in psychotherapy, gradually drifted from these understandings and became ever more absorbed in the role of sexual repression in the formation and maintenance of neurosis. Correspondingly, he moved more and more in the direction of dealing with the symbolic content of patients' concerns rather than with the affective in psychotherapy. Helen Block Lewis's (1981) close examination of the cases treated by Freud during his extensive clinical career led her to the conclusion that Freud's declining success in psychotherapy over the years, which he himself acknowledged, stemmed from his abandonment of affect as a key factor.

In the current clinical literature, there is growing recognition that paying attention to affect should be a primary consideration in psychotherapy (Emde, 1980; Orange et al., 1997; Krause, Steimer-Krause & Ullrich, 1992; Strupp, 1993; Tansey, 1989). This concern is usually couched within concepts such as transference, countertransference, empathy, and projective identification. Despite the very obvious affective content embedded in these analytic constructs, to date there has been minimal systematic research directly targeting the study of the ebb and flow of emotions in the psychoanalytic process. This is largely attributable to the fact that the analytic literature has not yet elaborated a formal theory of how affect works in human personality (Emde, 1980).

Within the field of developmental psychology, up until the end of the twentieth century, there was only sporadic and superficial treatment of the emotions and their role in human development. Early observations of infants' emotional expressions were unsystematic and inadequately controlled; consequently, researchers came to the erroneous conclusion that emotions were undifferentiated and probably "learned" behaviors

(Magai & McFadden, 1995). As recently as twenty years ago one well-known researcher seriously argued that emotional signals were essentially arbitrary. He cited the behaviors of snarling and punching and claimed that these ostensibly aggressive expressions could index happiness and greeting. Much evidence has since accumulated to dispel that idea definitively. The behavior of snarling and punching *pulls* for physiological change and readiness to action as well as galvanizes particular patterns of thought. Such behavior readies the body and mind for attack, even though symbolization of these behaviors could be used to designate some idiosyncratic code dissociated from attack, as in a secret society's greeting ritual. However, even such a symbolic greeting would still carry some of the innate attack-readiness intrinsic to the gesture.

Developmental studies such as John Watson's provocation of fear in "Little Albert" led to the idea that emotions were simple conditioned reactions that interfered with more sensible and rational behavior. Watson managed to extend Albert's fear reaction to a variety of innocuous objects, demonstrating generalization of the response. Later, others showed that there are in fact limits to this phenomenon; it is notably easy to extend fear to living, moving things such as bugs and difficult to extend it to nonliving entities such as door posts.

Nevertheless, Watson's behavioristic formulations at least admitted some type of emotional function; this admission was more than many of his successors could allow. For several decades, the exciting research in psychology lay outside of the realm of emotion – in the study of cognitive abilities and their development. This trend continued in spite of the seminal work of the mid-century Swiss psychologist, Jean Piaget, who attributed a central role to emotions in mental life. Ironically, the aggressively successful cognitive-developmental movement of the 1960s and 1970s, which had been originally inspired by Piaget, left little room for the emotional component of development.

Piaget regarded affect and cognition as two sides of the same mental coin – processes that were intrinsically joined and indissociable from one another. Although he attributed more influence to affect than would his followers in the United States where positivism was deeply entrenched, his concepts were still limited. He proposed that affect represents only the energic force in mental life, whereas cognitive activity supplied the "content." This formulation seriously underestimated the influence of emotion on mental life.

Most contemporary theories of human development treat the emotional events of infancy as pivotal in personality development, if not "critical periods," with lifelong ramifications (Ainsworth, 1989;

Bowlby, 1969). Although the strong form of the critical period thesis has been decisively challenged by animal and human research (Thompson & Grusec, 1970), it is still safe to say that early socioemotional experiences leave important residues. One example inheres in attachment patterns. Early relationships may affect the degree to which individuals are comfortable with intimacy later in development (Hazen & Shaver, 1987). This is not to say that early patterns are immutable (the strong form of the critical period thesis) or that later developmental experiences will not modify or elaborate early patterns.

Our model is more dynamic than espoused by most developmentalists and is decidedly more dynamic than current social and personality models. It is a theory of emotion across the lifespan. In this work, we look for paths of development and entertain the thesis that small effects may grow, even after a long time; that large effects may divide and become distributed across time; and even that events can lose their original purpose or meaning (Lewis, 1995). Certain events, including perhaps the intellectual insights of therapy, encountered in the exploration of remembered trauma may produce new paths that were largely unpredicted by the trauma. Intersubjective memories, present events, general knowledge, and emotional resonance or bias interact to produce new configurations as well as periodic repetitions. Emotional events work within ideoaffective or motivational systems and have a special role both in changing the larger system and in maintaining it, depending upon the emotion and the elements it has attracted. Emotion is especially critical because emotions are contagious among people; thus, a great many opportunities for interpersonal challenge to preexisting structures and for change exist. Every type and level of emotion is critical for this approach. No one emotion is, strictly speaking, "positive" or "negative," desirable or undesirable. As we shall illustrate in the lives of Rogers, Ellis, and Perls, even the typically avoided feelings of our culture play important roles in the creative process. The shame, anger, and contempt of Rogers, Ellis, and Perls are pivotal aspects of their unique contributions.

In these men's lives, affect shaped and framed the content of thought and the processes of thinking and problem solving. Their emotional biases were patently evident in their actions, as revealed, for example, in the filmed record of *Three Approaches to Psychotherapy*, and in their thoughts, as can be sampled from their theoretical writings. Mostly, affect is the missing link in making their developmental histories more apprehensible and real. It provides the more holistic grounding to each personality as it develops across a lifespan. Thus, affect does considerably more than simply supply energy to the cognitive apparatus. It organizes experience (thoughts, memories, perception) and is played out in multivariate splendor in the many repetitive, mundane, and not-so-mundane activities of daily life.

Tomkins wrote that affect becomes "structuralized" in personality over the course of development. The idiosyncracies of each unique personality depend on the particular affective circumstances of an individual's life just as much as on the people and the events of that life. According to Tomkins, emotional dispositions – what Malatesta-Magai (Magai & McFadden, 1995; Malatesta, 1990) has termed "affect biases" – serve as the filters and regulators of information and experience. They predispose individuals to perceive the world in certain emotionally framed ways and to assimilate information to preexisting affect-laden schemas. They also may prepare a particular course of action. Each person evolves particular patterns of emotional bias in the course of development. We, as authors, are not as enamored of "structure" as Tomkins was because we focus more on change and development; nevertheless, the concept of stability needs to be continuously evaluated.

An ideoaffective bias simply may involve the dominance of one particular emotion, as in the masked hostility of the Type A personality pattern. Many people who manage to fall into this category have a constellation of emotions and ideas that make many of their daily life events meaningful because they are linked to stressful achievement. Such persons, while denying that they are "emotional" are very willing to admit to being "stressed" because that word captures their drive and need for achievement and success. In this particular construction, however, success is gained only through "stress." Unstressed people are not valuable or successful. However, the stress comes because part of the ideoaffective scheme expects achievement to be difficult and blocked. The block leads to frustration and anger, which is also blocked since its actual expression has been construed to lead to further frustration and lack of success. The "stress" felt by the blocked hostile person is the result of the self-defeating ideoaffective structure. But taking away the stressful ideoaffective structure can leave an intolerable hole in the identity of this person. A "cure" is difficult if this structure is central.

In another example, depressed people are known to give meaning and connections in their lives through a sadness–guilt link. Early losses of very meaningful people or experiences are linked to depression. Then later losses acquire deep meaning by their depressive association. In order to cope, an opposing force is sometimes brought to bear. It becomes imperative to establish ideas of permanency (in opposition to loss), even if, paradoxically, the permanency is death itself. The thought of death, or the sound of waves beating on the shore, or the "eternity" of deep space can all be longed for and made glorious in a depressive ideoaffective structure. To take away the depression can be to take away the very foundation of personality. To give an example, the author Virginia Woolf lost one member of her family after another to illness and death when she was an adolescent and young adult. This was deeply distressing, of course, but it gave rise to ideoaffective schemes in which valuable relationships have to be "hot" – defined by possession and by loss. The looming potential loss gives meaning to the relationship and makes intimacy possible.

Even where there is no "pathology," ideoaffective structures are detectable. However, note that while the so-called pathology of the hostile or depressed person, as described earlier, can make life difficult or eccentric, it may do so without making it uninteresting or impossible. Rogers, Perls, and Ellis each had particular ideoaffective structures. Their ideoaffective structures are critical for understanding the creation of theories such as the ones they elaborated and are important for understanding how they actually conducted the practice of psychotherapy. They are also, of course, important in understanding the lives that they led. In other words, the understanding of ideoaffective structure is important in understanding the personality of the individual; but it goes even beyond that toward an understanding of the individual's most abstract thought and most productive works.

To make Tomkins's case for affect as the organizing, generative force in mental life, we have tried several approaches in previous efforts. In one approach, Malatesta (1990) aggregated individual empirical studies supporting the thesis that affective biases influence information processing; this work demonstrated that existing research could be readily organized to show the effects predicted by theories of affect development.

Another approach we have used is the narrative analysis of personal documents, for example, Haviland and Kramer's (1991) study of Anne Frank's diary. The emotion words in that document and the style of intellectual presentation were found to correlate, showing that there is a coherence between emotional focus and thinking style.

In yet another merging of affective information, Malatesta-Magai and Dorval (1992) analyzed the text and affective expression of a single twenty-four-minute family conversation. Here an analysis of the emotional postures of family members was combined with an analysis of their sociolinguistic expressions to show the coherence of postural and gestural affect with more linguistic indices of personality. Similarly, Kahlbaugh and Haviland (1994) used facial and bodily emotional indicators to show changes in emotional posture during adolescence that appear to be related to changes in adolescent identity.

In each analysis, whether a critical review, a narrative approach, or an examination of emotional posture, we were constrained by either the logico-deductive method itself or by the limited nature of material available for analysis. What we were searching for was the more compelling example of individual human lives played out in full. The eventual choice of our subjects – Rogers, Perls, and Ellis – was not dictated by the fact that they were therapists or that they were highly successful. As indicated earlier, we could have selected more ordinary subjects. After all, everyone has intuitions, reads nonverbal cues, and has interesting personal ways of using emotion.

What was particularly appealing was the very variety of the material available to us – detailed records of their lives and samples of their ideas in their own words, along with visual, moving images of them – and the fact that there were similar data on all three individuals interacting with the same client, Gloria. Using these materials, we hope to show that each man's personality was a set of complex, constantly evolving, emotional strategies for coping with the diverse experiences of life. We also want to show how the particular emotional strategies that developed within them over time shaped the quality of their thought processes, for example, as illustrated by each man's unique therapeutic ideology. And finally, we explain how the conduct and content of their clinical approaches is reflected in their particular emotional skills.

Rogers, Perls, and Ellis were skilled therapists who drew upon their own emotional resources in their life's work. Each had his own particular emotional biases but used them in differentially skilled ways. Perhaps this is true of all talented therapists, that they bring their own biases to bear in fruitful methods. By emotional talent we refer to a certain keenness of emotional intelligence. Salovey and Mayer (1990) described this kind of intelligence as involving the "recognition and use of one's own and other's emotional states to solve problems and regulate behavior" (p. 18).

The three men featured in our analysis of the impact of ideoaffective organization on thought and behavior are individuals who have had a substantial though sometimes forgotten influence on psychotherapy practice. Rogers's research on the real and ideal image of self founded an important domain of self psychology. Perls's views of gestalts (whole constellations) in personality has had a lasting influence on several integrative modes of psychotherapy (Greenberg, 1993). Ellis's use of structured cognitive interventions had a direct influence on the whole cognitive-behavior school of personality and psychotherapy, even though his own work has been somewhat marginalized in recent times.

Ellis, Perls, and Rogers each developed an approach to psychotherapy that was informed by a striking departure from conventional psychoanalytic theory and practice. Because all the approaches, including psychoanalysis, regard affect as a mediating variable in neurosis and in its amelioration, each therapist places affect in a particular position with respect to its role in mental life, the importance of attending to or subjugating affect, and the relative importance of affect versus cognition in the healing process. Thus, each man in his theory presents a unique ideology about affect. Nevertheless, it appears that none of the men were able to appreciate fully the role that their own affect played in the formation of their ideologies. Neither did the crucial role of affect in the psychotherapeutic process itself necessarily become part of their theory, or if it did, it was not particularly complete or accurate. However, the focus on communion in the writings of Rogers, the intrusive drama and fantasy of Perls, and the forceful rational challenge of Ellis all came from their own basic ideoaffective positions. These positions are clear in their biographies, in their action – posture and expression – and in their theoretical formulations.

We wish to acknowledge an important source of inspiration for our project, namely the seminal four-volume work of Silvan Tomkins – *Affect, Imagery, Consciousness* (1962, 1963, 1991, 1993) – the bulk of which comprises his "affect theory." We have taken some of the more important constructs and expanded upon them as well as extended the basic ideas of his theory in applying them to an understanding of therapist and client personality and interpersonal dynamics. Our backgrounds as developmental psychologists also promoted an emphasis on a dimension that was not well elaborated in Tomkins – that of lifespan development and change. We are not especially taken with the idea of "structuralization" or of "repetition compulsion" as the sine qua non of human development and personality dynamics; rather, we view personality as an evolving developmental process in the direction of wisdom in work and in relationships. We also bring new theories of intellectual growth and of attachment processes to the older affect theory. We illustrate how the therapeutic strategies developed and evolved across the lives of Rogers, Ellis, and Perls can be seen as creative and meaningful extensions of particular strategies for dealing with their own affective experiences, some of which are not personal in a strict sense but are affective experiences of their work culture and of the broader European and American cultures that formed their backgrounds.

We also expand the study to include an examination of how emotions affect interpersonal styles and how they, in turn, have an impact on interactions with clients or other people. Although it seems intuitively obvious that the success or lack of success of any one particular strategy will depend on its fit with personality structure and emotional dynamics of the client, this idea seems not to have penetrated psychotherapy theory or practice very far. In the present work, we have the opportunity to investigate this possibility, since the same patient, Gloria, is seen by each of the three men, as recorded in film.

Before proceeding further, let us pause to consider why the availability of both film and narrative text makes for a particularly adventitious combination of source materials for the present project.

Working Documents of the Project: Use of Narrative and Film Material

This project relies on autobiographical and biographical materials as well as film to reconstruct the lives of our subjects. (The coding protocols and inter-rater reliabilities are found in the appendix.) Both media have relatively limited histories of use within mainstream experimental psychology, though presently there is a surge of interest within personality and developmental research and some new and exciting applications as well.

Wiggins and Pincus (1992) in their review of the literature on personality research for the 1992 edition of the *Annual Review of Psychology*, noted two rather recent developments, namely (1) that the field has returned to its roots in its use of personal documents and notions of traits, and (2) that it was once again "okay to study the 'whole person'" (McAdams, 1992, p. 1). Methods employed to study lives were found to include variants used in Block's classic *Lives Through Time* (1971) and variations on psychobiographical analysis.

There has also been renewed interest in the relevance of narrative material in developmental psychology. In fact, within the lifespan literature, there is growing recognition that biography and the study of individual lives may be one of the best places to look for developmental principles, and one of the best places to confirm or disconfirm some of our most cherished developmental precepts (Datan, Rodeheaver & Hughes, 1987).

This approach to the study of human development was originally championed by Charlotte Bühler (1933) earlier in the century. Indeed, she conducted some of the first fruitful uses of biographical technique to explore adolescent development (1934) as well as adult development (1935). In approaching the prospect of understanding the stretch of human development *beyond* the childhood years, Bühler and colleagues availed themselves of existing biographies and other archival sources, as well as conducted their own set of extensive biographical interviews. These data led Bühler to propose the field's first stage-linked lifespan theory of human development; it is also noteworthy that she went on to help found the "third-force" of humanistic psychology. However, in her construction of the psychology of the developing human, individuals were motivated by *personal goals*, and there was little attention to the *interpersonal* context of development. Nor did her theory explore the role of emotion in the development of particular kinds of goals, in the structuring of personality, or in its transformation over time.

Erik Erikson was another early developmentalist who was an important contributor to the evolution of a lifespan developmental psychology. His theory of psychosocial development was a stage theory as was Bühler's, but it had additional elements, specifically, notions embracing the idea of what we call "developmental divergence" and of what Erikson termed "epigenesis," a concept originally derived from embryology. The idea of developmental divergence had to do with the notion that the developing individual confronts developmental junctures that pose new tasks and potential crises, which can be resolved in a variety of ways. That is, there are various opportunities for growth and divergence in personality. Thus, development is viewed as a product of a uniquely emergent organism–environment interaction. It is also epigenetic; that is, it consists of developmental continuity in the midst of change. As such, in Erikson's view, a view incidentally that we share, personality as it develops, becomes a modification and elaboration of earlier structures, rather than the creation of an entirely new structure.

Erikson spelled out these ideas in a rather straightforward and academic fashion in what is now regarded as a classic work, *Childhood and Society* (1950). But what is important for our discussion here is that

Erikson's ideas were more vividly and persuasively brought to life in his psychobiographical works, *Young Man Luther* (1958) and *Gandhi's Truth* (1969). Regrettably, however, during this era, Erikson was almost unique among his peers in daring to use qualitative material and a narrative approach to the explication of theory. Scientific thought had became dominated by positivistic paradigms and approaches by the 1950s.

Nevertheless, the pendulum had begun to swing the other way once again by the late 1970s with the emergence of a strong stream of research on the socioemotional aspects of children's development. Additionally, in cognitive developmental psychology, the post-Piagetians began to experiment with qualitative data and to discern new ways of thinking about thought. For example, Bruner (1986, 1990) began to differentiate between propositional and narrative modes of thinking, the former characterized by linear, sequential patterns of thought and the latter more infused with subjectivity and *affectivity*.

Within psychoanalytic circles, Spence (1982) made an important contribution to psychology when he distinguished between historical truth and narrative truth. He was influenced by both the analyst's penchant for the storied approach to human experience, as well as scientific psychology's growing awareness that the human mind is not a passive recording device. Rather, the mind takes events experienced over time and weaves them into meaningful themes that have personal significance. This understanding had even broader ramifications. Historical truth, the standard bearer of scientific credulity, is indexed by criteria of verifiability and inter-rater reliability. Narrative truth has a different set of criteria. Although narrative truth may not always be faithful to events as they actually unfold over time, its "veracity" lies in its relation to a person's private identity, in its ability to encapsulate personal meaning, *and* its ability to predict future events (Polkinghorne, 1991; Ruth & Kenyon, 1996).

The implication of this view for the human sciences, and especially lifespan developmental psychology, is of great import. It suggests that psychologists should take special note of biographically elicited material and of autobiographical memories as a unique window on personality rather than as a particularly suspicious, potentially contaminated, and likely "invalid" source of information. Instead, personal experience and personal construal of meaning – whether recorded in diaries, in confessional poetry, in autobiography, or in interview with a recording observer – yield material that is particularly accessible to analysis, rich in meaning (a thickening agent for the relatively thin data of "outside" observation), and, from our perspective, a slice of personality that is perhaps particularly close in quality to providing very pure forms of an individual's ideoaffectology.

What is different about today's psychobiographical approaches in personality research and developmental studies is that they do not rely exclusively on Freudian theory but are guided as well by Tomkins' script theory (Carlson & Brincka, 1987; Carlson & Carlson, 1984; Magai & McFadden, 1995), the personalistic tradition of Murray and Allport (Alexander, 1988; McAdams, 1992), and Erikson's epigenetic approach (Stewart, Franz & Layton, 1989). There is growing recognition that narrative material, especially when sampled over time, may provide a unique means of testing theories of personality. As time passes and individuals mature, the story of the self may or may not be modified; the changes or lack of changes in personality may be observed by others at some remove in time (Ruth & Kenyon, 1996). Researchers such as Caspi (Caspi, Bem & Elder, 1988; Caspi, Elder & Bem, 1987) and Skolnick (1986) started to mine narrative data in the form of interview records archived at the Institute of Human Development a decade ago to test theories of developmental continuity and change. One could use other kinds of narrative material, accumulated over time, in a similar fashion, as demonstrated by Haviland (1984) in her analysis of the diaries and writings of Virginia Woolf. The theoretical writings of social scientists ostensibly lend themselves to such purpose as well; this idea is exploited in the present volume.

Film and audio records provide yet another means of sampling personality. Tomkins (1963) suggested that individuals' micromomentary changes in facial expressions provide an ongoing source of information on emotional state, a glimpse of personality organization, and even data for biographical/historical inferences – as we will see particularly clearly in the case of Rogers.

Film and narrative records should be viewed as complementary sources of information. They tap different channels of interpersonal communication and emotion expression. Narrative texts provide a window on an individual's *affect lexicon* – the variety and types of words used to describe, dampen, or amplify feelings. To this, film adds facial expression, bodily posture, and paralinguistics. To a large extent, affect is overdetermined; that is, it is present simultaneously in several channels – face, voice, posture, and choice of words, though sometimes they tell a slightly different story, especially in grown individuals, and especially if the individual is particularly practiced in one or another channel. But for the most part, as we will see, all the expressive channels have a tendency to fit together to tell the same ideoaffective story, though they do not completely replicate each other. As a matter of fact, there is a combination of cross-talk that is much more interesting and informative than replication, as we will see in our analysis.

Summary and Overview of the Volume

The central aim of this volume is to reveal and explicate the relations among feeling structures, ideology, and praxis in the lives of three emotionally interesting individuals. We will propose a developmental model that implicates a dynamic relation between affective experiences and affective organizations, between affective organizations and emotional strategies, and between emotional strategies and individual ideology, personality, and behavior. As such, we will have cause to examine the life histories of each of the three men toward the goal of reconstructing critical socialization experiences.

In analyzing the emotional organizations of Rogers, Ellis, and Perls, we draw from several sources of material. Autobiographical statements and biographical accounts of each man provide basic historical data. Videotapes, audiotapes, and written transcriptions of the three therapists with the same client, Gloria, provide confirmatory data on affective organizations and emotional strategies through all the expressive realms of posture, facial expressions, vocal quality, and word content. We analyzed individual essays and whole volumes written by each man promoting their ideas and methods to derive the links between emotion and thought in each individual. In addition, we tracked changes in thought and emotion (confirming, usually, changes forecast from biographical material) over a long period of time over the corpus of each man's theoretical output. In the present work, then, we address three basic questions:

1. How do ideoaffective structures develop in childhood and change across the lifespan?
2. How are ideoaffective structures seen in virtually every movement of the individual – in the face, voice, posture, and bodily attitude? And how do these expressive behaviors influence other people?
3. How are ideoaffective structures integrated into intellectual work to provide focus on certain content areas, to motivate styles of problem solving, or to block discovery in some areas?

To answer the question of how ideoaffective structures develop, we formulated specific emotional profiles for Perls, Ellis, and Rogers. We analyzed biographical and autobiographical accounts of their lives. These materials yielded important data concerning the men's personalities. Not only were we particularly alert to statements by those who knew them, with respect to the men's emotional strategies and self-presentations, but we also studied the men's own autobiographical statements, looking for general tone, affective themes, and self-referential descriptions of personality. We examined their use of or avoidance of different kinds of emotion words and the quality of their self presentation as a means of analyzing the kinds of emotional experience that were most salient and the experiences that they most defended against.

A theoretical lens that was useful for Magai's analysis of the biographical and autobiographical material was that of attachment theory. Although the bulk of the current work on attachment has been centered on documenting different attachment styles in children and relating them to early experiences with caregivers, some writers are beginning to analyze adult styles of interpersonal relationships from the perspective of attachment theory. We find that attachment theory offers instructive insights into early interpersonal dynamics. However, although the attachment style constructs of security, avoidance, and ambivalence have the grace of parsimony to recommend them, the system is constrained by its very simplicity and, as we will see, does not provide quite the perfect fit to describe the attachment profiles of the three men considered in this volume. Magai's treatment extends the work she began in "Tolstoy and the Riddle of Developmental Transformation" (Magai & Hunziker, 1993), which attempted to integrate and expand upon affect theory, attachment theory, and Erikson's lifespan model of psychosocial development.

An analysis of the tapes and transcripts of the psychotherapy session with Gloria also yielded information on affective organization, which was useful in the biographical account. Here we examined Rogers's, Perls's, and Ellis's working affective lexicon. We also searched for the client, Gloria's, affective terms and themes and the kinds of emotions provoked in her by each therapist.

The second question asks how ideoaffective structures are seen in the posture, expression, and tone of a person. For this, the videotapes of Perls, Ellis, and Rogers are extraordinarily revealing. Using fairly standard coding procedures for detecting very small changes in expression (less than a second), we went through the tapes at several levels. The emotions portrayed on each man's face during the sessions as well as in their explanations after the therapy session with Gloria are presented. In addition, we examined Gloria and how she changes from one therapist to another. Of course, some aspects of her persona are stable, and we find out how each therapist reacts to her established emotional postures as well as participates in creating unique interactional exchanges. Each posture is related somewhat to the content and other qualities of the session.

Finally, the third question requires an analysis of the writings of Rogers, Perls, and Ellis. All three are "intelligent" as the world ranks intelligence. Nevertheless, the intellectual style of their writing varies tremendously, both among the three therapists and even within individuals across time. Samples are taken from several volumes written when each was young, middle-aged, and old. These excerpts are analyzed systematically for the use of emotion words and also for intellectual style. Sometimes absolutistic (argumentative) styles are used; sometimes more integrative and inclusive styles are used. How well each man can reach his goals in his writing also depends upon his emotional skills. Whether Rogers, for example, finds some area fruitful, worth continued work and worth the focus depends considerably upon how passionately he is able to address that area. Some issues just do not fit within a person's ideoaffective structure and fall to the wayside of intellectual life.

We have not oriented ourselves equally to the material at hand. We came to the project with slightly different insights and background, though with much in common as well. Using our own intellectual and emotional foci, we have roughly divided the chapters by our interests so that Magai is principally responsible for the analysis of socioemotional development and Haviland-Jones takes on the analysis of the intellectual works, although there is considerable sharing of the rest. We profited from discussions with our colleagues as well, most notably Bruce Dorval, who engaged us in lively exchanges over an extended period of time.

In writing this volume in the collaborative spirit, we exposed ourselves to one another's overwriting so as to present a smoother document for the reader; however, there is something individualistic left to savor. Knowing full well that the technique we use in the present project can be applied to our own writings, we leave it to the reader to discern which parts are more exclusively written by one or the other author.

For years we have been fascinated by the three individuals we have taken on in this project and hope that our three questions are addressed to the reader's satisfaction. However, we have no intention of taking the mystery out of emotion; much remains to be discerned by other discriminating personalities.

We chose Rogers, Perls, and Ellis because of certain unique features in their "case material." We suspect that Perls, Rogers, and Ellis would be of two minds about our manner of pursuing our topic. On the one hand, they would probably applaud the concepts we are working with, at least from an intellectual point of view. On the other hand, they would each no doubt want to retain the right to be skeptical about our work and, in particular, individual interpretations. Each would want us to know that we are sometimes taking our data one step father than they would like, that sometimes our own biases and training are leading us to conclusions with which they might disagree. We have tried to be respectful in our writings, as one would hope that any psychologist would be with any case material or with any individual client. As often happens, we have come to a greater appreciation and, in some cases, admiration for these three psychologists with whom we spent considerable time. The more we delved into their lives, writings, and filmed interviews, the more we came to understand not only the workings of affect but also the minds and hearts of these unique and absorbing individuals.

We proceed to a more formal approach to our subject matter momentarily. However, before we begin, it may be helpful to situate the analysis of individual lives and their impact on psychology from within a broader sociohistorical context.

Being and Time: The Historical Context

History is more than the mere passage of time, and the human trajectory consists of more the mere passage *through* time. There is a dialectic and mutually influential relationship between history and humanity. Thomas Carlyle observed that "history is the essence of innumerable biographies" (*Critical and Miscellaneous Essays*), yet this is but one element of the great dialectic. Individuals shape the course of history to be sure, but history itself exerts considerable influence on human consciousness and its products. Epochal events such as war, famine, depression, Holocaust, and first walks on the moon leave an indelible imprint on consciousness. Less catastrophic and momentous events, but no less influential are the slower moving secular trends and gradual drift in sociocultural mores. The lives of the men we examined were indeed products of their time. That said, we recognize that the term is surely too passive to reflect the nature of their own significant impact on the history of psychology and the history of ideas about the nature of humanity; consequently, we have more to say about that later on. For the time being, we consider the larger historical context that permitted, even promoted, consideration of psychologies as radical as those offered by Rogers, Perls, and Ellis.

Let us situate the lives we examine within their own historical context. Rogers, Perls, and Ellis were all born in the opening decades of the twentieth century and grew to maturity mid-century. The psychologies they would elaborate – humanistic, Gestalt, and cognitive psychology – took root and ripened on American soil in the years immediately following the Second World War. Humanistic psychology, which was the first of the three new psychologies to gain recognition in the academy, was seen as so great a departure from the known psychologies of the time that it was called "the third force," the first two forces being psychoanalysis and behaviorism.

Psychoanalysis, as a formal system, was originally introduced to the American public in 1909 during a series of lectures Freud gave at Clark University at G. Stanley Hall's invitation. Freud's theory, which was rather inhospitably received in his native Europe, and which was actually marginalized for quite some time, found a contrastingly warm reception in America. Not only was it embraced by a substantial segment of the medical establishment – separate professional organizations rapidly evolved and sustained an increasingly large membership – but the American public welcomed it as well. Psychoanalytic theory placed the child squarely in the middle of a social matrix in which parental behaviors exerted a profound impact on children's development and, as Kagan (1979) observed, a pragmatic and egalitarian America was eager to believe such messages. Implicit in the idea of the infant's susceptibility to adult influence was the notion that parents and other sociocultural forces could exert a potentially beneficial force on the course of human development. In the idealistic American mind, the correct rearing of children could ultimately lead to a harmonious social order, free of conflict and strife. Of course, psychoanalytic theory also promulgated other less sanguine views, especially the version following the First World War, when Freud was in the throes of disillusionment about human nature. As he contemplated the genocide and devastation wrought by war, he concluded that human nature was essentially aggressive and destructive.

Moreover, psychoanalytic views of parental influence offered a double-edged sword. The very same parents who could serve as midwives to human perfection carried the equal and opposite threat of inflicting psychological deformity on the all too vulnerable child.

The second force, behaviorism, which began to exert its influence on the academy in the opening decades of this century, had an equally profound impact on the public mind. Watson's theory played on the democratic ideal and American fantasy that any individual could aspire to and achieve any station in life, provided the right environmental conditions prevailed. Again, parents stood to maximize their offspring's success if they but understood the right principles of behavioristic conditioning – all of which, suggested Watson after his ignominious ejection from the academy (Magai & McFadden, 1995), could be found in *The Psychological Care of the Infant and Child*, a how-to book for progressive parents who were interested in eradicating all "the unnecessary sentimentalism" with which old-fashioned parental practices were afflicted.

When the third force started to exert its influence on American consciousness, a whole era had passed and another had begun. First, it is basic to understand that the term "humanistic psychology" – with which Carl Roger's name is almost synonymous – did not spring fully grown from the head of this singular man. William James (1842–1910) and G. Stanley Hall (1844–1924) were two of this country's earliest scientific humanists (Sexton, 1983). During the 1930s, Gordon Allport and Henry Murray also challenged the positivistic streak of American psychology with their espousal of humanistic theories of personality. That Allport and Murray's peers regarded these theories as devious and subversive, even against the backdrop of the work of their esteemed predecessors, is signaled by the fact that both men were marginalized during their careers at Harvard (Anderson, 1988). So how was it that Rogers succeeded in surmounting the academic obstacles that stood in his path? What is especially astounding is that he succeeded in the face of what appeared to be a relatively uncharismatic persona. At this juncture, it is important to consider other historical factors that may shed some light.

During the time that Rogers would rise to eminence (the 1940s and 1950s), and Perls and Ellis would gain recognition as well, there were two contending tribes of psychology professionals: the scientific and the applied. Contrary to received wisdom that scientific psychology displaced applied psychology during the early days of the field, Mueller-Brettel, Schmitz, and Schoepflin's (1993) analysis of the psychological and sociological literature of this century indicates otherwise. Their bibliometric analysis reveals that between 1894 and 1930 the greatest increase in the volume of psychological literature was in applied psychology. "These quantitative data highlight the fact that applied psychology challenged scientific psychology, not the other way around" (Mueller-Brettel et al., 1993, p. 7).

The ascendance of applied psychology must have been seen as posing a threat to the academic establishment. And Rogers, entrenched as he was in academia (in a fashion that Perls and Ellis never were), appears to have played this card to his advantage, charismatic or not. One imagines that there must have been lively skirmishes over turf, students, and status within the groves of academe. Rogers himself is oddly silent on the matter. However, everything we know from the historiography of the time suggests that Rogers had to face conflict on an ongoing basis.

Counselors were soon in demand at the major universities in the States, stimulated by the great growth in psychology departments across the country in response to the boom in students who were choosing psychology careers. The counseling centers at the several universities where Rogers held professorships were in place largely to treat students with academic problems, and these centers proved to be a fertile ground for Rogers to explore some of his ideas on personal growth in a nonclinical setting, addressing the concerns of the normal, average person, the person who might be unhappy and unfulfilled but not gravely ill.

Rogers experienced active resistance and hostility when he attempted to bring together two forces – the clinical and scientific – on the same turf. He made several courageous attempts to open the door of the psychotherapy office to scientific research, he was dogged in his determination to have his work accepted on equal footing with that of his academic peers, and he made singularly unpopular attempts to democratize the educational process. The struggle with the rest of the establishment must have been intense and intermittently humiliating and angering. Counseling and clinical psychology simply were not highly regarded in such citadels of dust bowl empiricism as the great midwestern universities; they were the necessary but somewhat despised citizens of the university world. Rogers was fortunate that broader cultural factors favored a receptivity to his client-centered, person-centered, and student-centered philosophies and approaches.

Indeed, currents in the broader culture signaled a receptivity to a psychology that focused on the self, rather than the parent–child relationship, valorizing the self – and its mending. These currents made at least some segments of the society ready to hear Rogers and his message.

As Cushman (1992) demonstrated, modern psychotherapy practices with a focus on the sick or incomplete self would establish themselves and come of age during an era of great social upheaval, uncertainty, and doubt. Rent by two world wars and various powerful sociopolitical and socioeconomic forces, the individual in society was no longer tightly woven into the fabric of tribe, ethnic group, clan, or even family, but felt singularly isolated (Foucault, 1988; Kovel, 1980; Wachtel, 1989); the person in modern society had become the "alienated self," the "divided self," the "false self," and the "empty self." This isolated, fragmented, and empty self needed filling up by psychologies that addressed the interior life of thought and feeling. What the post–World War II modalities of psychotherapy – humanistic psychology and self-, Gestalt, existential, and cognitive therapies – supplied in numbers were "doctors of the interior" (Cushman, 1992, p. 22). Rogers, in particular, spoke to the need for emotional fullness and self-acceptance in an eloquent and timely way. Thus, in terms of Rogers's place in history and his exploitation of it, timing was critical.

Timing was also of moment for the present project in terms of the rediscovered film of Gloria and the three therapists, our own place in developmental time in understanding affect theory, and psychology's renewed interest in human emotion. We find ourselves in the interesting, if not unique, position of writing about an era that we lived through (we were both in graduate school during the 1960s and were exposed to humanistic thought in a personal way) but also with hindsight and from the perspective of a new era in psychology's evolution. The psychologies of the 1980s, 1990s, and the new millenium are much more intersubjective and interpersonal (Bowlby, 1980; Orange et al., 1997; Stern, 1985). It is from that newer vantage point that we analyze and interpret the material before us, although other perspectives will also be brought to bear.

2 Affect, Human Development, and Dynamic Systems

Historically, developmental theory has been captivated by two central romances – the notion of "early experience" (pedogenesis) and the doctrine of "continuity." Like most romances, both theories attempt to simplify lives and to make them a mythical whole, sometimes a heroic myth. And like most romances, there is a certain truth to them, but also a loss of complexity and depth that can border on untruth or at least limit the romance to a special case. To prepare the reader for our approach of examining lives with a new look at their complexity and depth, we need to present a short history of these compelling romances and then open the field of possibilities. This exercise will involve considering theories of complexity and chaos or dynamic systems and will require that the reader have some familiarity with the new vocabulary. Our analysis does not rely upon the mathematical intricacies of these new approaches; it, however, often relies on the hypotheses and explanations that are generated.

Both psychoanalytic models of development as well as contemporary attachment theory follow the early experience and continuity theories. In classic psychoanalytic theory, early experience and continuity through repetition are paramount. Personality is largely formed by the age of five, and early conflicts are played out successively in later relationships, with the individual in thrall to an unconscious but headstrong repetition compulsion. In attachment theory, continuity and early experience are required. Infants form highly specific, qualitatively differentiated attachments to primary caregivers. These earliest attachments consolidate during early childhood and generate templates for other relationships through the mechanism of mental elaboration or internal working models. Attachment researchers were at first impressed by the high stability coefficients obtained between successive waves of measurement of attachment style, finding that this coincided with theoretical formulations concerning the enduring nature of attachment relationships and their pervasive influence.

In the 1960s the primate research of Harry Harlow and colleagues offered a first serious challenge to the romances of pedogenesis and continuity. Harlow reared monkeys on a surrogate, wire-frame "mother." But the effects of this early experience were not as profound and irreversible as anticipated. Peer relationships, for example, could provide alternate patterns for attachment relationships. More recently, and with respect to research on human attachment, samples of disadvantaged children have been found to display quite significant alterations in their attachment patterns over time. Despite these and other challenges, the two classic developmental romances live on in much of the developmental literature, albeit in a more pronounced form in the early child developmental literature than in lifespan studies.

Child developmental research is, by nature, focused on only one segment of the lifecourse, and, as studied with a close lens, it is easy to see why practitioners would regard every nuance of this early development as momentous. Taking the longer view, and from the vantage point of lapsed time and evidence from longitudinal studies, lifespan developmentalists are prone to be somewhat more skeptical. Granted, some lifespan developmentalists still espouse a continuity model of adult development, but the evidence on which the position rests has more to do with reliance on tests that are temperamentally based – as in the Baltimore longitudinal study which used the Guilford–Zimmerman personality measure (McCrae & Costa, 1990). That temperamental variables show stability is not surprising, since they may have physiological boundaries that limit the influence of maturation and life history. However, when research is based on personality tests that rely on more complex constructs such as "identity" and "intimacy" and that are tested in sophisticated designs that control for cohort effects (i.e., one's historical time period), evidence for change is rather compelling. [See, for example, Whitbourne et al.'s (1992) twenty-two-year sequential study of psychosocial development in adulthood.]

The studies of complex personality features, as theoretically grounded and mathematically sophisticated as they may be, can seem quite pale, because the lives that are being described have been distilled as group data. We may know, for instance, that people in the third decade of life during the twentieth century usually experience increases in trust, intimacy, and identity (Whitbourne et al., 1992). This general knowledge gives us little idea of what this looks like in any single individual. More importantly, it does not tell us how or why such a pattern may exist, or where its exceptions lie. Neither does it tell us how, nor even if, one person's trust, intimacy, or identity resembles another person's. Nevertheless, such findings alert us to look for substantive change in lives and, moreover, to question the dynamics behind such change. Quantitative studies are singularly unedifying on these points.

In the next section, we briefly review early challenges to developmental theory in the human literature as relevant to the issue of continuity and change. We then turn to emerging trends in the field that draw on dynamic systems constructs, followed by a more expanded treatment of the latter body of theory; this material will serve as the foundation for ideas that are developed later on in this volume.

Scope of Developmental Psychology: Then and Now

One of the first epistemological challenges to the pedogenesis and continuity doctrines came from a psychoanalyst, one who trained with Freud himself – Erik Erikson. It was Erikson (1963) who recognized that lives are permeable to the influence of culture, history, and experiences beyond childhood. His psychosocial theory advanced two novel propositions.

The first proposition was that *lives show developmental divergence* as well as continuity. In Erikson's model, as individuals mature, they confront stage-specific, developmental periods or nodes, to use the new vocabulary, that pose new tasks and potential crises. Although Erikson proposed that the nodes themselves are universalistic, being propelled by biological and species-specific interpersonal demands, the developmental resolution of each change period or node is highly variable. Each developmental task occurs within varied historically and culturally defined contexts. There are also various opportunities for consolidation, regression, or reorganization and growth that extend well beyond the initial period, as Harlow's monkeys used peer relationships at a later time to reorganize their early attachments.

The second of Erikson's novel propositions was the notion that there is developmental *continuity in the midst of change*. Erikson argued that epigenesis or development is a process of building upon and modifying earlier structures, not the creation of an entirely new structure. As such, development involves change, but it also preserves a fundamental unity of identity and sense of self-continuity. This theory then not only retains some romantic elements of the old theory but also allows for more developmental divergence and eccentricity in individual lives.

One element that Erikson left out of his more contextually sensitive model was the influence of chance events. In Erikson's model, the individual is periodically beset by new maturational demands. A child of any culture, at any time, can count on eventually having to take personal responsibility for bowel and bladder control. The child will confront the need to become independent to a greater or lesser degree, to develop an identity separate from his parents, and so forth. These are common elements in the average life, and we can more or less set our clocks by them. However, the human lifecourse always and for all of us is punctuated by both scheduled and *unscheduled* crises, by both normative and *nonnormative* events. For some of us, an illness of a parent will force the premature assumption of responsibility for siblings. For others of us, a physical injury will derail a sports career or initiate economic setbacks. For everyone, unique and unscheduled, but important, life events exist. There is little in Erikson's theory to help us predict how unscheduled challenges may affect the individual and ultimately be resolved.

Erikson also failed to specify what accounts for developmental divergence. Why does one child emerge from his second Eriksonian developmental crisis or node with his trust in the beneficence of his demanding and overcontrolling parents shaken, and with new sullen resentment, while another child resolves a similar crisis with benign compliance? Moreover, of what use is it to know what comprises the emotional residues of these periods? Do they help us predict future developmental process? In our analyses, we will find that these gaps lead to a narrow understanding of human development. Even though Erikson was one of the few lifespan developmental psychologists to point to the importance of emotions in psychosocial development, he was not particularly focused on emotion. Additionally, the emotional aspects of the various developmental nodes were not especially well elaborated, even though he often used emotional words such as shame or guilt in his writing.

Emotion

In the chapters ahead, we will pursue the idea that ideoaffective organizations are the key to understanding both the power and the limits of our romances of early experience and continuity. A person's unique emotional organization is recruited during moments of crisis and transition to assist with coping and to provide meaning, a form of self-generated continuity. Old motivations, intentions, and feelings can then be applied to new experience with a kind of continuous transformation. Competing with this tendency for construction of continuity is the condition where strong emotions, previously either not experienced at all or considered to be incompatible with the events in question, precipitate a crisis and create enough chaos such that entirely novel and divergent paths in life emerge.

In studying lives, we have the opportunity to consider how an individual's emotional organization provides the fundamental super-structure for the interpretation and integration of normative and non-normative developmental crises and remains at the center of continuity of self. At the same time, we can also address what it is about emotional experiences that accrue during normative development and the emotionally salient experiences of unexpected events and encounters that may constitute situations of new learning with potential for personality transformation.

Biography

The use of biography is integral to our project. Within the lifespan litera-ture, there has been growing recognition that biography and the study of individual lives may be one of the best places to look for developmental principles, as discussed in Chapter 1. But biographies do not, by them-selves, illustrate developmental history or provide insight into the pro-cess of change. Each biographer uses a particular lens and looks through a particular window at the lives he or she studies. Usually, because of general tendencies in Western history, biographers have neglected people's emotional lives and intellectual development. Nevertheless, biographical or case histories have a notable place in psychological, and often in biological, theories. Within developmental psychology, the bi-ographical and case approach was first advocated by Charlotte Bühler (1933) earlier in the century. Bühler and colleagues availed themselves of extant biographies and conducted biographical interviews themselves. As ahead of her time as she may have been, Bühler's approach failed in two respects. First, an interpersonal perspective was missing in her theoretical treatment of adulthood; individuals were motivated by per-sonal goals, almost in an interpersonal vacuum. She also failed to rec-ognize the role of emotion in structuring and transforming lives. To be fair, her successors have not been particularly sensitive to this issue either.

Erikson (1950) also used biographical and case material to create his lifespan developmental theory. He used the concept of crisis (emotional stress) and developmental milestones that pivoted around certain emotions (autonomy versus shame, industry versus guilt, integrity versus despair). Throughout his life and writings, however, he was drawn more to issues of identity rather than emotion, and he did not understand emotional dynamics as they were later elaborated in affect theory (Tomkins, 1962, 1963). In its turn, affect theory also had limitations, namely its lack of attention to interpersonal issues.

White (1952) used biographical and case material as a way to introduce people to the study of personality and to extend our understanding of personality. In this famous book, he presented the *Lives in Progress* of three students when they were college students and then five or ten years later. As we will do, he combined the insights of biography with some of the insights of objective testing common to social scientists. Also, as we will do, he embedded his cases in varied forms of scientific inquiry from the biological to the social and cultural. Once again, as had so many psychobiographers, he concluded that "[w]e have repeatedly found that general concepts did not help us to understand process or change, which always had to be described with reference to many particulars" (p. 327). White's conclusions prepare us for the study of the three cases that we will present with more modern analytic tools. He concluded that normal and healthy development is one of continuous change, with a block to continuous change constituting an emotional pathology. He concluded that there are multiple possible responses to any situation and that the person is constantly selecting, sometimes quite by chance. This act of choosing of a single path from the many available to any one of us determines the path. His last points were that people constantly change within their environment as well as change the environment, and that the environment – at whatever point it is looked at – is the prime reality for the person. To know the person one needs the details.

Attachment theory, which emerged during the late 1960s and early 1970s and subsequently inspired several decades of intensive research, redressed the absence of attention to the interpersonal in human development. Within this framework, affect, in the form of biobehavioral signals, served as a vital link between child and caregiver early in development. But emotions were hardly central to the theory. Nevertheless, attachment theory provides an important *apercu* with respect to human development. We will examine and extend some of the very useful constructs of attachment theory to our treatment of issues around socioemotional development in the coming chapters.

Another model we want to bring to bear on the issue of affect and its impact on personality over time is that of dynamic systems theory. Since this theory is less well known to most developmentalists and personality theorists, we provide a more extended introductory discussion. We will be using the vocabulary and style of thinking about causes and effects that emerge from this approach.

Dynamic Systems: Background and Conceptual Terms

Theories across all the natural and social sciences are showing signs of being transformed as we enter the twenty-first century. Though these theories of systems offer many new ideas, they also tend to show the limits of such romances as early experience and continuity, which we have been bounded by for so long. Dynamic systems theory evolved within the mathematical and physical sciences in response to the need of scientists to better describe and comprehend complex systems that could not otherwise be understood using familiar but limited linear systems approaches. Two branches of dynamic systems evolved during the latter half of the twentieth century – that of the Brussels school, which is closely associated with the name of Prigogine (1980) and his work on self-organizing systems, and that of the American school, which is known as chaos theory. Dynamic systems theory is also sometimes called complexity theory; however, this term often implies subtle differences in the types of systems being considered.

Linear systems are those in which input is proportional to output. Without some obvious input or cause, there is no output; if the output changes, it is influenced by a change in the input. However, many examples from life and science depart from these simple linear models. Dynamic systems tend to be governed by nonlinearity as well as other properties that were first modeled in mathematics and were then found to have many remarkable and powerful applications. In nonlinear systems, input is not proportional to output, as in the well-known dose–response curve in pharmaceutics – increasing doses of medicine do not result in a corresponding increase in effect. Additionally, in dynamic systems, small inputs (effects) can elicit large and ramifying outputs, as in isochronic iterative equations. Also in dynamic systems, chance interactions may lead to shifts in patterns or to entirely new and unpredictable patterns.

A linear systems perspective and notions of equilibrium have dominated the physical and social sciences for most of their histories. The notion of equilibrium is closely associated with early Greek mathematics and Galilean and Newtonian physics; notions of equilibrium are also found within psychology, most notably in psychoanalysis, Lewinian field theory, cognitive dissonance theory, Piagetian theory, and, most recently, attachment theory. These historical facts help explain why models of human development have been dominated by causal models of development, a preoccupation with issues of stability, and the utilization of inferential statistics based on linear models. In spite of their long, historical lineage, these approaches do not lend themselves very well to the articulation of change processes; hence, they are limited in describing human development, which is all about change.

Prigogine, the Belgian chemist, proposed the novel construct of "far-from-equilibrium" systems that had surprising characteristics, namely the fact that they were self-organizing. His first demonstrations of the self-organizing process was in the realm of chemical and heat transfer systems, but he later extended the notion to other systems. The far-from-equilibrium construct in the social sciences, as an alternative to equilibrium thinking, has a number of interesting implications for the understanding of processes of change in living systems, a point to which we return later on.

Self-organization theory and related notions from chaos theory provide exciting possibilities for discovery in psychology because these ideas enable us to examine and model both stability and change in human development and states in between stability and chaos. Chaos allows us to understand the mechanics of stability and change in physical terms; self-organization provides the important additional element of energy flow. In order to incorporate these notions into a developmental psychology of personality, we must consider the human being as a system with dynamic energy flow – and we must also consider interdependent systems – because human beings are highly interactive. Systems – whether they are physical systems such as tornados or whirlpools, or living systems with concepts of "self," identity, and consciousness – can emerge originally from chaos. Over time new forms can evolve as the system self-organizes in real time responding to both internal flux and flow and the perturbations and turbulence of surrounding systems. Even stable systems may have phase transitions in which further chaos is created, leading once again to new self-organization and new emergent forms – or to chaos again, of course.

The notion of chaos in living systems is transforming our notions of physical health and mental health. Although the layman's sense of chaos is that of dysadaptive disorganization, the science of complexity indicates that chaos and instability may be at the heart of successful adaptation in complex systems. In terms of mental health models, the old model based on equilibrium theory suggested that when a psyche is disordered the therapist must act to restore order so that health is regained. Newer thinking suggests that dysfunctional social/psychological patterns are dysadaptive because they are so stable and resistant to change. Therefore, therapy must consist of producing measured doses of chaos.

Similarly, in medicine, equilibrium models were standard assumptions behind concepts of physical health for much of the 20th century. Now however, dynamic systems-tracking of organic and suborganic systems indicates that the healthy body is chaotic. Strictly periodic behavior can signal the onset of disease or even death. Work on electrocardiography has led to challenges in basic assumptions about the way the healthy heart works. The equilibrium model proposed that cardiac rate hovered around a normal average (point attractor), which varied in a cyclic manner with circadium rhythms (periodic attractor). Goldberger (1991) objected to the equilibrium model and proposed that normal heartrate is best modeled as a chaotic attractor with three or more dimensions. Within a short period of time, Sabelli and colleagues (1995) even identified a virtual alphabet of normal cardiac patterns associated with the action patterns of different emotions. Porges, Doussard-Roosevelt, and Maiti (1994) studied human learning and emotion regulation as related to vagal tone; higher vagal tone and heartrate variability are associated with appropriate and adaptive behavioral and emotional responses to environmental and social stimulation. What we are learning then is that variability is not just an intrinsic feature of living systems and their biological processes but also essential to adaptation. Trying to produce simple stability may be fatal, rather than curative.

In the realm of personality and human lives, we often fail to demonstrate that linear systems are the most accurate. Esther Thelen and Alan Fogel, infancy researchers, were among the first developmentalists to comprehend the importance of dynamic systems theory for developmental psychology. Behaviors and habits that appear to be simple and that were long thought to be laid down by biological blueprints (e.g., stepping, crawling, reaching, clapping, walking) were described by Thelen as being constructed within a dynamic systems model. Thelen (1990) was also persuaded that the individual is the proper unit of analysis for psychology, coming once again to the theme first developed by Gordon Allport when he designated personology as the study of the unique personality and emphasized the morphogenic approach to measurement some seventy years ago.

Thelen's thesis goes beyond the recognition that everything in nature is unique. Her conceptualization of the individual emerges from a newer understanding of developmental process. Given that human growth and development is quintessentially a dynamic system – responsive to its own internal variability as well as environmental perturbations – group analyses will obscure the dynamics of self-organizing processes. Suppose that the emotion of interest was always necessary to bring about learning, but that the point at which it was essential might be individually variable – at the beginning for one, in the middle for another, and so forth. If one only measured interest at a single point in time, just a small proportion of the sample would show the effect, and it would appear to be unreliable. If every person's time line were studied individually, the effect might be very clear. We would still see a linear model, but the model itself would require dynamic procedures.

The study of individuals, formerly dismissed as too narrow and non-generalizable, is coming to be seen as the proper and most legitimate way of closing in on essential developmental principles. Though human life trajectories may resemble a "random walk" with no foreordained or predictable path or terminal state, the phenomena under inspection are completely deterministic in the sense that each output along the trajectory or the random walk or of the individual human life is a function of or conditioned on each preceding input. Nevertheless, we can still learn about developmental principles or about types of outcomes by studying the individual. Thelen argued that understanding individual outcomes can be apprehended only by studying individual trajectories. Once individual developmental paths are identified, and in sufficient numbers, we may be able to cluster individuals not only with respect to outcome but also with respect to route and process. Thus, like Allport, she advocated that we should pay attention to morphogenesis or pattern. Chaos theory understands patterning to be intrinsic to both living and non-living systems that have the capacity to respond to change, or what Murray Gell-Mann (1994) referred to as complex adaptive systems – those systems that evolve or develop over time in response to acquired information.

Alan Fogel (1992a, 1992b) used dynamic system theory to understand communicative behavior of dyads, specifically the behavior of mothers and infants in face-to-face interaction. Tracking the development of synchrony over time, Fogel noted that the behavior of dyads gradually became coregulated as the two individual systems "exchanged information." Thus, one organized system interacting with another system experiences the perturbations produced by proximity to the other, alters its behavior in response to the other, and vice versa, such that an intersystemic and suprasystemically stable pattern of behavior can emerge that neither can present when alone. Of course, the system does not have to stabilize but can stay chaotic; nevertheless, organisms tend toward self-organization.

Other researchers (e.g., Kunnen & Bosma, 2001; M. D. Lewis, 1995, 1996, 1997) have begun to model personality development as a dynamic system in particularly creative ways, drawing from the work of Prigogine and self-organization theory. In the present work, we also use dynamic systems theory in conjunction with attachment theory, and complementarity in our analysis of the three lives before us. However, dynamic systems is contentless in and of itself. It takes its particular form given the context of understanding – planetary systems, meteorological events, solid-state physics, and so on. In the human system, our content will be different than that found in physical systems (Van Geert, 1994).

Chaos theory therefore offers enormous heuristic potential for the study of lives and human development. After sporadic attempts by individual psychologists to grasp the grand principles of human development by studying the whole individual – notable attempts include Freud's case analyses, Block's *Lives Through Time*, Erikson's Gandhi and Luther, White's *Lives in Progress* – the field essentially abandoned such efforts as offering little in the way of generality. There appeared to be no regularities in lives per se, only regularity in smaller psychological phenomena such as event-related potentials, syntactic parsing, and neonatal startle patterns. Lives were seen as too hopelessly complex. However, the recent lessons from chaos theory and self-organization theory indicate that even things as complex as lives and as simple as a heartbeat are better understood with nonlinear systems.

Emotion

The emergence of dynamic theories has been critical to furthering our knowledge of emotional process in lives. Emotions are seldom continuous. Rather they are constantly fluctuating. Even though there is a degree of continuity in emotional behavior, it is supremely responsive to changes in the surrounding "reality." As long as we were constrained by romantic theories of continuity and early experience leading to repetition, emotions were perceived as troublesome and largely unimportant. Now that we are looking through a new lens, emotions begin to appear to be the driving force in a variety of processes. Emotions in human development may function as magnets or gravitational forces function in the physical sciences. A distinctive feature of emotions is their tendency to become attached to things that are in their vicinity. Thus, the reason that certain couplings – emotion–cognition, emotion–emotion, or emotion–behavior – cohere and make patterns is the result of the intrinsic property of emotion. Emotions make things matter; they make us notice our environment. In fact, in differential circumstances, they make us notice our environment in differential ways and respond in differential ways. According to Tomkins, who was already working within a cybernetic and systems framework in his 1962 and 1963 volumes of affect theory, *emotions amplify the gain of a system* – a good beginning for our examination of the work of emotions.

That emotions are involved in phase shifts in the lifecourse is patently obvious from examination of biographies. In Tomkins's terms, when chance events are emotionally magnified or amplified, they have the potential to disrupt old stabilities and initiate a course of different organization within the personality. This event corresponds to a phase shift. Such shifts do not have to be carefully planned and scripted. In an engaging piece on chance events and the lifecourse, Bandura (1982) noted the long-standing bias against studying opportunistic environmental events because we believe so strongly in continuity and accord them trivial status; however, as he documented, chance encounters play a prominent role in shaping the course of human lives. Paul Watkins, a talented teenager with a close family and a bright future, came into contact with the Manson "family" purely by chance in their early days; he fell under the influence of this group and his lifecourse was permanently directed toward violence. In another kind of chance encounter, Nancy Davis, an actress, found herself the recipient of mailings concerning communist meetings that were intended for another woman by the same name. Fearing that her reputation would be harmed if this became known, she approached the head of the Screen Actors Guild, who at the time was Ronald Reagan. The rest is history. We all can think of instances like this in our own lives. One of the present authors happened to take a course in psychology taught by Jerome Bruner. Bruner's passion was so contagious that she changed her major from math to psychology. Even Freud made room for chance and emotional connection, saying that small things are decided by the strictest application of logic, whereas more momentous decisions are made on the basis of feeling or intuition.

In his article, Bandura (1982) pointed out that though the lifecourse is deflected by "random" events, it does not mean that they do not contain lessons for a developmental psychology of the lifecourse. Random events do not all have an equal impact; that is, some chance encounters have a profound impact on lives, whereas others have an inconsequential effect. In this original work, Bandura suggested three factors that have to come into play to effect change: (a) chance events, (b) affective response, and (c) personality predispositions. In the present work, we elaborate on the notion that emotion plays a significant role in the phase shifts that occasionally herald changing life trajectories.

Dynamic Systems

The trajectories of lives may be quite unpredictable in advance. As Kierkegaard noted, lives can only be lived forward and can only be understood backward. However, life trajectories are completely deterministic in the sense that each step in the life trajectory is conditional on the preceding steps, and conditionally coupled random points lead to an overall macrostructure. It is a commonplace to observe that two individuals sharing much of the same genetic potential – children from the same family – will have widely differing interests and personalities. They even differ biologically in systems that continuously interact with the environment such as the immune system. As we progress with dynamic systems, we also find that many genetic processes are also nonlinear. These differences can now be understood as determined by inherent tendencies for self-organization and reorganization, the unpredictability of intersystemic perturbation, and the law of sensitive dependence on initial values.

As originally described by Poincaré (1952), sensitive dependence on initial conditions means that tiny differences in circumstances within a chaotic system may be amplified over time into a prodigious difference. Things grow and ramify. While behavior is bounded within certain parameters, details are quite unpredictable. This tendency may explain why the application of parametric statistics in psychology has enabled us to at times predict what the average person will do; however, our success in predicting what individuals will do has not been stunningly good. Our prediction from infancy to later periods of development has also not been very robust.

Small differences in initial conditions, combined with unpredictable perturbations, can produce quite divergent courses. Even if there are two nearly identical dots of chocolate in a white cake batter that are only an inch apart, one stir of the spatula will create two quite different swirling patterns. Two stirs will add further complexity and divergence to the pattern, and so on. Or one can think of a trajectory traced over the branches of a tree. At each branching, one is faced with one of several choices. Each succeeding branching point offers still other choices, and so on for an infinite number of choice points. Therefore, if we think of personality development as swirls in an environmental batter or branches on the tree of life, even if two people start off at nearly the same point, with nearly the same characteristics, they can wind up with very different patterns and at widely disparate places on the tree. On the other hand, they can end up even closer than they began without necessarily following the same path. Despite these divergences, each point along the trajectory is completely determined by the preceding point. As such, life pathways can be nonlinear but deterministic in a point-to-point sense.

Dynamic systems theory also leads one to expect that although we may not be able to predict individual lives, we may be able to discover "patterns" that repeat themselves, either within individuals or across individuals. In the physical and biological sciences, activity that on the face of it appears to be random or erratic is often disclosed to have underlying order and pattern. People may even share the same patterns of behavior or personality but not because they share the same "blueprints" – nor because there is a prescription or formula laid out. Patterns can emerge by assembling various units, none of which contains a "command center," because, in the case of living organisms, order and regularity are a fundamental consequence of their thermodynamics; they are open systems that use energy flow to organize and maintain stability. This means that unlike machines, biological organisms can actively evolve toward a state of higher organization (Bertalanffy, 1968; Thelen, 1987). Elements within the system "self-assemble," as the neurophysiologists say, because of energy gradients, simple association in time or place, or preexisting patterns. In the present work, we claim that the dynamic energy of emotion organizes systems and maintains stability.

Growth and development may be seen as an emergent product of a complex, chaotic system. The order that emerges in an initially chaotic condition is holistic in nature and derives from mutual effects. Within a system or between systems there may be an interdependence of variables with push-and-pull vectors that co-affect components, driving them to settle into a coherent pattern over time. In terms of human personality development, there will be the push and pull of co-affecting motor, cognitive, physiological, and emotional subsystems within the individual. There is also the co-affecting push and pull of interpersonal systems. Over time, these mutual effects settle down into recognizable patterns of activity that we identify with intrapersonal coherence or personality.

Self-organizing changes in a system occur spontaneously in far-from-equilibrium conditions, not under conditions of equilibrium. Energy flow plays a crucial role in the creation of order and of chaos. Energy flow effects are found to occur in the physical world (e.g., weather systems) as well as in living systems (e.g., colonies of ants) and supraliving systems (e.g., urban cities). Each is an entity, with a figure and ground, bounded by energy flow within. The reason that emotions may be one of the keys to understanding development within a complex system is that emotion is the concept we use when we want to consider energy, motivation, and movement. Describing a type of emotion is a way of describing a particular flow of energy – its directions, rate of flow, boundaries, and so on.

We must consider the elements and dynamic flow of energy not just within a person but also in the interpersonal environment and, eventually, in the broader ecology of life. For example, when two people meet for the first time, when a mother receives her baby shortly after birth, or when two people meet one another on a blind date, there is transient chaos. Soon, however, they then settle into patterned activity, a new pattern that neither possessed previously, that had no blueprint. This settling occurs through interdependent dynamics of coupling or entrainment. Studies involving slow-motion photography of movement patterns of mothers and infants in face-to-face play show how mothers and infants became entrained to one another's rhythms within the opening weeks of life (Stern, 1985). Many examples of entrainment can be found in both mechanical and living systems (e.g., the self-synchronization of cuckoo clocks whose pendulums are set at random and the synchronization of menstrual cycles among women who live together in dorms). Certain kinds of flocking birds such as starlings also show a kind of spontaneous but synchronous pattern of flight in response to perturbations in their environment; in response to a shot from a gun, they emerge from their roosting places in all directions, but instantaneously form a collective whole, veering off into space.

One of the advantages of nonlinear systems is that they can demonstrate qualitative changes in state. For example, Piagetians have documented the shift from nonconservation cognition to conservation cognition among children. Children first have a system for understanding quantity that is perceptual – if it looks taller, it is "more." In the next stage, children separate how the quantity "looks" from its measurement. These cognitive systems are qualitatively different. Another example of state shift involves the shift from walk to trot and trot to gallop in horses. Different patterns are not just more or less of each other; they are quite different organizations. As Van Geert (1994) has shown, conditionally coupled events – intrinsic to dynamic systems – naturally show sudden changes or a shift in state.

When beginning to study the three lives described in this book – the lives of Rogers, Perls, and Ellis – it will at first seem that order and stability and linear systems are emphasized. At first it will seem superfluous to consider chaos, complexity, and change. But as we proceed, the importance of change and even of chaos, certainly of complexity, will begin to emerge. What seems like opposites, both stability and instability, may coexist. Such paradoxes of duality, complementarity, and coexistence were recognized early on by William James (1890; see his discussion of coexisting strata of consciousness in Chapters 8 and 9). Niels Bohr (1950), having read James (1890), imported the term complementarity into physics, although as used in physics, it has a very technical meaning as it relates to laws of physics at the quantum and Newtonian levels.

Similar complementarities and paradoxes exist in living systems. For example, the existence of a conscious mind within a corporeal body is a matter of different strata. A theoretical resolution of this seemingly intransigent puzzle has been offered by contemporary biologists. They have proposed that a qualitatively new state – in this case, consciousness – emerges when a system reaches a certain level of complexity. However, this proposal entails a paradox because it means that consciousness or mind is reducible to physical matter. Several physicists regard this resolution of the mind/body problem as bordering on absurdity and have suggested that looking for physical building blocks of mind in matter would be as ludicrous as looking for quarks in a tornado (Dossey, 1989). Alternative views can be considered in the context of chaos and with respect to complementarity; as such it is not necessarily contradictory that mind and matter are dual, coexisting processes, inherent in living systems, irreducible to one another.

Physicists working with chaotic systems have found that, despite the fact that a system appeared to be random and erratic on the surface, there was often a pattern or form underneath. Moreover, chaos theory has contained within it an intrinsic duality. The theory specifies that there is both hidden order in chaos and incipient chaos in order. That is, one property of chaotic systems is that the fluctuations that occur within the context of disorder permit new forms to emerge. Chaos is a main source of the adaptive possibilities that allow organisms to be innovative, to produce originality, and to survive in the long run. At the same time, systems that appear to be quintessentially stable, such as objects within the orbiting fields of planets, sometimes suddenly break loose and fly off into space. Iterative growth patterns are also chaotic, now recognized as the period-doubling effect. That is, biological populations grow and shrink in response to the size of the food supply; many populations show an oscillating pattern between periods of growth and decline. A period is the time it takes a system to return to its original state. Robert May, the physicist turned biologist, discovered that the time it took for the system to return to its starting point doubled at certain critical values of the equation; then, after several period-doubling cycles, the population shifted to random activity. In sum, chaos leads to order and order leads to chaos.

What about chaos in such human interdependent systems as mother–infant dyads, lovers, or therapists with clients? In the process of attraction two originally independent "systems" are intensely drawn to one another and in the process become a couple. They are still two individuals and retain their individuality, but coupleness, a new state, emerges from their association. In the early stages of the relationship, where the forces of merger are most pronounced, individuals may struggle to avoid feeling engulfed, becoming entirely "coupled." So there is a push and pull in the relationship that makes the early stages of the relationship more chaotic, which derives from the periodic attraction of competing tendencies to merge and remain separate. Eventually the system settles down, and the coupleness is sustained by the history of the relationship.

Self-organizing systems are both deterministic and nondeterministic. Certain constraints are imposed on the system because of inherent properties of the system. For example, if a person is born male, he will not gestate a fetus. However, there are the open areas where the system responds to changes elsewhere in the system or to the activities of other systems. Self-organization is a property of both living and nonliving systems. An example from the latter is mechanical self-organization. The standard keyboard, known as the QWERTY system for the way that the letters are organized on the second tier of the keyboard, emerged from efforts of the designers to avoid key locking related to three interacting facts – that certain letters are used more frequently than others, that the two hands have differential skill, and that the individual fingers of the two hands have differential facility. Even though word processors have taken over the work of manual typewriters, the QWERTY keyboard is still the standard across the English-speaking world.

Emergent forms are seen in living systems as well. Newborn male cowbirds only have the tendency to develop what will become the distinctive song that they use as mature birds at mating time. Their song is perfected in the context of responses of female siblings; female cowbirds provide positive feedback when they lift their wings to the notes that come closest to the preferred species-typical tune. If a male cowbird has only male siblings, he will acquire only a weakly attracting song and will not be favored by females during mating time. If the cowbird has only female siblings, he will become a cowbird song impresario; however, though such a bird will be greatly favored by females, he will incite his male competitors to peck him to death or at the very least drive him away.

In personality development, some innate temperament traits and physiognomic characteristics may set the initial boundaries for a particular course of development, but after that there will be an infinite array of developmental outcomes depending on the dynamics of self-organization and environmental contingencies. Certain preferences for thoughts, feelings, and activity will develop over time; in dynamic systems terms, these are called attractors. Similarly, the system will also develop certain aversions for particular thoughts, feelings, and activities; in dynamic systems terms, these are called repellors. As the preferences and aversions develop over time, they appear to follow a trajectory. In dynamic systems terms, a system has a state space, which is a boundaried mapping of a system. State space is often represented by topographic maps, maps that convey the multidimensionality of the space. A nice visual metaphor here is provided by Lewis and Douglass (1997): if we think of personality in structural terms as a landscape, and the state of the organism at any time as a ball rolling around on the surface, we can visualize the state of the system as tending to gravitate to depressions in the landscape and to roll away from elevations. A system's phase state is the location of the system at any given point in time. Phase states are described as having pathways over which they course. A dynamic system is defined by a vectorfield of various tendencies of the system to change given any one of its ranges of states. The system moves through a succession of states after a given initial state is specified. The resulting path is its trajectory. The aggregate of all such trajectories is referred to as a phase portrait.

The landscape of a system is populated with attractors and repellors, regions that the system is either drawn to or deflected from. These evolve in real time in response to internal fluctuations as well as in response to perturbations from without and the inherent tendency of the system to self-organize. We will discuss three types of attractors in our studies of Perls, Rogers, and Ellis. Point attractors are stable places on the state space; they form an equilibrium pattern with tight trajectories occupying a relatively small area of the phase space. Periodic attractors show relatively small cyclic trajectories around the center of the phase space; they are sometimes also called limit-cycles. Chaotic attractors show large irregular trajectories that appear to be random or erratic. In one study of such attractors, Sabelli et al. (1995) examined mood shifts between anger, fear, and sadness in depressed and nondepressed people. Their phase portraits indicated that nondepressed subjects tended either to have point attractor patterns with respect to anger, fear, or sadness (this varied among subjects), or to show the pattern of periodic attractors, oscillating in a regular pattern between two of the emotions. In contrast, depressed people showed the chaotic attractor pattern, bouncing around among anger, fear, and sadness in no discernible pattern. We can conclude that depressed people are unstable emotionally but also poised for change.

In this book, the three patterns of attractors as exemplified in emotion traits and logical systems are very useful. In brief, we will find that Albert Ellis often provides a model of the point attractor system in personality. Carl Rogers's pattern is closest to a limit cycle, whereas Fritz Perls's pattern conforms more to the chaotic system. We will see that these particular forms are related to intrinsic properties of the particular affects that each man prefers, avoids, or ignores.

People, as well as a wide variety of other organisms and even ecologies or mechanical systems, may change and become qualitatively something other than they were when they began. In dynamic systems, variations around a central tendency (called fluctuations) are part of the system's intrinsic activity. Bifurcation in development occurs when some aspect of the system undergoes qualitative change at a "phase transition." Mathematicians consider two kinds of phase transitions. First-order phase transitions involve a sharp change from one state to another. An example in chemical systems is the phase change that takes place when water turns to ice. In living systems, the sharpest phase transitions are at birth and death. Some psychological state changes, such as those found in psychotic breaks, religious conversion experiences, or loss of consciousness, also have the quality of abrupt qualitative changes. Second-order phase transitions take more time to occur and are less well defined. Examples include personality change in the course of psychotherapy or the acquisition of "wisdom" over time in certain individuals (Baltes & Smith, 1990; Baltes & Staudinger, 1993). In our studies, Rogers will come to be seen as the best example of a person who undergoes such a transition. This mode of development has been difficult to conceptualize in linear systems with their romance of early continuous experience.

Change within a system or intersystemically can also involve periodic oscillations. In physical terms, two oscillators can be shown to demonstrate periodic complexity in their activity. Similarly, two persons can be shown to demonstrate periodic complexity over time; we will refer to this as interpersonal complementarity. Two people who have become a couple over time are at once single individuals operating within a bicomponential system. In a later chapter, we will discuss this relationship in the context of complementarity of personality structures during therapy as we study Perls, Rogers, and Ellis with the same client – Gloria. These oscillations can result in both stability and change.

In human systems, social feedback is one of the more important elements for change. And it is at these sources of feedback, with their unpredictable nature, that more "choice points" are encountered in the branching lifecourse. One of the authors attended a workshop on Gestalt therapy techniques during the 1970s that doubtless was one of the seeds for her original interest in facial expressions of emotion. After participants had gotten to know one another, they were asked to disclose their inner subjectivity in the context of a rather simple exercise that involved describing objects that the participants especially liked or disliked in the richly and exotically furnished room in which the exercise took place. The session was videotaped and played back to the participants. This feedback was a mirror of oneself, not entirely unlike the mirroring that some therapists such as Rogers or Perls might provide.

The author was greatly taken aback by her own segment. She was struck by how relatively inexpressive her face appeared to be; the weak facial activity was at variance with her inner experience and her intent to communicate her feelings. Subsequently, she became quite conscious of her facial activity and started to deliberately behave more expressively. This session occurred years before the author got involved in emotions research. Elsewhere we have suggested that being "struck" as she was, being surprised, in the context of disconfirmed expectations may serve as a control parameter activating a phase shift in personality or behavior (Magai & Nusbaum, 1996). It was not only the change in knowledge that was important, but also that it provoked a motivational change, one was "struck" by the knowledge.

Though the feedback in the preceding example was mechanical feedback in the form of viewing a segment of videotape, it occurred within a social context. The author had also sought out this kind of encounter and knew it would be socially and intellectually stimulating. That is, she placed herself in an environment where system's elements could conceivably couple in new ways and intersystemic processes would likely be brought into play. Other, less socially oriented individuals, would not likely seek out such experiences. In fact, one of the features of introverts is their virtual isolation from social feedback. The fact that they are characterologically deprived of this kind of intersystemic perturbation means that the personality is likely to fall into a state of suprastability. After our analysis of the three men, we return to the idea that certain systems, and certain interpersonal systems, may be more fundamentally stable than others. Ellis has, in many ways, a more stable personality, and, fittingly, he is socially the most isolated of the three men, the one who guards most against being "struck" with surprising events.

People are constantly providing emotional feedback to one another though they may not always be consciously aware of it. This feedback constitutes some, if not most, of the source of flux in personality systems making them more or less stable under dyadic conditions. A simple demonstration of this continuous feedback can be done with most people. One of the authors noticed one form of emotional feedback some years ago while preparing a training tape for instruction in the coding of discrete emotion using herself as the actor. When she viewed the resulting videotape some time later, she was amused to see that she had confirmed an observation made by the other author of this volume. The latter had once commented that quantitative scientists as a rule had some background contempt in their facial expressions, possibly emanating from their belief that the world is a messy place, in need of quantification and measured organization. In examining the training tape, the author found that she fulfilled the description of the contemptuous, anti-mess scientist. Despite the fact that, from a coding point of view, the expressions she posed were easily recognized and had high prototypicality, there was a subtle but discernible leakage of contempt to a few expressions. It was not very pronounced – none of the students in the course she was teaching noticed it until it was pointed out to them. The point we wish to make, however, is that such expressions can provide feedback and information to people. From her expression, one could, if very emotionally intelligent, infer that she is a person who would prefer organization, would be caught up in making the unclear, clear, and so on. However, a more pronounced expression might unintentionally repel people. One colleague at another university, who has a much more crystallized facial contempt, once complained that he could not get any students to work with him. He had a reputation for being forbidding and unapproachable, although by staying away from him, students did not get to learn that he was indeed eager to interact with them.

Let us consider the notion of *interpersonal attractors and repellors* a bit further. These are relationship states that dyadic partners either gravitate toward or away from in the development of superordinate systems. They seem to rely rather heavily on specific emotions rather than general emotionality. For example, a recent paper on complementarity and subjectivity in the therapeutic process (Magai & Papouchis, 1997) shows that a person high in trait contempt (one who has what we will call a deep contempt attractor) tends to see shame in others. As we will see later, when Ellis was working with Gloria, he focuses on her "shyness." Ellis himself expressed a fair amount of contempt. It is easy to see why the contemptuous person should think others often display shame; if they repeatedly display contempt, they will indeed see others turning away in shame. To the extent that contempt is an automatic elicitor of shame and shame involves a turning away or hiding, it is an interpersonal repellor. But, of course, as with Ellis and Gloria, there may be a good degree of preexisting shame and someone like Ellis may just become very sensitive to it.

Anger, disgust, and contempt also may be interpersonal repellors with their own specific dynamics. In one study (Magai, Hunziger, Messias & Culver, 2000), preoccupied attachment was associated with displays of facial disgust: These findings are of interest in light of the fact that preoccupied individuals report frustration in their attachment aims (Bartholomew & Horowitz, 1991). The literature suggests that it is the excessive demandingness that drives others away. However, these data would seem to indicate that disgust repellors are also at work.

The case for anger in setting an emotional climate may be much more complex. Anger is a much less distancing emotion than disgust and contempt because it contains within it a duality – at the same time that it repels, it also engages – as in Perls's case. It is a hot emotion, rather than a "cold" emotion. It is also a more turbulent emotion, offering intersystemic perturbation, a chaotic condition in which new forms of relatedness may emerge. In the film, *Three Approaches to Psychotherapy*, Gloria is treated to Perls's contempt. This creates in her anger, which aids in connecting her to Perls. She attempts to elicit anger in Perls, but he resists this and plays with her anger leading to increased frustration. Perls stated that this frustration was his goal, necessary for provoking change.

These complex interactions may help explain why dismissive individuals often pair with preoccupied individuals for purposes of emotion regulation (Magai, 1999a). There is little information on whether these relationships are stable or unstable. Research examining length of relationship as a function of attachment style (not dyadic relationship) indicates that people with a preoccupied style have more unstable relationships than people with secure and dismissive styles; people with a dismissive style have less stable relationships than people with a secure style. However, we have little empirical data on stability of pairings, though biographical analyses suggest the pairings may be both conflicted and stable (Magai, 1999a); moreover, they may be particularly prevalent among artists and other creative people. Dismissive people may need preoccupied individuals to constantly stir the caldron of emotion to shift the dismissive *system* out of its ultrastable state.

What about the emotions that function as intersystemic *attractors*? Joy and interest are clearly attractors as the work on extroverts has shown. Shame shows a more complex pattern. Kaufman (1989) and Tomkins (1963) described shame as the one negative affect that has the most positive interpersonal effects in that shame can only grow in ontogeny under conditions of relatedness; shame occurs when an interpersonal bond has been disrupted; but because the person cares about relatedness and knows that the bond can be repaired, the individual stays within the interpersonal frame. The relationship between shame and connection and contempt and disconnection also suggests that it may be hard to shame an individual with a dismissive pattern. Recall, for example, the apparent lack of embarrassment displayed by Richard Nixon as he resigned from office in the aftermath of the Watergate scandal. Since shame has a push-me–pull-me effect intrasystemically, the within system turbulence suggests that shameful individuals should be more capable of growth and organized elaboration than contemptuous individuals. Chapters 7 and 8, which deal with intellectual systems, show how Rogers's increasing emotional elaboration over time and Ellis's increasing addictive script bears this out. Perls' inability to sustain shame speaks to the other side.

Finally, we consider the aspect of chaos theory that concerns fractals. While we can think of the state of the system over time as the process, we can regard its structure at any given point as showing features of fractal geometry. One principle of fractals is known as self-similarity. That is, the form of the structure is replicated at lower and higher orders of magnifications. For example, a cauliflower has a cruciform shape as a whole. The smaller florets that comprise the cauliflower have the same shape at their own level, and subsections of the florets also show the same form in the diminutive. That is, the form is preserved, at any level one wishes to examine it. Here we contemplate the idea that self-systems may show the principle of self-similarity. Individuals reproduce themselves not only biologically but also psychologically. And there is perhaps no clearer example of this than the relationship between personal history and personal psychological theory, as Atwood and Tomkins (1976) showed in their discussion of the psychology of knowledge. In that work, they provide illustrations from the work of Freud, Adler, Jung, and Rogers, which show that "every psychological theory arises from a background of personal factors and predisposing subjective influences" (p. 170). In the present work, we will show that not only do each of the three men's biographies considered here relate to their distinctive theoretical formulations, but also that their own historical attachment patterns are reproduced in the context of the style of psychotherapy they conduct. That is, Rogers recreates an emotional climate for secure relatedness, Ellis recreates the emotional climate for detachment to emerge, and Perls recreates a climate for the turbulence of disorganized attachment leading to rapid change and potential phase shifts.

Generalization from Cases

To raise a more generic question, will anything of what we learn about the emotional dynamics of the three therapists we examine in this work be generalizable to other personalities? Perhaps. One of the ideas that dominated the work of Perls was the notion of polarities; this notion is also found at the heart of Silvan Tomkins's work, as well as that of Jung. This observation suggests that it may be fruitful to look for similar ideoaffective organizations and attachment backgrounds in these three very different men. Thus, as Thelen (1990) suggested, the study of individuals may be more than an interesting but ultimately frustrating diversion. Instead it may be *the* most fruitful activity. In gathering various observations that on the face of it seem unrelated, we may discover the coherent and recognizable patterns we know intuitively to exist but heretofore have been unable to identify. In the present work, and in our examination of three lives, we profile three patterns of affect expression that resemble types of dynamic systems; we also show how these patterns may in themselves predict how stable or discontinuous particular lives may be, that is, how permeable they may be to the incursions of random and unexpected events.

PART II

Emotion as the Integrative Link in Social and Personality Development

3 Lives Attracted to Shame and Longing

Carl Rogers

I can see what is perhaps one overriding theme in my professional life. It is my caring about communication. From my very earliest years it has, for some reason, been a *passionate* concern of mine [italics added].

Carl Rogers (1974, p. 121)

In his professional life, Rogers was devoted to helping others release their potential for growth and discovery. Individuals whom he treated in psychotherapy found the capacity to achieve growth in the context of the warm, supportive environment that he created. What is less readily recognized is that this same medium satisfied certain longings that Rogers had as well, and that the specifics of client-centered therapy, as an ideology and as a practice, were integrally related to the specifics of his affective organization. One of the more consistent themes in his life revolved around finding and elaborating emotional communion with others, as indicated in the opening quotation. This longing for communication, and the experience of communion that it promises, had very early roots.

Before we begin with the detailed chronology of his life, we should consider the historical context in which he came of age professionally, for it raises a basic enigma about his life and personality.

Overview

When Carl Rogers began to develop what would eventually become client-centered psychotherapy, the only other existing clinical model of therapy was that of psychoanalysis, and its practitioners were almost exclusively medical doctors – psychiatrists. Psychotherapy as practiced by psychiatrists was focused on the details of diagnosis, the interpretation of symbolic process, and, on occasion, the use of medication. Rogers was to emerge as an advocate of a new way of relating to patients that made attention to the emotions and emotional processes essential in psychotherapy. At the same time, he opened up the therapeutic profession to practice by nonmedical practitioners and literally created a new field within psychology.

Rogers was also the first to record and analyze the process of psychotherapy – to expose it to the scrutiny of the scientific method and to validate its usefulness. He encountered thoroughgoing resistance along the way from the psychiatric community as well as from academic psychologists, but he persevered, nevertheless, as a lone but ultimately persuasive voice of dissent and was rewarded generously by professional recognition during his own lifetime. Among other emblems of professional recognition, he was a recipient of one of the American Psychological Association's (APA's) first three awards for scientific contribution (the other two awards went to Wolfgang Koehler and Kenneth Spence), was chosen president of the American Association for Applied Psychology (AAAP), received APA's Distinguished Professional Contribution Award, and was elected president of the APA.

What was it about Rogers that led him to pioneer a method of psychotherapy that departed so radically from that which was known at the time? What was it that gave him the tenacity to persist in the face of myriad professional and personal obstacles? Where did the inspiration for the philosophy embedded in the therapeutic technique come from? The general developmental models of our day do little to inform or explicate the aspects of Rogers's life that made Rogers unique because general developmental theory is not centrally concerned with issues of individual difference. Here we will argue that the answers to these and other questions are to be found in the ideoaffective structure of his personality and in the significant socioemotional experiences of his early and later life. We go beyond this general and somewhat banal psychobiographical statement that life experiences shape personal biography to the more radical claim that emotional events of a particular type produce emotional residue in the form of ideoaffective structures. These structures, in turn, result in particular patterns of information processing and particular patterns of coping with emotional experience that have ramifications for the content of a person's philosophy of life and work. In the case of Rogers, these structures are graphically present in all materials that we would wish to examine – his thinking, his emotional expressivity, and his pattern of relating to people.

In examining Rogers's life, we encounter what appear to be various inconsistencies and contradictions. For example, by all accounts, Rogers was a caring husband and father and a sensitive and empathic man in his interactions with clients. He also had a large and devoted student following. However, to many of his colleagues throughout his long and varied professional career, he was an irritant of monumental proportions – especially if they happened to be part of an entrenched establishment. He often got embroiled in political fights with members of his department and with administrators. Many people regarded him as interpersonally reserved and distant. How then, do we characterize Rogers, as warm or aloof?

What about his attachment patterns? Attachment theory (Bowlby, 1969, 1973) suggests that if individuals have secure attachments with their primary caregivers, they will show certain dispositions to respond in a trusting, noncontentious way with other social partners. From the biographical and autobiographical materials that we examined, it appears that Rogers's primary attachment relationship was secure, versus avoidant or ambivalent. Yet, his interactions with other social partners could be fractious, as indicated earlier.

Rogers could also be painfully shy, and yet he was drawn to people and even did group encounter therapies. He often made others the center of his existence. He was also often in conflict with others, but he was not a particularly "angry" or hostile man.

How do we reconcile these various descriptions of Rogers's personality? Was he aloof or warm? Caring or attacking? Social or shy? Mild or angry? General personality theories do not seem to help us understand such unevenness. Prevailing models typically render the description of individuals in terms of attachment patterns or particular personality dimensions, for example, along the dimensions of extroversion/neuroticism/psychoticism (Eysenck, 1953) or in terms of a guilt versus a shame orientation (Lewis, 1971). Granted, Rogers can be readily characterized as more secure than avoidant or ambivalent, more introverted (shy) than extroverted, and more prone to shame than guilt. But these characterizations fail to do him justice, and they do not in and of themselves account for certain important details of his adult life and work, such as his outstanding achievements, his midlife crisis, his therapeutic ideology, and the specifics of the differential manner in which he related to family, clients, and colleagues.

In the following discussion, we attempt to capture Rogers's life and persona in a way that preserves the inherent complexity of his personality. Emotion is the link between the events of his life and the development of his personality or ideoaffectology (Tomkins, 1963). Emotion links his attachment patterns with the rest of his social and intellectual world. Before proceeding to a detailed socioemotional analysis of his life, we provide a brief synopsis of his ideoaffectology.

In terms of attachment theory, Rogers's primary attachment relationship during infancy appears to have been of the secure quality, although subsequent developments qualified this. Nevertheless, as predicted from theory, this early security was to lay the foundation for the capacity for intimacy in his closest interpersonal relationships. Going beyond this, and adding ideoaffective texture to the basics, we discover that his affective organization was an admixture of differentially developed emotions, the most dynamically important ones being joy, interest, shame, disgust, and anger. Snapshots of Rogers' emotional configuration can be gleaned from both his own reflections and those of others who were intimately acquainted with him.

Rogers presents the following picture of himself in his autobiography:

> As a person I see myself as fundamentally positive in my approach to life; somewhat of a lone wolf in my professional activities, socially rather shy but enjoying close relationships; capable of a deep sensitivity in human interaction though not always achieving this; often a poor judge of people, tending to overestimate them; possessed of a capacity for setting other people free, in a psychological sense; capable of a dogged determination in getting work done or in winning a fight; eager to have an influence on others but with very little desire to exercise power or authority over them (Rogers, 1972, p. 29).

The tendency to be socially shy and a "lone wolf" extended back to early childhood. Helen, the woman who became his wife but who also knew him in youth, described the boy of her childhood as "shy, sensitive, and unsocial" (H. E. Rogers, 1965, p. 94). Moreover, Rogers as an adult had a nonverbal self-presentation that made him appear tentative, somewhat shameful, and a bit unsure of himself, as we will see later.

Rogers also described himself as a person who had difficulty with the expression of anger. Though he often found himself embroiled in conflict, he tried to avoid "open combat" and would often work hard to bring warring parties to a point of conciliation. Although this trait may have been useful in his sparrings with academic colleagues, it caused periodic difficulties in his personal life, and, among other things, precipitated a midlife crisis, as described later on.

> I regret it when I suppress my feelings too long and they burst forth in ways that are distorted or attacking or hurtful. I have a friend whom I like very much but who has one particular pattern of behavior that thoroughly annoys me. Because of the usual tendency to be nice, polite, and pleasant I kept this annoyance to myself for too long and, when it finally burst its bounds, it came out not only as annoyance but as an attack on him (Rogers, 1980, p. 18).

And later in life,

> I am often slow to sense and express my own anger. Consequently, I may only become aware of it and express it later. In a recent encounter group I was at different times very angry with two individuals. With one I was not conscious of it until the middle of the night and had to wait until the next morning to express it. With the other, I was able to realize and express it in the session in which it occurred (Kirschenbaum, 1979, p. 333).

Other family members also provided affective portraits of Rogers. Once, while in a critical mood, his daughter wrote him the following:

> I feel that I have a right to point out to you, although this may be dirty words in your language, since I'm your daughter and have grown up under your parentage, that both as parents and grandparents, you *say* you want people, including children I surmise, to express their feelings; but you reward with love those who keep their angry feelings to themselves (Kirschenbaum, 1979, p. 362).

By the time he was seventy-five years old, Rogers believed that he had made some progress in his ability to deal with anger, though he still found it hard "to confront with negative feelings a person about whom I care deeply" (Rogers, 1980, p. 85). In other basic aspects of his personality, he felt that he had remained essentially unchanged.

> It seems to me that I am still – inside – the shy boy who found communication very difficult in interpersonal situations: who wrote love letters which were more eloquent than his direct expression of love, who expressed himself freely in highschool themes, but felt himself too "odd" to say the same things in class. That boy is still very much a part of me (Rogers, 1980, p. 80).

On the basis of these and many other descriptions of his personality, and in light of our observation of his actual behavior as he interacted within the emotionally charged climate of a psychotherapeutic interview, we found we could summarize some of the key features of his personality in emotion terms. Among the positive emotions, *interest* and *joy* are "up front" in Rogers; they dominate his social persona and are present fairly continuously. Another emotion that is fairly characterlogic but tends to hover in the background of his personality is *shame*, which is related to shyness and social anxiety (Gottschalk & Gleser, 1969). These three emotions are well developed in Rogers. They are key in the way that he presents himself socially – happy to be in your presence, interested in what you are saying, unassuming in appearance, hesitant in manner, and dysfluent in speech. Other emotions in Rogers are less pervasive and seem secondary, such as *disgust*, which is seen in selected interpersonal aloofness (along with contempt, a closely related emotion, which occasionally manifests itself when Rogers is in the process of analyzing non-Rogerian systems of psychotherapy). *Anger*, for Rogers, is "undeveloped" (Malatesta & Wilson, 1988); undeveloped emotions are those for which there is low tolerance and little expressive aptitude (Malatesta & Wilson, 1988). We will enlarge upon these and other points as we examine the details of Rogers's life.

We begin with an account of his early life and some of the important developmental influences of that time and then turn to other significant developmental sequelae. In his early life the several emotion themes mentioned above are already present: joy and interest within the attachment relationship, and anger and shame within the broader family dynamic. As we will see, in Rogers's family system, anger is particularly suppressed whereas shame is given expression and is multiply reinforced by siblings, religious doctrine, and social experiences. Disgust emerges as a latent possibility in the context of the attachment relationship and in religious training.

Rogers's Early Life

Carl Rogers was born on January 8, 1902, in Oak Park, Illinois, a suburb of Chicago, to an upper-middle-class family. He was the fourth of six children, five boys and a girl. Both of his parents had come from agricultural families and his father, who had a graduate degree in engineering and quickly established a thriving engineering firm early in his career, later became somewhat of a gentleman farmer, buying and supervising a prosperous working farm. Carl's mother, also from a farming background, had two years of college education, which was relatively unusual for a woman at that time, but she did not pursue a career; instead, she primarily concerned herself with raising her family and assisting on the farm.

Carl was the baby of the family for over five years. As a young boy, he was sickly, and his parents feared that he might not survive childhood. He recalls his relationship with his mother as having been warm. In attachment theory terms, he was probably more securely than insecurely attached, though being sickly most likely tempered the relationship, in ways described later on. (One basis for inferring a secure attachment in infancy comes from later biographical material. Attachment theorists look at the quality of intimate relationships in adulthood to inform understandings of attachment style in childhood; secure children are able to develop relatively unconflicted relationships in intimate partnerships. In Roger's case, as we will see, his relationship with his wife was described as intimate by both of them.)

Carl's relationship with his father was probably less central and more distant inasmuch as the elder Rogers was often away from home on business trips. One does not get the impression that the father was cold or remote, simply consumed with affairs of business and not often at home, and he apparently did his best to try and compensate for this. Carl's brother, John, relates, "'Since he was away so much of the time during World War I, this [particular outing with the family] gave him an opportunity to further enjoy his children. If he couldn't stay home, he'd try to take someone with him when possible'" (Kirschenbaum, 1979, p. 7). Carl especially remembered the time that his father took him along on an extended trip to several construction sites in the south and east; it was while he was in the eighth grade, and Rogers remembers it as the time he got the closest to his father.

In considering the father's relationship with his children, remember that this is the first decade of the twentieth century and the Parsonian split between the affective and instrumental for men and women of that time was the norm rather than the exception. We will see that Ellis's and Perls's fathers were also largely "absent" in their early lives; however, the circumstances were quite different from that of Rogers's and involved much more active neglect and mixed affective involvement. Rogers apparently regretted not being closer to his father, for his relationships with other men in adult life were distant if not combative. At the age of seventy-five, Rogers reflected on his growing ability to get close to men:

> I have developed deeper and more intimate relationships with men; I have been able to share without holding back, trusting the security of the friendship. Only during my college days – never before or after – did

I have a group of really trusted, intimate men friends. So this is a new, tentative, adventurous development which seems very rewarding (Rogers, 1980, p. 84).

Analysis of Rogers' Earliest Life

From a developmental point of view, an infant's earliest and perhaps most significant affective experiences occur within the context of how his or her cry of distress is answered (Tomkins, 1963; Bowlby, 1969). It is in this context that the child learns that distress does not need to be interminable and that other human beings can assist in the alleviation of distress. Under less favorable circumstances, he may learn an altogether different lesson – that distress is something he has to cope with on his own, or even that distress may be intensified in the presence of another.

The quality of attachment that a child forms to a caregiver – secure, ambivalent, or avoidant – has been shown to be largely, though not exclusively, associated with different styles of caregiving. When the caregiver is warm and sensitively responsive to the infant's emotional signals, he is likely to develop a secure attachment to that figure; the primary features of security are a trust in the availability of the caregiver and a general lack of fearfulness (Ainsworth et al., 1978).

In our present analysis, we find that Rogers most likely experienced his earliest encounters with his mother as rewarding, and therefore he probably was successful in establishing a basically secure attachment to her. Although attachment writers cautioned early on that attachment styles not be confused with personality traits, the literature has begun to treat them as such. Indeed, the secure attachment style has acquired a halo effect in the literature, to the extent that it is viewed as a relatively enduring disposition that confers ongoing security in development and whose attributes coincide with optimal mental health (Magai & McFadden, 1995). In fact, the term secure attachment, as applied to Rogers, may be useful in distinguishing the more basic qualities of Rogers's relationship with his mother – in contrast to the kind experienced by Ellis and Perls, whose relationships conformed more to an avoidant pattern and a mixed avoidant/ambivalent pattern, respectively. However, we believe that other circumstances of Rogers's early life and other developmental sequelae moderated this pattern in substantial ways.

Affect theory (Tomkins, 1962, 1963, 1991) places a great deal of emphasis on the child's experiences with reference to his or her cry of distress and on the child's feelings of love for the caregiver and ultimate disenchantment as formative developments. During the earliest period of infancy, the child comes to find that other human beings, apart from their role in helping to alleviate distress, are (or are not) gratifying in other regards. Under fortunate circumstances (i.e., where the caregiver takes pleasure in the infant and communicates this), the child falls in love with her/him and experiences a deep sense of "communion" (Tomkins, 1962, 1963). The term "communion" is interesting in this context; it at once connotes something spiritual and almost magical about the relation between mother and infant, an aspect that is sometimes mentioned by mothers when nursing their infants, but it also manages to convey the idea of dialogue – in this case a nonverbal, affective dialogue. Beyond these earliest experiences, the infant's encounter with minor and brief separations only help to heighten the positive value of the caregiver for the child. According to Tomkins, the very nature of the affective system makes the human being particularly vulnerable to psychological addictions, and the attachment relationship – engendering as it does both intensely positive and intensely negative experiences, fulfilling communions and distressing separations – qualifies as one of those addictions. If, on balance, the experiences of communion and joy predominate in his experiences, the individual will seek to reestablish similarly gratifying states of communion with others later in life. Young Carl may have been particularly vulnerable to the psychological addiction of attachment and communion given his precarious health. His cry of distress would have been more anxiety-provoking to his parents than that of a healthy child and may have resulted in particularly attentive caregiving, which magnified the affective salience of partings and reunions.

This description helps us to understand Rogers's "passionate" interest in communication, and the intensity of the empathic experience he is able to achieve in the context of the psychotherapeutic encounter, as discussed in more detail later on. However, Rogers's basically secure attachment and his delight in communion as an infant are no guarantee of an uncomplicated childhood or later adulthood, and, indeed, the assumption of a secure attachment profile does not help us understand certain complexities of his life.

The idealized descriptions of Rogers's early development fail to accommodate the actual details of his infancy – an infancy that was marked by fragility and illness, which conceivably altered the nature of his subjective experience. The circumstance of being the sick and closely watched baby of the family probably made him more precious to his parents than he might ordinarily have been. One can readily envision an anxious and vigilant mother, overly involved and perhaps overly intrusive.

What are the consequences of heightened maternal attentiveness? Conceivably, such conditions intensify the gratifications of communion, as suggested earlier vis à vis the psychological addiction theory of Tomkins. However, if the attentions are experienced as out of the infant's control, the child could feel threatened with engulfment, necessitating the learning of defensive avoidance strategies. Thus, security could be tinged with insecurity, and a sense of omnipotent narcissism might be tinged with tension and the need for vigilance. Such conditions create a more complex experiential world, one that would be more consistent with the developmental complexity we see in Rogers both early and later on. At the very least, the presence of an anxious, hovering caregiver must have heightened the infant Carl's sense of vulnerability, which may have been a factor in his reticence to join in play with other children later on. It is germane to note from developmental research that infants who are sick in the sense of being born prematurely show a clear pattern of behavioral inhibition and reticence with other children as early as age three (Malatesta-Magai, 1991).

In summary, Carl's early experiential world was one of both vulnerability and specialness. He was the center of his mother's attention during infancy, a circumstance that must have been basically gratifying, even if the attentiveness occasionally bordered on intrusiveness. His siblings also apparently doted on him, teaching him to read at home by the time he was four. That he was treated in a special way for a prolonged period of time is suggested by the fact that he did not enter grammar school until he was almost seven, despite the fact that he was reading at the fourth grade level by then.

We have introduced the notion of a complexly textured secure attachment. But a basically secure attachment is no guarantee of a secure childhood. Nor is an infancy of fragility in itself any guarantor of a shy or retiring childhood as we now know from research on Kagan's "behaviorally inhibited" infants (Kagan & Seidman, 1991; Kagan, Snidman & Arcus, 1992), some small fraction of whom overcame their shyness as they matured. Thus, it stands to reason that Carl's experiences of vulnerability and specialness had to be developmentally reinforced to sustain emerging behavioral tendencies. Other aspects of the personality organization can emerge and compete for representation as new developmental demands are made on individuals, as family circumstances change, and as children enter the larger community in which their families live. As Tomkins put it:

> Particularly during infancy and childhood, it is the case that we do not understand what has happened to us until it happens again and again with sufficient clarity and intensity that stable objects and relationships between objects can be constructed. One of the consequences of such a view of the nature of early learning is that one can never specify whether any particular experience will or will not have consequences pathologic or otherwise in the life history of the individual, since this will depend on the extent to which later experience amplifies or attenuates the significance of the earlier experience and the cognitive constructions which are placed upon the entire set of experiences as they are lived and experienced in memory and thought (Tomkins, 1963, p. 78).

The Early School Years

Did entry to school coincide with an important developmental transition in terms of Rogers' affective experiences? There is much to suggest that it did. In permitting young Carl to attend school at the age of seven, it seems likely that his parents felt that he was finally out of danger and now ready to handle the new developmental demands that would be placed upon him. From Rogers's autobiography, it is clear that he began to experience multiple strictures on his behavior not long after that. He was no longer the darling baby of the family (another child had been born), no longer at risk, and love became contingent on good behavior. His siblings, who had earlier been attentive and solicitous, were now prepared to treat him more like a peer, which amounted to extended roughhouse and barrages of taunting and teasing. "Margaret [Carl's sister] remembered how 'those boys nearly tore each other limb from limb in their arguing, but after they were over with it they were good friends again'" (Kirschenbaum, 1979, p. 5). "[M]uch family humor . . . very often had a cutting and biting edge to it. We teased each other unmercifully, and I did not realize until I was adult that this was not a necessary part of human relationships" (Rogers, 1972, p. 30).

Both parents had a deeply ingrained work ethic and were steeped in religious fundamentalism. The parents and children constituted a close-knit and closed family system, distrusting the larger community and being committed to the religious ideals of a simple life devoid of temptations. Most social activities involving people outside the family were forbidden. His parents were "in many subtle and affectionate

ways, very controlling of our behavior" (Rogers, 1961, p. 4). "It was assumed by them and accepted by me that we were different from other
people. . . . We had good times together within the family, but we did not
mix" (Rogers, 1961, p. 5). Carl could attend school, but he was to come
directly home afterward; he was not to play with other children.

Rogers's life had changed indeed – from beloved infant to duty-
bound child and butt of sibling teasing. In light of such dramatic re-
versals of fortune, young Carl must have experienced an emotional revolution of Copernican proportions. Tomkins (1962, 1963) believes that
"disenchantment" has been seriously underestimated as a psychological
force in development. Disenchantment results from the gap between the
ideal and idealized parent of infancy and the frustrating, disappointing
parent of childhood, between the parent who gives love unstintingly and
unconditionally and the parent who exacts terms and conditions and,
even more disappointingly, the parent who may squander attention on
a new sibling. Disenchantment poses a critical threat to communion and
to identification with the caregiver. The idealized parent is unmasked as
imperfect, as deserving of contempt, and the child's emergent identification with the parent undergoes revision. As a consequence of the fact
that early adoration for the parent is now colored with disdain for this
imperfect object, the child experiences shame and alienation both within
himself and with respect to the caregiver. The experience of disenchantment also provokes some of the first salient psychological experiences
of disgust. According to Tomkins (1991), disgust is a reaction that is generated when something "that was once good turns bad." The physical
prototype occurs in the context of taking in food that is subsequently
found to be distasteful and is then ejected. At the psychosocial level,
it involves the rejection of the formerly good object. Normally, disenchantment is balanced by the experience of continued nurturance, and
disgust is submerged in consciousness, remaining only as a latent possibility. However, in Carl's case, disgust must have been magnified in two
ways. First, because his sickness and fragility necessitated greater solici-
tation by his parents and more frequent and gratifying interventions, the
transition to normalized parental behavior as he became well must have
been more acutely disappointing. Second, oversolicitous parental care
can feel intrusive. Turning away – a prototype of the disgust response –
is one of the few effective avoidance strategies available to babies. Given
all these considerations, the potential for future disgust recruitment was
well established. However, the response still remained relatively latent,
awaiting further intellectual and experiential developments.

The experience of a particularly intense disenchantment may also have laid the groundwork for heightened sensitivity to other "discrepancies" that had an affective component. In Rogers's later and more mature theoretical expositions (see Chapter 7), he was drawn to the idea of "ideal" growth and "idealized longings." For Rogers, one task of human growth was to close the gap between the real and the ideal self through the process of growing self-acceptance. The idealized self, like the idealized parent, could not help but disappoint, leading to feelings of shame and self-disgust. With a more realistic and accepting view of the self, such unpleasant sensations could be avoided.

If we are right in our analysis, Carl's imperfectly secure attachment to his mother, while ensuring a basic trust in humanity and an ability to sustain intimacy in a primary relationship, was tinged with latent distancing defenses that enabled him to escape from overly intrusive encounters when necessity dictated. In addition, attachment security is only one significant component of personality development; consequently, as Carl grew into the larger interpersonal world of his family and community, he learned a new set of emotional equations. As he matured, he confronted the everyday disenchantments common to children maturing from infancy to childhood, compounded by the arrival of a younger sibling just as he was entering childhood. His developing experiential world was further complicated by the discovery of restrictions on behavior that were idiosyncratic to his family. As Carl observed with reference to his parents' treatment of his siblings, it was clear that anything that could be construed as exciting – cards, movies, dancing – was forbidden. Worst of all, that most exciting object of all – another human (if outside the immediate family) – was strictly out of bounds; the family simply did not mix with others.

As such, Carl's early interest and excitement in others, previously a source of communion and deep gratification, was now sharply restricted. Any time Carl felt excitement stirring at the prospect of meeting others, he also experienced an accompanying sense of anxiety, an anxiety that could be felt in the very pit of his stomach, one consequence of which was ulcers at an early age. Since discussion of feelings was also not something with which the Rogers family felt comfortable, he was often left to struggle on his own with feelings of internal distress. Eventually, however, and despite the discomfort and dread he often experienced in meeting others, something deeper, more archaic, and more fundamental drove him forward. Once out from under the careful eye of his family and on his own, Rogers began to take risks.

The great experiment of his young adult life was to put to the test whether his bids for intimacy would be met with the ridicule he experienced with his siblings and the "punishment" threatened by his parents, or whether he would be able to recapture the communion of infancy. As Tomkins noted, "Disenchantment with the primary identification figures is perhaps the most serious threat to communion to which the human being is vulnerable. . . . The outcome of disenchantment is ultimately a renewed quest for the lost love object" (Tomkins, 1962, p. 450).

The issue of punishment and its consequences requires some discussion. Tomkins stressed that repeated exposure to specific kinds of emotion, as experienced in the self or in others, leads to a consolidation around these emotions. The question of disciplinary practices is especially germane to the issue of emotion socialization. Discipline encounters between parents and children constitute repetitive, salient, emotionally charged events that cannot help but have a profound impact on the character of a child's emotional development.

Rogers's autobiography made it very clear that his experiences were partly those of love-withdrawal, practices that are thought to provoke anxiety and guilt. Also, given the family's intense religiosity, their avoidance of strong emotion, the parents' high level of education, and all the emphasis they placed on the practical and pragmatic, it is likely that the parents also relied on induction, which emphasizes the nature and consequences of misbehavior and is associated with the development of a strong conscience. Rogers's parents both gave much love and used it to induce conformity. They were "devoted and loving"; they were also "masters of the art of subtle and loving control." Power assertion techniques were not the order of the day: "I do not remember ever being given a direct command on an important subject" (Rogers, 1972, p. 30).

Considering the environment Rogers grew up in, he should have been a generally obedient and responsible child; as an adult he should have demonstrated a strong superego and been relatively responsive to guilt inductions. As it turns out, Carl's early childhood was indeed characterized by steadfast obedience; he came directly home from school, attended to whatever chores there were that had to be done, and, as instructed by his parents, kept away from other children. As a result, Rogers "had no close friends . . . all through elementary school" (Rogers, 1980, p. 28). His primary escape was into literature; he became a voracious reader making his way through anything and everything within reach, even going so far to read his father's heavy scientific tomes on the latest approaches to agriculture. "I was buried in books – stories of Indian and frontier life to the extent that I could lay hands on them, but 'anything' was grist to my mill. If there was nothing else, I read the encyclopedia, or even the dictionary" (Rogers, 1972, p. 31). He was especially drawn to nature books and mentions the "Girl of the Limberlost" series by Gene Stratton-Porter as a particular favorite of his.

Rogers's absorption in books substituted for human contact for the time being. As he grew older, the yearning for human companionship became keener and more insistent, and he was eager to make social contact with others. However, family moves caused him to change high schools three times, and he was unable to establish any enduring social bonds.

Rogers's preadolescent and early adolescent years provided further material for the repetition of earlier themes of social isolation and aloofness and for consolidation of shame/shyness and disgust. While other children were practicing social skills, experimenting with extrafamilial sources of social intimacy, and otherwise having fun, Rogers worked, read, and daydreamed. During this time, he continued to be exposed to a religious doctrine that emphasized special privilege, purity, and avoidance of the contamination of sinning and of sinners.

> My mother was a person with strong religious convictions whose views became increasingly fundamentalist as she matured. Two of her biblical phrases, often used in family prayers, stick in my mind and give the feeling of her religion: "Come out from among them and be ye separate"; "All our righteousness is as filthy rags in thy sight, oh Lord." (The first expressed her conviction of superiority, that we were of the "elect" and should not mingle with those who were not so favored; the second her conviction of inferiority, that at our best we were unspeakably sinful.) My father was involved too in the family prayers, church attendance, and the like ... (Rogers, 1972, pp. 29–30).

Such a religious doctrine inherently engenders disgust. Tension is created when the disgust that would normally be prompted by a religiously inspired exclusionary identification is at the same time blocked – because to acknowledge or act on disgust would be to reject others, which is also antithetical to religious doctrine. In time, Rogers developed a loving acceptance of certain individuals (family and needy clients) and a disdain for others who did not subscribe to his particular brand of epistemology. In his case, the targets for his disdain were many of his work colleagues – bright people with PhDs, MDs, and positions of authority but who, if we may be permitted to put words in Rogers's mouth, could otherwise be regarded as nincompoops.

Period of Rebellion

During late adolescence and early adulthood, certain threads of thematic continuity occurred in Rogers's life, but there was also one dramatic departure. Somewhat paradoxically, aspects of his affective organization helped account for both phenomena. To recapitulate, at this point, shame/shyness was a well-consolidated feature of Rogers's personality, anger was grossly underdeveloped, disgust was latent, and affiliative needs loomed large. During Rogers's period of relative social isolation, social shyness was magnified, but there was another consequence for Rogers's subsequent intellectual development. In individuals who are intellectually inclined, intellectual resources can be used to buffer the sense of isolation. Being comfortable with time alone and the tendency to introspect, analyze, and engage in flights of fantasy are skills that can be applied to an array of intellectual endeavors that require concentration and originality. These resources also engender escape and coping strategies for loneliness and isolation. As such, Rogers was well fortified not just to stake an original intellectual course but also to endure any temporary rejection he might experience from his family, as he did when he broke with their religious doctrine for a much more experimental one of his own choosing. The period of rebellion in late adolescence also prefigured the rebellious streak he would display throughout his later professional career, as he exercised intellectual originality, endured social isolation from individuals he could dismiss as misguided and unenlightened, and satisfied affiliative needs in other arenas.

Erik Erikson (1963) asserted that one of the more important tasks of late adolescence and young adulthood is the achievement of identity, which requires individuation. The task of individuation is a difficult one, since the crystallization of a unique sense of ego necessarily entails a differentiation of self and separation from others. It also engenders the threat of loss of love and communion. However, according to Tomkins, if the original experience of communion is sufficiently gratifying, then the "loneliness of individuation can be better tolerated and the achievement of a sense of one's own identity is thereby favored" (Tomkins, 1962, p. 111).

As Rogers graduated from high school and entered college, he began to take his first tentative steps toward establishing his own separate identity. Though he enrolled at the University of Wisconsin as family tradition dictated, the expanded world of individuals, ideas, and opportunities drew him further and further away from the more provincial attitudes in which he had been indoctrinated at home. He began to develop important social relationships with other young men at the YMCA dormitory where he resided and to reject the idea of an agricultural career, and started leaning toward a religious vocation. However, during his junior year, he was selected to join a delegation of students and professional workers from the YMCA to travel to Peking and other parts of the orient on a program of intercultural exchange. During the six-month trip, he was exposed to a range of liberal religious and political philosophies, which greatly expanded his awareness of a range of options. These ideas so changed his outlook that he could no longer uncritically espouse the views he had absorbed from his family. During this time, which Rogers refers to as his period of rebellion, he established his own independent views and broke with his family's traditions. This rebellion was not accomplished without conflict, since he developed ulcers, which were diagnosed upon his return home and required hospitalization and intensive treatment for some six months; he temporarily withdrew from classes and worked part time.

Though Rogers broke with the religious fundamentalism of his family, particularly the content of their ideology, he did not abandon religiosity per se, nor that aspect of religiosity that emphasizes man's essential humbleness before God. He could rebel against the religion of his family and could tolerate the tension that this generated because he was reassured by a fundamentally secure attachment and because he was comfortable with intellectual idiosyncrasy. As such, this particular discontinuity in his life, the rejection of a conservative religious philosophy, did not lead to affective reorganization, as did Perls's adolescent rebellion. In Rogers we see the continuity of affiliative and shame themes. In the case of Perls, shame was transformed into contempt.

During the same time that Rogers was experimenting with his religious ideology, he was able to keep up contacts with a classmate, Helen, with whom he had become enamored. He graduated in June of 1924 with a degree in history and married Helen two months later. Together they headed for New York and Union Theological Seminary, a school with a liberal orientation, much to the chagrin of his fundamentalist parents.

We pause here to comment on Rogers's wife, his relationship with her, and his relationship with his children, since these issues are germane to the thesis that Rogers's basic attachment style was of the secure type.

From various sources it is apparent that the relationship Rogers had with his wife throughout their long marriage was one that was a fundamental source of intimacy and gratification for both of them, which is not to say they did not have their periods of difficulty. In describing her husband, Helen painted a picture of a man who was openly communicative and empathic with her: "We were able to establish a free communication with each other, never allowing misunderstandings or hurts to fester. It gave us a basis for growth and closeness which has lasted through the years. His ability to listen and be empathic was there in the very first years of our marriage" (H. E. Rogers, 1965, p. 95). From other accounts, it was clear that Carl was a loyal and caring partner, though he and Helen had their difficulties toward the end of her life when she became ill and dependent and when she began to regret the early subordination of her own career to his.

In terms of his children, we see a replication of apparently secure attachment relationships. As a father, he clearly enjoyed the recreational time he spent with his children – building boats and mobiles with them and engaging in other joint activities – although Rogers was often away from home because of professional obligations. It is obvious from the children's accounts (as adults) that he inspired love and admiration in them. Both David and Natalie reported being able to talk readily and fairly openly with their father in their early years. They apparently got even closer to him after the family moved to Chicago. In terms of careers, both children pursued professions that closely reflected their parents' interest in people and art; David trained as a physician and became a successful administrator, becoming successively the chair of the medical school at Johns Hopkins, the head of medical research at Johnson and Johnson Pharmaceutical Company, and most recently the head of the National Task Force on AIDS. Natalie earned her masters degree in art therapy, became very involved in intensive small group work, and sometimes co-led encounter groups with her father.

We return now to the period of early adulthood. During his second year at Union Seminary, Rogers began to take courses at Columbia Teachers' College where he came under the influence of the educational philosophy of John Dewey and the clinical inspiration of the psychologist Leta Hollingworth. Shortly afterward, he left Union Seminary in favor of a full schedule of classes in clinical and educational psychology at Columbia Teachers' College.

In 1926 he applied for and received a fellowship at the Institute of Child Guidance where he undertook his doctoral research – which involved developing a test for measuring the personality adjustment of children – and was exposed to a broader eclecticism than he had found at Teachers' College. After graduation, he accepted a position as a psychologist in the Child Study Department of the Rochester Society for the Prevention of Cruelty to Children. He remained there eight years, rising to the position of director. The job was somewhat professionally isolating, but it gave him an opportunity to develop his self-confidence. In addition, certain experiences galvanized him to begin thinking about counseling and therapy in ways that would eventually cause him to break with tradition.

Between 1937 and 1938, the Rochester Guidance Center was formed with the intention that the Child Study Department, of which Rogers was the head, would be at its core. The psychiatric community was committed to ensuring that a psychiatrist headed the center. Rogers was of a different mind. He fought for his claim to the directorship and eventually won. He published a well-received book during that time – *Clinical Treatment of the Problem Child* – and soon was lured from Rochester to Ohio State University where he assumed duties as a full professor.

From here on out Rogers's star rose quickly. He began formulating the ideas that would become the emblem of client-centered psychotherapy, published and lectured widely, and within five years was invited to establish a counseling center at the University of Chicago. During his Chicago years (1945–57), he taught at the university, established the counseling center, did research on psychotherapy and personality change, was elected and served as the president of the American Psychological Association, published his now-famous book *Client-Centered Psychotherapy*, and received APA's Distinguished Scientific Career Award. He also developed innovations in educational methods and in graduate training in clinical work, with emphasis on equality, freedom, and creativity. The years at Chicago were exciting and for the most part happy ones, save for two circumstances – one involving ongoing difficulties with the psychiatrists at the university who were in general opposed to his unorthodox teaching and counseling techniques and another involving a client that culminated in a period of great personal distress. The latter event is particularly illuminating with respect to affect dynamics and, in particular, Roger's own complex emotional organization. We will return to this event momentarily.

Rogers next received an attractive offer from the University of Wisconsin and moved to Madison in 1957, where he and his family remained for seven years. Part of the lure of Wisconsin was that he would have dual appointments in the departments of psychiatry and psychology. Although the conditions at first appeared to offer even further opportunities to develop his therapeutic ideology, advance his career, and further his ideas on humanistic education and therapist training, Rogers regarded the psychiatric residents as being of disappointing caliber. One can envision Rogers contending with ever-increasing tides of disgust over time. He also met with considerable resistance from the psychology faculty in response to his ideas concerning teaching and graduate education. Rogers's radical ideas and unconventional style of teaching – "facilitating" rather than lecturing, clashed with the traditional "rigorous" curriculum that was well entrenched at Wisconsin. Rogers did battle with those who opposed him, but he eventually resigned from his appointment in the psychology department in frustration, retaining only his appointment in psychiatry. While at Wisconsin he was also engaged in research on process and outcome in psychotherapy, especially in the context of work with more deeply disturbed clients.

Rogers spent a year as a visiting fellow at the Western Behavioral Sciences Institute in California from 1962 to 1963; this was a humanistically oriented nonprofit organization devoted to the study of interpersonal process and constructive change. He found it a stimulating and congenial place to be, and when he was invited to join the staff, he did so in 1964. Here he was able to promote his humanistic ideals and practices in the context of an interdisciplinary milieu with like-minded, progressive colleagues. He was able to pursue his interest in promoting growth in normal people by using what came to be known as t-group or encounter group process. He described his time there as personally invaluable.

When the administration changed to a more structured one several years later, the more humanistically oriented members, including Rogers, split off from the Western Behavioral Center to form the new Center for Studies of the Person in 1968. This small group of individuals, who collectively spanned several different fields of specialty in the behavioral sciences, constituted a warmly supportive psychological community dedicated to enhancing the continued experimentation and growth of its members. For Carl Rogers, it turned out to be the ultimate and perfect resolution of his search for the environment that could nurture communion with others while still fostering growth of the self.

An Analysis of Rogers' Career and Adult Life: Prominent Themes

In the introductory section, we noted that Rogers presented somewhat of an enigma to the extent that he was seen in quite different lights by the various people who knew him – as warm, caring, and empathic by some but as aloof and somewhat combative by others. This apparent contradiction is rendered less of a paradox when one considers the nature of his communion/disengagement experiences as well as the elaboration, in development, of certain pivotal emotions. Here we will pursue the line of argument that the developmental juxtaposition of an unusually satisfying and protracted period of communion with his mother, followed by a rather severe disillusionment and disenchantment, laid the grounds for joy and interest on the one hand (affiliation) and disgust and shame on the other. His religious training and social isolation led to further feelings of separateness and social ineptitude. In adulthood, experience with rejection – in the context of the exposition of his original and iconoclastic ideas – magnified the grounds for shame, and, as good social objects turned bad, for disgust. However, given his religious training, the disgust is ambivalent and functions only as an intrusion affect (Tomkins, 1963); that is, it is only intermittently functional. The ambivalence, in turn, leads to a splitting of his affiliative investments (i.e., between family and clients on the one hand and rivalrous colleagues on the other). It also led to a further distinction between occasions to be separate and aloof and occasions to be tender, caring, and absorbed. All of this had far-reaching ramifications, as seen in his career development, the depth of his commitment to it, and even specifics of the therapeutic ideology.

Commitment to Healing

Roger's choice of psychotherapy as a career appears to have been multiply determined, but certainly one ingredient must have involved psychological disenchantment as formulated by Tomkins. Disenchantment took place somewhat later for Carl than is the case for many children because of the family's concern for his fragility. However, when he was judged to be out of danger, he also confronted a rather more prohibitive environment than many of his contemporaries. In addition, he was subject to the tauntings of his many siblings and had few other social experiences to buffer or substitute for the harshness of his new circumstances. Such conditions must have made for a rather profound disenchantment. There is evidence that Rogers was somewhat moody as a child/adolescent, and one speculates that he must have nursed a serious disillusionment and disaffection with his new circumstances. In his autobiography, he related that he was considered a "dreamy" youngster and had earned the sobriquet "Professor Moony."

Despite the unwitting perpetration of this set of illusion-shattering experiences, Rogers's parents were not particularly punitive. They did not use power assertion methods in disciplining him and they were apparently not likely to engage in practices that would cause escalation in negative affect since there was such a premium on self-containment in the family. Affect theory suggests that one of the outcomes of disenchantment is a renewed quest for the lost paradise. The search for a lost paradise can take any number of forms including the idealization of another adult, coming to the belief that one has been swapped as a baby and really belong to other parents, or, in adult life, in philandering or constantly changing partners. In Rogers's case, his quest for communion could be satisfied within the context of idealized communion in psychotherapy.

Before Rogers, psychotherapy emphasized the therapists' authority and placed a premium on remaining neutral, even distant and frustrating in the context of the therapy session. In contrast, Rogers emphasized the importance of warmth and acceptance on the part of the therapist as critical ingredients in promoting psychological health. As such, the therapist recreates the conditions of interpersonal communion and intimacy. Research later reinforced Rogers's thesis that creating such a climate was in itself conducive to client improvement. Rogers was perhaps more skilled than most in generating the atmosphere of communion in psychotherapy, and, to all appearances, both he and the client were beneficiaries of this healing climate. It was precisely this kind of context in which he could act out his identification with the nurturing, satisfying, empathic, nondemanding mother of early infancy and receive the adoration of the client in return. At the same time, he could also act out his identification with the omnipotent mother of childhood, who had the power both to give and to withhold love and who could control how and when affection was expressed. As Tomkins noted, "Identification with a parent who combines nurturance with dominance will produce an enjoyment of being together with others so long as one can tell them what to do and when and how to do it. Such a mode of enjoyment of communion is not uncommon among men of the cloth and among educators" (1962, p. 454) and, we might add, certain kinds of psychotherapists. Although one might not think of "non-directive client-centered" psychotherapy as involving telling the client "what to do and when and how to do it," it does indeed involve shepherding the client in specific ways, as our later analysis of Rogers's session with Gloria illustrates.

It is perhaps no accident that Rogers would make "unconditional positive regard" the centerpiece of client-centered psychotherapy. He had experienced its gratifying consequences as well as known its revocation. Although Rogers's mother and father were well-intentioned and caring parents, they displayed a conditional rather than unconditional positive regard. Love, at least beyond the infancy period, was conditional on conformity to family values (including distrust of and separateness from others) and the work ethic. His mother was apparently particularly controlling. Apropos of this, it is of more than passing interest that Rogers singled out the "Girl of the Limberlost" novels by Gene Stratton Porter as an example of his love for nature and books as a youngster. (The only other book mentioned specifically by Rogers in his autobiography as having been of influence in his childhood was, interestingly enough, "the heavy scientific tome by Morison" on agriculture, entitled *Feed and Feeding*.) While the books in the Limberlost series deal significantly with a young girl's intellectual quest and fondness for nature, the more overriding theme is one of interpersonal alienation and subsequent reconciliation. Elnora, the protagonist, is a young farm girl who lost her father early in life and is being raised by her mother, Kate. The mother is portrayed as an emotionally reserved, even cold, controlling, and somewhat antisocial individual who is struggling to support her family and hold on to the farm. Elnora is a nature-loving, book-loving girl who is somewhat shy but who wants to have friends, even though she is thwarted in this by her mother and the exigencies of their hard life. There is little substantive communication between the girl and her mother, and it is later revealed that the mother harbors resentment toward her because she believes her pregnancy prevented her from saving her husband's life during a freak storm. Elnora chafes under her mother's controllingness and aloofness but strives to win her affection nonetheless. She secretly rebels against some of her mother's strictures and comes to form a bond with a local naturalist who is admirable because "she can do anything she wants." Eventually Elnora and her mother are reconciled to one another in an emotional epiphany when the mother is able to express and expunge her anger toward her daughter.

The themes of absent father, misunderstanding and controlling mother, and unarticulated anger have their obvious counterparts in Rogers's life, and the themes of alienation and reconciliation were played out not only in his personal life but in his professional life as well. At a very fundamental level, Rogers wanted to recapture the communion of early life before the fall from grace, but he did not wish to sacrifice his personal autonomy. The close-binding love that his mother offered simultaneously fed the need to be loved, and restricted the sources of nurturance, making love conditional.

By transferring his affiliative needs to others in late adolescence and early adulthood – to his school companions and later to Helen – he found the means to break free of the emotional deadlock his family had on him as well as the binding cords of their conventionality in a manner that he frankly saw as rebellious (rebellion is mentioned seven times in the autobiography). Rogers's rebellion, however, is mixed with conflict, and he takes considerable care not to injure others. True, he broke with the religious fundamentalism of his mother and the career designs of his father. However, even though he did not pursue a religious vocation, he subsequently ended up in another helping and guiding profession, and even though he gave up agriculture as a career, he went on to nurture growth in people in the practice of psychotherapy. He did not renounce the value of education (both parents were unusually well educated for their time) but exceeded their accomplishments by going on for advanced degrees. Rogers's parents were well educated, but they were practical and "anti-intellectual." Rogers himself placed great store in being "real" and writing clearly; he eschewed mystification. The family emphasized not showing any sexual interest; Rogers maintained a monastic appearance as well as conducted himself in a rather quiet, desexualized manner. The parallels and contrasts are numerous. His descriptions of his parents indicates that he not only loved and cared for them but also recognized that they had stifled his potential through their "subtle and loving control." Despite his criticisms of his parents, Rogers did not scandalize them in the way that Ellis did, (who portrayed his parents as neglectful and morally degenerate). Thus Rogers's rebellion and subsequent individuation was gentle and respectful; however, it was also firm and determined.

In summary, Rogers both loved and sought to be free from his parents. He wanted to restore the idyllic time when love was not conditional, and he wanted to be the one who would control its sources and duration and the character of love given and received.

The theme of commitment to healing is not unrelated to commitment to achievement, although it may not at first be apparent. Achieving affiliation with others was clearly a central motive for Rogers. However, it was somewhat less central than that of other themes. A thematic content analysis was applied to the narrative material in Rogers's autobiography (1972). The coding protocol is found in the appendix. In brief, this analysis indicates that, at least in terms of sheer frequency of themes, Rogers's description of himself and his life's work is organized along four central axes: Control/Power, Separateness, Achievement, and Affiliation. The Control/Power dimension incorporates themes of fighting/rivalry, weakness or lack of control, power or its denial, leadership/influence, and control, collectively accounting for 23 percent of all themes that were coded. The Separateness dimension incorporates the themes of independence/dependence and individuation, accounting for 22 percent of the themes. Themes of Achievement (success and lack of success) amount to 15 percent of the total themes coded. The Affiliation axis (affiliation and lack of affiliation) accounts for another 17 percent of the themes.

Here we will argue that the themes of Control, Separateness, and Achievement are integrally related to one another and contribute to the part of Rogers's persona that is emotionally constricted and problematic. The Affiliation dimension is also dynamically related but seems to occupy a different location in Rogers's psychological state space. The dimension of Affiliation permits Rogers to express the loving, longing, affectively engaged part of his personality. The themes of Control–Separateness–Achievement relate to Rogers's social discomfort around others (shyness, shame), his avoidance of contamination by unenlightened people and his aversion for disappointing others (disgust), and his need to avoid being engulfed by double-binding love. They also serve to organize (and suppress) his anger experiences – though one aspect of his anger is observed in the conflict he generates around him. In this section we consider Rogers's commitment to achievement and its relation to power.

Commitment to Achievement

The experience of an intense and protracted period of gratifying communion followed by severe disillusionment and disenchantment also helps to explain the strength of Roger's achievement drive, his lack of discomfort with being different, and the manner in which he pursued his goals, although other factors were at work as well.

It is clear from Rogers's career trajectory as well as from the sheer number of achievement themes that appear in the autobiography that Rogers had high achievement motivation. According to Tomkins (1962), one unintended consequence of socialization experiences that are predominantly intensely rewarding in early development is an overwhelming desire to excel, which results in an overachieving personality; a close link between achievement motivation and sociophilia is also a byproduct. The interesting thing about Rogers is that although issues of achievement and control are prominent in Rogers's autobiography, he explicitly and repeatedly disavows interest in power. This contradiction provokes the perplexing question of how a person who was genuinely disinterested in power could ever have become president of the American Psychological Association. Obviously, any nominee for the position would have to covet the position at some level and be perceived by others as embodying power in order to have achieved sufficient endorsement and ultimate election. And then there is the matter of his various challenges to the authority of those in power above him, many of which were successful. Was Rogers just a hardworking, tenacious, and obdurate person – a kind of junkyard dog with a lot of stamina – or is there more to his protestations concerning power than meets the eye? In our earlier chronicle of Rogers's professional advancement, we specifically addressed the dynamic elements of his rise to fame and recognition. Here we pause to consider what elements of happenstance, personality, and ambition may have been operating to pave the way for such impressive achievements.

In his autobiography, Rogers repeatedly referred to conflicts with others, most notably with psychiatrists, academics, and administrators (i.e., those in power). He also made a considerable number of career moves, and although these were framed as being largely at the service of allowing him more satisfying opportunities to pursue and test his evolving theories, one forms the impression that he left when interpersonal rivalries and power conflicts became too intense. Rogers portrayed himself as someone who is disinterested in power and who achieves through hard work and luck: "I see myself as . . . capable of a dogged determination in getting work done or in winning a fight; eager to have an influence on others but with very little desire to exercise power or authority over them" (Rogers, 1972, p. 29). Despite this disclaimer, he always seemed to end up drawing "skepticism and opposition" and inevitably found himself embroiled in conflict. One is provoked to consider whether the conflict and turmoil Rogers managed to attract was simply a product of his challenge to establishment psychology and orthodox psychiatry or whether elements of his own personality were more deeply implicated.

Although Rogers denied that he wanted power, he did acknowledge the need for control over his own life, and he managed to exercise a great deal of control over those in his immediate surround. In the domestic sphere, it is clear that his own desires controlled the fate of the family. His wife, Helen, led her life basically as a somewhat servile adjunct to Carl's own ambitions, though she was able to achieve some personal identity in the domestic sphere and in her avocational interests involving art (H. E. Rogers, 1965). Helen had been well educated and had shown promise of developing a successful career in commercial art, but she put this aside when she married. Given the standards of the day, and the expectation that women's activities should be subordinated to those of men, Helen may not have offered much resistance when Carl made decisions for both of them. It was only much later in life that she was able to articulate her negative feelings about having subordinated her career aspirations to her husband's professional development and to express her anger toward her husband. Although Rogers's need to dictate his wife's activities meshed with her own comfort with sex role standards of the day, as she became more discontented with this position, their marriage began to look less and less ideal to both of them in later life.

Rogers also acknowledged his need to influence others outside of the family sphere, but this was framed in the context of altruistic motives – his goal in psychotherapy, he maintained, was to promote "growth" in others and to help release their potential. Moreover, the way he deployed his own personal power was more classically feminine than masculine; he made considerable efforts to avoid appropriating the autonomy of the other, and the power that he did exert was "softened" by the evident respect with which he treated others and his ability to express empathy. Nevertheless, exerting control, or "influence" as he would have it, is a power-based motive.

As French (1985) suggested in her compelling analysis of men's and women's access to and use of power, power is motivated by the human desire to control one's destiny (i.e., to avoid being controlled by nature or by other human beings). Although success in controlling nature is notoriously elusive, humans can attempt to influence and master the actions of others. French made an important distinction between two kinds of power: "there is power-to, which refers to ability and capacity, and which connotes a kind of freedom, and there is power-over, which refers to domination" (p. 505). Moreover, French noted that the need for power and the urge for domination can spring from self-aggrandizing motives, but that it may also emerge from idealism and the desire to bring about some common or specific good to others. The distinction that French makes is especially important in our consideration of Carl Rogers. The power motive in Rogers appears to engender more power-to than power-over, to be generally noncoercive in nature, and to involve more idealism than self-aggrandizement. However, it would be a mistake not to recognize how much issues of control and power played in his life and work. First and foremost, Rogers needed to ensure that no one would ever again exercise the degree of controllingness and stricture he experienced in his family and their adherence to religious fundamentalism. Interestingly enough, the model of power with which he himself identified and which is clearly in evidence in his style of psychotherapy is a maternal and ecclesiastical one. It is maternal in the expression of concern for others (i.e., in his skilled deployment of empathy), and it is protective rather than domineering and humiliating, a therapeutic "strategy" often used by Perls.

In accord with this thesis, it is interesting to note a striking curiosity about the way that Rogers used facial expressions of emotion during interpersonal contact. Rogers's affect, at least as seen in *Three Approaches to Psychotherapy*, had certain salient features, most notably an idiosyncratic and habitual use of the brows which involved oblique gathering of the inner corners. In most facial coding systems, this particular configuration would be regarded as indexing or symbolizing sadness. What is peculiar about Rogers's use of this expression is that it does not seem to consistently index sad affect, at least as judged by vocal indicators and the verbal content of his speech. Instead, it appears to coincide with expressions of empathy and general concern. Interestingly, this is precisely the kind of interested concern expressed by mothers in interacting with infants in distress, though it tends to be displayed only briefly, thereby circumventing the threat of contagion and escalation of infant distress (Malatesta & Haviland, 1982). To this extent, Rogers's use of it is a very maternal gesture. We will have more to say about this expression and its relation to other aspects of Rogers's biography and personality later.

The ecclesiastical aspect is seen in his conception of himself as having privileged views on matters psychological and in his eager attempts to convert other practitioners to client-centered psychotherapy. The clerical identification is also revealed in some of his nonverbal mannerisms and gestures as observed in the film, which are ceremonial in nature and frequently convey the sense that he is "blessing" the other or conferring grace on the other. His frequent avowal of wanting to understand the client from the inside and to move around in their world betrays that he entertains a sense of potential omnipotence and omniscience, inasmuch as the ideology assumes that one can actually come to know another fully. He also assumes a classically religious, and in this case somewhat grandiose, stance in asserting a posture of humility:

> Placed in the perspective of billions of years of time, of millions of light years of interstellar space, of the trillions of one-celled organisms in the sea, of the life struggle by billions of people to achieve their goals, I cannot help but wonder what possible significance can be attached to the efforts of one person at one moment in time. I can only do my part as one infinitely small living unit in this vast ongoing universe (Rogers, 1972, p. 76).

And elsewhere, "[w]hen I was informed of this I wept with joy and surprise. I couldn't understand how or why they would have chose *me*" (Rogers, 1972, p. 37). We will have occasion to revisit the issue of Rogers's attraction to and exercise of power later in the volume. For now, we turn to an examination of Rogers's emotional organization and its relation to affective themes.

Affective Themes and Their Dynamic Interplay in Personality

Let us summarize at this point the aspects of Rogers's personality that seem particularly noteworthy in terms of emotional organization, based on his history, and then endeavor to determine how this particular organization manifests itself dynamically in therapeutic ideology and practice, in expressive behavior, in the management of distress, and in interpersonal relating. In presenting data from our analysis, we hope to show more concretely the basis of the conclusion that Rogers' ideology and practice are products of a personality organized around attractor states of conscious shame, repellor regions of anger, the pursuit of interpersonal excitement, and the release of joy.

We begin with a rather simple accounting of the frequency with which Rogers used various emotion terms in both narrating his autobiography and as deployed in session with Gloria and also examine his facial and vocal displays during the film. We then turn to two particularly revealing episodes from his life, which we examine in some detail, and which serve to substantiate in a dynamic and fairly vivid way, impressions gleaned from quantitative analysis. They are particularly illuminating with respect to affective dynamics. One episode has to do with a simple expressive gesture that occurs fleetingly in the course of an expostulation and explanation of his therapeutic interventions, and the other involves a particularly distressing encounter with a client and subsequent midlife crisis.

As we proceed, and as appropriate, we consider what both attachment theory and affect theory have to say about particular developments and configurations. In doing so, we wish to advance the discussion of emotional organization and attachment from the more general to the more personalistic, from the notion of the secure or balanced personality to a description of personality that sheds light on individuality and character.

Attachment theory has emphasized that secure personalities are characterized by the ability to invest in intimate relationships and to place trust in them. Such individuals, as adults, can endure occasional distress, even outright adversity, without retreating into either denial or other repressive coping mechanisms or collapsing into a state of abject hopelessness. Securely attached individuals are portrayed as valuing attachments and being capable of intimacy. We might also imagine that they would dislike interpersonal strife, though not necessarily avoid it, and would develop strategies for resolving conflict. Rogers shows this profile to a certain extent. He is able to achieve intimacy, and he values his family life. Though his theoretical iconoclasm prompts conflict and rejection, he is usually able to avoid open warfare by soft-pedalling his approach or, in instances where open conflict cannot be avoided, by leaving the scene to take another job. However, there is more to Rogers than the maintenance of a stable domestic relationship and the avoidance of conflict in work. If this were all there were to Rogers, he would be a rather bland character as an adult, not very distinctive, and certainly not very much of an individual in the personalistic sense. Fortunately, Rogers is more complex than this, and affect theory allows us to come to terms with some of the complexity.

Emotional Profile of Rogers

Several sources of data concerning Rogers's emotional organization are available to us – his autobiography, the biography by Kirschenbaum, his theoretical writings, and the film of his encounter with Gloria. Even though these different types of information do not always reveal the same picture – one would not really expect perfect overlap given the very different sources of information and contexts of disclosure – there is enough coherency across sources to give us confidence that we can gain a fairly good perspective on Rogers's emotional organization.

One first impression, derived from viewing the videotape, is that Rogers's affectivity is generally muted, especially the negative affect component. He seems shy and tentative, interested, but with a weak affectivity. (If you have not seen *Three Approaches to Psychotherapy*, a likeness can be had by picturing the Mr. Rogers of the children's program, *Mr. Rogers' Neighborhood*.) The impression of dampened affectivity is confirmed by noting the number of discrete words such as "happy" or "mad," versus undifferentiated affective terms such as "feelings," in both the session with Gloria and his autobiography. In the session with Gloria, he uses 3.8 times more nondiscrete terms than discrete terms (the corresponding ratios for Ellis and Perls are 0.17 and 0.28, respectively).

Beyond the overall dampening of emotion, we observed other patterns that are related to specific affects. As indicated in Chapter 7, a frequency count of the number of discrete emotion words in the fifth chapter of Rogers's book, *Counseling and Psychotherapy*, was revealing. Anger was the prevailing emotion mentioned by Rogers in the course of discussing the steps involved in nondirective counseling. In terms of sheer number of discrete affect words, words in the anger category were most frequent, followed by fear. However, as pointed out, the emotions were not randomly distributed over the twelve-step progression that Rogers used to describe clients' progress through psychotherapy. Few emotion words appeared in the early phases; then negative emotions (largely anger words) were portrayed as being in conflict with "generally" positive emotions, with the gradual emergence of more specific positive emotions later on. Elsewhere, Rogers expressed his view that anger is only defensive and needs to be circumnavigated so that one can find the real issue; as indicated in Chapter 7, Rogers clearly does not intend to work with anger.

Other sources of data indicate that Rogers avoided or worked around anger in his own life as well. In the opening pages of the present chapter, there are several selections from Rogers's own writings that demonstrate his awareness of the difficulty he had with anger expression. Other more quantitative analyses sustain the thesis that it is important for Rogers to avoid expressing and dealing with anger. In a frequency count of discrete affect found in Rogers's autobiography, there were only four instances of anger words, which made this the category with the lowest frequency for any emotion, positive or negative. In the interview with Gloria, Rogers referred to anger only once out of a total of fifteen discrete affect words. We also asked a class of graduate students in clinical psychology to view *Three Approaches to Psychotherapy* and to specify the most dominant "background" affect of each of the three therapists and then the next most dominant affect. A tally of the results indicated that Rogers received zero attributions for the categories of anger, contempt, and disgust – the three emotions mentioned by Izard (1972) as belonging to the "hostile triad." In contrast, he received sixteen attributions for interest, seven for joy, and five for shame (these three emotions, it turns out, are also pivotal for Rogers, as is discussed later). Another class (see Chapter 7) coded discrete affects on the basis of muscle movement patterns linked to discrete emotions. They found that sad and happy expressions predominated and that they were frequently mixed. As discussed earlier and will again be discussed later on, what appear to be expressions of sadness are enactments of concern and interest.

From these examples, we can see that Rogers shuns and avoids angry affect. Nevertheless, he is still sensitive to it in others, thus making it possible to circumnavigate or avoid anger more efficiently. On occasions where he attempts to express it, it has a flat and half-hearted quality, as in the two filmed records we have of him interacting with clients (Gloria in *Three Approaches to Psychotherapy* and Nancy on another occasion). We thus can say that, in terms of Rogers's overall profile, anger is one emotion that constitutes a repellor region on his emotional landscape. In some ways, this is surprising given that we know Rogers was frequently in conflict with work colleagues. Of course, we cannot know whether he expressed anger overtly or not. It is certain that co-workers and theoretical rivals provoked anger experience, but it is doubtful, given all the preceding information, that he allowed himself to express it overtly or in very strong form. One guesses that he "worked around it" as he did with his clients, or had occasional "eruptions."

Other interesting aspects of Rogers's emotional profile emerge in the course of the several quantitative analyses. One such aspect is the prominence of positive, affiliative affect in his constellation of "developed" affects. The positive affects of joy and interest, and to a lesser extent, surprise, constitute attractor regions in his personality landscape as indexed by the sheer number of times he uses terms in these affect classes in his autobiography and in the session with Gloria.

There is, finally, one negative affect that is well developed in Rogers, and that is shame. Although he does not use words in the shame/shyness class very frequently in his autobiography, they are more frequently referred to than most other negative affects including sadness, anger, guilt and disgust. Only fear and contempt are mentioned with any greater frequency. In his session with Gloria, he did not use any shame/shyness words, whereas he did use one anger word, made five contemptuous comments, and used two fear words and three guilt words. From these two sources, one would gather that shame was not undeveloped as an affect, but that it was not a very prominent aspect of his personality either. However, it is helpful to note that shame is not an affect that individuals feel very comfortable articulating. As Sheff has noted (1984, 1987), there is a taboo associated with shame in our culture; it is considered shameful to either express shame or notice the shame of another. However, shame is one of the more frequently provoked emotions in human social interchange, and its presence can be detected in so-called "hiding behaviors" – covering the eyes or other parts of the face, hanging or averting the head, and averting the eyes (Retzinger, 1991; Scheff, 1984, 1987) – and in paralinguistic aspects of speech.

Two kinds of shame have been discriminated. Shame that is shunted from consciousness is detected in fast, propulsive speech and has been termed "bypassed shame" by Helen Block Lewis (1971). Shame that an individual is aware of shows up in speech dysfluencies (ums, uhs, false starts, repetitions, etc.). When our students were asked to judge the background affect of Rogers based on their viewing of *Three Approaches to Psychotherapy*, shame was the most frequently cited negative affect for Rogers. Moreover, when we counted the number of speech dysfluencies, in each of the three therapists' introductory speeches in the film, they constituted 3.55 percent of Rogers's speech sample, whereas they accounted for only 1.17 percent of Perls's and only 0.52 percent of Ellis's. We also note that Rogers and his wife describe him as having been "shy" as a youngster. Biographically, there were multiple early and continuing sources of shame, including parental socialization based on shame (see later discussion), restrictions on his autonomy (see Erikson, 1950, on autonomy versus shame and doubt), experiences with critical others including parents, teasing and derision from his siblings, lack of social skills, and, finally, curtailment of excitement. With respect to the latter, Tomkins (1963) argued that the incomplete reduction of joy or interest is itself an automatic trigger for shame. It is clear that Rogers had not surmounted the basic shame he experienced even by late adulthood. It is of more than passing interest that Rogers describes the purpose of client-centered psychotherapy in his introduction in the film as being that of *moving from disapproval of the self to greater acceptance of the self*, and it is surely no accident that client-centered therapy is a "self" psychology (see discussion of Rogers's "self-system" as articulated in several presentations of his work in Chapter 7).

In summary, Rogers appears to be organized around his conscious experiences of shame (and less so, disgust), the avoidance of anger, the pursuit of joy, and the expression of interest – the latter in the context of affiliative goals. He is able to find and release positive emotion in the context of psychotherapy, as plainly seen in the transaction between Rogers and Gloria. Gloria herself is aware of this as well. The filmmaker invited her to comment on her experiences with each of the three therapists following the final session:

> I: Did you see Gloria different, somehow . . .
> G: Yes.
> I: . . . with each of these guys?
> G: Yes, very much. I was surprised to see . . . I felt my, uh, more lovable, soft, caring self with Dr. Rogers. And, uh, I even felt more free openly, even about sex, and I was surprised with that. And, uh, and Dr. Ellis I just, uh, I'll almost say I felt more cold toward Dr. Ellis. I didn't have enough feeling. I was so busy trying to think with him that I didn't have enough feeling there. And I feel the most, uh, oh, uh, the – the biggest amount of emotions came up with me and Dr. Perls.

The aspects of Rogers's emotionality already noted not only have a bearing on what he was able to accomplish in psychotherapy but also reflect on his preferred modes of thinking, as examined in Chapter 7. The controlled affectivity appears to be related to his parents' emphasis on self-containment (especially of anger and other warlike feelings) and obedience to family values and religious fundamentalism, aspects that seem to support the absolutistic form of thought observed in some of his writing. The joy/interest aspect of his affective organization and ideological emphasis on self-acceptance as a therapeutic goal and the inventive strategies he applied toward the overcoming of shame and self-criticism appear to be related to and commensurate with the more creative and flexible aspects of his thought – more prominently found in his writings.

We turn now to a brief consideration of how Rogers's emotional configuration originated in early life experiences and in later developmental accretions, and then we examine the affect dynamics that might explain them. When we merge our affective and thematic analyses of Carl Rogers's autobiography, we are left with the impression that two of his most powerful affective issues have been the tension between excitement and anti-excitement impulses and the struggle between disgust/contempt and shame, between the impulse to feel proud of himself and superior and the countervailing impulse to control the contempt with humility, which is amplified by his equally strong feelings of shame and convictions of inferiority.

Excitement and Interest

That excitement and anti-excitement are important affective impulses for Rogers is borne out by an affective and thematic content analysis of the material found in his autobiography. The majority of affective expressions are in the interest–excitement category; he not only asserted interest and excitement the most frequently of all discrete emotions but also denied interest and excitement more than he denied any other affects. This tendency to emphasize (or deny) the exciting appears to have roots in early childhood experiences, particularly those forbidding such exciting activities as dancing, movies, and drinking along with the interpersonal. The themes of control and rebellion, freedom and independence, come up with a fair degree of frequency and are both directly and indirectly related to the previously described prohibitions. And yet Rogers was drawn to the exciting things in life, especially the interpersonal and social. In adult life, he was able to actualize his interest in relating to others. He was excited by human contact and the possibilities of communion and intimacy as this is played out on a moment-to-moment basis in the context of psychotherapy. And he was also excited by the effects he was able to produce in the course of therapeutic intervention. However, he also continued to be on guard against *undue* expression of excitement.

A dramatic illustration of this dynamic occurred during Rogers's session with Gloria. A person's face is not just the locus of both fleeting and sustained emotional reactions but also an historical document, revealing lifelong patterns of emotional expression and inhibition (Darwin, 1872; Malatesta, Fiore & Messina, 1987) and the dynamic interplay between historical events and learning experiences (Tomkins, 1963). Humans learn to inhibit expression of emotion through conditioning experiences as well as through voluntary hiding of emotions that are proscribed and for which punishment is expected. Since experiences with emotions and their expression are repetitive, salient, and highly motivating, individuals acquire well-ingrained habits with respect to emotional expression, sustained by defenses. However, as Tomkins noted, these defenses are not always effective, and the affect that is suppressed may break through in times of stress or excitement. At such moments "we see simultaneously the original affect and the specific defense" (1963, p. 268). We have argued that Rogers was both attracted to and defended against excitement. Furthermore, we have seen that Rogers expressed the interest end of the interest–excitement continuum in an idiosyncratic and peculiar way. In most people, interest is typically expressed with raised and arched brows; this is the innate pattern as observed in young infants who are as yet untutored in the ways of culture-specific emotion expression and as yet unconditioned by experience, and it is the pattern typically observed in adults (at least in Western cultures) expressing interest either intentionally or more spontaneously. Rogers, however, tended to express interest via oblique brows, which imparted an element of distress or sadness to his face. However, there is one instant in the *Three Approaches to Psychotherapy* film, in the course of an unguarded moment of excitement, that strikingly revealed the historic dynamics behind Rogers's idiosyncratic use of the brows. That context follows. Rogers had finished his session with Gloria and had been given a period of time alone to relax and reflect on the interview. He had just now returned to the camera to share with the viewer some of his thoughts about how the session went. Although Rogers was ostensibly nervous and self-conscious during the opening moments with Gloria and was intensely engaged throughout the encounter with her, in the postinterview session he was more visibly relaxed. It is clear from his demeanor and what he said that he felt basically good about the session. He still exhibited speech dysfluencies, indexing his ever-present background shame, but now he seemed more spontaneous in both his comments and nonverbal behavior, which led to a temporary lapse in his guard.

At this point, he commented on how client-centered practices promote growth and drew attention to his own success with Gloria. "When I'm able to enter into a relationship, and I feel that this was true in this instance . . . " (voice rising). He was being spontaneous here and the excitement and proud pleasure he was experiencing mounted. At the height of this juncture, the configuration of his face changed into a more open and unguarded one, and at this point we see the only "pure" prototypic interest expression (brows raised and arched) of the whole film. Furthermore, what happened at this juncture is even more revealing. The raised brow lasted only a flicker of a second before the muscles controlling the outer brow were drawn into play to pull the outer corners down, thus creating the sad brow with the oblique configuration, (though the inner corners were still raised in interest. Thus, the probable affect dynamic was revealed. If it is dangerous or forbidden to express too much excitement, pulling down one corner of the brows is a successful camouflage; it may also be somewhat reactive, given Tomkins's general principles of affect expression (see later discussion). Having to curtail excitement is "punishing" to use Tomkins's vocabulary – it is distressing. Other dynamically revealing aspects of Rogers's nonverbal behavior relate to another of Rogers's major affective axes – that of shame. We turn to the dimension now.

Shame

Rogers described himself as having been a "shy boy," and themes of the desire for closeness, on the one hand, and the denial of the need for closeness, on the other, figured prominently in the autobiography. Sources of shame included parental shame induction as a socializing practice, teasing by siblings, and periodic inculcation regarding the value of humility and biblical reminders of basic human inferiority. In the part of the autobiography dealing with the accomplishments of his mature adulthood, Rogers the observer hovered over Rogers the narrator and surveyed what he had written with a critical eye; he then gave expression to the inner conflict engendered in the task of writing about the self and the self's achievements without undue self-congratulation. He caught himself at what he called smugness and is of two minds. On the one hand, he wanted to expunge it from the autobiography (he was ashamed of it); on the other hand, eliminating it would mean rejecting an authentic part of himself, and philosophically and ideologically, he could not accept that kind of resolution. Consequently, he allowed his more prideful statements to remain. At the same time, he was equally convinced of his smallness, worthlessness, and insignificance in the larger scope of things. A viewing of the videotape of Rogers confirms the impression from the autobiography that adulthood had not enabled him to resolve issues of shame and shyness. There was a considerable residue of shame/shyness, as marked by various nonverbal behaviors. Not so coincidentally, his ideological preoccupation was revealed to be centered on liberating the self from conditions of nonacceptance.

How did Rogers resolve the conflicts engendered in excitement–anti-excitement impulses, and the tension between shame and pride? Although rebellion against the family and, later, against the established order of clinical practice is a frequent theme in his life, the keen work ethic is one family ideal that Rogers did not reject. By working hard and achieving success and recognition, he was entitled to experience pride, and this pride in accomplishment was somewhat of an antidote or buffer to shame. At the same time, it was a reminder that acceptance is contingent on good behavior and accomplishment. At some level, Rogers must have wished to be allowed to crow about his accomplishments; he would probably also have liked to be accepted no matter what his accomplishments. It is no accident then that his recommendations for therapist behavior involve unconditional positive regard and a prizing of the individual in his or her own right.

Application of Affect Theory

Let us turn now to a more detailed discussion of affect theory to see how it may be applied to a fuller understanding of Rogers's personality. In Tomkins's (1962, 1963) formulations, people tend to be characterized by individualistic ideoaffective organizations that are unique constellations of emotions and cognitions. An ideoaffective organization serves two very important functions in personality. First, it acts as a selective filter during the intake and processing of information, interpreting incoming information for its relevance to a particular affect or set of affects. Second, it encompasses a set of strategies for dealing with affect-relevant goals and, thus, effects behavioral dispositions. Ideoaffective organizations tend to be organized with relevance to particular emotions that have figured prominently in development. They constitute "affect theories," which may be either weak or strong. Strong affect theories are so massively dominating that they involve significant distortions of reality and are ultimately maladaptive – as in the monopolistic fear of the paranoid schizophrenic. Weak affect theories involve ideoaffective organizations that color the cognitions and perceptions of the individual and affect the particulars of their behavior in distinctive ways; thus, they impart "character." Such affect theories are adaptations and tend to involve successful emotional strategies; thus, the term "weak" does not imply that the organization is ineffective or insignificant.

According to Tomkins, humans are motivated by four key goals with respect to affect, namely the minimization of negative affect, the maximization of positive affect, the minimization of affect inhibition, and the power to maximize achievement of the first three goals. The latter achievement is often rendered difficult because, as an outcome of socialization, some of these goals may be placed in conflict with one another. For example, the cost of minimizing negative affect in the extreme may be the minimization of positive affect as well. For our discussion of Rogers, the third goal is particularly important. The goal of minimizing affect inhibition relates to the intrinsically gratifying nature of affect expression; when it is thwarted, there are penalties. According to Tomkins, the inhibition of emotion expression under certain conditions tends to produce residual affect; the original emotion gets both heightened and distorted and will have punitive (affectively unpleasant) consequences.

There is evidence from the autobiographical and biographical accounts of the Rogers' family that strong expression of emotion – either positive or negative – was not something that the parents felt comfortable with or tolerated in their children. In general, it appears that shaming and rational persuasion rather than power assertive techniques were the prevailing modes of socialization to family standards of behavior, as indicated earlier, and that this applied to the socialization of emotion as well. We will argue that one of the byproducts of these early experiences around emotion resulted in the general muting of emotionality in Rogers. Given Tomkins's third general principle – the need to minimize affect inhibition – we have the grounds for conflict over emotion expression, one consequence of which might be a heightened motive to create conditions in which emotion can be liberated, though perhaps not maximized. Consequently, we have another motivation for Rogers's attraction to a career in psychotherapy.

There is a second consequence of shaming as a primary socialization tool, and that is the creation of a significant shame theory. Shame is a complex emotion, and we will argue that it is a core affect organization in Rogers – shaping his own emotional profile as well as affecting his preferred mode of thinking and his therapeutic ideology in significant ways. Consequently, it will be useful to spend some time describing the dynamics of this particular emotion. We also suspect, though the evidence is more circumstantial, that within the family milieu there was an especially great premium on the avoidance of anger affect, and that this is related to the shame dynamic.

In the parent–child relationship, shame is elicited in the child by the experience of defeat or as a result of any number of contemptuous communications by parents, including derogatory, derisory, belittling comments or tone of voice and physical displays of disgust and contempt (Tomkins, 1963). In other interpersonal contexts, shame is induced by the process of comparing and competing with peers and by experiencing insufficient deference, regard, respect, or equality from one's partners (Scheff, 1987). Tomkins noted that the use of contempt to induce shame is one of the most common and powerful means of achieving control over social behavior; it also has the most negative side effects, especially in the context of childrearing since it is so punitive, rejecting, and distancing. In summary, shame can be induced by various verbal and nonverbal communications but is most ubiquitously and effectively induced by contempt expressed by a social partner, whether that partner is a parent, peer, or other intimate.

According to Tomkins, children acquire personal styles of learning to deal with parental shaming. One pattern involves the child learning to fight back, to get angry, and to counter contempt expressed *by* the parent with contempt expressed *toward* the parent. Or, it may be the case that the parent's contempt for the child's actions is incorporated as an aspect of the child's self such that one part of the child (identified with the parent) can have contempt for another part, so that there is a part that is contemptuous and condemnatory and a part that is shamed. Where there is self-contempt, there can be contempt for others. Another pattern involves developing a unified shame for the self. Here we would not expect there to be contempt for others but rather an acceptance of the self's shamefulness before others. Rogers's profile most closely coincides with the latter resolution and helps to explain the particular pattern that his therapeutic ideology and clinical principles will take, as we demonstrate momentarily. The developmental profiles of Perls and Ellis, who also experienced shame in the context of childrearing, are quite different and conform more to the first two resolutions; moreover, their therapeutic ideologies also bear the stamp of their particular strategies when contending with shame, as discussed in later chapters.

Child or adult, shame is an especially painful affect because it is most closely associated with personal identity; it is the emotion that is most acutely associated with the self as critically observed and judged (Tomkins, 1963) and is often accompanied by shyness and social anxiety (Kaufman, 1989). As such, from a developmental point of view, parental reliance on shaming to bring behavior under control may have inadvertent and negative consequences over the long run. Repetitive experiences of shame, especially if unalleviated by more positive, self-affirming experiences, may leave in its wake a residue of self-doubt and a compromised sense of self-esteem. Such a unified shame complex means that the individual will be vigilant for further shame experiences and develop strategies to avoid or cope with this affect. Some developmental adaptations to shame can have positive consequences, rather than or in addition to negative sequelae. Earlier we argued that shame is an important part of Rogers's emotional organization. It is every bit an example of emotional giftedness that Rogers was able to convert a potential liability into a resounding career success. In development, shame experiences provoke intense self-scrutiny and self-consciousness; if they are not too extreme, they can foster useful introspection and an ability to utilize self-awareness. Given Rogers's own shame organization, it is perhaps no accident that client-centered psychotherapy is a "self"-focused psychotherapy. It capitalizes on the human desire to experience self-affirming self-acceptance; in the hands of a skillful therapist who exercises accurate reflective listening and genuine unconditional positive regard, the client is drawn into a more positive, self-accepting stance toward himself.

Affect, especially shame affect, is in general very contagious. Shame markers were very much in evidence during the filmed session with Gloria. One cannot help but suspect that some of Rogers's success with Gloria, as well as with other clients, resided in the shared shame affect that accrued in the context of therapist shame and client contagion. Once shame is induced in the client, it has the capacity, by virtue of its phenomenology, to foster or enhance self-consciousness and self-awareness. One imagines that this would be particularly effective with clients whose personality state space gravitates toward defensive contempt. Contempt can serve as an anti-shame strategy; as an aspect of personality, it tends to deflect self-scrutiny. However, once the contempt defense is rendered impotent through contagion of shame, renewed opportunities for self-awareness and self-evaluation are opened up. In *Three Approaches to Psychotherapy*, Gloria showed various dynamic as well as crystallized signs of contempt, which came out massively in the session with Perls and almost not at all with Rogers. Indeed, Gloria seemed to have contracted or absorbed some of Rogers's shame, since she produced more of it in the session with him than with the other two men; moreover, the shame appears to have neutralized her contempt and led her to greater introspection and self-disclosure. In passing, it is probably also worth commenting that the shame component of Rogers's personality probably had additional interpersonal benefits, especially in confrontation with colleagues who were or might be rivals. In an ambitious person such as Rogers, shame can serve as protective coloration in interactions with potentially hostile interactants.

Obviously, shame is a powerful motivator of behavior both personally and interpersonally. It is a central organizing affect that can be incorporated in various ways into the personality. More typically, it is an affect
that is often mixed or bound with other affects. As such, other affects
can become the activators of shame or shame can become the activator
of other affects, making for complex organizations of personality. For
example, shame and anger are dynamically linked, according to affect
theory. In interaction, the experience of shame, whether provoked by
the self or the other, triggers the experience of anger, often at the other
party because one experiences the shame in the presence of the other. In
fact, it is difficult not to feel that the shaming is coming from the other
(even if it is not) and that one is being scorned.

If a child's socialization history involves the use of shaming to contain emotional expression, shame becomes bound to the affects that are
shamed. If the emotion in question is anger, then the child develops
an anger/shame bind such that whenever anger is elicited, shame is
provoked, and the anger is inhibited. In the case of the Rogers' family, we deduce that not only was there a general taboo on expression
of emotion, but that the expression of anger was especially frowned
upon. This deduction suggests that within Rogers's personality shame
and anger are not only prominent organizing affects but may be linked
in a shame/anger bind. One specific incident in Rogers's life gives particular credence to this supposition. Although the significance of the
incident is somewhat downplayed in his autobiography, and certain
crucial details are missing – from the perspective of affect theory – the
specifics both sustain the thesis as well as reveal the complex topog-
raphy of this deeply embedded and ramifying aspect of his emotional
organization.

The incident took place in Chicago, between 1945 and 1957, and is
referred to in Rogers's autobiography under a section entitled "Period of
Personal Distress." While he was at Chicago, a deeply troubled woman
whom he had treated in Ohio renewed her therapeutic contacts with
him. His account of this episode reveals much about Rogers's emotional
organization, his emotion strategies, and a peculiar deficiency.

> I see now that I handled her badly, vacillating between being warm and
> real with her and then being more "professional" and aloof when the depth
> of her psychotic disturbance threatened me. This brought about the most
> intense hostility on her part (along with a dependence and love) which
> completely pierced my defenses. I stubbornly felt that I *should* be able to
> help her and permitted the contacts to continue, even though they had

ceased to be therapeutic and involved only suffering for me. I recognized that many of her insights were sounder than mine, and this destroyed my confidence in myself; I somehow gave up *my* self in the relationship. The situation is best summarized by one of her dreams in which a cat was clawing my guts out, but really did not wish to do so. Yet I continued this relationship, destructive to me, because I recognized her desperately precarious situation, on the brink of a psychosis, and felt I *had* to help (Rogers, 1972, p. 57).

Feeling himself on the verge of a nervous breakdown, Rogers convinced a colleague to take over the client's treatment. The termination with her must have been rather abrupt, for he reports that she "burst into a full-blown psychosis" within moments, complete with delusions and hallucinations. Overwhelmed by this outcome, he raced home and convinced his wife that he had to escape; within an hour they were on their way, and they stayed away for "two or three" months. He discusses this event as a period of personal anguish and uncertainty, during which he questioned his fitness for the profession and his whole adequacy as a person. He eventually returned, sought personal counseling with an understanding colleague, and emerged a more fully realized person, according to his account. "I . . . gradually worked through to a point where I could value myself, even like myself, and was much less fearful of receiving or giving love. My own therapy with my clients has become consistently and increasingly free and spontaneous ever since that time" (Rogers, 1972, p. 58).

What are we to make of this episode in his life? Was it merely a transient situational disturbance of no great magnitude or consequence, or was there more to this than at first meets the eye? There are certain curiosities about Rogers's recounting of the episode. In the first place, it was never localized specifically in time; it merely took place "while I was at Chicago," which turns out to have been an interval of time that spanned twelve years. The significance of the event was also downplayed somewhat in the way that he treated it. However, on closer analysis, it appears that the event actually constituted something like a fairly severe midlife crisis. Though he said that he returned to his home and work two or three months later, elsewhere he indicated that the impact was of much longer duration, encompassing "two years of intense personal distress" (Rogers, 1972, p. 57). In addition, several years later, after he moved to Wisconsin, he inaugurated an ambitious and programmatic study of the uses of client-centered psychotherapy with schizophrenics, which, when taken in light of this episode, has all the feel of an attempt to master an egregious failure. It is likely that his experience with this client stimulated the interest in such an application, but then oddly enough, the book that resulted from the program did not mention the woman or the episode at all.

Here we argue that the precipitation of the episode and the manner of its expression are intimately related to Rogers's affective organization. The two elements we believe to have triggered the episode and the consequent distress and flight revolve around issues of responsibility and failure. The two most important affective aspects related to these themes are shame and anger, emotions that figure prominently in his personality, as already discussed; in this instance, the episode provoked a particularly flammable mixture of immensely magnified shame, an occasion of hostility, and the lack of emotional strategies for modulating the hostility such that the imminent combustion could be averted.

We know how important achievement and recognition were to Rogers's sense of self-esteem. Themes of success and failure figure prominently throughout his autobiography. Experiences of pride are clearly linked to work and success, and are perhaps the main means of keeping the more interfering aspects of shame at bay. Experiences of failure are, by their nature, occasions for shame, and to fail at one's chosen occupation, even in a single instance, might in itself be occasion for feeling ashamed.

This experience notwithstanding, it might seem odd that the failure to manage a particular case would have such a catastrophic effect on a mature and seasoned therapist like Rogers. We suggest here that the experience of failure was magnified for Rogers because it also involved confrontation with previously undeveloped aspects of the self, in this case, a forbidden and powerful emotion. Rogers's description of the client's behavior, and the dream he singled out as symbolic, included allusion to extreme hostility. Given the unstable nature of the condition of this patient, the outbreak of psychosis and attendant hostility must have been quite frightening to Rogers, who characterologically did not like to work with anger and whose basic underlying affect was that of shame. Individuals who have a well-developed shame organization tend to have permeable self boundaries (Lewis, 1971). Permeability of the self permits merger with others, which can be both an asset and a liability in psychotherapy. Therapists who have permeable versus rigid self boundaries are more readily able to experience empathy with others, which, at least according to Rogerian theory, is desirable. On the other hand, such a condition offers little protection from the contagion of emotion, unless, of course, one's emotions are generally subdued. Affect tends to recruit more of its kind once it is activated (Tomkins, 1963), but if there is less available to begin with, the risk is reduced. In Rogers's case, his muted emotionality served adequately in the past as a buffer against the undue contagion of emotion. However, it is doubtful that he had ever encountered such intense hostility before. His family's avoidance of anger meant that Rogers would be deficient in all the defensive strategies and modulatory skills necessary to circumvent contagion of anger or to regulate the experience of it; thus, it is understandable that he would feel overwhelmed by this intense and unfamiliar affect. Moreover, he had not had sufficient opportunity to observe angry outbursts and their resolution to have understood that occasions of such intensely negative affect need not be catastrophic.

Thus far we have described a man who was confronted with a client who responded with anger rather than gratitude to his therapeutic strategies. It appears that he failed to avert a psychotic episode – or perhaps even precipitated it due to an inept or unwise intervention. This reaction is disturbing and worrisome, indeed. But one ponders whether or not such conditions would have been, sui generis, of sufficient magnitude to have unhinged a man of Rogers's vast experience, maturity, and competence.

One element that seems to be missing from the account is the full nature of Rogers's relationship with the client and any complications that may have been experienced therein. Although it is sheer speculation, there are various reasons for suspecting that Rogers came close to a real or imagined transgression with the client, one which would have heightened his sense of shame, guilt, and vulnerability to a critical mass. Clients frequently fall in love with their therapists, and the very texture of client-centered psychotherapy as practiced by someone of Rogers's convictions and style of relating may have been particularly vulnerable to such developments. Rogers consistently stressed the importance of communicating to the client unconditional acceptance, positive regard, prizing, empathy, and total understanding – conditions that are seductive in their own right, more so, one suspects, when they are encountered in a male–female relationship and where it is the male who is the sensitive, responsive listener. It is, after all, an ancient complaint of women that men do not understand them and do not make an effort to understand them. Rogers clearly made such efforts and basked in the gratitude he received in return from his clients. In *Three Approaches to Psychotherapy*, we see the intensity of Rogers's absorption in the client, his warmth, and his intense caring, and he was rewarded by Gloria's frequent smiles, and, at the end, the confession that she would have liked him to have had him as her father. In the wrap-up session, Rogers positively glowed at the success of his encounter with Gloria, and he was clearly delighted about the part of being "able to move around in the world of the client."

In the case of the client involved in Rogers's episode of personal distress, an attachment had apparently been formed to Rogers during the time that he was still living and practicing in Ohio. Rogers must have agreed to see the client in Chicago, in advance of her moving there. The fact that she pursued him across state lines, combined with the fact that Rogers granted her permission to do so, indicates that he may have been attracted to her as well, or that he was astoundingly naive about the seductive overtones to such an agreement and about the potential for her to misconstrue his intentions. In any event, Rogers was of the age that would have made him just about ripe for the sort of midlife experimentation that middle-aged men frequently fall prey to. It matters not whether he acted on such temptations or merely fantasized about them – as we know from the confessions of President Jimmy Carter, even highly scrupulous men can entertain such thoughts in their heart of hearts. Thus, the conflation of shame affect, unfamiliarly hostile emotion, and the dread of exposure could have been the right mix of circumstances triggering emotional collapse in Rogers. Let us discuss the dynamics behind this from the perspective of affect theory.

As we argued earlier, Rogers experienced multiple and continuing sources of shame socialization; shame for him was not only archaic but also reinforced by later experiences and thus constituted a deep attractor region on his personality landscape. Because of recurrent experience with this affect, we can assume that he would have a certain sensitivity to shame recruitment but that he would probably also have fairly well-developed defenses against it. In this light, it is easy to see why he would be particularly vulnerable to shame experiences in adult life but why he did not break down in a catastrophic way until certain additional precipitating conditions were met. One ingredient would involve his confrontation with hostility. The experience of unfamiliarly intense negative affect (through the process of contagion), for which he had not developed sufficient defenses and modulatory coping strategies, created the potential for system instability and a phase shift in the organization of the self. Second, he was likely shamed by his inability to contain the schizophrenic woman's psychotic episode. Other sources of shame were also attached to this episode; some were real, some were imaginary, but all were equally powerful and evidently additive. One guesses that the potential for shame was magnified by a recent experience of public exposure – he had just published *Client-Centered Therapy* (1951) and a number of papers that contained a precisely articulated statement of his whole theoretical position, which had been widely distributed and subsequently published in a key chapter in Sigmund Koch's prodigious series, *Psychology: A Study of a Science* (1959–1963). Perhaps, consistent with his newly published ideology, he was now trying to perfect the practice of what he preached – being especially genuine (transparent) and empathic (permeable to others' affect). Shame is experienced when one feels exposed (Kaufman, 1989), and it can make a person especially vulnerable to anger, as indicated earlier. Intense shame can be expected when one is especially vulnerable because of lowered defenses.

We also need to recognize that Rogers may have been under a great deal of other stress and have felt even more exposed than usual owing to the fact that he served as president of the APA in 1947. As he noted, these "were years of great change and expansion in psychology following the war, and I was deeply involved in formulations regarding clinical training, the formation of the American Board of Examiners in Professional Psychology, and the continuing attempt to resolve the *tensions between psychiatry and psychology*" [italics added] (Rogers, 1972, p. 56). If Rogers were in fact sexually involved with the patient, or even just sexually tempted, he may finally have realized how closely he was courting ultimate public shame and disgrace – a scandal he would bring upon both himself and his profession if, as the president of APA, he were found to be involved in an indiscreet, not to mention professionally unethical, relation with a client. The relationship would have been even more scandalous if that client went on to have a psychotic break. The cumulative "exposure" experience and any further threat of exposure of failure could easily have precipitated a catastrophic shame experience and the resultant flight into hiding. The fact that Rogers needed to escape and go into seclusion following the episode with the client are emblematic of a profound shame experience, hiding being a quintessential marker of shame. However, it is doubtful that the episode by itself, even in conjunction with his national visibility, would have alone produced the crisis, had Rogers not had a particular sensitivity and vulnerability to shame by virtue of his affective organization.

Summary and Concluding Thoughts

In this chapter, we attempted to come to an understanding of Carl Rogers's emotional organization, his personality dynamics, and their developmental origins. An analysis of his early life experiences and consideration of his affective profile as an adult suggested some of the reasons for the type of career he chose, his dedication to it, the therapeutic ideology he developed, and his mode of implementation. Chapter 7 deals with the latter two matters in greater detail and further relates these aspects of his life and work to the affective profile mapped out in the current chapter.

This chapter also illustrated one very essential feature of affective organizations. Emotions and their idiosyncratic organization in personality are not intrinsically disorganizing or dysadaptive – a position that has been advanced down through antiquity, echoes of which one still finds in contemporary psychology texts. Emotions serve creative as well as disruptive forces in life (Getz & Lubart, 1998; Piechowski, 1991). Life experiences are various, unpredictable, and alternately uplifting and unsettling. For the most part, people are fairly well served by their emotions. Emotions organize experience, motivate, and direct behavior. They organize experience and behavior in ordinary life and in crisis. In times of crisis, they can appear to be maladaptive, but even this is an illusion since emotions are the servants of adaptation. With respect to Rogers's period of personal distress, it is helpful to remember that, although he had a catastrophic shame experience related to an undeveloped aspect of his emotional profile, his lack of narcissism (acceptance of shame) also permitted him to turn to others – his wife, his colleagues – in this time of crisis. In so doing, he was able to release the positive affiliative emotions, which were so healing for him. We also observed that Rogers's underlying affective structure – with its attractor regions of shame, interest, and joy – as it was cognitively elaborated over time, gave rise to the generative lessons and legacies that the corpus of his work – and own example – set for generations of psychologists to come.

4 Lives Repelled by Fear and Distress

Albert Ellis

Albert Ellis, unlike the other two men who are the focus of this volume, is still alive today. At the age of eighty-nine, he is a seasoned therapist who remains professionally active. During the 1960s, he was most well known as a sex educator who promulgated progressive views. Later on, he became renowned as the developer of Rational Emotive Therapy (RET), which can be considered the forerunner of cognitive-behavior therapy.

Ellis's influence in the field of clinical and counseling psychology has grown considerably over the years. Although many psychologists regard him as eccentric and at odds with more traditional clinical practice, the notoriety of his public persona does not seem to have tarnished the evaluation of his historical contribution. In 1982, no fewer than three journal articles accorded him special acknowledgment. The *American Psychologist* ranked him as the second most influential psychotherapist in the world at that time. The *Journal of Counseling Psychology* determined that he was the most frequently cited author in professional journals since 1957. The *Journal of Marital and Family Therapy* cited him as the fourth most influential theorist. Consistent with these important signals of recognition, in 1986 he received APA's Award for Distinguished Professional Contribution.

In his work at the Rational Emotive Institute, Ellis remains an extraordinarily active psychologist. A 1988 biography of him described a seventy-five-year-old Ellis putting in an eighty-five- to ninety-hour work week, daily from 9 A.M. to 11:00 P.M. Over his lifetime, he published dozens of books and hundreds of articles. In a recent essay in which he reflected on what he had learned as a psychotherapist, Ellis (1996), at the age of eighty-three, could still inform his readers that certain of the ideas he discussed in the present article would "be the subject of several of my subsequent books" (p. 151).

As a trainer of therapists, he has a substantial and dedicated following. A volume of reminiscences by former students and colleagues on the occasion of his seventy-fifth birthday (DiMattia & Lega, 1990) is replete with anecdotes that describe Ellis warmly as an idiosyncratic but admired mentor and peer. The flattering adjectives abound; he is thoughtful, caring, gentle, patient, tender, kind, sensitive, generous, and supportive. Of course, celebratory occasions necessarily invoke the most positive images from contributors; adversaries and misanthropes are assuredly not invited to the festivities. Yet one still is struck by how well liked a man he is.

Ellis provided other, less warm, views of himself in various autobiographical musings, as did Daniel Wiener, his biographer, who is a long-time friend and colleague. The Ellis of Wiener's biography is a man who is more remote, self-contained, and temperamental. He is also an unreconstructed workaholic, as might be gleaned from earlier paragraphs, with rather remarkable energy, drive, and ambition. To read Ellis on himself, he is the quintessential self-made man – a redoubtable pioneer, a bold entrepreneur, and an American success story par excellence. This interpretation of his life is, of course, only one of many, and we will offer other analyses later. However, there is a way in which Ellis's portrayal of himself as the quintessential self-made man is a keenly penetrating insight, and perhaps even more laden with meaning than he himself suspects, as discussed in a subsequent section.

To be sure, Ellis's early life was hardly a charmed one, but he made it seem almost adventitious. Writing in the heroic mode in his autobiography, he told the story of young boy, adrift with little parental guidance, a de facto "orphan," sickly and shy, who re-created himself through his intellectual efforts and hard work. Indeed, his personal tale is one of stoicism and cleverness triumphing over what others might construe as fairly wretched early circumstances – economic hardship, multiple dislocations in residence, parents who were patently neglectful. As the tale unfolds, we find that young Albert almost single-handedly battled forces of neglect, superintended his two younger siblings, and, later in development, cured himself of painful shyness, social inhibition, and sexual ineptitude. Ultimately, he triumphed over not just the hard knocks of early childhood and adolescent angst but professional marginalization in his early career as well.

Though he indeed overcame an array of adverse circumstances and has been eminently successful at his chosen work for years, an underlying bristliness and anger still emanated from the narrative material that constituted his autobiography as well as even the most recent works (Ellis, 1996). Ellis himself was aware of this at some level, for he mentioned his tendency toward "irritability," which he believed he inherited from his father. He also thought that he had this innate streak of temper fairly well mastered, though others may have a different impression. Indeed, he appeared to be unaware of how much anger affect had become an integral part of his ideoaffectology. An underlying irritation and anger was also obvious in Ellis's voice and posture when he spoke – even when he was not ostensibly angry at some immediate circumstance – and it was also found in the structure and quality of his language. Indeed, whether in oral or written narrative, Ellis's language was "colorful," being inflected with crude street talk and profanity. His language was also combative, forceful, aggressive, and, on occasion, even assaultive. Certainly, some readers may be repelled by this kind of raw, aggressive language. However, and notably, this very self-same angry and contemptuous disregard for convention propelled the forcefulness of his delivery on the lecture circuit and was at the heart of a writing style that commanded strong reactions – curiosity and interest in some and repulsion in others.

But there is more to Ellis's personality than the sharp edge of anger and characterlogic scorn. If this were all, it is doubtful that he would have had the following that he attracted over the years and the ability to cultivate warm sentiments in others. It is also doubtful that he would have had as sanguine a personal life as he felt he has had. How is this possible? A rebellious streak and barely sequestered anger is never far from the surface in Ellis. How is it that such an angry, rebellious individual gave the world a fruitful and effective form of psychotherapy, instead of, say, the ranting rhetoric of a Central Park agitator or, at the extreme end, the murdering venom of the Unibomber?

Obviously, Ellis was able to channel the anger in constructive ways. Moreover, he was able to keep at bay another kind of affect – shame – which might have created a more combustible mix, through strategies that we will examine later on. However, another useful and successfully deployed emotion for Ellis is interest. Indeed, Ellis can be seen as having fairly prominent interest affect. Part of what clients and students warm to in Ellis is the intensity of focus and concentration that he marshaled when listening to people's problems and the rather adroit skill that went into crafting unique solutions for their difficulties. Finally, fear was a dynamically important partially warded-off affect in Ellis. It was often hidden, but not entirely concealed from view. This affective quality tempered, to a degree, Ellis's austere and dauntingly self-reliant personality and then softened it with a modicum of appealing vulnerability. This warded-off aspect of self was a dimly visible part of him; developmentally, we will argue that the highly shielded fear behind the facade was the driving force behind his self-reliant ideology and the emergence of thematic ideas that grew into Rational Emotive Therapy.

What do we make of all these portraits of Ellis? They seem somewhat at variance with one another. Was he the rude, abrasive, crude, callous, and unfeeling man that some of his written material suggested? Or, was he the intensely interested, gentle, patient, generous, and supportive individual that many of his clients, friends, and colleagues described? We found that both portraits reveal important elements of his personality, aspects that we learn more about from accounts of his early socioemotional development.

Early Childhood

Albert Ellis was born of Jewish parents on September 17, 1913, in Pittsburgh. He was the eldest of three children; his brother was two years younger, and his sister was four years younger. Ellis's father was an entrepreneur who failed as often as he succeeded at a succession of business ventures; he demonstrated little emotional involvement with his children and was often away from home on business trips during their early childhood. In his autobiography and biography, Ellis characterized the mother as a self-absorbed woman with somewhat manic and depressive features. On the one hand, according to Ellis, she was a "bustling chatterbox who never listened. She expressed strong opinions about everything, but without explanation or substance. She'd simply expound, then go on to something else" (Ellis, 1972, p. 41). On the other hand, there appeared to be a great deal of basic neglect, and it is apparent that she was often emotionally and physically unavailable to her children. Ellis recounted that she usually slept well beyond the time that he had to leave for school and was rarely at home when he returned in the afternoon. Rather than remember the loneliness, distress, and resentment that must have attended such circumstances, Ellis remembered his own resourcefulness and adultlike responsibility. Young

Albert woke himself and his siblings in time for school – and this with the aid of an alarm clock he purchased himself, he points out. He, rather than the parents, fed and dressed the other two children and otherwise looked after their needs. Ellis recounted that the family lived without much financial strain until the arrival of the Great Depression, at which point the children went out to work and were able to provide for their mother. Much of this narrative is devoid of emotional tone or content. En passant, Ellis converted a tale of parental neglect and involuntary role reversal into a matter-of-fact tale of filial respect and care.

Although parental supervision of the children was largely absent in this family, when the parents did intervene, discipline was typically authoritarian and power-assertive. The mother favored the use of spanking as a corrective to bad behavior and demanded compliant behavior. "He [Ellis] thinks this may have reflected an authoritarian attitude of their culture. She seemed to suffer no doubts nor remorse once she decided what her kids should be doing. Her assurance – and her husband's, the little he was around – opened little opportunity for debate with their children" (Wiener, 1988, p. 16).

Ellis was apparently weak and colicky as an infant and sickly up until adolescence. However, there were no major health problems until the age of five when he developed a kidney ailment that required hospitalization. Ellis reported that he did not remember much about the illness, but from all accounts the circumstances surrounding it must have been fairly traumatic. Originally admitted to the hospital for tonsillitis, he developed a severe strep infection that required emergency surgery to save his life and culminated in nephritis. Afterward, he had recurrences of the nephritis and developed pneumonia for which he was hospitalized once again; all told he was admitted to the hospital seven or eight times between the ages of five and seven. On one occasion, he was hospitalized for almost an entire year. Notably, his parents provided little psychological preparation for what to expect of surgery and anesthesia, nor did they prepare him for the pain he would experience afterward. On the occasion of the year-long hospitalization, his parents seldom visited him; he was left alone for days and weeks at a time. In recounting this experience, the narrative flattened to atonality; Ellis reported that he was able to adjust to the circumstances that confronted him, and that he "developed a growing indifference to that dereliction" (Ellis, 1972, p. 22).

Ellis was first sent to school at the age of four – during an era in which this was an unusual practice. There was apparently little psychological preparation for this early separation, and he reported that he did not know what was expected of him in school. Though Ellis disliked his first experiences with school (this changed later on), his feelings did not appear to matter, and there was little room for discussion. Young Ellis also was aware that it was dangerous to cross intersections unassisted by an adult as he made his way to school before the age of five, but he makes little of this in his autobiography.

Not long afterward, the family moved to New York and moved again two more times in the course of three years. These various dislocations must have exacerbated the trouble he had making friends; Ellis suffered from acute shyness and was essentially a loner except for his relationship with his brother and one neighborhood friend.

Ellis's family was neither close nor demonstrative. Manny Birnbaum, Ellis's childhood friend, recounted that "it was a cold bunch, the whole family, showing very little feeling." Ellis agrees that his family was not particularly emotional, except for his mother's flashes of anger and his sister's bouts of depression. Everyone "went their independent ways, seldom confided in each other, and rarely visited after they left home" (Wiener, 1988, p. 14). Although Albert shared a room with his brother growing up and maintained that they had a "harmonious" relationship, as an adult Ellis never visited with his brother in his home in New Jersey, though he himself resided nearby in New York.

Ellis's parents led lives that were relatively independent of one another and eventually divorced while the children were approaching adolescence. Although Ellis knew few of the details, he was aware that the divorce was precipitated by his father's affair with his mother's best friend. The dissolution of the marriage was accompanied by little rancor, according to Ellis, a claim that is difficult to accept in its entirety; even more remarkable is Ellis's claim that he was relatively unaffected by the event. His biographer reported that "for a long time Albert did not even know of the divorce since his father's absence was about the same, and neither his father nor his mother acted any differently" (Wiener, 1988, p. 45).

Developmental Analysis of Childhood and Adolescence

Two contemporary developmental theories – attachment theory and developmental self-organization – help us to make sense of the impact of Ellis's early childhood experiences on his personality development.

Attachment research has established that securely attached individuals are able to describe their early experiences in a coherent, organized way and are able to evaluate the impact of their experiences on their lives as a whole in a realistic and insightful manner. Most securely attached individuals have the common experiences of having had supportive, nurturing parents who fostered a sense of self-acceptance and trust in others. Alternatively, in certain cases, the secure adult may have had difficult experiences involving neglect or rejection during childhood, but worked through these experiences intellectually and emotionally. Such a resolution is relatively uncommon, but it is regarded as "achieved autonomy." The hallmark of achieved autonomy is the individual's ability to talk about the negative experiences of his or her childhood in a coherent fashion without notable contradictions or affective disconnection.

Albert Ellis clearly had a difficult childhood, which could have been resolved through later life experiences or through the mitigating impact of some other important social influences. This does not appear to have been the case. In fact, what is striking about Ellis's autobiography is that it is missing the hallmark features of achieved autonomy; instead, it is marked by some of the key features of insecure attachment. Within the autobiography, for example, there is clear evidence of the disconnection between descriptions of the circumstances of his family life and his feelings about it, and a number of inconsistencies in the narrative leave a less than coherent picture of the family.

Let us take up the first point. The experiences he described as a young child would have filled most youngsters with considerable anger, fear, and distress: anger at the parents' autocratic exercise of power and role reversal with respect to caregiving, fear over the danger he often confronted in navigating the perils of city life on his own and in his several life-threatening illnesses, and distress at the neglect and multiple abandonments and separations he experienced. And yet, Ellis's descriptions of these events and experiences have a cavalier and often flippant quality to them. "As if all this parental neglect were not enough, I had a few other problems as a child. When I was five, I almost died of tonsillitis and suffered, as a sequel, acute nephritis or nephroses (the doctors are still arguing differential diagnosis about this)" (Ellis, 1972, p. 105). And "[d]espite all this, I somehow refused to be miserable. I took my father's absence and mother's neglect in stride – and even felt good about being allowed so much autonomy and independence" (Ellis, 1972, p. 105).

There were also a number of startling inconsistencies in his autobiographical statements about himself and his family. In one place, he described his mother's neglect ("dereliction of duty") in graphic detail, and yet he told his biographer that he was "the apple of my mother's eye because I knew how to humor her" (Wiener, 1988, p. 43). Ellis disavowed that his childhood had any impact on him as well as avowed its tremendous influence. "I do not believe that the events of my early childhood greatly influenced my becoming a psychotherapist, nor oriented me to becoming the kind of individual and the type of therapist that I now am" (Ellis, 1972, p. 103). Elsewhere, he asserted that he began to develop strategies to cope with life that were the forerunners of RET tenets in childhood. Ellis himself does not appear to be aware of these and other inconsistencies.

His personal relationships with intimate others in later life – two marriages that ended in divorce and a late-life "partnership" in which the two partners, to this day, lead relatively independent lives – adds to the emerging picture of a man whose attachment profile conforms more to the insecure than secure pattern. In Main's system (Main & Goldwyn, 1984), of the two insecure styles, Ellis's profile would seem to resemble the dismissive style more than the preoccupied. Within Bartholomew's four-category system (Bartholomew & Horowitz, 1991), Ellis shared features of both the fearful-avoidant and dismissing. The dismissing style of attachment includes compulsive self-reliance, independence, emotional control, emphasis on achievement, and emotional detachment. The fearful-avoidant individual is drawn to people but avoids forging close connections due to fear of rejection.

Ellis clearly showed the first three features of the dismissing style, but the last quality is somewhat questionable. Was he emotionally detached in his interpersonal relations or merely somewhat avoidant due to fears of rejection? On first examination, Ellis appears to have displayed a yearning for human relatedness, as reflected in his amply documented multiple attempts to forge human connection sexually, romantically, and therapeutically. From his autobiography, we learn that as a young man Ellis wanted desperately to overcome his akwardness around girls and women; in fact, many of the ploys he devised for meeting young women and getting dates admittedly originated as directed efforts at overcoming his social insecurity and fear of rejection. He married twice, and although these two marriages failed, the more extremely dismissive individual might have avoided marriage altogether. Moreover, his late-life partnership with fellow therapist Janet Wolfe has endured many years. These observations would seem to suggest a conflicted need for relatedness, which is more consistent with the fearful-avoidant than dismissive attachment pattern. On the other hand, Ellis emphasizes the sexual motive over the intimacy motive behind his romantic alliances. In several places in the autobiographical and biographical material, he indicated that he thought he was "sexier" than others (i.e., more sexually driven than others); elsewhere he indicated that intimacy is an overrated preoccupation.

In his work as a therapist, Ellis was patently interested in his clients and deployed his own creative emotional skills at the service of helping others contend with their emotional problems. He oriented to his students and clients in an intensely focused way and remembered the minute details of their circumstances. They, in turn, appeared to be equally drawn to him, as demonstrated by the large following he has attracted among former graduates of the RET training program and among current and past clients. These circumstances should make us wary of attributing a purely dismissive attachment style to Ellis. In Ellis's case, the features are more mixed or equivocal than attachment coding criteria would lead us to believe.

Finally, the dismissive individual does not typically recall overt neglect or rejection by caregivers, and Ellis painted a fairly clear picture of this on the part of both parents. However, the intermittent periods of separation and abandonment Ellis experienced while in the hospital as a youngster surely provided the grounds for a partial detachment response, much like the children described by Spitz (1965) and later Bowlby (1973).

In summary, Ellis's attachment profile resembles the dismissive style most closely, though some aspects of the pattern are not entirely consistent. What is especially problematic about the dismissive formulation is the observation that one does not generally expect dismissive individuals to be drawn into the helping professions. Moreover, there is a startling bifurcation in Ellis's career path that is unexpected and unexplained. To be specific, as we learn later, Ellis pursued accounting and business as an undergraduate but then turned to clinical psychology as a graduate student. There is very little in the way of an explanation for such a major shift in orientation – neither the deflection from business nor the attraction of psychology. Possibly he left business because he dreaded the possibility of following in his father's failed footsteps, or perhaps during his several initial business ventures he found out that he was not a very good salesman, though his later enormously successful marketing of RET seems to rule out the latter supposition as a leading contender. Further, what circumstance of life or of motivation propelled Ellis to undertake training as a psychologist? One might generally assume that those who go into the helping professions are motivated by altruistic and empathic concerns, but, obviously, other motives may also be at play. In Ellis's case, the opportunity to conquer fear may have played a particularly important role, as discussed later.

Attachment theory suggests that adult patterns of relatedness and even work patterns (Simpson, 1990) are expressions of internal working models of relationships based on the experiences of childhood, but the preceding observations bring into question the adequacy of attachment formulations to account for all the features of a given personality or life trajectory. In that same vein, attachment theory does not help us understand the prominence of certain emotion traits in Ellis or the aversion to certain emotion states.

One developmental perspective that is particularly helpful in understanding the impact of early experience on Ellis's personality, and specifically early emotional experience, is self-organization theory, which is related to nonlinear dynamic systems accounts of complex behavior. According to this thinking within the developmental sciences (Fogel, 1992a, 1992b; Lewis, 1995, 1997; Thelen & Smith, 1994; Van Geert, 1994), the human being is a self-organizing system. In other words, the elements of a developing system in maturation have the inherent tendency to assemble themselves in a process that results in the emergence and consolidation of novel forms. However, self-organizing systems are both determinate and indeterminate, and a number of structural and contextual constraints influence the infinite ways in which new forms can assemble. Many readers will be familiar with the notion of developmental constraints, originally elaborated by embryologists (Thompson & Grusec, 1970) and eventually by cognitive developmentalists in the 1980s. Features such as the connectivity and modularity of the cortex constitute structural constraints on neural self-organization (Gunnar & Maratsos, 1992). Likewise, limits on early social resources constitute contextual constraints that influence the self-organization of cognitive-developmental pathways (Keating, 1990).

These kinds of constraints impose their force from outside the developing individual. Other forms of constraints reflect indeterminism, however, and emerge as a *consequence* of developmental self-organization whose elements proceed to influence further self-organization. These emergent constraints, coming from within the individual, have a cascading effect in that each emergent form of development goes on to influence the formation of the next, narrowing the developmental pathway over time by increasingly specified out-comes. As ontogenesis proceeds, the prespecified constraints, such as physical limitations, genetic endowment, and sociocultural contexts, do not act directly on developing forms but *through* the action of emergent constraints. Thus prespecified and emergent constraints are in ongoing interplay developmentally as individual pathways evolve (M. D. Lewis, 1997).

These ideas from dynamic systems theory are fully, if not quintessen-tially, applicable to the development of human personality and inter-personal process, as M.D. Lewis (1995, 1997) so eloquently described. Constraints endowed by genes and culture are matched by the oppor-tunities of indeterminism as well as the emergent constraints of self-organization. The biographical material on Albert Ellis makes for a par-ticularly good model for dynamic systems theory because the emergent features constitute a clear pattern that is highly crystalized. To be sure, Ellis has highlighted some aspects of his development and shorn it of the more equivocal features because his narrative was written in the heroic rather than prosaic mode. The heroic mode tends to deliver the didactic lessons of the day in a clear and unambiguous way, though it sacrifices some of the finer shadings and complexities of life and human development. It is also worth pointing out that the heroic mode is also antiphobic in that it is incompatible with the acknowldgment of fear and distress, which has particular meaning in the case of Ellis.

The part that Ellis underplayed and is, therefore, very revealing (Alexander, 1988) is the frightened distress of a child who is a de facto orphan and whose worries are unarticulated or fall on deaf ears. These early terrors have clearly been silenced but surely still play a role in his personality because of the repetitive and chronic nature of the fear and uncertainty Ellis must have experienced as a youngster. One has only to imagine the plight of a four-year-old child dropped off at school with little psychological preparation and thrown in with older children, a child left to cross dangerous intersections on his own, a child who must face the uncertainties of surgery with little preparation and support, a child who is left to deal with virtual abandonment in the anonymous corridors of a big city hospital for a prolonged period of time. Ellis was a weak and sickly child, as was Carl Rogers, but lacked the attention and solicitude that Rogers's parents and siblings provided.

Fear (fright, terror, anxiety) is a particularly toxic affect, according to Tomkins (1963). This emergency emotion, when chronically activated, is physiologically enervating and can be ultimately deadly (Selye, 1956).

Young children have only the most primitive means of protecting themselves against such toxicity, and parents play a vital role in shielding
children from such experiences. In fact, they play a most important role
in the broader context of "emotion socialization" (Cassidy, 1994; Lewis &
Saarni, 1985). Optimal emotion socialization involves helping children
avoid circumstances of undue distress as well as teaching them how
to cope with their emotional experiences. Normally, parental vigilance
and protectiveness ensure that children do not often confront circumstances that are unduly frightening. Later, children are taught how to
cope with feelings of anxiety when circumstances that provoke these
feelings cannot be successfully avoided. Absent these conditions, a particular child may fall upon whatever strategies or adventitious circumstances provide some escape or relief from the toxicity of his or her own
fear.

One such strategy might be to self-distract, another to dissociate,
and another to engage in some form of behavior that removes the self
from danger. These alternative strategies may be differentially successful under different circumstances and environmental conditions. Young
Albert managed to avoid being struck by a car when he crossed busy
intersections on his own. Did he learn to be careful and, gaining confidence, overcome his fear? Or did he route the threat from consciousness
and escape injury and death only by sheer luck? Did he squelch his fear
in school by absorbing himself in books? (Ellis taught himself to read
by the age of five and read voraciously all through his childhood and
adolescence.) If so, this could easily have led to his great absorption in
literature, his discovery of the Horatio Alger stories, and his later fascination with philosophy, especially the writings of the Stoics of ancient
Greece. His interest in reading clearly was not a model set by his parents; indeed, Ellis's family was hardly one that placed a great emphasis
on the life of the mind.

One can easily imagine that as a young boy forced to deal with danger
and neglect on a chronic basis, Ellis might have begun to formulate the
first of a set of counteractive strategies for managing fear, strategies that
Tomkins (1987) referred to as detoxifying scripts. A script in Tomkins's
system constitutes a set of rules for ordering, interpreting, evaluating,
predicting, and controlling affective scenes. One large set of scripts are
"antitoxic" scripts; these involve scenes of particularly intense emotion
such as terror and experiences that cannot be tolerated for any length of
time and perforce must be avoided, escaped, attenuated, or eliminated.
Scripts evolve over time as a consequence of trial-and-error learning

and may take many forms such as "when in danger, seek the caregiver" or "when in danger, withdraw" or, in a more cognitively inclined individual, "when in danger, reframe." Failing all else, denial, repression, and dissociation will also serve.

Interestingly, Ellis asserted that in childhood he began to develop strategies to cope with life that were the forerunners of Rational Emotive Therapy tenets. He claimed that, around the age of four, he began formulating and drilling into his head these rules:

a. Life is full of hassles you can't control or eliminate.
b. Hassles are never terrible unless you make them so.
c. What does happen could always be worse.
d. Making a fuss about problems makes them worse.
e. Wait before you panic.
f. It's interesting to seek solutions.
g. Fight to overcome troubles, but accept failure when necessary.
h. Use your head in reactions as well as your heart (Wiener, 1988, p. 18).

What is interesting about these rules is that they are virtual anti-toxic scripts. If one but makes the assumption that these scripts were originally directed at toxic scenes, the original scenes, deduced from the earlier list, might have consisted of the following:

a. Things are terrible (frightening).
b. They could even get worse.
c. They are uncontrollable.
d. Complaint and supplication do not help; there is nobody there to help.
e. Panic is imminent.
f. Do something quickly, and if it works, use it again.
g. Fight if need be – anger is effective at deflecting aggressors.
h. If it works, relief; the world is not really as bad as it seems.

Whatever Ellis's original strategies, and we can only infer them at this point in time, his strategies later in development seem to have consisted of both active coping and cognitive strategies such as positive reframing and denial. These solutions were evidently quite successful in coping with the circumstances of immediate distress. However, "successful" emergent forms tend to be repeated and to have cascading results that constrain other developmental options. Over time, there are fewer opportunities to experiment with other forms of relief from fear and distress, such as finding a responsive adult who could intervene and/or teach alternative strategies in coping with fright, or learning how to complain effectively. Indeed, the latter is the strategy that Ellis's younger sister apparently fell upon in her own self-organizing developmental pathway.

Ellis described his sister as a compulsive "whiner" both as a child and as an adult, although his friend Manny did not feel that the tendency was all that pronounced. Given the fact that Ellis had no surrogate parent in the form of an elder sibling (as was the fortune of his younger siblings), he was left with little recourse in the face of parental neglect; complaint would have been a patently unsuccessful strategy, reinforcing a sense of impotence. In the sister's case, since she was in effect being parented by Albert, some of her complaints were heard and attended to, providing her with a means of contending with distress that was at least partially effective.

The two different strategies the siblings adopted for contending with fear and distress not only are good examples of how emergent constraints are the very stuff of developmental self-organization but also illustrate how emergent constraints interact with prespecified constraints to temper or consolidate the developmental pathway in self-organization. Additionally, they illustrate the principle of branching pathways in which deflections of the lifecourse are conditioned on preceding developmental contingencies. In young Albert's case, his native physical/genetic endowments, which included a frail, ectomorphic body and innate keenness of intelligence, functioned as prespecified constraints. If we are correct in our assumptions, he was drawn to literature early on as a medium of self-distraction; this developmental option became autonomously fulfilling as he cultivated his mind and sought academic achievement. These developments, in turn, became valuable sources of self-esteem. They also furnished a sense of personal satisfaction that served as an alternative to fulfillments that other children enjoyed in the context of friendship with the more sports-minded and athletically inclined children of Ellis's working-class and middle-class neighborhood. As such, he became ever more drawn into the world of the mind, self-reliance, and, to a degree, social isolation.

In the case of Ellis's sister, the circumstances of gender were a prespecified constraint, which may have acted to further her development as a complainer or supplicant. Given the day and age in which she grew up, one can readily imagine that a young girl with a feminine identity would never have taken advantage of the "freedom" that parental neglect permitted – to roam the streets, for example, as Albert did. As such, she would not have experienced some of the more potentially positive concomitants of premature self-reliance – compensatory self-confidence forged out of assertive behavior and independence.

From one perspective, Ellis's evolving self-organization was creative and adaptive, but from other perspectives, the emergent constraints and cascading effects that followed were at the expense of other options. From an attachment theoretical perspective, he would increasingly forego the closeness and intimacy provided by secure attachments. From an affect theoretical perspective, he would suffer the consequences of un-expressed, "backed up," or blocked affect. According to Tomkins (1963), backed-up affect runs counter to human nature and thus constitutes an innately dissatisfying state of affairs. What results is "affect hunger" and a (mostly unconscious) longing for affective expression. Backed-up affect is dissatisfying to the person whose emotion is blocked as well as to others who come into contact with the individual because the sup-pressed emotion tends to leak through despite efforts at its containment. The leaked affect has a disturbingly distorted, warped quality to it. For example, a person whose distress and anger are backed up tends to carry a "whine" in the voice, as did Ellis's sister. (Note that the extent of the whine may have been exaggerated, and Ellis may have been overly sensitive to it in his avoidance of affect contagion.) Interestingly, there is also a nasality and pleading quality to Ellis's own voice, although it is masked for the most part by other, more authoritative speech patterns such a fast, staccato delivery.

In Ellis's case, fear and distress are most noticeably warded off, and this is key to understanding some of the larger issues of his life and prac-tice. In growing up, Ellis developed detoxifying scripts that relied on distraction, denial, and positive reappraisal. These strategies certainly enabled him to cope with the exigencies of the moment. But emotion that is subverted, rerouted, and otherwise derailed, as noted earlier, remains dynamically active. It can find an outlet in leaked affect; in Ellis's case, it found expression in his face and voice and in psychosomatic disease, or what is today called stress-related illness. The use of the term "stress" is interesting; it covers a multitude of types of blocked affect that can have both systemwide and/or organ-specific health consequences (Traue & Pannebaker, 1993). It is perhaps not coincidental that Ellis suffered from headaches and insomnia throughout his life. This is not to say that he could have found alternative strategies that would have been less tax-ing on his physical condition and emotional well-being. He may have done the best that could have been managed by anyone under the circumstances. But it does point to a pattern of emergent constraint over developmental time.

According to Marc Lewis's (1995, 1997) theory of self-organizing personality development, feedback and coupling are at the heart of both emergent forms (change) and stabilization or consolidation. Positive feedback involves activity in a system that produces change that is fed back into the system's state and sets up a new starting point for subsequent activity. The developing system continues to adjust to its own history and revises its present condition, building on itself as it goes. Through the ongoing process of positive feedback, coactivated elements adjust to one another and become coordinated within the overall system's activity.

In the course of this mutual adjustment, the coactivated elements become coupled or entrained to one another. Elements that do not participate in this activity drop out of the feedback cycle. Those elements that work against the activity are inhibited or turned off and become coupled with other remaining elements in a negative or competitive manner. Recurrent coupling among cooperative elements create attractors in the system's state space. Given a range of starting conditions, the system prefers and gravitates toward these states. Recurrent coupling among competitive elements creates repellors, which are states that the system tends to avoid. Attractors and repellors promote stabilization within the system as activities tend to converge or diverge around these preferences. New attractors can form, and old attractors can fade as patterns of coupling change; however, change becomes less likely over time because structural changes in the underlying system take place, and these in turn resist reversal.

In human personality development, the subsystems that participate in the processes of feedback and coupling are emotional patterns and related cognitive activity (Malatesta & Wilson, 1988; M. D. Lewis, 1997). Each of the basic human emotions (joy, interest, sadness, fear, contempt, disgust, shame, guilt, and anger), when elicited, produces a particular and distinctive pattern of activity within the self system, including distinctive neurophysiologic, physiognomic, and phenomenologic changes. The recurrent activation of certain emotion states within individuals leads to a tendency to stabilize around these states in development through the reciprocal activation of congruent perceptions, appraisals, and interpretations. Certain cognitions are naturally associated with or congruent with certain emotion states. The emotion of fear elicits appraisal of the self-endangered and associated appraisals of the need to escape. With recurrent activation of fear, the organism develops preferential behavioral patterns, and the cognitive apparatus becomes sensitized to the detection of circumstances signaling danger. In development, the more primitive appraisals associated with the self-endangered become increasingly elaborated as the cognitive apparatus matures. The elaborated cognitions recruit similar cognitions, and over time they become coupled in an ever-expanding network of associations. Elements within the elaborated network, even the more remote associations, eventually become capable of provoking the emotion state with very little cuing, unless, of course, other attractor areas evolve and offer alternative constellations for the coupling of elements.

In the case of fear, the cognitions associated with the self-endangered become attractor states for the identification of threat. When individuals become sensitized to danger, they develop an acute sensitivity to cues of danger, no matter how remote. After these dangers are identified, they trigger the emotion state and the justification for feeling that the world is a dangerous place mandating vigilance. In this way, emotions and cognition become coupled and sustain each other in a recursive loop. In the preceding example, we stressed the kinds of natural emotion/cognition coupling that are a product of evolutionary adaptation. However, specific couplings between cognition and emotions may evolve in quite idiosyncratic ways, depending on idiosyncratic social input or out-of-the-ordinary experiences. For instance, the emotion of guilt can become variously coupled with themes of aggression, narcissism, and even good fortune (i.e., survivor guilt).

Over time, and as the cognitive apparatus becomes increasingly elaborated, recurrent cognitions cluster into emergent meta-themes that have a certain self-perpetuating activity of their own. Tomkins called these themes ideoaffective organizations. Ideoaffective organizations have two features, a tendency to scan incoming information for relevance to a particular emotion, and a set of strategies for coping with a variety of contingencies specific to that affect in order to avoid, attenuate, or activate it.

In Marc Lewis's (1995, 1997; Lewis & Junyk, 1997) model of self-organizing personality development, emotion traits are considered attractors in the landscape of personality. Emotions that are defended against are conceived of as repellors. Although anxiety is identified as the quintessential repellor, and the emotion state that stimulates the creation of other emotion repellors, Tomkins (1963) argued that shame functions in much the same way. Indeed, in Chapter 5 we show how shame functions as a repellor in the case of Perls. Nevertheless, Ellis's socioemotional organization appears to offer a particularly rich illustration of the origins of a defensive fear repellor and of the ramifying effects of this repellor on the life trajectory. Additionally, it illustrates the development of and ramifying effects of an interest attractor.

Young Albert's experiences with neglect – and the attendant feelings of fear, distress, and anger – could readily have become coupled with images of the self as unloved and endangered. Moreover, he might have withdrawn into a life of passivity and helplessness. Instead, they became coupled in his case with appraisals of the self as a coper, nurturer, and thinker. These images are not, in popular and literary culture, associated with weakness, despair, and impotence but with more powerful images of the achiever, the physician, and the philosopher. As these more powerful images became cognitively elaborated in the long hours Albert spent alone with his books in virtual social isolation, they evolved as attractors. Inasmuch as images of the self as weak and sickly, abandoned and unloved, worked against the more positively coactivated elements, they remained uncoupled with these elements and got inhibited or turned off, becoming coupled with other "inconsistent" elements in a positive coupling of their own. Thus, images of the self as strong became negatively coupled with images of the self as weak, causing competition between the two "teams."

Negatively coupled elements contribute to negative feedback, inhibiting the formation of patterns with which they compete. As indicated earlier, recurrent couplings among competitive elements create repellors. In this way, we can imagine that by the time Ellis had become an adult he would be drawn to circumstances that continued to reinforce the image of himself as strong, helpful, and accomplished and avoid circumstances that reminded him of weakness, inadequacy, and/or rejection. In emotion terms, if we consider Ellis's personality as a dynamic system responsive to his and others' affective states as they occurred in real time, our analysis suggests that any hint of weakness or sense that the system was approaching the vicinity of fear or distress would generate enough instability in the system to drive it into the attractor regions of anger and/or interest.

It is interesting in this light to view the principles of RET as representing Ellis's affective ideology writ large, in fact, a form of self-similarity. As we hope to show later on, RET, at least as practiced by its innovator, is a tightly knit and relatively unassailable fortress of mostly congruent and elaborately coupled cognitions that enable the exclusion of threatening emotions and cognitions thematically related to vulnerability.

With this illustration of the principle of developmental self-organization in the realm of personality, we can begin to perceive how Albert Ellis is indeed a self-made man. He did "invent" himself and his system early on in the sense that he successively responded to the circumstances of his early environment as well as to his own adaptations to these circumstances over time, gradually evolving, elaborating, and crystallizing a personal coping strategy as well as a larger metatheory.

Let us examine more closely Ellis's ideoaffectology, that is, the particular constellation of ideas and feelings that became coupled in his development. Here are three assertions that appear fairly frequently in Ellis's voluminous writings on RET:

1. Humans are inherently frail and prone to dysadaptation.
2. Negative affect is something we create ourselves.
3. Distress is both a ubiquitous and a *needless* state of the human condition.

Ellis argued that negative emotion is not a product of our past, nor a product of interpersonal process. Other people and circumstances do not cause people to be upset; people upset themselves. In Rational Emotive Therapy, therapists help clients "see how they are basically causing their own disturbances and are not truly disturbed by what happened to them many years ago or by contemporary environmental conditions" (Ellis, 1982, p. 209). The individual person creates his or her own problems and is capable of solving them – with the assistance of the educator/therapist who teaches the method of cognitive reframing. The educator/therapist may not even need to be in the room with the client. Self-help manuals with the RET principles provide the raw material for change. This is essentially a one-person model of human development rather than a two-person model, to use vocabulary from the field of modern intersubjectivity theory (Kahn, 1996); the self is the ultimate source of causation.

Ellis also argued that human distress and misery are a needless condition and can be actively corrected through the procedures of RET. Here we pause to consider that Rational Emotive Therapy is a philosophical extension of Ellis's own ideoaffectology. Ellis had what Tomkins might have described as a strong and well-elaborated *anti-distress ideology*. Indeed, the title of one of his autobiographical pieces is "Psychotherapy without Tears." Ellis could not tolerate distress in himself or in other people. In his autobiography, people, including himself, are never described simply as crying or being sad. There is either a strong negative valuation, with distress described as an irritating condition ("whining," 6 instances), or depicted as being extreme – i.e., people are "miserable" (2), "suffering" (6), "depressed" (6), or "morose" (1).

Ellis's disdain of and repulsion by distress in himself or others was markedly evident in much of his writings, although he could occasionally also be more whimsical about his disparagement of distress and those who would complain about it. Here is a verse composed by Ellis (to be sung to the tune of "The Whiffenpoof Song").

> I cannot have all my wishes filled –
> Whine, whine, whine!
> I cannot have every frustration stilled –
> Whine, whine, whine!
> Life really owes me the things that I miss,
> Fate has to grant me eternal bliss!
> And if I must settle for less than this –
> Whine, whine, whine! (Wiener, 1988, p. 136)

Ellis was particularly sensitive to the whine of his sister's voice, though it apparently was not very pronounced. Perhaps that which we most abhor in others is that which we find most abhorrent in ourselves. If one is frightened by distress, as we believe Ellis was, the distress of others would also be disturbing because of the threat of contagion. One solution to others' distress is to avoid people altogether. But if one also finds them appealing or interesting, then a conflict is engendered: How does one stay engaged but avoid the contagion of their distress? Ellis developed a system that worked for him and works for many other people as well, to judge from the rapidly growing forms of cognitive behavioral therapy. At this biographical juncture, let us pause to examine some of the experiences of Ellis's adult life and the eventual systematization of his ideoaffectology into Rational Emotive Therapy.

Becoming an Adult: Adolescence and Young Adult Years

The account of this period of Ellis's life is sketchy and devoid of the kind of substance that makes for gripping biography. Though replete with circumstances of life that must at times have been frightening, exhilarating, shaming, and enraging – elements of real human drama and emotion – one is treated instead to a rather dry, almost vapid and nonreflective account of several decades of his life that must have had ramifying effects on developmental self-organization. In a fairly standard linear narrative, he takes us through the several junctures of his life at this time. Unlike Fritz Perls, whose agonies are piercingly, if somewhat disjointedly, detailed, Ellis recounted what amounts to an emotionally unannotated account of what was possibly quite an interesting *Bildungsroman*.

As a young man of Jewish parentage, Albert followed one of the ancient traditions of his family's faith, becoming bar mitzvahed at the age of thirteen. What is interesting and of special note, and never detailed, are the circumstances of this coming of age and why he abandoned his religion for atheism later in life. Ellis's parents were second-generation immigrants. His father's side came from Russia and his mother's, from Germany. The religious practices of his father are not mentioned in the autobiography and may not have been of much consequence given his virtual absence from the family. His mother belonged to reformed Judaism, and she attended temple weekly; however, these outings seemed driven mainly by her craving for a social outlet. Like many second-generation Jews, the Ellis family may have been ambivalent about their religion and origins, choosing to assimilate rather than cling to old customs – perhaps as a means of deflecting anti-Semitism. Indeed, the father changed the family name to Ellis from the more Jewish-sounding Groots. Ellis reported that he underwent a bar mitzvah ceremony only to please his mother. However, preparing for this ceremony entails a considerable investment in intellectual and socioemotional resources, including learning Hebrew – a difficult language with foreign characters – and foregoing the pursuit of other activities; instruction is intensive and involves after-school classes usually taught by part-time instructors who typically can be very demanding. Ellis managed to fulfill the rigorous demands of this instruction and ceremony. That he did so for his "mother's sake" indicates more of an emotional connection with her than he otherwise indicated. To identify with and display his Jewishness at a time during which the family lived in a mostly gentile, and possibly anti-Semitic neighborhood of the Bronx, to please his mother, may belie the dependence he still felt on her. His later rejection of Judaism is interesting in this light. It suggests that he no longer needed the meager emotional support she provided. Moreover, the fact that he did not merely renounce Judaism but became an outspoken proponent of atheism while his mother was still alive indicated not only that accommodation to his mother's goals had been abandoned, but that he could also perhaps express his anger against her in another form. Here, as elsewhere, there are disjunctions in the narrative of his life that raise issues with respect to attachment and to the kinds of ideoaffective scripts that he would evolve as a young man, a point to which we return a bit later.

As it were, the young Albert soon found another source of "spiritual" guidance. As early as the age of sixteen, Ellis was reading a wide variety of philosophical works that included the writings of Epictetus, Spinoza, Kant, and Bertrand Russell; he related that these early intellectual forays formed the basis for several of his later views on solving human problems. At the time, however, they may well have served to foster an intellectual identity to replace that of Judaism, one that permitted a more perfect assimilation and shored up what was still a fragile sense of self-esteem.

Ellis's immersion in these philosophical works and his self-contained intellectual world, however, were interrupted by the exigencies of life at this time. Ellis's parents had already been divorced for some years when Wall Street collapsed in 1929, ushering in the Great Depression, a time of severe economic hardship that was felt at all socioeconomic levels. With the onset of the Depression, his mother's savings rapidly dissipated. Moreover, the family's economic plight was compounded by the fact that she did not receive alimony payments. Ellis reported that he and his brother were able to find odd jobs to help support the family while he was still in high-school, but there is little description of the hardscrabble life they surely led during this time, as so vividly depicted by other writers of the era. Instead, he quickly glossed over the economic hardship, thereby depriving the reader of any kind of empathic response or identification with the author. Ellis simply "became concerned" about money and decided that he should consider pursuing a business career.

With this plan in mind, upon graduation from high-school at age sixteen, Ellis enrolled in City College's Baruch School of Business and Civic Administration, where tuition was free to city residents. In college he studied to become an accountant because he believed that this would lead to a secure and steady income at the end of four years. His brother and friend continued to pursue the business profession after graduation, but Albert stayed in business about ten years, just long enough to put himself through graduate training in psychology.

As Ellis revealed in the autobiography, his real passion was for writing, though he apparently was not very polished and lacked the proper connections during his first efforts during his twenties. Ellis wanted to become a "famous" writer for the express purpose of "having lots of women and sex"; he also expected that it would permit him to retire from business at thirty. He tried his hand at virtually every literary activity, producing over twenty manuscripts before he entered graduate school eight years later at the age of twenty-eight. The works were quite diverse including novels, plays, poetry, musical lyrics, and nonfiction pieces on politics, philosophy, and sexual mores. One was a socialist primer, presenting Marx's theories of communism to the public. Another was *The Art of Never Being Unhappy*, which was his first book on self-help therapy. None of this early work was ever accepted for publication.

After college, and before beginning graduate school, he joined his brother in business selling men's trousers for a few years. He also worked as a paid organizer and propagandist for political groups and even joined his father in a couple of the latter's abortive business ventures. During this time, Ellis continued to live at home with his mother and siblings and to provide some economic support. Although he was called up for the draft, he was rejected because of diabetes, a dislocatable shoulder, and a history of kidney trouble.

Ellis entered graduate training in clinical psychology at Columbia University in 1941 at the age of twenty-eight and earned a master's degree by the end of the academic year. He saw clients in a small office at his mother's apartment. Before Ellis developed his own therapeutic philosophy, he had rather classical training, as well as training in some of the most modern techniques of his day. During his time at Columbia, he experimented with Carl Rogers's client-centered psychotherapy, but he regarded this kind of therapy as too passive for him. It is also possible that he was made uncomfortable by the need to absorb and reflect feelings, permitting clients to express emotional distress in its many acute and chronic varieties. It is quite evident from the earlier discussion of Ellis's socioemotional background that the kind of empathic responding called for in client-centered therapy would not come easily to him.

Ellis continued to work and see clients during graduate school and completed his doctorate in five years. Soon thereafter he took a job as a psychologist at the Northern New Jersey Mental Hygiene Clinic, based in Morristown, and began training to become a psychoanalyst. His own personal analysis lasted two years, and he credited it with reducing some of his irritability and compulsivity. One wonders what kinds of interpretations his analyst offered for Ellis's dispositional anger and what Ellis was able to do with this explication in therapy; there is little evidence that he had any kind of dynamic understanding of it. Ellis did, however, conclude during this time that his irritability was irrational and that he required active efforts to control it.

In three years' time, he advanced in standing at the clinic to become chief psychologist of the central diagnostic center and spent the next two years as chief psychologist for the State of New Jersey's entire psychological program. During these early years of employment as a psychologist, Ellis must have led somewhat of a frenetic life, working full time in New Jersey, living in New York, having analysis two to three nights a week in New York, and conducting a clinical practice on the side as well. He was also writing at a fast clip during this time and starting to get his works published. He published research reports on an odd assortment of issues including mongoloids, hermaphroditism, women's attractiveness, and people with peculiar names. His first published book was *The Folklore of Sex* (1951), followed by a number of other publications involving advice on sexual matters. In his autobiography, he explained that his career as a sexologist began by reading all the literature he could get his hands on and his own active experimentation and personal data collection, which he then passed on to friends, clients, and other interested audiences. To read of this, one comes away with the impression that the women of Ellis's social world provided little more for him than a laboratory for his experimentation. Was he really as callous as this sounds? To some, yes, but one can also read between the lines to envision a sexually inept and thoroughly frustrated young man who converted the disasters of his early romantic and sexual encounters into fantasies in which he was the ultimate conqueror, although the conquered entities were not only his rejecting dates but also his own anxiety over performance and intimacy.

Ellis become known for his avant garde approach to sexual counseling, typified by advocacy of free sex and nonjudgmental attitudes toward behaviors that were conventionally regarded as loose, immoral, or even perverted, that is sexual behavior between unmarried individuals, adultery, or homosexuality. This work is discussed in greater detail in Chapter 8. As is well known, Ellis eventually moved away from this area of concentration to that of RET.

Ellis left the New Jersey office in 1952 after five years, apparently because of some dissension in the ranks over his having a clinical practice in addition to his state job, and because he lived in New York rather than New Jersey. He also alluded to rancor created by a dispute over the order of authorship of a book. His clinical practice had grown over the years and was now able to sustain him. He was practicing as a psychoanalyst, although he grew further and further away from classical analysis as he began to experiment with a more active problem-solving approach for which he would later become famous. In fact, by the time he left his New Jersey position, he was ready to give up on psychoanalysis and practice his own brand of therapy. He thus shed four years of analysis and training and five years of analytic practice and asked his clients to refrain from calling him an analyst. He began to make direct interventions and to set specific goals for clients. Moreover, he began to write critically about traditional analytic practices. During this time, he also began to refashion his personal image, shedding some of the facade he had previously adopted. Most notably, he dropped the British accent he had cultivated earlier and reverted to what some of us know as Basic Bronx, accompanied by authentic street talk and vulgar language. This shift in persona had the effect of drawing even more attention to his unusual views.

In terms of professional activity, this period in his life was also the most productive as a writer and counselor on sexual matters, permitting him to turn out books and articles by the score. By the time he was sixty, he had written hundreds of books and articles on sex. By middle adulthood, however, he was also elaborating his theory of Rational Emotion Therapy.

Ellis Formalizes His Therapeutic Ideology

The scheme for dealing with the emotional problems of life that worked for Ellis is called Rational Emotive Therapy, originally simply Rational Therapy. This theory had its intellectual roots in Stoicism, hedonism, and behaviorism. Stoicism taught that emotions must be eradicated; hedonism, that pleasure was better than pain; and behaviorism, that one could engineer one's life by design. It was Ellis's unique contribution to focus on the training of thought patterns and to do so in a systematic, formulaic, and easily replicated manner. Considered as an oeuvre, Rational Emotive Therapy, at least as practiced by Ellis, was the ultimate system for finessing negative emotion. Some of the rules for this system, as illustrated in examples from Ellis's own life, are given here. The rules are simple and straightforward, as Ellis points out to initiates. These rules have obvious roots in his own practical solution to the one-person psychology of self-reliance.

How to Finesse Negative Emotion

1. *Cognitive Reframing and Denial.* Positive reframing looks for the silver lining in the dark clouds of painful, stressful, and tragic life circumstances. Denial ignores the dark clouds altogether. Both are types of coping strategies, though denial would appear to be less healthy. According to Lazarus (1996), the uses of denial have been sorely underestimated; he wrote instead that denial may at times be necessary and life-promoting. Denial may indeed at times be necessary, although it may be attended by certain costs. Denial and positive reframing can bring immediate respite from circumstances that are at the moment uncontrollable; however, as regular defenses, they risk tuning down the emotional life to a considerable degree and, as such, may invite affect hunger and/or stress-related illness. Ellis himself was faced with the early need to preserve a sense of the self that did not seem to be constantly endangered. Despite the apparent neglect he received at the hands of his parents, Ellis remembered only a happy early life except for a period of hospitalization. In his autobiography, he reframed his early experiences as merely a set of challenging circumstances. He neither expected nor wanted pity or empathy from others. Additionally, in his practice of RET, he weaned clients away from self-pity and "catastrophizing" – that is making too much of one's pain or anxiety.

2. *Substitution.* Substitution of emotional responses is another means of averting negative experience. In Ellis's case, interest became an attractor in his personality state space, one that he said he actively cultivated. In truth, he may indeed have learned to mobilize interest to deflect his attention in the face of recurrent terror during his early years. A particularly revealing anecdote in Ellis's biography suggested developmental antecedents. The story may be apocryphal, but it is still illuminating.

During his bouts with nephritis, Ellis's ankles, legs, and belly would swell. Once just before his seventh birthday, his abdomen became so bloated that he was hospitalized and the doctors were forced to operate. As his biographer relates,

> They reassured him that his stomach would be just slightly punctured and then drained, all so painlessly that he could stay up and watch. Again he thought of objecting, but decided not to. So he squelched his fear, saw the large needle with tube attached stuck into his belly, and observed a huge amount of milky fluid drain into a basin on the floor. He remembers consciously deciding to ignore his fears and compel himself to become

interested in the strange procedure. He forced curiosity to be his primary emotion. He actually enjoyed the experience: the attention, the relief, the exoticism, deciding once more that he did not have to suffer from anxiety if he did not choose to (Wiener, 1988, p. 24).

As bizarre as this explanation seems, there may be a modicum of truth to it in the context of understanding emergency coping. Indeed, a reinterpretation of fear as interest may be a rather constructive and adaptive solution to the problem of fear in the short run. As a long-term strategy, however, it has its liabilities. If generating "interest" becomes a goal in its own right it may take on a life of its own as an antidote to accumulating waves of negative affect. To keep such tides at bay, interest affect must be maintained at all costs, for to risk the loss of interest is to invite the mood of boredom. Boredom is an emotional state or vacuum condition that is little described in the theoretical literature but typically experienced as a negative mood. Thus, boredom may be the first inroad to ward off negative affect. Hyperactivity in the form of overcommitment to work and the stress that accompanies it may be less distressing than the possibility of boredom and the wellspring of negative affect that it threatens to unleash. Ellis is described as a workaholic by most who know him – his work so interests and compels him, and he is filled with such zeal for his mission to share his discoveries with everybody that he works almost continuously, living in the same building as his institute and working from 9:00 A.M. until 11:00 P.M. Obviously, something other than commitment to a vocation is at work here. In this context, interest becomes self-amplifying as cognitions and emotion enter a cycle of positive feedback. The emotion of interest leads to exploration and analysis, which deflects attention from occasions for negative affect.

What is of note about this pattern of emotion substitution is that it is a particularly effective strategy in Ellis's work with clients. In our later analysis of material from the case of Martha, one of Ellis's clients, we see that Ellis found the client's dream – a dream that evoked fear in her – "interesting," rather than frightening, and eventually persuaded her to shift her own focus to the interesting elements.

3. If All Else Fails, Dissociate. Dissociation can take a number of forms, from the simple disconnection between thoughts and feelings, and between different experiences, as noted earlier in the context of our discussion of Ellis's account of his life, to the severe dissociations documented in patients with chronic mental conditions (Magai & Hunziker, 1998). Ellis's dissociations were of the milder sort. Since these kinds of mild dissociations and the two other strategies for circumventing negative affect noted earlier were evidently so successful for Ellis, he was able to retain a kind of simple equilibrium over the long course of his life, reinforced, one guesses, by his daily immersion in teaching the tenets of Rational Emotive Therapy to others.

This rule appears to be a viable means of coping with the distresses that Ellis endured, but the features of this system share some of the same hallmarks of the repressive coping style described by Schwartz (1990). One consequence of the repressive coping style is somatization of emotional distress, which may find an outlet in any number of stress-related diseases or afflictions. Hence we might expect that Ellis suffered from some such complaints. In fact, as indicated earlier, throughout his life he had been plagued with headaches and insomnia, though the former problem has diminished over time. The sleeping disorder remains the "most of his unwanted behavior" (Wiener, 1988, p. 23).

Another kind of dissociative consequence has also been described in the context of our discussion of Ellis's attachment style. This brings us to a fuller discussion of the place of intimacy in Ellis's life.

Ellis and Intimacy

In terms of the social circumstances of his adult life, Ellis married twice. One marriage ended in a strangely depicted "annulment" (Wiener, 1988), and the other broke up "amicably" after just a few years; neither relationship resulted in children. In the meantime, there were various liaisons fore and aft that he relishes relating.

Ellis's earliest romantic involvements were tumultuous and unstable. He appears to have been attracted to women who had a flair for the dramatic and who tended to be intense but emotionally unpredictable; some of the women had histories of emotional instability or led lives that were somewhat marginal or precarious. Ellis's relationships with these women were turbulent and did not last very long. However, these relationships also provided material that he later used in his books of human sexuality and the problems that might be encountered in the course of relationships.

Later in life, Ellis met and formed an enduring relationship with a different kind of woman, Janet Wolfe, whom he describes as his "companion" and who is portrayed as more emotionally controlled, independent, and self-reliant. Although Ellis and Wolfe lead relatively independent lives, they have lived together for over thirty years and appear to share a certain kind of warmth and humor between them. More recently, in recognition of the fact that Ellis and Wolfe are not married and Ellis will, in all likelihood, predecease his much younger partner, he made special provisions for her in his will. As an aside, we note that attachment theory in its present form does not yet adequately deal with this kind of mix of independence and considered concern, nor does it deal with changes in the preference for types of attachment objects over the lifecourse.

Let us return, however, to the basic premise that Ellis is a man who is not very comfortable with interdependence and intimacy. In our thematic analysis of his autobiography, only 6 percent of his coded themes were about affiliative relationships, in contrast to 11 percent for Rogers. There are two other sources of data on Ellis and his stance toward human attachments and intimacy that we bring to bear on the issue.

The first is an essay entitled "Intimacy in Rational-Emotive Therapy" (Ellis, 1982), written for an edited volume on the theme of intimacy. After opening with a dictionary definition of the term, Ellis cited the need to distinguish between healthy and unhealthy forms of intimacy and warned against the tendency to idealize the construct. He then proceeded to disparage "authorities" (his quotation marks) that overemphasize the significance of attachments; his position, in contrast, was that even though attachments may be one of life's more enjoyable pursuits, "it is hardly the be-all and end-all of existence" (Ellis, 1982, p. 204). He further noted that "millions . . . live most of their lives in a distinctly nonintimate and nonloving manner, and yet some of them are extremely happy" (Ellis, 1982, p. 204).

The next section in this article considered intimacy between therapist and clients. Ellis came out clearly and strongly against sexual intimacy, listing the various reasons it should be condemned; he then raised the question about other kinds of (nonsexual) closeness and warmth between therapist and client. Even though he at first acknowledged the reputed advantages of a therapist relating closely or warmly to clients, he quickly pursued a much more extensive elaboration of the perils. For one, offering closeness and acceptance to individuals may reinforce the core of their disturbance, since "almost all seriously disturbed individuals tend to be perennial babies" (Ellis, 1982, p. 204). In Ellis's opinion, emotional disturbance is "largely self-indulgence, lack of discipline, and childish demandingness" (Ellis, 1982, p. 205). Moreover, in this view, giving clients acceptance and warmth can and has in many cases exacerbated clients' problems and fostered their continuing dependency and disturbance. Other risks of a close relationship are that the client will become frustrated, hostile, or disillusioned and embittered about the limitations of the intimacy or "pseudointimacy" offered by the therapist. Ellis also suggested that by fostering dependency through closeness and extending the course of treatment, the therapist may be acting more on the basis of his own needs for intimacy than the clients', or even purely for monetary gain. Thus, therapist warmth was evaluated with some suspicion and looked upon as largely dangerous to the client.

In the next section, he contrasted healthy and unhealthy kinds of love and intimacy. One expects Ellis to review both close-binding, demanding relationships and compulsive self-reliance as forms of unhealthy attachment. However, here the concerns were almost exclusively with the former kind. Unhealthy love involves partners who "demand, dictate, insist, or command," intimacy (Ellis, 1982, p. 211). The following relatively long section amplified the theme that unhealthy love is found in clients who are obsessed or fixated with a lover and ultimately leads to client feelings of "anxiety, jealousy, depression, inertia, hostility, and feelings of worthlessness" (Ellis, 1982, p. 213). The article concluded with lessons on how RET may be applied effectively in dealing with unhealthy attachments of the close-binding or dependent kind.

If we interpret this disquisition on intimacy as reflecting on Ellis's own internal working models of relationships, it is clear that intimacy is a scenario fraught with risk. He expected that closeness with another individual (client, partner) would result in that partner's dependency and anger. In dealing with such a partner, he would feel a whole host of turbulent emotions: anxiety, jealousy, depression, inertia, hostility, and shame. The bulk of these feelings are repellor emotions for Ellis.

One of the things that is noteworthy about the text on intimacy is that it is filled with dismissive and contemptuous evaluations. In particular, it is riddled with derisive comments about dependency (e.g., "perennial babies"). Although contempt is salient in almost all of Ellis's written work, it is especially dense in this chapter. This attitude suggests to us that contempt may have evolved in Ellis's ideoaffectology directly in relation to feelings of vulnerability with respect to dependency. To be dependent on the inept mother of childhood would have been terrifying. Contempt then, for Ellis, is a safe emotion; it allows him to interpose the kind of distance he requires so as to avoid encounter with the vulnerable emotions associated with dependency.

We get another sampling of Ellis's views on attachment and a clearer picture of how he deals with individuals presenting with problems of intimacy at a public demonstration of RET he conducted in November of 1989 at the Rational Emotive Institute. This was one of the famous Friday night workshops open to the public that Ellis has been conducting for over two decades. The volunteer, let us call him Enrico, was prompted for a problem. After some hesitation, Enrico picked a problem he was having with intimacy. Specifically, he told Ellis that he had "difficulty in getting close to women without relating to them sexually." As the dialogue on stage evolved, Enrico revealed that he was afraid of dependency, feeling that if he got intimate and became dependent, he would be vulnerable like a child, and would lose control. Therefore he runs away.

Since this may have been one of Ellis's early fears as well, we listened attentively to Ellis's reply. Ellis pointed out that Enrico was not going to solve his problem with intimacy by avoiding it; instead, he must try to get closer. On the face of it, this recommendation seemed somewhat surprising coming from Ellis based on what we already know about his credo concerning intimacy and its perils. However, this recommendation was followed by another which was that if the relationship does not work out, abandon it. "[Y]ou always have the choice of changing, stopping, getting some other person to be intimate with," and "becoming intimate with a woman" doesn't mean that "you have to remain so with that same woman for the rest of your life." Furthermore, "there's no necessity for any humans to bond and millions of them don't bond at all in their life; some of them lead very happy lives, like Emmanual Kant, who was a great philosopher. He never bonded with anybody and led a good life."

Later in the session, Ellis provided a bit of desensitization therapy followed by homework assignments. "Imagine that with your wife, or some other woman – it doesn't matter, but it could be with your wife that you really get desperately needy and that she doesn't need you, see – it's not reciprocal – that you need her very much and she can easily live without you. Can you visualize, imagine that, that might happen?" Enrico could; then Ellis asked him how he felt, and the man described terror, fear of being abandoned. "Alright, get in touch with that. Make yourself really terrified, really afraid to be abandoned. That's good.... Now ... change it to feeling only sorry, only disappointed." The man reported that he was able to change his experience in the way that Ellis suggested.

Once again we see that for Ellis the danger of closeness is dependency and the threat of abandonment – a very terrifying thought indeed. The treatment Ellis conducted was applied to the fearful feelings, not the circumstances that could be causing the dependent behavior of the other individual. The fear was downgraded to sorrow or disappointment. The threat of abandonment was dispensed with by dismissing the importance of the other to the self and by empowering the weak, fearful individual to abandon the hurtful person. Enrico was told that people do not die of unfulfilled intimacy needs, that people do not have to remain with the same partners all their lives, that people who are intimate don't have to stay together. "[L]ove is very satisfying, it's very good if ya don't need it and what's more, as we said before, when you desire it with one person and that doesn't work out, there are many other fish in the sea."

Ellis was trying to show Enrico that he had many more options than he felt he had and that he did not have to feel as "stuck" in his problems as he thought he was. In spirit, this is the kind of message that any therapist would like to impart. However, given that this was only one session, and given the particular solutions that were recommended to Enrico – a man we have little background information on – we pause to consider its impact.

Enrico was a relatively responsive demonstration client; he seemed to absorb the lessons that Ellis offered and was ostensibly grateful for his session with Ellis. There were several key messages embedded in the session: intimacy does not necessarily mean dependency; people can live without intimate relationships and be quite happy; one can abandon bad others just as others can abandon the self; intimate partners can be replaced. While one cannot dispute any one of these ideas in the sense that they can apply to certain individuals in certain situations, what is missing is the personalized context in which therapy usually takes place, and perhaps takes place with Ellis as well when he is not on stage. One does not know which of these messages were more salient to the demonstration client. Enrico showed some key features of the fearful-avoidant individual – ambivalent feelings about closeness and fears of rejection and abandonment. Ellis's desensitization exercises and counterphobic homework assignments may have been some use to Enrico in that a drop in his guard against his wife might have actually led to an improvement in the intimacy of their relationship. On the other hand, if the message that got through to Enrico was the interchangeability of partners and the ease with which relationships could not only be forged but also dissolved, then another consequence to the relationship can be imagined.

In summary, Ellis's biographical and theoretical writings revealed a somewhat dismissive stance toward attachments; it is also fairly certain that this stance was a defense against fears of abandonment that have very early roots. Moreover, he showed the feature of compulsory self-reliance that is a hallmark of that attachment style. Still, he is a shade too emotionally elaborated for that, and it appears that dismissivness is mixed with another attachment style. That is, he also showed signs of fearful avoidance, although it is very muted. One usually thinks of the fearful-avoidant individual as deeply vulnerable. Ellis worked fiercely at mastering this latent vulnerability. Although he seems self-confident and self-possessed, there are telltale signs of his continuing vulnerability – the slightly skittish look to his eyes in an otherwise masklike face as seen in the film, his apparent yearning to be related to and helpful to people. One doubts that "pure" dismissives would either go into, or be successful in, the helping professions. Moreover, there is the incontrovertible fact that a significant number of colleagues are drawn to working with him. He managed to attract a fair number of romantic partners as well, perhaps those who could discern the little motherless boy behind the facade of cynicism and bravado. Even in middle age, encounters with him still leave one with the feeling that one is interacting with a stoic little boy who has not quite graduated to a comfortable feeling about himself. His language is still adolescent, sprinkled with curse words and adolescent braggadocio. It does not require penetrating Freudian analysis to discern that he still has many unmet needs for acceptance and love, though, of course, he would be the last to admit it. And, like the brave "bad" child whose attempts to bluster through an uncomfortable situation is so obviously a cover up of his own deep shame and who gets everyone's sympathy and help rather than their anger, Ellis's underlying vulnerability buys him fans.

In the article on intimacy (Ellis, 1982), Ellis disparaged the need for close human attachments. There was great self-consistency in his behavior in that he routinely insulated himself from having much contact with others outside of work. Though others regard him as a social recluse, Ellis considered himself as being in the grand tradition of the self-sufficient Stoic of the ancient Greeks. Of course, it is helpful to reflect that stoicism may be a sterling quality when it comes to coping with certain critical crises in life, but if one remains stoic under circumstances that do not require stoicism and avoidance, and if one continues to harbor unmet needs for intimacy and acceptance, it is unlikely that these needs can ever be met, thus producing the effect of cascading constraints on the capacity for intimacy.

This observation raises the provocative question of Ellis's potential for success in psychotherapy. No matter how one evaluates his metatheory and therapeutic techniques – as occasionally useful, as the best thing since gefilte fish, as superficial, or as inconsequential – it cannot be gainsaid that Ellis has helped many clients with a variety of problems in his long career as a psychotherapist. Let us be clear that he has not accomplished this because he has a great capacity for connection. And, for the most part, he has not accomplished this by emphasizing the setting of a warm, accepting climate, like Rogers, or in establishing a therapeutic alliance based on empathic resonance (Strupp, 1993) or empathic enquiry (Orange et al., 1997). He was not particularly concerned with establishing the Winnicottian "holding" environment that provides a safe place to explore the darker and more split off aspects of the self.

In some ways, Ellis's style is more akin to the detached assessment of the classical analyst in which an authoritative shaman, sui generis, divines the objective reality of the patient's being (Kahn, 1996). However, Ellis went quite beyond the classic analytic stance in both his active directiveness and in his communication of very focused and intense interest – a talent that helps to convince clients of his sincerity and involvement. Although Ellis is probably not the most ideal therapist for a variety of individuals, he may be an extraordinarily effective one for others. At this point, we introduce the notion of complementarity as a facet of therapeutic process and examine its meaning in the case of Ellis and RET techniques, exploring it in the context of attachment styles and linking it to our notion of emotion traits. Here, however, we consider emotion traits as interactive elements in interpersonal process. As personality psychologists from the interpersonal school (Tracey, 1994; Wiggins, 1982) pointed out, personality traits or dispositional tendencies are only that – tendencies. Although they lend a certain defining feature to individual personality, they are essentially stochastic in nature, responding to the different base rates of behavior in different individuals and to alterations of state during ongoing interchanges.

"Complementarity" is a term that is found in diverse disciplines, from physics (Bohr, 1950) to personality theory (Wiggins, 1982) to psychotherapy process (Tosca & McMullen, 1992). In each instance, complementarity refers to a coexisting duality of states or processes. According to the interpersonal school of personality theory, each person's behavior constrains or elicits behavior from the partner with whom he or she is interacting. Individuals relate to the personality traits and behaviors of others in either a complementary or reciprocal way depending on the dimension in question. Interpersonal interactions are typically reciprocal on the affiliation dimension and complementary on the power/status dimension. That is, a smile by one person tends to elicit a smile in the partner; a hostile gesture tends to elicit a hostile comment in return. In terms of power, a dominant individual tends to elicit submissive behavior in his or her partner and vice versa. There is also evidence that dating partners may be attracted to one another on the basis of complementarity of affect or attachment style (Magai, 1999a).

A slightly different version of complementarity has been assumed by Tracey and Hays (1989) and Krause and colleagues (Anstadt et al., 1997; Krause et al., in press; Villenave-Cremer, Kettner & Krause, 1989) within the clinical context. Krause proposed that successful therapy is predicated by responses from the therapist that compensate for dysadaptive client social and affective processes. For example, a complementary response to client shame emitted in the context of relating an incestual seduction might elicit therapist horror or disgust rather than reciprocal shame. In terms of relational styles, Mahoney and Norcross (1993) suggested that there may be an optimal amount of "contrast" between therapist and client, but that neither the amount, nor particular dimension, of fit and contrast needed is as yet clear. In considering Ellis and his clients as related through complementarity in therapy, we turn to a discussion of both his trait emotions and attachment style.

By Ellis's admission and our own inspection of the live material of the film and from transcripts of other sessions, anger is a salient background affect for him. It is one of the two negative affects that he is not on guard against (the other being contempt), having been exposed to eruptions of anger in both parents on occasion and being personally convinced of its rootedness in genetics. As an interpersonal emotion, anger is a double-edged affect in the sense that it can be used both to keep others at a distance and to engage them in an intensely confrontational way. Intrapersonally, it is also an effective way of handling anxiety. Assertiveness trainers know that if they can mobilize a sense of frustration, resentment, or anger in the client, they can use this affect to overcome the timidity that feeds into self-defeating passivity.

If we are right, Ellis works best with those who are fearful, and especially those whose presenting problems have more to do with anxieties that interfere with work success than for those who present with anxiety problems involving intimacy. Thus, those individuals who are anxiety prone, but not necessarily fearful-avoidant in the attachment sense, would adapt well and profit from RET's homework assignments involving the practice of assertive behavior and gain from making incremental steps at being more self-assured and self-assertive.

Earlier we introduced the notion of expressive aptitude and expressive tolerance as aspects of trait emotions. In this context, one could say that Ellis had an expressive aptitude for anger, which had multiple consequences. Ellis's prickly demeanor put others on notice that they did not dare trespass on his highly guarded privacy or penetrate the barriers against intimacy. At the same time, it probably was an affect that was easy for him to model and express in the psychotherapeutic context, in a compensatory way, giving expression to an affect that might have been difficult for certain clients. The case of Martha is a good example. In fact, one suspects that Ellis was particularly effective with anxious clients whose temerity interfered with the ability to express their own needs, defend their own self-esteem, and deflect intrusions, in other words, to express anger, resentment, and hostility.

Martha is a twenty-three-year old client whom Ellis described as presenting as depressed, almost suicidal, with deep and chronic feelings of unworthiness. Ellis presented a verbatim transcription of the therapy sessions as well as his own commentary. Despite the salience of her depression and shame in the opening sessions, Martha's working affect lexicon was almost exclusively localized around fear; anxiety was a highly elaborated dimension of her personality, which was experienced in most aspects of her life, including those involving her family, her love-life, work persona, moods, and both important and mundane tasks. In the course of their sessions together, Ellis was able to work effectively in helping her to expand her expressive language to affects beyond fear and to mobilize her anger and a more assertive approach to her family and work situations. He forged an alliance with the client early on by acknowledging and elaborating on her emotional position. He then introduced and modeled hostile and angry postures for her, which she was able to absorb and follow in work outside of therapy to a limited extent. He supported the activation of anger to counter fear in instances where she was immobilized by anxiety; he was adept at provoking and scaffolding separation – in Martha's case in the context of abusive family control and enmeshment. Thus, his ideoaffective posture of anger worked as a complementary and compensatory turbulence for her established attractor of fear, promoting a destabilization of her affect system and, at least potentially, new and more adaptive patterns of behavior.

In terms of attachment styles, one surmises that those with a dismissive attachment style would find Ellis's brand of psychotherapy less threatening than other kinds of therapy. This is not to say that such individuals would work well with, or overcome, certain types of problems, or even enter psychotherapy on their own. Ellis is not going to make demands on the client to make emotional connections, a capacity for which neither he nor the dismissive client have particular facility. Although this state of affairs may be comfortable for the client, to the extent that a certain degree of tension or an expansion of affect has to occur in a relationship to prompt change (Magai & Nusbaum, 1996), RET with dismissive individuals may be only a quick fix for certain problems and less effective in dealing with long-standing issues of self-awareness or relatedness, for example.

In the same vein, it is of interest to note that much of what Ellis does in therapy is to amplify and elaborate on the client's expression of emotion, as in the case of Martha. He uses exaggerated versions of emotion terms and successive iterations of terms connoting the same affects. That is, things are not just regrettable or unsatisfying, they are "terrible," "horrible," "awful." Use of such evocative language is not merely striking in this context; it is the kind of vocabulary one might expect if Ellis were dealing with individuals having a relatively restricted range of affective expression. Ellis not only uses this kind of emotionally evocative language but also uses it in a fusillade. Ellis's use of escalated affect terms conceivably helps clients with point attractor or monopolistic emotion styles or clients whose emotion regulation strategies consist of routing negative affect from consciousness – most notably those who have a dismissing attachment pattern – find the words for their deeply sequestered and conflicted emotions. Thus, we surmise that Ellis may attract fairly well-defended individuals, who nevertheless stand to gain something in the way of achieving more effective behavior in task-oriented, goal-defined sectors of their life, and possibly even an expansion in their affective vocabulary.

In terms of the kinds of change in personal functioning we may anticipate from this kind of psychotherapy and with this kind of client, we surmise that it is likely to consist of changes in what personality psychologists call "characteristic adaptations" – views of self, patterns, and habits of everyday life – rather than changes in personality traits (Costa & McCrae, 1994, 1996) or real change in the depth of interpersonal relatedness. This is not to denigrate the substantive personal gains that can be had from RET in terms of more effective everyday functioning.

It is simply to say that this is probably not the kind of therapy, at least as practiced by its innovator, that is conducive to solving problems in interpersonal intimacy where the goal is to accept dependency and interdependence.

One might also imagine that those with a fearful-avoidant attachment style would be initially drawn into work with Ellis but would ultimately find it unsatisfying. As already indicated, Ellis's stance is that achieving intimacy is not the most important goal in life. Although he can supply the client with tools to overcome shyness around potential romantic partners and get them to advance to the first stage in the intimacy process – getting physically close – there is less likelihood that he can help them overcome the deeper anxieties about letting go and exploring the roots of their fears of intimacy. Still, he may be able to equip them with the tools to overcome behavioral distance while dampening the painful experience of anticipated rejection through the cognitive reframing exercises in which he specializes, an antidote that may prove helpful at least in the short run. This is the tack he takes with Gloria, the client in *Three Approaches to Psychotherapy*. In the film, we see her listen attentively to what he has to say. It is apparent she has already read some of his advice on sexual and dating problems, specifically *Intelligent Woman's Guide to Manhunting*, and thinks something can be gained by his methods. However, at the conclusion of the sessions with Rogers, Perls, and Ellis, when she is asked whom she would like to continue to see if she were to continue in treatment, Ellis was the last on her list. As deeply conflicted as she was about her dependency needs and wishes for intimacy, she intuitively grasped that she would be better off with one of the two other therapists.

To summarize at this juncture, in terms of Ellis's ideoaffectology and attachment style as it relates to psychotherapy process and therapist – client fit, it appears that Ellis may be rather effective, at least in the short run, with two kinds of clients: those who are either too anxious or too inexpressive. For those who are too anxious, he provides the cognitive skills (denial, emotion substitution, and dissociation) to break through the cycles of disabling anxiety; with those who are too inexpressive, he provides a working vocabulary that may help bring to the surface problems in adaptation that then can be addressed, and addressed in a relatively quick and nonthreatening way. The case of Martha provided a particularly good example.

In terms of attachment complementarity, it is of interest to note that this case, which is one of Ellis's more successful cases, involved a woman whose attachment style was a mixture of fearful avoidance and preoccupation; that is, there were two sides to her attachment profile – one interfaced her romantic longings and the other, familial enmeshment. Martha showed an ambivalent attitude toward romantic involvements, wanting a relationship but fearing rejection; this is characteristic of the fearful-avoidant individual. However, at the same time, she was trying to break free from an emotionally abusive relationship with respect to her family in which she felt trapped. She was not hoping to establish a more intimate relationship with her parents.

Ellis was apparently quite effective in helping Martha separate from her parents. However, he was less effective when Martha turned to a discussion of her fear of men, which involved the dual dread that she would become dependent on a man with whom she became romantically involved and that he would leave her. Ellis attempted to have her reinterpret her problem as one of poor self-esteem and the tendency to catastrophize; he was ineffective in engaging her at this level, although he made several attempts. Perhaps he did not succeed because he could not acknowledge the depth of her longing for romantic intimacy. To do so would permit her to express her dependency needs, and what he wanted for her instead was independence and self-reliance. Thus we see that Ellis is effective in areas that involve assertion of separation needs but relatively ineffective in areas that involve expression and understanding of dependency needs.

According to complementarity theory, dismissing individuals, such as Ellis, and those with a fearful-avoidant attachment pattern, such as Gloria, may be expected to mesh best with those having a secure or even a preoccupied rather than a fearful-avoidant attachment style. Indeed, at the end of the three sessions, Gloria indicated that she was most drawn to working further with Perls, who showed features of the preoccupied/ambivalent attachment pattern. The dilemma for Gloria, however, if she did enter treatment with him, is that his own trait contempt is so well matched by her own dispositional contempt that complementarity processes would not be called into play. That is, we suspect that the complementarity in attachment style would be overpowered by the lack of complementarity in emotion style, leading to a relatively ineffective treatment.

Indeed, complementarity theory suggests that Gloria should do best over the long course with someone like Rogers, who offers a complementary, secure style to her insecure style, and who offers joy, sympathetic distress, and shame as the complement and the compensation to her repertoire of defensive contempt. In fact, during the filmed session, Rogers made particularly rapid progress in dissipating Gloria's strong contempt bias, though it recovers by the end of the session. Interestingly, although Gloria, who has had substantial therapy before this particular demonstration film, chose Perls over Rogers as her preferred therapist on first being queried, she later changed her mind. Many years after the filming, as she reflected upon the experience once again, Gloria concluded that she would have had more to gain from Rogers, and that Rogers had indeed been able to establish a connection or a promise of connection with her in that limited half hour that still impressed her years later.

Summary and Concluding Thoughts

To summarize the key features of Ellis's affective profile, interest, anger, and contempt are attractor states and fear and distress are repellor states on his personality landscape. From a developmental perspective, the biographical analysis as well as the analysis of his own written works (see Chapter 8) suggest that the attractor regions are so deep and the repellor regions so unscalable that there are very few occasions for system instability, turbulence, and consequent change. Indeed, there appeared to be little in the way of personality development or change over the course of the adult years; the contempt and almost adolescent braggadocio discerned in his earlier works was still present in his mature works. Moreover, there is little evidence of theoretical evolution over the course of his professional life. It is our assessment that these two aspects of Ellis are integrally related. Perls will also be shown to have a substantial contempt component to his personality (Chapters 5 and 9); however, the tension between two strong attractor regions – contempt and shame – is such that there is movement in moods and cognitive states that generate conditions of system instability. This movement may account for why Perls's work is more generative and why he has moments of brilliant creativity. This creativity is not sustained, to be sure, and a good deal of the writing that is original is inchoate and rambling if not disjointed.

Ellis's attachment style can best be characterized by a combination of dismissing and fearful-avoidant elements. We have surmised that he probably attracts clients with anxiety issues, and those who may have dismissing and fearful-avoidant features. Whether he keeps them very long in therapy is another matter, as is evident in the case with Gloria. Then again, Ellis is not interested in long-term therapy, in developing a therapeutic alliance and establishing interpersonal bonds with the client. He would like for his clients to become self-reliant, like himself. This brings us to a discussion of several observations that emerged in our examination of Ellis's profile, which may be useful to those working from an attachment theoretical perspective.

First, as indicated earlier, Ellis showed an admixture of attachment style elements, as did Carl Rogers, the client Martha described earlier, and the client Gloria. Consequently, the dimensional approach of Kirkpatrick and Davis (1994) and Bartholomew and Horowitz (1991) may provide greater latitude in understanding and characterizing individual attachment styles than the categorical practice utilized by many developmentalists. In Ellis's relationship with his partner, Janet Wolfe, we see the avoidance of interdependence on the one hand being blended with the expression of concern for her in various indirect ways, such as the provision for her wellbeing after his death (Weiner, 1988).

The attachment literature suggests that attachment patterns will remain relatively stable over developmental time, though revisions of internal working models are accorded possibility in the context of new relational experiences. Still, attachment theory does not yet adequately characterize attachment trajectories over the lifecourse, nor does it account for alterations in choice of attachment partners. There may be a variety of patterns. In the case of Rogers, we saw that his attachment profile underwent a change from infancy to adolescence. In contrast, Ellis's attachment style in terms of his working models of relationships did not appear to change over time. However, we noted a change in his choice of partners. Over the course of his adult life, Ellis appears to have moved away from the flighty, emotionally demanding women of his earlier romantic liaisons to a more emotionally controlled and self-reliant type of woman. The length of time that the relationships lasted also changed – from short-lived affairs to a stable, long-standing partnership. Thus, Ellis seems to have settled into a relational pattern with which he was more comfortable. His earlier relationships occurred during his daring-to-do-anything experimental phase in which he was actively trying to overcome his acute shyness around women. The emotional demands of these more turbulent women, rather than generating forces that could soften or round out his relational contours, may instead have activated defenses against the threat of too much intimacy and the associated feelings of vulnerability. If we construe the earlier romantic relationships as involving women with a more preoccupied or ambivalent leaning and his present partner as reflecting a more autonomous disposition (there are no data that would allow us to judge whether the autonomy is grounded in secure attachment, avoidant attachment, or some mixture of styles), it appears that Ellis shifted from a more complementary to a more reciprocal partnership.

However, other relationships showing the complementary pattern can be quite stable as found in the marriage between Edward Hopper, the great American painter of the mid-twentieth century, and his wife, Jo Nivison (Magai, 1999a). In that case, the pattern was one of avoidant dismissiveness on the part of Hopper and preoccupied attachment on the part of his partner. However, their turbulent partnership lasted over forty years and appears to have provided creative grist for Hopper's artistic mill. In our analysis of that relationship (Magai, 1999a), which appears to reflect a not uncommon pattern, we speculated that dismissive individuals are attracted to preoccupied or ambivalent partners because their own constricted emotionality creates conditions of what Tomkins (1963) called "backed up affect." Since the need to express emotion is part of the human motivational blueprint, suppressed or backed up affect generates intrasystemic tension in the individual who suffers from constricted affect, as is the case in the dismissive individual. We speculated that the attraction between avoidant and preoccupied individuals lies in the fact that each partner provides an interpersonal system for the regulation of mood. The dismissive suffers from too little affect and consequent affect hunger, and the preoccupied suffers from a surfeit of roiling emotions. If Tomkins was right about the human need to minimize affect inhibition, the avoidant individual requires others to stimulate emotion expression and thereby reduce affect hunger. The preoccupied person, on the other hand, has a maximizing strategy – he or she is hypervigilant to distress and engages in heightened emotional expression. Thus, in the context of an avoidant/preoccupied relationship, the boredom of low affect can be transformed by a certain kind of partner into an exciting hell.

If these formulations are correct, how do we account for the fact that Ellis fled from the women with more unrestrained affect and settled down with a partner with an affective profile more similar to his own? Perhaps Ellis found the ideal solution for himself, just as Hopper found the ideal mate for his own situation. As an isolate and a recluse, Hopper had little social life that was not brokered by his partner. For an artist, a life of sheer reclusion would not seem to offer much in the way of inspiration. The artist's life's work, which is focused on the canvas, in itself could be conducted in a lonely garret, but he would need outside agents for stimulation. For Hopper, the fiery agitation provided by his spouse helped enable him to stay alive to life and his work. In the case of Ellis, however, his life's work brought him into contact with people on a daily basis. Moreover, Ellis derives his ongoing stimulation from his clients. Unlike Hopper who had to wait for creative inspiration, clients present new challenges to Ellis on a daily basis. This relation leads us to an understanding that intersystemic turbulence can derive from the immediate social network as well as from sources outside the network. Ellis found the ideal solution for himself. He found a helpmate who did not profoundly challenge his interpersonal style of relating and a profession that offered him emotional stimulation without risk. Hopper channeled his interpersonal angst into masterful artistic scenes of austerity and disquieting loneliness. Ellis found other gratifications that led to a more perfected theory of cognitive-behavioral psychotherapy.

5 Lives Repelled and Attracted by Contempt and Shame

Fritz Perls

Fritz Perls's name is inextricably linked with Gestalt therapy and the movement it inspired during the 1960s. In a moment of uncharacteristic modesty, Perls once maintained that he was not so much the founder of the movement as the "finder." Indeed, Perls was somewhat of a theoretical magpie, borrowing from whatever he needed at the time and whatever suited him to inform this new therapy. Later he was to suggest, in a more characteristically brash manner that he might just be the "creator of a 'new' method of treatment and the exponent of a viable philosophy which could do something for mankind" (Shepard, p. 1, 1975). This modesty/immodesty split was but one of the many splits that typified Perls's world and his writings and that got imported into the theory and practice.

Gestalt therapy, as it was articulated over time, rested on strands of philosophy and psychology from phenomenology, Zen Buddhism, depth psychology, psychodrama, holism, existentialism, and a theory of perception articulated by a small circle of German psychologists in the opening decades of the twentieth century, which was known as Gestalt psychology. Despite its hybrid nature, Perls' Gestalt therapy is most closely associated in many people's minds with German Gestalt theory, though this notion was thoroughly repudiated by the Gestalt psychologist and historian Mary Henle (1978) in an excoriating piece on the distinctions between the two bodies of thought. Henle noted that Perls's writings constituted a hodge-podge of ideas unrelated to original Gestalt theory, and, moreover, that the body of work associated with Perls's Gestalt therapy hardly comprised an adequate theory of neurosis, therapy, personality, or anything. We take issue with this conclusion and argue that even though Perls's work is not a coherent and well-integrated body of thought, it was indeed a system of belief

146

and practice that constituted a theory, albeit a personalized theory; the theory was largely about emotion and the role of emotion in life and psychopathology and it was Perls's own affect theory (cf., Tomkins), that is, a magnification of his own emotional biases – although Perls himself did not appear to have recognized this any more than Rogers or Perls.

Gestalt therapy was launched at about the same time that Rogers and Ellis were developing their own programs; in Perls's case, however, a number of other writers made substantial contributions to the emergent body of theory and practice, including his wife, Laura (Lore Posner), Kurt Goldstein, and Paul Goodman. Nevertheless, people invariably think of Fritz Perls's name when they think of Gestalt therapy, partly because he was its most flamboyant practitioner, and partly because he took his "show" on the road all over the country as well as abroad. The form that Gestalt therapy took changed over time; successively, Perls moved Gestalt therapy from the inner sanctum of the clinician's office to group encounter, from group work to public demonstrations, and finally from group work to the foundation of a Gestalt kibbutz.

Fritz and Laura Perls developed and applied Gestalt theoretical concepts to their work with patients as early as the 1940s and 1950s. However, aside from a close circle of friends and practitioners, the work was largely ignored by the therapeutic community during these early days. Gestalt therapy attracted a greater number of followers during the 1960s while Perls was in residence at Esalen Institute in Big Sur, California. The philosophical underpinnings of Gestalt therapy, with its anti-intellectual and antirationalist bias and emphasis on self-expression, articulated well with the emerging countercultural values of the 1960s and may even have helped to amplify the messages of the then current political and cultural Zeitgeist. In a critical analysis of the epistemology and values inherent in Gestalt therapy, Cadwallader (1984) maintained that Perls carried out a Nietzschean "transvaluation of values" and that at least five of the major value claims of his psychotherapeutic theory and practice were in fact dangerous half-truths, which in themselves have contributed to the rapid dissolution of the social fabric Americans used to know.

Although Gestalt therapy gradually made its way into cultural consciousness and attracted a large popular following, Perls was denied professional recognition by most of the psychiatric community up until the very end of his life. One of the things that made Gestalt therapy appear revolutionary and earned him the animadversion of the psychiatric community was that it attacked some of the fundamental principles of psychoanalysis and pointedly eschewed most of its rituals. Instead of probing the patient's past for the sources of neurosis, Perls demanded that his patients stay in the "here and now"; instead of taking a detailed history, Perls directly observed and reported what the patient's behavior in the session revealed. Instead of the remote practitioner who sat out of view and avoided eye contact with his patient, Perls moved the patient from the couch to the "hot seat" and engaged him in confrontation.

Despite the therapy's early renegade status, Gestalt techniques have since quietly entered the mainstream, and centers of Gestalt therapy continue to survive, if not flourish. There is a *Gestalt Journal*, a number of widely subscribed Gestalt institutes in Europe and the United States, and, most recently, Web sites devoted to Gestalt therapy and Gestalt theoretical writings. Several eminent therapists have incorporated Gestalt techniques into their own programs, among them Leslie Greenberg (1993). Moreover, a recent review of the scientific literature on the efficacy of different therapeutic modalities showed that two of the techniques developed by Perls had the highest efficacy outcomes from among an array of techniques that were evaluated (Orlinsky, Grawe & Parks, 1994).

As such, Perls's work cannot be readily dismissed, as it was by many of his contemporaries. Moreover, those who saw Perls in action during group sessions and public demonstrations give evidence that they were impressed by his clinical acumen, the subtlety and acuteness of his observations, and his ability to produce rapid insights and behavioral changes in clients. Ann Halprin reported that "he could see subtle, subtle messages in your body. He could read expressions in your eyes, in your mouth, and all around your cheeks that were uncanny, they were so perceptive" (Shepard, 1975, p. 131).

It was clear to many that there was something of the great emotional intelligence at the base of Perls's work (Stoehr, 1994). There was widespread consensus among therapists who knew him that he had a tremendous capacity to read body language and facial expressions and to deploy these observations skillfully in therapeutic encounters. Among those who were taken with his impressive skills was Everett Shostrom, the psychologist who would eventually produce *Three Approaches to Psychotherapy*. Shostrom studied Gestalt therapy with Perls during Perls's California years; he also later worked with Gloria in group therapy for some time before he made the film. Thus, it was not accidental that Perls was chosen as one of the three psychologists sought to illustrate contemporary psychotherapies along with Rogers and Ellis, although according to several accounts Perls's session with Gloria was not among his premiere performances (e.g., Dolliver, Williams & Gold, 1980).

Among the three therapists under discussion in this book – all of whom experienced an uphill battle in gaining recognition for their work – Perls encountered the most thoroughgoing hostility and resistence. The reasons for his marginalization were theoretical and political as well as personal. One source of animosity toward Perls and his system, at least among academic psychologists, had to do with his use of the term "Gestalt" as applied to his therapeutic approach and the equation of Gestalt therapeutic principles with the principles of Gestalt theory as articulated by Wertheimer, Koffka, Koehler, and other early Gestalt perceptual psychologists. The classical Gestalt theorists and their students were disdainful if not downright contemptuous of what they felt to be Perls's misappropriation of their work and his distortion of Gestalt terms and principles (Arnheim, 1974; Henley, 1978). Perls himself admitted that he had read little of the original works of the Gestalt theorists; he had read none of the textbooks and only a smattering of the papers by Lewin, Wertheimer, and Koehler. Of these readings, the idea that had the most appeal for him was the concept of the unfinished situation, the incomplete gestalt, and he made this concept a cornerstone of Gestalt therapy.

Another source of Perls's marginalization had to do with the old Cartesian split between mind and body and the fact that Gestalt therapy was privileging the body over the mind at a time that the former, along with the emotions, was in deep trouble in psychology. In Perls's system, unlike other prevailing systems, the mind was not the core of the person and the locus of all that was distinguished in man, but rather the seat of dishonesty – the part of the psyche that ran interference with the strivings and momentum of the organism and that was in large part responsible for the neurotic condition of contemporary life. According to Perls, the human psyche consisted of an "animal self" – the original organic being with needs, primitive functions, and feelings as well as four other layers emergent from social development and the influence of Western civilization. In the healthy person, all these layers would be integrated; however, this has been subverted in modern man. Therapy consists of routing out the repressed, warped, hidden, and conflicted emotions so that they may be integrated. In restoring the body and emotions to the human equation and rejecting the thoroughgoing mentalism of the Freudians, Perls certainly did not win any friends among psychoanalysts.

Finally, Perls's own personal excesses drove many people away, and indeed there were a number of unattractive aspects to his personal and professional life. He was patently neglectful of his children and disdainful of parenting; on the rare occasions when he was around, he was rejecting of his children's overtures and insensitive to their feelings. He passed some of his wife's writings off as his own (Gaines, 1979; Stoehr, 1994), was a notorious womanizer, and used people for his own gain. By many accounts he was a monumental egomaniac. Rollo May found him an "authoritarian boor" (Gaines, 1979, p. 36). He violated established ethical standards in sleeping with his patients. All said, there is a great deal that is troubling about Perls's personal habits and ethics. Here we face the dilemma of separating the man, Perls, from his contributions to a body of work. This task is not unlike that involved in the controversies surrounding the Belgian deconstructionist Paul deMann and the existential philosopher Martin Heidegger, although these two examples are perhaps more malevolent on a broader level because of their association with fascism. (However, see Cadwallader, 1984, on the inherent dangers of the value system inherent in Perls's philosophy and therapeutic ideology.)

Nevertheless, an examination of the life and work of Fritz Perls adds to our accumulating database on the link between affective organization, thought, and action, and provides an interesting contrast to the other two therapists in this project.

Socioemotional Development

In composing a socioemotional portrait of the development of Fritz Perls, at least in terms of his early life, we have relied largely on two sources to reconstruct the events of his life. One is his own autobiography, *In and Out of the Garbage Pail* (1969a), which was published when he was seventy-five years old, and the other a biography by Shepard (1975), *Fritz*, which was published six years later. Both accounts were written relatively late in Perls's life. In the case of the biography, most of the information came from Perls himself or his immediate late-life family. Information from others who knew him in early life was unobtainable. His only surviving sister, who had suffered a stroke, could not provide any coherent information on his early life; his other friends and family members had been lost to the holocaust; those who saw him in psychoanalysis were no longer alive. Much more is available on his adult life. Jack Gaines's book, *Fritz Perls: Here and Now* (1979), which is a collection of reminiscences by a wide assortment of people who knew Perls, fleshed out and cross-validated impressions of Perls's personality distilled from his autobiography and biography.

It may be useful to start with the autobiography itself because the form it takes tells us a great deal about the psychological content of Perls's experiential life. As Allport (1942) noted, personal documents provide rich narrative material for psychological analysis. Here, it is not the details of the traumatic events and conditions of Perls's early life that are so revealing but the form that the narrative takes – its expository style, its thematic preoccupations, the way he uses language, the nature of his affective vocabulary, and the way the text alternates between hiding and exhibitionism. It also predates the biography by six years. Hence we begin with an analysis of Perls's autobiographical self-presentation, which will set the stage for material that is developed in the Shepard biography.

In his autobiography, Perls takes us on an excursion through his stream of consciousness; in doing so he allows us to glimpse what appears to be a fragmented, disorganized, and unstable subjectivity. "Kaleidoscope of living. Went to the lodge, Breakfast. Nixon won on the first ballot. Anybody interested in politics? We live in another world. Very peculiar morning" (Perls, 1969a, p. 171). Is this his authentic "here and now" experience? For a man whose holy grail was "integration," it is apparent that he had not been able to reach his goal even in old age.

In Perls's autobiography we have only the sketchiest of information on the important events of his childhood and adolescence. This dearth of information appears due to his lack of access to memories of early development as well as a certain reluctance to explore this terrain. Moreover, the few spare details that are provided are related in an unconventional and essentially obfuscatory narrative style. Nevertheless, a qualitative analysis of the material sheds a great deal of light on his character, which we take up presently. A more formal content analysis is discussed later.

The striking metaphor in the title of his autobiography, *In and Out of the Garbage Pail*, was meant to grab the reader's attention and tell us something of how he sees his life; an introductory poem that repeats the theme of the garbage pail reveal that Perls regarded his life, emotions, and creativity as smelly trash, but trash from which he hoped to be able to create some existential meaning.

If we take a page from his own technique and focus on the behavior rather than the words in this autobiography, we find that Perls imparted more of himself than he perhaps intended. In essence, he indicated that he is both afraid of the reader's prying eyes and has contempt for them. To begin with, the document is unpaginated; here he is flaunting convention and being difficult. He is thumbing his nose at the publishing industry, the reader, and anyone who wants to cite his work. He also disregarded autobiographical conventions in terms of the style and content. Ordinarily, the reader looks to an autobiography to learn the details of a life and the author's interpretations. Although this particular autobiography is quite long – some 282 pages according to our count – there is little in the material that is about the substantive details of his life. Instead, the occasional biographical note is interspersed with long disquisitions on science, philosophy, psychoanalysis, art, the laws of gestalt dynamics, and so forth, almost as though he feared to establish a focused train of thought. Alternatively, he may have just been trying to keep the reader off the scent of the trail. In any case, the whole work is really quite remarkable for its lack of biographical content and frustrating evasiveness.

Additionally, the form of the text itself makes it difficult for the reader to readily assimilate. Unlike Ellis and Rogers, who wrote their autobiographies in the familiar and conventional way starting with early life and progressing in a linear chronological fashion up through adolescence and adulthood, Perls's autobiography is much more chaotic in nature. While Rogers and Ellis followed traditional narrative style in their emphasis on chronicity and linearity, which, according to Herbert Leibowitz's *Fabricating Lives* (1989) is basic to human experience and the most instinctive way of organizing material, Perls's autobiography is almost studiously nonlinear. The work itself is idiosyncratically organized – ricocheting from present to past to present. It is riddled with incomplete thoughts, themes, and fragments of narrative and interspersed with bits of poems and artwork haphazardly strewn about. Perls assumed different voices throughout the text – professor and student, self and projections, good Fritz–bad Fritz, the haughty voice, the sniveling voice.

It is certainly possible that Perls deliberately wrote in this fashion in an attempt to stay in the "here and now" and to be congruent with the philosophical tenets of Gestalt therapy in which unprocessed thought and feeling are prized in their own right. It is clear that Perls wants the reader to think that he or she is being treated to the "unedited" Fritz. However, if this is the case – though we doubt that any recorded material is totally uncensored – we have an interesting look at the way in which Perls's psychological world is organized. If we take it at its face value, it is rambling and disjunctive, probably not just a stream of consciousness.

In many ways, Perls's autobiography constitutes the narrative equivalent of his renowned disheveled personal appearance in that it reads like unedited, unkempt ruminations. As indicated, he meanders from one point to another in what appears to be a random way, but we take this path to be driven by contradictory motivations. The end result is that the reader does not have a clear picture of the important events of his life. Whether intentional or not, the obfuscatory prose style succeeds in concealing Fritz from the reader.

The distorted chronicity of the autobiography, we will argue, rather than comprising a deliberate and prescient postmodern approach to narrative, was a consequence of the need to avoid connecting with a painful past, as well as a means of distancing himself from the reader and of preventing the reader from connecting with him in any meaningful way. There is a parallel in the physical realm. In the film we see that he hides much of his face (the face being one of the two primary organs of communication aside from speech) with thick facial hair and the idiosyncratic way that he holds a cigarette, obscuring the whole lower portion of the face.

Paradoxically, although these mannerisms suggest a need to hide from others, Perls the writer and man also assaulted the senses in a number of ways that made ignoring him difficult. As a physical presence, he was a striking figure, bulky and overweight but somewhat magisterial, taking up more than the usual personal space. In his autobiography as well, his personality sprawls all over the place with rambling ruminations, accompanied by sketches consisting of multiple bearded personae of himself. He was an olfactory presence even when one could not see him; a lover complained that he was not very scrupulous about his bodily hygiene. Finally, in the event that a person had the audacity to ignore his physical presence, his acid and provocative remarks in face-to-face encounter guaranteed that he would not remain invisible for long.

What are we to make of this apparent simultaneous need to hide and to be seen? That Perls had ambivalent feelings about drawing attention to himself is clear, but is there more? One could argue that Perls's slovenly behavior both on and off the page had less to do with the need for attention than for disregard of the other. This interpretation is not inconsistent with additional facts we learn about the way in which he related to others interpersonally, as discussed later in the section on his attachment style.

The duality of Perls's self-presentation is emblematic of the splitting that constituted his working phenomenology and is manifest on many

levels – most notably in his theoretical writings, his personal relationships, and the therapeutic techniques he developed within the Gestalt
program. Perls did have some insight into this and had occasion to remark on his "schizophrenic layer." Here we explore more of what is
known of his life as gleaned from the material developed in the biography by Shepard (1975), and from a few other available sources.

Early Life

Friedrich Salomon Perls was born July 8, 1893, the third and youngest
child (two girls and a boy) in a lower-middle-class family living in a
Jewish ghetto just outside of Berlin. The Perls considered themselves
modern Jews, that is, Germans, although they preserved certain limited
religious traditions. For example, the family went to temple, the children learned Hebrew, and Fritz was bar mitzvahed; however, the father
secretly studied to become Grand Master of the Freemasons, even going
so far as to start his own lodge after he was rejected by existing lodges.
When Fritz was three years old, the family moved to a more fashionable
part of Berlin, where they resided for about twelve years. However, as
moderately assimilated Jews, the family was "nichte here, nichte there"
to use a Yiddish expression – that is, they did not fit neatly into either the
German or Jewish world. Perls's biographer suggested that like other
modern Jews they were ashamed of their Jewishness; but they were also
uncomfortable in the non-Jewish Aryan world.

According to his sister, Grete, because Fritz was the youngest of three
children and the only male, he was spoiled by his mother, who placed
few demands on him in terms of his behavior or in taking his share of
family responsibility. He was said to be a wild and unruly child, and he
himself seems to have gloried in being an "enfant terrible." He often did
things deliberately to spite his mother and teachers and clearly relished
their emotional distress. These provocative behaviors were designed to
get their attention and to have them focus on him, for his own emotional
distress went unnoticed.

Perls's parents were alienated from one another even before Fritz's
birth, and he evidently witnessed many bitter arguments including
physical fights. The father worked as a "Chief Representative" of the
Rothschild Company, which imported Palestinian wines. As a wine
merchant, he was often on the road, and took advantage of this to
indulge his interest in other women. Perls's mother had a vehement
dislike of her husband and the children came to despise him as well.

Perls admitted that he hated his father and his "pompous righteous-ness," but he also reported that his father could be warm and loving. Of the latter, however, Perls provided no specific examples. Moreover, he remembered that his father called him a "piece of shit" (stück scheisse). Fritz maintained that he hated his father and that they were not on speaking terms when Fritz was growing up. Both parents used power assertive methods of discipline and often threatened to send him to a reformatory.

Perls's mother is a particularly murky figure. Nothing is known of her own mother. Her father came from relatively obscure origins and worked as a tailor. Despite this, she pursued interests in art and espe-cially the theater and cultivated her children's interests in these areas. We are told that though the family was often strapped for money, she saved a bit from the household expenses so that she and the children could have standing places at the Kroll Theater, an annex of the Impe-rial Opera and Theater. Here Perls could both escape from his abusive father and observe his mother in a state of happiness. It is no wonder the stage held a fascination for him in adolescence and later on in his own professional life.

Perls related that his mother was very ambitious for him but that she was "not at all the 'Jewish mother' type" (Perls, 1969a, p. 174) and appeared happy that his mother showed no such inclination. What are we to make of this backhanded compliment? There was little further contextualization for the disclaimer. We do know, however, that "Jewish mothers" of ethnic literature are typically portrayed as overly solicitous and/or overbearing. Is her departure from the cultural norm of Jewish mothers a reflection on the fact that her behavior bordered on neglect or remoteness? Or was she in actuality quite overbearing and intrusive – that is, is his denial a signal that he protests too much? In any case, the mother was described as heavy handed in disciplinary style, using whips and carpet beaters on her unruly son.

There is some suggestion that Perls may have been attached to one of his grandmothers. At one point in his autobiography, as he takes on the topic of tears – real and phoney – he admitted that he himself could be just as phoney and manipulative as others could. As an example, he related that he once conjured up the image of the loss of his grand-mother to produce tears that would mollify the person about to mete out punishment and that he was successful in this manipulation.

Like most other things in his life, Perls polarized feelings toward his two sisters, one of whom he liked. This sister, Grete, was one-and-a-half years older than he and was somewhat of a tomboy; he disliked the other, Else, intensely and described her as a "clinger." This sister, who provoked uncomfortable feelings in him, had been legally blind as a child and apparently absorbed much of the mother's time and attention, prompting intense sibling jealousy on Fritz's part. She later died in a concentration camp; Perls reported in his autobiography that he "did not mourn much" when he learned of her death. The other sister married a violin repairman and the two fled to Shanghai after Hitler came to power; they subsequently moved to Israel, and finally, after Perls had moved to the United States, he helped get them into the States. She was described as a high-strung, garrulous woman, who maintained contact with Perls over the years by sending him marzipan and other sweets.

As a child, Perls took an avid interest in theater, and this interest dated back to some of his earliest memories. In his autobiography, he reported that he fell in love with a circus horseback rider when he was four, that he looked forward to Punch and Judy puppet shows, and that he took delight in the little plays that a neighbor used to produce in the Perls's large living room. It may be somewhat telling that what impressed him most about the actors was that they could be something other than what they were, that is, that they could turn themselves into something different. Given the marital discord in the family and Fritz's second- or third-place status with respect to his siblings, the ability to escape from himself and become someone else might have been quite appealing. In later years, of course, he focused on roles that people play in everyday social intercourse and the masks that they wear; his work in group therapy involved stripping away these masks, props, and roles with the goal of returning the individual to his or her real self. Concerns with masks, real and false selves, phoniness, and authenticity turned out to be preoccupations that he carried throughout his life.

Perls's experiences in school were quite mixed. He could read and knew his multiplication tables before he entered school. Work was easy for him, he was eager to please and to learn, and the elementary school provided a warm and secure environment in which to learn. At the age of nine, however, he began studies at the Mommsen Gymnasium, a local high school that emphasized discipline and may have been particularly punitive. To make matters worse, there were only four Jewish children in the class, and anti-Semitic remarks were common enough to make him feel uncomfortable. After a while, Perls became rebellious and unmanageable in school, his schoolwork deteriorated, and he had to repeat the seventh grade, only to fail again and finally be expelled.

Adolescence and Early Adulthood

Perls remembered his adolescence as one in which he had been a "very bad boy" (Shepard, 1975, p. 20). After dropping out of school, Perls became an apprentice to a soft goods merchant, but he was quickly dismissed for playing pranks. At the age of fourteen, he found another school to enroll in, the Askanische Gymnasium, which was very liberal and had humanistically oriented teachers. Given his early interest in theater, he sought and secured a position as an extra at the Royal Theater at mid-adolescence. Later he became acquainted with the director of the Deutsche Theater, Max Reinhardt, who made a great impression on him. Under the influence of the new, more liberal school, and that of Reinhardt, his grades improved, and upon graduating he entered the University of Berlin to begin medical studies.

However, Perls's studies were interrupted by the outbreak of World War I. With the general mobilization of the country in 1915, he volunteered for Red Cross work because he was not among the most fit for combat; for a while then he remained in Berlin and continued his medical studies. With the worsening of the war and the army's loosening of standards with respect to the medical and physical conditions of recruits, Perls and a friend, Ferdinand Knopf, were able to enlist in the German army.

Later Perls described his war years as constituting the most difficult period in his life. He appears to have suffered considerable stress and several traumatic shocks at the time. He spent nine months in the trenches before his first furlough, sustained lung damage during the gas attacks, was wounded at one point, came down with a severe bout of influenza on another, and narrowly escaped death in Flanders. He saw many of his colleagues killed, and also lost his only friend, Ferdinand Knopf. By 1917 he was showing signs of detachment and depersonalization and was found going about his tasks in a trance, exposing himself to danger without apparent concern. Later he blamed his war experiences on his loss of inner imagery and fantasy.

Given his several traumatic experiences and the description of his symptoms, he may have suffered post-traumatic stress disorder, which is associated with psychic numbing, affective blunting, emotional turmoil, and personality change. One common pattern identified by Bradshaw, Ohlde, and Horne (1993) in the course of treating some 1,000 Vietnam War veterans – the heart of darkness syndrome – is typified by feelings of invulnerability, grandiosity, and an absence of empathy.

These features of personality can be seen in Perls's need to be the center of attention, his need for emotional "explosions," his sense of self-importance, and his relative insensitivity in the face of what he saw as weakness and dependency in others. However, it is impossible to sort out which personality traits were precipitated by his war experiences and which predated his combat years.

After the war, Perls resumed his medical studies and received his MD from Frederick Wilhelm University in Berlin in 1921. Soon thereafter he started to practice as a neuropsychiatrist. By 1923 Germany was involved in a period of runaway inflation, resulting in extremely volatile economic conditions and eventually a deep depression. Perls, who was thirty at the time, took the opportunity to travel to New York in 1923 where he found work in the Department of Neurology at the Hospital for Joint Diseases and continued his work in neuropsychiatry. Not much is known about this time, but it must have been somewhat of a trial. He had difficulty with the language, and his heavy accent would have made him conspicuously German during a time, following the first world war, when there was strong hostility toward Germans. These factors probably compounded his inability to connect with others – a problem that had arisen from, or been magnified by, his war experiences and had resulted in psychic numbing and emotional isolation. As such, he found himself adrift and alone. To add to his problems, he faced obstacles in establishing himself independently in America because his medical degree from Germany was not recognized in the United States.

With these difficulties, and feeling isolated, alienated, and lonely, when the economy in Germany stabilized, Perls returned to his homeland, and, at the age of thirty-two, resumed living with his mother and sister. Benumbed by his war experiences and at somewhat of a loss as to the direction of his life, he had a period of emotional somnambulism. His biographer indicated that Perls suffered from a pervasive sense of worthlessness, that he had always felt like an "ugly toad," and that he had grave self-doubts and worried about his sexual potency (his first sexual experience during adolescence had been one of humiliation). All this changed when he met and had a passionate affair with a married woman who was a distant relative of his mother; Lucy restored his sense of self-worth and vitality, but the affair led to other complications. Indeed, it was the beginning of an unconventional and stormy relationship that included experimental sexual activities including group sex and homosexual encounters. This wide cast of the sexual net suggests that there was a desperate search for love and relationships at this stage in his life. Subsequently, he entered psychoanalysis as a means of coming to terms with the clashing of intense emotions – "love, lust, guilt, surprise, shame, jealousy, and desire." Interestingly, his experiences with this treatment itself led to a change in the direction of his career, as he eventually left neuropsychiatry behind in favor of clinical work and psychotherapy.

In his treatment with Karen Horney, he worked on resolving some of his confusion about his goals, sexuality, and problems with his memory. He also spent some time in treatment with Clara Happel, but when his money ran out, she recommended Perls have a training analysis and undergo supervision of his own cases, which he did under Helene Deutsch and Edward Hitschmann. He also later undertook analysis with Wilhelm Reich, whose emphasis of working through body armor impressed him enough that he later borrowed some of the ideas and techniques for Gestalt therapy.

In the meantime, Perls became Assistant to Professor Kurt Goldstein at the Institute for Brain-injured Soldiers in Frankfurt and, in the course of his work there, met his wife-to-be, Laura Posner, who had been doing experimental work for several years with Goldstein's brain-damaged veterans of World War I. Laura came from a wealthy family and was well educated. Her father was a successful jewelry manufacturer and sent her to a classical gymnasium, which was unusual for a girl at the time; in fact, she was the only girl in her class at first. She later went on to earn a PhD.

Laura must have had a formidable intellect for it was unusual for a woman to pursue doctoral work during the early part of the twentieth century, perhaps especially in Germany. It was probably helpful that she came from a well-to-do and cultured family who were possibly influential in helping her overcome obstacles she might have encountered in her pursuit of advanced education. She read Greek and Latin, studied the classics in Gymnasium, studied modern philosophy including the works of Husserl and Heidegger, and took courses with Paul Tillich and Martin Buber.

Perls and his wife gave conflicting reports of how they came to be married. Perls alleged that she sought marriage and pursued him, whereas she denied she had her sights set on marriage and that the idea had been his. In any case, the couple was married in 1930, despite the disapproval of Laura's parents, who disliked Perls and never did come to accept him. By this time, Laura had finished her dissertation on visual perception and had attained her doctorate. She was then in training for psychoanalysis with Frieda Fromm-Reichmann and Karl Landauer.

Later Adult Life

Perls continued his studies at various psychoanalytic institutes in Berlin and Vienna up to 1933 and had private practices in Frankfurt, Vienna, and Berlin. At this point, with the stirrings of fascism in his country, Perls, Laura, and their two-year-old daughter made plans to immigrate to Holland for political reasons having to do more with the Perls' leftist political activities than because they were Jews, although anti-Semitism was already very open and threatening to intensify. Fritz had been teaching at the Workers' University, and he and Laura were members of the antifascist league. He had to leave the University of Freiburg because of leftist activities.

In April 1933, Perls crossed the German–Dutch border with 100 marks (the equivalent of about $25) hidden in a cigarette lighter, leaving his wife and daughter behind to stay with his in-laws; they were to join him a few months later. Leaving Germany meant that Perls's training as a psychoanalyst had to be interrupted; he broke off his analysis with Wilhelm Reich and his supervision under Otto Fenichel and Karen Horney. In Holland he resumed supervision, this time from Karl Landanner, who had been his wife's analyst in Frankfurt. In Amsterdam, neither he nor his wife were permitted to work so they had to live on charity. The family settled in to live with other refugees in a house provided by the Jewish community; the other refugees included an actor and a young married woman with whom Perls proceeded to have an affair. Fritz and Laura did not remain in the house in Amsterdam long because conditions were crowded and primitive and they must have still feared for their safety.

As it happened, Ernst Jones, Freud's friend and biographer, received a request for a training analyst in Johannesburg, South Africa, and referred Perls for the position. In Johannesburg, Perls and his wife both set up practice, and Perls founded the South Africa Institute for Psychoanalysis in 1935. The couple's practice did well, a son was born, and the family prospered materially. However, Perls was still restless, and the marriage was undergoing strains. He had not wanted a second child and when Laura got pregnant again, he wanted her to abort, a decision she fought. Perls had shown some interest in Renate as a baby, but at the age of four, when her brother was born, she began sucking her thumb, wetting her pants, and showing other signs of regression. At this point, Perls turned from her in disgust; helplessness and dependency were revolting to Perls. As the family and marital relationship worsened, Perls shut himself away in his practice and wrote. Other relationships also soured at this time. He had attended the International Psychoanalytic Congress in Vienna in 1936 and was deeply aggrieved to find that his paper on "oral resistance" was not well received and, in fact, elicited strong disapproval from his peers.

Perls must have nursed his injury for some time, for it was not until 1947 that he published *Ego, Hunger and Aggression*. The work included a stinging critique of psychoanalysis and introduced concepts derived from perception and the work of the Gestalt psychologists. According to Taylor Stoehr (1994), the work might never have seen the light of day had it not been for his wife. Laura actually wrote some of the chapters and contributed a great deal to the ideas in the book; of the two, she was the scholar and was well-acquainted with Gestalt psychology having worked with Professor Kurt Goldstein and having earned her own doctoral degree in the field. Two of the chapters were primarily her work, and she had written drafts for several of the chapters. It is likely that the rest of the material also involved considerable input from her and possibly heavy editing, since the book was published only after Fritz and Laura had shared over a decade in intimate collaboration. Because of Laura's close involvement with the book, it is hard to say how much of the intellectual property was hers and how much his.

Despite the fact that the book was a genuinely collaborative effort, involving descriptions of theory and practice by both Perls and Laura, Perls did not share authorship. Moreover, although he gave Laura credit in the preface of the first South African and British editions, he substantially downplayed her part in the later American edition. The acknowledgment in the first editions contained note of her "considerable contribution" and even mentioned the particular chapters she had had a hand in. Perls rewrote the introduction for the later edition, reducing the acknowledgment of her contribution to that of "stimulation," "encouragement," and "discussions."

Although it is generally difficult to dissect Perls's thoughts from Laura's in this book, there is considerable evidence that the chapters on "emotional resistance," "oral resistance," and "dental aggression" are largely Fritz's contribution and contained ideas that he would expand upon later on. Even at the start, aggression was a strong ideological motif in his writings, and he enacted it himself in therapy. According to the theory of dental aggression, man's aggression had a biological basis but was linked to biting and chewing. If it were deflected from its natural outlet, it led to projection, paranoia, war, death, and destruction. Thus he recommended verbalization of anger and use of "concentration therapy," which utilized fantasy and visual imagery acting out of the aggressive instinct. "If you are afraid to hurt people, to attack them, to say 'No' when the situation demands it, you should . . . imagine yourself biting a piece of flesh out of someone's body" (Perls, 1947, p, 195). Perls was a master of dental aggression in person, using confrontational techniques to draw patients out. As Stoehr (1994) noted, "you had to see him in action, eating his patients alive, to understand what dental aggression was really all about. All the better if his patients bit back" (p. 134).

For the next five years, Perls served as a psychiatrist with the South African Army. During this time, he became increasingly concerned with what he saw as the rising tide of fascism. When the South African prime minister Jan Christian Smuts retired from office and Perls foresaw that a right-wing regime might come into power, he sought another place to live. In 1946, in his early fifties, he immigrated to the United States.

Perls first came to Manhattan where he soon established himself with a bohemian group of artists, writers, and therapists. He actively sought out a meeting with Paul Goodman (the social critic who is perhaps best remembered for *Growing Up Absurd*), whose article on Wilhelm Reich he had read in a journal called *Politics* back in South Africa; they quickly struck up a relationship that subsequently resulted in the publication of *Gestalt Therapy*. Goodman was originally conscripted to be Perls's editor; however, the fee he received for the project was enough to pay his rent for two years, which suggested that Perls even originally intended him to play a bigger role in the project. Perls, by nature, was more comfortable in the role of performer than he was as scholar. He wrote and published relatively little given the length of his career. In fact, as the work progressed, Goodman added substantially to its development and he and Hefferline, a colleague at Columbia, were acknowledged as co-authors when the book was published.

Perls had been told that it would be easy to establish a practice in Manhattan, and he and Laura proceeded to set up private practices as well as get connected with other groups. Shortly after Perls had come to the United States, he struck up a relationship with Clara Thompson, who was among the leading faculty members at the William Alanson White Institute, which was New York's premiere psychoanalytic training institute. The group at White were "neo-Freudians" – they adhered to Harry Stack Sullivan's theories, which stressed the importance of interpersonal relations. While this group was somewhat more accepting of Perls's challenges to Freudian orthodoxy than analysts in Europe, his own unorthodox therapeutic and personal habits gradually earned him their disapprobation; they never granted him full membership, and he finally left their company.

Perls turned more and more to group work and to his collaboration with Paul Goodman, which, in 1950, resulted in a first draft of their book. Perls deliberated over the choice of what to call the book; he had not yet used the term "Gestalt therapy" as a description of his treatment, instead using the term "concentration therapy," because it included exercises in inner fantasy and intense concentration on bodily awareness. Shortly after the draft had been completed, Perls and Goodman both left Manhattan. Perls went to Los Angeles, where he received an honorary degree, and subsequently returned to Manhattan. When Goodman returned from his own excursion, they worked together to complete the book; it was published a year later as *Gestalt Therapy* (Perls, Goodman & Hefferline, 1951).

By that time, Perls was even more thoroughly alienated from family life and from his wife, and thus Laura and Perls essentially separated. In his autobiography, he alluded to a certain competitiveness between himself and his wife over who was more accomplished. He related that he "could not possibly win" and that he "always got clobbered." Perls returned to the West Coast with some of his followers, and Laura remained in New York where she ran her training group. However, within a year, he returned to New York, leaving a colleague to terminate clients who could not follow him, a behavior of questionable ethics that earned him the disapproval of a number of his peers. However, as Stoehr (1994) pointed out, Perls was being true to form; he never formed strong attachments to his patients nor did he encourage strong attachments on their parts.

Perls decided to start his own Gestalt Institute in 1952. The members of the Institute met weekly at the Perls's apartment, and it functioned as a training group for the discussion of cases, an exploratory seminary where the theory and practice of Gestalt therapy was crafted, and a group therapy session. During the years 1950 to 1964, Perls led a peripatetic life, giving workshops and establishing Gestalt institutes across the country: New York, Cleveland, Los Angeles, Miami, and San Francisco. He also had private practices and did some consulting for hospitals.

In 1956 Perls once again decided to leave Laura, and in fact moved to Miami; however, the couple never actually divorced. He continued to see her from time to time, even staying at her apartment during occasions that he visited New York. Once in Florida, Perls found himself lonely and isolated for a good length of time. However, in 1957 he met and fell in love with Marty Fromm, a married woman whose trouble with her daughter caused her to seek treatment, first for her daughter and then for herself. At the time Perls was sixty-five and Marty was thirty-two; in the course of individual therapy with her, Perls initiated sexual contact. They had a very intense and at times tumultuous affair, during the course of which they experimented with mood-altering drugs, including LSD. Perls barely managed to stave off psychosis. Six months later, when Perls got an invitation to go to Columbus, Ohio, to train psychiatrists at a mental hospital there, he picked up and left with relatively little afterthought and was clearly unconcerned about Marty's distress at his leaving her behind.

In 1963 Perls experienced a painful angina attack and contemplated suicide. There is also evidence that he may have contemplated suicide earlier in his life as well; certainly his incessant smoking can be viewed as another form of slow suicidal destruction. In 1964, however, at the age of seventy-one, Perls discovered Big Sur and Esalen Institute. Here he found the blossoming of the human potential movement and a community of free-thinking, ready-to-try-anything people, who more or less accepted him.

Perls remained at Esalen for five years where he honed his Gestalt skills in a group context, leading various workshops and holding group demonstrations of Gestalt techniques. By 1966 Perls had achieved name recognition, and Gestalt therapy was on the map. During that year, he also participated as one of the three therapists in the demonstration film *Three Approaches to Psychotherapy*. These must have been heady times for him; he had gained the recognition that he had always sought – was almost a star of sorts – had plenty of admiring women to sleep with, and reveled in the thought that the word was out that "nobody kisses like Fritz." However, he was quite testy during the first year as he attempted to find out just where he fit in. During his early phase at Esalen, Perls displayed a short-tempered, introspective nastiness, which lasted through most of 1965 according to Shepard. Over the years, however, he was said to have mellowed. Initially brazenly rude, rageful, and envious of others at Esalen who earned earlier recognition and bigger reputations, the aggressivity receded somewhat toward the end as he came into his own fame. Alan Watts recalled, "I can't quite remember. But suddenly I ran into this vastly patriarchal character with a big beard. And he was a very affectionate man. He wasn't stand-offish. He was warm. He would embrace you; he would touch you" (Shepard, 1975, p. 159). Watt's perception of Perls as a warm fuzzy bear of a man was only one side of the persona at the time. Transcripts from group sessions of this era indicate that he could still be cold, cruel, and rejecting. Dick Price, who was another colleague of Perls during the Big Sur years, disliked Perls's predilection for

> putting people down and having very little patience. If someone was obviously disturbed and came to see him and Fritz wasn't interested, I'd see him just turn away. It was almost brutal. But [in contrast] in the context of the group I saw him as loving and patient and sensitive. It was just like a coin turned around. All the things I thought he was utterly without, in the course of a group he had with a richer degree than anyone I had ever witnessed (Shepard, 1975, p. 124).

After a while, however, Perls grew restless once again. He found it difficult to share the spotlight with other Esalen personalities such as William Schultz, the author of *Joy*. Moreover, his sensitivities to fascistic trends led him to feel discomfort when Richard Nixon was elected President of the United States and Ronald Regan was elected Governor of California. Envisioning a rising tide of conservative backlash and anti-Semitism in the United States, disillusioned with Esalen, and restless once again, he made plans to emigrate to Canada.

He researched the area around Vancouver Island, British Columbia, and, at the end of 1968 bought an old motel on Lake Cowichan. In late 1969, at the age of seventy-six, he moved there with a small coterie of staff and acolytes where he proceeded to build a Gestalt kibbutz, which he called the Gestalt Institute of Canada. Here he gloried in having uncontested authority over everything in his immediate surround, enjoyed the relatively unalloyed admiration of his band of followers, and blossomed into a more giving, grand old paterfamilias (although he banned animals and attempted to ban children). His joy was to be short lived. On March 14, 1970, he died at the age of seventy-six. There is the story, which may be apocryphal, but somehow has the right ring to it, that Fritz died true to form. In the hospital, for an ailment that turned out on autopsy to be cancer of the pancreas, a nurse tried to stop him from getting out of bed and disturbing the medical paraphernalia attached to him. The nurse insisted that he lie down once, and then again.

The second time, "He looked her right in the eye and he said, 'Don't tell me what to do,' fell back and died." (Shepard, 1975, p. 192).

Content Analysis of the Autobiography

Perls began his autobiography during his Esalen years; it was published in 1969 during the transition to Lake Cowichan. Because this personal document was written by Perls in advanced age, near what was to be the end of his life, and at a point at which he was feeling most acknowledged and accepted, it offers us a unique opportunity to see how Perls had come to terms with his fragmented self-image, feelings toward his parents and siblings, and negative image of himself. Because the autobiographical material produced by Perls was of much greater volume than that of Ellis and Rogers, we analyzed a random selection from the autobiography sampled over the entire book, with the condition that it be equivalent in length to the other two autobiographies.

A frequency count of all emergent themes in the material revealed twenty-four main themes: Acceptance (25 instances), Achievement (21), Affiliation (29), Aloneness (11), Boredom (10), Control (38), Danger (31), Death (28), Exhibitionism (34), Fighting (3), Honesty (20), Inadequacy (12), Jewishness (14), Luck (2), Mystery (15), Phoniness (33), Polarity (13), Power (14), Rebellion (14), Rejection (36), Sex (29), Sickness (12), Self (24), and Trust (7).

This material and the prevalence of key themes and clusters of themes allows us to grasp what Perls's central preoccupations were. The material indicates that Perls's subjectivity revolved around certain concerns related to a fragile sense of self, a devalued and rejected self, and threats of fragmentation. The themes of Rejection (second highest ranking theme) and Acceptance (eighth highest) are related. The Rejection category includes descriptions of being rejected, being criticized, being disliked or disliking someone, and being a bad boy or black sheep of the family. The Acceptance category includes a search for or receipt of approval, recognition, and acceptance. This is closely coupled with the Exhibitionism theme, which includes being admired or wanting admiration, boasting about the self, exhibiting pride or vanity, and showing off. The experience of rejection and desire for acceptance also seem related to efforts to protect a fragile sense of self (Self, Danger, Death, Sickness). The Self theme category includes issues of selfhood, selfish thoughts, self-esteem, and self-actualization; the Danger category includes risk, danger, struggle for survival, threat of death, being in jeopardy, and the precariousness of life; the Death category includes explicit references to death or allusions to killing; and the Sickness category refers to various kinds of illness and indisposition.

Another cluster of themes relates to polarities, which in turn are linked to issues of fragmentation and the immanence of annihilation. People reject him or praise him (rejection/acceptance) alternatively, making him feel ambivalent, split, marginal, and at risk. Narcissism appears to be his defense against the threat of annihilation. For Perls, the world exists as disjoint polarities: body–soul, yin–yang, male–female, right–left, topdog–underdog. Although the frequency count for the theme of Polarity (13 instances) seems to indicate that this is only a moderate preoccupation, this count does not reflect the true incidence of his reference to polarities because he often mentioned polarities in long strings. (In our system of enumeration, a string of polarities counted as only one instance unless interrupted by another theme.) The threat of annihilation comes in the form of death preoccupation and in the looming of Boredom, which is equated with being vacant and "dry" and which he tries desperately to escape.

Yet another cluster of themes has to do with interpersonal relatedness or lack thereof. The fragmented sense of self and preoccupation with polarities appears to reflect his ambivalent (split) representational system (good mother, bad mother; good father, mostly bad father; wanting to be cuddled, wanting to be released). Perls simultaneously sought union/communion with others through sexuality, love, and the enjoyment of others' company (Sex, Affiliation) and rebelled against social constraints and interdependence (Control, Rebellion). Narcissism (Exhibitionism), which, as noted earlier, was a prominent theme in the narrative, appeared to be at the service of reassuring himself of his worthiness, a condition that he fundamentally doubted. Perls had a deep distrust of others and, in the therapy sessions he conducted, was preoccupied with unmasking that which was phoney and dishonest (Trust/distrust themes, Phoniness, Honesty, Mystery).

We also undertook another kind of content analysis, this time examining the types and frequencies of affect works used in the autobiography. On a strictly quantitative basis, we found that expressions of contempt dominated the text, accounting for fully 24.3 percent of the affect words/phrases in the narrative. On a more qualitative basis, we discerned an interesting pattern related to affect regulation. Throughout the text, Perls gave evidence of having poor affect tolerance, which led to alternating periods of containment and "explosion." The ability to modulate affect was severely compromised, leading to bouts of "nothingness" on the one hand or "emotional explosions" on the other, sometimes accompanied by no clear sense of their origins. "We visited the grave of Lore's [Laura's] father and I had a grief explosion.... I don't understand the outburst either. My father-in-law and I were never close." (Perls, 1969a, p. 223). He is buffeted between the threats of too little affect and too much. Too little affect threatens "nothingness," and too much affect signals feelings of helplessness and the threat of annihilation.

There is an ambivalent struggle with respect to the capacity to feel. On the one hand, Perls has considerable difficulty tolerating his own negative affect, and seeks flight from it: "I can do this. I can 'forget' myself completely" (Perls, 1969a, p. 3). However, the absence of affect is also experienced as punitive: "Boredom drives me . . . to be obnoxious to people or to do some 'gloom-casting' or to start flirting and sexy games" (Perls, 1969a, p. 7). He is aware that he provokes people as a means of keeping himself stimulated, not bored, not depressed. Fighting the impulse to flee the "dead point" (a term from Russian psychology to which he was drawn), he tried to harness the experience and use it constructively as an aid to psychological integration. Perls referred to this as going into the "fertile void" – the term itself a metaphor of clashing images – but, for the most part, he fought off these feelings. To escape from nothingness, he continued to harass and goad others into states of intense distress or anger; at other times the solution was to pack his bags and find another environment. "I don't like this dryness, lack of involvement. I like myself much better when I think or write with passion, when I am turned on" (Perls, 1969a, p. 34). This explanation helps clarify Perls's need to be provocative in therapy, to take psychoactive drugs, and to experiment with abandon in the sexual realm. It also helps to explain his almost single-minded preoccupation with staying in the "here and now." The alterative to being here and now, of course, was to be nonexistent and nowhere.

The picture that emerges from the autobiography is of a man who had what today's clinical psychologists would call narcissistic and borderline characteristics. He was ridden with feelings of fragmentation and alternated between abject shame and grandiosity. As a psychiatrist, there is a good chance that Perls had some basic understanding of his own disturbances, although at the time he was writing, narcissistic and borderline personalities were not yet well understood and not well articulated at a theoretical level. At an intellectual level at least, Perls could see that he vacillated between two deep attractors; narcissistic self-absorption was one magnetic basin, and narcissistic injury was the other. "As with every psychological phenomenon, self-esteem is experienced as a polarity. High self-esteem, pride, glory, feeling ten feet tall, opposes the low: feeling down, worthless, abject, small" (Perls, 1969a, p. 4). Of course, the public tended to see more of Perls's narcissistic pride than the narcissistic injury. "Shall I now draw the conclusion that self-glorification is the genuine interest for which I live, that I slave and labor in the service of the image of the Great Fritz Perls?" (Perls, 1969a, p. 7). However, if we view contempt as a counteractive dynamic designed to control shame, it is striking that the deep shame that haunted Perls all his life was still in evidence. The picture here is complicated. Because contempt was deployed in therapy deliberately as a means of challenging and confronting the patient, and because it was such an effective stage device, we gather that it became ever more crystallized in his personality over time. We will have more to say about affect dynamics in a latter section. For the present it is worth noting that splitting and fragmentation are features of Perls's personality even in late life at the pinnacle of his success. Perls's vaunted therapeutic tools – role play, body awareness, concentration on the here and now, and two-chair techniques – evolved as a means of promoting psychological integration in patients; however, at the end of his life, Perls was still striving for his own integration.

In summary, the thematic content analysis of the material from Perls's autobiography indicated that he was plagued by experiences with rejection, doubts about his own self worth, a keen need for approval and admiration, a fragmented inner life, and difficulty with affect regulation. Because affect regulation is so closely associated with attachment patterns, let us proceed to a more extended examination of his attachment style.

Attachment Style

Before we begin, we want to make it clear that there is insufficient biographical material on Perls's infancy and childhood life to make anything but an educated guess about his early attachment style. However, the picture that emerges on his adult attachment style based on his romantic involvements, his therapeutic ideology, and his relations with patients, all seem to point to a mixed pattern of avoidance and ambivalence, as elaborated later.

As a start, let us take a somewhat unconventional approach beginning with ideology and proceeding backward to personality and developmental experience. We have proposed elsewhere that there is an intimate link between psychological theories and personality. Let us first approach Perls's ideological stance toward human relatedness and connection. According to other psychologists (e.g., Ainsworth, 1967; Bowlby, 1969) of the mid-twentieth century, human attachments are fundamental to healthy psychological development. In the course of early development, the attainment of a secure attachment relationship with the primary caregiver is a necessary prerequisite to successful exploration and mastery of the environment; in adulthood, the healthy individual is able to keep needs for both connection and self-actualization in balance. However, according to Perls, affection and attachment are goals that are secondary, or even in conflict with, personal autonomy.

At the heart of Perls's version of Gestalt therapy was the insistence on the primacy of independence and self-reliance. The "child does not want affection, it even hates being suffocated with it. The child wants facilitation, that is the opportunity and assistance for his development" ("Planned Psychotherapy" http://www.gestalt.org/planned.htm). And elsewhere, "to grow up means to be alone, and to be alone is the prerequisite for maturity and contact" (Perls, 1969b, p. 179). Furthermore, "the child needs the environment to take care of him, and as you grow up, you learn more and more to stand on your feet, to provide your own *means-whereby* to live" (Perls, 1969b, p. 139).

The quotations tap a broader Weltanschauung or epistemological stance with respect to Perls's view of the relation between the individual and the social matrix in which the individual is embedded. According to Perls, in the course of development, individuals introject or interiorize "shouldisms" that are societal and parental proscriptions and prescriptions for behavior. The compliant individual naively adopts these roles, rituals, routines, and games that represent a subversion of the person's authentic and unique development and the warping of the individual's natural vitality. The individual then stays ill by maintaining this "phoniness" and game-playing routines. The task of therapy is to expose these facades, dismantle resident defenses, uncover the original inner vitality, bring closure to long-standing holes in personality, and integrate the various split-off aspects of the self.

Perls favored what he called individual responsibility over interdependence and social responsibility, which he regarded as closely linked to interpersonal manipulation. Dependency, neediness, and vulnerability, as expressed by others, were despised behaviors that interfered with the pursuit of one's own individual freedoms. Furthermore, Perls promoted a view that redefined personal responsibility, transforming it from "responsibility for the welfare of others" to "responsibility only for one's own self and welfare" (Cadwallader, 1984, p. 193). Indeed, in Perls's own words, "responsibility is the ability to respond and be fully responsible for oneself and for *nobody else*. This is, I believe, the most basic characteristic of the mature person" (Perls, 1969b, p. 107).

Now, although there is much to be said about the virtues of independent thought and action, and a certain degree of self-sufficiency, Perls's prescription for personal development goes well beyond this to the single-minded valorization of self and separateness at the expense of otherness and connection. Of course, individualism and autonomy are part of a dominant ethos in American culture (Kagan, 1979) and perhaps reached its apotheosis during the so-call countercultural revolution of the 1960s. Ironically, however, it took a German emigre, Perls, to take this peculiarly American ideal and glorify it in new and idiosyncratic ways.

The Gestalt Prayer, which is found in *Gestalt Therapy Verbatim* and in his autobiography, can be considered the epitome of social nihilism and personal disconnection. "I do my thing, and you do your thing. I am not in this world to live up to your expectations and you are not in this world to live up to mine" (Perls, 1969b, p. 24). That Perls was resonating to the thematic preoccupations of then current generational "forerunners" (Troll, 1975) is clear; that he would become one of the standard bearers of the new banner was unforeseen. This codification of a demand for freedom from restraint by others must have seemed particularly liberating to the generation of children who had grown up in the toned-down, buttoned-up Eisenhower years and the era of gray flannel suits. The Gestalt Prayer was subsequently turned into a mass-produced poster and its first line became a popular slogan of the 1960s. However, we can also see the Gestalt Prayer contains Perls's own antitoxic script for his "dreads," just as RET contains within it antitoxic scripts for Ellis. The parallel antitoxic scripts for Perls might read as:

1. I do my thing.	1. I am alone in this world.
2. You do your thing.	2. You ignore me.
3. I am not in this world to live up to your expectations.	3. Yet you demand too much of me.
4. You are not in this world to live up to mine.	4. We can never connect.

Perls went well beyond the idea that society was evolving in new ways during this time; he celebrated the break from traditionalism, custom, and manners. As it happened, Perls transformed what was a culture-specific ideal and secular trend into a universalistic and pan-cultural norm in asserting that autonomy and self-reliance are the preeminent goals for healthy human development. The cultural anthropologist and historian can readily provide us with instances of other times and cultures that would refute this normativeness. In fact, in many other cultures from agrarian and pastoral peoples of earlier times up through some present-day industrialized societies, such as Japan, interdependence is the sine qua non of existence. Even in our own culture, we do not practice a thoroughgoing individualism; adults take responsibility for the rearing of their children, and people exchange goods, services, and resources with one another throughout adulthood and provide care to the old when the elderly are no longer capable of looking after themselves. Attachment theory has underscored the relevance of interrelatedness not only for children's development but also for survival of the human species (Grossman, 1996). Psychologist Carol Gilligan has written eloquently on the importance of connection in moral judgment and in many other spheres of life.

Perls's theory not only emphasized the social origins of neurosis and the necessity to free individuals from the yoke of interdependence but also proposed techniques whereby the therapist could enable the liberation from interdependence. In some ways his pronouncements and proposed interventions for others sound very much like a prescription for Perls's own psychological rehabilitation. For Perls, other humans were the source of his deepest humiliations. The lion's share of his mother's attention had gone to a handicapped sibling, and his father openly scorned him. His schoolmates derided him for being Jewish, his platoon was openly anti-Semitic, and his country's government codified a politics of hatred toward Jews that even threatened his physical existence. His wife challenged his intellectuality and scholarship, and her family treated him with disdain. His colleagues in the psychoanalytic movement rejected his first tentative theoretical formulations, Freud himself dismissed him, and former mentors Goldstein and Reich offered him a lukewarm reception when he first came to the United States. The Gestalt theorists and their students sneered at his misapplication of Gestalt concepts. As late as 1947 he was still reeling from his various professional rejections, though he put his face-saving spin on it when he delivered a talk at the William Alanson White Institute in the late 1940s. "In South

Africa, I was considered a megalomaniac rebel for daring to contradict the words of the master; in Canada, a fool for doubting the sacrosanct reflex arc; in New Haven, a stray dog for wanting to do psychotherapy without a medical license, and, what's more, without belonging to an established group; in New York a plain lunatic for having abandoned a secure economical position. . . . [I know that] I cannot attack the roots of a man's credo and, at the same time expect to be accepted, but I knew that I was not merely destructive, but constructive and instructive as well" ("Planned Psychotherapy," http://www.gestalt.org/planned.htm). He expected to be more well received at the White Institute but was ejected from their society in short order.

Having suffered various kinds of neglect, rejection, reproach, and derogation, Perls must have experienced deep feelings of humiliation and rage. Unsurprisingly, these experiences did not sensitize him to the crippling effects of human cruelty. Indeed, Perls could not tolerate any signs of weakness in others, preferring to support the individual's pursuit of self-sufficiency and autonomy, even if he had to be a bully to do it. In a way, Perls could not afford to connect with the plight of helpless others. Sensitivity to other people's vulnerability, the contagion of "weak affects" expressed by others – sadness, fear, feelings of helplessness – would only have magnified his own feelings of marginality and insignificance and threatened a fragile ego. It was much more empowering to be the party doing the rejecting, to express disapproval and contempt toward others, to be dogmatic and authoritarian without penalty. Here he had turned the tables in the power equation. Now he was the one who was aloof and inaccessible and had the power to command and control. Perls did not, and likely could not, nurture his patients or cultivate a warm therapeutic alliance; he could not sustain long treatments with patients. What most therapists might have seen as real vulnerabilities in others, Perls defined as interpersonal manipulation. He badgered his patients in a way that left them no recourse but to capitulate or to leave treatment. He worked with patients only on his terms, and his terms meant that they must become self-sufficient. In his therapeutic encounters, he constantly warned others that he would not tolerate their fragility or helplessness. At a dreamwork seminar he told the participants, "So if you want to go crazy, commit suicide, improve, 'get turned on,' or get an experience that will change your life, that's up to you. . . . Anybody who does not want to take the responsibility for this, please do not attend this seminar" (Perls, 1969b, p. 95).

Relatively early in his career he retreated from one-to-one psychotherapy. It is fairly obvious that this kind of close, intimate work was too emotionally demanding of him and, on occasion, too boring; at times it was even too much of a temptation for him – his autobiography documents at least two instances of individual therapy that led to the seduction of the patient. By mid-career, Perls had virtually abandoned individual therapy and was conducting his therapies in the context of groups of individuals.

However, even in the group context, the therapeutic process was enacted in a rather spartan fashion. The essential material for therapy in working with Perls was supplied by the individual herself feeding off her own dreams or own nonverbal behavior at the moment as it was drawn to her attention, or in shuttle-work between different aspects of the individual's persona. The fact that the person was in a group environment was almost irrelevant, and it appears that Perls's penchant for groupwork had more to do with certain of his own exhibitionist needs than any belief that there was special benefit to be gained from the inclusion of other people. An added attraction for Perls of groupwork was that the presence of others meant that he could pick and choose with whom he would work and that he could terminate a therapy abruptly – which he often did – if the patient was not cooperating in the way he wanted and proceed to engage someone else.

With the exclusive focus on the person's own material and on the here and now, he worked with the individual as though he or she not only existed in an interpersonal vacuum but was isolated in time as well. The demonstration patient was truly the individual removed from all contextualizing circumstances – his or her social context, historical context, goal context. Thus, Perls reproduced his own experience of being "cut off" from others earlier in life and kept his patients socially marooned during the therapeutic process.

Perls preferred to work with certain kinds of patients – those who were not seriously ill (he did not want the responsibility for their welfare and did not like working with patients over a long period of time) and those who were fairly submissive and who did not challenge his judgment of what was best for them. He also browbeat them into submission by refusing to work with them if they questioned his interpretations or called him on his rudeness or condescension.

The emphasis on autonomous self-sufficiency applied in Perls's own personal life as well as his professional activities. He spent little time with his children, brushed off their overtures for intimacy throughout his life, and belittled them for their various failings. Both children ended up resenting him intensely. His daughter, Renate, spoke about her father with a great deal of bitterness. The few memories she retained of him in childhood do not portray him in a favorable light. Once, she recounted, he got angry with her and locked her in the garage for the whole afternoon despite her terrified protests. Nor did he display much warmth or attention toward his grandchildren. His daughter was sorely aggrieved that he never took notice of her children. "The last time Allison, my eldest daughter, saw Fritz, she was there with a girl friend. He went over to the friend and said 'Hello Allison'" (Shepard, 1975, p. 135). He rejected conventional monogamy, having a series of affairs throughout the early years of his marriage as well as a legion of short-lived affairs after he separated from his wife. He was capable of abruptly breaking off relationships, even with Marty Fromm, the one woman he felt had the greatest emotional impact on his life. Finally, he used sarcasm and dismissal as the weapons of choice against anyone who displayed signs of neediness or dependency (e.g., his sister, daughter, friends, patients).

The preceding descriptions of Perls's preference for keeping an emotional distance from his family and patients and his theoretical exaltation of an exaggerated self-reliance as the ideal of healthy functioning suggests a picture of a psychologically and emotionally detached individual, someone whom we might regard as showing features of the avoidant attachment style. Moreover, this profile is consistent with Perls's lack of clear early memories and the presence of internal inconsistencies in the autobiographical narrative. In addition, his intrusive therapeutic style in which he confronts and hectors his patients can be seen as something he may have modeled from an intrusive, insensitive mother. This points to a denial on Perls's part when he relates that his mother was, thank God, not too much of a Jewish mother, if he is referring to the stereotype of an overinvolved, overbearing mother. Now, obviously, no ethnic group has a monopoly on intrusiveness, Perls's crude stereotype notwithstanding; however, intrusiveness is a feature of the maternal behaviors of mothers whose children develop avoidant attachment patterns (Belsky, Rovine & Taylor, 1984; Belsky & Isabella, 1988; Malatesta et al., 1989). It is our thesis, to be developed more fully later on, that therapists, at least as evidenced by the three individuals who are the subject of this project, tend to reproduce their attachment environments in the therapeutic context.

To conclude that Perls had an avoidant attachment style, however, only does partial justice to this emotionally complicated individual.

In point of fact, a number of aspects of his emotional profile contradict this conclusion or add a more complex texture to it. As indicated in earlier parts of this volume, the dismissive individual shows a predilection for emotional control and a preference for routing negative emotion from consciousness. Perls, in contrast, amplified awareness of the nonverbal affective messages of others (i.e., brought them forward into the foreground for scrutiny) as well as showed a heightened emotionality himself from time to time. He was quite comfortable with anger and contempt and sometimes used these emotions skillfully in therapeutic encounters. He also had periods in which he had emotional eruptions – which he called "explosions" or "outbursts," emotional storms that he apparently sought and valued. Charlotte Selver, who had given private body awareness sessions with him in New York, once said that she had never seen a man weep so much in the work (Shepard, 1975). He had periods of jealous rage – some with Laura, some with Marty, and to a much lesser degree with other women. He had a restless and relentless quest for the next emotional fix – a new passionate affair, a new drug high, a new patient to challenge.

The picture then that emerges of Perls's adult attachment style based on his therapeutic ideology and manner of conducting therapy is of a man who vacillated between an avoidant and an ambivalent pattern. On the one hand, he provoked intense emotions in his patients and was often given to emotional explosions in himself. On the other hand, he was often withdrawn and detached. There were also disjunctures between his prescriptions for patients and the application to himself. Perls avowed an interest in and a valuation of honest and direct communication and demanded it of his patients. He relentlessly probed their nonverbal behavior in an effort to get them to drop their masks. "If you wear a mask, you are in touch with the inside of the mask. Anyone trying to touch you with eyes or hands will merely make contact with the mask. Communication, the basis of human relationships, is impossible" (Shepard, 1975, p. 37). However, Perls rarely dropped his own mask and never risked exposing himself; he was a master of control in his demonstration workshops.

These kinds of inconsistencies, dualities, splits, and ambivalences get played on in his personal life as well. Even though Perls was a negligent father and absent husband, he was resentful that he did not command more of his family's attention and admiration. At the same time, he could not tolerate the demand for reciprocity that is implied by mutually giving interpersonal process. He experienced his family as threatening him with "clutching, symbiotic relationship[s]" (Shepard, 1975, p. 47). Elsewhere in the autobiography, Perls described Laura as acting as "The Supreme Giver and Comforter" and the daughter, Renate, as "The Perpetual Taker and Sufferer"; with these "honorifics," he managed to elevate them and deride them simultaneously. He begrudged the closeness between his wife and Renate, resented the birth of the new child, and was not at all pleased by the attention Laura gave to the children.

What is of interest in the current discussion is the reasons behind Perls's single-minded emphasis on separateness. Perls certainly lived his life congruently with his ideology of self-sufficiency. He was an independent, free spirit who took risks and dismissed convention. He was a lone wolf whose sexual escapades were less in the service of intimacy than they were in the service of avoiding a vacuous deadness of self. He was clearly ambivalent about human connection, constantly involving himself in affairs of short duration with both women and men. He was prone to jealous rages as well as abruptly terminating relationships with little regret. There is no evidence that he ever achieved a deep, long-lasting emotional connection with another individual, despite his frequent sexual couplings.

Even in group work, the detachment is fairly prominent. This attitude is not especially evident at first blush because there is a lot of "affect" that transpires. However, there is a real division of labor in this emotional work. It is the patient who provides the charged affect; Perls remains remote and emotionally out of reach. Gloria, in the film, puts her finger on this early on, articulating her frustration at getting so little emotional reaction from him. It is of interest that Perls isolated the patient both from the group and from his or her historical socioemotional context as well as galvanized intense affect. What this accomplished, in the process, was an intensification of the individual's dependence on the therapist and a sea of "hot" emotion that offset the gravitational pull toward emotional numbing that always threatened Perls. Fritz Perls had a deep dread of boredom, nothingness, implosion into darkness. Here we will argue that he needed the affect of other people to fend off his own sense of emptiness and the existential void. The real trick here for Perls was to stimulate the expression of affect in others and yet remain free and under control of the situation and of his own affect.

We do not discover much about the details of Perls's early developmental history, but there is some suggestion of a fair amount of deprivation. He received little affection from his father who was often absent and fairly neglecting. This was true of Ellis's father as well. However, what differentiated the fathers, and their son's experiences with the paternal figure, was the fact that Perl's father was actively rejecting. It is fairly likely that young Fritz, the "piece of shit", felt insignificant and worthless in his father's presence. Although Perls's few remarks about his mother indicate that he was able to obtain more emotional sustenance from her than from his father, she was probably available only inconsistently. The mother showed her son a certain degree of indulgence (Grete described him as "spoiled"), but she was clearly more absorbed in the care of his visually impaired sister. Perls's tendency to bait his mother and to play the "enfant terrible" probably was a tactic he learned to help him secure more of his mother's infrequent attention.

In adulthood, Perls does not appear to have resolved his feelings toward his parents. Nowhere does one find expressions of sadness or loss with respect to his mother. Although we discover, almost accidentally, that his mother died during the holocaust, nowhere in the autobiography or biography do we learn of the circumstances or timing of her death; nor do we learn when and how Perls heard of her fate or his emotional reactions to it. We are able to discern little of his feelings toward his father in later life. There is no direct expression of bitterness, on the one hand, or resolution of anger toward this punitive and rejecting figure, on the other. We do learn that Perls did not attend his father's funeral, but we know nothing more of how and when the father left Germany (if he did), when he died, and under what circumstances.

All in all, these features of Perls's personality in terms of attachment style make for a curious mixture of avoidant and ambivalent features. This kind of inconsistency is not identified as a discrete pattern in adults, nor was it found in the original work on attachment in children, although certain children who showed a mixed pattern of behavior in the early studies were regarded as "unclassifiable." In later work, however, Main and colleagues (1985, 1986, 1996) found that the attachment patterns of these earlier unclassifiable children could be subsumed within a new category that they have come to call the disorganized style. The latter is characterized by confused and disjointed behavior and internal representations. Although Main identified the pattern in infants and in six-year-old children and found that there was substantial continuity over time, there has been virtually no discussion of what the adult counterpart to the disorganized child might be, although adults have been studied in the context of work with children. The Adult Attachment Interview (George, Kaplan & Main, 1984) was developed to explore the internal working models of mothers of secure and insecure children.

Although most mothers' transcripts revealed working models of attachment that could be described as secure, dismissive (avoidant), or preoccupied (ambivalent), some protocols, which were deemed unclassifiable because of their mixed pattern, showed histories of unresolved mourning. Though there is no clear adult counterpart to the disorganized pattern seen in children, some of the patterns identified with the latter seem recognizable in Perls, as discussed presently.

In their seminal research, Main and colleagues found that children classified as disorganized often showed role-reversal behavior in the context of the Strange Situation reunion, consisting of a well-articulated effort to control the parent, mostly through punitive behavior, but sometimes through caregiving. Following reunion with the parent, they often took the lead in conversation; however, they also demonstrated strong dysfluencies in discourse. Additionally, photographs of the family shown to the children as part of the protocol elicited disorganized behavior sometimes accompanied by depressed affect.

Another curious finding in the work with disorganized children is worthy of comment. Although each of the original three attachment patterns – secure, avoidant, and ambivalent – involve coherent strategies that either allow the child to maintain a balance between attachment and exploration motives or to maximize one at the expense of the other, disorganized children seem unable to maintain a particular strategy. Moreover, as a group, they are a heterogeneous collection of children in terms of the manner in which they deal with separations and reunions. It is as though disorganized children function in a far-from-equilibrium state with respect to the negotiation of the biobehavioral instincts linked to attachment and exploration and are thus vulnerable to the push and pull of whatever circumstances prevail at the moment.

Several other features of the disorganized attachment pattern in children resemble certain behavioral characteristics seen in Perls. One remarkable feature of these children is a simultaneous display of contradictory patterns of avoidance and contact with the parent. They seek to remain in proximity with the parent, but at the same time they display avoidance. In most cases, however, the strength of the proximity-seeking instinct sufficiently overrides aversion so that the child can retain some contact with the parent. This interpersonal emotional configuration, one that we could describe as "within-range-but-distant," seems to fit Perls's manner of relating to patients and family and may explain why people were fascinated with him despite his often unlovely behavior. His treatment of Gloria may be emblematic. Although the verbal content of his communications to Gloria were filled with contempt, his tone of voice was mellow and even somewhat warm. This mix of messages is seductive and confounding, a mixture that clearly confused and upset Gloria. Perls appears to have sent the same mixed messages to his family. Despite his neglect and generally dismissive behavior, all members of his family tolerated him and even sought to retain contact. His son pursued contact and reconciliation with his father on a number of occasions – despite all odds that his father could muster the kind of paternal warmth and attention that the son so craved. The son even became a psychotherapist, possibly so that they would have a forum for communication. His daughter also continually sought to engage him despite his cruel behavior toward her and her family. Additionally, Laura, his wife, never divorced him; instead, she maintained intermittent contact with him over the years, even appearing at his bedside at the very end of his life. In ways, his family's ambivalence with respect to contact with Perls are reminiscent of the plight of battered women. The literature demonstrates that what battered women have in common is not so much a personality type as being married to a common type – a man who mixes brutality and abuse with protestations of love, seductive promises of reform, and gestures of appeasement. This intermingling of positive and negative sentiments and behaviors sets up a confusing matrix of pushes and pulls that can immobilize women from taking action to end the relationship.

Perls emitted mixed signals of warmth and rejection toward patients and family; and it is this unexpected, rather surprising blend that kept them intrigued but emotionally confused and ultimately frustrated. In the context of these relationships, Perls could remain in contact to a sufficient degree to feel connected, while protecting his emotional flank from too much or too little connection. It is our speculation that he feared two things: warm acceptance, on the one hand, with its implicit demand for reciprocity, and lack of attention. Both threatened abandonment and loss of self.

Another feature of the disorganized child is incomplete or undirected movements and expressions, including incomplete expressions of distress and anger. A child might strike at the parent's face but do so with weak, almost undirected actions. Or the child might move away from the mother during reunion but then stop dead still and begin crying, but without turning toward the mother or initiating approach. It is of interest that a major theoretical centerpiece of Perls's therapeutic oeuvre is the incomplete gestalt. As early as *Ego, Hunger and Aggression*, Perls maintained that the organism is motivated to seek a state of balance or homeostasis. Events that impinge on the organism throw it temporarily off balance, causing a residual charge that motivates the individual to seek to restore balance, to "complete the Gestalt." Situations that are not resolved constitute "unfinished business." These ideas are, of course, knock-offs of the Gestalt notion of closure and the social psychological construct associated with Bluma Zeigarnick's name.

One of the most marked expressions of confusion and apprehension found among disorganized children is a hand-to-mouth gesture that appears to index shame and apprehension and occurs during emotional junctures, for example, at the initial return of the mother. Perls displays a similar gesture repeatedly during the several segments of the Shostrom film, although we do not know how characteristic of him this gesture may have been. To the extent that it was fused with the peculiar way in which Perls held a cigarette, and to the extent that he was an inveterate chain smoker, we can assume that it occurred with some frequency.

Hand-to-mouth apprehension and "behavioral stilling" are quite common in the disorganized child in the context of reunion with the parent. As the mother returns, the child becomes rooted to the spot, accompanied by a dazed or depressed expression or an unfocused, "dead," blank look. Some children stare into space as though completely out of touch with self, environment, and parent. There is no way of knowing the internal state that accompanies such behavior, though it does suggest emotional numbing and a confusion so deep as to immobilize the self. Is this the kind of inner experience that Perls so dreaded and sought to avoid? In the strange situation, the child has no control over the reappearance of the mother, and the child's apparent anxiety suggests enormous fear of the uncontrollable, a possible symptom of abuse.

Although we can only speculate at this point that Perls's attachment style may represent an adult counterpart to that of the disorganized child, the very fact that Perls's style does not conform to the traditional secure, avoidant, or ambivalent patterns and that he shows unresolved mourning suggests that Perls's case might provide us with a model that could be tested in subsequent work with adults. Here we speculate that disorganized adults might not only show mixed and inconsistent patterns of approach and avoidance with respect to interpersonal relatedness, flee from experiences of shame and apprehension, show emotional numbing, express emotion in incomplete form, and attempt to control important others, but also show other features that accrue with the accumulation of adult relationships and complex adult professional roles.

For example, we suspect that adults with the disorganized attachment style may seem more unconventional than others in their professional lives or appear to be unscrupulous in their interpersonal relationships because of their lack of commitment to common ideals of responsibility. They may also seem more unconventional because their internal working models of relationships are unstable, giving rise to an unstable experience of self and other and a fragmented sense of identity, with a concomitant inability to form stable interpersonal commitments. Such individuals might even appear to be more creative than individuals with other attachment styles because they are less rule-bound, have fewer well-organized social schemata (Forgas, 1982), and take more risks, or because there is greater instability to their thought processes – rather like random walk mathematics applied to mentation. Moreover, given a probabilistic world, they will sometimes actually produce novel and useful meanings and solutions; the context will be of great importance for such people.

Disorganized individuals may show more sheer change versus continuity in their relationships, theoretical works, and behaviors than individuals with other attachment patterns, even in the absence of life crises. We will have an opportunity to examine this possibility as we turn to an examination of Perls's patterns of thought and logic over the course of his theoretical works (Chapter 8). At this point, we turn to a deeper consideration of the unique features of Perls's affective organization.

Affective Profile

There are three areas we want to discuss in this context: (a) Perls's emotional organization, one that we will characterize as consisting of an overt veneer of hostility with a hidden attractor of despondency and shame; (b) his theory of emotion, and (c) how he used emotion in psychotherapy.

The Perls Affective Persona

One of the most salient aspects of Perls's affective profile was hostility. Those who knew him, almost to a person, described a man who was cynical, bellicose, contemptuous, and selfish. Jim Simkin, a friend and former student, described him as a difficult man, often angry and belligerent. Arthur Gold, his son-in-law, reported that "he was very disdainful of me, looked down on me, and would shit on me every chance that he had" (Shepard, 1975, p. 135). Ann Halprin noted that she had never seen a man "who could be so sarcastic, so belligerent, so nasty, . . . " (Shepard, 1975, p. 131).

Hostile affect is also prominent in the session with Gloria. The single published study of an analysis of the Shostrom (1966) tape that looked at both therapist and client (Kiesler & Goldston, 1988) found that both Ellis and Perls had more hostility than Rogers, but that Perls was also colder, while Ellis was more friendly (nurturing, agreeable, and affiliative). Our own affective content analysis of the session indicated that contempt expressions were the dominant affect expression, accounting for 54 percent of words or phrases expressed in the session related to discrete emotions.

A more detailed analysis of Perl's affective posture with Gloria is discussed in Chapter 10, but in the context of our present discussion, we turn to a brief summary of some of the salient affective highlights of that session and with the additional filmed material that consisted of an introduction to his theory and a wrap-up analysis of his session with Gloria. In the introduction, Perls held a sheaf of notes from which he read. He sat forward on the chair in a somewhat combative pose with massive shoulders positioned forward and one hand propped on the thigh in a forbidding hand-on-hip posture. His signature facial expressions throughout the introduction and session with Gloria were those of deeply furrowed brows and lips often pressed together in a taut, somewhat contemptuous, configuration. The communication of distance and aloofness was heightened by his failure to make eye contact with the camera. In one of the rare instances in which he looked at the camera, his gaze was interrupted by a micromomentary flinch from which he quickly recovered by reverting to his notes. However, in this instant, we have the opportunity to view, however briefly, a miniaturized signal of fear. In this one brief flash, Perls appeared to betray an underlying anxiety. Additionally, Perls's speech was quite dysfluent (typically an index of shame and social anxiety), despite the fact that he used the prop of notes. Thus, these opening segments of our view of Perls are quite revealing. We glimpse an underlying apprehension mixed with shame, fairly well masked with an aggressive bodily posture and somewhat hostile facial demeanor. One is reminded of the apprehension and shame that is briefly leaked by the disorganized child who faces and is observed by the returning mother.

During the actual session with Gloria, Perls was confrontational and hectoring, though the tone of voice was often bland, even soft. In the session, he accused Gloria of being phoney and manipulative and was successful in igniting her anger. In the closing minutes of his session with Gloria, just when she had her guard partially lowered, and in the context of expressing feelings of vulnerability, Perls abruptly broke off the session, which still had about seven minutes to go. "I think we came to a little closure, a little understanding. And I think we finish this scene now." He waved his hand dismissively to signal the end of the session, and while this news was still registering with Gloria, who remained seated and looked somewhat stunned, he got up and exited.

In the wrap-up session, Perls seemed confident and triumphal and his hand was once again at his hip. In a self-congratulatory summary that revealed a basically contemptuous view of Gloria, Perls reviewed how he successfully challenged Gloria's "manipulations." He seemed especially delighted to dwell on the contradictions between her verbal and nonverbal behavior. Ignoring her assertions of discomfort and anxiety, he challenged the sincerity of her protests, concluding emphatically that, "a frightened person does not smile." Finally, in an interaction that takes place off stage at the conclusion of the day, Perls turned to Gloria. Confused for a moment as to his intention, she held her hand out to him, at which point Perls dumped the ash from his cigarette into her palm, treating her hand, and by extension, herself, as an ashtray. Many years later she still felt angry at his humiliating treatment of her.

Despite the fact that Perls dominated her during the session and subjected her to an intense and difficult twenty-four-minute session, Gloria was able to assert her opinions and offer her own interpretations from time to time; moreover, she had intuitive skills of her own, suggesting that Perls himself had a soft emotional underbelly, which was only partially obscured by his gruff exterior and assaultive verbal behavior. Though she might not have been able to characterize this vulnerable layer as consisting of shame, she did perceive that he shared some of her own dynamics, notably defenses around feelings of vulnerability and inferiority.

Silvan Tomkins, whose theory of affect has already been mentioned in the context of our discussion of Carl Rogers, had a well-articulated theory of shame. In fact, his second volume on affect theory (Tomkins, 1963), devoted expressly to the "negative affects," was primarily a theory of shame. Tomkins understood this emotion intimately, especially the dynamic relations among shame, anger, and contempt, and the varied ways that these affects could relate to one another developmentally and temporally. One dynamic pattern described by Tomkins seems to fit the adult Perls rather closely, and that is the pattern in which contempt is the dominant affect in personality with shame playing the role of an intrusion affect that emerges in consciousness intermittently. In Perls, the occasion of intrusion shame seemed to threaten chaotic collapse into depression and/or the nullity of psychic numbing, which meant that it had to be carefully monitored. Perls could not afford the relative luxury of bypassed shame (Lewis, 1971). Indeed, Perls's hypertrophied awareness of shame and vigilant defense through contempt came to saturate his consciousness. In fact, this may also explain why both shame and contempt figured so prominently in his therapeutic teachings and practice.

Much of Fritz Perls's inner struggle was between what he called his topdog and underdog, with topdog representing the internalized authoritarian and judgmental parents who demanded conformity and moral perfection and underdog representing the weaker child who threatened the outbreak of instinctive impulses toward self-gratification including that of dependency. Although Perls did not put it in these terms, he had an acute understanding that the underdog is the recipient of topdog's contempt and all the attending shame that this inflicts. Indeed, he often found himself in one or the other role and had a basic and organic understanding of this class distinction. Even though he appreciated the fact that topdogs typically humiliated and defeated underdogs, he also knew that underdogs did not have to tolerate their condition. They could rise up in rebellion, though the rebellion needed to be fomented in some way. Whether he could articulate this or not, Perls understood tacitly that shame is a tabooed emotion, remaining largely silent and hidden in Western culture. As an unexpressed, unacknowledged emotion (Perls would have described it as an "unfinished" emotion), it lay dormant in the personality and could be cultivated and brought to flower only through special methods of which Perls was the supreme master. Indeed, in sessions with patients, he was the master craftsman of humiliation. By subjecting patients to his contempt for their manipulations and weaknesses and by hounding them with his relentless scorn and derision, he was able to provoke the shame/rage spiral and the attendant release of tremendous emotional energy. In fostering the conversion of shame into anger and by supporting patients' tentative movement toward self-assertion, he taught a liberation politics of emotion for underdogs.

As such, there was a kind of method to his madness in his group interventions, despite the fact that he could seem utterly uncaring at times, even brutally cruel. True enough, he regularly confronted, browbeat, and bullied his patients, especially early in the session(s). Afterward, however, he had them play out the rivalrous polarities of topdog and underdog within themselves both with him and in the context of the two-chair technique. It is quite possible that the patient's enactment of conflicting needs to dominate and submit, humiliate and rebel, permitted Perls to identify with the patient, which then elicited more of a sympathetic response from him as well as supportive reinforcement when the intensity of their anger earned them a new-found sense of self-expression and power.

If we are correct about Perls's need to monitor sensations of shame, he would have been especially sensitized to its expression in others, though not necessarily sympathetic. Interestingly, Perls detected a deep vein of pathological shame in Freud. According to Perls, Freud was so immobilized by shame that he rarely left his home. "Such pain he had to cross the street, what pain to talk to any person. He was so embarrassed and so self-conscious" (Perls & Clements, 1975, p. 22). In fact, Perls hypothesized that it was Freud's inability to stand his own feeling of embarrassment – Freud did not like patients staring at him – that caused him to resort to the use of the couch during the analytic hour. Perls, of course, eschewed this approach early on, preferring to adopt a posture in which he faced the patient. He believed that the use of the couch allowed the patient as well as the therapist to avoid the awareness of embarrassment and shame. Avoidance or repression of shame was countertherapeutic.

The conditions supporting the development of shame and humiliation in Perls himself were manifold and included multiple sources of rejection throughout his life – parents, peers, teachers, colleagues, and mentors. He felt ugly and had grave doubts about his sexual adequacy. Perls's biographer, Martin Shepard, noted that Perls suffered a "pervasive feeling of not being worth anything" (Shepard, 1975, p. 32). Fritz struggled to overcome these deep feelings of worthlessness and ached to achieve recognition as the man who might "really contribute something." He was already practiced at making the best of the meager attention he got at the hands of his parents. As the mischievous, naughty boy of childhood and rebellious youth of adolescence – who played pranks and did things for spite – he became the bete noire of the family. As the scandalous lecher of middle and ripe old age, he enjoyed a roguish reputation in which he actively reveled. One might ask how the prominence of these emotions found their way into his theory of affect. These emotions, it turns out, were part of a more comprehensive theory of affect, although because he wrote so little, and his manner of presentation was both so dense and scattered, the extent of his impact on the field is difficult to evaluate.

Perls's Theory of Emotion

Perls had one of the more complicated theories of emotion at a time when emotion was not much of a topic of psychological discourse. The theory of emotion must be understood in juxtaposition to its counter-part – the "dead point" or void, a terrain of psychic numbness and ultimate emotional stilling. Perls himself was powerfully motivated by the fear of emotional numbness, lack of fantasy, and depleted vitality. There is some circumstantial evidence that he might have been exposed to conditions that fostered a disorganized style of attachment early in life; the disorganized style is marked by a tendency to experience confusion and immobilization. This nascent trend may have been magnified by post-traumatic stress disorder in the aftermath of horrendous war experiences toward the end of his adolescence. He gained some help for his sense of worthlessness and emotional deadness through therapy, especially perhaps in the work with Reich, who specialized in diagnosing body armor and in breaking through bodily resistances. Perls rapidly incorporated the insights he gained from this experience into his own work with patients in the form of concentration therapy. Perhaps he reflected that what worked for him might just be the antidote for others and provided a further means of mastering his own conflicts. In some ways, this is not unlike the young child before the stage of mature empathy, whose contagious distress in response to another's distress prompts an intervention. In an egocentric fashion, the child may offer the same stuffed animal that makes him or her feel better when similarly upset. Indeed, Perls constructed a whole system of psychotherapy that revolved around central psychological problems with which he was on intimate terms, most notably, shame, blunted affective ability, and lack of psychic integration.

From an early date, Perls was concerned with emotional resistances and numbness of spirit. Moving quickly beyond theory to practice in his first volume, *Ego, Hunger and Aggression*, he became engaged in the practice of "concentration therapy," or what would later be called training in sensory awareness, and the relation between psychic numbness and blocked affect. Perls intuited a basic conflict between the mind and the body, given the fact that Western culture privileges the intellect over the corporeal body. And yet for Perls, the intellect was a "pallid substitute for the vivid immediacy of sensing and experiencing" (Perls, 1975, p. 11). Life without affect and sensory awareness and sensation was tantamount to death. Even in his more mature work (Perls, 1973), affect was the means of resurrection for mankind. "Modern man lives in a state of low-grade vitality ... he has become an anxious automaton. ... He does not approach the adventure of living with either excitement or zest" (Perls, 1973, p. xiii). "He is usually either poker-faced, bored, aloof, or irritated" (Perls, 1973, p. xiii). The goal of Gestalt therapy, with its emphasis on the here and now and the fully engaged sensorium, is to return to life "previously robotized corpses" (Perls, 1975, p. 15). Health is impeded by an "implosive layer" of the psychic structure, in which there is a fear of being, with a "basic contraction or freezing" (Perls & Clements, 1975, p. 24). It is characterized by behavioral rigidity and the experience of being stuck at an impasse.

According to Perls, the center of personality is an emotional core, but conventional socialization encumbers it with thick layers of insulation, which deadens the spirit and fundamental vitality of the human body. Therapy consists of bringing the emotions back into psychic life. Perls maintained that emotions are always connected with somatic manifestations; he saw the somatic behavior as indexing an unfinished action, which was in turn "hardly differentiated" from the unfinished emotion. In therapy, he constantly drew attention to nonverbal behavior. Without labeling the behavior as emotional in nature, he simply pointed out contradictions between speech and the nonverbal signals emitted by the body and voice. In this respect, he was quite skillful.

Attention to the contradictory in body language was one of Perls's prescriptive routes to the recovery of vitality and integration. The other route was the stimulation of "emotional explosions" or "outbursts"; these occur when the organism that has been in emotional hibernation begins to stir again. Perls does not expect individuals to find their emotional centers *gradually* and begin to articulate their full range of emotions slowly. Only the extremes of psychic somnambulism or emotional paroxysm seem to exist. There is apparently no middle ground in which the individual retains the capability of feeling and expressing his or her emotions while observing the social conventions that make for mutually respectful and sensitive social intercourse.

At the grossest level, Perls tells us, emotions can be classified as positive and negative affects and complete and incomplete affects. Note that even here, polarities dominate his world. Complete emotions are those that involve intense emotional convulsion. Although he granted that emotions can be controlled, he did not believe that they could be fully repressed. He maintained that they would always find a mode of expression, whether this was in the form of nonverbal motor discharges or in miniaturized expression – incomplete emotion expression such as pouting, whining, worrying, or acting sad. Sadness, he claimed, only becomes complete when there is an emotional explosion with an outburst of crying.

Perls wrote about four basic kinds of emotional explosion: sexual love, anger, joy, and grief. He himself had little difficulty with explosions into anger and was quite practiced in arousing such outbursts in others. He also maintained that the one emotion easiest to reach is grief because it is one of the more socially acceptable outpourings of emotion. Interestingly, he thought that the most difficult expression was explosion into love and that joy was the hardest for the neurotic. In sum then, grief, anger, love, and joy are developmentally strong and empowering emotions, whereas sadness and worry are incompletely developed emotions.

Another set of affects also fall outside of the range of complete emotions. They are not only incomplete, but might even be considered anti-emotions in the sense that they block the more empowering emotions and act as barriers to integration. Perls's list includes disgust, embarrassment, shame, anxiety, and fear. It is of interest that embarrassment is mentioned separate from shame, even though most theorists (Ekman, 1984; Izard, 1971; Tomkins, 1963) recognize the latter as belonging to the family of shame, and that anxiety is mentioned as separate from fear, though most identify anxiety as a variety of fear. Thus, we might infer that shame and fear are particularly important to Perls. Shame for Perls is associated with emotional immobilization, the inability to think, the inability to move, and deadness. In passing we note that apprehension and shame are noted as concomitants of behavior of the disorganized child, which includes motor stilling and a blank look, under conditions of interpersonal stress.

The emotion of shame received greater elaboration from Perls than any other emotion. According to Perls, shame may itself be suppressed, an activity that in itself leads to arrogance and exhibitionism. "The exhibitionist is permanently busy with suppressing his shame" (Perls, 1947/1969, p. 179). In a later work, he links sexuality with self-esteem, thinking that he had discovered a fundamental truth appreciated neither by Freud, who was deeply interested in sexuality, nor Sullivan, who was deeply interested in the self system. He equates impotence or detumescence with shame and erection with self-esteem.

Shame was a deep and abiding experience that Perls tried somewhat unsuccessfully to combat. Because he felt that successful conversion of shame involved transforming it into self-expression via exhibitionism, we have some indication why Perls was such a strutting egoist and "monumental boor"; he may have understood quite clearly that the alternative to exhibitionism for him would be the fatal descent into the void, that he would be vaporized into a mist of nothingness.

In light of the density of shame affect in his psychological architecture, it is perhaps not so surprising that he made focusing on the here and now a requisite of therapy with him. Much of the shame was linked to his developmental past – the shame of rejection by his father, the shame of his unattractive appearance, the shame of being subordinate in an authoritarian home and an authoritarian culture, and the shame of his Jewishness in an anti-Semitic state. As such, his own feelings of significance must have been severely challenged. By focusing on the here and now, he kept this painful affect from consciousness. Anger and contempt are the antithesis of shame. By maintaining an angry and contemptuous posture, he defended himself against his own shame; by provoking anger in his clients, he provided them with empowerment to throw off their own sense of effacement.

Perls was not unconscious of shame in others, and it was only partially warded off in himself. We surmise that though shame was a painful affect for him, it served a utilitarian function of screening another more toxic affect, that of fear. The psychological numbness he described and the "void" he sought to escape seem more closely related to terror than humiliation – terror of annihilation. For Perls, shame is more intermittent and thus more under his control.

Indeed, according to Perls, shame as well as fear and disgust act as forces of repression with respect to the other emotions; they are auxiliary to the containment of emotion. Interestingly enough, Silvan Tomkins, writing some twenty years later, also regarded shame and disgust as auxiliary emotions associated with truncated emotion and behavior. Disgust was a drive auxiliary that evolved to protect the human being from coming too close to noxious-smelling objects; later, through learning, disgust acquired a psychological dimension and a turning away from noxious ideas and values. Therefore, disgust is associated with a shutting down of the senses. Shame was also an auxiliary in that it was associated with the reduction of joy or interest.

In Perls's view, the emotions of shame, disgust, and fear, to the extent that they acted as forces of repression, were the primary means whereby neurosis is produced. Therapy, therefore, necessitated helping the patient avoid suppressing these emotions and the associated actions that give rise to them. In effect, what Perls recommended came close to supporting what we would today call affect tolerance. "The awareness of, and the ability to endure, unwanted emotions are the conditio sine qua non for a successful cure" (Perls, 1947/1969, p. 179).

Affects in Psychotherapy

One of our working theses is that psychotherapists commonly deploy affects in therapy with which they are most comfortable and avoid those that generate discomfort. Perls was clearly skilled at working with client anger and at liberating shame; however, he had little tolerance or aptitude for dealing with anxiety or depressed affect. A colleague, Abe Levitsky, reported "an overemphasis on the issues of autonomy and selfsupport which, I feel, he was almost obsessive about and reflected his own unresolved problems of dependency. This probably had a great deal to do with his rejection of my depression when he worked with me. Or anybody's depression. It made him impatient" (Shepard, 1975, p. 120).

It was generally obvious that Perls had a talent for working with anger. He kindled it deliberately. And for some people at least, he used his skill at eliciting anger as a stimulus to change. Perls was particularly sensitive to the detection of anger, one might even say hypervigilant for anger. It was the emotion that he looked for beneath every surface emotional gesture. He was adept at detecting its hidden manifestations – guilt is resentment, hurt masks anger, worry is repressed anger and aggression. He also expressed anger facially almost constantly, providing material for contagious conversion. Finally, he used contempt (his own) to elicit the shame/rage spiral in patients. As soon as he succeeded in creating the hostile climate, he felt at home. This environment was familiar, and he knew how to navigate in its presence. One guesses that the reproduction of his own affect in others also allowed him to feel relatively stable and to repel other feelings associated with disorder. It is not surprising that he recreated angry affect in therapy, nor that it was reproduced in the context of his family and other interpersonal relationships. This tendency to create a familiar emotional environment by reproducing particular affects is certainly salient in Perls, though we see it in Rogers and Ellis as well. We might call this kind of pattern the fractal geometry of affect. This is a line of thought we pursue and expand upon in Chapter 6.

In summary, Perls knew, understood, and cultivated anger in psychotherapy; it was an intrinsic part of his program. What is less obvious is the deliberate way that he worked with surprise; here was an interesting distinction between the three therapists of this project. Rogers was relatively comfortable with this emotion but did not actively seek it out, and Ellis actually avoided that which was surprising or unpredictable. Perls, however, showed a particular appreciation of novelty and the unexpected, noting "all my life I hated drill, overdiscipline and learning by memorizing. I always trusted the 'aha!' experience, the shock of recognition" (Perls, 1969a, p. 35).

He also cultivated the emotion of surprise in therapy. Although he may not have thought of it in terms of its dynamic properties (Magai & Nusbaum, 1996), he valued it and thought that "the 'aha' experience of discovery is one of the most powerful agents for cure" (Perls, 1973, p. 67). His patients experienced this directly; as one recalled, "when you were in therapy with Fritz, it was kind of like an event. It had a suspenseful quality. You didn't know what was coming up next" (Gaines, 1979, p. 52).

Indeed, Perls engaged in a number of practices that were unconventional and surprising to clients, the least of which was his attention to the nonverbal and to the emotional content of communication. Unlike his contemporaries, who focused on the historical and symbolic in therapy, Perls zeroed in on the unspoken bodily tensions, nervous twitches, and contradictions between the client's verbalizations and their nonverbal signals. It is probably safe to say that most people are unconscious of their body language a great deal of the time. As part of our early socialization, we all learn to disattend to the nonverbal, to ignore signals of shame, discomfort, anxiety, and the like. To have someone draw attention to these background signals would have been unusual in any context and at any time, but perhaps especially so during the era that Perls began practicing. By focusing on the nonverbal, Perls brought patient discomforts and contradictions out into the open. This unanticipated exposure had to be somewhat disorienting and startling at first encounter; it allowed Perls to have a meaningful device that others did not have.

Perls also ignored other customs and conventions of polite social discourse such as the exchange of pleasantries on introduction. Indeed, these kinds of civilities were dispensed with immediately. Perls did not wait to develop a therapeutic alliance or establish trust before he tackled patients' defenses; rather, he seemed tuned to people's vulnerabilities. We see this immediately in the film with Gloria. She is nervous and wary; perhaps she has been warned about Perls in advance by Shostrom, the producer of the film who once had been a student of Perls and who had been her own therapist. Ignoring the obvious defensive posture she has reflexively raised to protect herself, he immediately tells her that she is "phoney" and he succeeds in eliciting distress and anger. This accusation is hardly what one expects from a therapist, especially in the initial encounters when both parties are getting acquainted with one another.

Although such transactions can be initially unpleasant, surprise is often accompanied by a sudden expansion of awareness or jolt of consciousness (Magai & Nusbaum, 1996). It involves a temporary interruption of thought processes and clears the sensory channels for the reception of new information (Tomkins, 1962). With the customary modes of thinking suspended, the individual is temporarily more receptive to new thoughts and perceptions, often leading to an excited sense of discovery or insight. This may explain why Perls's demonstration sessions were so hypnotic to observers and why he seemed at times a genius or wizard (Stoehr, 1994). Patients would take the platform, have angering and surprising experiences, and subsequently come to what appeared to be new insights; this in turn led to excitement and pleasure, all within a relatively short period of time. In catching the client offguard, Perls was able to disarm prevailing defensives temporarily, creating a greater openness to warded off aspects of the self.

Perls's ability to startle and unsettle the expectations of others was also emblematic of this behavior outside of therapy. Once when a reporter was interviewing him for an article on Gestalt therapy, he refused to be interviewed in the traditional way. Instead, he insisted that she play the role of a patient and present her own fears and worries; she complied and in short order had a revelatory experience (Bry, http://ourworld.compuserve.com/homepages/gik_gestalt/fritz_perls.html).

Concluding Thoughts

Perls gave the world an interesting set of formulations about affect and a framework for a new form of psychotherapy. It is difficult to tell how lasting his overall contribution will be and to what extent his ideas will continue to be incorporated into several of the more well-established therapeutic practices. In a way, Perls's reputation suffered from not only his personal excesses but also from the Gestalt movement's association with the cultishness of Esalen and the whole counterculture movement of the 1960s. However, one of Perls's contributions is really quite profound – his analysis of nonverbal behavior and affect during an era of thoroughgoing mentalism. His was a singular voice in drawing attention to the nonsymbolic, nonverbal axis of behavior as a crucial arena for analysis and treatment. In this sense, he made an extraordinary contribution to therapy. His attention to affect during the period of academic psychology's virtual neglect of the emotions was also avant garde and may have been one of the small but significant preludes to a new consciousness of affect in the field.

As far as Perls's personal therapeutic style is concerned – as a model for emulation – we have substantial reservations. Although Perls used emotions such as surprise and anger to good advantage in therapy with certain individuals, he had a relatively limited repertoire. To be sure, he was skillful in eliciting anger and self-assertion in patients who were timid and insecure. He was an ace at detecting every possible conversion or subversion of anger and ferreting it out. The ability to acknowledge and tolerate anger is a valuable resource in a well-balanced personality, and Perls's ability to liberate repressed anger in patients must have been experienced by many as fresh and empowering. However, liberating anger without addressing the whole spectrum of emotions and the larger life context in which the individual is situated can be dangerous at times rather than therapeutic. Perls showed no aptitude for dealing with sadness and anxiety, feelings of helplessness and dependency. In some ways, Perls was like the carpenter who only has a hammer – everything begins to look like a nail. Clients with only anger at their disposal would have been at a disadvantage. Like the sole hammer, anger in isolation from other affective sensibilities is a relatively blunt instrument.

In summary, Fritz Perls was a master of the nonverbal, sensitive to hidden, blocked, and distorted affect but somewhat restricted in his range of affective responses and his ability to tolerate certain emotions in others. The curious reader might wonder what precisely led Perls down this particular path and not another. Given Perls's level of immersion in psychoanalysis and training, and his supervision by some of the great names in the field – Helen Duetsch, Karen Horney, Wilhelm Reich, and Otto Fenichel, among others – it is perhaps surprising that he broke from psychoanalysis so completely and later became one of its most hostile critics. On one hand, given his familial background, it was perhaps to be expected. Although it is a somewhat hackneyed interpretation that many of those who broke with Freud – Adler, Jung, Rank, and Erikson, his theoretical sons – acted out Oedipal issues, Perls's case may have been a particularly clear instance of it. But Perls's break with the psychoanalytic school was not the most remarkable of his excursions from the traditional and may have had more to do with the analytic school's absorption with symbolism to the exclusion of corporeal experiences. For Perls, the world of the body and state of emotions was what was real and compelling, as well as disturbing and troubling.

For Perls, the inner mental life was at times a confusing maelstrom of disconnected experiences and vague, unsorted, emotional turmoil; at other times, it was an empty, dead space. Many of the things that most of us take for granted – the solidity of the body, and the regular and sometimes not-so-regular highs and lows of emotional feelings – often eluded him. He struggled to overcome a deadness of spirit and to bring his fragmented experiences together by a technique he called "withdrawal into the fertile void." Going into the fertile void entailed "experiencing [one's] confusion to the utmost . . . hallucinations, broken up sentences, vague feelings, strange feelings, peculiar sensations" (Perls, 1973, p. 99).

One gains a sense of the instability of his affective landscape from another of his theoretical formulations. For Perls, an intrinsic aspect of emotions was their malleability or convertibility. Disgust could be converted to discrimination; anxiety, into a specific interest; and embarrassment, into self-expression. The transformability of emotion was thus a salient aspect of his theory. Perls's discussion of affect transformation reveals the fluidity with which he viewed the shift from one affective state to another and reinforces our sense that instability of affect was likely a part of his everyday subjectivity. The emotions of others were also often suspect in terms of their reality and stability. Others' emotions were not always what they seemed. Guilt commonly masked resentment. Hurt masked anger. Anxiety was really blocked interest. Boredom was lack of interest. "Crying is not crying is not crying" (Perls, 1969a, p. 221). Boredom/impatience would eventually produce anger and rage. "Crying is a very well known form of aggression" (Perls, 1969a, p. 148).

This unpredictable inner life – sometimes dead and sometimes in turmoil – is conceivably a sufficient explanation for Perls's fascination with the nonverbal evidence of incomplete emotions and actions. Alternatively, it was his inability to trust others – their motives, their real inner feelings, their acceptance of himself. This basic mistrust may also have been amplified by the very real sense of the historical persecution of the Jews, as well as that which he himself experienced in gymnasium and the army. The person who doubts other peoples' trustworthiness and intentions, who feels that others may be less than honest, may well be vigilant for dishonesty and need to search for the reality behind the words.

This mistrust must have posed a difficult existential quandary for Perls. If emotions are this fluid and transformable, how is one to trust either oneself or others? In our view, this was a central dilemma for Perls and may account for both his fundamental distrust of others and his acute sensitivity to the nonverbal signals of emotion. If things are not what they seem, one must be vigilant for underlying intentions and sentiments; one must read beyond the masks and words of others. One must try to find the emotional center of oneself despite the chaotic flow of emotions. It is of interest to note that the last line of his autobiography raised the poignant query, "Will I ever learn to trust myself completely?"

PART III

Emotion as the Link in Intellectual Work

6 Wisdom and Passion

In the next sections of the book we turn from the large sweep of life as it has been portrayed in the socioemotional analysis. Now we examine some smaller emotional behaviors, the habits of expression in writing and behavior. We show that these are much more than disconnected habits; they form meaningful bits of the structure of personality. They are like fractals – small versions of elements with similar forms making up a larger form. Some critical behaviors are like crystals in that they are made of elements that resemble each other and then form a larger structure. The larger form resembles the elements, and, psychologically, the resemblance may be both meaningful and symbolic. These small pieces of behavior are what the broader categories of attachment are composed from or result from. We have already been integrating the forms of specific emotions such as shame or anger into the portrayal of attachment styles, but now we will go in a different direction with the same intent.

It is in the small, significant bits of behavior that people such as Silvan Tomkins, a founder of emotional analysis, or Perls, founder of Gestalt therapy, erratically form their often surprising insights about the larger wholes. From subconscious uses of expressive emotional words to the larger patterns of intellectual organization, the tendency toward emotional wholeness of the person is always building, adapting to new circumstances, and then rebuilding on the old foundations. Even when the personality is framed with elements that oppose each other, a form of discontinuity, that opposition in itself becomes a paradoxical organizing feature with interesting limiting or boundary features in personality, as it is in art forms. The "fit" does not have to be simple; it may range from the mechanical to the symbolic. It is the variety of the patterns that has eluded us and may yet continue to baffle us for years, but some general principles are emerging. In this chapter, we show how an analysis of these elements is performed. In the following chapters, we learn how the small elements constitute a changing whole.

Emotional processes are like cognitive processes in that they are processes of change, not simple reactions. Some emotions note, promote, or accelerate change and the assimilation of sensory information. Other emotions note lack of change and the stability of events and tend to promote that stability, assimilating new material that maintains it. Yet other emotions prevent change; they preserve some internal state, blocking information. These ideas are not new, but are part of the tradition in emotional theory dating from Tomkins in the middle of the twentieth century. As various people who study or work with emotions have written in many different ways, what we call emotions is our sense of how we perceive the world. If we understand it to be changing too rapidly to take it in and to be out of our control, all our sensory and information processes react accordingly. We may call this sense or feeling something like fearfulness, but the sense of fearfulness is a summary of the fit between the world and the person who tells us how the world is being perceived or processed by this person. It is as much a statement of cognition as it is anything else, but as a summary, it may seem to be all one thing, one state, one sensory feeling. However, it is much more likely that we are usually just not aware of processing capacities that we have. Most of them move too fast and too subtly for awareness. Nevertheless, as we note changes in states of emotion, we are summarizing changes in physiological processes, cognitive processes, and social preferences. As emotional states become individualized and become personal habits or traits, so also do physiological processes and cognitive processes. In what follows we will outline in some detail three patterns of emotional processes becoming or representing cognitive and personality processes.

We will turn first to the stylistic elements of theoretical work in the books and other writings of Perls, Rogers, and Ellis. Later we will turn to the application of that work in the stylistic elements of therapeutic practice. We will discover several things from studying what seem at first to be minor idiosyncrasies. Emotional habits and values support significant larger issues, even such large and seemingly unemotional issues as the emergence of a major psychological theory. For example, we will see that Ellis's emphasis on rational emotive rules is not separable from his small habits of attending to and correcting or enduring fearfully uncontrolled bits of life. But emotional habits and values, because they are so numerous, so influenced by unpredictable cues ranging from Ellis's childhood hospitalizations to political ideologies of the 1960s, are also a potential source for change. We will find that in nonlinear and surprisingly interactive ways, little changes in emotional habits may precede larger personality shifts and intellectual changes. Such changes on the individual level constantly interact to produce changes in institutions or in history. Stabilities in emotional expressiveness may indicate deep, difficult-to-change areas of life and deeply held but unexamined beliefs both for individuals and for cultures.

These aspects of the self apply to us all, of course. Whether the work is studying psychology or driving a truck or leading seminars or practicing medicine, the way that our work is done reflects the person doing it. It will reflect our larger beliefs about life's important values.

People who claim that their own fractal habits have nothing to do with their convictions or moral values are stating a value, not a fact. They have decided that large and important events such as starting an economic war are separate and acted upon differently from their habitual modes of handling tiny personal power plays. When this is true, then the separatist belief or value would also be supported with separatist types of fractal-like habits. Such people would have areas of life split off from each other at all levels. They would be biased toward the emotions supporting separatists positions such as contempt. Someone such as Gandhi, who seemed so nonaggressive in his politics but who was reported to abuse his own family, is an example of such separation. As we will see in more detail when looking at Gloria, the client interviewed by Rogers, Perls, and Ellis, the fact that emotions and other habits are not coherent may indicate a lack of coherence in personality, itself a defining feature of the person.

The relations among fractal habits and larger forms would inevitably also mean, as naive psychology tells us, that particular kinds of work or home life or any context, finally, may be influenced by personal styles. Why else is there a stereotype of the absorbed computer whiz or the narcissistic actress or the rigid military person? It is not because these are requirements of the work in an abstract sense, but because the style of the work and the people doing it have created an historical workplace synchrony. These synchronies also create predictable patterns of problem solution and bring with them predictable motivations for the work.

When someone enters a workplace who has a different personality from the usual people framing the space, then not only are there clashes in small habits and styles but also in larger personal and intellectual ways of understanding the work. Hence, people with new styles for a situation often work on the edge of a field, productively or not. For example, when women enter a field dominated by men or vice versa, the larger view of the work may change. A male secretary may define and perform his job differently from a female secretary. A female gas station attendant may perform her job differently from a male attendant. Often chaotic eddies form around these marginal people, whether they intend it or not, and whether they can formalize philosophic positions or not, resulting in larger changes or in a building of defenses against change.

Our three clinical psychologists bring very particular emotional habits to their adult lives and work. In the next section, our task is to show how we discovered unexpected synergistic connections between the content and development of the theories and the sometimes minute, emotional expressions of the three. This will also illustrate three (out of uncounted numbers) possible ways for adults to change and develop, depending upon their emotional habits and values that emerge early in life giving foundations for particular organizations and predictable modes of change that will interact with the contexts and opportunities that come later.

The major developmental theories of this century and years past tend toward very simple descriptions of change. One of the insights that emerges from the work that follows is that adult development may take a multitude of trajectories. The early foundations of personality are important boundary conditions on the types of change that might occur, but there is not a single trajectory or mode of change. It is even possible to not change in any noticeable way across decades. It may also be the case that we have exaggerated the commonalities even of early development across individuals, much less later development (Van Geert, 1994). The fact that people begin at one place and end at another does not tell us that the path between is common to us all.

Why did each man, as an individual, become the kind of psychologist that he did? When in their lives did they become Client-centered or Rational Emotive or Gestaltist? Why are their theories different? It cannot be the historical time period because they all emerged in approximately the same period. It cannot be gender differences because they are all men. It cannot be discipline of study because all three are psychologists. It cannot be fame because all three are famous. It cannot be social class because all three emerged from the middle class. All three married, though the relationships within the marriages differed.

Two of the three had children and again the relationships with the children differed. Only one followed an academic career but in late life left it for an experimental institute. The other two founded their own institutes, though their relationships with their foundings also differed. In most broad respects, these men have much in common. Only a few differences emerge in the larger sociological aspects of their lives. Two grew up in the United States and remained there all their lives. The third grew up in Europe and settled in South Africa before moving to the United States to found his institute and achieve fame there. One grew up practicing the Protestant religion and considered a career in the ministry. The other two grew up in Jewish families but were apparently not devoted to the practice of their religion. In nationality and religion of origin there are differences, but it is the relationship that each man has with the religious or marital or work institutions that differs most strikingly.

The answers to questions about the process of personal change with a particular historical epoch do not lie on the surface of major sociological events, nor do they always lie in the large or peak events of an individual life. A single great gift or great trauma does not in itself have to determine much of development. As Virginia Woolf (*A Room of One's Own*) argued in her brilliant description of Shakespeare born female, it is not just the gift of poetic genius, but the continuous opportunities to experience life, to learn, to have freedom for creativity, and to have acclaim that all must come together for a Shakespeare as we know him or her to develop. We do not hold the medieval belief that a Shakespeare or a king exists as a homunculus at conception.

It is our theory that, to understand personality development, we need to attend to factors that we usually ignore when looking at historical and biographical material. We want to understand not only what Rogers, Perls, and Ellis write about their ideas, what they hold as important truths but also *how* they express their beliefs. It is here in the modes of expression that effects emerge and build and produce order or chaos as they would in any human interaction. A view that a single event or idea is the sole cause of developmental change may occasionally be true, but it is more likely that such events only symbolize, in a particularly vivid way, the smaller events. One might claim, for example, that a divorce occurred because one partner pushed the other, resulting in serious damage. The supporting picture would tell us that there were repeated "pushes" in words, in emotional expression, in the structuring of mutual responsibility, in sexual relations, and so on. At the same time, there were probably contexts in which no pushing at all occurred.

We know well that the same spouse who abuses at night may tenderly bring flowers when he visits in the hospital the following morning. The shifting of context can then obscure the regularities that do exist and confuse us if we expect linear simplicity.

Since we do not ordinarily attend to small habits of expression, we must make a special effort to be attentive to emotional expression and then to patterns of organization. For example, we need to ignore at one level *what* the three founders of clinical schools wrote and focus on *how* they wrote it and with what motivational or emotional emphases. We need to orient ourselves to the process of becoming Rational Emotive or Gestaltist or Client-centered with a systematic approach. Certainly the "becoming" is connected to the kinds of relationships discussed previously, but how they are connected can be shown at yet another level. It is to this connection that we turn next.

Following work that we and others have done previously, we will introduce two techniques for uncovering motivational patterns. At first we concentrate on the emotional words a person uses regardless of their context. This tells us the emotional ingredients that a person has access to. Then we look at how they are organized. In this second regard, we are going to focus on intellectual or cognitive organizations. We will find how the process of thinking about theoretical and applied psychological processes is associated with emotions.

In the remainder of this chapter, we explain how we use these techniques of analysis and give examples that would enable the reader to make similar excursions into written material or dialogues so that fractal-like expressions of personality contained in emotion and cognition can be detected anywhere. First, we explain how we came to propose these techniques. Then in the following chapters, we show the results of the analyses done for Rogers, Ellis, and Perls demonstrating the personality information that is in everyone's movements and words.

Emotional Patterns

Until very recently we have not taken emotions into account when considering cognition or intelligence except as an interference problem. We have suspected that emotion interferes with logic or with healthy behavior. This bias reflects centuries of Western philosophy in which rationality is a high function and emotionality is a lower function. Western philosophic and scientific beliefs about the basic emotions imply that emotions are more negative and damaging than they are positive and constructive, a belief not shared by Eastern cultures. The study of feelings and emotions in Western culture is found in the study of animals, children, and women, but even these studies reflect an ancient history. As long ago as early biblical writings, Job complains that it is not right that he, a righteous, moral man, should feel grief. Grief is for women and beggars, whereas powerful men have judgment in its place. It is not right nor fair in Job's mind that he should experience grief. It makes him fear being ill, irrational, and dependent. Such beliefs are deeply entrenched and found everywhere in Western culture so that we hardly notice their pervasiveness.

Even the briefest of historical overviews of the science of emotions will show that in the early part of the twentieth century the concentration of research that was at all related to emotion employed as subjects animals and children or mental patients. Most of the mental patients were women. Students were employed to make intellectual judgments of emotion communication in the middle of the twentieth century, but their own empathic and emotional experiences were not studied. Only at the end of the twentieth century did the science of emotions begin, and it is still hampered by long-held beliefs about the domain of emotion.

In contrast, the Chinese and Indian cultures present in their philosophies and art highly refined and admired emotions that are difficult to produce except by the most skilled and talented people (Shweder, 2000). These are the sorts of emotions that can live in the rafters of one's home and influence the entire emotional balance of a household in a direction of refinement and awareness of nuance. There are difficult and complex levels of emotional experience that one might attain with devotion, practice, and good fortune. Compare this to the very limited view of emotions in a Western scene. Little attention is paid to creating an emotional tone that would be conducive to particular tasks. Most of the effort lies in the direction of banishing emotion. Under "emotional" circumstances, a person's best rational self might not emerge. On the other hand, to get an athletic team or squad of soldiers "primed," their coach or captain is likely to use emotional language and postures. In the physical and competitive realms, emotion may be legitimately used. Again the connotation is largely negative, as sports and fighting are not viewed as intellectually challenging activities. Similarly, film stars may work with emotion, but their expressive control is not expected to make them wise or refined.

Very recently, and still considered radical, there has been some appreciation of emotional intelligence – the aspect of intelligence that uses culturally relevant emotional knowledge. That is, if one has skills in decoding signals of emotion or has a rich vocabulary for feeling states that is highly differentiated, then one would be more emotionally intelligent. If one has methods for controlling emotional expression, one might be more intelligent (Salovey & Mayer, 1990; Goleman, 1995).

In spite of our cultural history, it is quite possible for individuals to pay attention to people's emotional patterns. Perls, for example, was very adept at watching people's movement in order to interpret their feelings. Rogers also wrote about the usefulness of listening to his clients' emotional words in order to be empathic to their feelings. An "effective approach was to listen for the feelings, the emotions, whose patterns could be discerned through the client's words" (Rogers, 1980, p. 138). Although Ellis makes little claim for his abilities, he too listens carefully to emotional words and then may use the client's own emotional terms in his responses. What becomes interesting is that, without a systematic approach, each man has a bias toward hearing certain emotional words and not others. Most people notice emotional cues "intuitively." Hatfield, Cacioppo, and Rapson (1994) have research evidence to show that if an actor tells us that he is happy, but gives voice, face, and postural cues for sadness, we may report the stated happiness for the actor, but report that we, ourselves, feel sad. We know at one level that sadness is appropriate in the context, but we do not know what the cues were. Hatfield and her colleagues suggested that we misinterpret the cues and believe that we have generated them ourselves. Originally, the context was sad, not the person watching. The cues are contagious, but often people do not know what has happened.

It is not actually a mystery to decode emotion; it is just difficult at first to pay attention on more than one level. Training is helpful, but some types of listening remain difficult. People may even have a general bias toward the meaning of words and away from nonverbal emotional material, learned or not. We know how confusing it is to identify correctly the color a word is printed in when the word itself is a name for a color. When the word is "red," for example, but it is printed in a bright green color, will we say "green" or "red" and will we know when we have made an error? Perhaps we also find it confusing to read emotions that are different from the spoken or written meaning, and we may have a bias toward the words.

With written material, the repeated emotional cues can be searched for, although even that seems an alien mode of reading at first. For example, in reading the biography of the Nobel Prize winner Barbara McClintock (Keller, 1983), we repeatedly find that she expresses "surprise." In a journal article, she writes "it would be surprising indeed if controlling elements were not found in other organisms." In talking personally about a difficult time, she says "It was just a surprise that I couldn't communicate; it was a surprise that I was being ridiculed."

McClintock's biography is titled *A Feeling for the Organism* because she remains open across a very long career to the unexpected and improbable stories that each individual seed and plant might tell her. She is constantly prepared to be surprised or biased toward surprising events. By listening to her emotional words, we find that her emotions themselves are small versions of her larger values. In dynamic systems terminology, we would infer that this is a sort of fractal – the whole is made of parts that resemble it. A personality trait that expresses openness to the novel events of the world with an expectation of learning but not being able to predict what is around the next corner and repeated minute expressions of "surprise" are forms of each other on different levels of processing. We can all learn to attend to repeated words of emotion if we choose. We can also learn to attend to repeated emotional gestures or expressions that seem to operate in much the same way as words.

The first way that we listened to our three therapists was to look at their emotional words and phrases. We literally counted types of emotion words and made charts for them. Even we were not expecting the first results that quickly emerged from listing emotional expressions. As we will see in the following chapters, Rogers used words related to anger (the client's, not his own) more than any other emotion expression in his early books about therapy. He even has titles for cases such as "The Angry Adolescent." We did not expect this prevalence of anger from the kindly humanist who mythically lived in our imaginations when we began this project. Ellis used words related to fear (again, the client's fear, not his own) more than any other in his early books and articles. By the time we coded his work, we were more prepared for the paradox that the emotion most attributed to others may predict patterns of self-control that emerge as major values or theories. So we were less surprised that our vision of the audacious New York performer of therapy is concerned with people's fears. But this observation was only the beginning and one of the simplest, though powerful, effects.

The most highly developed systems of measuring emotion deal with bodily and facial expression or simple word definitions. There are few studies of the typical meanings of expressed emotion in writing or speech, but it is apparent that there are associations between the use of emotion words and personality. For example, depressed people use depressed emotional terms (Beck, 1967). Emotionally repressed people are sparse in their emotion vocabulary. Gender differences occur in usage. A manic-depressive such as Virginia Woolf shifts rapidly between polar opposites (Haviland, 1984). So it seems likely that the written emotion statements can symbolize a variety of motivational states.

We expect that when we focus on simple emotion words, alone and in combination with other psychologically and sociologically important elements, we can find evidence for emotions that are predominant at particular times or in relation to particular people, events, or thoughts. We will find that sections of writing can be dominated by particular emotions and can be dense or sparse in the variety of emotion. This information provides important clues to personality development and change.

We assume that the use of emotion terms reflects a number of things in addition to personal style. They indicate individual sensitivity to cultural gestures and immediate emotional crisis, both conscious and subconscious. Writing about emotion is not the same as the experience itself. Much of an emotional experience is not easily accessible and may be distorted. The mood of the individual at the time of reporting may color the report of previous feelings. It is inevitable that a great deal of variance in emotion usage will occur. Nevertheless, patterns of usage will also emerge from the writings over a period of time if we look patiently. It is a form of projective testing, and we know that reliable inferences can be made from multiple sources through projective testing (Lillienfield, Wood & Garb, 2000).

In order to proceed with our work, all the emotion words in the parts of the texts that we used were identified. All the words gathered are matched to the dictionary lists provided by Izard (1971) to form nine general categories. Within the categories, the degree of emotion may vary. The anger category, for example, varies from expressions of annoyance to expressions of rage. The categories include words meaning some degree of interest, enjoyment, surprise, sadness, disgust, anger, shame, or fear and a category for nonspecific moods or feelings. This last one accounted for words such as "moody" or "feelings" or "emotion." We did not search for colorful or idiosyncratic usages; we stayed with common dictionary definitions.

Organization Analysis

Once we have an idea about emotional preferences and gaps in emotional expression, we turn to the associations of emotion to modes of intellectual organization. Going back to the example of McClintock, who often expressed surprise, we study how she thinks when she is surprised. Is there a particular intellectual organization that lends itself to solving surprising problems? Does the bias toward surprise enter into a pattern of thought that could lead to a Nobel Prize, as it did with McClintock? If we know that Ellis has a bias toward expressing fear, does this have something to do with how he thinks about therapies for anxiety and neurosis? When Rogers is enjoying himself, how does he think? Is it different than the way he thinks when he is facing hostility? How is emotion integrated with the type of thinking or problem solving that we do?

In recent years psychological theories about thinking have been changing rapidly as a result of discoveries converging from several areas of psychology. They all lead to the idea that intellectual skills are many, not singular. The notion that one has a unique, singular, and stable "IQ" is being questioned on all sides. One theory suggests that thinking is dualistic, that we have "right" and "left" brain problem-solving abilities, and that we can be "linear" thinkers or "holistic" thinkers. Even though the evidence for this theory is hotly debated, it at least demonstrates the perspective that people have more than one mode for organizing and using information.

In the realm of intelligence testing, both Sternberg (1977) and Gardner (1983) pointed out that intelligence can be composed of many different abilities – some social, some organizational, some spatial, and so forth. One might be musically talented or empathically talented, for example. Once again, we find that the direction of discovery is moving us away from the belief that there is a general intelligence, a single factor that determines whether one is absolutely clever. Such discoveries move us culturally and philosophically away from serious consideration of "pure" reason toward modes or styles of reasoning.

The direction of this trend toward expanding and defining different types of rational process is related also to the critical work of the epistemologist Piaget earlier in this century. Piaget (1951) was trying to answer the philosophical question, "How do you know that what you experience as a real object, is actually there in the form that you think it is?" Piaget demonstrated that even the youngest child has a system of knowledge that leads it to explain events in the world according to general principles. The basis of the child's philosophy is not the same as the adolescent's or the adult's; however, it is still a logical approach of its own. Piaget hoped to demonstrate that as the child's system evolved into the adult system it would incorporate more object–events in a systematic and successful way. For Piaget, intelligence is a form of adapting to a context successfully.

Piaget's important contribution, for our purposes, was to lead researchers to consider that the acquisition of knowledge is less learning bits of information, an encyclopedia sort of view, and more a joint project of the information available and the mode of thought that is used to organize the information. All the theories Piaget studied explain how things work to a degree, but the processes and assumptions vary among theories. They are all "rational" in their own context even if some seem more limited than others. Inadvertently, Piaget also managed to demonstrate that we are not aware of how our theories work and that they differ among people and change over time and contexts. Curiously, we all tend to assume that our own system represents *the* singular rational system. In a way, Piaget continued the trend begun by Freudians to show how there are kinds of knowledge that we are not usually aware of. Even our beliefs about how we know things are not likely to be absolutely true. How to retrieve and remember even simple associations, for example, is a complex matter. Our beliefs about how it is done bear little resemblance to the actual process.

We will assume that Rogers's, Perls's, and Ellis's intellectual lives were not made up only of bits of knowledge but of organizations of thought or of theories about psychological processes. They were not aware of these organizations any more than any other person might be. For the better part, they knew the same bits of scholarly, psychological information or at least they had the opportunity to know the same sorts of things. Nevertheless, their ways of using the information differed markedly.

Not only do individuals prefer different modes of thought, but even different scientific and philosophical theories reflect different modes of thinking and use information differently (e.g., Pepper, 1942). There is not a single mode for scientific or philosophic theories either. Once again, there are multiple styles of thinking, all potentially quite different and yet successful in their contexts.

Coding the organization of information is fairly complex (see Haviland & Kramer, 1991). However, the gist of it is possible to grasp without extensive training. Again, it is a matter of listening for aspects of self-expression that we ordinarily ignore. If we do not hear someone clearly we usually ask *what* was said. We seldom, if ever, ask *how* it was said. But it is in the *how* that we find our cues to motivation and thought.

Originally the modes of thought or organizations of information that we will be using came from the categories of organization in major philosophies (Pepper, 1942). These categories have also been adapted to examine the different types of formal, logical thinking that develop in adolescents (Basseches, 1980; Blanchard-Fields, 1986; Broughton, 1978; Chandler, 1987; Perry, 1970; Sinnott, 1984) and later in life (Kramer & Woodruff, 1986).

Absolute Logic

The first style of organization we looked for is familiar to us all and taught in many educational settings. It is called many names but we will use the term "absolute" to describe this style of organization. Absolute thinking or logic posits a belief in a fixed, stable world. According to this system, we can know the world through reflective abstraction or scientific experimentation (Kramer, 1983). The absolute thinker is prone to categorize people using traits and types seen as inherent and fixed and to think in terms of absolute principles and ideals. The mode of thinking probably develops in early adolescence. For example, the adolescent Anne Frank wrote in her diary, "You only really get to know people when you've had a jolly good row with them. Then and only then can you judge their true characters" (Frank, 1953, p. 31). The absolute quality of these sentences comes out in the assertion that there is one way to get "true access" to someone's "true character," indicating also the belief that people actually have singular real characters to be discovered, just as they might have a true, eternal IQ or a true, eternal temperament.

Absolute logic is a linear process. With this style, we can start with an hypothesis, next describe the elements of the problem, and finally show that the elements either add together or that one leads to or causes another. Having discovered this or shown it, we present the conclusion. From this approach, general rules or principles are derived. Contradiction is logically impossible; only one approach or principle or rule can ultimately be correct because there really is only one truth. If there are two answers, there must be a flaw in the analysis.

Rogers in one early book presents a list of events that always occur in the process of therapy. This is an example of absolute thinking. He breaks the process down into units that follow logically one from the other. Alternative pathways are not predicted. Rogers figures out how the elements fit together, how each element leads to or causes the emergence of the next element. When thinking absolutely, Rogers assumes that such blocks will be finite and stable, that what happens for one case will happen for any other.

The reader can probably call to mind several theories of science and social science that are constructed in the style of absolute logic. Such theories are likely to assume underlying traits or forces, perhaps inherited, or in some way "given" that we could discover. Then the theories look for mechanisms to explain how these traits or forces operate. It is a sophisticated and thoughtful approach to many problems and situations. It is the primary mode of thought taught in twentieth-century science and technology. We use this style to solve problems, but we also look for problems that fit this style. In spite of the present preference for absolute logic in technological cultures, there are vast cultures and historical time periods in which this mode has not been preferred. Even presently among scientists, there are prominent people who use other modes.

We will find that Ellis is overall the most adept of the three men with absolute styles of organization. For example, in describing a case, he wrote,

> The beauty of the rational-emotive approach is that no matter what the client seems to be upset about, the therapist can quickly demonstrate that there is no good reason for her upset.... So if RET is consistently followed, *any* emotional problem may be tracked down to its philosophic sources...and these philosophies may then be challenged, attacked, changed, and uprooted. (Ellis, 1971, p. 256)

Just as we described earlier, Ellis holds that what we can know about "upset" is a representation of an underlying "true" event that can be discovered. No matter what the client claims, Ellis will find the irrational aspects of it and, in a causal chain of analysis, show the false aspects. There is never going to be an exception. Unlike McClintock, the Nobel biologist, he is not going to be surprised or expect to keep finding things he cannot explain.

Although absolute logic is probably most common, we are becoming more familiar with another style of logic as postmodern relativism expands its horizons. Absolute logic does not always seem to be the most complete method. Sometimes we know two things about our problems. One is that the perspective we take on them or the level at which we approach them defines the problem and ultimately the solution. Therefore, there are two or more logical ways to solve a problem or to understand a relationship. They may seem to fit with each other or even to oppose each other, but both are logical, and each provides a solution that is unique. The second thing we often know about our problems is that we change the elements of problems when we try to understand them. Our mode of thinking does not always remain separate from the problem being studied.

Relativistic Logic

When we consider these alternative aspects of a problem we are using a relativistic logic style. Relativism is an intellectual organization in which we are aware that reality is continuously constructed with the very tools that we use to examine it. A simple approach to the Heisenberg principle will probably come to mind – in measuring the speed of a small particle, you will necessarily alter its movement and thus cannot know the present speed. You only know what it was at the moment of measurement. Your measurement inevitably changes it. There are even some forms of physics in which an object apparently exists only when it is observed. This is also relativistic; there is no underlying reality independent of the context.

Relativistic thinking derives from the assumptions of Pepper's (1942) contextual world view, which posits a changing, unknowable world. Consequently, all knowledge is subjective and constantly changing within fluctuating contexts. Some understanding and use of relativistic logic emerges during early to middle adolescence.

Social reality is often viewed relativistically, although the style works perfectly well with physical reality. Knowledge of social reality creates the reality, but it is a changing reality. Even the description of one's knowledge may alter its validity. Suppose a father continuously finds his child underfoot in the kitchen when he is preparing dinner. If the father takes the relatively amorphous tendency to be around the preparation as an interest in cooking, he may indeed influence the emergence of a chef. The elements of "chefness" might have existed at some level, but they are organized by the father's observation, thus creating certain reality from an uncertain potential.

Ellis's theory sometimes can be viewed as a relativistic theory, even though particular issues are usually resolved with an absolute style. In writing about the philosophy behind his theory, he wrote about one client, "Even if real, overt hazards exist in her life (such as the possibility of dying of some disease), she can learn to convince herself that 1) she probably won't suffer in the worst ways she can imagine" (1971, p. 259). The assumption Ellis used here is that two views of reality are possible. Even impending death can be viewed irrationally and catastrophically or rationally and noncatastrophically. The view that one takes then creates a reality, in particular, an emotional reality, that can guide behavior in significantly different ways. When we find logic like this we label it relativism and note that the writer considers alternative approaches to a subject. However, the writer may recognize this relativity and then still return to an absolute style, as Ellis repeatedly does. Ellis, in this same case, then argues that one reality is better or truer than another and that the realities are contradictory. In other words, he allows for two realities but then compares them and finds that only one is rational and worthwhile and that the one can substitute for the other.

The basic assumption in a strong version of relativism is that there is no actual reality that is, in a logical sense, better or more real than another, nor is it the case that one can merely be substituted for another. In this sense, Ellis is not really using a complete relativistic style; he resolves his relativism with absolute logic.

In some of his writings, Perls is quite relativistic. For example,

> The *how* is all we need to understand, how we or the world functions. The *how* gives us perspective, orientation. The *how* shows that one of the basic laws, the identity of structure and function, is valid. If we change the structure, the function changes. If we change the function, the structure changes (Perls, 1969b, p. 47).

The last part of this excerpt gives a good example of relativism: "If we change the structure, the function changes." Perls is aware that the position from which he makes his argument forms the argument.

Patterned Thought

There is yet another style of logic that is very infrequently used. Occasionally one sees a style that moves from showing the step-by-step logic of several systems and to searching for a pattern, not necessarily a linear one, that relates the separate systems. One form of this has been called a dialectical style. In dialectical logic change occurs through the conflict that emerges from opposing systems or knowledge bases. From such differences emerge possible new events or problem solutions that tend to resolve the previous contradictions (Kramer, 1989). Knowledge through resolution of contradiction is seen as evolving through increasingly integrated structures characterized by emergence (novel features) and reciprocity (systemic characteristics).

Most researchers using this dialectical style of thinking consider dialectics to be a form of "wise" thinking that emerges in adulthood, often quite late in life. It is usually easiest to find examples of patterned styles in the areas of expertise or mastery that people develop over their entire lifespans. If that is so, then examining the work of three theorists is likely to show some development over time in their areas of mastery.

We want to broaden the concept of the dialectical style and will call it patterned thought to indicate that it includes dialectical styles but does not simply require the resolution of opposites. In a patterned style, knowledge is always in a state of flux and must always be considered in particular contexts. Even so, change and relations among events occur in certain systematic but not necessarily strictly predictable ways among systems. Patterned styles may develop from attempts to integrate absolute and relativistic concepts in order to find continuity within change or they may be independent. Like relativity, the patterned style construes all phenomena as changing and potentially contradictory at one level.

The patterned mode of comprehending problems is a newly emerging one. Recently a renowned physicist tried to explain to an interviewer how he came to change his theory of quarks. He claimed that he immersed himself in all aspects of the problem and stayed with them until a pattern emerged in which each of simpler systems he had been considering had a place. A similar claim was made by the people who first realized that DNA forms a helix. After extended immersion in all aspects of the problem, the pieces fell into place forming a pattern that contained the various relationships in a new way. Many psychohistorians make the same claim for their styles of problem solving. They immerse themselves in all aspects of the person and historical time period in which they will write and wait for patterns to emerge from the material. Possibly even when we play word games we use some form of the immersion method. After guessing letters according to frequency in the language, we start to make models of possibilities. We "guess" possible words, that is, patterns of letters, little models, that might be tested. Of course, much of the new dynamic systems or chaotic systems (see Gleick, 1987) are forms of pattern analysis. It appears to be becoming a better formed intellectual thought process in recent years. The existence of such models or patterns can be tested in various ways, but the initial ideas emerge from the patterned mode of thought.

It would have been difficult for Rogers or Perls or Ellis to produce fully formed versions of patterned thought because it would have been obscure during their historical period, having no name or clear examples. They may well, however, at least considered that opposites may create coherent systems, as this is very common to psychoanalytic and some psychological styles of working. For example, Rogers had a description of the release of feelings in therapy that is a primitive version of a patterned style. He described negative and positive feelings balancing each other and together bringing forth a wondrous new product – insight. It is primitive or undeveloped in that Rogers has not made clear how "insight" brings the positive and negative feelings into accord within a single system. But it is clear that he sees the value of both positive and negative feelings in therapeutic process and that one feeling cannot substitute for the other. He has gone slightly beyond simple relativism by intuiting a new system emerging from and containing seemingly opposing elements.

For a better example, consider Perls discussing the existential position and trying to explain the difference between the Western and Eastern concepts of nothingness:

> When we say "nothingness" there is a void, an emptiness, something deathlike. When the Eastern person says "nothingness", he calls it *no thingness* – there are no *things* there. There is only process, happening. Nothingness doesn't exist for us, in the strictest sense, because nothingness is based on awareness of nothingness, so there is the awareness of nothingness, so there is something there. And we find when we accept and *enter* this nothingness, the void, then the desert starts to bloom. The empty void becomes alive, is being filled (Perls, 1969b, p. 41).

Perls is confronting a dialectical paradox in that nothingness is something. The apparent opposites are not independent but form a unit. The fusing or the realization viewed from a certain standpoint is that they create each other and together create something more and different from each considered separately. Nothingness contains a necessity of somethingness which creates a "bloom." Perls does not tell us how these opposites "create," so it is not a completed dialectical system, but, as with Rogers, patterned thought is beginning.

When Perls in a group session responds to a person who says she is afraid, Perls suggests that she might become "comfortable" with her feeling. Then he says "Mmmmhhmm. Now, try to get more of the rhythm of contact and withdrawal. Of coping and withdrawal. This is the rhythm of life. You flow towards the world and you withdraw into yourself. . . . So this rhythm goes on and on, I and thou, together form a unit" (Perls, 1969b, p. 130).

In this therapeutic instance, Perls speaks of opposites forming a unit. His conceptualization is the dialectic pattern – the creation of new forms out of apparent contradictions – rhythm being the unit that comes from opposing directional movement. Here Perls is in his element – good description, good imagery. Perhaps the dialectic mode is most easily used by Perls. On the other hand, all these examples come from Perls's last works. He was at the end of his life and work but also at the height of it. Perhaps the dialectic is his pinnacle, and earlier writings might be different.

For the last example, consider Rogers writing about the transcendental aspect of therapy. "We breathed together, felt together, even spoke for one another. I felt the power of the 'life force' that infuses each of us. . . . [I]t was like a meditative experience when I feel myself as a center of consciousness, very much a part of the broader, universal consciousness. And yet with that extraordinary sense of oneness, the separateness of each person present has never been more clearly preserved" (Rogers, 1961, pp. 129–30). Again, as with Perls, the transcendental experience emerges from apparent opposites, both the sense of shared universal consciousness with its opposite, the sense of separation.

Descriptive Writing

Finally, not every piece of writing has a discernible thought system embedded in it. There are pieces of exposition in every book that either are entirely descriptive by design or do not set out enough elements of any of the thought systems for one to detect a logical organization. When Rogers describes his data tables, for example, we just classify this writing as descriptive. It is possible that someone reading the material aggressively could see behind the descriptive mode, one of the thought styles, by making a few assumptions. A good deal of Rogers' data, for example, emerge from the absolute style of modern statistical psychology. However, in the chapters that will follow, such descriptive statements are not interpreted as formal modes of thought.

Conventions or Personal Style

Although we are suggesting that each person has different intellectual organizing styles for addressing particular problems, one must also consider that the style may be imposed. Many sorts of narratives have their own conventions. Scientific and clinical psychological writing are not exceptions. Because of these conventions, it is legitimate to question how much of a personal thinking style can be extracted from professional writing.

There is more than one way to think about conventions. It is possible that conventions might mask personal modes, but there are at least two reasons not to think so. On the one hand, the conventions of a profession can attract individuals. The conventions accepted by the group would be the very ones the individual prefers. Therefore, an analysis of the style or mode is the person's "own" as much as the group's. On the other hand, within almost any convention there is room for variation, and individuals may make exceptions to a rule. One may work at teaching as if it were advertising, for example. When the exception is made it is likely to demonstrate the unusual strength of the individual preference. This tendency makes it important to note variations and to consider their source.

Logical Organizations and Emotions

We do not want to be left only with a sense of how frequently the three therapists use certain emotional expressions. Neither do we want only to know what style of intellectual organization each man uses. Both these pieces of knowledge are useful in and of themselves, but the more important aspect is the dynamic of these in personality change over a lifetime. It is important for our ideas to make some connections. What aspects of personality are contained in emotional expression, what aspects in intellectual organization, and how do the two connect to provide potentials for change and for stability?

We will be offering several new interpretations after we have worked with the writing of the three psychologists. These will follow from our work and are not always predictable from the older ideas about how emotion and intelligence and personality connect. However, it is still useful to review briefly a few hypotheses that are considered seriously by people in this field because each contains interesting and pertinent information. The question is less one of which is absolutely correct and more one of how the different pieces of information fit together.

The Traditions: Genius of Emotion as Oxymoronic

One older idea, common to much of Western philosophy and psychology for centuries, has been that passion and complex thought are in opposition. Within this tradition it is not even possible to analyze genius in emotion. It is not hard to understand why there has been a tradition of belief that emotion and logic are opposites. Being passionate about something is not clearly a recipe for "rational" behavior or flowering insight. A fit of rage when one's wife has been raped will excuse a person who then kills the rapist. The excuse is that he was overcome with emotion and was not rational. Anxiety when taking a test is an excuse for not performing well on the test. Again, the high anxiety is thought to interfere with normal memory or problem solving. In all such cases it is assumed that if the person were not "emotional," he or she would think differently – better, in some way.

Further, passionate individuals sometimes are deemed unworthy to make important decisions in political, business, or scientific realms. These working realms are considered to be nonemotional and explicitly rational. In tests of word associations, these realms are related to traits of masculine and dominant, as well as rational. It is so common to believe that emotion and rationality are separate that we associate even the words with different aspects of life. Emotion is feminine; rationality is masculine. Emotion is dependent; rationality is independent, and so forth. But is it true in some abstract sense that these are completely separate? Would it really be "rational" to not be enraged at the rape of one's wife or to not be anxious when one's career is in the balance? Is it essentially the emotional aspect that opposes the rational aspect?

What is dangerous about extreme emotional behavior is not that it represents the absence of thought. Extremes of emotional behavior probably recruit and support repetitive or ritualistic single thought systems. It may become hard to "break set" or to assimilate different information or to accommodate to different forms of logic and information. We will find even with our sophisticated three psychologists that when they use a particular emotional set exclusively, they are less adaptable to complex situations and more likely to use formulaic responses. On the other hand, we will find that when the three psychologists are passionate in general – using a wide variety of emotional words discriminately, they tend to be more complex in their logic. It is too simple to only consider emotion and logic to be separate and in opposition.

Another problem with extreme and single-minded emotion is that it is contagious to other people and will tend to attract similar emotional scenes from others. Some emotions may be more contagious than others. For example, Hatfield, Cacioppo, and Rapson (1994) argued that when there is a social or political climate for the suppression of an emotion, then a group contagion can release the pent-up emotion. This leads to escalating group emotional effects. What causes one to stop and reconsider the emotion versus logic argument here, though, is that the suppressed emotion seems most vulnerable to contagion. A suppressed emotion is, by definition, an emotion with which one has little conscious and thoughtful experience. It is not clear that this applies to more acceptable emotions that one is aware about, however. Nor does it tell us whether the same emotion, not suppressed, would still be "irrationally" contagious.

In the opposite vein there is a minor tradition that allows us to question the wisdom of ideas stated without emotion. When a person enters therapy and initiates the interplay with descriptions of "what is wrong," the astute therapist is sensitive to the "intellectualized" issues, the ones from which emotion has been withheld or in which emotion is suppressed. These issues, presented so rationally, can be the most problematic for the client. Leonard Woolf, in speaking of the occasional violent insanity of his wife, the writer Virginia Woolf, wrote "What tends to ... reduce one to gibbering despair when one is dealing with mental illness, is the terrible sanity of the insane. . . . Virginia's . . . power of arguing conclusively from false premises was terrific" (L. Woolf, 1963, pp. 163–4). In such cases, "knowing" solutions intellectually and without passion that one is aware of is thought to be the death-knell to deep understanding. So it seems that traditional beliefs about emotion and logic can be argued either way.

There are some known historical variations in how acceptable or rational emotions might be. This fact also reminds us that our views about when emotion is rational or not are tied to our experience as well as our awareness. Stearns (1988) has found that, in preindustrial times, the expression of many forms of sorrow and grief was acceptable and encouraged. People thought it more rational to grieve when your neighbor stole your pig than to show a fit of temper. Of course, people did engage in terrible rages over thievery, but this was considered irrational. Presently, most people in the Western world find it more rational to show a bit of temper and "hit him with a law suit" than to sorrow and pray for divine assistance. Those emotions of sorrow are no longer rational. Even so, many people probably are grieved and probably do resort to divine assistance even today.

Emotion can occur at different levels of awareness. This leads to confusion. One of the reasons that many students of emotion claim that emotion is omnipresent whereas many other people claim that they are "not emotional" is that the person who studies emotion is referring to several levels of emotional expression, not just the one that we are aware of. On the one level, which shows partly in postural expressiveness, there is a physical reaction and preparedness that occurs in response to events. But this type of response can occur without awareness. So a person could seem emotional to a companion and claim on another level to be unemotional.

Speech habits also can express emotion in a way that the speaker is unaware of. If you listen carefully for emotion words, in addition to learning to decode emotional postures and gestures and facial expressions, you can detect emotional biases that the individual (including oneself, of course) is not quite aware of. Some people will even deny them. But a person who uses fear words, for example, saying in reference to ordinary physically repulsive events – I was afraid to look at her cut – and then later about amusements – It was a great movie, I was scared to death – and still later about people – Who likes her? She is totally phobic – is making a statement about fear. What type of statement is not clear immediately, but the person has a bias toward connecting events with fearfulness. Just as if one constantly looked around fearfully, or sat tensely and ready to dart out of the chair, the constant words for fear are indicative of motivations that are fear-laden. People have biases for different emotions, as anyone can show just by picking up any two books and comparing the uses of different emotions. In the cases of our three studies, Rogers overused anger, Ellis usually overused fear, and Perls often overused shame. We will find that these emotional signatures are parts of families or patterns of emotion, thought, and behavior. As we will see, these biases are not irrelevant to organizations of thought or to the content of their theories or to their behavior in therapy.

Thus we are becoming aware that it is overly simple to think of ourselves as "rational" at one point and as "emotional" at other times. One must begin to ask what type and level of rationality is being used in addition to the type and level of emotionality. Then one has to ask about the relationship between them and their stability. One needs to attend to blends and sequences and so forth. This is part of what we will explore in Rogers's, Perls's, and Ellis's writing. This is the new psychology of emotion and thought.

Another common and ancient theory of emotion and thought has held that a moderate amount of emotion can be conducive to thought, but not extremes, either too little or too much. Moderation is the key to all rational and proper behavior in this philosophy. There is, for example, a tradition of research in educational psychology concerning reports of anxiety that support this prediction. Students who report a moderate degree of feeling anxious are more likely to do well in test situations than students who report high or low levels of anxiety. This may be true without indicating that there is a general rule for all situations and emotions, however.

Differential Emotion and Thought

Yet another approach to emotion and thought holds that there is a whole system of emotions, each with its own domain of activity. For example, psychophysiological researchers (e.g., Panksepp, 1992) argue that structurally different areas of the brain process different types of emotional information. Others argue, not as much for structurally different areas of the brain, but more for different processes having differing chemical properties (e.g., Ohman, 1999). Different emotions each have their own place or mode of operating.

Researchers who study the facial and postural expression of emotion such as Ekman and Izard have shown that several emotions have their own expressive systems that are universal across cultures. We rely upon these expressive systems to describe the emotional/expressive postures of Perls, Rogers, and Ellis in later chapters. Again, as with the physiological evidence, the evidence for motor movement shows that different emotions do not operate the same ways at basic levels. Lang et al. (1980) and Leventhal (1984) argue that there are hierarchies of motoric, cognitive, and physiological systems that are related differently to each emotion. Leventhal further points out that the type of emotion will be likely to influence susceptibility to different illnesses or to the progress of illness just as we will argue that each type will influence susceptibility to ways of organizing or processing information.

Isen (1990), Teasdale (e.g. Teasdale & Barnard, 1993), and many others also note that the type of emotion is related to ways that information is categorized, to the likelihood that one will remember certain types of information, or to the likelihood that one will solve unusual problems. With respect to memory, certain memories might be facilitated by paying attention to emotion. For example, if fear has been overwhelming and is blocked, then the memory that goes with the fear is also blocked. The assumption is that the fear, if brought back into experience, would facilitate retrieving the memory. A similar case is made for any traumatic feeling state. One might say as much for returning to the scene of the memory or the scent of the memory. Emotion is just another feature of the memory in this theory.

Another perspective on this issue of emotion and its elaboration in memories and experiences is presented by Schwarz and Weinberger (1980), who have some evidence that the particular emotion being remembered is significant. When investigating the relationship between specific emotions and the contexts in which they arise, they found that certain emotions elicited a greater degree of complexity in terms of both the situations with which they were associated and the other emotions that they recruited as part of the emotion experience. These studies suggest that when a person specializes in a particular emotion, a complexity and elaboration of experience develops with it that goes beyond a simple association of an emotional experience with a scene.

Taking one more step away from the simple association of emotion and a thing remembered, Malatesta and Wilson (1988) argued that adults specialize in certain emotions and have biases to use them frequently. This tendency, in turn, influences the kinds of memories that they have. For example, if a person has become "specialized" in sadness, more memories will become associated with that emotion, and thus, when sadness is felt, the person will have access to a wide variety of thoughts that he may use creatively and flexibly or not (Malatesta & Wilson, 1988; Malatesta,1990). They argued that emotional reactions can become habitual, and thus part of the defining features of personality. Even William James had similar reflections more than a hundred years ago. "Past emotions may be among the things remembered. The more of all these trains an object can set going in us, the richer our cognitive intimacy with it is" (1890, p. 477).

Tomkins (1975) went further than believing that emotions set "trains" of thought going. He proposed that having a bias toward certain emotions would bias one in major ideologies. For Tomkins, a personal ideology is born from emotional biases. He suggested, for example, that there are two poles in political ideologies, at one end the humanistic and at the other the normative. The humanistic position presents people as essentially good, creative, and self-determined, while the normative position presents people as conforming, passive, predetermined, and struggling against evil. Each set of beliefs predicts who will favor a particular political party or political candidate. According to Tomkins, these basic postures are acquired early in life via the socialization of emotions within the family and the culture. Humanists originate from families and subcultures that maximize positive affects, whereas normative thinkers originate from families that maximize negative affects. As a consequence, humanists are more affiliative with people, and normatives are less so. Tomkins used this simple polarity to describe sweeping differences. Positive and negative emotional biases were related to humanistic versus normative philosophies, to Western vs. Eastern political systems, to historical time periods, and to lability in political power. And yet, when Tomkins turned to individuals, he also found that this simple dichotomy seldom accounted for the complex differences and life trajectories. He was forced ultimately to expand his theory and propose many patterns for different personality types.

Tomkins was not alone in believing that emotional preferences figure in people's ideologies in unsuspected ways. In yet another approach to people's emotions and what they value, Rozin, Markwith, and Stoess (1997) examined the change from having a mere preference to having a strong moral value. People who hold that vegetarianism, for example, is moral have it aligned with a large family of elaborated thoughts and feelings. It is an ideology in Tomkin's terms. Within the elaborate chain of thoughts about feelings, one feeling stands out. Rozin and colleagues claimed that feeling disgust at the thought of meat is a crucial emotion for transforming a preference for vegetables into a passionately held belief that eating meat is wrong. Violating the belief is repugnant and disgusting. It is not enough just to have a good argument for ecology or health, but the strong feeling of disgust seems to be needed as well. Rozin and colleagues, like Tomkins and ourselves, took a step beyond the simple idea that emotion is only a link between memories and suggest that disgust as a particular emotion organizes and changes the value of events or people.

Examining the cognitive – emotive relationship from another perspective, Haviland and Kramer (1991), in their analysis of Anne Frank's diary, found that different emotional situations resulted in specific modes of analysis even within the writings of the same person. For example, Anne's expression of anger was found to be related to absolute causal thinking. This is best illustrated when Anne has an altercation with her mother and later writes in her diary that her mother is to blame, that her mother is completely at fault, while she herself is completely innocent. On the other hand, situations in which fear and sadness are expressed led Anne to use a more relativistic mode that allowed her to see another's perspective as well as her own and to be concerned that she respect their right to have them. Anne's diary shows that families of emotions may facilitate different intellectual approaches and goals.

It may be that when people have a bias toward or away from certain emotions, they may therefore have a bias toward or away from certain intellectual styles, as well. For example, if Ellis is biased toward eliminating fear, perhaps he has a bias concerning the elimination of relativistic thought as well.

Our initial position is that each emotion will tend to create a probability for a certain family of cognitive patterns, just as each might for ideologies. Emotions do this in much the same way as they create a probability for physiological and behavioral patterns. Emotional biases and habits form a context in which different thought organizations are more or less likely. The combinations of emotions and thought patterns form a context for particular personalities to then emerge. The study of Rogers's, Perls's, and Ellis's emotional and intellectual development helps to uncover aspects of the new visions in personal and relevant ways.

Coding

Following a tactic that is fairly consistent across the the writing of Ellis, Rogers, Perls, we selected several chapters from several books for careful analysis, chapters that allowed us to make comparisons across the books and therefore across the lifespan of each man's writing life. We can use this to examine lifespan change in cognitive style.

Examining each page, we look for evidence of description or of absolute, relativistic, or patterned thought. The unit of analysis could be a phrase, a sentence, or multiple sentences. When an absolute assumption is embedded in a passage expressing a relativistic or dialectic assumption, only the relativistic or patterned assumption is counted. If a relativistic assumption was embedded in a patterned assumption, only the patterned is counted. Because patterned thought is usually less frequent than relativistic and relativistic thought is less frequent than absolute and absolute thought is less frequent than descriptive, we adopted a rule of thumb to maximize noticing the infrequent categories. The summary of coding goes page by page for convenience. It is possible on one page, for example, that both evidence of absolute and descriptive thought patterns appear. However, we noted only the absolute. We assume that there was also some description, since it occurs nearly everywhere. So the method is sensitive to less frequent categories. In a sense, this strategy gives the benefit of the doubt to Perls, Rogers, or Ellis when more complex patterns show themselves.

In all the selections we then ask, "What emotional vocabulary is used and where?" This is merely the process of "listening" most carefully to what Rogers, for example, says, even when he is not listening to himself with awareness of his emotions – the days of joyful writing, of hateful writing, of anxious writing. Then we move on and try to discover the differences that hours or days of joy or anxiety make in patterns of thought. What kinds of leaps in understanding come during joy, which during anxiety? What happens when there is no acknowledgment of emotion?

We will find many changes from the analyses. For example, Rogers changes in midlife, incorporating and solving problems related to previously suppressed emotions and shifting his intellectual process toward the midlife endeavors that Labouvie-Vief (1994) sees as the formal emergence of "symbolism" as a mode of thought. Ellis seems stable across the years both in terms of emotion and thought. He demonstrates the possibility that one can have a system that primarily assimilates material but does not change or accommodate its pattern of analysis to new material. Perls achieves a kind of balance in change by swinging between exaggerated opposites, but the exaggerations and the precariousness of the balance remain a lifelong pattern. He moves along through extreme oscillations often resulting in chaos, as one might predict from general theories of oscillations in patterns.

7 Cognitive Stages and Joy, Surprise
Carl Rogers

> When the individual's *negative feelings* have been quite fully ex-
> pressed they are followed by the faint and tentative expression of
> the *positive impulses*. There is nothing which gives more *surprise* to
> the student who is learning this type of therapy for the first time than
> to find that this *positive expression* is one of the most certain and pre-
> dictable aspects of the whole process. The more violent and deep the
> *negative expressions* (provided they are accepted and recognized), the
> more certain are the *positive expressions* of love, of social impulses, of
> fundamental self-respect, of desire to be mature [italics added].
>
> Carl Rogers (1942, p. 39)

This lengthy quotation is a succinct and eloquent description of Rogers's
approach to his therapeutic work in the middle of his career. It can be
read as instruction to the eager beginning therapist. It can be read as
an introduction to Rogers's theory for the interested general reader. But
it also reveals the man himself and his stance in relation to his work.
This last reading is the one we are interested in – the man himself. In
particular, we concentrate on how he and his work develop over time
as a function of his emotional and cognitive growth.

The fact that Rogers is specific about some emotions and general
about others, even when he is not explicitly thinking about emotion,
is important. Note that the beginning therapist specifically will be
"surprised." We learn that Rogers knows that the beginner's expectations are going to be challenged, that the beginner is going to make
discoveries that are contrary to previously held opinions, and that he or
she is going to have an emotional reaction – surprise.

"Surprise" tells us something about Rogers as well as about his ideas.
Rogers knows and appreciates the challenge of the contrary. He knows
and appreciates his own "surprising" ideas. He is not aware of being
repulsed or attacked by new or contrary ideas. He wants and implicitly

expects his beginning practitioner colleagues to have the same attitude. He is not anticipating active resistance or anger to his ideas and the experience of therapy that he has arranged, only surprise. We anticipate, even without further information, that he is not even prepared for attack or rejection by his colleagues. We anticipate that he searches for new, creative experience.

What about the client's emotional experience in Rogers's view? The client will have faint and tentative positive emotion that will be more certain if his or her expression of negative emotion has been violent and deep. Here Rogers does have a strong intellectual theory of general emotion in therapy. In fact his theory of emotion expression has had a profound influence on several schools of psychotherapy. Rogers expected that the expression of violent negative emotion would eventually lead to the expression of positive emotion, even if tentative. The fact that he was not specific about the type of negative emotion (fear, sadness, or anger, perhaps disgust) as Ellis would have been with his listings (fury, guilt, or annoyance, for example), or even the type of positive emotion (joy, interest, or surprise), is significant. It is noteworthy that when he was demonstrating his emotional patterns in vivo rather than writing about them, he was much more exact, but unaware of his specific emotional expectations.

At other places in his theory, around midlife, he would tell us that having negative emotional feelings and not expressing them deeply inhibits the expression of positive feeling and, furthermore, limits insight. In other words, Rogers had expectations about emotion that involved the depth of expression as well as its positive or negative quality. He also had expectations about the relation of emotion to insight in therapy. He would probably be surprised and delighted to know that present-day research has begun to confirm his suspicion that insight arises from emotional origins, his own insights included.

Ways of expressing emotion and beliefs about emotion influenced Rogers's work in ways that he was aware, as well as in ways that he was not aware. Over time his professional writing reflected the changes in his inner emotional life just as clearly as it reflected change in the content of his abstract ideas.

The basic premise of this chapter is that work, even, perhaps, particularly, highly theoretical or scientific work, is driven and, in certain critical ways, ultimately defined by emotion. Furthermore, the development of that work is an interweaving of earlier problems that remain emotionally alive as well as present-day pressures and opportunities in the working environment that are emotionally alive. It is even more broadly interwoven with historical and cultural pressures or opportunities, which contain emotional aspects that interact with the individual's own sensitivities.

The use of emotion words is itself a revelation of inner life, something like the "slips of the tongue" described earlier in this century by Sigmund Freud (Haviland & Kramer, 1991; Haviland & Goldston, 1992). Emotional words, their frequency, their explicitness, their intensity, all tell a story about the speaker or the writer. Since the seminal work of Tomkins, Izard, and Ekman, as well as newer research by ourselves, Krause, Schwartz, and D. Keller, we have come to see that the facial and gestural expressions of people clearly relate to their immediate emotional reactions as well as to long-held emotional attitudes. Words may hold something of the same qualities.

Expectations for Affect Structures

In previous chapters, we demonstrated that a psychobiographical approach to Rogers's ideoaffective personality dynamics revealed specific affective patterns. We can expect that these patterns, which developed across Rogers's life, will be not only descriptive of personality but also determinants in the style and content of his professional work. We showed that the key dynamic elements of Rogers's personality can be described in terms of joy, interest, shame, disgust, and anger. Will examination of the fractuals of words and gesture also show that these are the dominant elements in Rogers's professional and intellectual life? What has happened to surprise or fear, for example, which appeared so readily in the opening quote?

Interest and Joy as Information Filters

Chapter 3 argued that "interest and joy constitute a 'strong affect theory,'" and that they comprise "the prevailing informational filter" for Rogers. The other emotions are "intrusive" background emotions. If one is interested in "interest and joy" as intellectual filters, exactly what is one looking for? What is an emotional "filter"? Is an emotional "filter" a focus point or obscurant, both or neither? In other words, is it even a strength? Can examination of Rogers's work at least reveal how the question may be reasonably asked? As the reader will note, we take the position that no one emotion is a significant strength, but that flexibility with emotion provides strength, while singular filters provide focus, at best.

Undeveloped Anger

The psychobiographical analysis in Chapter 3 also revealed that Rogers's anger was "undeveloped" in that there is "low tolerance and little expressive aptitude" for it. Does this mean that anger plays little role in Rogers's intellectual work or does the undeveloped affect actually play a significant role, defining an emotional and intellectual "shadow" side of Rogers intellectual life? Is the view that is presented in the psychobiography also colored by the fact that it was written late in Rogers's life? Was he always the same?

Flexible Emotion

The brief presentation of Roger's emotional expectations and thinking in the quoted paragraph at the start seems to say that individuals have an emotional signature – that "surprise" is an emotional signature for Rogers, for example. However, this idea of emotional signatures is too simple and too static. The work on wisdom – the thought processes that demonstrate overarching, integrated modes of thought – has already demonstrated that wisdom increases with age. The notion of wisdom advancing with age is a concept very different from established academic concepts of intelligence. Intelligence as it is captured in intelligence tests, for example, is a summation of knowledge and problem-solving skills as they exist in young adults. It is biased toward quickness, lists of memorized items, and absolute (static and singular) definitions. These types of thought have been known for many years to peak in late adolescence and young adulthood. Some adults, as they age, lose some of these skills, others do not seem to be much affected. However, more recent interest in intelligence has centered on the intelligence that comes *after* the descriptive quickness of youth; this has come to be called wisdom. Rogers's facility with anger in his personal life changed somewhat due to challenges of his middle age. People like Rogers change over their lives, not just intellectually, but also emotionally. It is important to note that the intellectual change goes hand-in-hand with the emotional change. The purpose of presenting several of Rogers's works spanning his life is to demonstrate evolving change toward wisdom, even though some relationships hold for long periods of time.

Emotional Processes in Thought

To show how emotional processes operate in intellectual contexts this chapter is organized in sections; each set of material examines a particular aspect of Rogers's emotional experience in intellectual contexts. These sections follow an introductory definitional section. The main points raised by the autobiographical material are organized here as three hypotheses:

1. Nonpassionate ideas: When only one emotional attitude or no clear emotional attitude was held toward some intellectual issues, blocks and twists occurred in Rogers's thinking.
2. Passionate ideas: The ideas and relationships that Rogers was passionate about, that he had many emotional approaches to, were the issues about which he was clear, decisive, and creative, becoming wise.
3. Lifespan changes in passionate associations: Rogers's emotional experiences and awareness changed across his life leading to change in his work and intellectual awareness about particular issues.

Blocked, Silent, and Singular Emotions and Thoughts

When only one emotional attitude or no clear emotional attitude is held toward some intellectual issues, it is intellectually inhibited or constricted. Blocks in thinking occur under these circumstances. Reflection on emotion is reflection on and acknowledgment of motivational processes. Emotion is always an implicit part of the approach to a question or a judgment; however, when awareness of emotion is *explicit*, emotion comes directly into the context of a decision. It triggers thoughts about the process of observation and problem solving. Whether the emotional process leads one to the gripping, archetypical example or to the tedious, controlled experiment or to questioning leaps, it influences the probable types of alleys to be followed or dead ends to be endured.

One of the puzzles for us in thinking about Rogers's intellectual life is how he became involved in his particular areas of specialization, and how he avoided other areas. As the preceding proposition suggests, we suspect that some topics, while interesting to other psychologists of his day, met with emotional silence or lack of emotional development. Some topics that Rogers wrote about in the earlier books, such as the components of diagnosis, are nowhere to be found in the later books.

Other topics, such as research approaches to therapy evaluation, evolved and became slightly more passionate through contact with more basic emotional Rogerian issues.

As we have seen, Rogers's hostile emotions were undeveloped and caused him difficulty in his personal life. If there is some continuity given by emotion to different scenes – attachment scenes as well as intellectual problems – we should find that, when emotion is missing for Rogers, it is probably related to hostility and, furthermore, the ideas as well as the emotion will be undeveloped or even faulty. This may strike some readers as peculiar, if they regard anger as an undesirable emotion in itself. But why should any emotion be undesirable unless it is warped and maladaptive? This concept will be clearer when Rogers's intellectual difficulties with anger are revealed.

Book 1

Rogers's first book, *The Clinical Treatment of the Problem Child* (1939), was a remarkable achievement in some respects. In it he attempted to organize the tremendously varied approaches to diagnosing and treating childhood disturbances as they existed in the 1930s. These approaches spanned individual treatments such as play therapy and family therapy, as well as social or institutional treatments such as foster homes or institutions. His goal for the book was to provide enough organization to the field of child psychopathology that one could begin to see what factors needed to be studied in order to discover what treatments were most effective and for whom. On the surface, it is a relativistic approach to the science of diagnosis and treatment. He is not overly critical of any treatment plan but tries to give each a fair, but skeptical, assessment. He is critical of the field as a whole for neglecting a scientific approach to treatment.

Seemingly quite un-Rogerian, this early work was a gift to the field of child psychology at this time because it allowed one (in the abstract) to take any case presented, find the factors of the problem, and suit a treatment to the problem. In this way, it cut across the specific disciplines of treatment as they existed, and still do, including psychoanalytic, behavioristic, social welfare, family treatment, or institutionalization. Rogers wanted to maximize the effectiveness of intervention by trying to determine which approach would yield the maximum benefit within a given time period. This is a strikingly pragmatic and business-like orientation to labyrinthine psychological services.

Even though the thrust of the first book is component analysis, Rogers's chapters on component methods were not presented with passion nor were they remarkably abstract. The type of thought was largely descriptive and somewhat absolute (see Chapter 6). Further, we know from looking back on Rogers's writing that he never picked up the threads of component methods of diagnosis or treatment again. This topic was finished for him. Finally, he had little impact on the diagnosis and practice of child psychology, at least in comparison with the impact made by his other work. It was silent and undeveloped in many ways. Yet other psychologists worked passionately on factor approaches.

As an example, consider the central, passionless chapter entitled "Basis of the Component-Factor Method." This chapter presented Rogers's organization of the field of diagnosis and treatment. Here Rogers was primarily interested in specifying boundaries. "The method contributes to the field of treatment the concept of *limitations*, which is conspicuously lacking in other modes of analyzing or diagnosing behavior [italics added]". (Rogers, 1939, p. 57). Was this the same man who would later discuss "man's tendency to actualize himself, to become his potentialities" (Rogers, 1961, p. 351)? This is an amazing early view of the Rogers who will in later life write, "Life, at its best, is a flowing, changing process in which nothing is fixed.... It is always in the process of becoming" (Rogers, 1961, p. 27) and even more to the point, "The more I am open to the realities in me and in the other person, the less do I find myself wishing to rush in to fix things." (Rogers, 1961, p. 21). Perhaps the apparent difference between boundaries and potentialities has something to do with Rogers's age and his struggles as a young man with limitation and with potential, as well as with hostility.

When Rogers wrote *The Clinical Treatment of the Problem Child* he had been working in a clinic for problem children. Over the years he was there, we know only a little about his professional growth. One problem does emerge in the biographical data; Rogers had to fight with colleagues in the psychiatric schools to achieve leadership in the clinic. Perhaps this first book partly grew out of his struggle to climb to the top of his profession as a psychological counselor. This fact would begin to account for his concern with boundaries and territories. Rogers's continued insistence over his professional life on evaluation and accountability in therapeutic treatments may have stemmed from early hostility between him and his psychiatric colleagues. For us, however, this also means that the presentation of the book and its "component method" is based on the implicit emotion of hostility or anger. We may guess that Rogers is somewhat hostile, but, if so, he has masked it well. The anger is silent.

Rogers introduced eight factors that must be diagnosed when a client is present. These were the hereditary factor, the physical factor, mentality, family environment, economic/cultural factors, the social factor (companionship group), education/training outside the home, and the child's own insight. Rating scales were provided for each factor reflecting the judgments related to adjustment that were common to the historic period. For example, the heredity factor included at its higher end "parents college graduates;" family atmosphere at its worst occurred when the mother is immoral and the father is weak and alcoholic. However, overall, the descriptions were very pragmatic and have stood the test of time relatively well. Rogers presented the reliability of the ratings then made by experienced clinicians and found them to be satisfactory and easy to use. Next, he turned to the plans for treatment in relationship to the diagnostic factors.

Using the diagnostic chart with its eight factors, Rogers claimed that one has "the total picture of the child's situation . . . not only in general terms as to whether each factor has been largely destructive or constructive, but also in specific terms of the conditions, attitudes, and relationship which are responsible for that summarized judgment" (Rogers, 1939, p. 51). It was here that the limitations aspect became so clear. For example, "The hereditary factor can never be changed, mentality, but rarely" (Rogers, 1939, p. 51). On the other hand the examination of the categories would bring to light the factors that are most amenable to change, as in "family attitudes, or in the realm of social adjustment or self-insight" (Rogers, 1939, p. 51).

Rogers proceeded to give an example of a case using the component factor analysis chart. This was followed by a chart that estimated which factors were most amenable to change and to what degree. Given the limitations for the child presented in the case, Rogers summarized again emphasizing the limitations: "We cannot expect a thoroughly normal adjustment, and our prognosis should be moderate and cautious" (Rogers, 1939, p. 56).

The final pages of the chapter argued for general, "common-sense, realistic" use of the component approach to avoid biases and to better understand the limits of treatment. He was careful to say that diagnosis should not be mechanical, nor should it be replaced by a device. (However, twenty-five years later Rogers would actually argue that diagnosis is better performed by a clerk with a set of instruments and a statistical table than by a clinician.)

This quantitative and categorical chapter is not passionate. Rogers referred only once to the "smugness" of the intuitive approach used by psychiatrists. He used very few specific terms even to describe individuals in particular cases, terms such as "happy," "unhappy," and "jealous" (twice). He used general terms such as "emotional" only five times and the words "interest" and "surprise" twice. As we will see, in comparison with other samples of his writing, this is strikingly sparse in emotional vocabulary. Except for "jealous" and "smugness," it clearly has no hostile vocabulary, which will also turn out to be unusual in Rogers's professional writing. Either the hypothesis put forward earlier, that Rogers was writing in part to defend his territory in counseling, is wrong, since there is no claim from Rogers for anger or its derivatives, or Rogers simply does not put emotion words to his experience of hostility.

What was his thought style in this early quantitative chapter? According to the categories of thoughtful style described in the introduction to this section, a third of the chapter is straight description. It has no propositional analysis at all. He describes cases or data. Another quarter of the chapter presents only absolute types of thinking mixed with the description. As defined earlier, this sort of thoughtful analysis assumes a real structure made up of separable elements, only waiting to be discovered. Here Rogers hypothesized that if one aspect of his analysis is true, then another part will follow – that one part predicts another. The last 20 percent of the chapter has some vague, but codable, aspect of relativistic thinking mixed with the absolute. That is, credit is given to different approaches having some merit within their own realms. There is no dialectical thinking at all, no mode that would merge different approaches.

In Rogers's attempt to provide components or factors in treatment and diagnosis, there are strong elements of absolute thinking. The components were treated as elements, the sum of which will describe wholly the universe of diagnostic issues and treatments. He had some hope that basic truth could be uncovered – a very absolute sort of hope – but still he had a relativistic concern that there might be different treatments for different diagnoses. He resolved the relativism with the rather absolute belief in the power of "science" to find the truth of the matter as if there was, after all, a single best answer.

An example from the summary chapter of the book shows the brevity of the presentation of thinking style. In this chapter, he resolved the relativistic thinking into absolute. First, he wrote, "Certainly so far as diagnostic techniques are concerned, there is no best method" (Rogers, 1939, p. 60). This is an example of a relativistic tendency; he suggested that many methods might be equally appropriate, perhaps dependent upon circumstance. But then he wrote, "There are only methods which need testing and experiment and revision" (Rogers, 1939, p. 60). In other words, he did not actually hold that the methods are equally valid, only that we do not yet know which one is correct. This finalization implies that none of the methods are known to be the best because data are lacking. When this omission is corrected, the absolute truth of how to use each approach will emerge, the best will also be known, at least for each case.

Book 2

Roger's second book, *Counseling and Psychotherapy* (1942), was the first full-length presentation of his new approach to counseling and a highly personal statement. It introduced the nondirective process and was incredibly passionate, full of emotional expression. However, there are also chapters that are as stark as dead volcanoes in the relief of Rogers's emotional landscape.

Chapter V "The Directive versus the Non-directive Approach" is an emotionally silent consideration of possible objections that one might raise to Rogers's newly created nondirective therapy. One expects a defensive or combative chapter – this chapter pits one approach against another even in the title. Given the dread with which Rogers appeared to approach his own experiences of hostility, this chapter offers an opportunity to discover how he confronted opposition in his profession and how it affected his thinking.

When faced with the potential for experiencing anger or contempt himself, for becoming a defendant, Rogers became emotionally mute once again. Except for mentioning the client's fears and anxieties once in a list of directions and saying "it is of interest" one time, there are *no* specific emotion terms in the entire chapter. There are certainly no directly hostile, annoyed, irritated words. Even the use of nonspecific terms, such as "feelings," is very restricted relative to other chapters or writings or speech patterns.

In this chapter, Rogers proposed that someone might object to his nondirective approach because it would be impossible to believe that counseling could "solve the client's problem" or be successful if the counselor takes "no responsibility for directing the outcome of the process" (Rogers, 1942, p. 115). To answer this objection, Rogers presented data to demonstrate that the counselors in nondirective and directive counseling actually differ from one another in their techniques. In other words, as in the first book, this is a chapter with a more "scientific," data-oriented approach. It is quantitative and gives tables of information, charts, and so forth. It comes closer to the journal article presentation of professional psychology even though it is embedded in Rogers's first major book length statement of his own theory and practice. This documentation is not necessary for this type of book, as neither Ellis nor Perls include this sort of information nor do they revert to the style of a scholarly journal.

Rogers demonstrated with data and with excellent case excerpts that nondirective therapists did less talking overall and in their talking were much more likely to "recognize...the feeling or attitude which the client has just expressed" and much less likely to have asked "highly specific questions, delimiting answers to yes, no, or specific information" (Rogers, 1942, p. 123). Directive counselors did just the opposite. Therefore, Rogers concluded that "the directive group stressing those techniques which control the interview and move the client toward a counselor-chosen goal, the nondirective group stressing those means which cause the client to be more conscious of his own attitudes and feelings, *with a consequent increase in insight and self-understanding* [italics added]" (Rogers, 1942, p. 123).

It only takes a moment's thought to realize that Rogers did not answer the objection he raised himself and did not demonstrate the validity of the conclusion contained in the preceding quote (see italics). Rogers directed himself to another question. He answered the question: is there a demonstrable difference between the speech of counselors trained in nondirective versus directive counseling, and, if so, what is the nature of that difference? He did not in this chapter show that nondirective counseling was successful. He did not present evidence that there would be an increase "in insight and self-understanding." He seemed to assume that, if we believed that the client talked more, had his feelings reflected back to him, and was less directed toward the therapist's goals, then we would subsequently believe that the client was clearly becoming more self-understanding, but he presented no evidence.

The whole chapter on directive versus nondirective counseling is a pathetic example of the directive process in action when Rogers is doing the directing. This directive process misfired just as Rogers predicted it would, although Rogers was unlikely to have intended this. That is, Rogers argued that the directive counseling process misdirected because directive counseling did not allow the client to follow her own true thought and feeling process. Instead the counselor diverted the client with his own thoughts and feelings, suppressing the client's feelings and problem-solving abilities. This is just what happened to distress us in this chapter. The question supposedly posed by the hostile critic was misdirected, and the author never answered it. As a literary metaphor of the directive process in Rogers's hands, this chapter is illuminating.

In Rogers's own terms, what happened in this chapter on directive versus nondirective methods? First, he did not reflect upon the real concerns of the question poser; whether that person was hypothetical or not is of no matter. He did not provide a context in which the question poser's feelings would emerge. Why did the questioner ask this question? What were his feelings about the question or the context itself? Rogers was highly directive and sidestepped those questions and behaviors. Instead, *he* directed the chapter to his own goal, that of further defining and describing the nondirective process. Behaving just like the implicitly derided directive counselor with his client, he assumed further that his own client, the reader, would share his values and interpretation of the issue. What became very clear was that he had little "sympathy," no interest or concern to express for the directive counselor with objections.

What has happened here? In our terms, Rogers was working from a single emotion system – anger and contempt, a hostile system. He was not sympathetic, empathic, or even interested. Even the hostile system was undeveloped in that he did not express his angry feelings clearly. The single system, combined with the inhibition of emotion, led to restricted thought processes and lack of the logic needed.

To extend the line of argument we are pursuing here, we looked at the codes for thought that are applied in this chapter. Regardless of the relationship between the questions posed and answered, what type of thought process was found in this particular chapter? Compared with the other chapters in this book, this one contained the most straight description (54 percent), the least amount of explicit theoretical awareness, that is, the least amount of insight. The very few dialectical explanations (23 percent) occurred when he described his own theory, the pure description occurred when he described the directive counseling.

Again, the silence in his emotion was reflected by silence in logic. When he might have been considering the assumptions and system of directive counseling, he was not. He treated his knowledge of directive counseling as a "pure" perception – he saw directly what it was. For critical colleagues, there was a severe inhibition of clear thinking relative to their concerns. He was more aware of the processes involved in his own proposals for therapy, and the analyses showed this. When discussing his own approach, he became clearer. Paradoxically, this demonstrated Rogers's own point about the importance of reflecting emotion in counseling or even education.

The analysis of the two first books suggests that the assessment and evaluation domain was an emotionally hostile and difficult one for Rogers. When Rogers felt attacked or was he, himself, attacking, even though he contained his expression of hostility, he moved into a journalistic style and provided charts of data and categories of information. He was not particularly able to hit the mark with this method, though. This leaves open the question of why research was associated with hostility at all. Why is Rogers using research defensively and not creatively? What inhibits him from asking an open question instead of using research merely to bolster an opinion he has already become certain of on the basis of clinical experience?

Does the nature of scientific research deal with defense and the aggression of ideas and ideological territory or does it illustrate the problem encountered largely by Rogers in the research domain? The relationship between the personal and the professional seems important. Modern historians of science are persuasive that Western Baconian science is based on a domination model of man and nature. In this model, which dominates scientific enterprises (see Keller, 1983), man uses science to extend his power over nature and over fellow human beings. All scientific problems are in need of conquest; answers are "tortured" out of nature. However, there are exceptions. McClintock is one of the more notable ones in our century. In describing her Nobel Prize-winning research in genetics, she emphasized the empathic relationship that develops between a scientist and her subject matter and nature's capacity to reveal itself to a trained scientist.

The answer to this question is probably that Rogers's attitude and his aversion reflect an existing cultural tendency within psychological circles. However, he may have been particularly vulnerable to certain aspects of it. A general aversion among researchers for clinical evidence and among clinicians for laboratory or survey evidence has accumulated throughout this century. The use of caselike demonstrations or even personal introspection on the part of an "expert thinker" formed the basis for most early scholars including philosophers, biologists, and physicists. One has only to recall "Cogito, ergo sum" (a single-case proof by the expert thinker, Descartes) or gravity demonstrated by dropping the objects off the tower of Pisa (a single-case demonstration) to remind oneself of this.

In this century, the single case and the general case often are at odds. Not only is the difference in methods important, but so also is the difference in emotional and empathic investment, which can cut across methods. There is so much professional hostility that some clinicians such as Miller (1982) stated forcefully that quantitative research is dangerous in psychology and destructive in its devotion to mechanistic solutions: it "[c]an contribute to the more rapid, comprehensive, and effective soul murder of the human being" (p. 277). On the other hand, quantitative researchers counter with "anything" can be proved with a case, by which they mean in an odd contradictory sense, that nothing can be so proven.

Rogers's avoidance of distancing emotions in general, anger as well as contempt and even disgust, fits our distinction between quantitative researchers and qualitative researchers. The quantitative researchers tend to be comfortable distancing their subjects from themselves and using distancing tools; they prefer to work with distancing emotions such as contempt over other negative emotions, especially shame or sadness. On the other hand, the qualitative researcher tends to immerse himself or herself in the subject, not keeping it at a distance. These researchers avoid distancing emotions such as contempt or anger in favor of sadness, grief, or shame. It seemed that Rogers as a young man and even into early middle age was working outside his area of greater emotional sensitivity when he attempted confrontation.

Book 3

Twenty years later after the changes of Rogers's middle age – presidency of his most respected professional organization, prestigious academic positions, opportunities to expand the application of his ideas, personal antagonisms with colleagues, flight from a disastrous client, beginnings of exposure to optimistic and humanistic philosophies – is Rogers the same man? Or, to limit the question, does he have the same problem with hostility and quantitative research?

To examine the older Rogers's approach to research, Chapters 10 and 12 in *On Becoming a Person* (1961) are very useful: "Persons or Science? A Philosophical Question" (Chapter 10) and "Client-Centered Therapy in Its Context of Research" (Chapter 12). Even the titles of these later articles suggest some type of change with regard to research.

In *Counseling and Psychotherapy* (1942), the earlier chapter used the word "versus" in the title; these later ones use "or" and "context," obviously a more contextual or relativistic mode of analysis. But what has changed, only the words? Even if Rogers's own deep emotional experiences with failure, success, anger, and guilt have emerged from silence, how has he learned to work with them?

Chapter 10 was composed in an interesting, antagonistic way. In the introduction, Rogers described the chapter directly as a drama with two protagonists, a conflict, and a resolution. The chapter had an early section ("Protagonist One") which described the experience of therapy. It was juxtaposed in the middle section ("Protagonist Two"), which described the purpose of science relative to therapy – the science section. Finally, a summary section attempted to show the reader how science and therapy speak to each other.

Each section contained many statements that contradict the content of the other two sections. Rogers was now forthright about the conflict between research activity and clinical activity. This was, obviously, a major change. In earlier writing, the possibility of conflict in his own research and clinical activity did not arise. In this *On Becoming a Person*, he faced the problem directly. This late-life chapter demonstrated that hostility no longer needed to be cloaked. Rogers was able to state that there was conflict and that it could be used. No doubt this reflected an internal emotional transformation for Rogers, now embedded in his work. Now that he is aware of conflict and can introduce it, can he follow through in the essay with the drama and the anger or is the acknowledgment as far as he could go?

The first protagonist of this dramatic essay presents Rogers's later thoughts on the therapeutic process in a fully passionate manner, but with little reference to the impact of "science." The second protagonist presented "the essence of therapy in the terms of science." Now the antagonism has a chance to surface.

At the outset, Rogers, as the second protagonist, was careful to note that nothing absolute was learned through scientific method, only probabilistic relationships. Also he noted relativistically that the product of science was unlike the object it examined: "If the science in this field followed the course of science in other fields, the working models of reality which would emerge (in the course of theory building) would be increasingly removed from the reality perceived by the senses" (Rogers, 1961, p. 206). Having presented the boundaries of science – science is removed from sensual reality and only probabilistic in the end – Rogers then offered a counter for science. He proposed that science is a measurement system – anything that exists can be measured in an absolute theoretical approach.

Having given "science" a measurement role, Rogers presented the reader with a set of testable hypotheses about therapy that science could measure. He described methods for operationalizing the hypotheses so that they could be measured. When this was accomplished, he asserted that science offered an "exact description of the events...and changes....It can...formulate...laws....It can offer replicable statements" (1961, p. 208). It did not become clear how science remained probablistic with reference to sensual reality and yet gave an *exact* description of events.

Throughout the description of the scientific approach Rogers again wrote with almost no affect terms. He ended the section with his first affect term – "antagonistic" – and then proceeded to argue in summary as if science and the experience of therapy were not cooperative but in mortal conflict. He shifted again from the opening contextual or relativistic statements back to the absolute: "Hypotheses can be formulated and put to test, and the sheep of truth can thus be separated from the goats of error" (Rogers, 1961, p. 210). But one wondered what will be separated – the sheep and goats of therapy, the sheep and goats of science, or the sheepish therapy and the goatish science?

Rogers managed to bring his scientific thought to his therapy, but, ultimately, he did not bring his therapeutic thought to his science. He personally always used science aggressively, to confirm his own position, or to batter others, not to be surprised or amazed. Herein lies the chief differences between science in his hands and science in the hands of others. Even though Rogers acknowledged the existence of personal hostile feelings late in his life and even though this was a significant change, his sensitivity to where hostility exists and how useful or terrible it might be remained constrained.

It must be acknowledged, in spite of the serious difficulties apparent in the early research reports in his books, that Rogers was a real innovator in clinical research. Rogers was one of the first researcher–clinicians to audio-tape his sessions regularly and to have his student–practitioners do the same. These transcripts were the source of much of his quantitative work. He and his students analyzed different aspects of the transcripts to show the differences among particular techniques and the changes in the interaction across therapy. Later in his life, Rogers and his students also used various measures of change for his clients including Q-sorts and questionnaires. In a few notable instances, he participated in studies that controlled for the influence of therapy by assigning clients to nontherapy conditions for a period of time. He also participated in follow-up studies on the long-term influence of therapy.

In his later research work, Rogers became bound to the concept of the ideal self (see Rogers, 1961). This concept was also tied to his therapeutic goals of bringing experience into the emotional here and now. Where did this come from? It seemed divorced from his other measurement concerns in therapy, and perhaps it was. This later research concern was an attempt to verify that there were sustained individual changes in therapy. He and his research colleagues developed a technique for computing the distance between the "real self" and the "ideal self." This was the change aimed for in therapy – the unity of the real and ideal selves. His measurement system and the many variations that have been spawned by it in the past fifty years are still a mainstay in personality research.

The distinction between good self and bad self, idealized self and actual self in present-day personality research has its roots in the psychodynamic, clinical work from earlier in the twentieth century (Horney, 1950). Horney wrote about the good self as a construction used to fend off rotten and horrid experiences. It tended to split off and lose its reality because of its purity. Horney emphasized reuniting the selves, acknowledging the greater importance of the whole, rather than aiming to achieve the good self.

In this later research, used to demonstrate the effectiveness of nondirective therapy, Rogers chose to show that the true measure of personal change was a movement toward uniting the ideal and the actual self. A person who felt that his best self was not being "realized," but whose real, daily self was pitifully inadequate was the person needing therapy. When he felt that his ideal self (changed a bit from the original idealization, no doubt) and the actual self (now perceived as much more adequate and valuable – prized in fact) merged, the person had successfully completed therapy. As has been pointed out, Rogers ignored the bad or undesired self (see Ogilvie, 1987). In the same sense that Rogers believed that inhibited hostility kept one from expressing real feelings and evolving positive emotion but was not interested in hostility itself, he was concerned with the leashed self – the idealized self, not the evil self. He consistently denied the power or the reality of the evil in people and dismissed the dread of it.

Rogers and his colleagues also developed a prototype "healthy" picture of the actual self and showed that the person emerging from nondirective therapy had moved in the direction of being and valuing this prototype. So he demonstrated that one of the changes of therapy was the client's acceptance of a healthier view of himself. This change was somewhat important as it harked back to the question raised by Rogers in the first book about the goal of therapy. In *The Clinical Treatment of the Problem Child*, Rogers pitted the individual's wish for happiness against the therapist's goals for social acceptance. At that point, the young Rogers had seen the issue as philosophically unresolvable. Obviously, the older and wiser Rogers is not even persuaded that there is any controversy. He had a larger view.

Although the older Rogers had taken steps to bring his therapeutic and research goals into closer contact, he remained aggressive in his use of research. Even late in his life, Rogers believed that he needed to be defensive about science, to claim that it was not destructive. He could just as easily have claimed that it was not irrelevant. Why did he focus on hostility except that it was emblematic of his own battle with hostility?

In this later defense, Rogers argued (still without passionate words) that only people are destructive; science is not destructive. In an oblique way, he managed to place science, a system and language of ideas, into the category of attack weapons, and then he found that he had to deny its potential hostility. He used the same specious argument that "weapons do not kill people, only people kill people," as do people who want to persuade others that weapons are only neutral tools. He insisted that people invent scientific problems and methods and communicate the scientific results. Angry people may be aggressive, but science, reified, is nonaggressive. "Science can never threaten us" (Rogers, 1961, p. 222).

In the sense meant perhaps by Foucault (1973, p. 353) when he wrote, "The human sciences thus occupy the distance that separates (though not without connecting them) biology, economics, and philology from that which gives them possibility in the very being of man." Psychology is the link between our ideas about the physical world and the symbolic world. Science, whether it is a human science such as psychology or not, is a symbol and, as such, is a manner of communication. Any manner of communication can be destructive as well as it can be constructive. It is not possible to exempt science, and an attempt to do so shows that Rogers intended to diminish the power of science in psychology. In so doing, the dark side of the scientific mode of symbolizing is hidden.

Present-day scientific methods have a strong orientation toward making ideas, feelings, and behaviors containable and linked in causative, mechanical manners even when it is not at all clear that they work that way. Is intelligence the sum of certain measured traits or correct answers? Are emotions and thoughts separate, parallel processes measured with physiological instrumentation? Can computers without motivation be said to have thought that is compartmentalized and connected?

The symbol system used in "science" defines, destroys, ignores, and creates because it is part of the broader human symbol experience that also defines, destroys, ignores, and creates. It is as much a part of emotional expression and driven as much by experience and feelings as any other symbolic yell, scream, or exultation. It certainly has no ultimate truth in it which ultimately measures truth or "verifies"; it only verifies anything that is inside its system, as does mathematics or law or even therapeutic practice. Once again, Rogers denied the shadow side of thought and denied the full humanization of science, leaving a gap between therapy and science. He tried to emphasize one absolute side of science, weakening it and his argument.

To give a more complete view of Rogers than the one visible in midlife, it is important to quote the even older Rogers: "If the university psychologist accepted the latter (humanistic) view, he would have to admit that he is involved, as a subjective person, in his choice of research topics, in his evaluation of data, in his relationship to students, in his professional work. The cloak of 'objectivity' would necessarily be dropped (Rogers, 1980, pp. 57–8). Not only did Rogers later clarify the subjective nature of science, he later also saw the dark side of mechanistic science, writing, "I am not being dramatic when I say that humanistic psychologists, emphasizing the essential freedom and dignity of the unique human person, and his capacity for self-determination, would be among the first to be incarcerated by such a (behavioristic science led) government" (Rogers, 1980, p. 59). It is quite likely that by the end of his life Rogers had come around to a fuller appreciation of both enlightened science and its shadow side.

All this examination of Rogers in confrontation across many decades shows that Rogers did not continue to pursue concepts considered in his quantitative and muted hostile style early in his life, neither did he argue very clearly or persuasively when he was motivated by hostility. We are attributing this disconnection to the undeveloped hostile emotions. Rogers's inability to express, modulate, and apply anger or contempt in

life scenes successfully led to eruptions and disconnections in his friendships and working relationships as well as in his thought processes. In
this sense, he was lacking not only in emotional intelligence but also in
intellectual pursuit more narrowly defined.

Passions are important, perhaps necessary to intellectual processes.
Not only are we arguing that passion is critical for intellectual endeavor,
but we are also arguing that the maligned negative emotions, including
anger and contempt, are critical for full intellectual flexibility. A person
who uses anger as a single focus is not going to have much intellectual
flexibility, although he may be able to use angry argument cleverly. On
the other hand, a person such as Rogers, who cannot use anger flexibly,
will be handicapped by the attention given to translating anger with
inevitable losses into more personally acceptable emotions.

From an analysis of only the biographical material, one might have
concluded that the undeveloped hostile emotion played very little role in
Rogers's life. From an analysis of his unemotional writings, one might
have concluded that his silence in the face of hostility was crippling.
Yet when we look further into his work, we find that hostility played
an essential role in creating a personal thought style for Rogers at many
levels. Theories of personality must account for this type of motivational
"salience" – an odd combination of sensitivity, avoidance, and explosion.

Hostile emotions were salient for Rogers because they were a paradox for him. He did not move easily in a hostile world, and he had
grave difficulty perceiving the positive role that confrontation, hostile,
distancing motivations may play in a caring, thoughtful, and creative
life that blinded and cast shadows rather than light. As a paradox, it
remained a burning bush in his life. He could not see into it clearly, yet
it always drew him back.

Joy Alone

Although the biographical evidence presented in Chapter 3 showed that
Rogers was undeveloped in anger, he seemed to have had a generous
capacity for joyfulness in writing about his life achievements and his
lifetime relationships. This occurrence gives us an opportunity to study
a second emotion that seems to work somewhat independently, to find
out how joy as a focus emotion was used by Rogers. Instead of looking at
a suppressed emotion, one can look at a clearly expressed single feeling.
Rogers often developed whole chapters or sections of chapters around
general "positive emotion" or around happiness, more specifically. This

use of joyfulness as a focusing lens had some intriguing consequences in his theories.

Book 2

The first example in Rogers's books of a lengthy piece of writing with a joyful focus was one of the later chapters in *Counseling and Psychotherapy* (1942), called "The Achievement of Insight." (There are no lengthy sections in his first book associated with positive emotion. As we noted previously, the general tone of the first book is one of unexpressed anger and contempt.) At this point in *Counseling and Psychotherapy*, Rogers had taken us through several steps in therapy, including the "release of expression," and now he argued that the next step or achievement in therapy related to insight. Insight was the next-to-the-last phase of counseling. The closing phases resulted when the client fearfully and tentatively began to act upon the insights gained. One can see then that the process elements needed for therapeutic change were (1) negative emotion expression (most usually of mixed hostile emotions), (2) positive emotion expression, (3) insight, and (4) action (accompanied by fear mixed with other emotions). These steps had a necessary order for Rogers. He had an orderly theory of growth and change that still maintained a place for the unexpected and the surprising.

What were Rogers's insights then? "They are learnings with deep emotional concomitants, not learnings of intellectual content, and hence may or may not find clear verbal expression" (1942, p. 175). Some insights were contained in actions, then, and not in words. Some might never be expressed clearly. Where does insight come from? "The answer is bound to be a disappointing one to the overeager. . . . The primary technique is to encourage the expression of attitudes and feelings . . . until insightful understanding appears spontaneously. Insight is often delayed, and sometimes made impossible, by efforts of the counselor to create it or to bring it about" (Rogers, 1942, p. 195).

It is because Rogers proposed such a simple linear relationship between the client's positive emotion and insight that much of his thinking in this chapter is of the absolute style, almost concrete. It is, in its structure, as simple as a stimulus–response theory: (1) release hostile emotion, (2) leading to spontaneous positive emotion, (3) leading to spontaneous insight. Rogers took very little time to inform the counselor about the nature of insight. He gave very few examples or cases. He had no warnings for the counselor about difficulties in identifying real insights. He had little suspicion that the counselor could be misled. The worst that the counselor could have done would have been to apply "effort" to create insight.

Rogers's advice in this particular set of writing for achieving insight is primarily to work on achieving release of feelings. Insight takes care of itself. It never seemed to cross his mind that the release of some feelings might lead to partial or misleading insights. The relativistic or dialectical dark shadows of emotional feelings were suppressed in his theory of insight or denied outright. Rogers was clearly no advocate of analytic interpretation nor was he an advocate of behavioral reinforcement. In fact, this lack of concern with the content of insight is an indirect challenge to analytic interpretation, although Rogers never introduced it in that way.

Rogers's writing and its absolute style can be compared with other writing that is about happiness. In other narratives (Haviland & Kramer, 1991) when joy is expressed, it is often in the service of rewarding an achievement. That is, joy is not always a preceding condition for coming upon solutions, but merely a rewarding glow, a lingering nice taste, that follows upon success. Not everyone thinks of positive emotion in this way, but people who do are oriented to conflict and the achievement of difficult goals (e.g., Haviland & Goldston, 1992; Stein & Liwag, 1997). The contrasting view given, for example, in Isen's research (1990) demonstrates that giving people a happy glow with something simple such as a piece of a sweet candy will lead them to be more creative thinkers when presented with unrelated problems. Isen, then, like Rogers, argues that the state of happiness sets people up for a creative mode of thinking, not that happiness is restricted to being the successful aftermath of a struggle.

Rogers's chapter on insight has the goal-oriented narrative style, beginning with its title – "The *Achievement* of Insight." One could, of course, consider insight to be the problem, not the achieved solution. One could consider the process of becoming insightful to be conflictful or discouraging, less overtly rewarding. One might even consider that the achieved insights would be cause for dismay, not cause for rejoicing. But little of this occurred to Rogers. His presentation of insight only with general positive emotion gives a focused and simple view of insight, not one that is has much depth.

On the surface, it is paradoxical that insight would be presented by Rogers with less creativity and flexibility, even insightfulness, than emotion expression. It is almost like a magic trick: wave the baton and in a cloud of smoke, out pops insight. Oh, joy! One might anticipate that a so-called higher ordered process such as insight would require a more flexible and integrative discussion than a so-called lower ordered process such as emotion expression. It reminds one of the psychologists' jokes about people who study creativity having no creativity in their method or people who study memory forgetting the paths previously trod, and so forth. One could hardly say that Rogers had no insight about insight, but he certainly had a singular and light-hearted view of insight and its emergent properties.

Even beyond the consideration of insight, there was another anomaly in Rogers's theory. There is no analytic, narrative perspective at all in his therapeutic endeavors, no developmental history. He never appeared to take an interest in the client's insights into her early history or the story of her life. In part, Rogers himself attributed this to a reaction against the rigidity of Freudian interpretations that were available when he entered the profession. That may be partly true, but it does not account for his never creating a new narrative approach, as did the postmodern psychoanalysts. Even in the second book, it was not entirely clear what Rogers aimed for in therapy beyond the release of suppressed hostility. It was clear that he eschewed analytic interpretation, but what the alternative might have been was less clear. Later, Rogers would present a fuller picture in terms of relationships, one still aimed at the achievement of joy.

Book 3

The clinical scene as described by the older Rogers was one that had the goal of having "all associations of experience, feeling and thought unified in an instant." This is what Hudson et al. (1992; see also, Haviland & Goldston, 1992) call the moment-in-time scene or narrative. In our studies of children's and adults' stories about emotional scenes, happy stories are most commonly of the moment-in-time variety.

To construct a happy, single-affect narrative, the story teller brings together all the elements that allow one to have a complete but elegant picture of what exists at the moment or, to slip into Rogers's terms, what it means to "be" at a particular instant. Creative and poetic happy stories for many people are picture or mood narratives with no essential chronology or plot; they are a narrative of being and living in the moment. Creating a consistently happy and peaceful narrative is not simple; it is considered one of the most difficult tasks of people who write children's stories, the so-called mood stories, or of those who write poetry, perhaps Haiku poetry. Some narrative authors can produce it beautifully in novels, writers such as Willa Cather, but it is rare in Western literature.

When the older Rogers began to describe the relationship of client and therapist in *Becoming a Person* (1961) he moved into the moment-in-time narrative style. This style is not typical of clinicians but is rather especially a Rogerian insight. Rogers hardly ever presented a plotted clinical narrative. He never gave us tales such as the tales of Oedipus or Narcissus; he never even gave us memorable cases such the Wolf Man or Erikson's Gandhi. All these clinical presentations are notable for their plotted narrative, for the scene setting, for having direction and movement, conflict, resolution, and, often, morals, or truths in a nutshell. Throughout his career Rogers avoided this model. He stayed with the moment-in-time, usually happy, narrative.

This revelation about Rogers's happiness ideology also helps to explain why his later writing, in particular, avoided more narratives of self-exploration in therapy. The absence of cases in his approach is very curious in the history of therapists, until viewed through the emotion lens of happiness. Most forms of psychoanalysis and related forms of therapy focus on reconstructing the developmental psychohistory of the client. Some theories of analysis go so far as to say that the process of therapy is first and foremost a particular kind of storytelling. In the course of therapy, the story is both discovered and constructed by both the teller and the therapist listener (e.g., Ricoeur, 1981; Schafer, 1981; Spence, 1982). But it is also the case that these narrative histories are aimed at uncovering "highpoints" – points of crisis and frustration. The very methods used to elicit the stories are based on a controlled frustration. The frustration of the client's wishes by a therapist is expected and honored as much as the narrative technique itself.

Very modern philosophies of narrative in therapy reflect how retelling biographical stories necessarily changes the story. For example, a young child has limited knowledge even of its own interpersonal world (e.g., Stern, 1985). When telling about early childhood as an adult, two things immediately change. First, the structure of the story is clarified because the intellectual and pragmatic demands for storytelling are well known to adults but are more fragmented for young children. Second, knowledge about the situation has changed over the years. The adult "knows" that the "crocodile" that appeared on the ceiling when the light was off was not at all dangerous. And major changes occur such as knowing about contexts, for example in appreciating the demands on parents while caring for an ill grandparent. All these elements interact in the narrative construction of a life. These are attempts to reconcile the philosophical conflict between the real life boundaries on the possible understandings of self that an infant or young child could possibly have and the complex narratives that an adult could construct about her own interpersonal and intrapersonal early stories. In some sense, one can never tell the true story of how one actually felt at an earlier time. In spite of this fact, even the most modern of the analysts relies on standard narrative in therapeutic practice. Potential life narratives as created by Freud, Erikson, or Klein would obviously all differ, but they all would share a conflictful orientation to therapy. Rogers is very unusual in not creating conflictful narratives but instead developing being and moment-in-time descriptions. He does not comprehend the usefulness of major conflictful narrative.

It is quite likely that the emotions Rogers has had a history of *not* developing, the hostile ones needed for dramatic plots, must have played a role in his curious and unique perspective as well as his singular focus on joyfulness. It is the early, happy family years that Rogers seemed to relive and reconstruct in his timeless moments. Although the emphasis has been on happiness, it should be noted that a shared, timeless experience itself is as much the goal as the achievement of bliss. "When there is this complete unity, singleness, fullness of experiencing in the relationship, then it acquires the "out-of-this-world" quality, . . . a sort of trance-like feeling in the relationship" (Rogers, 1961, p. 202) "Consciousness . . . becomes the comfortable inhabitant of a richly varied society of impulses and feelings and thoughts, which prove to be very satisfactorily self-governing when not fearfully or authoritatively guarded" (Rogers, 1961, p. 203). Note once again what is to be avoided, even in the older Rogers – fear and the authoritarian guard. Even though he has made many changes, the younger divisions still govern some thoughts.

In *Becoming a Person*, as expressed in the preceding quotes, Rogers presented an experience of good therapy that emphasized a fusing between the client's and therapist's experiences. Here he avoided the conceptualization of the client as emotionally separate or separating from the therapist and potentially hostile to him. However, the ideology of emotional fusion was not transformed into the practice of fusion (see the chapter on the practice of therapy). In fact, Rogers explicitly referred to the necessity for the therapist to have a solid sense of self and self boundaries in order to be helpful in making the blissful connections. The merging was both frightening in its ability to reveal the experiences of the client or the therapist and maximally rewarding. Never did Rogers mention that the merging itself might contain or lead to any type of distancing or hostile feeling other than fear of exposure, (i.e., shamefulness). This fear of exposure was not an acceptable goal but itself needed to be overcome with further provision of security.

Many Passioned Ideas

The ideas and relationships that Rogers was passionate about, that he had many emotional approaches to, were the issues about which he was clear and creative in contrast to the issues that were aligned with single emotions.

Book 1: Emergence of a Passionate Therapy

Rogers abandoned his component factor approach to studying clinical treatment after this first book. Why did he abandon a factor approach that heralded the common use of modern factor-analytic statistics? We suggested previously that the component factor approach was an idea born of suppressed hostility, not an idea that was multiply emotionally elaborated for Rogers. At first it appears that he may have abandoned a promising experimental and diagnostic career. Alternatively, maybe he barely escaped being drawn into an intellectualized science, never to make his major contributions to the process of therapy for which he is fondly remembered. But then, on the other hand, why did he turn to the expressive therapies? We think it was because they brought together all his emotional abilities. Some of this will remain a puzzle, but some of the roots of this development are to be found even in the first book and will continue to surface in later writings.

In Rogers's first book, *The Clinical Treatment of the Problem Child*, there was a high rate of emotional expression in the chapter on expressive therapy. There is an enormous difference between this chapter and the one reviewed previously on component analysis. This chapter is very passionate (146 emotion words coded), whereas the other is not (10 emotion words coded). Of course, superficially, one is about a "scientific" method of diagnosis and the other is about the "art" of therapy, but that does not reveal the significance of the difference. Even science tells a story and can be passionate, as any devoted scientist or mathematician can affirm. But to someone who is not passionate about science, it is desiccated. To Rogers, quantitative and compartmentalized science was not a fully passionate endeavor.

Even this first book showed us that Rogers was passionately invested in "expressive therapy." There was passion, even though he stuck this chapter near the end of the book and did not tell the reader of its importance directly. Does more passion mean less thought, then? Very little of this chapter was simple description. There was a small amount of patterned thought and a great deal of relativistic thought. The last page in the chapter, which had some patterned Dialectical thought, also had the most emotion and the most variation in emotion – "jealous," "fear," "hate," "guilt," "feeling," "emotions." The words were largely in the hostile category, which also differentiates them from the other emotion words in the scientific work, but they were diverse. Expressive therapy is going to grow into a problem that Rogers will happily chew on for many years, getting everything out of it that he can. The passion and the complex thought with which it was originally invested should have told us that.

There were hints throughout the early work that Rogers had a strong respect for individuals and the relativistic context in which their problems developed. Although this respect was embedded in his early concern with absolute boundaries and limitations, it also demonstrated a respect for a more relativistic approach. For example, in describing the limitations of family therapy, he presented a case in which the father's punitive, authoritarian attitudes toward his son contributed greatly to the child's problems. However, Rogers did not expect the father to have sufficient motivation to change. Rogers recognized that, if the father were to change in his attitude toward his son, he would have had to change a similar pattern of behavior toward his wife. Further, the power and status that his behavior accorded him within his family offset the losses he had faced in his career, where he suffered from punitive supervision himself.

Rogers questioned the father's motivation to enter family therapy and found it unlikely that he should want to change. To do so would have required changing many or all of his other relationships, which were not in jeopardy and would probably have brought him face-to-face with his career disappointment. In this case, Rogers recommended that the efficient intervention clinic, intent on helping the child, would elect to work with some tactic other than family intervention. In other words, without denigrating family intervention, Rogers focused in a contextual or relativistic style on the practical limits of the technique, as he did with each and every approach in his first book.

If the hypothesis about many emotional expressions being related to more complex intellectual work is correct, then of all the topics addressed in the first book, expressive therapy is the one most likely to provide long-term interest to Rogers as indeed it was. This preference was not obvious strictly from the way in which he described expressive therapy; he did not extol it. He referred to the expressive therapy as an interesting experimental attempt being made by a few colleagues of his. He did not describe his own cases or attribute the method to himself. He even had a word of caution concerning the cases for which it is "most valuable" – "when there are strong guilt feelings on the part of the child, particularly when such guilt feelings arise because of hostile feelings toward another" (Rogers, 1939, p. 321). However, he believed that this approach had great promise because he concluded by saying that the method could be adapted for any age group, although he apparently had no experiential grounds for this statement.

One has to wonder, since this young man, Rogers, was still quite embedded in his childhood history, whether the emotional appeal of the individualistic expressive therapy was not related somewhat to his own situation. Perhaps, he, too, felt some unreleased hostility toward his family, and the consequent guilt, yet yearned to retain his self-respect and his socially benign behavior. Perhaps there were feelings unresolved from his childhood and adolescence that were reflected in this passionate embrace of the expressive therapy. It would be reasonable to presume that Rogers's attraction to this expressive therapy originated in conflict that he was still struggling with in young adulthood. Unlike his strangled struggle with his psychoanalytic colleagues, however, this one was based on multiple emotions – hostile ones of guilt, of self-respect, and pride and positive ones of joy and contentment. He was not stuck with a single emotional approach here, as he was with other intellectual issues.

Overall, Rogers's style of thought was fairly typical of a young intellectual in the first book. He did not use much integrative thought in the first book; he had no integrating statements to make. Instead, he relied on finding the elements of problems and working out logical combinations of the elements to find the best and most conclusive solutions. When he acknowledged uncertainty or diversity, he did so in a relativistic mode, allowing each solution to have its own space and largely denying that any one solution might be preferred over another in an absolute way, only in terms of the problem to which it might be addressed.

Only in describing expressive therapy was there a hint of more integrated, evolutionary theory in his first book and even here it was so fragmented as to be merely a promise rather than a fully developed theory or position. However, it was in the arena of expressive therapy that there was both passionate involvement and evidence of continuing creative intellectual work.

Book 2: Linking Emotions to Stages in Therapy

Counseling and Psychotherapy (1942), Rogers's second book, as described earlier, was a sophisticated first statement of his own theory. It contained descriptions of research that could be used to justify his own approach, many brief case examples, and a lengthy Rogerian case transcript with commentaries. It contained no overview or organization of types of therapies and little statistical analysis. It was a highly personal work, very different from the first book, but it still did not quite present the humanistic, person-centered Rogers that appeared in his later work.

The second chapter, "Old and New Viewpoints," is one of the most emotionally dense and, hence, passionate chapters in *Counseling and Psychotherapy*; it put his theory of nondirective counseling most elegantly. The emotion words are so dense that, unlike the first book, it begs for analysis according to the types of emotion, as well as emotion terms in general.

One section of *Counseling and Psychotherapy* described the process of nondirective therapy from the initial meeting of client and therapist to their final meeting in twelve steps. The emotional elaboration of different ideas in this chapter were not distributed randomly, rather different "steps" seemed aligned with the expression of different emotions. In step one, the client came for help. There are no emotion words here. Rogers asserted the importance of nurturing a client's responsibility for taking the first step. In step two, the helping situation was described to the client; it was "defined." Here one client was fearful of therapy and another was surprised at the therapist's description. As was typical in these early descriptions of therapy, neither the feelings nor the behavior of the therapist were described; only those of the client were detailed. Thus, the second step was emotionally described or elaborated in terms of "novelty" emotions – fear and surprise in new situations.

In the third step of counseling, the therapist encouraged the "free expression of feelings." The therapist was described as interested, whereas the client was seen as being hostile, anxious, concerned, guilty, and violent; some of these terms were used more than once. One notes immediately that Rogers was pointing to the first task of the therapist as the exploration of negative feelings, not any delineation of thematic content or other regular definition of the problem as one might do in more behaviorally or cognitively oriented therapies. This section was the most emotionally elaborate with the most different kinds of negative emotion in it and the first hint of subjective emotion; that is, the therapist has an emotional experience. This subjectivity is rare throughout *Counseling and Psychotherapy*, although Rogers developed a more transactional, integrated, and subjective approach later in his life.

In the next step of counseling, the therapist should *accept, recognize,* and *clarify* the client's negative feelings. (We will return to the point that Rogers is not, as he is often portrayed, merely urging the therapist to reflect or mirror feelings – nothing so simple.) The feelings referred to were hostility, guilt, fear, hopelessness, and despair. This section ended with a poignant description of a client "wailing." In both cases, the negative emotion was diverse and rich, but there was still a strong preference for hostile feelings. As Rogers wrote, "Note the fact that the counselor's sole aim is not to impede this flow of hostile and critical feelings" (1942, p. 39). We also note again that the therapist had no recognized feelings of his own.

Although it is true that Rogers was here referring to a particular case, one gets the impression from the preponderance of hostile emotion words throughout these sections that Rogers generally expected to encounter hostile feelings in his clients. He did not emphasize anxiety other than in the introduction to therapy, and he did not emphasize depressive feelings, either of which might be stressed in another psychologist's writings. Ellis, for example, usually describes anxiety or depression in his clients.

In the next two steps of therapy, after the acceptance phase, positive feelings emerged and were then also accepted and clarified. Rogers viewed this as a natural rule: "Positive expression is one of the most certain and predictable aspects of the whole process" (1942, p. 39). He did not seem to perceive any intervening process or conceptual need, only an absolute certainty that this would happen, even that it will "surprise" the beginning therapist with its predictability. This seems to suggest to a beginning therapist that no particular analysis or conceptualization of the themes or issues in a client's case is necessary for transformation. It is only a reflection of the natural order of things that needs to be "released." As was reflected in the previous discussion of joyfulness, this section in Rogers's writing was poorly elaborated with emotion in comparison with the earlier sections. When Rogers expanded his theory into chapters, there was no chapter specifically on the emergence of positive feelings, so this whole arena was neither emotionally nor intellectually developed by Rogers. The emergence of positive feeling and its singular emotionality led only to singular modes of thought about the issues involved. One might contrast this direct approach with that of Ellis. Ellis described the process of confrontation, practice, and imagery that he requires of his clients in order to reach a point of pleasure in their experiences. In Ellis's experience, this process is neither a simple nor a naturally evolving sequence.

When Rogers described the point at which positive feelings emerge, no specific positive feelings were identified; they were only "positive feelings." Unlike the sections on negative emotions, which described the therapists' behavior a bit and described the varieties of negative emotions to be encountered in the clients in some detail, this section had a vague tone in both emotion designation and in cognitive solution. Again the specific feelings mentioned are the negative ones from which the positive feelings will emerge – violence, antagonism, aggression, guilt, and defensiveness – but there was still a heavy preference for hostile feelings. This inclination occurred, in part, because Rogers emphasized the conflict that emerges between negative and positive feelings, which may at first seem like a "war."

It is somewhat unclear when Rogers described emerging changes in the client whether he was presenting an absolute view of the nature of mankind, one in which we are all basically good and happy, or whether he was presenting an integrated theory of psychological process in which there is a balance between opposing processes, in this case, hostility and positive feeling. This question represents a real vacillation in Rogers' analyses. On some issues, he was quite absurdly dictatorial, on others he considered the balance of factors and the possibility of unexpected creativity in a complex process of integrated change. This flux in the type of thinking Rogers used will continue to emerge.

In the next several steps, following the emergence of "tentative positive impulses," the client moved toward insight and action based upon the insight. As in the previous section, when positive feeling arose spontaneously, the emergence of insight was also miraculous. "Insight and self-understanding come bubbling through spontaneously" (1942, p. 40). In terms of the emotions, once again fear came to the fore as it did at the beginning of therapy. The client expressed the specific feelings, and they were recognized and clarified by the counselor. Once again, the feelings that Rogers mentioned were fear (several times), hatred, terror, and jealousy. Only in the final phase did Rogers mention interest and enjoyment as client feelings. Still, at this point, they were mixed with fear as the client attempted new undertakings.

This analysis of the therapeutic process as described by Rogers in *Counseling and Psychotherapy* suggests an implicit description of the prototypic client for Rogerian therapy. It is clear that Rogers did not have in mind a client who was principally aware of being terrified or anxious, for example. His prototypic client was conflicted and paralyzed by the inhibition of negative, hostile emotion. (This is not to deny, of course, that an anxious individual might also be paralyzed by the inhibition of anger; it speaks only to the voiced concerns of the client.) In many ways, the prototypic client is the seeming antithesis of Rogers's portrait of himself that he would write later in his life.

In contrast to the writings that pertain to Rogers's later description of his own, the emotions used by the younger Rogers when describing this nondirective therapeutic process were very dense in negative, hostile emotion. The largest single category that occurred in describing the therapeutic process was the hostile–anger category. Anger and fear together account for two thirds of the specific emotions described in this chapter on the process of therapy.

As we saw in analyses of Rogers's biographical material, which dates from the last decades of Rogers's life, the older Rogers very seldom described himself or his own life with hostile emotions. Perhaps Rogers found that his own most dreaded self was the hostile self and that he projected this perception upon people seeking help. It would make sense that a person in deep pain and requesting assistance from a therapist would experience a dreaded side. When thinking about this processing in the abstract, when writing, Rogers may have been projecting his own most dreaded self upon his imaginary client. When he did this, he saw a person suffering from hostile feelings – unexpressed hostile feelings. It was apparently important that the hostility existed but that it needed to be developed and clarified by the therapist, perhaps transformed. From this process emerged positive feelings and spontaneous insight.

Another way of viewing this split between Rogers, the man, describing himself and Rogers, the professional, describing a client is to point to the intellectualization of Rogers's own problem. He did not perceive his *own* problem very clearly in emotional terms, but he had an intellectual grasp of how such a thing could be a problem for someone else. The emotional block was also an intellectual block of sorts.

One might erroneously assume from this discussion that we mean to argue that Rogers's entire theory of the therapeutic process could be reduced to a defense system. Such a position would be terribly oversimplified. Here we are only making a very small, but possibly important, point that a diverse, even superficially oppositional, use of emotion in narrative and thought can lead one to discover the significant motivational biases and patterns of any individual. Emotional patterns then lead to deeper understanding of logical patterns and intellectual choices. Our position is more active and positive than defensive.

The next few chapters in *Counseling and Psychotherapy* expanded the issues raised in the introductory chapter. We used analyses of them as a corrective lens through which we could reevaluate the initial presentation of Rogers's theory. For example, if the hostile emotion in the middle phases of therapy actually came only from Rogers's thinking of a specific case, then the presentation of more cases in the longer exposition would not show the same correlation.

The chapter entitled "Releasing Expression" is the most thoughtful and most intellectually sophisticated one in this book; it also contains a fair amount of controversial text. Here Rogers opened the doors on his conduct of therapy and allowed us to follow him as he showed his greatest talent, the talent for "responding to feeling in clients," or, "releasing expression." Releasing expression implies both feeling and thought, of course, and Rogers meant that we should be aware of that. As he pointed out later, he was not discussing "catharsis" or the release and clearing out of feelings to provide space for some other process, but the whole process of disinhibiting awareness and understanding emotions. Because this chapter is complex, it will be helpful to go through it in sections.

Throughout the chapter, Rogers insisted on the importance of responding to the feeling and not the intellectual content of the interview. Even though this admonition hit again at the "deeper therapies" with their insistence upon "insight," it had a positive side as well. It corresponded to his position that if clients needed instruction, they did not need therapy, they needed tutoring. Therapy is about feelings for Rogerians. Rogers presented, brilliantly, several examples of some therapists responding to the problem-oriented aspect of the session and other therapists responding to the emotional attitude aspect of the situation. In all the cases Rogers presented, the response to the emotional attitude preceded the clients' expanding the information on the topic. The response to the problem-oriented content preceded the clients' changing the topic or denying the validity of the therapist's remarks. One should note also that Rogers made his argument with examples from cases, not with tables or charts or "quantified" information.

Rogers presented a classic example (1942) of the difference between responding to feelings as opposed to responding to problems first. The client came in for the first time and said, "I've always realized that my methods of study…are wrong…but I don't think I am as stupid as my grades indicate" (p. 32). The directive counselor responded with, "Well, how bad are your grades? I thought they were pretty good" (p. 32). Fairly soon the conversation was directed by the counselor into a discussion of one major course of study versus another.

In the contrasting nondirective example, the client brought the problem that he could not tell his parents about his declining grades. He asked, "Would you advise me to tell them about it?" This nondirective therapist did not ask how bad the grades were, neither did he answer the question. Instead, he reflected the feeling saying, "It will be fairly hard for you to tell them." This led the client to talk about the conflictful situation that existed within his family of which he and his grades were just a part. As Rogers pointed out, the grades themselves were not the concern of the counselor, and if the client wanted information about improving his grades, he would have done better to visit his professors. However, the conflict about grades arose with respect to the family's attitudes. As it turned out, this conflict had an indirect bearing upon the student's grades and could be fruitfully addressed with Rogers's approach.

Rogers went on in the chapter to discuss the temptations that the counselor would face to do something other than reflect feelings. He believed it was terribly distracting or alienating to the client if the counselor succumbed to these temptations. This is distinctly not a simple, absolute chapter about spontaneous process but rather a technical and integrative approach to his theory. For example, he discussed the need that a counselor would naturally have to deny a client's negative feelings about himself and gave many examples of the real helpfulness of affirming the client's statements of his negative feelings – even when they were about himself. This sort of reflection might make a cognitive-behavior therapist such as Ellis expel a deep, rejecting breath. Most of the these modern cognitive therapists believe that they must challenge the depressed client's "irrational" negative descriptions of himself, not accept them.

Rogers also discussed the importance of fully reflecting the client's feelings even when they were contradictory or ambivalent. If the client was both hostile and loving to a parent, Rogers did not claim that one side only should be responded to, or reinforced, again as some modern behavior modification therapists might argue. Instead, he again provided examples showing that acknowledging the contradictory feelings led to the client's own resolution of the conflict. Having the counselor emphasize one side of the conflict led straight to denial with an inhibited anger in his case presentations. Unlike Ellis, Rogers was not sensitive to events that eventually might follow the inhibited anger and denial – a working through of the denial process because of confrontation between the client and therapist. He took another path.

Throughout this emotionally dense section, Rogers's main avenue of thought was integrative or patterned. He did not suggest single-minded, linear solutions; he offered no absolute right answers. There were not even absolute, linear questions. The entire context and evolution of the client's problem-solving abilities and sense of self-understanding were at issue. He aimed for nothing less than that the client becoming capable of integrative problem solving and questioning. It is a brilliant exposition, weaving among the different emotional approaches of clients and allowing for the surprising and rewarding emergence of solutions from clients.

Toward the end of the chapter on releasing expression, Rogers even discussed the pitfalls of his own nondirective method. It was quite clear that he viewed it as a method requiring intense training and practice for a serious therapist, not just an agreement to be sympathetic or supportive to people. He was full of information about the problems encountered by novice practitioners. For example, he pointed out that in reflecting feelings the counselor should only reflect feelings that have been verbally expressed. He argued strongly for his position, using many examples.

Rogers was chagrined at the ways that his therapeutic advice became distorted and popularied. Many of us have met "Rogerians" who repeat the last four or five words one says, never adding anything. Such people claim to be "reflecting." It is maddening. But paying a modicum of attention to Rogers's writing shows that he never had anything like this poor imitation in mind. He wrote late in his life that he despaired of this second book on the releasing of feeling and the ridicule it evoked when untrained practitioners tried reflecting.

However, as Rogers may have been aware, other therapists disagreed equally strongly with his "reflecting" caveat at a deeper level. For example, Fritz Perls and other members of the Gestalt therapy schools believed that reflecting the unstated, nonverbal expression was very important. As we will see in later chapters, Perls was often confrontational and produced emotion in clients that they were not aware of. Pointing out that one is saying one thing and expressing another in tone of voice or way of sitting or facial expression highlights the conflict within an individual as well as emphasizes the implicit confrontation between the naive clients and the knowledgeable therapists.

In that Rogers did not have a place for confrontation to develop and become permanently useful, only to become transformed through expression, it was also becoming clear that he did not want to create a place for it. He warned therapists against the creation of conflict. In treating the "client who demands an answer" as well as the hostile client, Rogers believed it was the counselor's responsibility to avoid escalating the conflict or the hostility. Rogers believed that this type of confrontation would inhibit the release of expression within the client and possibly lead to discontinuation of the therapeutic contacts.

Rogers was very clear and directive in telling the counselor what approach to take with confrontational clients: "Yet the principle of dealing with them, the principle which is consistent with the whole hypothesis of this book, is simple and clear-cut. It is to recognize understandingly that the client would feel great satisfaction in finding an answer to his problem but that the only realistic answer that can possibly be found is in terms of his own abilities and desires to deal with the situation" (1942, pp. 162–3).

In practice, Rogers seldom left a client's request for an answer without redirecting the client back to a consideration of feelings. Rogers presented the case of a mother who asked him how to respond to a disobedient child who would not get her some ink when she asked him to and, in fact, said that he would not do it. Rogers said, "'Well, I doubt that there is any one set, particular answer to – that would fit all cases like that. You – you were probably pretty much upset by the time it was over, too'." Not only did he not answer the mother's question, but he clearly redirected her back to reflecting upon her own feelings about the incident. In a sense, Rogers was directive. The mother had said that the *son* was "upset – he was almost hysterical" (1942, p. 163). She did not make any remark about her own feelings. Rogers was directing her to do so, not explicitly reflecting her own assessment of her feelings. If

Rogers was aware of directing clients to reflect upon their feelings, he did not report it.

Just how nondirective is nondirective therapy? Perhaps it is not the nondirective quality of it that is successful, but the emotionally directive quality. Even further, perhaps it is the specific emotions to which the client is directed that make the therapy successful. Although Rogers may have been directing his clients to think emotionally, since he instructed his practitioners to reflect emotion, there may be some differences between the master Rogers and the disciples. He only partly explained precisely what he was doing as a therapist.

As one would expect, the chapter on releasing expression in this early boom on nondirective counseling contained a great many references to emotion. It had an exceptionally large number (88) of nonspecific emotion words such as "feelings," "felt," or "emotion." Relative to the other chapters it also contained a large number of references to hostile types of feelings (31), but every category of specific emotion expression was available. Once again this general type of analysis shows how often Rogers anticipated that the client, who would be counseled in nondirective therapy, was a client who needed to express hostile feelings rather than a client who needed to express feelings of sadness, misery, guilt, or self-consciousness. To be certain, the minority depressive (6) or anxious (13) feelings were mentioned, making it a fully passionate chapter.

What is the meaning of the prevalent hostile emotions attributed to clients by Rogers? Does it mean that, in fact, he was overexposed to clients with emotional inhibitions in the hostile realm? Does it mean that Rogers was overly sensitive to the counseling difficulties posed by hostile emotion whether or not the client has a particular difficulty with hostility? The answer to this question is important because it is relevant to developing a theory of the role of emotion in therapy. And the same question must be considered in the cases presented by Ellis and by Perls. Not only do their techniques differ from Rogers, the thoughtful style of their theories differs and the emotional problems of their clients also seem to differ.

If Rogers's experience with clients was restricted to particular types of clients, is this indicative of his success with a particular range of client problems and lack of success with other types of problems? If the client's own emotional problems are irrelevant, then does it even matter that Rogers focused on hostile emotion in his theory? Clearly, Rogers's focus suggests that he viewed unexpressed hostile emotion in his clients as problematic, in need of solution and care, in a way that he did not view other emotions. But if a client viewed a different set of emotions as problematic, did the "reflective" aspect of Rogers's theory compel him to follow the client's lead in addressing other emotions, or did Rogers elaborate the hostile emotions in spite of the client's needs?

To give more credit to Rogers, his writing preceded any research on the behaviors and thoughts associated with different emotions. He could not have anticipated that anyone would interpret his subconscious emphasis on hostile emotions to mean that he was focusing on a particular type of client. He certainly never said that the nondirective method was to be used for clients with a particular emotional history.

If we stand on Rogers's shoulders, to use an awkward metaphor, and let his intuitive sense of the client be our guide, then our hypothesis would have to be that – at this point in his professional life – Rogers believed that he had worked well with clients who had inhibited their feelings of hostility. The lack of emotional understanding that Rogers perceived in these clients reached into the realm of their cognitive understanding. Being unable to perceive or process their own hostile reactions and motivations, his clients were unable to understand how to solve their constellation of daily problems. Rogers argued that providing cognitive input before emotional input was of little use in these cases. The emotional realm contained the immediate inhibitions, and only subsequently the cognitive.

It is equally clear from Rogers's descriptions of the therapeutic process that he "reflected" but did not "share" his clients' hostile feelings. (In later books, Rogers did portray the client and therapist sharing blissful states of communion.) Rogers did not advocate at this point that any emotion expressed by the client actually become contagious to the therapist. The counselor, while reflecting something in the verbal content of the expression, responded with interest and sympathy in his own nonverbal behavior, no matter what the client did. That is, the counselor took the hostile feelings out of the behavioral scene with which they would ordinarily be associated – a scene of distancing, confrontation, loss of control, and judgmental thought – and put them into a scene of sharing and understanding.

Rogers claimed to "prize" hostile feelings, prized them as a significant part of the client's being. Even here, though, there are questions that arise about the actual prizing of hostility that Rogers might have done. How much prizing of anger is being done if anger is never allowed into the good therapist's repertoire? It is not much of a prize if it is not wanted by the therapist. He might not have reflected hostile emotion even though he intellectually recognized the problematic nature of hostile emotion. On the contrary, he might have helped the client move the hostile perception of the problematic scene to a perception of it through other emotions – discouragement, interest, self-consciousness, guilt.

How common is the unspoken assumption that the therapist must be sensitive to others' moods but not affected by them? Rogers seemed to believe that he could reflect equally well any emotion without having the emotion become contagious to him. He was unable to perceive that the therapist's role, as he defined it, called for a certain history of skill in emotion management. When faced with contempt and anger, the therapist had to have had the power to mute or inhibit a corresponding rage and respond with a "good" behavior such as sympathy. However, this hypersensitivity to managing others' feelings had the consequence of leaving his own hostility unacknowledged.

Some recent commentary on analytic therapists has some bearing on Rogers as a clinician. Apparently, most therapists did not have perfectly attuned emotional relationships when they were young. As Miller (1981) described the typical person drawn to therapy, she or he had somewhat insecure infant and childhood relationships. However, in spite of the insecurity, a facade of good, even perfect, connection could be preserved by the child if he politely managed his real feelings, if he responded only as the adults required. Such children are rewarded with parental love for their own sensitive, undemanding, attentive behavior toward the parent. By attending so carefully to others, they develop a seductive, sometimes grandiosely lovable facade, but retain a sense of having lost contact with their own negative feelings.

The unexpressed childish self has a strong potential for being the heavenly self or the hellish self, both of which remain undeveloped, but tantalizing, like any unsolved puzzle or any treasure almost within one's grasp. This must be the story that Rogers is not telling about his family roots, largely because he did not know it. Rogers was probably the child who did not whine when he was sick, but was kind and brave, who did not have tantrums when frustrated as a toddler, who did not laugh tauntingly when his brothers slipped and fell, who was "politely thankful" when he did not get the present he most wanted, who was most "understanding" when others told him what was good for him.

The loving parent who searches for self-validation in his or her own good child is not the obvious target of public reprimand. In fact, parents who manage so excellently to produce well-mannered, obedient

children are idealized. This idealization can easily turn into a disappointing, perpetual motion machine so that the child of such parents
also grows up to forever look for approval and love from his or her own
children (or adopted children – clients or students), love that he or she
can sense only when their positive empathic response is attained. Rogers
gave his parents unconditional regard and love although inhibiting his
own feelings and self. Then he expects others to do the same for him to
restore his feelings and sense of self. When they do become empathic
with him he is rewarded and rewarding. Eventually someone questions
the absolute goodness of relationships built on the manipulation of feelings and polite misrepresentation. What is really being sought in such
relationships? The contrast of Rogers with Ellis or with Perls will be
striking. Neither Ellis nor Perl, although still rather grandiose, has the
same willingness to subsume all personal negative emotion to create an
affirmative relationship. However, they both had life histories of manipulating certain other emotional stances to achieve their aims, as do
we all, of course.

Rogers conformed too readily to standard pictures of the good child,
the good therapist, the good father, the good husband, the good researcher, allowing us to doubt all this goodness. What did this human
being do with his feelings of contempt for snide colleagues, his frustration with slow students, and his desolation at not being welcomed by
other schools of thought such as the psychoanalytic? What did he do
when he failed with a patient, and badly failed?

The biographical material showed us that when the younger Rogers
occasionally failed to reach the Himalayan peaks of his self-appointed
heights, he was completely shamed and ran. When cornered or when
his frustration snuck up on him, he attacked but was also shamed by
this weakness, this inability to express and control his fury. This problem
reached crisis proportions in middle age. Although he told us little about
it, there was clearly a turning point for him. He failed with a client. She
turned on him in a rage, and he fled. He was sought by loving colleagues
and family, entered therapy himself, and emerged a slightly changed
and wiser man; in fact, he emerged after his tranformation most fully as
the humanistic psychologist who is written about in the textbooks.

Book 3: Integrating Passion and Being

What about Rogers's later books? Are the emotionally rich chapters
still creative and thoughtful? How has Rogers's conception of therapy

changed after his own emotional tranformation? What new issues engaged him late in life? *On Becoming a Person* (1961) is a collection of speeches and essays written by Rogers from 1951 to 1961, late in midlife. It covered many of the same topics that were raised in *Counseling and Psychotherapy* (1942); yet there were differences in how these topics were approached and given meaning, as well as in the emotional environment which contained the topics. These essays of Rogers give us some of the best evidence we have ever had to see wisdom as a late-flowering virtue related to the integration of emotional experience.

In this late-life book Rogers returned to the same themes. In Chapter 7 of *On Becoming a Person*, we find again a discussion of "the process of psychotherapy." This was now a seven-step description of stages in psychotherapy (not twelve, as earlier) with apparently similar goals to the one appearing in the earlier book. In the first stage, the client had a "fixity and remoteness" to "feelings." The specific emotions were not mentioned, and it was the orientation to emotion itself that Rogers focused upon, not the negativity or the type of the emotion. Further, Rogers was not starting with "everyman" in therapy as he did in the previous list. Here he was distinctly writing about a particular client who presented himself at this first stage. He stated that another client might enter therapy at a different stage. The stages did not precisely refer to a stage in therapy as much as they referred to a type of interaction that the client was prepared for.

Even in the opening of this later chapter on psychotherapy, we can detect two interesting changes in Rogers. There is a change to person-alize both the client and the therapist that did not seem to occur to him in his earlier presentation when therapy was often a more rigid and ab-stract idea. Second, there is more clarity about the roles of emotions in therapy, going beyond releasing them.

In the second stage of therapeutic interaction, feelings were discussed by the client with the therapist, but their focus was external to the client. Emotion may have belonged to others or to the past, or it may have been an intruder. Again the specific emotion was not noted in Roger's presentation; however, the targeted client, used as an example, was ex-periencing depression. This fact was mentioned twice. Again this was an important change in Rogers. He was much more aware of and rela-tivistic about the process of using emotion. Also, significant to us, he had not yet been drawn into considering conflict or hostility. Instead, he mentioned depression in a client, a state that did not receive attention in either of the earlier books.

In the third stage, the emotions were more the focus of the therapy as the client began to examine them reflectively, contradictorily, evaluatively – still, usually, as past events. Responding to the client, Rogers was also more specific in describing this stage, mentioning almost every shade of emotion – smile, gruff, shame, guilt, fear, cheerfulness – and many references to feelings in general. One might note in contrast to *Counseling and Psychotherapy*, we again had, so far, no references to hostile feelings and no generalizations about fearfulness and entering therapy.

The descriptions of each and every stage tended to be more broadly emotionally elaborated rather than connecting each stage to a particular emotion. In other words, more of the stage interactions were associated with more types of emotion. It is as if each of the processes in therapy was fuller for Rogers, fuller of diverse feelings and fuller of diverse thoughts as well. Earlier, except for the release of negative expression, most stages were associated with a particular emotion and the clients' thoughts about emotion were obscure, even irrelevant.

In the fourth stage, clients began to express presently held feelings. They colored their emotional sharing with ambivalence and even fear or distrust. In this fourth stage, the feelings described by Rogers were both varied and specific. He mentioned hopelessness, fear, blame, mad, cry, amusement, embarrassment, and sadness. Although feeling "mad" finally emerged, the depressive and more self-conscious feelings were numerous and salient. In the fifth stage, more precision about present feelings emerged as the client looked for clarity in labeling emotion and connecting it with personal constructions. There was more awareness that a feeling is a real part of the perceived experience and, hence, necessarily acceptable as "what exists." The verbal expression of emotion continued to become more intense, but the reflected reaction to the experience and examination of feelings remained somewhat fearful.

Following the description of the client again in the fifth stage, Rogers mentioned even more specific emotions. General feelings were mentioned twelve times, fears four times, sad related feelings nine times, surprise three times, enjoyment five times, and irritation once. Again the specific negative ambitions mentioned were related to sadness or, in second place, fear. This relationship was reversed in the sixth stage. Here he mentioned fearful emotions ten times and crying three times. General feelings were mentioned seventeen times, and shame and amazement each came up once. In this sixth stage, feeling became less self-conscious, "self as object begins to disappear" (1961, p. 147). "The incongruence between experience and awareness is vividly experienced as it disappears into congruence" (1961, p. 148).

In the final seventh stage, feelings were easily and clearly described and used freely as symbols and referents for personal behavior and beliefs. Here again there was a diversity of feelings specified – from fright to happiness – and a better representation of hostile feelings – frustrate, obnoxious, anger, hostility (twice), resent. This range represented an interesting switch. In this sequence, the hostile feelings finally emerged at the end. The inhibition of conflict that Rogers wrote of directly before was now transformed and only included implicitly as part of the sequence of learning to vividly experience or "be"; it was no longer explicitly a goal in therapy to release inhibited conflict, nor was it an early achievement of therapy, but a later one.

Obviously, this writing is rich in emotional expression, but what about the thought processes? Did Rogers become more emotional and less wise? Even in this later version, the process of therapy was linear in that there was a clear direction for it to take, one that the therapist continued to facilitate by providing a secure environment. However, it no longer had a highpoint, a point such as the release of negative feelings, and it had no sudden achievements such as spontaneous insight. It was more clearly a process in which even the stages were merging into one another and in which there was an expected amount of back and forth among the stages. It was a more cognitive therapy because the focus now was on the awareness, labeling, and construction of feelings in scenes rather than on the release of inhibited expression.

In this book, Rogers was somewhat less an absolute thinker and less Platonic than he was as a younger writer. In the earlier construction, there was always a suggestion that the already present, very real, but hidden, healthy person would emerge if he or she could only be released from inhibitions. That expectation can still be found here and there in the older Rogers, but it is easier to perceive a more constructive orientation as the person actively changed "cognitive maps."

The focus on positive versus negative emotions was gone altogether in the later writing, as the possible dialectics have been expanded and woven together in a more integrated fashion: subjective and objective, feelings and cognition, present and past. The dialectic was less concrete and more fully developed, not restricted to "positive versus negative." The emotional and cognitive flexibility occurring with growth during therapy was more easily grasped in this later theory – there were fewer of the spontaneous insights.

This change to a clearer, richer, integrated theory and a less mechanistic or absolute theory comes in parallel to the rich emotional environment provided in the narrative. As noted earlier, most of the stages were fully emotionally elaborated. The variety of emotions associated with most of the stages involved most categories of emotion, specifically mentioned. Previously, there was more compartmentalization of stage and emotion and in the intellectualized version of therapy a strong insistence on hostile feelings as key to the process. The reader should remember that this change was not complete, as remnants of the focusing of happiness and the restrictions on anger remained.

The skeptical reader might question the stability of the apparent changes in Rogers. Had Rogers's emotional reasoning changed and become broader, wiser? It would be risky to base an important point about Rogers's emotional and cognitive development on a single chapter. It is essential to assure ourselves that a change has occurred. Two additional chapters in this collection expand upon the therapeutic process. As was done with *Counseling and Psychotherapy*, counts of the emotions to establish the emotional context and coding of each page for the type of cognitive style allowed us to cross-check the impressions of the process described in the short-listed version against a more expansive version written at a different time. It lends some credibility to the argument that a substantial change really had taken place from the earlier book to the later one when the essentials of the change can be found in several instances.

Chapter 2 was called, rather awkwardly, "Some Hypotheses Regarding the Facilitation of Personal Growth," and Chapter 3, "The Characteristics of a Helping Relationship." Both were originally written as talks, one in 1954 and the other in 1958; however, their content and style were quite similar. Both dealt with the relationship constituted by therapy and were concerned with the role and task of the therapist as well as with characteristics of the client.

In much the same way as in the earlier book, Rogers focused on the behavior of the therapist that would promote the best outcome for nondirective counseling. In *Counseling and Psychotherapy*, the explicit emphasis was on reflecting the emotional content of the client's expression and the implicit emphasis was on providing a secure situation in which the client would release her own hostile emotional content; the emphasis in *On Becoming a Person* is somewhat different. In his later writings, Rogers was far less explicit in describing the directive and nondirective behaviors of a therapist and more concerned with the general presentation or attitude of the therapist. Rather than focusing on a specific therapist behavior – reflecting feelings versus asking directed questions or giving advice – he noted that the primary requisite was having a relationship. He did not refer just to the ability of the client to express his or her emotion but also to the ability of the therapist to be aware of and expressive of personal feelings to make them clear to the client.

In his later descriptions of therapy, Rogers presented a more interactive message than he had earlier. Here the relationship required that both the therapist and the client express their feelings, not that the client express and the therapist reflect. Here, there was an implication that communication and sharing, overcoming loneliness and estrangement were essential. This ideological emphasis is even more complicated when observed in the actual practice of therapy as was apparent in the films with the client Gloria (see Chapter 10).

Examination of the information gathered on moods and feelings mentioned in the text to provide the emotional environment does support the prediction that Rogers became more emotionally elaborated as he aged. The analysis of the types of thinking in these chapters also showed that Rogers had moved toward a more integrative or dialectical theoretical orientation. This thought pattern is presently labeled "wisdom" by researchers working on thinking in older people (Baltes & Staudinger, 1993; Labouvie-Veif, 1994).

The "Integrative Process of Changingness"

Rogers's emotional experiences and awareness changed across his life, leading to change in his work and intellectual awareness about particular issues.

Book 1

In his first book, *The Clinical Treatment of the Problem Child* (1939), Rogers did his journeyman work, not his original contribution, although there was much that showed promise. Like a Caesar facing Gaul, he divided and sorted the field of clinical psychology, preparing a space for his own work, as well as covertly putting the prominent "deeper therapies" on the defensive. He gave a pragmatic, egalitarian, American descriptive organization to the field of child diagnosis and treatment without presenting much that was new in treatments or diagnoses.

A reading of the first book through the lens of emotion revealed a paucity of emotion devoted to the methods of organizing and analyzing the field. The covert hostility of the book made it a bit tedious in the enormity of descriptive rationalization throughout, which may well account for its lack of popular appeal. A diversity of emotion was discernible only in a section of a short chapter on expressive treatments.

Although the book did establish boundaries, overall, it had the deceptive appearance of an exceedingly egalitarian American approach. It harbored the American melting pot approach to therapies. As a theoretical style, the idealized American melting pot hypothesis can emerge either as a relativistic approach – every method considered separately has good and bad aspects, none is best – or as a dialectical approach – the whole is more than the sum of its parts and together provides a more dynamic system. In Rogers's first book, the tendency was distinctly toward the relativistic.

A second emerging trend, also culturally a very North American point of view, is one of the right of each person to pursue his or her own eccentric goals. At the very end of the book, Rogers wrestled with the problem of the rights of the individual versus the rights of the group. "On the one hand are those who strive to bring the child and his behavior into conformity with generally accepted standards of conduct" (Rogers, 1939, p. 354). But "we find a second school of clinical thought which maintains that the goals of therapy are within the individual. The aim to be achieved is the comfort of the child, or the child's happiness, or the child's inner growth, . . . whether or not it leads to social adjustment" (Rogers, 1939, p. 355). "All this, however, is a problem for the philosophers and for each individual to solve" (Rogers, 1939, p. 356). In other words, there are two sides, but Rogers, as a young writer, had no integrative solution. The positions were in irremedial conflict and one decision was as good as another – a purely relativistic, almost cynical, position. Ultimately he hoped for truth to emerge from the gathering of data and, then, quantitative analyses.

Rogers, therefore, was not only a pragmatic young writer but also a very American pragmatic writer. It was not for him to consider the role of Jungian yin and yang or the collective unconscious or the existential anxieties of man in society – not yet in any case. The importance of the unconscious was minimal, the hermeneutics of personal narrative were never mentioned. The important questions were the practical arrangements to be made when problems are faced; the pragmatic cost effectiveness of different strategies for repair. Any technique that worked was valuable, if quantifiably verified. What each contributed was considered without prejudice. He seldom questioned the values that any individual may have had, even when they conflicted with therapeutic aims. Every individual had a "right" to his own aims. He had some concern for "destructive" aims, but this was rather naively conceived, and there was some presumption that any reasonable person would know a destructive aim when he saw it. There was not much need to dwell on psychological defenses and similar constructions.

Rogers did not directly challenge or malign the dominant psychiatric claims to therapy; he subtly embedded them in the mass of treatments. Completely egalitarian, he did not even pause to acknowledge the status differences between the social worker and psychiatrist. Whether he actually believed in his youth that this approach would enable him to avoid controversy is hard to know. Even silence on these matters would have to be treated as a challenge. His own position on hostility was so clearly suppressed at this early stage in his life, that he may have been strongly persuaded to feel guiltless by his own intellectualized egalitarianism. Overtly, he was too respectful to be hostile. That this is a personal emotional orientation and not just a function of age is obvious when contrasted with Ellis. Ellis's earliest books on sexual attitudes are *overtly* contemptuous of prevailing norms and authorities.

Rogers was not only embedded in the American cultural approach, using particularly American tactics as a writer, he was also a young writer in cognitive terms. Wisdom demonstrates a shift from the more absolute modes of thinking to more integrated and dialectical modes of thinking. We call Rogers a young writer in this first book because he used mostly Description, a bit of the Absolute and Relativistic thinking modes and very little integrated Patterned thinking.

This first book was rather different from Rogers's later books in that its ostensible goal was to organize the existing field of child treatments, whereas his later books created a new therapeutic approach. On the surface, this first book was more intellectual, abstract, and rational and less personal than his later books. It dealt with second-order issues in treatment, such as diagnostic categories or process elements in one therapy that appear to resemble process elements in another therapy. It was impersonal and passionless for the most part – supposedly meeting a scientific ideal in writing. Somewhere in all this intellectualization was Rogers's passion, however. As it emerged in our analyses, the issue lay in expressive therapies or the role of certain emotions in therapy. Here in the more impassioned presentation, more sophisticated thought tantalized the reader and a lifelong interest in expression or emotion was born for Rogers.

Although Rogers began to develop a position on emotion expression in his first book, his construction of the position of emotion in therapy built very slowly across his life. His scholarly position on emotion was very much embedded in his historical period. Though he was enormously creative and challenging to others in the intellectual fields related to psychology, he was only on the edge of the period in which emotional processes themselves were named and examined (see Magai & McFadden, 1995, for an historical review). His ability to delineate theoretically the processes of emotion was sadly restricted by limitations of his academic milieu. The suspected influences of emotion on adults' lives in his time were limited to the influence of infantile "conflict" or genetic "temperament."

"Unresolved infantile issues," as a concept, never proved fruitful for Rogers. For example, unresolved infantile "Oedipal" issues might influence a businessman's drive and competitiveness by having him repeatedly challenge authority as he had, in some sense, challenged his authoritarian father. This "unresolved issues" approach to emotionally salient material is derived from the psychoanalytic movements and remains a powerful analytic tool. However, Rogers largely eschewed the unresolved-issues approach in his own work. He preferred to work in the present with his clients, not in their past. He absolutely refused to be drawn into idealizing interpretative therapies, even though in his practice he used many techniques from these therapies.

The other approach to emotion in Rogers's time was the "temperament" one. For example, one might argue that an active, expressive person would enjoy work in open spaces and might like variety. This very general approach to emotion in temperament was acknowledged by Rogers in his earliest work cataloguing dysfunctions, but it never became an important issue. Overall there was very little appropriate theoretical context for his working model of emotion in therapy. Rogers is not often acknowledged as one of the heralds of emotional processes in psychological practice, but he deserves a few accolades. He was able to use his clients' emotion expression successfully for a long period without knowing precisely how to describe the process. In one of his last books, he wrote of his early experience: "A little later a social worker ... helped me to learn that the most effective approach [in therapy] was to listen for the feelings, the emotions, whose patterns could be discerned through the client's words" (Rogers, 1980, pp. 137–8). He had very little to work from, just hints from colleagues, and his own intuitions, when it came to prior theory or practice. Given the point at which he must have started, it is amazing that he was able to make the critical leaps for which he is famed. From listening to his clients in his professional practice, he developed subtle awareness of how emotion worked in general terms.

The early Rogers displayed more of certain aspects of his childhood emotional life and leanings than was at first suspected. Although he claimed to have left behind his parents' religious views and decided against the ministry as a career, he had by no means left behind the standard emotional beliefs of his childhood. It took a few more years before his own views began to emerge out of his work in the context of therapy and many more years before his views developed a more philosophic breadth. Rogers was not aware of how his own emotional experience influenced his expectations and practice and was unable to be completely specific about the emotional forces at work, although as he matured he became more aware and more specific on both issues.

Book 2

Turning to *Counseling and Psychotherapy* (1942), we can see Rogers as a person becoming more distinctly aware of emotion in his writing and in his theory, much more so than in *The Clinical Treatment of the Problem Child*. He was open to emotions of novelty – interest, surprise, fear – in himself, the therapist, as well as in his clients. He did not perceive them to be problematic. He viewed depressive emotions as playing a background kind of role. Positive feelings were seldom specifically named, but when they were, they were a focus point, as previously discussed. The singling out of happiness was probably related to his singular focus on the process of transformation in insight. It was also a drawing point for focusing on the "here and now," the moment in time when feelings are shared and loneliness is overcome. But this focus did not emerge clearly until late in his life.

On the other hand, hostile emotions were polarized for him in his personal life, in his therapeutic practice, and in his professional writing. By the time the second book was written, this emotional issue had crystallized. He was extremely sensitive to the problems that clients may have had with inhibited hostility; he himself was probably experiencing just such problems. He, like his clients, lacked subjective awareness of the power that mute hostility had in his own writing and thinking. Rogers appeared to have had an undeveloped anger function, and, as much of his early writing demonstrated, Rogers dreaded confronting hostility directly. As the biographical analysis demonstrated, Rogers had difficulty recognizing his own anger by his own admission. However, he did not have any difficulty in recognizing and attempting thereby to change the anger of others. He was in the personal position of having anger build until it was explosive and destructive. In his autobiographical material he seldom used hostile vocabulary. In his theoretical descriptions, he objected to confrontation. He avoided directiveness in his ideology, even though he was often directive in practice. He valued spontaneity. Yet he perceived anger in his clients quite readily.

The confrontational chapter in the second book on his own nondirective approach versus the directive approaches represented the intellectual difficulties that Rogers had to overcome when forced to work with hostility. This chapter could not follow through with a consistent argument, paralleling Rogers's inability to follow through with angry feelings. It attempted to cover the fact that it was confrontational, again paralleling Roger's shame and need to hide when he did become angry.

There was a clear strength in what Rogers was able to do theoretically at this point in his career with impassioned ideas, but there was also a clear weakness. In terms of the theoretical approach, saying that Rogers had an undeveloped sense of anger–rage motivation led us to anticipate that he would have difficulty focusing in confrontational situations. When writing, he would not value confrontation or argument, even in scientific debating circles. Taking yet another step, it might lead one to suspect that he would not value much of the work that experimental psychologists admire because so much of the kind of work requires a distancing, often confrontational, emotional stance.

Rogers's failure to present his own theory in a confrontational mode may also have been related to his general lack of success in circles of research psychology that strongly value the confrontational, linear approach. To such scientists Rogers's brand of motivation and thoughtfulness evoked contempt. Yet to writers and thinkers who valued more relativistic or integrated modes of thinking and more loops in their information, Rogers was an important colleague and theorist.

Book 3

Most of the early inhibited rage and its accompanying inhibitions in logic would show dramatic change across the years of Rogers's middle age. Comparing the chapters on the process of therapy from *Counseling and*

Psychotherapy to those from *On Becoming a Person* brings the changes into surprising relief. Even when the explicit therapeutic steps are outlined, the change is clear.

Both books list the steps to be traversed in psychotherapy and counseling. The earlier book lists the twelve steps in psychotherapy and counseling. In reviewing them it became clear that each step was aligned with its own set of emotions. To simplify, one began therapy with fearfulness; progressed to a point of releasing negative, largely hostile and conflictful feelings; moved to releasing more positive, but usually unspecified feelings; and then commenced with more joyful insight. Finally, changes in behavior were again experienced with some trepidation. In the expansion of this outline in several chapters, it was the release of hostile expression that Rogers explored the most extensively, both in terms of emotional elaboration (the number and density of different types of emotion) and in terms of dialectical and relativistic types of theoretical consideration.

The intellectual style of the early theory for the twelve steps was mixed in that there appeared to be a linear progression with a certain amount of mechanistic connection; the theory appeared absolute. On the other hand, Rogers referred continuously to the dialectical importance of opposing factors that led to change and growth and that interacted in bounded, creative ways. This aspect of the theory was more dialectical or integrated, but it was still static. Although there was evolution and it did not come from a simple, causal pattern, the type of opposition that moved the development was related only to positive and negative affect, one of which was more acceptable than the other. There was no recognition that both positive and negative emotion have valued aspects that are permanently necessary.

Thus, in the earlier writing, Rogers did not recognize the positive in the negative or the negative in the positive. Also his solutions progressed on a one-way time line, as did his therapy. It was clear to him that change would progress in a particular good, achieving direction. Rogers was still caught by the alternate release and capture of hostile forces, which ultimately tended to return him to the absolute, Platonic solutions.

The sense that one gathered of the younger Rogers as a person bound by hostility in subtle ways and struggling to resolve conflictful issues was largely dissipated in the later writings. The mature Rogers who spoke of client-centered therapy, the fully functioning person, and creativity, in short the Rogers who wrote about becoming, emerged late in middle age. But this mature voice was not merely repeating old messages. Rogers had been developing and changing.

The emotional emphasis had clearly changed from the earlier description of the process of psychotherapy to the later ones. Although Rogers remained sensitive to his clients' fears about feelings across the years, he was less directly concerned with releasing inhibited conflictful or hostile feelings in his later writings; in fact, he was less concerned with conflict in general. Instead, Rogers focused on the integration of what he earlier called insight and what he now called awareness of a "continuing changing flow of feelings" (1961, p. 157). "From construing experience in rigid ways which are perceived as external facts, the client moves toward developing changing, loosely held constructions of meaning in experience, constructions which are modifiable by each new experience" (1961, p. 157). "He has changed, but what seems most significant, he has become an integrated process of changingness" (1961, p. 158). Clearly not only the client, but also Rogers, had become more "an integrated process of changingness."

This development in Rogers's description of therapy was remarkable. Let us look at Rogers's depth of change another way. If instead of thinking of a client and middle-aged therapist, we visualize an adolescent and his parents, the change can be dramatized.

Adolescents are often confused about their emotions and thoughts. Their painful awareness leads to an obsession with controlling both thought and emotion as well as behavior. They intellectualize the most mundane events as well as the most glorified. They dramatize successes and failures equally. Faced with such an adolescent, sensitive Rogerian parents might respond to their child's "warring" approach and avoidance as expressions of fearfulness and hostility and to his intellectualizations as defenses against passions.

As the younger Rogers did, sensitive parents would provide a secure place for the fearful adolescent to approach them and release his hostility. They would perceive the hostility as confusion about growing up, adapting to social demands, coming under pressure at school. They would perceive it as something that needed to be "let out" so that the child could go on to positive feelings, having "worked it through." These very idealized parents would not take the adolescent's hostility personally nor would they respond in ways that would increase his shame and insecurity. Eventually they expect that their child would have more insight and perspective on his life, that he would spontaneously and joyfully "grow up."

There is no doubt that parents acting in much the way that the younger Rogers recommended would be unusually open to their child's conflicts and probably quite helpful parents. However, one can sense that these parents are themselves a little afraid of confrontation and separation, perhaps to the neglect of other issues. Further they expect themselves only to "hold fast" to their nondirective principles and insights, while the child changes. They do not expect to be directly involved in the changing themselves.

If parents perceive the changes in their family a bit more like the older, wiser Rogers, they are no longer centered on managing conflict. Instead, the older Rogerian parents attend to sharing their child's growing realization that the intense feelings (from excitement to depression) about sexuality, about entering into intimate partnerships, or about the workings of one's own mind are appropriate and wonderful. The parents' participation in this emerging sense of self will awaken in them a fresh and still wiser understanding of themselves and their experience as parents.

In the older Rogerian plot, the task of the parent is to share with, be a companion to, the adolescent as he or she leaves the externalization of ideas and feelings common to childhood and begins to give emotion and thought a more complex place in identity. The awareness of sharing and mutual exploration of the growth process, the awareness of looking at it from two personal sides and from many emotional angles, is the integrative and significant part of the therapeutic development. In Rogers's plot, the adolescent and parents who share this will emerge with a sense of being themselves that would be different from the sense of identity that would emerge in the path walked alone. From this shared "changingness" emerges "new cognitive maps."

This sharing of present, moment-in-time experiences in therapy is the essential mark of the late Rogerian. It strongly differentiates Rogers from other therapists of the same time period. For example, Erikson, who was almost contemporaneous with Rogers, is the guru of the adolescent identity crisis and is as delicately sensitive to emotion and attachment as Rogers. However, Erikson (1963) always portrayed the chaotic changes of adolescence as a personal crisis, embedded in a distant cultural milieu. The strong interpersonal aspects of identity processes are denied by Erikson as he separates intimacy and identity issues. He makes sharing an issue that can be solved only after personal identity is solid. For Rogers, in contrast, the self discovered in a shared experience was a different self than one established without intimacy.

While the mature Rogers seemed very wise and passionate about sharing feelings in the moment, there remained, nevertheless, an extremely telling omission. He gave very little attention to standard human problems. This was an increasingly pressing puzzle presented in Rogers's theoretical work as it emerged. Plots or narratives in his approach were absent. Rogers had no landscape that included particular types of relationships such as Oedipal ones. He had no crisis concerning achievement or identity or sexuality. Sexuality, itself, along with social relationships, had no particular place in his theory.

For Rogers, people were not in counseling because of a problem with other people or with life tasks. People were in therapy because they had a problem with the process of understanding and experiencing their own emotion. Clients were not functioning simply because their emotions had not been expressed productively. This is something of a simplification because Rogers had been clear all along, as he was in his first book, to state that some types of problems, while real enough, were not the province of the therapist or counselor. Problems that reflected poor health, a destructive family that one could not leave, and denigrating education were not problems for the psychologist.

Even so, the actual content of any encounter was never of clear interest to Rogers; he never focused on it or explained it to his readers. Take his case of "the angry adolescent." This young girl had been acting out in some delinquent fashion and was brought to Rogers. It is clear from the case material that there are several problems. Her mother was seriously ill and hospitalized. The adolescent was being treated in sexually suggestive ways by her stepfather. Rogers, as usual, focused on the importance of the girl recognizing her own feelings. When she recognized her own ambivalent feelings and therefore ambivalent behavior toward her stepfather, the case was resolved. In real life, such happy, simple endings are somewhat rare. Rogers does not address the complexities of incest, only the relationships between the girl's inhibited hostile feelings and acting out behavior. Even though Rogers made crystal clear the latter emotion – behavior relationship, the possibility that the threatening and real problems of incest or an ill, possibly dying mother could have created new emotional problems, and demanded new defenses continuously, did not occur in the case material. Rogers focused on the client–counselor relationship, not the client–family relationships, and he definitely avoided the content of the case.

Rogers's clients clearly did not experience sorrow to have a fuller sense of life and death, anger to propel achievement, happiness to encourage a child's nearness, or fear to make real the holocaust. Roger's clients experienced emotion to exist fully – just to exist. The visible danger was not the problem, rather it was nothingness, no feelings at all. Nothingness was the danger addressed by psychology; other professions could take on the concrete problems.

At some level, Rogers's desire for and "prizing of" real feelings, experiences, and an actualized self stated the problem most clearly. In modern psychoanalytic views (Kohut, 1971; Miller, 1981; Winnicott, 1964), the vacillation between grandiosity and shame or contempt begins to be resolved only when one recognizes that one's inner self has not actually been accepted, or "prized" as Rogers put it. This recognition is accompanied by feelings of loss over the illusionary life one imagined one lived and the kind of sadness or mourning that is distinct from depression.

What kind of person finds mutual sharing of emotional experiences the highpoint of existence? What kind of feelings and thoughts propel desire to merge the ideal and the real self? What feelings or lack of feelings propel a person to spend his entire life searching for "realness" in life and relationships? Rogers began to touch on the issue of the inner self through the process of prizing emotion. But the singleness of emotion begets a one-sidedness in the fusion experience. Here, also, his ultimate inability to resolve the prizing dilemma emerges. Rogers described only pleasurable sharing of emotional experiences. This singleness of emotion is matched by a search for a fusion of the ideal and the real self. The range of sharing in human emotions can obviously include many painful and rejecting feelings, just as the sense of self can contain many unsought aspects of personality. Rogers was still trying to recover an imaginary perfect relationship even though he understood that the road to this actually imperfect relationship was fraught with many difficult emotions.

Rogers was living in his time problems that would not be clearly identified by psychology for many years to come. Yet his own, unacknowledged, suffering led him to propose solutions to emotional problems that were no doubt germane to many people of his generation. For many of his solutions, he owed his emotional sensitivity.

As usual, the most intellectualized forms of Rogers's concerns about self emerged in his research. There was always a curious pioneer spirit about Rogers; he was always looking to growth, sensation, insight, creativity – always heading toward some idealized way of being and relating that took him above the mundane terrain of everyday problems and encounters. It seemed rather abstract and unworldly and highly intellectual, even though it was concerned with earthy feelings. Just how earthy are these feelings? They were rather ethereal in their being experienced for themselves rather than as part of a narrative. Nevertheless, and by a circuitous route, Rogers's research dilemmas even more than his therapy practice led him to the central problem of being.

Rogers's interweaving of anger, joy, and shame provided a unique lens through which he did his work. With respect to his anger and shame, Rogers was always using his writing and his research to "prove" something or define something. At first he used the component factor method to prove that the most effective way to improve children's lots in life was to work on family and social relationships. Most of the other factors were not easily susceptible to improvement or change. He established at the beginning that his pursuits in psychology were worthy of his ambitions. However, emotionally, he was not at home here. Emotionally he was off investigating the expression of inhibited and forbidden hostile feelings. The solving of this problem kept leading him to enjoyment and spontaneous bliss.

In *Counseling and Psychotherapy*, he proved, in an excruciatingly inadequate manner, that expressing inhibited and forbidden conflictful feelings is good therapy. Again he was not at home emotionally in the barren land of defending expression with antagonistic research. Even more than before, he was deeply involved in understanding how to control and encourage passionate experiences. And he was better able to insert the profits of joyfulness – in insight.

In his later writings, he proved that client-centered therapy, which strives for the continued realization of expression in feelings, brought one closer to merging real identity and ideal identity. At last the research and the expressive therapy began to find a common emotional home. He finally was able to merge the real and ideal self in the actualized self. This "real" self was about as close to undesirable emotions as Rogers came.

In a frontier, eyes-on-the-horizon type of culture such as has existed in the United States, the notion of becoming in the sense that Rogers used it in *On Becoming a Person*, combined with the concept of the prized and ideal self, presented a seductive package for Americans. Rogers, of course, was embedded in the midwestern, Protestant ethic culture of the United States and was terribly vulnerable to the poisonous as well as to the sustaining aspects of that culture.

The striving for an ideal self, while an innocent enough idea in an upwardly mobile society, has long been held up in European psychoanalytic circles as a potential example of a false self. The ideal self can be a defense against the experience of a bad, split-off, undesired worst self. This idea of a false self has been hard for Americans to accept. In the American manner of denying the shadow side of idealism, Rogers also fell into facing only the positive.

Americans have felt more comfortable with Erikson's description of the immigrant identity. Here one moves from an unexamined, immature early self to a culturally mobile, peer intimate, generative self. Neither the early self nor the later self were truer or more ideal than the other; they were just different steps on the path to maturity. The dread for the Eriksonian is abandoning or denying the reality of the search and constructing a mature self; one does not dread blocks on the road or moments of indecision.

Even though Rogers appears to have ignored most demons in his own life and theories, he had the ability to listen sensitively to the actual words and, in addition, the unstated feelings of people who come for help in therapy. His lack of attention to the negative in his ideas did not seem to extend to his behavior. His skill was likely to have developed in a more balanced, less idealistic manner. There is a great deal that is punishing about practicing the therapeutic professions. For hours, the therapist is alone with desperate, unforgiving, almost hopeless people. He or she must listen to their grandiose and frightening histories, their nasty perversions and petty or great cruelties, and their inadequacies and furies and empathize with their furies, rejoice with their achievements, and offer forgiveness when disaster strikes. This is not the most pleasant or easy of occupations. And yet Rogers gravitated to this passionate profession.

For Rogers, both the acknowledged and the unacknowledged emotions played roles in his skills. The balance of dark and light, known and unknown, also provided the paradoxes and devotions of his career. One must not paint an overly bleak picture of Rogers or any other therapist, for that matter. He allowed his feelings to express themselves in his pursuit of nature and in reading nature-oriented, sentimental stories. He and his siblings teased each other, so some amount of contempt must have been tolerated. But he obviously grew up quite lopsided – sensitive to others' feelings and his own to some extent, easily shamed, conforming, intellectualized, desperate to continue proving himself but not sure who he was or what he was worth, inhibited, and occasionally hotheaded. For various reasons, he needed to be the person who achieved the control of feelings. He proved his own worth by controlling feelings, his own and others. Many of these qualities appeared to serve him well, others not so well, but the entire network propelled him toward his unique career.

In issues of research and in clinical practice, Rogers did achieve a synthesis late in life. From the vantage point of several decades, we may see untraversed areas in Rogers's own experience. Some of these untraversed fields are visible only in light of more recent work in psychology and philosophy. The importance of the negative emotions was only slightly visible to Rogers; he usually denied the destructive sides of human nature. Having denied or suppressed the losses, loneliness, and authoritarian-derived shame in his own childhood and life, he never knowingly mourned their reality.

Rogers turned a blind eye to the dark side of his roots while keeping his good eye on the optimistic horizon. He perceived that his road to becoming a real person was through the moment-to-moment experience of feeling and thought working together, and he had terrific insight for the emotionally connected rather than intellectually directed environment that would foster such sensations. This insight occurred in a historical time when emphasis was – is – primarily on the opposite. It was an achievement of and longing for better balance in visible forces.

8 Cartesian Logic and Anger, Fear
Albert Ellis

Like stoicism, a school of philosophy which originated some twenty-five hundred years ago, RET holds that there are virtually no legitimate reasons for people to make themselves terribly *upset, hysterical,* or *emotionally disturbed,* no matter what kind of psychological or verbal stimuli are impinging on them. It encourages them to feel strong appropriate emotions – such as *sorrow, regret, displeasure, annoyance,* rebellion, and determination to change unpleasant social conditions. But it holds that when they experience certain self-defeating and inappropriate emotions – such as *guilt, depression, rage,* or feelings of worthlessness – they are adding an unverifiable, magical hypothesis (that things *ought* or *must* be different) to their empirically based view (that certain things and acts are reprehensible or inefficient and that something would better be done about changing them [italics added].

Albert Ellis (1973, p. 56)

As we began in the previous section on Rogers with a single paragraph, we can begin with a single paragraph to orient ourselves to Ellis's ideoaffective positions in his theoretical work as well. A little appreciated facet of personality is that people express their personality in everything they do. The way a person moves his face or body, the words he or she chooses, the context in which the expressions occur – these are all aspects of personality. Therefore, even a single statement can reveal essential features of a person.

It should come as no surprise that a well-chosen paragraph could provide almost as much information about the personality of the writer as a standard personality test, sometimes more. The standard test gives scores to indicate how much we are like each other on a few dimensions that the majority of people share. Such a standard task actually makes a major mistake if the purpose is to understand individual differences and processes. The key lies more in unique features or in how the features are organized, less on variations in shared features or traits considered singly. Unique features will never show up on standard tests because they simply are not there. So, there are times when the unique production of the individual tells more about personality than a standardized test. In this very typical quote from Ellis at about age 60, the core emotional modes and the principle mode of thought that he uniquely employed quickly emerge, if we know how to access them. The principle, unique feature in Ellis's writing here and, in most examples, was the abundance of emotional terms. Unlike Rogers and Perls, who used emotional words relatively sparingly, Ellis's use of emotional words was dramatic and in multiples – sorrow, regret, displeasure, annoyance or guilt, depression, rage or upset, hysterical, emotionally disturbed. He bombarded the reader with emotional language even as he argued for moderation in emotionality. He was both creating an exaggerated emotional environment and urging control of exaggeration. There was a seesaw of emotionality – high, low, high, low.

This paragraph tells us that Ellis perceived a great danger that emotions could overwhelm people, presumably both himself and his patients. The overwhelming emotions were many for Ellis: guilt, depression, rage, and feelings of worthlessness, as well as terribly upset ("terrible" is itself an emotional derivative from the word "terror," something that would dominate Ellis's thoughts and writing), hysterical, and, finally, emotionally disturbed. These overwhelming emotions were to be managed through systematic distancing and rational analysis.

Ellis presented a rich emotional landscape with variation in types of emotion and degrees of emotion. Further, he was not as concerned here with the contrast between positive and negative emotions (as was Rogers) as he was with the "appropriate" and "inappropriate" negative ones. Ellis held emotions at a distance and was critical, even contemptuous, of many emotions. For Ellis, good and bad emotions are not just feeling good and bad. Emotions have social values.

As we will see with further examination, Ellis was quite dictatorial about his dichotomy of emotions. This attitude is further evidence that his views of emotions were strongly held values. It was intuitively obvious to him and intuitively logical. He would no more question his judgments of emotion than he would question whether water is wet, whether red is a color, or whether time passes. He appeared to accept as part of the definition of guilt, rage, and so forth that they are inappropriate, just as other emotions are appropriate and even socially useful (i.e., rebellion – though it is definitely unusual to conceive of rebellion as a common emotion).

Ellis's abundant use of emotional terms persuades us that he was highly sensitive, even hypersensitive, to emotion cues just as Rogers was hypersensitive to hostility. Given the abundance of emotion he projects and basing our predictions on previous studies of emotion and cognition, we ordinarily would expect an abundance of complex thought as well. Is it just that simple, or will we find that the type of emotion, the context of emotion, and the dynamic relations among emotions are of equal importance? An examination of Ellis's work allows us to test and expand our ideas.

Even though particular emotions such as anger or fear do not stand alone in the exemplary paragraph, there are hints of the primacy of anger or contempt and fear in the structure of the writing. Oppositional and dualistic propositions occur. Positions needing defense, as well as attack, were used as examples – verifiable versus nonverifiable, appropriate versus inappropriate. Even the paragraph construction in the example was oppositional. The first sentence expressed a negating thought ("*no* legitimate reasons"), the second a supportive thought ("*encourages* . . . appropriate emotions"), and the third another negating thought ("experience *self-defeating* emotions"). This argumentative – back and forth between negation and support – mode of thought will occupy much of our attention in this chapter. It brings forward a form of ideoaffective process that relies on oppositional affects such as anger, fear, and contempt to fuel and focus it. It also suggests a style of writing that was almost disconnected in its choppy opposition, its approaches, and its avoidances.

The logic or style of thought in the writing in the introductory paragraph is absolute and linear – what is often called "strong" writing. In this writing the truth is there to be uncovered and verified. There is truth and untruth, verification versus magic. There is no wish for, or expectation of, surprise or spontaneity or development, as there is in Rogers's writing, and no evidence of exciting changes as there is in Perls's writing. The inappropriate emotions such as guilt or rage, mentioned by Ellis, led to feelings of worthlessness in contrast to "verifiable" and "efficient" feelings such as rebellion or determination. The perceived truth was so clear to Ellis, as it is to anyone who argues in this style, that it was unlikely he would propose relativistic alternatives or consider a dialectical system in which emotion and rationality dynamically evolve to form new patterns. Given the intuitively obvious nature of his propositions, it also was unlikely that Ellis would be driven to do empirical research that would verify the proposals. There was simply not enough doubt expressed in any form.

To some extent, Ellis may have relied upon perceptual and concrete logical processes rather than the more formal absolute logic in his writing. Sometimes, he just *saw* things as obvious and did not work through the solution with propositions and proofs. We will find in later analyses that he often was contemptuous of people who did not see what he saw. This contempt was not expressed directly, but could be seen in his derisive style of taunting names, for example. Although the linear writer appears to be extremely rational in the cause-and-effect simple propositions and proofs that he chooses, he relies upon his own expert logic as "proof" and believes that his reasoning about a case takes the place of evidence. Ellis relied on this "strong," debating style.

From this first glimpse of the intellectual mode in which Ellis expressed his working theory, we can hypothesize that Ellis wanted control and predictability of emotion. We infer this desire from both the content and the style. He was working with a style that demonstrated strength and single-mindedness. He expected to meet opposition in his own thinking, as well as in other people and the norms of society. He expected other people to have competing emotional systems – the inappropriate and the appropriate. These systems do not work together, but rather one replaces the other when the wrong one is exposed; this is typical of linear, absolute or even mechanistic thinking styles in which correct solutions are discovered and replace incorrect ones. Some implied hostile (through the oppositional challenge) emotions were used elegantly – both in construction and logic. Ellis used oppositional, propositional logic to express himself, urged empirical tests, but did not present evidence around these issues. Usually this would also mean that he avoided or defended against fear or surprise, the emotions marking an appreciation of novelty, but his use of multiple affects as well as the ideational content with its advocacy of rebellion suggests some playing with riskiness and daring.

Stated Philosophy

Ellis's stated philosophy late in his life was very much in line with the interpretation of this work as it was illustrated in the emotional and cognitive bits of the opening paragraph. Ellis acknowledged the Stoic philosophy as his ideal model. Certainly, the one aspect of Stoicism that

Ellis admired and used constantly is its reliance on reason to provide a calm outlook and to certify self-worth. Although numerous philosophies exhort people to avoid excess to avoid anxiety, Stoicism relies upon the direct perception of logical processes to provide this tranquility more than any other philosophy.

There is a traditional, relevant distinction between the definitions of Stoic and the more Rogerian and Perlsian Epicurean philosophies. This brief quote from the *Encyclopedia Britannica* eloquently speaks to the distinction: "The walls of the Stoic's city are those of the world, and its law is that of reason; the limits of the Epicurean's city are those of a garden, and the law is that of friendship. Though this garden can also reach the boundaries of earth, its center is always a man." The distinction between the laws of friendship and the laws of logic will prove most relevant to understanding Ellis's work. As we will see, this dichotomy played itself out in two distinct threads of Ellis's life work in his writing: books on sexuality and books on Rational Emotive Therapy.

Expectations for Life's Work from Socioemotional Development

When looking at the family picture of Ellis's early years, one notes immediately the ambivalence of attachment, as the study of Ellis's attachments showed (see Chapter 4). This detachment is no doubt related to his adult preference for the Stoic over the Epicurean philosophy. The bonds of friendship or of any relationship were of dubious value. But in many respects Ellis's early story is less captured by mother–child attachment themes more captured by the Freudian Oedipal story. His interest in and involvement with sexual issues led us to this metaphor. The Oedipal story is a heterosexual family and community tale of fear, distrust, neglect, and tragedy, a story in which attachment is an often neglected underlying theme.

When told that their son would be fatal to them, Oedipus's parents sent the child away from them to grow up in ignoble circumstances. There were no secret side trips to admire him and no requests for reports with any personal detail. There were no special gifts or other signs to young Oedipus that would give him a clue about the personal qualities of his parents. The fear that close attachment might lead to tragedy – or at least that preventing close attachment would prevent tragedy – is significant for the story. If either parent had observed the child Oedipus, knew what he looked like, or understood his personality, no part of the tragic story could have emerged. One cannot ignorantly kill the father one knows or marry the mother one would recognize anywhere. The parents would have recognized him at the critical junctures, or he might have suspected them.

In the Oedipal story, Freud focused on the fact that Oedipus replaces his father in his family and kingdom, and that fact is significant in Ellis's life as well. However, Freud ignored the initial neglect necessary for creating the Oedipal tragedy and in so doing diminished the problem of care and the development of attachment. In the Freudian version, the "feminine" concern with care and development is seldom noted, in contrast to the well-analyzed, "masculine" issues of power and sexual attraction. It is still a good metaphor for masculine power or control and sexual themes, however. In that respect it is relevant to Ellis.

The Oedipal story arose initially in connection with our wondering why Ellis was so fascinated in his early professional writing with sexual behavior. (The core of this insight came from conversation with D. Ogilvie, PhD.) In the Freudian script, the interest of the Oedipal child in uncovering matters sexual is now legendary, if debatable. However irrelevant Oedipal conflict is in some families, it is part of Ellis's family story. He unfortunately "won" the father–son contest; he got possession of his mother and siblings. He was duly contemptuous of his "prize" in his autobiography, but he never abandoned his family – of course, neither did Oedipus.

Ellis, while still young, believed himself the chief care-taking male to his family when his parents separated. According to Ellis's account, his mother was stereotypically feminine in her intrusive and histrionic manner. Unlike the stereotype of the mother, however, she does not appear to have devoted herself to her children, behaving more like a lonesome child herself. Similarly, Ellis's father exaggerated one version of masculinity of the time. He seems to have been a womanizer and devoted to his business, probably a workaholic, as Ellis would also be. He had little interest in his children, only to take them on very infrequent excursions. Together the parents presented a strong sexual dichotomy in emotional styles, but both seem to have been relatively neglecting and to have had difficulty managing their caring behaviors.

Ellis wrote that his father was known for his uncontrolled rages, and his mother, for her inability to stop talking. Both parents were uncontrolled in Ellis's eyes, a lack that appeared to Ellis to be an emotional problem, though it has obvious cognitive and practical difficulties as well. His characterization of his mother's behavior leads one to suspect a degree of manic and depressive episodes, a general inability to solve family or childrearing problems and yet to display an outgoing charm and "acting" ability. Ellis would be repeatedly drawn to women with these characteristics of charm and neglect. His even briefer description of his father in his autobiography, and later when he wrote about his own need to control anger, presented a picture of an angry, distant person, a person who fled from an unmanageable family scene. And yet he presented a desirable, if not kingly (per Oedipus), image of self-sufficiency with his business success and separate apartment and woman friends.

Not only did Ellis grow up with these ambivalences and dichotomies between his parents, but one suspects, even though he did not mention it, that there were broader social problems as well. The community might have looked askance at the family, and Ellis may have felt some shame at the critical glances. He reported his own childish efforts to keep his siblings in school, on time, and fed. Obviously, he was sensitive to social pressures for appropriate behavior, even if his parents were unable to cope. His later rebellion against ordinary family values seems to reflect an anger against the shame and neglect that led to his too-early responsibilities and the distress at being abandoned to cope with them.

Not only is the Oedipal story related to attachment and, therefore, to emotional preferences, but it has also been related to logical styles by postmodern writers of the twentieth century. For example, feminist theories have related the Oedipal themes to problems in twentieth century scientific thinking. In this interpretation, metaphorical "mother" nature is the primitive and seductive challenge to the scientific man. The modern scientist identifies with rational "fathers" and conquers nature with rational tools, each scientist replacing his scientific mentors (fathers), while also being seduced by the exciting chaos in "primitive" (mother) nature. Science masters nature and is, at heart, both seduced by and contemptuous of its possible virtues. At a slightly deeper level, scientists are afraid of mother nature – this is why the mastering is so imperative. It becomes important to conquer nature within oneself as well as without. To lose the battle is to give way to nature, to become emotional, intuitive, and, above all, irrational. There is no sense of partnership with nature just as Oedipus has no sense of partnership with his parents or sexual peers. (See Labouvie-Vief, 1994; Elshtain, 1981.) Using this postmodern interpretation of scientific thought, one would form the opinion that Ellis might defend himself against attractive, emotional, and irrational people and thoughts, even though they are attractive. The weapons would be the traditional linear and absolutely rational system, the same ones that mechanistic science relies on.

Although psychological threats and defenses, such as the Oedipal, are always interesting and helpful, it is important not to neglect the obvious in learning to appreciate Ellis's emotional biases and consequent cognitive style. In Ellis's early life, he suffered from several direct and largely uncontrollable physical threats that could have been directly related to his concern with emotional control. In Chapter 4, we pointed out that there were many risks in his young life, but his repeated and serious medical problems with surgeries and long hospitalizations, during which periods he seldom saw his family, were central. In an apocryphal childhood scene, Ellis reported being praised by his doctors for his scientific or intelligent attitude while his abdomen was being surgically probed and pus was coming out. This stoical little boy controlled his fears with a rational attitude and was praised for this by authoritative and, hopefully, caring adults. Ellis reported this scene as an example of his early rationality and lack of anxiety, but it can easily be turned around and might as well be a shadow scene of extreme terror. In either case, paradoxical as it seems, threats *and* rational control form a repeating scene for Albert Ellis. This paradox leads us to Ellis's ideoaffective processes.

Intimacy and Emotionality Emerge as Problem Areas

When we began examining Rogers's writing, we proposed three straightforward hypotheses about emotion influencing intellectual behavior. First, we proposed that blocked or singular emotional investment in certain ideas leads to blocked or singular intellectual examination of those same issues. In very concrete terms, when you do not know much about what you feel, you do not know much about what you think either. In Rogers's case, for example, we found that his singular elaboration of intimacy with the singular affect of happiness led to the one-sided drive to increase the utopian moment-in-time communion of the therapist and his client. This consequence is not necessarily negative; however, if it is narrow, it is narrow because the use of happiness as a singular emotion also was associated with a singular type of thinking – a holistic, nonlinear one. In Ellis's case, a focus on the terror-ible or on fear may also lead to a single logical stance.

Blocked affects, such as Rogers's blocking of anger, led to serious flaws in the logic of issues about which he was clearly angry. Rogers would begin to use a linear logic when angry, but fail to carry through, blocking his own argument, just as he blocked his anger expression. Since Ellis has consciously blocked several of the major emotional systems, claiming that feelings such as panic or guilt are irrational, we can anticipate that his intellectual commitment to solving some emotional issues will be similarly blocked. It is also likely that he blocks some emotions that he is not consciously aware of. Later, we will propose that contempt operates in this manner, as a blocked and silent emotion for Ellis.

Second, we proposed that the elaboration of certain ideas with a wide variety of emotions leads to commitment to explore those ideas and represents a person's best intellectual and creative efforts. In Rogers's case, once again, the elaboration of play therapy with many emotions indicated an abiding interest in solving the riddles of an expressive therapy, an area in which he developed over his lifetime. Here, Ellis will present a significant challenge to our earlier proposition. Ellis had a high density of emotion referents – about emotion – in much of his writing and speech, as shown in the opening quote; however, these referents are used in blocks, not separately. The complexity provided by multiple emotions comes from their differentiation and their organization, not their sheer numbers. Ellis had many emotional referents, but he did not differentiate them, nor are they differentially organized according to themes. His cognitive complexity was thereby significantly limited. When there is a high rate of emotionality that is not focused or differentiated, a second or corollary proposal has to be formed to deal with this more complex situation. Magnified, undifferentiated emotions act much as blocked emotions. Both magnification and minimization constrain intellectual work. Other clinicians have noted that when emotional expression is magnified, it can be used to block anxiety. What may look, at first glance, like an expression of feelings may actually be a mechanism to block feelings. Therefore, we will amend the second proposal to say that multiple emotions only when differentiated and organized with differing themes will lead to complex cognitive development.

Third, we proposed that changes in emotional experiences lead to or are interrelated with intellectual changes and changes in the issues that require commitment. In Rogers's case, his late-life efforts to develop processes related to anger were related to continuing changes in his intellectual accomplishments. There were epochs of significant emotional confrontation with developmental stages emerging. With Ellis, there is again a challenge to the original simple proposal that there is continuous development in a stagelike manner. By middle age, Ellis's ideoaffective structure operated in a self-sustaining, closed system. Apparently the closed system developed here makes late adult developmental change highly unlikely. A system that does not have sufficient randomness and openness is resistant to developmental change. Thus, much of this chapter will be devoted to the accumulative ideoaffective posture. In this chapter, we will emphasize this new idea. Not every adult, even one who contributes greatly to society, continues to develop cognitively or emotionally across the lifespan.

The Singular Emotion of Fear: Continuity Across a Life and Across Themes

Fear is detected as a motivator at the very beginning of Ellis's psychological career. Ellis's first article (1950) on psychoanalysis, published in the *Genetic Psychology Monographs*, was an essay on "dangers." The article has twenty-three sections, nineteen of which begin with "The danger of." These dangers include, for example, "The danger of psychanalytic theoretical biases," "The danger of psychoanalytic topologies," "The danger of psychoanalytic developmental theories," and "The danger of psychoanalytic concepts of research." Ellis was attracted to writing about psychoanalysis not because it was annoying, surprising, interesting, or amusing, but because it was dangerous. Guarding against dangers in all forms, he included the intellectual and clinical dangers of analysis at the juncture of his life when he was learning about analysis and was not far from being in analysis.

Even though the overall motivation is danger, the general topic Ellis addressed was that of science in relation to psychoanalysis. His early work appears to be a nice example of the feminist argument with its emphasis on the danger of nature, even human nature, and the use of scientific objectivity to counter the danger. But Ellis's approach was unusual. He argued that objectivity is dubious for the person who conforms to society:

> Another set of biases . . . is that represented by vested interests which . . . prejudice their therapeutic and public formulations. Because he usually has a wife and family, the analyst must watch his step when he speaks or writes about marital and family affairs. . . . Because he wishes to publish his papers in regular psychoanalytic journals, he must to some extent conform to the philosophies of these journals. . . . Because he comes from a certain socio-economic class in his society, he may tend to look upon

his patients and evaluate them in terms of the standards of this particular class . . . *the more he heeds this pressure to conform, the less scientist is he.* [italics added] (Ellis, 1950, p. 166).

Ellis pinned the lack of scientific objectivity on analysts' social conformity. For Ellis, the problem was one of being hemmed in by potential disapproval. There was a dread contained in his beliefs, the dread that the avoidance of disapproval in relationships – family, marital, socioeconomic, or even professional – would lead to nonscientific irrationality. Danger was everywhere. The analyst with a spouse cannot speak truthfully about marriage. The analyst connected to a particular journal cannot with authenticity speak about the material he will publish. For Ellis, there was a fearful, dangerous threat in human connection. Relationships and commitments were dangerous and bred irrationality. Giving way to danger, conforming, was contemptuous.

Ellis's earliest writings on psychological theory indicate that the thoughts contained in the opening quote were pervasive. This is particularly true in his books on sexuality, but as the preceding quote shows, it is not restricted to the books on sexuality. The focus on sex merely highlights the threat that intimate relationships had for Ellis.

This opening article on psychoanalysis laid a stylistic groundwork for much of Ellis's writing that was extended in longer texts. *How to Live with a Neurotic – at Home and at Work* (1957) is one of Ellis's first books that was related to his psychological theory. He had published a book on advice about dating and sexual behavior or attitudes, which we will attend to later, and had written several manuscripts, both fictional and nonfictional, earlier but did not find a publisher. This first book on therapy was for a general reader. It did what the title promised and gave information about treating or surviving neurotic people. In this first popular book, we will find pieces of Ellis's Rational Emotive Theory as it came to be known later.

Ellis defined a neurotic person as one who is governed by unreasonable and exaggerated emotion, emotions such as fear, anxiety, or depression. The content of a neurotic person's thought or behavior was of little or no interest to him. "Thus, if you say, 'I want A to love me very much,' and A does not love you, you can make yourself appropriately sad, sorrowful, regretful, displeased, unhappy, or even miserable. But if you say 'I *must* have A love me; I find it *awful* if she or he doesn't . . . ' you make yourself depressed, anxious, despairing, self-downing, and possibly suicidal." (Ellis, 1957, pp. xvii–xviii), It was not the need for love that Ellis acknowledged (the content of the complaint) but the emotions created in this or any situation. Ellis focused on the control of emotional reaction in this book, setting an unchanging pattern that can be seen in all his books.

One has to admire the initial control that this sidestepping of content relevant to relationships gave Ellis. His childhood was one in which neglect rather than care was prominent and in which threat rather than security held rein. He told an amazing story of discovering a "solution" to these problems at the age of seven. He realized, he wrote, that he could decide not to feel what he did not want to feel. This conviction that he could control his own feelings was an epiphany. The simple idea that a thought process is concretely something to perceive and to have exist in a stable and predictable way is peculiar to the concrete thinking of school children (e.g., Elkind, 1969). When children form an explanation for some puzzling event, they tend to ignore contrary evidence or to recast it to fit the "elegant" solution. What they do not originally know is that their solution is one of many and that it may be suited only to a singular situation. Children do not set up experimental designs to test alternatives and to cover an entire field of possibilities. Of course, the thought control solution often does work efficiently – it is not entirely untrue. And given Ellis's childhood circumstances, it is a near miracle that he discovered it. That it enabled him to be kind as well as collected was the greatest good fortune. That it became one of his most important beliefs, his life story, the narrative of his success, is less then surprising.

At the beginning of *How to Live with a Neurotic*, Ellis briefly presented a very decent sketch of neurotic defense mechanisms from the standard psychological literature. He described neurotic people as torturing themselves with their thoughts and behavior. He advised their relatives and work comrades to give them clear directives, to praise them when praiseworthy, to ignore their failings, and to help them plan to be successful at their tasks. When the neurotic person acts unreasonably, Ellis urged the relatives and colleagues to consider that they *are neurotic*. This consideration was supposed to provide a rational distance that preserved those of us who are not neurotic from the contagion of irrational emotional reactions. One can be annoyed or frustrated or even sorry about neurotic behavior, but having accepted that it exists, one plans around it in some rational manner. This plan might include the manipulation of the targeted neurotic person, but it is in their best interest apparently. Considered in the light of Ellis's own neurotic family, this description is probably how he maintained emotional distance.

When we start to take a close look at emotional expression in *How to Live with a Neurotic*, the first thing that we note, as usual with Ellis, is the sheer mass of different emotional referents used. Ellis used more emotional words relative to other types of words in this book than any other professional author we have examined. One might be tempted to conclude the obvious: that he was a very open hearted, expressive person. However, he noted in his autobiography that his personal expression of emotion at this time in his life was stilted. The magnification of emotion in his writing was the opposite of exuberant expression in his relationships. Even though he perceived an onslaught of emotion in his world, he did not contribute much emotionally, as far as he knew.

Although the overall rate of emotionality in the writing is enormous, not all emotions are used extensively. Given Ellis's history, our preview from the opening quote, and the initial article using "danger" as a key, we are not surprised to find the most frequent emotional referent, one and one half times more frequent than any other emotion, is to fear. Ellis used many different words to connote fear, including fear, anxious, worry, terrify, horrify, panic, phobic, fright.

Not only was fear mentioned very frequently in *How to Live with a Neurotic*, it also applied to diverse contexts indicating its centrality to Ellis's thinking. Fear is a major organizing feature in his writing. He wrote, "Most neurosis seems to consist of irrational or exaggerated fear" (1957, p. 73). Then he described two types of fear. "We often rear our children to think that getting love or approval has enormous value and that striving for self-acceptance has less virtue" (1957, p. 74). The social disapproval is not a minor inconvenience, but is "terrible, horrible, awful" when considered "irrationally" (1957, p. 75). On the one hand, Ellis used fear in the most common way, to describe neurotics' unreasonable fears and phobias of death, people, illness, and so forth. "People commonly fear physical injury and social disapproval" (1957, p. 73). But Ellis also used fear when he might have used words referring to embarrassment or shame. When he described the neurotic's fear of failure, he might have said that the neurotic person tries to avoid embarrassment. But he used fear again. We noticed earlier that he even found ordinary conforming behavior such as marriage to be "dangerous," a rather unusual construction again demonstrating that fears are the common denominators in a great many categories.

It is not actually unusual that Ellis should have used fear in both the social failure sense and the concrete physical sense. There is a long history in psychology of studying people's fears. One of the more

interesting results of these studies is the knowledge that has accumulated about how the content of fearful experiences tends to change with
age. There is a regular progression from early childish fears of animals
and the dark to older children's fears of physical attack, illness, and
death and finally to adolescent's fears arising from social occasions –
fears of crowds, of loneliness, of ridicule. Whereas young children will
tell their most frightening stories about monsters, adolescents will tell
their most frightening stories about being the focus of attention. These
developmental changes in the content of fearful stories are also seen
in phobias and pathological fear reactions (see Haviland, 1991). The
developmental history of fearful stories suggests that Ellis had a full
repertoire of both physical and social fears and that he had continued
to accumulate new scenes within his fear repertoire as he grew.

Fear is, of course, the most toxic of emotional states. In the short run,
it requires a great expenditure of energy and rapid cognitive processing.
Fear allows one to dodge dangerous objects quickly, to hear the slightest
noise, to see movement in the near dark, to run faster than imagined,
and to move heavy objects. But in the long run, chronic fear leads to
stress, apathy, and illness. Ellis is not wrong about the need to guard
against chronic fear, but he is hypersensitive to cues to the point of
being anxious, even phobic, and this comes across in his writing.

People with an early and persistent negative history with any particular emotion are liable to lack sensible moderation including intellectual
moderation in the context of that emotion. Just as Rogers with his history
of blocked anger had difficulty with modulating anger, and Perls with
his history of shame had difficulty moderating his "topdog, underdog"
complex, Ellis probably would have difficulty with fear modulation.
People needing to block an emotion such as fear or anger have learned
to be hypersensitive to minor events that just might evoke the dreaded
emotion. Because of this vulnerability, they are liable to block versions
of the emotional experience that are not lethal and that might even be
beneficial. Ellis would need, of course, to control terror, but even relatively positive forms of the novelty emotions such as surprise, awe, or
wonder might often be blocked, if he were overly sensitive. Ellis's capacity for being charmed by the mysterious or for playing with surprise
might be undeveloped, and his tolerance for change inhibited.

Multiple Emotions – A Second View

Occasionally, especially at the beginning of chapters, Ellis grouped
emotions providing sets of feelings rather than single emotions. One

frequently used set referred to the emotions he freely associated with regret: (a) sorry, frustrated; (b) sorry, regret, annoyed, displeased, sad; (c) sorry, annoyed, sad, irritated, frustrated; (d) sorrow, regret, frustration. Another set was more associated with depression: (a) depressed, anxious, self-hating; (b) depressed, guilty, anxious; (c) depressed, hurt, hostile, anxious. But the most frequent sets were associated with fears (1) horrified, terrified, and angry or (2) anxiety, rage, guilt, and depression. Such a set of emotions defines neurosis: "we usually label as 'neurotic' those whose feelings seem so inappropriate and whose behavior appears so ineffective or disruptive that they often feel anxious, depressed, hurt, or hostile" (Ellis, 1957, p. 1). But when one has a more rational "belief, and really believed nothing more than this, she would tend to feel quite sorry, annoyed, sad, irritated and frustrated – but hardly hurt and depressed" (Elllis, 1957, p. 1). Ellis ran the emotional possibilities together, not stopping to think of them independently. It was not sufficient to be only anxious; a whole cascade of emotion came along with it or almost any other emotion.

Another example of emotion sets occurs in Ellis's description of a couple with a neurotic son, "Your problem basically consists of changing the ... referents, ... so that whenever you think of ... your son's continued neurotic behavior, you will feel appropriately sorry, sad, regretful, displeased, and annoyed, but not inappropriately horrified, terrified, angry and self-downing" (1957, p. 142). Emotions were undifferentiated and clustered. This case almost seems autobiographical. One needs only to reverse the actors so it is not parents with a neurotic son, but a son with neurotic parents. As a child, Ellis may have found that one emotion in his parents led to another, escalating into the terrible domain. Often the only recourse for a young child is to turn away or to shield the eyes and ears. Ellis appeared to need to block emotions or to miniaturize their expression. Ellis may not wish to look too closely at individual emotions because any one of them may be a signal for the escalation of emotion. If Ellis initiated the emotional barrage, then he might be in control of it. This multiplication of emotions gives the sense of such a strategy.

When diagnosing clinical problems, McWilliams (1994) described the hysterical personality as that of a "small, *fearful* and defective child coping as well as can be expected in a world dominated by powerful and alien others [italics added]" (p. 310). Such people may "magnify their emotions in order to get past their anxiety and convince themselves and others of their right to self-expression" (p. 311). McWilliams wrote that the hysterical person often copes by being controlling and manipulative, which can optimally translate into "rescue operations." Such personality types tend to manage other people in order to "achieve an island of security . . . , to stabilize self-esteem, to master frightening possibilities by initiating them, to express unconscious hostility" (p. 310). It seems peculiar to imagine that Ellis has characteristics of the hysterical person when so much of his personality seems antihysterical (though he claimed his mother had such symptoms). However, he wrote as if the management of hysteria were his chief need. Furthermore, as a child he reported that he consciously manipulated other people and cared for others, both characteristics of this coping strategy. Whether Ellis fully understood his emotional motivation or its relation to family issues is uncertain.

Cognitive Style in the First Writings Related to Fear and Magnified Emotionality

Just as it is rare to find a page of text without emotional words, it is equally rare to find a page of text that is not formally logical. It was rare for Ellis to describe something about neurosis without proposing a mechanistic, causal explanation for the event. Much of his writing was of a tacit nature – if a, then b. He intended to be, and actually was, extremely logical in absolute causal logic. That is, his logic usually assumed that there is an underlying best or right answer and that it can be discovered by a logical chain of analysis. In his case, discovery came through the use of logic and was presumably tested in the fire of emotional response as one of the "outcome measures." If the emotional response appeared to be nonneurotic to him, then the logic and the consequent behavior were correct. Although rational, this is also egocentric.

The method we used for counting types of thought process generally tends to obscure the strength of Ellis's linear, absolute logical system. This is the most frequent and simplest one, for Ellis in general. Because it is so common, we did not count it on a particular page if there was evidence of any other system. Therefore, we counted the less frequent modes of thought as the thought system for an entire page rather than counting all modes on each page. This approach gives the advantage to the infrequently occurring systems – as it was intended to do – but it still has drawbacks. In slightly more than half of the text coded (every other chapter), the *only* mode of logic Ellis used in *How to Live with a Neurotic* was the absolute linear one. In another third, the mode coded was that of a limited relativism, but it does not follow that there is no absolute logic on the pages with some relativism.

Where Ellis used relativism or contextualism, he was acknowledging that alternate systems of analysis exist or that different procedures might result in different conclusions. The high rate of relativism might make it appear that relativism was nearly as important to Ellis as absolute modes of logic. The deceptive part of this counting system is revealed in the text, however. Ellis used a partial relativism to compare the erroneous possible views with the only logically correct one, and then he rejected the possibility of relativism (just as he rejected fear). For example, he wrote, "Children almost always take criticism as disapproval.... Whereupon he or she usually begins to believe in and profoundly feel this no-goodness" (1957, p. 66). Here Ellis was indicating that children have an (illogical) system of "no-goodness" – but, at least they acquired the illogical system in an understandable manner; it was based on habit. Ellis resolved this "illogic" by claiming that children's interpretation of criticism as disapproval, although understandable, was "nonsense." In this way, typical of his thinking, he presented a partial relativistic position – two forms of thinking existed – but then he concluded with the absolute because it was clear to him that one of them was nonsense and the other absolutely correct.

Ellis's use of relativism was linear. He described a line of possibility that ranged from least to most correct. Degrees of incorrectness might exist, nevertheless, they are still incorrect. This methodology is actually relativistic thinking described, rejected, and then resolved by absolute thinking. A more thorough relativism acknowledges that alternate approaches exist and are equally true because they are true within their own parameters or procedures – the old, what tickles you, might pain me. Ellis does not accept that in *How to Live with a Neurotic*. In that sense, he is rarely, perhaps never, completely relativistic, and our coding of so much of his writing as relativistic is possibly misleading.

The rare indication of dialectical transformation of thought processes comes forward in cases, as had most instances of relativism. In one instance, a client came to Ellis because she had problems with a dominating mother-in-law. Ellis convinced the client that her mother-in-law's apparent overdecisiveness "masked this woman's [the mother-in-law's] weakness and indecisiveness." This case is evidence of a dialectical logic system because Ellis pointed out that, paradoxically, overdecisiveness and indecisiveness are likely to be part of the same system, not exclusive modes of being one of which substitutes for the other. When the client understood her mother-in-law better – as being most "decisive" in appearance when she was feeling her "weakest," she stopped resenting her. Even more interesting, at a later time, the client reported a significant transformation of her understanding when she recognized in her own behavior that *her* indecisiveness led her to "bully" her child into doing homework with the goal of having the child be more decisive. Her understanding of a particular instance of unconscious motivation leading to contradictory behavior became a larger system of understanding paradoxical psychological processes in herself, as well as in her troublesome mother-in-law. Thus it was apparent that the client had established and was able to use a rudimentary dialectical system.

Ellis received credit in our coding system for presenting dialectical material in the mother-in-law case. His analyses and presentations of analytic defense systems indicated that he found such material understandable. Ellis's ability to follow relativistic or dialectical arguments in other people's repertoire was excellent. It simply did not fit into his own emotional-cognitive schemas. In that sense, he did not fully understand it or use it flexibly. He may have actively disliked the dialectical system, as most people who are absolute in their thinking do. For Ellis, it was as if this relativism and dialecticism were equated with illogical bad habits. In his final analysis, Ellis found the mother-in-law client to be substituting a single correct idea for a wrong one. In the end, Ellis did not argue (as he would have to in order to complete a more dialectical perspective) that the client was evolving a system in which seemingly contradictory elements are actually parts of the same theme, although he had the information to do so. He argued that the client merely came to see that her resentment of her mother-in-law's bullying was irrational. The irrational thought was simply replaced with a more rational one. Ellis oversimplified his own presentation by making it, in the end, merely a simple, mechanical process.

Emotion and Logic – Fear and Absolute Thinking

Fear appears to drive Ellis's overwhelming use of absolute logic in *How to Live with a Neurotic*. On the surface, we have a book whose logic is absolute and whose primary emotion system is fear. Beyond this surface association, there is a deeper one. The partial relativistic passages are closely linked to fear, even panic. Almost three quarters of the pages coded as having some example of the partial relativistic thought, limited though it is, contain the word "fear" or its near neighbor in meaning such as "terror" or "panic." This frequency might not be surprising since "fear" is such a prevalent word in Ellis's writing, but on pages that are purely absolute or descriptive in their logic, fear words occur less than one quarter of the time. In other words, fear-connoting words were not randomly or evenly distributed. When Ellis presented relativistic alternatives, the emotional context would frequently be the dreaded fear. When he was absolute in his arguments, he avoided or had resolved his thoughts about fear, terror, and panic.

The occurrence of fear is associated with relativism in this book, but Ellis had incomplete or blocked relativistic thoughts. Relativistic thought in itself appeared to be dangerous. "What ifs" were not playful trains of thought to Ellis but multiplications of threats that could not be completely anticipated. It is fairly clear that Ellis would regard the alternative pathways as "irrational," not alternately rational, and he would not eagerly follow them just to see where they led. Switching to absolute and mechanistic styles of logic banished his fear.

We are not stretching our argument for the connection in Ellis's writing and thinking between the emotion of fear and absolute thought. Late in Ellis's life, the emotion–logic connection evolved from a process that can be detected by analysis of the fractals of emotional and cognitive behavior into a thematic certainty. He consciously and deliberately relied upon his preferred logical style to alleviate fear. Evidence for such a fear–logic association occurred repeatedly. For example, in one of Ellis's stories from his autobiography, he described going into a diabetic coma at work. When Ellis regained consciousness in the hospital, he was under restraints, disoriented, and alone. He reassured himself that it was not reasonable to be panic stricken. One could, with premises different from Ellis's, claim that it is logical to be afraid if one has a potentially fatal illness, loses consciousness, and wakes up alone and under restraints. But Ellis found this fear to be unacceptable and therefore called it "irrational," rather than just saying that fear might drive him over the edge. By this time in his life, he directly perceived fear to be irrational and the antidote to fear to be an absolute assertion that it is not reasonable.

In one instance of unquestioned premises in *How to Live with a Neurotic*, he gave an example of a neurotic neighbor who was (verbally) abusive. He pointed out that one might feel afraid (unreasonably) if such a neighbor leaned out a window and began to curse. He argued that if the cursing neighbor were in a mental institution, we would understand that her abuse was not personal but a symptom of her illness. If we regarded the neighbor as mentally unhealthy, as we rationally "should," then we would also not be afraid. By this line of logic, Ellis could demonstrate that there is no rational excuse for fearing the neighbor and that fear is irrational. However, we could use different premises; if we did, we might actually be alarmed. Ellis neglected to note that an institutionalized person is quite literally less of an immediate threat than one's unfettered neighbor. It is not simply the mental state of the individual that is in question but also her real ability to harm. The curses may be threats, and the threats may be a prelude to attack. In that case, a reasonable degree of fear might lend itself in Ellis's writings to self-protection. There are many instances of argument much like the cursing neighbor, and all are unquestioned.

Research on trauma and panic provides some general insight into the problems associated with fear: fear is usually perceived as transitory and normal, whereas panic and associated trauma are usually perceived as abnormally rare. People who experience a trauma are vulnerable to posttraumatic stress syndrome (Foa & Riggs, 1995). A traumatized person would usually experience some or all of three types of symptoms. The fearful person might have flashbacks or nightmares, might attempt to avoid all reminders of the event and have trouble being expressive when actually around the reminders (this might extend to a lack of feelings about other people), and, finally, might have periods of high anxiety with irritability and hypervigilance when scanning for tiny cues relevant to the feared events.

There are reasons to believe that Ellis had some of the symptoms common to people with a history of trauma and fear. On the one hand, there is no evidence in his autobiography that he suffered from recurrent nightmares or flashbacks about traumatic events. With respect to numbing of feeling, this is more questionable. Ellis's insistence that fear is unreasonable and that one might instead be only "concerned" points to a de-escalation of fearful thoughts. This switching from fear to concern might lie close to numbing depending upon how it is applied. The symptom of hypervigilance is very prominent in Ellis's writing. He could not escape from heightened fear terminology. He was constantly on the lookout for fearful instances of behavior and belief so that he could minimize them. Of course, being hypervigilant, he was always able to find instances of fearful belief and behavior. He had recurring opportunities to de-escalate fearful events successfully and these occasions tended to reinforce his habit of scanning for potential fearful events. The problem this approach creates is that he could never relax his vigilance. The state of near-fear was always present.

The way that fear worked for Ellis is not very different from the way that anger worked for Rogers. In both cases, they were hypervigilant for the frequently cited emotion, saw it in their clients, and denied that the frequent emotion was of much concern to them personally. Eventually, in mid or late life, Rogers became partially aware of the personal significance of anger, but Ellis has not yet reported a growing awareness of the effect that fear might have had on him. Rogers found that he avoided anger expressions until they "exploded." One wonders if Ellis's control also waned on occasion and if he was similarly afflicted. Some reports from colleagues that Ellis had fears about travel might be an example of this phenomenon. He was somewhat of a recluse, seldom going beyond the walls of a familiar environment, which also might speak to the same problems. On the other hand, one might be puzzled by the fact that Ellis exposed himself to popular opinion on a stage where he did public therapy and in print where he did little to shield himself from criticism. Of course, Rogers did little to avoid confrontation in his professional life, and the number of people who found him abrasive was legendary – as were the number of people who found it difficult to imagine him being abrasive. There are probably many people who find it difficult to imagine Ellis fearful as well. The problem with a prominent emotion system is the constant need to balance over- and underreaction. The lack of balance gives rise to the apparent paradox that the same person, at different times or with different people, exhibits the extreme ends of the particular emotional continuum. Rogers could be extremely non-angry or he could explode. Ellis can be extremely brazen, but probably the opposite is true as well.

Given that Ellis was hypersensitive to fear, one wonders whether his theraputic process would be considered appropriate for trauma. There are differences between modern emotional processing approaches and Ellis's approach, but they may be a matter of semantics and timing. The modern therapist has the patient recreate the fear and reexperience the trauma in a safe environment. This procedure allows for some integration and avoids dissociation. Reportedly, people who express more fear during the process recover faster. Ellis actively encouraged people to immerse themselves in their anxiety causing situations to overcome the anxiety. In treating fears of rejection, for example, he would give homework assignments in which the fearful person entered a situation that might very well lead to rejection. On the other hand, Ellis told us unequivocally that experiencing terror about past events was irrational. In this position, he almost certainly differed from therapists who advocate emotional processing. There is perhaps a difference between description of fear in his writing and description and practice of rational emotive therapy, especially as it evolved over Ellis's lifetime. While Ellis disclaimed fear as an acceptable label for emotion, he did not encourage anyone to avoid their fearful situations. Though sometimes Ellis may write or speak as if he were advocating dissociation, he usually practiced as if he believed that the reexperiencing were necessary. This is a complex approach and seems to involve more processing of emotion in its practice than appears at first blush.

Later Books on RET Therapy

Humanistic Psychotherapy (1973) is a collection of papers and talks given by Ellis from 1965 to 1973. It is representative of Ellis's writing fifteen or so years after the early book on neurosis. It is mature work done after he had accumulated several awards and editorships and was directing his own Institute for Rational Living. In this book, we catch a glimpse of the successful therapist and theorist at work. We can ask whether he changed in his emotional preferences and avoidances in these years, being especially concerned about his orientation to fears. Also, we can follow his intellectual maturation.

In *Humanistic Psychotherapy*, we find a chapter called "Therapy with Psychotics and Borderline Psychotics" that parallels in some ways the earlier writing about neurotics. Our coding of emotional biases shows that the fear category was still the most frequent, if one includes the words "terrible" and "horrible" (because of their derivative from "terror" and "horror"), but it was nearly balanced by the hostile–anger category. Previously the hostile–anger category was also the second most frequent one. There was an equally large category of unspecified negative emotion, such as references to emotional disturbance; several references appear to happy, interest and excitement, and sorrowful emotions. Guilt is barely mentioned; surprise, shame, and contempt are not mentioned at all. This is quite a well-elaborated chapter in terms of its emotional breadth, even though it still shows a bias toward fear-related issues and away from shame or contempt. Ellis did not change his early orientation, although there is somewhat more breadth to the emotional spectrum.

The slightly expanded elaboration of emotion in this later work would lead us to suspect a somewhat more elaborated system of thought as well. In fact, relativistic or contextual thinking occurred somewhat more frequently than earlier, being found in more than half the chapter. Concrete description and absolute thinking without relativistic thinking account for the other half. This reflects a slight tendency toward more relativistic logic given that the proportion previously was closer to one third. There was, however, still no instance of dialectical or patterned thinking.

An interesting feature of this chapter is its presentation of ten ideas people diagnosed with schizophrenia must have according to his theory (Ellis, 1973, pp. 242–3). Presumably these ideas would be symptoms of a very severe disturbance. Among these disturbed thoughts are the ideas (paraphrased) that it is a necessity to be approved by every significant person in the community, that one should be thoroughly competent to be worthwhile, that some people are wicked and should be severely punished, that it is *awful* when things do not go as one wishes, that people can do little to control their sorrows and disturbances, that one should be *terribly* concerned about something that may be *fearsome*, that history indefinitely affects present behavior, and that it is *catastrophic* when the perfect solution to human problems is not found. These irrational ideas that psychotic people presumably hold are nearly the same as the ideas that afflicted neurotic people in the earlier book, perhaps stated more clearly and vehemently. The content of Ellis's therapeutic thinking seems not to have changed over the fifteen- to twenty-year period, even though it is applied to new types of patients.

Fearful, awful, terrible, and catastrophic events still were central in the older Ellis's thinking. Another major issue still at the forefront was judgment and evaluation by oneself and the community. The evaluation content suggests shame and contempt in the background without specifically mentioning either, as well as a continuation of previous schemas (see the next section on contempt). Overall, the listed items seem to discourage absolute or single solutions, but the list was presented as absolute rules. Ellis saw the value of contextual processes in a few situations; nevertheless, he tended not to adopt that mode for his own theoretical presentation.

By this later date, Ellis had added more contextual material but had not changed his own primary mode of analysis. Once again, he rarely documented his assertions or his premises. How would we know whether the ideas listed are the defining features of psychosis? We must accept Ellis's assertions. We might see slightly more relativistic thinking and slightly more diversity of emotional consideration; however, earlier concerns, feelings, and ways of thinking were still the most prominent.

Ellis often asserted that where others saw change in his theory, there was little or none. His own assessment, then, parallels our analysis. In *Overcoming Resistance* (1985), a book probably written when Ellis was in his seventies, over ten years after *Humanistic Psychotherapy*, he wrote, "Although some critics of RET assume that it was almost entirely cognitive when I first created it in 1955 and that it later jumped on the emotive and behavioral bandwagons that started rolling in the 1960s, this is not true. RET has always been . . . a unified-interaction approach to psychotherapy . . . that includes cognitive, emotive, and behavioral techniques" (Ellis, 1985, p. 73). Ellis then went on to quote his earlier works from 1958 to 1962 to demonstrate this assertion – in a rare instance of documentation.

However, Ellis alluded to one sort of change – focus or intensity: "As RET developed, it emphasized the *strength* of ideas even more strongly, and it began to use even more emotive-cognitive methods than it used during its first few years" (Ellis, 1985, p. 85). To understand this consider that "From the start, it [RET] pointed out that what we call emotion largely consists of strong, vehemently held cognitions, while 'pure', dispassionate thought leads to behavior but not usually to what we call intense or disordered feeling" (Ellis, 1985, p. 85). In Ellis's mature theory, then, thought is everything. Disordered thought is called "emotion." Emotion does not have here an independent definition. Pure thinking without emotion leads to appropriate behavior but emotion or, rather, disordered thought leads only to disordered feeling. Although Ellis's late theory is called Rational Emotive, the Emotive part was not meant to lead us to expect that emotions were skills or talents. Emotion must be managed and controlled. Most emotions were painful for Ellis, and this quote from his late-in-life work was one more strike in a continuous war against them.

In spite of very strong continuities in some basics of the theory and style, both emotional and cognitive, there were some pockets of change at this latest age for Ellis. The circumstances of Ellis's life had changed. He had a steady life partner who shared his work as well as his personal life. Whatever chance or sought-for events led to this major change, it had to share a part in his somewhat more relativistic and emotionally elaborate thoughts. His emotions and consequent patterns of thinking were so closely tied to his familial attachment style that any changes in close attachment would be likely to lead to substantial change elsewhere. He had a loving partner as well as working colleagues and students who shared his interests and admired his work. The existence of such relationships would be a node for other kinds of change. It opens up possibilities for close collegial relationships in general and should be related to a curtailing of the defensive and silent contempt at least around colleagueal relationships. Although the contempt was still clear in many places, there were many longer exceptions. There was an increased referencing of other theoretical points of view and a directing of his own disciples to study others. At one point, for example, he recommended using the techniques of Rogers for listening and responding to patients having difficulty with a supportive relationship. However in Ellis's case, the cognitive changes seemed to remain fragmented or as occasional additions rather than as transformations of cognition.

A good example of how Ellis had changed toward the end of his life in respect to acknowledging the feelings and thoughts of others comes in a statement about treating sociopathic people. Embedded in a list of more traditional Ellisian prescriptions is the addition of this remark about empathy: "Try to help them see the pains and troubles of others and to become more empathic. Dramatize what some of these victims go through and how pained they may be. Show them some of the social ramifications of their acts – how they lead to widening rings of human suffering" (Ellis, 1985, p. 149).

Remarks like the one on empathy were more frequent in the later books. The feelings emphasized were a step away from Ellis's usual concern with the fearful and showed more concern with distress and suffering. However, the style of thinking had not changed. He was suggesting a substitution of correct behavior, empathy, for inappropriate behavior that caused pain. There was no appreciation or explanation of the systemic transformation across major systems of thought and feeling that might occur if the sociopathic person were to actually become empathic.

Even though Ellis had increased his perception of distress in some cases, he did not reduce his contempt and emphasis on separateness in other cases. For example, in *Humanistic Psychotherapy* (pp. 222–3), Ellis reported on his dialogue with a phobic client. He reported saying to her, "look at that drivel you're telling yourself." He continued to use disparaging words like "drivel" perhaps not to describe the client, but to challenge her thoughts, as he might have said. His modes of thought were very slow to change, but they did slide gently away from wholesale contempt and absolute types of thinking toward a more sparse and focused relativism in certain instances.

Another example of both continuity and change could be seen in the last chapter of *Overcoming Resistance*. It is a recursive chapter on the therapist: "Your Most Difficult Client – You." This chapter was most likely to have reflected problems that Ellis experienced himself or with training young therapists. Again when the focus was on the therapist, there was a strong influx of fearful (panic, horror, anxious) emotional states. The change was that there was an equal number of positive ones (humor, enjoy). As has been the case in most of Ellis's writing, absolute types of thinking and relativistic thinking coexisted. However, they were no longer separated clearly by emotion functions as they had been for the younger Ellis where fear was associated with relativism. The alternating style was pervasive and largely independent of emotional context.

Ellis, if anything, in his later books had perfected the model of opposing multiple negative affects against multiple positive affects and presenting the transformation as the result of cognitive disputation. Note this quote from the later book, *Overcoming Resistance:* "Extensiveness in psychotherapy means that clients can be helped not only to minimize their negative feelings (e.g., anxiety, depression, rage, and self-pity) but also to maximize their potential for happy living (e.g., to be more productive, creative, and enjoying). Where 'intensive' therapy usually deals with pain, inhibition, panic, and horror, 'extensive' therapy also deals with exploring and augmenting pleasure, sensuality, and laughter" (Ellis, 1985, p. 129). The oppositional debating style – an opposition of good and bad components to the whole paragraph and the opposition of good and bad emotions – was clearer than ever. There was still a major emphasis on fear-related overwhelming emotions – anxiety, panic, horror. There was still a fair amount of bundling negative emotions together rather than considering them as having separable functions. However, there was also a real elaboration of the positive side with pleasure, sensuality, laughter, and enjoyment. Here, as elsewhere, pleasure was not just mentioned in passing; it was emphasized more equally with terrible, negative emotions.

The argument in the preceding quote that there are two types of therapy – intensive and extensive – each of which might offer some benefit, was also a move toward more relativistic thinking, as was also slightly more typical of the aging Ellis. Research on older adults (Kramer & Woodruff, 1986) usually shows a gradual increase in relativistic and sometimes dialectical thought. Ellis's gradual migration in that direction is not unexpected. He was, however, very slow and tentative with this mode of thought. Even here, the two therapies – intensive and extensive – were not really equal. One was more negative, and the other was more positive. Ellis was probably arguing that "intensive" therapy, possibly depth-oriented psychotherapies, extend and intensify negative feelings. Ordinarily, Ellis seemed opposed to this approach. He was not one to argue with Rogers that the deeper the feelings of negative passion, the deeper the emergent positive feelings, and the more creative the solutions to the underlying problems. This is a nice example of "almost" relativistic thinking. It shows that Ellis still found tolerating two equally good solutions difficult.

Fearfulness appeared not to decline with age, but other emotional sides of Ellis did grow somewhat, particularly the positive. This is a way of saying that it looks as if Ellis did not change the basic organization or ordering of his emotions and thoughts, but as if he added new components.

The Silent Emotion: Contempt

We turn from examining Ellis's most frequently expressed emotion of fear to the emotion that is least explicitly expressed in his writing – contempt. (Here we distinguish between lexical terms of contempt in contrast to contemptuous utterances – as coded in the treatment; see Chapter 10). This change in focus brings us from the emotion he most needed to manage to the one he least needed to manage in his written and in his nonverbal expression. Eventually we will see that fear and contempt are not entirely separate but form two aspects of the same system.

The examination of contempt takes us back to Ellis's earliest published writing, the writing that focused on sexual problems. Of course, it was his devotion to sexuality that led us to consider the Oedipal themes in his personality in the first place. *The Folklore of Sex*, his very first book (it preceded books on therapy), reviewed sexual attitudes in the media of the 1950s. He found the accepted 1950s sexual mores to be irrational. Another of his books was a married couple's guide to extramarital sex (*The Civilized Couple's Guide to Extramarital Adventure*, 1972), an activity that he found to be rational and valuable. A third book, *The Art and Science of Love* (1960), was more directly oriented to sexual behaviors. Clearly, this was an area of continuous interest.

Ellis claimed that he began his entire psychological career with marriage and sex counseling. He wrote in his biography that he wanted to be a rebel in the arena of family and sexual behavior. He even attributed being drawn to psychology by his success at solving the sexual problems of a friend. Perhaps it was often himself whose problems were amenable to management by psychology.

The Folklore of Sex (1951) was published when Ellis was a year away from forty. As far as we know it was not the first book he had written, just the first published. In his autobiography, he wrote that he had twenty book-length manuscripts prepared before he went to graduate school – both fictional and nonfictional. Since he was twenty-eight when he went to graduate school, he had considerable writing experience by the time this first book appeared. He also had considerable experience with sexual issues. He had been married and divorced himself. He wrote that he had done an enormous amount of research on sexual issues for his own interests before he received this particular book contract. There is ample reason to expect a knowledgeable, balanced presentation, but that expectation would not be fulfilled.

The introduction to the book is especially interesting because Ellis presented an abbreviated autobiographical history of its beginnings. He had heard the Kinseys speak on Americans' sexual practices and fortuitously rode home from this event on the train with a psychiatrist who had connections with publishers. This man and Ellis discussed the need for research on sexual matters, but Ellis had doubts about getting support for a book on the topic. His companion offered to have publishers contact him. Ellis wrote "knowing the usual value of such vaguely voiced promises, I did not take him too seriously" (Ellis, 1951, p. 12). Sometime later a publisher did contact Ellis. Then Ellis expressed doubt about the publisher's sincerity in publishing a scholarly book rather than a "salacious," salable book. "Having once worked for a book publisher myself, and knowing full well the pressures which induce publishers to present shoddy but salable rather than profound but unpopular volumes, my confidence in the scientific soundness of book hucksters is not high" (Ellis, 1951, p. 12). At each step he was deeply skeptical and contemptuous of his fellows. He welcomed the fact that his suspicions were not fulfilled, but he did not expect it.

We see that Ellis expected very little of people; he was the sort of middle-aged man who was prepared to be ignored or treated badly. At the same time, he was obviously attractive or persuasive to people he met. The psychiatrist on the train and the publisher must have seen promise in him; not everyone gets such offers. This encounter suggests an attractive quality in Ellis that is less than obvious in his description of himself except as he contemptuously described his ability to manipulate other people by appearing successful and helpful.

Finally, Ellis and his publisher decided to "make a study of American attitudes toward sex, love, and marriage as these are expressed in popular mass media." For not only could such a study be done "with limited ... financial resources, but it would also provide a great deal of valuable material for ... other research procedures" (Ellis, 1951, p. 13). Even here Ellis had foremost in his mind, the limited resources that the world provided.

This whole introduction was purely descriptive and assertive in its mode of thought. In comparison with other later writing on other subjects, it was sparse both in emotional terminology and logical process. The highest frequency of emotionally related words is "interest' as when he describes how people will be interested in the book or his views. The only negative emotion specifically mentioned was, of course, fear – "our *frightfully* popular publications" (1951, p. 14) and the little bit of work that can possibly be done on sexual attitudes "loses its ability to *terrify*" (1951, p. 13).

Although Ellis's use of emotion terms in the introduction to the book on sexuality was sparse and there was no direct mention of contempt, derision, or any related term, there were many indirect suggestions of contempt. Instead of writing that he was "contemptuous" or that someone was "ridiculed" or that he saw a "sneering" face – words that we would have coded directly as contempt – he used derisive colloquialisms to express his contempt. His contempt came out in names, such as "hucksters," or in mock surprise that promises have been met or, yet again, that publishers might be intelligent.

Ellis's mockery and doubtfulness of others was matched by a daring and perhaps defensive lack of *self*-doubt. He might have doubted his fellows' scientific objectivity, but he did not examine his own: "Which thing to do, patently" (and he gives the "patently" clear answer). "In other words, I, as the originator of this study, feel that the media examined were truly representative." There was no possible question about the representativeness of his media, only his own expressed confidence. "What media? And the obvious answer seemed to be: Mass media, of course" (Ellis, 1951, p. 14). Again, the answer to his question was, "of course," obvious – to Ellis.

Given the times in which Ellis was writing and the nature of the book's content – sexual attitudes – one might expect a certain defiance against the social norms. Sexual matters have usually been matters for privacy if not shame in the United States, particularly in the middle of the twentieth century and particularly in scholarly publications. Was Ellis demonstrating the "head held high" of the person publicly shamed but righteously undaunted? Perhaps he was acting contemptuous of others before they had an opportunity to be contemptuous of him. Perhaps this is another example of fending off fears.

The format of each chapter in *The Folklore of Sex* was to give examples and ample quotes from the mass media regarding topics such as adultery or pregnancy. In the last few chapters, the frequencies of attitudes – conservative, liberal, or salacious – in each publication were tabulated and listed in the text. As we examine emotion in this book we find more emotional usage. The introduction is not entirely typical. In the chapter entitled "Scatology," for example, there were more emotional words, and, not surprisingly, there was much more of an attempt to present a reasoned argument, rather than the pure description of the blocked emotional introduction. Nevertheless, the chapter retained the contemptuous assertions: "That the great majority of twentieth-century Americans seem to consider scatology to be, at one and the same time, (a) dirty, filthy, wicked, and unclean and (b) gay, titillating, clever, and exhilarating. That in consequence, American attitudes, feelings, thoughts, and actions in relation to scatology are incredibly *chaotic, childish and confused* [italics added]" (Ellis, 1951, p. 125). The writing followed a simple propositional style, but it was derisive as he called his readers' attitudes "chaotic, childish and confused." Although the analysis is propositional, it is not argued completely or conclusively. One must accept Ellis's premise that to be of two minds is to be childish. Ellis's last words – "chaotic, childish and confused" – left no doubt that his feelings about American attitudes were contemptuous. Once again, the contempt was contained in the adjectives he used to describe people, not in a direct expression of his own feelings. Peoples' attitudes were not organized or mature or rational. On the contrary, that one might see two sides of a question and perceive that the direction to go depends upon the circumstances was simply not acceptable to Ellis.

The primary coded emotion that found its way into the scatology chapter directly is the happiness category – in words such as "humorous." The "humorous" references also contained some element of contempt as well as happiness. And as one might expect in a discussion of scatology, there was much reference to disgust, and some reference to shock, interest, and shame. Still, only about half the chapter shows even partial evidence of a problem-solving orientation. As in *Overcoming Resistance* (1985), the one contextual presentation is on the page with reference to shock. This is a reminder that when the younger

Ellis entered the fear (panic, shock, anxiety, etc.) realm, he was rather consistent in using relativistic logic, though he would quickly defend against both the feeling and the mode of thought and would not support the relativistic presentation. As we find generally, the emotions preferred by a person lead to valuing a mode of logic that he will use in such a way that the logical style seems exclusively correct.

The consistent relationship between emotional thoughtfulness and intellectual style within the individual can be further demonstrated by choosing another chapter. Scatology might appear to require both contemptuous humor and disgust, but the topic of romance does not. So we turned to the romance chapter to challenge our prediction about consistency. Once again, the contemptuous humorous emotional category was paramount. General emotionality and the guilt/shame categories are equally in second place. Even disgust and sadness are mentioned. However, once again, there was no coded contempt, though there is a very high level of mockery, which is implied contempt and can easily be taken as an insult. Consider just the opening paragraph: "Whoever enjoys sex pleasure with a mate he or she does not love, is, according to this view, a *crass, low-living, soulless apology* for a human being [italics added]" (1951, p. 192). Ellis is not claiming that he would ever say that a person who enjoys sex without love is crass and so on, but he believes that other people have this insulting attitude. He anticipates other people's contempt and finds it rampant in the "garden-variety" of humankind. This is a less than profound example of seeing the speck in someone else's eye but missing the large blind area in one's own.

Once again in the romance chapter, there is evidence of both relativistic and absolute styles of reasoning throughout the chapter, but Ellis's use of the logical styles was again flawed – as is apparently common when the principal emotion, contempt in this case, is obliquely projected onto others and denied for the self. His approach to romance was just about as contemptuous as his approach to scatology both in emotional organization and intellectual consistency. For example, all the media evidence that Ellis claimed he used supported the view that sex *with* love was much preferred. Ellis was forced by the unanimity of his sources to conclude that there was "no serious contemporary opposition, since stories, plays, movies, or nonfictional works in which men and women consciously enjoy sex without love and do not suffer any dire consequences are quite rare" (1951, p. 196). Unlike the evidence in other chapters which Ellis found to be contradictory, the sources here were not contradictory, but Ellis did not accept them.

When the data did not support Ellis's own beliefs, he inferred irrational "unconscious" contradictions. "Once a sex act that is still psychobiologically urgent is banned, it is bound to cause mental anguish and conflict... we will tend to build up (largely unconscious) feelings of doubt, anxiety, and depression" (1951, p. 277). Ellis thought that this argument was obvious. He provided no evidence that sexual matters are psychobiologically urgent enough to require adultery, scatology, and other behaviors he saw as nonconformist and possibly desirable. If we wanted to argue with Ellis, we might ask how we would know that mental anguish stemming from sexual desire led to neurotic outbursts. Ellis sounded logical because he proposed a causal sequence, but at each step we must accept his assertions of connection without evidence. His argument was incomplete. There was no evidence in his media data about anguish or depression. We may even believe Ellis's assertions from other evidence such as psychoanalytic cases, but Ellis left that argument up to us. He used a causal sequence to describe his information and believed that he was scientific and logical, but he did not examine the process of his logic. He concluded in his final paragraph that "the average American frequently enjoys it [sex] on a fairly non-loving or neutral basis, the result is inevitable; namely, a piling up of an enormous burden of guilt and regret that will tend to destroy sexual pleasure... and perhaps physical-health of the common-garden-variety human being who should not, but obviously still does, like his sex affairs with little or no love" (1951, p. 197). He had no evidence for these assertions from his media data. The point is that Ellis, when using contempt in this oblique and blocked manner, shifted the base of his argument to suit his own beliefs. His logical argument became every bit as flawed as Rogers's argument when he was blocked by his silent anger.

Ellis had no interest in the process by which people might come to their sexual beliefs. That his nonconformist opinions were his own was unacknowledged. Because the contemptuous feeling was unacknowledged and silent, the logic of his experience was silenced. Note that Ellis lived up to his personal convictions about the importance of not conforming. He spoke against conservative family values, virginity, monogamy, and so forth. Finally, he laced the book with ridiculing remarks about both experts and the "garden-variety" person. Ellis clearly despised conformity in sexual matters and perhaps in family matters. This commitment was deliberate as we find in his own words from his autobiography, "Since my socioeconomic beliefs were partly shared by a great many writers who were effectively propounding them in print...,

I was determined to devote a good part of my life to promulgating the sex–family revolution, which most of my fellow radicals were sadly neglecting" (1972, pp. 109–10) To conform was equivalent to being irrational, unscientific, and vulnerable to overwhelming emotionality.

The battleground on which Ellis seemed compelled to avoid conforming and to take risks was that of human love and sex. As far as we know, he was not risky or nonconformist with automobiles, drugs, or athletic adventure. His risk taking was limited to social risks – both in sexuality and in the intimacy of therapy. Even when working with clients, he was opposed to ideas that he found conformist. It was here in the area of closeness that he most needed to be in control. In discussing a man depressed about his wife's heart disease, his affair with a "lower-class" woman, and his daughters' disapproval, Ellis writes that this man "was needlessly flagellating himself and refusing to push through convention-shattering approaches to his difficulties" (1972, p. 173). Ellis found that the guilt that this man felt was inspired by conformity and was an irrational problem.

A careful reader of *The Folklore of Sex* might contend that the "statistical considerations" section would necessarily be objective and thoughtful and that we should look here for Ellis's more mature thinking. Ellis presented tables of percentages of each type of media (e.g., professional medical journals versus men's magazines versus popular plays). He organized his data according to his own view of whether the attitude presented in each type of media was a liberal, conservative, or salacious view of sex. However, Ellis alone made the decisions about the typing of each piece of evidence with no doubts about whether other social scientists might agree with him. The text was still purely descriptive and did not in fact demonstrate a more mature form of logic (similar to Rogers when he described tables and data – the amassing of data does not necessarily promote logical processes). In this case, Ellis did not present alternatives, nor did he develop a train of logic that built from evidence. There was sometimes a simple cause-and-effect type of argument, but it was circular. It took the form: if there is censorship, then there is less salacious material. But this reasoning is circular since the definition of censorship is the enforced reduction of salacious material, so the connection is tautological. There is nothing new emerging.

In *The Folklore of Sex*, Ellis was distinctly uninterested in how people come to have their attitudes about sexual matters or any other moral issue. His position was not endemic to his time period. As a contrast, one might consider that, at about this same time, the psychologist Kohlberg

(1964) was investigating the development of moral decision making. In the arena of adolescent moral decisions, there are many "logical" contradictions, just as Ellis found 'logical' contradictions or irrational positions in his media data. Kohlberg's approach was to find a system of analysis that would make the apparent contradiction an important part of an evolving pattern or maturation. Kohlberg found, for example, that there comes a time when moral behavior is considered contractual. People who use contractual models hold that there is no single best answer to the moral question, but that rules for agreement are needed. It is in this mode that codes such as "my word is my bond" arise and may be held to be important honors. In this mode of thinking, the speed limit, for example, might not be logical, but its logic is not necessarily the reason for accepting it or violating it. It rests upon people's views of whether they have "contracted" to obey it or whether they have a silent contract to drive "in tune" with other drivers. The emergence of abstract principles of moral judgment is a later stage that develops from this earlier one. Not just Kohlberg's approach but many other psychological approaches recognize that the connections among behavior, thought, and feeling are not linear. This does not mean that they are intrinsically irrational. It only means that a simple, additive, and linear model does not always explain the reasoning of the person making the judgment.

Ellis often relied more on direct perception than on analysis in spite of his many claims to logical objectivity. He saw certain types of logical contradiction, described the extent of the contradiction, and then went no further. He did not inquire about the process of decision; he only noted that, as it was not rational in his terms, it was necessarily irrational. Judgments were black and white. Appearances of contradiction were a source of disorder, not of development. As he wrote, contradiction leads to confusion and is dangerous because it leads to emotions that are undesirable – to Ellis.

In spite of Ellis's desire for scientific objectivity on sexuality, *The Folklore of Sex* is not a sophisticated, logical book overall, no matter whether we look at scatology, romance, or data tables. It is rather descriptive and concrete, somewhat immature for a person of Ellis's years. However, it is charming in its "cheeky" remarks, both the outrageous and funny quoted ones from "men's magazines" or from Broadway musicals and the remarks original to Ellis himself. Ellis could find nothing beautiful, tragic, or complex about Americans' attitudes toward sexuality – "the true picture of the proverbial average American should be that of an individual whose sex attitudes are woefully addled, straddled, and twaddled" (1951, p. 246). Ellis's emotional biases were behind the type of logic that he used, where his family attachment biases were behind the content, although he was unaware of and often denied these biases.

The content of Ellis's early writing is as typical of adolescents as his logical or cognitive style. In adolescence, an essay on public sexual attitudes would be likely to be a defensive intellectualization of personal sexuality. The defensive quality of the adolescent intellect would be clear from the intrusion of personal views, as it is for Ellis. The contemptuous references to the general public and to public leaders such as science writers or religious leaders, combined with his often unsubstantiated assertions, reflected a grandiose desire to place them in a low position and himself in a higher one. His bravado masked any uncertainty that he might have had about his personal acceptability in a sexual attachment just as it lacked objective consideration of other people's experience.

Because this book on sexuality appeared when Ellis was nearly forty, it clearly reflected more than a passing adolescent interest. That it is, in many respects, still an early book becomes clear when we examine one or more of Ellis's later books on sexuality. Even though we will not do this in depth, we do not want to leave the reader with the notion that Ellis remained so young in his approach to sexuality. In *The Art and Science of Love* (1960), published about a decade later, several things changed. First, there are many references to work done by social and biological scientists in the field of sexuality. Ellis no long required the reader to trust just his own opinions, and perhaps he found that he might trust the work of colleagues. Second, and not unrelated to the first change, he was more respectful of people's personal attitudes, even when he disagreed with them. And finally and perhaps most critically, he had developed an approach to reciprocity that bordered on relativism: "This means that you should want your mate to succeed at intercourse because you *love* him or her and, through love, want his or her good. By love, here, we...mean...the mature wish for another individual's growth and development for *his* sake, even when his desires do not precisely jibe with yours" (1960, p. 121).

The more mature Ellis did not abandon entirely either his contemptuous writing or his dread of worry and fear in the sex books. He just found a few more occasions to use alternate approaches. For example, in describing the application of his new therapeutic principles to sexual problems he revisited his earlier approach: "Their sex symptoms almost always are derivatives of these idiotic general creeds or assumptions;

and when their basic beliefs . . . are ruthlessly revealed and analyzed to show how ridiculous they are, and consistently attacked, discouraged, and rooted up, their sex problems . . . are at least much more susceptible to specific re-educating instructions" (1960, p. 236). Note the reference to "idiotic general creeds," "ridiculous beliefs," and the "ruthless" analysis to be used against them – "attacked, discouraged, rooted up." There is a nonrelativistic and hostile certainty that Ellis, the expert, had the right answers and would "re-educate" people who had wrong answers. The respect and relativism was not always present. Ellis still could be found ridiculing people and asserting his own expertise.

In the same later book, there also were many sections that showed the characteristic Ellis orientation to fears and dreads: "If, however, he continues to tell himself how *awful*, how *frightful*, how *terrible* his premature ejaculation is, . . . he will almost certainly make himself . . . worse and worse [italics added]" (1960, p. 218). Once again, Ellis was certain that *terror*-ible problems had a single, correct answer and cure. Sometimes he would be right, of course, but he would not be likely to have examined contextual factors or wondered about alternatives.

In another ten years, the sixtyish Ellis advanced further yet in adding certain apsects of contextual or relativistic thinking but without changing his original position. In *The Civilized Couple's Guide to Extramarital Adventure* (1972a) a few examples will illustrate the slow change. Ellis described his own reaction to an affair that his girlfriend had. "At first, I had something of a rough time. I wrongly concluded . . . that if my beloved couldn't find me one hundred percent satisfactory sexually, there must be something wrong with me, and that was pretty awful!" (1972a, p. 117) But his reading of Epictetus, Marcus Aurelius, Spinoza, Bertrand Russell, and others taught him that there was no "need to upset oneself seriously about anything." A different reading of Russell might have led to a slightly different conclusion. Russell was fond of tweaking the Stoics for their passionless position, one that he claimed was of no use to anyone with depth. Bertrand Russell aside, Ellis used the Stoic philosophy to find advantages in his beloved's philandering. For example, he argued that he could work later at night while she was with another lover. His logical and stoical analysis revealed to him that "there was no reason why, with her nuttiness, she *had* to be any different." The outcome was that "I was able to greet my paramour quite agreeably when she finally returned, be genuinely interested in her outside adventure . . . and have more enjoyable sex with her that very night" (1972a, p. 117).

Ellis's solution reflected both his persistent emotional and logical biases. He began with the "awful" part, moved to the silently contemptuous, and ended with the agreeable and interested. He did this in a linear and causal style. The situation at first seemed awful, but his girlfriend was "nutty." Such a comment was indirectly contemptuous. She was not a whole or sane person, but a "nutty" one. The contempt moved Ellis away from considering his girlfriend's feelings equally with his own (her thoughts were probably irrational under this black-and-white construction) and their interaction in their relationship. Considering a relationship might have necessitated relativistic thinking. He turned instead into himself alone and to his usual dread of feeling awful. He worked on his own feelings until he could feel some degree of agreeableness but without making any important changes in the relationship. This is a fairly lonely approach to a relationship problem, but Ellis was pleased with it.

Ellis did not expect or require that people care about him. He did not tell his girlfriend that her being intimate with other men made him feel awful and worthless. He asked for nothing from her. He was still interested in her and their sexual relationship, even though it was flawed. He did not ask himself why he had a girlfriend who had such a limited degree of commitment. Ellis wrote as if the full solution to this romantic and sexual problem lay within himself, not as if it was a mutual problem. In focusing on the dread, alone, he missed recognizing that he might feel sorrow at being abandoned and question the meaning of love, feel angry at being neglected and question his beloved's motivation, feel proud at being so independent and question his beloved's independence, and so forth. He missed the relative and meaningful context of the relationship. Ellis particularly missed knowing what his girlfriend might have been feeling and thinking. She may even have been trying to get him to express his feelings to her with her provocative behavior. Perhaps, the more he withdrew into his "logical" position, the harder she tried to elicit some statement of his feelings from him, even if that statement was negative. Although Ellis worked on himself to stabilize the relationship, his girlfriend was blocked out of the process. Ellis had not explored the relationship with the full range of emotions, and he had not explored it relativistically.

Many of the descriptions of Ellis' early romances had themes that rejected a need for care. When making love and feeling lazy, for example, he did not tell this to his partner or ask for her help. He exerted himself to renew his own activity. When his family neglected him, he did not ask that they become responsible, he cared for them. The title of his autobiography was "Psychotherapy Without Tears." One might as well say "Ellis' Life Without Tears." Sadness and empathy for sadness were hard for Ellis to accept. That sorrow was needed to contemplate unsolvable human dilemmas was not within his agenda, and there were no unsolvable human dilemmas that he could attend to. When we note the absence of sadness or grief or themes of loss, we also note a certain lack of sympathy for suffering and little or no acceptance of great tragedy. His turning away from people apparently with a degree of contempt may have been due to intense suffering when identifying with his own parent(s) and, later, other people he cared for. We have seen with infants whose parents are too overwhelming, a turning away. Turning away is the only defense for the very young. Hiding or turning the other way is often the first defense of the terrorized.

Nevertheless, in the later volumes, there were many examples of advanced contextualism when Ellis moved away from his own concerns with awful and terrible feelings and focused on his clients. For example, Ellis wrote, "Not every couple has the same tastes, preferences, and habits. . . . Just as these extremely different conditions can exist in a conventional monogamous marriage, and both partners seem to be happy with the way things are working out, so can extramarital arrangements be exceptionally diverse" (1972, p. 126). He is even more relativistic in the section on basic rules for making ground rules: "1. Start with your own feelings. . . . 4. "Don't . . . make absolute promises to your mate or to any of your lovers, and don't be afraid to admit that your feelings can and do change radically over the years" (1972, p. 126). The recommendations that feelings might change and that absolute ideas may not be wise are examples of a tendency toward contextual thinking, although, as usual, these are presented as absolute assertions. There were still weaknesses in the relativism.

The contextualism of the later books on sexuality was definitely more complex than the simple absolute thinking of *The Folklore of Sex*, but it was not getting close to dialectical or systemic thinking. There was no hint that different contexts may themselves constitute a system, even a simple one. Mutual interactions and growth still were obscure. Although there seems to be a general tendency for people to become more contextual and systems oriented as they mature, Ellis is an example of a person whose system of emotion and thought resists such change. We have been arguing all along, of course, that this was not due to any restrictions on his general intelligence, but was the result of boundaries that resulted from his particular emotional development.

Layers of Information

"Thus, an autobiography can be read in at least three different ways: literally, to obtain factual information; critically, to check this information and to expose distortions and omissions; and interpretatively, to discover its principles and account for its biases" (Vidal, 1994, p. 5). To the three readings proposed by Vidal, we added a fourth: analysis and synthesis. We treat the text as having separable parts to be analyzed and synthesized, as in chemical analysis and synthesis. This is the process of considering the psyche in its component parts and their relation to each other. In synthesis, one subjects the text to tests to determine the interactions or the products that result from the various ways of combining the compounds or ingredients. Synthesis describes the process by which separate elements are brought together to form wholes. In our case the chemical elements are the emotional words, the motivational referents of the writer. The compounds in intellectual traits arise from the way that emotional referents relate to and organize thought process in interaction with events. These thought processes may then sustain the emergence of the same emotions again or of different emotions. They also may form and dissolve interactive self-sustaining or developing systems. The interaction of these emotional thought patterns then organize information from internal and external sources, providing a personal world view that is both emotional and cognitive in its wholeness.

We can use Vidal's literal, critical, interpretative manners or our analytic manner to read not just autobiographies but any type of organized information including behavior. Into this category of factual accounts we placed Ellis's books on therapy and sexuality. We can read *How to Live with a Neurotic,* for example, to learn the factual information provided by Ellis, a therapist-expert, about living with neurotics. We can read it critically, to note its flaws or to expound upon changes in the field of psychology with advancing knowledge. We can read it interpretatively to translate the original from one context to another, as in from one type of language to another type or from one intellectual arena to another or to abstract general principles. But we focus on analysis and synthesis to provide the perspective on Ellis's emotional elements that lend themselves to the synthesis of the theory and working blueprint that he intends to have guide his Rational Emotive Therapy.

Ellis's Challenge

Of the work of the three psychologists, Ellis's work presents the greatest direct challenge. He actively discounts and disputes, to use his terms, the approach we take toward the functions of emotion. In one of his first published articles when he critiqued psychoanalysis, he stated that "The analyst may be blinded and biased by his own *emotionalized* faith in analysis [italics added]" (1950, p. 167). This is but one short example of Ellis remarking on emotions as a negative bias in thought. Ellis could not conceive of functional scientific logic as always being organized by emotion. He was not alone in this belief, of course. Scientists have often argued that their logic and systems operate without or above emotion. Such a position is part of our Western philosophical and political heritage. Nevertheless, postmodern philosophy in general, and the modern philosophies of science in particular, have challenged this premise, and our work lends empirical support to the challenge (Elshtain, 1981; Solomon, 1999).

Ellis began his career in psychology arguing that emotional bias works against scientific logic and that scientific logic was the desired goal. He attributed the origin of this insight to his childhood belief that he could use rationalization to manipulate emotion. He never seriously considered the position that such a need was itself an outgrowth of emotion or that, similarly, scientific thought may be both as "emotional" and as "unemotional" as any other type of thought. Ellis seemed adamantly opposed to the very venture we have undertaken in this chapter – to examine the various ways in which emotional thinking influenced his own different types of logic – including scientific thought. Presenting Ellis's ideas as a system with our own tools of emotional and cognitive analysis gives rise easily to an oppositional set of feelings and the logic that goes most easily with oppositional affect – perhaps because Ellis intended for all readers to feel opposition to his ideas. In contrast to Rogers who expected his readers to feel surprise at the emerging change in their thoughts, Ellis encouraged opposition and then a substitution of one belief for another. But it is more than instructive to attempt to examine how Ellis's own position emerges. From our perspective, Ellis's own theory is driven by his emotional preferences and history. He was the least flexible, the most resistant to change, of our three therapists.

In our analyses, we found that Ellis too early-on became more of a parent than his parents and adopted many of their traits, only slightly transformed. He wrote that he was easily angered, like his father. He worked obsessively, like his father, and this was a target of his early therapy. Although he was initially shy with women, he advocated "open marriages" and casual sexual contact and was openly contemptuous of contemporary attitudes to sexuality, like his father. In his therapeutic work and personal philosophy, he was forever fixing the ravages of hysteria as he had worked to fix his mother and siblings at an early age. Yet he did not demolish either parent, and he never abandoned his mother or siblings. His early successful caring and rescuing of others from their hysterical feelings became a lifelong habit, one that enlarged itself and extended to the community. Ellis transformed what was, in some respects, a handicap, into enormous success in many realms of life. Ellis's story is not a simple repetition of childhood issues, however. Overcoming trauma, neglect, and difficulty led him to have a need to repair, not to produce problematic histories repetitively in his career work. The awful fears and terrors emerge as organizers of his whole self in quite productive ways.

Like Rogers, Ellis was little concerned with the origins or content of emotions. He mentioned that emotions have "stimuli," but mentioned nothing within the broad class of "stimuli" that was specific to any emotion. It is the emotions themselves that primarily concerned Ellis, not the losses and loves, illnesses or accomplishments that led to the emotions. This focus is remarkable given his commitment to sexual relationships. The complex and diverse loves, friendships, attachments, or infatuations of adulthood were never systematically explored. His therapeutic stance was oriented toward correcting emotional extravagance, just as Rogers was oriented to correcting emotional inhibition. Neither man, not surprisingly, at the middle of the mechanistic twentieth century, consciously attended to the systems that emotions emerge from and build within particular content areas or relationships. Neither anticipated complex organizations of ideas and feelings, the ways that emotions are embedded in history and events and relationships. Not only was the content not very important to Ellis but note that there was no hint that emotions operate between people as well as within the individual. His focus was on the emotion within an individual. There was seldom a suggestion that the person with anxiety might need to examine his or her human relationships directly because they were worthy of being anxious about. Ellis was not likely to consider the themes or scenes that might be important in personality – no Oedipal conflict, no intimacy crises, no dreams or wishes. Instead, Ellis focused directly on emotionality, particularly on fearful and awful emotions.

Ideoaffective Themes: Nontransforming Adult Development

In working with Ellis, it is necessary to unravel the apparent contradictions as far as we can. Why did he repeatedly set himself up for socially daring and dangerous situations when being afraid was a blow to his self-esteem and possibly even his identity or sense of self? Why did he put such distance between himself and others with his rationalization and contempt while clearly staying in the business of listening to people and helping them? Why did he repeatedly argue against absolute beliefs and demands in an absolute manner? The personality theorist who looks at repetitive scenes might say that the answer is clear – Ellis attempted to repeat the childhood scene in which he was frightened and repeatedly prove, as an adult, that this can no longer happen to him. Perhaps that is too simple.

After all our analysis of Ellis's writing over several decades, it is clear that the fearful, anxious, and awful feelings kept coming back. In other words, the threat of being overwhelmed by fear was omnipresent. Although he could make the frightening go away – he needed to make it go away and go away and go away. It had to be controlled not only in himself but also in other people. And fear had to be controlled not only in behavior but even in thoughts. Thoughts directly about awful things were obvious targets, but even thoughts about more neutral things that are not absolutely certain might be invitations to terror. This meant that his preferred cognitive style or habit was necessarily absolute and clear. To not be certain, to be relativistic, was to invite fear and anxiety and a whole cascade of overwhelming emotions. It was important to be certain and to avoid not being certain.

Some theories of emotion insist that people will always avoid negative emotion and seek positive emotion. Common sense observation tells us that this is a limited rule. Ellis's emotional life is not one in which he actually avoids negative emotion and seeks positive emotion. The dilemma is that Ellis repeatedly puts himself in situations in which he will find, perhaps produce, negative feelings. If repetition of punishing childhood experiences is not sufficient to understand this, perhaps we can get a better understanding from theories of emotional functioning.

Among the emotions theorists, Tomkins's (1966) work takes us one step beyond simple repetitions of childhood scenes and suggested how stable organizations are formed in a larger sense. Tomkins wrote about emotional circularity providing a basis for addiction in cigarette smokers. For Tomkins, the keys to unlocking an addiction in which one needs to smoke and needs to avoid not smoking provided both positive and negative emotion. A system in which the one is the prompt for the other gradually emerged. They did not require external experience but circularly relied upon each other. Ellis did not need an external cue or to pay attention to the content of his experience; he needed only to be aware of the circular negative and positive feelings.

In Tomkins's example, the positive affect smoker might have a cigarette after a meal to increase his enjoyment. If he decides to change his habit, he primarily needs to find an alternative source of pleasure. His pleasure could be flexibly attached to many things, and it is quite possible for him to change. The negative affect smoker has a cigarette when he is anxious or depressed to reduce his suffering. If he decides to change, he primarily needs to solve his problems or find other comfort. Again, his negative affect reduction could be flexibly attached to many things and can be changed from cigarettes to something else. The unfortunate emotionally addicted smoker has both a push and a pull. He enjoys his cigarette and he suffers when he is not enjoying his cigarette. When he is not smoking, not smoking in particular makes him anxious. Then when he smokes, he feels good and stops smoking. But soon, not smoking will again produce anxiety and so forth. Whenever he is away from smoking, he misses it and will miss it until he can smoke again. Using Tomkins's model of repetitive affective experiences, we argue that Ellis was addicted to controlling intense emotion. He did not just manage it in response to different events in a flexible way. If no emotion needed management, he searched for one and felt its absence in his life as an anxious lack of clear direction. The management of emotion itself is a driving force, independent of the situations providing meaning to his identity. For example, the absence of manageable ideas about sexuality, that is, the presence of beliefs that seemed contradictory to him, led to the emergence of terrible feelings. He was more aware of suffering from the cognitive and affective disturbance than from consequences of intimate problems. Unlike Rogers, who could face contradiction with an enjoyment of the mystery, Ellis was repelled by contradiction.

Fear and Contempt: A Particular Closed Organizing System

It is probably important that the particular emotions that Ellis managed were fear related. In each case as we examine the ideoaffective structures of Ellis, Rogers, and Perls, only a few emotions have come forward as very frequent for each man. Not only is it worth knowing that some emotions are more frequent than others for different individuals and that this is a fairly stable bias on each person's part, but the exact nature of the frequent emotions may be extremely important in giving insight into the variable relationships between emotion, thought, and behavior. In deciding whether an emotion is central to the personality organization, we have attended to the frequency of its expression, the variety of contexts in which it occurs, the emotions it might occur with, and whether it is an emotion the person actively avoids or seeks.

Of all the emotions, fear is the most toxic to us all (see Ohman, 1999; Tomkins, 1962). When it is unmanaged or unavoidable, it can contribute to mental and physical illness and death. Yet fear is necessary because it communicates emergency. Because of its necessity and its toxicity, there would likely be a multitude of ways to use, avert, and control fear. In Ellis's case, one method of control is oppositional. When fear is salient, he may both point it out and then make a mockery of fear. These two approaches are two sides of the same coin.

We often find the oppositional mode of controlling fear in young children, but it can be found anywhere. It would not be impossible for Ellis to have hit upon this defense as a child. It is fairly common among children of war, for example. Having been exposed to danger and having been the observers of agony and death, some children learn to be extremely vigilant. But the same children make up adventures and games that are dangerous; their vigilance toward outside risk paradoxically encourages them to initiate risk. There are reports of children playing games in which they dart in front of armed tanks or through firing ranges. This "daring" is well understood to be the children's attempt to control dangerous situations magically by initiating them, just as vigilance is another route to control. If they can "win," they repeatedly demonstrate their personal charmed invulnerability and cleverness. They learn to seek out danger to demonstrate that while some people may be in danger, they are not. On the positive side, such children may – when lucky – learn valuable coping skills for dangerous times. It is the dilemma of the "street-wise" child. When the risk-taking child "wins" – dares and gains, becomes the charismatic "Robinhood" of his or her time and place – then the charm and courage of the child are justly admired. However, if the child were not deeply afraid and defending against this fear, he or she would never demonstrate such daring. It is a comment on the world that child lives in. Although Ellis is a winner, too often, the danger-seeking child loses.

Background Issues: The Hidden Patterns Emerge

We would like to step aside from the description of Ellis at this point to make a general remark, one that will be elaborated later in Part V. We want the reader to recognize that what we are proposing here is quite new. We know of nowhere in the psychological literature where there is an expectation that a particular emotional bias will lead to a particular style of thinking, that the need to control fear would lead to a preference for linear logic, for example. Our present theories of intellectual change do not examine individual personalities or cognitive strategies in differing emotional contexts. Nevertheless, we know well that the developmental time course for cognition is highly variable and that many people get to a certain point and never progress or progress so slowly that we have no measure of it. We propose that this is governed by the individual's emotional history, which is, in turn, set in motion by early attachment history. The associations are ones of patterns of boundaries and fractals, not surface ones of simple associative chains of behavior.

That Rogers and Ellis can be shown to have a preference for certain cognitive biases because these biases are easily attracted to specified emotions is quite a new idea. The emotions arise at first from early attachments in the family and begin to attract supportive scenes and are changed by chance, by friends, by work, and by prevalent values of the time. They fit together and enhance each other's probability of occurrence. If we seem to belabor the relationship, it is to provide many demonstrations for this new concept. Emotions are embedded in thought, just as thought is embedded in emotion, and both are embedded in life events.

The development of relationships between emotion and cognition brings up general, broad questions about early childhood experience that have not been addressed prior to this new thinking about the organizational potential of emotions for cognition. Analysts such as Alice Miller (1981) have argued that political and economic conditions can influence whole nations in their childrearing such that the future of the vast majority of individuals in the next generation changes. She suggested in her analyses that the punitive and horrible experiences of Germans in World War I contributed to the emergence of shame scripts with obsessive and moralistic, intellectualized personality attributes. These attributes contributed to the next generation's susceptibility to extremist politics. That such characteristics might often emerge after a childhood of dealing with hostile fear is a distinct possibility. It is not entirely a repetition of previous themes of the family or culture, but an evolutionary response to old and new events.

Ellis's work and theory bring together his identity within his family and his identity in the American psychological community. Even though Ellis's early life was full of fearful times, it was not particularly hostile. He was also protected by his many opportunities for interesting successes. However, we agree with Miller's general point that emotional traits may emerge among large groups of people who are influenced not only by their family history but also by their moment in historical time.

One example of this cohesion of family and generation issues probably occurs in Ellis's orientation to sexuality. Even in the late adult writing, Ellis was still working on his family scene and transforming it into a therapeutic stance while finding his place in American society and history. He could not rely upon his family to care for him, and he continued to bring that fact into his adult experience as an example of his independence. The other side of that scene was that he could not help his family change, he could only convert himself. In his early childhood "conversion experience," he found that he could be dismissive of his family and believe only in himself and his own logic to control his dreads. He could live on the edge of his family. Ellis's dreads were minimized through contemptuous blocking or rejection of partners rather than through sympathetic intimacy or loving concern. He was, thereby, always self-sufficient. To solve the problem by oneself with contemptuous distancing was satisfactory, but actively creating distance required getting close first. He wrote several self-mocking portrayals of his early love experiences in which the loved one caused him great anguish, but he always dealt with his own feelings alone and never immersed himself in the relationships.

Ellis on the Frontier

As a working therapist, Ellis had no expectancies that the client might teach him something or even inadvertently add to his life, as did Rogers, and sometimes even Perls. He seemed unaware of the paradox that people leaned upon him to become self-sufficient. He conceptualized this as a learning experience, not as a relationship. These aspects of Ellis's approach may be the key to his enormous popularity in the United States. The idea that one can be educated to be self-sufficient and that in doing so one can minimize the need to be cared for or to care for others is important in the myths of frontier and immigrant America. The fears that come with this daring and lonely position are also seemingly minimized by Ellis's contemptuous and aggressive approach. This position is also appealing in an anxious society such as the United States. Ellis is an American phenomenon.

In respect to Ellis's historical time and his incredible popularity and influence during his lifetime, it is clear that Ellis's philosophy and therapeutic stance resonate in American culture. Many aspects of American culture arise from the feeling that people are independent pioneers and revolutionaries. Ellis's revolutionary ideas about sexual living were probably compatible with many of his peers in the sixties. Some observers of the American scene embed this whole period in the middle of the twentieth century and call it the "age of anxiety." Living independently whether it is on the edge of the wilderness or on the edge of culture is much valued in American views. Living on edges, tempting fate, and taunting those who seek more stable and traditional ground is intimately and necessarily woven into feelings of anxiety and fearfulness. Inevitably, fearsome things happen when one moves to unstable and undeveloped positions or places. Feelings of fearfulness and anxiety are apparently easily perceived, yet they are not acceptable. Ellis offered workable solutions to the anxiety but did not directly confront the values for living on the edge in an independent fashion that necessarily lead to the anxiety. Being a revolutionary or a pioneer is valuable for him and many of his peers. Solving problems independently is best. Aggressively controlling and managing one's anxiety by oneself is of the utmost importance. Again and again American thoughts return to these values.

Even in psychology, Americans have been singularly oriented to simple cause-and-effect solutions to learning, to distress, to anxiety, to hostility. These solutions favor "correcting" the attitudes or knowledge within individuals, not of examining contexts or of changing expectations. For decades, American psychology claimed that emotion did not even exist. Then when it became possible to study emotion and ideas about its functions changed, we moved into "managing" emotion within individuals. If there were emotional problems, they occurred within particular individuals who could be treated independent of their peer group or their working or political environment. As yet, few expect emotions to be talents, to be significant in the thoughts and attitudes of the powerful, or to be parts of the environment. At best they motivate when properly managed. In this system, there is no genius to emotion.

In the ongoing American tradition, Ellis has the core of many of the important values in his therapeutic approach. When asking college students to judge Ellis, Rogers, and Perls from films and to choose one as a desirable therapist, the majority of the students chose Ellis. They liked that he did not seem to probe and to look for things about themselves that might be hidden. They liked that he focused on observable behaviors and claimed to help people change any undesirable features that they, themselves might identify. Students felt that he shared their values, would respect their boundaries, and would be helpful in the limited way that they wanted help. Even at the beginning of a new century, it seems that Ellis projects beliefs that parallel the coming generation of North American adults.

9 Dialectical Logic and Excitement, Disgust, and Shame

Fritz Perls

Self-interruptions can readily be observed. The "er . . . er" and "uf" of any *self-conscious* speaker, the incomplete sentences, the gaps within sentences, may *irritate* you as much as an interrupted gesture. Your neighbor at the dinner table stretches out his hand for the sugar and stops it in mid-air, asking you whether you take sugar with your coffee. He looks at you and immediately interrupts the visual contact by withdrawing his eyes, for he begins to feel *embarrassed*. A very important interruption is interfering with the transformation of basic *excitement* into specific *emotions*. Again the interference is executed against the aware symptoms, since all the self-preaching ("now, don't get *excited*!") helps not one whit. Instead, one stops breathing, holds the diaphragm, diverts one's attention. And then one of the fundamental neurotic symptoms, *anxiety*, comes into being. Thus, *anxiety* is not repressed libido, or repressed aggression, or repressed death instinct, or repressed exhibitionism; or repressed expressionism; it is any one of these or other possibilities. It is, practically speaking, the inability to take the step to any *emotional* involvement. One is *anxious* to be oneself, but *afraid* to, for the self is the ever-flowing, ever-changing *emotional* engagement and disengagement with and from the world about us. Love, hate and peace; impatience, dread and interest; appetite, frustration and satisfaction; expectation, disappointment and appreciation; *guilt*, *resentment* and gratitude, are some of the triangles of our life; they are the dialectical opposites and their integration. . . . It is obvious now that the therapeutic procedure (which is the re-establishment of the self by integrating the dissociated parts of the personality) must be the teaching of "non-interruption"

[italics added]. Fritz Perls (From an unpublished manuscript: "Psychiatry in a New Key" written about 1950)

In this quotation, Perls bombards us with compelling ideas. One barely, if at all, grasps one point and he brings in another. It is up to the audience or reader to provide a context that might link the thoughts. But if the reader provides a context, it is possible to perceive a certain wholeness. Perls's writing is an example of his thought. He has multiple incompletions or mini-interruptions of himself as he rushes excitedly from one point to the next.

As one might expect for a person with discontinuities in his thoughts, Perls's principal emotions were in different spaces, and they are emotions that impose interruption. Perls began with shame and self-consciousness, moving to irritation. These feelings arose from interruptions of behavior and connection that he claimed the "self" created. He did not see them as formed *between* people as part of the dialogue of tentative approach. There was no continuous dialogue in which one would approach, look away, wait for a response, wait for the other person to hesitate or look away, and then offer more of an approach. If he had recognized the dialogue he might have been aware of a more continuous rhythm. Looking at each person separately separates the parts, and discontinuity appears. Perls, like most analysts of his time, saw the individual in isolation, not as participating in a dance in which partners alternate in their leading and following.

Anxiety/fear and excitement formed another pole in Perls's thoughts. They were not quite attached to the previous sugar-in-the-coffee scene, but they were a trio of emotions that occurred in an internal, private process. If one interrupted the excitement, one created anxiety. Was the self-consciousness in response to rising excitement as well? Perls had skipped a step here. Having done so, he then emphasized a need to establish continuity or cohesiveness, a flowing from experiences – "Love, hate and peace; impatience, dread and *interest*; appetite, frustration and satisfaction; expectation, disappointment and appreciation; *guilt, resentment* and gratitude [italics added]". Once again, Perls did not tell us how these feelings or perceptions are connected, only that they are. He picked out opposites for us, claimed continuity, but created opposition. Perhaps he believed he had presented two poles and their integration, but what he did is hard to grasp. Is appetite the interaction of frustration and satisfaction? Is guilt the integration of resentment and gratitude? Perhaps the pairing we chose was the one he intended, perhaps not.

Perls is often deep and complex, but he shows in this quotation, as in most of his writing, that he was extremely sensitive to interruptions – which are the cognitive side of shame. He was forever designing systems to overcome these feelings and thoughts. The systems of emotion and cognitive process are redundant and between them produce particular themes, as we saw earlier in our examination of Rogers and Ellis.

Perls's thoughts interrupt each other, his emotions do the same, and his thematic concerns are for the repair of such discontinuity.

As described in the introductory quotation, Perls was exceedingly ambivalent in his presentation of human interaction. Other people were attractive, but they provided occasions for irritation and shame – resulting in anxiety. On the one hand, he often argued that one knows oneself only in a context. So contact in interaction was highly desirable as a way of knowing oneself; however, he emphasized its contribution to knowing others less. Neither did he focus on the world that grows up on the boundaries of two or more people as opposed to the world that exists when each of them is alone, although he did believe that therapy needed to be in groups so that these boundaries could appear.

Perls revealed a key part of his life story or personality themes loudly and clearly in a single quote, just as Ellis and Rogers did; we just need to know how to recognize it. He portrayed people, including himself, as in danger of falling into confusion. This confused sense of identity arose from disintegrating due to constant self-interruption, constantly stopping contact and completion. He did not directly fear emotional overload as Ellis did, nor emotional inhibition per se as Rogers did, but he dreaded something more basic – that he might lose touch with himself. His creative solution to this dread was to become exceptionally aware of the minute, nonverbal expressions of experience. His detailed knowledge of people's feelings both gave him a power of knowing and allowed him to stay in an intense zone of experience himself. It also gave him an intellectual distance – as the analyzer – that reduced his potential for humiliation. He is the knowing observer. In this state of heightened awareness, the deadening aspects of interrupting emotions such as shame might not overtake him.

Looking at this introductory quotation, we see first that Perls was focused on what the person was *not* saying. Perls needed to know what is hidden foremost. The person expressed himself with stammering and interrupting gestures. Was Perls expecting us to be sympathetic to the person's dilemma? Perls rather believes that we will be *irritated*. The hesitations and "self-interruptions" provoked hostility.

Then Perls switched to another constellation. Perls interrupted himself (and us). We are not to know the outcome of the brief interaction. We were allowed to see only the single flash contact, or rather, the moment of incomplete contact. The dinner companion caught his eye and was overwhelmed by the intensity of the contact, looked away embarrassed. Perls again was not overtly sympathetic. He judged that the person was working from an old idea of "do not get excited," some ancient prescription about being ashamed of positive involvement. It was not possible that the looking away might sometimes be a regulatory device to keep experience and interaction at a balance. Perls implied that the embarrassment operated against self-awareness, that being humiliated split the self into an aware side and an unaware side; the person lacked wholeness. Perls noticed (one of his many brilliant asides) that embarrassment influences the process of awareness.

Again and again, Perls shifted his own attention and our focus – looking away from us, metaphorically, in his writing. Instead of following up on the question of how embarrassment, shame, or humiliation operated, he went on to another point. He now claimed that the embarrassment operated to produce anxiety because it had interrupted true knowledge of the emotional contact. The stranger was anxious *to* engage but afraid at the same time. The stranger blocked his awareness of a desire to make contact and felt only the anxiety. Again Perls offered a potentially notable insight, but left that topic, too, before providing us with the full picture. Perls was in danger of becoming what he seemed most to dread – an interrupter.

Perls moved ahead again to speak of the dialectic of experience, which involves movement through a variety of emotional realms without hindrance. Like Ellis and the younger Rogers, Perls had placed the solution of emotional problems internally. It is the experience within that hinders or enhances, not the prospects in the actual world. Perls did not see a sympathetic, helpful, supportive person in this contact, only people striving – at best – to see each other clearly. The problem was not perceived to be deliberate deception, but rather tentativeness and ambivalence.

What about Perls's cognitive or intellectual process in this opening quote? Not only is there likely to be redundancy across cognitive and emotional systems, but micro examples such as this paragraph are likely to demonstrate macro processes that we will later see stretching across decades. At first in this micro example, it seems that Perls was using concrete observation only. As an artist might, he looked at the world. He saw the world in terms of the fragments of expressions. He did not tell us how he saw this or how to pick out the significant from the insignificant. He did not tell us how to make sense of foreground and background.

Perls's simple observation of gestures and expressions obscures an approach to another logic. If one starts with the conclusion and works backward, one might find a causal logic: "It is obvious now that the therapeutic procedure...must be the teaching of 'non-interruption.'" Perls, as therapist, intended that the person not interrupt himself with contradictory gestures of which he is not aware, that themselves produce lack of awareness and that therefore lead to anxiety as the expressions are incomplete and presumably not focused on the desired task. To persuade us of the causal links, Perls used a simple example at the beginning. He gave us the data, though he did it before telling us what we were working on. He was not thorough in setting up a formal problem and showing that his solution was the most probable one, but he did use examples to demonstrate that his solution might exist.

We also see a hint of context in this long quotation; however, it is not a continuous pattern. Perls reminded us that "the self is the ever-flowing, ever-changing *emotional* engagement and disengagement with and from the world about us." In other words, he seemed to remind us that the world is contextual and that all things change. At another point, he reminded us that one behavior may result from many sources – "Thus, *anxiety* is not repressed libido, or repressed aggression, or repressed death instinct, or repressed exhibitionism; or repressed expressionism; it is any one of these or other possibilities." So this statement, too, has a distinct relativistic flavor to it.

There is also an apparent dialectical part to the quote. Perls claimed that there is a dialectic of movement that creates a pattern of behavior or of identity, one that moves backward and forward among opposing elements – "appetite, frustration and satisfaction; expectation, disappointment and appreciation; *guilt, resentment* and gratitude." For appetite, one swings between frustration and satisfaction; for expectation or hopefulness one swings between disappointment and appreciation. Guilt is a swing between resentment and gratitude although that is perhaps less intuitively obvious. Perls did not explain why these are dialectic nor why he chose these particular examples. In addition to Perls's statement that the pattern of a person evolves from these dialectics or opposing forces, he also showed some evidence that integration may evolve from the compositions of opposites. The process of moving between frustration and satisfaction and back again creates the idea of appetite. It is not just an additive process or a substitution process but an interaction that creates something new. This relation is further evidence of a dialectical process.

Although the form of argument is not as clear as one might like, and the thoughts in the paragraph are often fragmented or disconnected, the different types of thought that we have been examining are all present in this typical but complex passage. This quotation is as complex a passage as can be found in the more mature Rogers and contains more different types of thought and presentation than Ellis would use. Except for the fragmentation, the work is more purely creative and intellectual than any work by either Rogers or Ellis. Perls has varied command of the cognitive processes discussed earlier, but he fragmented their use and perhaps mixed them too much to form any coherent argument at times. It takes a devoted reader to pick up more than scattered gems of thought, but the gems are definitely there.

Tentatively we see some alignment of different types of thinking with different emotions in the paragraph. The shame and irritation occur with the observational reports. Anxiety and fear and excitement occur with relativistic modes, and when the dialectical emerged it was with the juxtaposition of positive feelings (gratitude and appreciation) and an extensive variety of negative emotions. The only emotion that was rather silent here is sadness.

Perls clearly had a history in which being allowed to feel his own feelings, to know himself had been problematic. Others deceived him by telling him what he felt. He had rebelliously known that they were mistaken, but had been powerless to do anything other than sense the interruption and feel the fragmentation and resentment. Further, he decoded the deception of others by examining their behavior, especially their expressive behavior. This ability allowed him to ward off or to control other people's intrusions that unbalanced his fragile world. Interestingly, anyone, including ourselves, who makes a lifelong business out of detecting unspoken messages and testing them is likely to share Perls's dilemmas.

With Perls, as with Rogers and Ellis, a single, admittedly well-chosen, microcosm of his writing reveals hypotheses about his macrocosm of personality and interlaces his personality with his theoretical and clinical work. Once again we will examine these hypotheses by looking at his work across several decades. Once again, the elements such as the specific feelings, the intellectual approach, and the specific contents are interesting and important, but the organization of the elements is most important. Simply knowing Perls's traits would not be a clear view into his macrocosm, but perceiving the organization of emotion, thought, and content makes it quite clear.

The Development of Perls's Ideoaffective Processes

When we examined Rogers's writing, we proposed three hypotheses. Looking at Ellis we were forced to change parts of the theory. At first we proposed that blocked or singular emotional investment in certain ideas leads to a lack of full intellectual work on the ideas. In Rogers's case we found that his focus on happiness in isolation from other emotions was related to a singular mode of intellectual analysis that was necessarily incomplete, though useful. Similarly with Ellis, his singular use of fear was closely associated with a singular use of one incomplete intellectual style.

A blocked affect, such as blocked anger in Rogers's case, resulted in flawed logic that led to a failure in following any intellectual argument to completion. Similarly with Ellis, his blocking of contempt often led to concrete perception with no system or to a faulty causality. With Perls, we find interruptions and incomplete interactions right on the surface of his writing. The incomplete thoughts also suggest blocked emotional processes. He actually addresses the dilemma of blocking but is still blocked emotionally and cognitively.

Second, we proposed that the elaboration of certain ideas with a wide variety of emotions leads to commitment to explore those ideas with the person's best creative and intellectual efforts. When applied fully, changes in intellectual power will emerge indicating that understanding of the ideas or experiences has matured. In Rogers's case, there was considerable evidence for this, but not in Ellis's. While Ellis had an extraordinary rate of emotional expression, he did not differentiate the emotions as to function, as Rogers had done. So we amended the second hypothesis to include that multiple emotions applied to an idea will lead to developmental change only if the emotions are differentiated and organized. Undifferentiated blocks of emotionality appear to function as emotional blocks. There are instances in Perls's writing when emotions appear to be differentiated and diverse. It is here that we expect his best work.

Third, we proposed that changes in emotional experience lead to or are interrelated with transformations in intellectual style. Even though this still may be true, the systems of transformation are not required to be linear. In Rogers's case, emotional change was related linearly to intellectual maturity. In Ellis's case, there was little evidence of emotional change and little evidence of intellectual transformation. Ellis added new material constantly and showed an assimilative style of growth rather than the transformative development that Rogers had shown. With Perls, we expect a possible new addition to our theory of adult emotional and intellectual growth. Perls's repeated self-interruptions and focus on a particular cycle of interrupting emotions – shame and contempt – lead to the formation of personality that is very susceptible to accommodation. Perls cycled in response to situational demands and opportunities, so he appeared to be flexible. However, an underlying lack of change in emotional or intellectual process resulted from his particular emotional abilities.

Work in the Early Years: Building and Exploring the Emotional Scripts

It is more difficult to confirm Perls's working characteristics than it was for Ellis or Rogers because we cannot be certain that all Perl's writing is his alone. Partly for this reason we chose the spoken example at the beginning. It is more likely to be entirely his own. Perls's principal contribution, *Gestalt Therapy* (1951), was co-authored by Goodman, Hefferline, and Perls. While Perls may have inspired much of the book, the exact contributions of Perls to the book are not clear. *Gestalt Therapy Verbatim* (1969b) seems likely to be faithful to his own expression, but it is edited. As the foreword states, the transcripts are essentially verbatim, but changes are made "to clarify meaning," and they are "selected" by the editors. The other book we examine, *Ego, Hunger and Aggression* (1947/1969), is controversial as to authors. In the British edition, Perls acknowledged that a major contribution was made by his wife, Laura Perls, but this credit did not appear in the U.S. edition. Laura Perls herself said that she and Fritz Perls worked together on the book and that her interest in infant feeding and weaning inspired the book. We are particularly ready to credit others with editing and smoothing out the writing because there is a contrast between manuscripts or talks that are more purely Perls and those that have been assisted. Perls by himself is a discontinuous speaker and writer, which is a problem for journal and book projects. Because of these problems with pinpointing Perls's independent writing, our analyses will be more tentative than with Rogers and Ellis. We will also just focus on one or two aspects of his emotional life that illustrate new ideas rather than attempting a broad approach.

Ego, Hunger and Aggression is an early book (1947/1969) by Fritz Perls and, as we noted, is undoubtedly heavily influenced by Laura Perls and possibly partly written by her. Reflecting upon it twenty years after the first publication, Perls wrote that it was "the transition from orthodox psychoanalysis to the Gestalt approach" (1969a p. 5). It does indeed introduce new Gestalt concepts and critiques some aspects of orthodox psychoanalysis. It is a more academic and, perhaps, intellectual work than Rogers or Ellis usually produced, although both Rogers's and Ellis's earliest productions were also more dense, even pedantic, than their later work.

Ego, Hunger and Aggression is composed of three parts. One is tempted to draw analogies to Caesar's Gaul and to pursue the famous quote "I came, I saw, I conquered." In the first section, Perls came to his problem via a historical and philosophical review. In the second section, Perls saw what his contribution could be to theoretical psychology and its applications, and in the third section, Perls conquered the illnesses of his patients.

The first part of *Ego, Hunger and Aggression* is called "Holism and Psychoanalysis." Here thirteen very short chapters address many traditional philosophical or psychological questions. They also set forth the premises and concerns of Gestalt psychology. The first section of the book reviews traditional questions pertaining to psychoanalysis and Gestalt therapy. Perls considered such traditional issues as the unconscious and the sex instinct, topics that Perls believed were overly stressed in orthodox psychoanalysis while it "underestimates or neglects" ego functions and the hunger instinct. Perls attempted to fill in gaps he perceived in the original theory and used an approach he called "holistic" and "semantic."

The second part of the book gives a more detailed presentation of novel Perlsian views on hunger instincts, resistance, emotional resistance, personality split, megalomanic-outcast complex, sensomotoric resistances, and related topics – what Perls "saw" in the field of psychoanalysis. It brings us closer to the creative focus of this book. There are chapters entitled "Hunger Instinct" and "Mental Food," a discussion of Perls's early description of the "dummy complex," and again a set of short reflections on traditional analytic topics. This section of the book reveals Perls's principal concerns in personality.

The final third of the book focuses on "Concentration-Therapy," the practice of therapy as Perls laid it out in the middle of the twentieth century. It consists of short chapters each of which is an exercise in becoming more aware or "ego-conscious." We read about "concentration" and, more specifically, "Concentration on Eating." Perls summarized the third section, writing that it "is designed to give detailed instructions for a therapeutic technique resulting from the changed theoretical outlook. As avoidance is assumed to be the central symptom of nervous disorders, I have replaced the method of free associations . . . by . . . concentration" (1947/1969, p. 8).

Overall, *Ego, Hunger and Aggression* is an intellectually dense and wonderfully challenging book, but not one likely to become popular as the later Rogers's and most of Ellis's books have been popular. There are references throughout to philosophical and psychoanalytic theories and theorists and nomenclature in Greek and in symbols made up by the author. It is written for scholars and, of course, for practitioners of psychoanalysis.

Emotional Content in the Early Years

The first chapter in *Ego, Hunger and Aggression* (1947/1969) that we analyze is called "Organismic Reorganization." Perls opened with dialectical opposition, a common Perlsian theme, as we already discovered in the opening quotation. Perls proposed that every theory will create a corrective countertheory. He believed, for example, that psychology and psychoanalysis naturally arose to counter the mechanistic thinking of the nineteenth century. These two approaches to knowledge, the mechanical and the analytic, represent opposite ends of a pendulum swing – if mechanistic thinking becomes ascendant then psychoanalysis rises to balance it.

Perls then moved to look briefly at the dichotomies created in similar pendulum fashion within psychoanalytic schools. "It is difficult to remain near the zero-point – not to be lifted to the heights of enthusiasm nor to slide down into the depths of despair" (1947/1969, p. 72). He saw the back and forth as a swing between *despair* and *enthusiasm* (not the usual positive–negative swing of sadness and joy, take note). Further, he believed that theorists on outer points of the pendulum swing *despise* each other. He, himself, was contemptuous of "those analysts who go fundamentally astray" (1947/1969, p. 72), analysts such as Rank and Jung, who did not take a whole-person approach to psychological problems but instead focused on "isolated problems." He mentioned that Adler and Riech at least offered complementary positions to Freud and thereby made a modest contribution. Perls was openly contemptuous of the battles between Freudians and Adlerians, their "pseudo-tolerant" and "uninterested" attitudes toward each other. His point for holistic or organismic approaches was that isolating problems rather than considering the whole person and his or her context is wrong. However, his own contempt for other psychoanalytic positions infused every paragraph. As a Gestaltist, he firmly believed that piecemeal solutions or piecemeal problems are worthless. Even though he obviously spoke of himself as well as his colleagues when he wrote that people from different schools "despise" each others' philosophies, he seemed to ignore the possibility that his own theory might have a counterpoint or that he might be intolerant or have a piecemeal solution.

Perls also described "dialectics." By dialectics Perls meant that opposites define a system rather than merely cancel each other out. In this manner, he defined psyche and body as opposing poles and later defined synthesis and analysis as opposing poles. In reorganizing the organism, Perls argued that all seemingly opposing aspects were needed. In viewing the development of psychoanalysis, Perls argued for a swing in the direction of the body and emotions to counterbalance the attention given to mental experience which he called psyche. In that body and emotion have been neglected, as well as the whole organism viewpoint, he intended to correct the imbalance with Gestalt theory by reintroducing body and emotion.

When dealing dialectically with theory and theorists involving issues of the mind, or psyche, Perls worked in an emotional context that emphasized enthusiasm and interest, swinging to despair and contempt with most emotions mentioned. The complex intellectual material was accompanied with complex logic and emotion. However, when he turned to describe issues of the body, his emotional content abruptly shifted to embarrassment. In particular, he was concerned about the lack of expression of embarrassment.

Perls's argument about embarrassment is interesting. As long as he treated it intellectually, his dialectical or oppositional thinking offered complexity. He argued that the orthodox psychoanalytic mode urges the patient not to suppress embarrassing material. Perls thought that a patient "eager" to cooperate would "force himself" to tell everything. "So he becomes shameless, but not free from shame" (1947/1969, p. 74). The patient has then developed a technique to avoid feeling shame or embarrassment. Perls promised to provide new therapeutic techniques later to overcome this form of resistance to embarrassment and also to disgust, fear, and guilt.

Perls, was, of course, not wrong. Urging someone to stop inhibiting is still a method of control that naturally inhibits free expression. If a child looks ashamed when told to do so by a parent, she does not express her own feelings, which maybe that she is ashamed to show shame. If the patient *must* talk about shaming things, then he might try to talk about them disinterestedly, objectively, or "clinically." Perls was correct in stating that to do so does not make such things less embarrassingly powerful.

At this point, there is a sudden break in the chapter, the first of several. Perls first dealt with highly theoretical issues, and then the issue of embarrassment, itself barely an issue embedded in the theoretic material. Then he shifted to an entirely new subject – anxiety. There is literally a space made in the chapter between the paragraphs, though there are no headings. If we were in analysis with Perls, we would question his need to avoid the discussion of embarrassment in favor of anxiety. We are aware that he has opened an issue but not finished it, interrupting himself. This self-interruption is a serious concern of Perls's and one that he is repeatedly subject to. Indeed, as we have already seen in the opening quotation, many years later in a different country and before an audience, Perls has a similar style of self-interruption, which was still organized around embarrassment.

We are in the same brief chapter entitled "Organismic Reorganization," having been introduced to a weighty topic in the context of a major theoretical attack on orthodox psychoanalysis and then exposed to a number of Perlsian gems of thought about embarrassment. Next Perls absolutely dropped everything he has introduced. In his writing, he turned away from the reader and the reader's interest. This shift creates a curious effect on the reader of being abandoned and made to feel stupid, a dummy, as Perls would say. Just as Perls drew us into his ideas, fascinating us, he left us. The reader must leap along, or limp along, ignoring his own needs for completion and trying to make a "gestalt" or a wholeness of this chapter.

Perls leapt into the phenomenon of anxiety. The previous section had no one dominant emotion, stretching across a wide spectrum of emotions and using complex dialectical logical systems; however, this next section created quite a manic emotional contrast. It raced along with anxiety and also excitement. In a mere six pages, Perls used the word "anxiety" more than forty-five times and the word "excitement" more than thirty-five times, but only one "rage" and one "despair" made it into this section of the narrative. Perls's writing gives an excellent example of how scholarly, written language can be as individual as nonverbal expression. It shows that scholarly and scientific writing overflows with personal expression, as well as learned convention.

Perls began this section on anxiety by once again presenting a selection of theories. In this first book, Perls was traditionally academic in presenting background sources before he presented his own ideas. He assimilated unusually broad categories of information and categorized them in unusual ways, which is characteristic of people who are highly creative. The particular theories used in this chapter were about anxiety, of course, and came from diverse areas of medicine (his source of bodily images, given his medical training) and psychoanalysis (his source of emotional images). On the one hand, he suggested that the medical practitioner comes across anxiety in connection with heart disease. Medical practitioners are also supposed to know that excitement is associated with heart attacks and warn their patients against excitement. On the other hand, orthodox psychoanalysts believed that anxiety neurosis is related to suppressed sexual impulse or suppressed aggression.

Perls suggested, anxiously and relativistically, that since several theories are in conflict with each other, a number of things might be going on. His argument appeared to be relativistic because he began by giving each of the theories some credence within the realm of things that it aims to explain and within the realm of its own expertise. However, as did Ellis in the context of fears and anxieties, Perls was quick to find a common single force underlying all the theories that account for them all. It is a somatic explanation for Perls, though for Ellis it was a cognitive solution. Both men, when thinking in the context of fears, used linear, absolute thinking, looking for cause-and-effect, single answers. That various sorts of things might lead to anxiety and that they might not be 100 percent predictable, but stochastic, did not occur to either Perls or Ellis in the final analysis. It is likely that fearfulness produces this cognitive approach in general. When we are afraid, we all may look for absolute, even magical, answers, without regard for complexity.

In every example he used, no matter what the origin, Perls argued that the problem in anxiety was breathing, or rather, blocking breathing. "Eliminating all the incidental factors we realize that excitement and lack of oxygen form the nuclei of the theories . . . and when observing an anxiety attack, we invariably find excitement and difficulty in breathing" (1947/1969, p. 76). Perls made a lightening-like leap here. We either follow him or we do not because he will not fill in his train of thought. Instead he claimed, grandiosely, that he has solved "a thousand-year-old riddle": how is excitement converted into anxiety? Some of us may not have known this was a thousand-year-old riddle, but Perls does not hear such complaints. For the answer to his own riddle, he turned first to a semantic analysis and examined the Latin roots of the word "anxious." He discovered that it refers both to high tension and to contraction or narrowing. It was then intuitively obvious to Perls that the word "anxiety" means to control excitement. When people get excited and suppress the expression of excitement, they reduce their oxygen by making their

muscular breathing system rigid. "In a state of anxiety an acute conflict takes place between the urge to breathe (to overcome the feeling of
choking), and the opposing self-control (p. 77). "Anxiety equals excitement plus inadequate supply of oxygen" (1947/1969, p. 77). This little
theorem is derived linearly from premises that are not examined at all.
If one accepts Perls's premises, then the conclusion seems clear. If one
does not accept his premises, then the conclusion may be logical, but
still false. As is typical of most simple linear analysts, including, as we
have already seen, Ellis, and the young Rogers, Perls seemed unaware
of the fly in the ointment of his argument.

   Because Perls had the genius to have taken a thousand-year-old problem and found a simple answer, using linear logic again, he naturally
was able to have a simple cure. "One can learn to overcome anxiety by
relaxing the muscles of the chest *and* giving vent to the excitement. Often
no deep analysis is required, but . . . concentration therapy may be indicated" (1947/1969, p. 78). He then asserted that he ignored details such
as the "carbon-dioxide content of the blood." This aside with reference
to pseudomedical jargon is part of the grandiosity. He finally "proved"
his theorem by presenting himself as a case. "My chest felt constricted so
that I could scarcely breathe, I would not stand or sit and was pacing the
building like a lunatic . . . I was practically speechless and shaking like
a leaf" (1947/1969, p. 79). Although this scene occurred when he took
his medical qualifying exams, he attributed the anxiety only to a problem with suppressed excitement and breathing. He took an emotional
problem that is usually conceived as having complex ideational roots,
as well as somatic roots, and reduced it simply to a somatic problem.

   As Perls moved away from the first emotionally and cognitively elaborated section in which many emotions catch his attention to the length-
ier section that is overwhelmed with anxiety and excitement, he became
more absolute in his reasoning. Perls searched for the single solution in
the second section. He found it through a convoluted logic. He discovered that the common denominator among the various theories is that
breathing is suppressed during excitement and that this suppression of
the mechanics of breathing results in anxiety.

   So after all the tentative dialecticisms and delicate balance of emotions in the first section of the chapter, we come to an abrupt shift, an
overwhelming emphasis on anxiety and excitement and a shift to mechanistic thinking. Even though Perls was clearly capable of dialectical and
balanced patterned thought, he was also clearly overwhelmed by ideas
and feelings about anxiety and excitement, so much so that he resorted

to the very flawed mechanistic thinking that he "despised" in the earlier section. Rather than achieve some kind of balance, integration, or synthesis between psyche and body, he threw his entire weight into the body side of the equation to deal with anxiety. This change occurred at the point of discussing embarrassment. There are at least two sides to Perls: he swung abruptly from one mode of analysis and emotional context to another and seemed unaware of this swing of the pendulum when it was happening, although such swings were a concern to him.

In the next chapter, called "Emotional Resistances," we learn more about Perls as a man as well as his theory. This chapter also has flashes of brilliance. It even forecast several seminal ideas that emerged later in Tomkins's (1962) theory of emotion. We are uncertain why the similarity between Perls and Tomkins exists, since Tomkins never referred to Perls. Perhaps they had similar training and personalities and independently developed common ways of thinking about emotion, or perhaps Tomkins just neglected his predecessors.

In this fascinating chapter, Perls first argued that Freud was overly focused on *intellectual* resistances such as justifications, rationalizations, and verbal demands of conscience and the censor. As before, Perls began with an academic review and an attack on orthodox psychoanalysis. He claimed that he wished to expand Freud's theory, presenting the importance of *emotional* resistances. In a previous chapter, he already went over somatic resistances. Perls presented a tripartite ("Such classification of resistances, is, of course, an artificial one" (1947/1969, p. 174) view of resistances and believed that individuals may specialize in one or the other, but that none should be neglected by the analyst.

Later in the chapter, Perls wrote that the behavior and emotion may not be different at all; "often the unfinished emotion and unfinished action are hardly differentiated" (1947/1969, p. 176). This is actually a substantial addition to orthodox psychoanalytic thought, one that is often overlooked. The Western reliance on rationality has dominated in nearly every sphere. Perls is one of the few who early recognized that much that is significant to a person's development and identity happens in noncognitive, nonrational systems. Even though Freud opened our eyes to subconscious and unconscious process, he still relied on conscious knowledge to unravel problems seemingly created by the very existence of the subconscious. Perls did not develop his thoughts – that would have been unlike him – but he did lay the groundwork for personality or identity to be composed equally of somatic processes or emotional processes. These somatic or emotional processes, when they are problematic, may be cured, according to Perls, through somatic or emotional means – without a need to track backward to intellect. Krause's (Krause, Steimer-Krause & Ullrich, 1992) work on the dialogue of disturbed people is a case in point. The disturbed person has somatic bodily gestures, and expressions that, while miniscule and seemingly irrelevant, and disconnected to his wishes and intentions, bring out disturbed expressions in other people. Patients with schizophrenic tendencies bring out contemptuous behaviors in others, for example. Perls might have argued that the cure for this reaction is to change the expression of the schizophrenic patient, rather than to cure his understanding.

As in the earlier chapter and the opening quotation, the chapter on emotional resistances is fragmented and open to various interpretations. The chapter is emotionally and cognitively diverse. There is no centering on one emotion, although there is a heavy reference to emotions in the school of shame and embarrassment (the emotion abandoned abruptly earlier in the book). There is also no centering on one mode of thought, but movement from absolute causal and mechanistic logic through relativistic or contextual presentation to an emerging dialectical logic.

Perls began his description of emotional resistances by classifying the emotions. There can be complete and incomplete emotions, positive and negative emotions, and finally, approach and avoidance emotions. There is a stop and a shift here in the chapter, typical of Perls. He did not tell us the route by which he gained the previous insights, nor did he elaborate on the insights he just provided; instead, he jumped to a new layer. Whereas he began with "incomplete" emotions, he moved abruptly to "autoplastic" and "alloplastic" emotions. The first is pleasure from destroying something such as crunching crisp food or from "running amok." Autoplastic is in the category of mourning. He gave us a brief aside on the benefits of crying, claiming that it is needed to "cure" having been hurt, presumably being the object of someone else's destructive emotion running amok. His written thoughts on this remedy verged on the pure descriptive or perceptual logic – he saw its truth and expounded on it, but he did not tell us how he knows it or what the alternatives might have been. It is at best an absolute set of statements, but more likely it is description of intuitively perceived situations. It is, in fact, tempting to consider that Perls told his own story and that he is only partially aware of it. He might be interrupting his own sense of fury and resentment with grieving, but does not see the connection – they follow with their own logic, like a slip of the tongue. Perls also ended this thought with somatization; he claims that the mourning sort of emotion has a "chemical nature." This may be so, but how did he deduce this? He did not present his path of logic for the reader, and the whole is hard to accept.

Once again, Perls started a new section on positive and negative emotions. He claimed that emotions that appear to be opposites are poles of the same dimension and vary as to intensity. Making any positive feeling too intense makes it negative. So increasing the intensity of pride brings one to shame, increasing appetite brings one to disgust, even intense love becomes hatred. And extreme elation is depression. Again, how he "knew" this is unclear. He argued from examples such as, "Children like to be hugged, but they will not like it if you 'squeeze the life' out of them" (1947/1969, p. 176). He calls it a "dialectical law." For Perls, positive and negative and low and high intensity are the same dimension. He follows this law with another law – that negative emotions cannot change back into positive emotions unless they discharge the high energy or tension that produced them. Attempting to suppress negative emotions is to suppress a high level of energy, which seems to be a doubtful possibility to Perls. Again, he baldly stated so many improbable things that it is hard to know just how to evaluate them.

Perls brought us next to consider the emotions of shame and embarrassment, which he called the "quislings" of the organism. The word "quisling" comes from the name of a Norwegian leader who agreed to govern Norway for the Nazis after Norway had been invaded in World War II. Quisling was therefore a traitor to Norway. For Perls, who suffered great losses in war, this is a powerful image. Among the emotions, shame is both a traitor and a ruler.

What is particularly striking about Perls's presentation of shame is his use of the powerful adult political metaphor – quisling – when the examples he provided were from childhood. The example Perls provided is that of the parent who does not praise the child sufficiently. The child becomes greedy for praise instead of doing the task at hand well for the pleasure of doing it well. In other words, the evil quisling traitor here is not identified as the mother, nor even the child, but an emotion that the child feels – shame. The separation of the feeling from the actors or the context is an old method of missing the point common to us all. We are all apt to say, "If only I were not so shy" or "If only I could control my temper" or "I hate it when I cry in front of the boss." We blame the emotion, as if it were a thing in itself, separate from ourselves, our history, and the immediate context.

There is clearly another story here for Perls. When Perls's playful child is being shamed, we know that the parents are not empathic to the child and may be punitive. It is not just that the child is not praised sufficiently, as Perls claimed – that would be the tip of the iceberg. The child is not attended to as a person who has feelings and thoughts of his own that need to be responded to in a graduated manner depending upon their nature. Perls described a child who when being hugged may be viciously squeezed, who when asking for praise may get neglect, and whose tea is made unpleasant by too much sugar. Perls claimed to be describing shame but was actually describing egocentric parents who do not read the child's emotional signals and who cannot modulate their own behavior, but who are intrusive or foul tempered. This is his own story, of course. In response, he compensated for the blindness and hostility of his parents, who could not see his feelings, by becoming a master reader of emotional life. No doubt he could avoid some punishment by anticipating his parents' moods. The possibility for shared empathy was not developed in this early period as it ordinarily would be (Stern, 1985). Empathy or knowledge of someone's emotions becomes a powerful separating function in Perls. He is knowing and others do not know. They do not know each other mutually.

Perls saw the solution to be the working through of the shame and the release of the exhibition. He seemed to miss that there is an underlying problem unsolved, which is the acquisition of a good relationship in which any feeling of the child, or in his case, the child grown adult, might be legitimate. Once again he left the discussion of shame unfinished or "undigested," to use Perls' phrase. He abruptly shifted to consider the behavior or the "physiology" of the emotion. The somatisizing that pervades Perls's writing has become part of Perls's creative contribution.

Perls further claimed (as did Tomkins, 1962) that shyness is a form of shame. Tomkins claimed specifically that shyness is an interrupter for intense excitement. Perls, as we noted previously, found that too much excitement, when interrupted, becomes anxiety. Both men were likely to have had experiences in which the swings in emotional dialogue with parents were too extreme and intrusive. Both were, no doubt, reflecting on their own regulation of this dilemma. Tomkins believed that the emotional dialogue got "too exciting" and that the child would look away and down to manage the excitement. Then he is able to return to the dialogue at a better level. For Tomkins, this was a strategy of managing the parent that resulted in renewed contact. This strategy appears to be more benign than Perls's, where the child who suppressed excitement with shame could not return to the dialogue at all but felt a building anxiety. It is more likely that the parent in Perls's case was not able to adapt to the reduced level but maintained a punishing level of intrusiveness and demandingness, or actually became entirely punitive when the child attempted any control strategy at all. Perls wrote about escalating child demands with the parent suppressing and condemning the child, whereas Tomkins wrote about the child as being in some control.

Once again, Perls moved to a metaphor that is power dominated and political, giving the example of a peasant girl who dressed in her finest but was then shamed by the contemptuous scrutiny of a "lady" who is more finely clothed. Perls was subconsciously giving us only examples in which there is a "master–slave" relationship. One person has absolute power to control people and resources and is contemptuous of the dependent person who can never be good enough. Perls gave yet another example. He pictured a child building a castle. The mother appeared and berated him for making a mess, saying "You ought to be ashamed of yourself." The image of a small person being bad in the eyes of a big person, even when doing good in his own eyes, is brought into being.

Perls wrote as if the emotions were the villains here. He did not focus on the master/parent or the "lady" or directly challenge them. It was the shame of the slave/child that was to blame for continuing repressions and lack of good psychological functioning. Perls went on to remind us that shame (and then also embarrassment and fear) is a quisling who might "identify with the enemy," though it is not clear who the enemy might be here. Perhaps the enemy is the parent, the shame, a tool of the enemy parent. Shame is the "tool" of repression and the producer of neurosis.

Perls was searching for solutions to a complex dilemma and wanted to find the pivotal element, a single aspect to hang the problem upon. He fastened upon the feelings of the child, rather than the whole experience and the people who might have been able to change the situation, the parents. The belief that a single element might be at issue in neurosis has been challenged repeatedly since Perls's time. For example, Tomkins (1987) (among others with related ideas) presented the contextual idea that the formation of scripts guide repetitive behavior patterns and expectations that we might call neurotic. A script requires feelings, of course, and shame might be important, but it attaches the emotion to people and situations. To acquire a powerful script (a script that seems to one to account for a large portion of one's existence (such as the optimist's "People are basically good"), one has to have repeated experiences of the basic story line seeming to be a general account of events that occur here and there and everywhere. Unraveling such a powerful script is not just a matter of dealing with the emotion but of acquiring another script in all its aspects that is equally powerful in accounting for the experiences one has had and is presently having. Accounts that apply to someone else's experiences are not acceptable.

When Perls adopted shame as a powerful metaphor, it was not only because he was shamed at some critical moment in childhood with his castle, but also because he had repeated experiences with power figures where he was unable to manage the situation and could expect no assistance or loving concern. No doubt his parents, his school masters, his army leaders, the German government, and so on produced scripts that he could interpret as "No matter how extravagantly you produce things for yourself, or for them, people who have power over you will misinterpret your intent, will see you as small and as a "mess maker," and will shame you." One must watch out for shameful feelings because they announce that one is alone and vulnerable in an unpredictable and vicious world.

If Perls could read emotions accurately, he could seemingly avoid his parents' mistakes and also be a powerful controller of situations in which he would have more knowledge than other people – someone else would be the mess maker. In many ways Perls was not much different from Ellis, who also faced difficulties with intrusive but, for Ellis, largely terrifying, scenes and who also tried to gain some mastery of the situation by blaming the emotions. Perls was less fastened on terrifying scenes and more involved with the suppression of feelings in general. He was more concerned with shame and humiliation as feelings that interrupt and control more authentic emotions.

Perls shifted to his analyst self then and agreed with much of what we have just written, without referring back to the particular examples he had just given. He was concerned that in analysis the patient bring "the complete situation; resisting emotions plus resisted actions" (1947/1969, p. 178). It is probably important that to define the complete situation he did not mention people but rather the individual's own physical action. For Perls, "whole" meant whole person, not whole scene, in spite of his claims.

Perls argued that to work effectively in analysis with expressions that have been repressed by shame, nothing should be forced from the patient. The patient needed to "endure" embarrassment in analysis, not move to a position in which nothing appeared to be embarrassing nor be allowed to hide his embarrassment. Perls believed that the "patient on the couch" approach is a way for the *analyst* to avoid embarrassment, a problem he claimed was serious for Sigmund Freud. Perls believed that both the analyst and the patient needed to admit shame and embarrassment to give release to the tensions shame produced in analysis. However, rather than exploring this idea with an example about shame, Perls instead provided examples about fear – fear of aviation and agoraphobia. If the agoraphobic patient fears to cross the street and we force him to "numb" or repress his fear in order to make the crossing, Perls believed that we leave the fear intact but provide the patient with a fragile grandiosity, which could be dangerous. Just as the child who is ashamed will act out and show off, the fearful person may brazenly dare danger. But that fear may in a roundabout way be justified. Instead, Perls believed that all the fears must be experienced and analyzed, even exaggerated for the person to return to normality. The fear of crossing the street is, therefore, a complex defense that Perls did not wish to remove prematurely. This is a very complex causal relationship surrounding fear with dialectical networks in its midst. We note that dialecticism occurs here in the context of fear rather than in the context of shame. Still, it is notable that shame itself was not discussed even though Perls had proposed to discuss shame.

This dialectical analysis of fear or shame was then moved into a consideration of disgust and of perversions. "Repression of disgust does not lead to the restoration of appetite but to greediness and stuffing. . . . Common to all these cases is the fact that the suppression of the emotional resistances absorbs most of the subject's energy and interest in life. Their endeavors in the long run are . . . exhausting and useless" (1947/1969, p. 179).

This system of emotional functioning is much more complex than either Rogers or Ellis suggested, even though each of them has a piece of Perls's hypothesis. For example, Rogers was aware of the effect of repressing emotions and the need for them to be released, which he believed automatically brought with it a release of positive emotion and even of creative abilities. But Rogers was not aware of the plethora of emotions that might be used to suppress expression or of the complexity of resistance against resistance. Rogers discussed only hostility as a suppressing emotion. On the other hand, if there is a Rogerian deep well of positive emotion waiting to spring up when the repressive emotions are released, it is not clear that Perls was aware of it or sought it. Perls did argue that the consciousness and endurance of suppressed emotion was the basis of a cure. Once again, even Perls arrived ultimately at a single solution, when a more relativistic one might have been expected.

At the end of the chapter Perls considered "the unemotional resistance which we call 'force of habit'" (1947/1969, p. 180). Once again, he ended a section, allowed a space, and shifted abruptly. Once again this happened just as he began to address some issue related to embarrassment. Once again Perls went from embarrassment to exaggeration, to a grandiose riddle: "The true nature of habit remains the darkest riddle of all" (1947/1969, p. 180). Why he found habits to be the dark side of humanity was not spelled out any more than he previously spelled out why excitement and anxiety composed an ancient riddle.

Rather than explaining why he had this belief about habits, Perls moved directly to give an example of curing these habits – this darkest riddle – with a somatic or bodily cure. He referred to the Alexander method in which the inhibition of movement is used before the habitual movement to make the habits more conscious. It is not as if Perls reviewed a variety of methods and presented the Alexander method as most fitting; it was presented as if he just had a stray thought about it. In any case, he found the Alexander method to be useful for people who are overly tense, who have a "hanging-on bite." For people with other problems, he was afraid that the meaning of the impulses would be neglected and that people might be happier "but emptier," not knowing the meaning of their behavior. Perls gave the example of a person who habitually paced to inhibit his feelings of irritation. Perls wanted him to express the irritation, not just inhibit the pacing. In this more relativistic analysis, he left his concern with embarrassment and fears and concentrated on the general idea of emotion, placing a great deal of emphasis on "interest" and some happiness.

In this chapter, as in the previous one, we are again impressed by Perls's depth and dialectical complexity in brief emotionally elaborated portions but also are struck by his abrupt changes and self-interruptions associated with shame and embarrassment and his egocentric tangents in response to the shame-related thoughts. He used a number of defensive writing strategies that emerged just when shame and embarrassment arose. He avoided shame by interrupting himself, he changed the emphasis to the somatic, even the medical/medical, or he shifted from shame to fears and anxieties. In no case did he stay with the embarrassment. Paradoxically, this is the precise problem he anticipated for clients in therapy – an inability to work through shame. Perls was aware of the problem in a general sense, clearly, but he was not aware that it pervaded his work.

To complete *Ego, Hunger and Aggression*, we chose two chapters from the third section on the application of Gestalt techniques in therapy. These two chapters toward the end of the book showed the contrast between emotionally elaborated Perlsian ideas or issues and nonemotional Perlsian ideas. The chapter entitled "Internal Silence" has only 1.5 emotion words per page, a low number for Perls. On the other hand, the chapter entitled "About Being Self-Conscious" has at least ten emotion words per page. For Perls, the chapter on internal silence is unusually descriptive and absolute in its logical style. Perls seemed to have found the answers here. He intended to tell the reader how to accomplish internal silence and exactly what the benefits would be. However, much of the chapter is incomprehensible. In the chapter with largely unemotional thoughts, we also find an absence of logic; it is nearly impossible to follow. This chapter illustrates the propensity for writing that is devoid of emotion to degenerate in its rational aspects even while it appears to its author to be intellectually clear. When people ignore or suppress their feelings, they are also ignoring the process of thought. For someone like Perls, who has a strong tendency to monitor and thereby interrupt his feelings rather than let them progress to some conclusion, this complete suppression of emotion is particularly devastating. It suggests that the whole topic of internal silence is both shameful and anxiety producing for Perls – so much so, that he cannot even get as far as acknowledging the feelings associated with it. This topic is difficult indeed.

The chapter began with the observation that children differ from chimpanzees because of their use of language. Perls admired language because it "unified" objects. As usual, with his turn for dialectical opposition, Perls then immediately wrote that language can be used to "conceal" and destroy. In this guise, language is a "deadly weapon." Perls did not set out to demonstrate or prove this to us; we must accept his assertion not only that these things are true but also that they should be in the foreground of our thinking about language. Of all the things that one might think about language, Perls thought of unification and destruction.

Words become insignificant and deceptive in comparison to a deep intuitive feeling that exists without words – this is genuine feeling. Perls used as his example the stripping away of language and intellect for a soldier. The soldier attends to his biological needs first and foremost. In some ways this example seems highly suspect, since in times of danger and emergency one might make contact with deeper feelings, but one might also block out feelings and not just with language. Perls did not pursue this example but used it somehow to introduce the concept of reaching one's genuine feeling. "There is one way by which we can contact the deeper layers of our existence, rejuvenate our thinking and gain 'intuition': internal silence" (1947/1969, p. 212). To become expert in internal silence, which is not defined here, one first learns to listen to one's thoughts. Perls was obscure here. He did not spell out exactly how this is related to revealing genuine feeling.

Although the reader was already left behind, Perls forged ahead to write about listening to our thinking. In solitude, one listens to the internal "babble" searching for the "'feel' of thinking, the *identity of listening and talking* [italics added]" (1947/1969, p. 213). He did not describe the "identity of listening and talking," nor is it clear what the internal "babble" might be or why it would be deceptive when the "silence" would not be deceptive. However, this situation is quite serious because occasional interruptions of the "incoherent language" make one feel "insane." Whether it is the content of the babble, its existence, the uncontrolled interruptions, or something else that leads to insanity is hidden. This chapter represents the very problems with language that Perls hoped to overcome. There is a lot of interruption and a fair amount of incomprehensible material that might be "babble." It is quite possible to feel as if there is something wrong with oneself – that the ideas Perls reaches for are just outside the reader's grasp. Perhaps the reader might think that one more reading, or more concentration, will reveal Perls's meaning. But the medium is the better part of the message. Without intending to, as we all do, Perls gave an example of what he most wanted to avoid.

This listening to internal silence, Perls claimed, will "reorganize" one's thinking. How this is going to happen is quite impossible to understand from the text. Next Perls leapt over to claiming that reorganization of thinking in this manner is essential to people who have difficulty making "genuine contact," including "timid, awkward or stammering people"as well as their opposites. Such people cannot "contribute anything amusing or interesting" (1947/1969, p. 214). This inability to contribute amusement seems banal in the face of feeling like one is going insane from the unlistened to babble in one's head. But not only will people be able to make genuine contact if they reorganize their thinking, but this process will also even lead to "a deeper knowledge, a 'psychoanalysis' of the characteristics of personality" (1947/1969, p. 214).

Next one attempts to suppress verbal thinking. The last sentence of the chapter is revealing: "Perhaps the valuable outcome of the training in internal silence is the achievement of a state beyond evaluation (beyond good and bad), e. g. a genuine appreciation of reactions and facts" (1947/1969, p. 215). Finally, we hear that the goal of all these nearly inexplicable exercises was to silence judgments of the self. Once again, Perls neglected to use any emotional language here, as he neglected it throughout the chapter. Nevertheless, the chapter comes across as a significant statement of the chaotic side of Perls's inner life. When his emotions were obscure to him, he believed he must make a great effort to find the genuine feeling (in isolation – away from potentially supportive people) and he must hear what his intuition told him – without language.

Perls's emphasis on bodily language was no doubt related to this deep distrust he had of the spoken or unspoken word. It is not just that people can deceive with language but that language could destroy the sense of knowing oneself, the inner unity of identity.

It is not that we could not make some sense of the chapter. However, the lack of context in this chapter as well as lack of personalization (it is full of generic "people") and lack of emotion elaboration makes this chapter highly intellectualized (in the worst sense) but not highly logical. We are clearly being exposed to some scenes that are critical for Perls, ones that he was unable to describe with much clarity or even to perceive with emotional description. More so than the other two therapists, Perls seemed to have continuing problems with knowing who he is at any point. He sensed this even at a somatic level, distrusting his body and his emotions to be genuine or to be easily knowable. It was a struggle for Perls to know himself. At very basic Eriksonian infantile levels of trust, Perls lacked a solid sense of giving himself trustworthy messages. Naturally, he was extremely vulnerable to messages from others, particularly criticism. He would also have been vulnerable to what Erikson (1950) called severe identity diffusion, a sense of not knowing who one is even insofar as one is aware of reality. Perls perceived schisms within himself that he attempted to mend by focusing and then by silencing the criticism, leaving only the bit that is aware without words and without judgment. One senses that Perls would not solve this problem, and that, at this point when he was writing his first book, he did not have enough knowledge or possibly enough help to solve this kind of problem. Whether he listened to himself here in this chapter is not clear. Of course, the paradox will be that his intense need to clarify the relationship between somatic, emotional, and cognitive signals will pursue him and potentially make him an expert on bits of these subjects.

The next chapter we considered, "About Being Self-Conscious," was quite different in that it was very emotional. Perls mentions a whole gamut of emotions from thrill and pleasure to annoyance and anger to worry and fear to ashamed and embarrassed. Once again, it also ran the gamut of logical processes, changing paragraph by paragraph. It naturally presented content that was essential to Perls's own personality, his own self-consciousness which is so severe that he continuously felt it as an interruption of some underlying genuine self experience. These great insights that Perls had about self-consciousness are probably quite applicable to many people – we do not see them as incorrect – but they apply first to him. And they apply in such a way that they are redundant. The emotion, the cognitive approach, and the issue redundantly tell the story, just different aspects of it.

Perls's ability to see particular psychological issues from differing emotional perspectives may be a necessary part of his intellectual creativity. In order of paragraphs, we first have three paragraphs with no emotional content, paragraphs in which the subconscious mind is defined. It is descriptive and assertive, full of statements such as "A middle-ground does not exist in the healthy mind" (1947/1969, p. 253). Perhaps not, but Perls threw out this assertion without considering any alternatives. Once he "saw" something it existed for him without question; he had a very authoritative side. In the next paragraph, he expressed himself emotionally and became more relativistic, giving the reader information. When emotion is inhibited, it is because there is a projected censor, acting as if the person was being criticized for feeling "annoyance or love or envy ... we are ashamed or afraid or ... embarrassed ... then we experience self-consciousness" (1947/1969, p. 234–5). In the next paragraph, Perls gave yet another example in which a person was unable to express anger and annoyance. Inhibiting this feeling of anger, the person felt awkward, and self-conscious. Perls had him act out his annoyance imagining the target to be present and responding. The symptoms cleared up.

A little later in the chapter, Perls pointed out that being self-aware, as opposed to self-conscious, brings a thrill and peace of mind owing to the sense of feeling "oneness." There is pleasure merely in self-awareness without self-consciousness. This idea is rather sophisticated.

Perls contrasted self-consciousness of emotion with self-awareness. When self-conscious, one monitors, criticizes, and manages emotion. When self-aware, one senses that the emotion, the experience, and the thoughts are in harmony. This is akin to a meta-emotion – a system of feelings about feelings. In the second instance, emotion is not beyond a person's control, but it is not in need of control. For Perls, self-consciousness is directed only at monitoring emotions. In so doing, it disrupts emotions and causes schisms. The need for congruency and "wholisms" that pervaded Perls brings him to consider that this self-consciousness is pathological.

The sense of self-consciousness is accompanied by a "censor." The censor is the projected critical voice of other people. The angry boss suspects that someone will criticize her if she does not suppress her anger. In other words, the self-criticisms that occurred in other chapters are back again, and the potential for humiliation and embarrassment exists but is prevented by the self-conscious behavior. So Perls has set up a cause-and-effect set of behaviors and consequences and is at least rather clearly absolute in his logical prediction. Self-consciousness results from self-censorship. Unless the original feelings are released somewhere, they lead to seemingly unrelated misbehavior such as accidents. The fuzziness of the other chapter is diminished or absent as Perls returns to the issue he knows best, both emotionally and intellectually.

The chapter on self-consciousness ends here with a description of the two poles of activity – the projected criticism and the felt self-consciousness. Perls noted that people try to silence one or the other but that both need to be recognized. One changes "the wish to be admired, the fear of being stared at, and the feeling of being the centre of interest, into activities of being enthusiastic, of observing and of concentrating one's interest on to an object" (1947/1969, p. 257). In the next section, we will find that these two poles of feeling or activity become sides of personality – they will reappear as "topdog" and "underdog" in the jargon of Perls in the 1960s, rather than the academic Perls of earlier decades.

Although we just gave an example of causal thinking in this chapter, the chapter as a whole relies heavily on relativistic thinking – where the context effects, even quite small ones, make a difference in the outcome. So when dancing, and feeling while dancing that all is in harmony, one might be pleasantly self-aware. When there is a disappointment in the dancing, then self-consciousness emerges. It is not a full exploration of relative possibilities, but an acknowledgment that single outcomes are uncommon. There is also a tendency toward the dialecticism that recognizes that opposites are often poles of the same system. Again, there were not full dialectical statements, but instead hints of them. The chapter, although still marked by incomplete thoughts, had a markedly different logic to it from the previous one.

Early Emotional Patterns

When we reviewed *Ego, Hunger and Aggression*, several emotions stand out and identify him, as different classes of emotions identify everyone. The younger Perls used one of several sets of emotions equally frequently and at a very high rate – shame or humiliation, fear or anxiety, and interest or excitement. These are in a dynamic pattern. Interest or excitement is the desirable emotion leading to Perls's goals for awareness and control of change. Interest and its related cognitive goals of awareness and focus are continuously interrupted with shame or humiliation. Shame is accompanied by its cognitive attachment of self-consciousness. The consequence of the constant shifting in consciousness is fear and anxiety. The inferred or silent emotion is contempt, which Perls described as self-criticism or others' criticism. Contempt directed toward himself or his creations drove his feelings of humiliation and anxiety. The more or less constant voices of contempt repeatedly interrupted his excitement even though he experienced it as humiliation and usually mentioned it only as an afterthought.

Perls used a second rank of emotions at about half the rate of these top three, but still with regularity – happiness, sadness, anger, general "feelings or emotions." These emotions do not form oppositional or dialectical patterns but seem to be quite appropriate just to the situation rather than to be repeating in the personality.

Unlike Rogers or even Ellis, the pleasant–unpleasant distinction did not hold for Perls. Whereas Rogers strove to detect and replace the hostile emotions with happiness and Ellis strove to detect and replace fear with happiness, Perls had a three-way complex. Perls was sensitive to criticism or contempt from himself and from others, always sensitive to detecting it so he could deflect it. To deter this sensitivity, he attempted to ascend to a grandiosely wise and aware position where he would be beyond contempt. Since he always monitored and criticized even his own awareness of his grandiosity, he always reproduced the self-contempt. Needing to monitor his feelings of excitement made him self-conscious, which was humiliating and finally led to overwhelming anxiety. To conquer contempt, humiliation, and anxiety, he searched for one more thing he could be wise about in order to excite himself, but the interest and excitement were brief. He had become his own intrusive parent, denigrating and interrupting his own play.

Perls had a complete repertoire of emotions several of which he used quite flexibly. Similarly, he had even in the first book a complete repertoire of cognitive approaches that he used intermittently. He had enormous capacity for theoretical work. On the other hand, he was, as a young to middle-aged man, less likely to follow any train of thought through to a complete explanation and conclusion. When he concentrated on academic and theoretical matters, his European background in existential and dialectical matters came to the foreground. When he concentrated on body or somatic issues and humilation, he lost the dialectical tendency and became more absolute, often in flawed ways.

Although Perls had the potential for tremendous creative and intellectual work, he failed to reach this potential for two major reasons. First, he was unable to take the reader's position and to anticipate the detailed explanation that the reader might need. Second, he constantly interrupted his own line of thought. He is often like the mythical mathematics instructor, who, when asked how he got the answer to a problem, says it is intuitively obvious, ignoring the questioner, and proceeds to yet another point, during which he stops midway. To whom is it intuitively obvious? We require of our wise men and women not only that they provide interesting or workable answers, but that they also provide a route by which the rest of us can come to the same conclusion. This expectation requires of them a knowledge of our knowledge and a respect for our process of understanding.

To be fair to Perls, he was aware of the difficulties he had in explaining complex or suppressed knowledge. However, his answers to people's questions often were the advice that they needed to learn for themselves through work on behavior as well as thought. This background is interesting, but the pattern of working was still obscure, and the dialogue of learning, omitted. Perls was not willing or was perhaps unable to tell how he came by his knowledge. He repeatedly gave anecdotes and provided insightful commentary as if he were pulling rabbits out of his magician's hat. He hid the process.

Perls as a Wild Man

The younger Perls is not alone in having both the tremendous potential and the particular flaws that he wrestled with. A portrait of similar men is described metaphorically by Robert Bly in *Iron John* (1992). Bly tells the story of the mythical maturing of Iron John. Early in his learning, Iron John found the "wild man" as mentor. As Bly writes the story, the wild man is not a savage or primitive individual but a metaphor for a wise man who lives in a natural connection with the world. "In part he resembles a rabbi teaching the Kabal; in part, he resembles a holder of a mystery tradition; in part he resembles a hunting god" (1992, p. 55). From the wild man, Iron John received tasks and gifts. In the end, he gained a realization of his great abundance of selves and his abundant desires. He became aware of multitudinous aspects of himself and of the world he lives in.

In many respects, Perls is a wild man for our times, and the older he grows, the more he will attempt the role. In adolescence, he lived the life of the boy searching for a wild man. He left home and the prescripted school. He found acting, he found his own school, and he became the star pupil after being the failed pupil. He went off to medical school and still succeeded. He was a "wild" wanderer with regard to his family and yet somewhat golden in respect to his goals and independence.

One might imagine that Iron John would be a wise king after his ritual days with the wild man, but the story tells otherwise. The boy in the story, a bit like Perls, "has been lifted up to what is great in him" (Bly, 1992, p. 56). There is a danger in this accomplishment that the wisdom of the story gives us. The golden boy is in danger of grandiosity – of ignoring his dark side to maintain the golden feeling. Bly wrote that such people "are open to terrible shocks of abandonment; they are unable to accept limitations, and are averse to a certain boring quality native to human life" (1992, p. 57). They are Peter Pans and Don Juans. They ask others to do the boring work for them. They do not complete conversations; they do not wash the floor or make their children a lunch or punch a company time clock. To cure this grandiosity, Bly wrote that such "ascendant" men need to follow the "road of ashes, descent, and grief" (1992, p. 56).

Is it possible that Perls was not matured by grief and by hard work in his life? He had opportunity enough. His terrible years in the war making impossible, heart-wrenching medical decisions about life and death seem like a qualifying experience. His time of fleeing from Nazi persecution and starting his career again was once again a possibility. His immigration to South Africa and then again to the United States, leaving his language, his home, his culture are other examples of a potential road of ashes in Perls's life. Actually we do not know much about

Perls in these times. It is quite possible that even when we see places he could have gone further down particular paths, we are not knowing how far he has come. We only know him after those times. Even so, the difficulties he had when we do know him were still those of the ascendant golden boy, and the difficulties he had were the resistances against the road of ashes.

Let us look more closely at this road of grief and its importance in development. According to Bly, after Iron John made wonderful discoveries about himself with the wild man, he found that he still had no life work or intimate companions. He cast about and could only find employment as a kitchen boy. He could not start his loves or his work at the top, but had to start at the bottom. He had to learn to chop wood and haul water, as the old saying goes. This is a time for recognizing and for enduring shame and anxiety even while learning. This is a time for Iron John to discover the darkness of his own soul, to be without worthy tasks, light, fresh air, or guidance.

In the story of Iron John, accepting one's limitations and doing constant hard work are important parts of maturation. He comes to know his own weaknesses and evil thoughts and dreads, to endure loss of everything he holds dear about himself, and still to go on. For Perls, this endurance of humiliating circumstances would have been the greatest challenge. Perls had enormous difficulty with humiliation and anxiety as he often told us. He had the least benefit of endurance and self-awareness in the depths of his dark self. This is clear from his constant concern with self-criticism. He could not accept his own dark, humiliating side and was constantly veering away from sustained contact with almost any idea that might lead him there. He might return later, but he could not stay with it. As Perls expressed this, he took things in, but then he spat them out. This metaphor for eating, hungering and going on to the next morsel is not sufficient for Iron John in the dungeon or basement. The basement work is a metaphor for continuing to care for things in all the mundane ways that life calls for, ingesting them and having them become a part of ourselves. Ideas and people must be carried around, sweated over, and explained in multiple ways. The perspectives of several people must be accounted for. People and things must be cared for in the day-to-day ways as well as in the great or challenging moments.

Perls would usually not let his dreads be dreadful, his weaknesses be weak, but he would insist that they have ascendant qualities. For example, when describing a nagging child, he focused not on the child's weaknesses but on the child's using nagging to manipulate powerful adults. It is true that such beseeching behavior is manipulative, but it is also true that it is despairing. It was humble despair that Perls denied, emphasizing instead a grandiose self-sufficiency. This would manifest itself in many ways, including the epigrams that he was known for later such as the prayer in Gestalt Therapy :

> I do my thing and you do your thing. . . .
> You are you and I am I,
> And if by chance, we find each other, it's beautiful.
> If not, it can't be helped. (1969b, p. 4)

There is no thought that anything other than "chance" might enter into the formation and cementing of relationships and no call to notice how much work and commitment might go toward making something from a relationship that is something other than two separate people perhaps "finding" each other.

Though Perls may well have been a man caught in the "golden" or ascendant phase, as Bly recounted it, reluctant to descend into his own drudgery or hells, we have to wonder why he avoided but also, as a medical doctor and as a therapist, was drawn to the descendant side. The early family problems probably made it difficult for him to accept support and guidance, and the war horrors of his early adult years may have made revisiting early as well as late traumas dangerous. In modern analyses of subjectivity, there are descriptions of people with problems like Perls whose problems arose from an early unfulfilled longing to have someone to mirror or admire them. When there is no mirroring of feelings in childhood when the child is trying to create a basic sense of who he is, he may compensate by finding an "omnipotent self-sufficiency." This is a psychoanalytic term for Blys's "golden boy." Focusing on the omnipotent self or the golden boy allows the person to dismiss the painful emotions of the humbled young self locked in the basement.

The sense of humiliation is a response to other pains, as Perls himself noted. To remove oneself from the humiliation is also to remove oneself from the other painful experiences. It is this underlying pain that the person believes is a "fatal flaw," the flaw that if revealed would condemn him to the disgusted reviling of other people, the flaw that explains why other people who should have loved him did not act in loving ways. "From early, recurring experiences of malattunement, the child acquires the unconscious conviction that unmet developmental yearnings and reactive feeling states are manifestations of . . . an inherent inner bad-ness" (Orange et al., 1997, p. 80). The grandiose self-sufficiency is actu-ally a "defensive self-idea . . . representing a self-image purified of the offending affect states that were perceived to be intolerable. . . . Living up to this affectively purified ideal becomes a central requirement for maintaining harmonious ties . . . and for upholding self-esteem" (Orange et al., 1997, p. 80). There is a split then into "conscious, noisy, imperious grandiosity" defending against a sense of a pained self that is totally worthless – Perls's topdog and underdog. Unfortunately, the person with such a history usually ends up identifying in part with the care-giver who maintained such a contemptuous attitude toward him as a child. Perls in many ways resembles his own parents who did not ad-mire him or mirror his feelings empathically, yet he wars against this identification, not wanting it to be him. However, his authoritarian as-sertions and lack of continuity and dialogue with his readers is one representation of this phenomenon.

Transition to Later Years

The question we examine in the next section concerns Perls's ability to develop, to move in his emotional dynamic – away from the childhood construction that pervades his first theoretical work and away from the intellectual qualities related to the early emotional pattern. We wonder about the presence and absence of humiliation scenes in Perls's later work as well as in his early work. When he is, to the world, a golden guru, will he have mastered a solution to the early problems of traumatic responses to his growing childhood self, or has the grandiosity phase just gained the upper hand in his personality and thoughts? As with Rogers and Ellis, we expect that the affective issues of his early adulthood, the concerns with humiliation and excitement, will, if not resolved, have be-come entrenched themes. They will lose their purely motivational quali-ties. Their emotional qualities will become "cognized"; in other words, they will become entrenched ideals or rules. Our search for emotion words may show changes, but the ideas will contain the emotions in a crystallized form.

Emotion dynamics move from childhood attachment scenes to crea-tive constructions for motivational and emotional expectations in life positions to a-emotional "knowledge" or values. This is not to say that such crystallized knowledge is necessarily incorrect, but it is incorrect to believe that such knowledge has evolved free from the emotional needs of its creator. Emotional truths are still true, but they may be more limited than the person who operates under their influence can recognize unless he or she can see the entire dynamic development of the ideas. The premise that one might understand the origins and path of one's own ideas and beliefs is a concept that is thoroughly twenty-first century (see Rozin et al., 1997). This transformation of feelings into moral declamations that then require their own feelings in order to support and validate the beliefs is a little-explored personality change.

In Perls's case, we will find that the ideas of his later years reflect the feelings of his younger years just as the feelings of his younger years reflect the family attachments he had as a child. It is not just the case that the attachments of childhood are repeated in adulthood, but that the feelings become broadly important in areas outside family and love attachments, even in work and thought styles. Apparently in young adulthood when identity issues are being sorted out; careers defined; allegiances formed to philosophies, communities, political ideas, and so forth, the feelings themselves are at the forefront. When the decisions have been made, the allegiances formed, and the beliefs committed, then the feelings are less salient, but only because they are incorporated into the commitments and values. In the next section, we will find examples of this transformation.

Perls Late in Life: The Gestalt Approach and Gestalt Therapy Verbatim

Some twenty years later, Perls wrote *The Gestalt Approach and Eye Witness to Therapy* (1973), which nearly parallels his early book. We can also check the possible transformation of Perls's motivations and ideas in transcripts of Perls's speaking in his Gestalt workshops, edited into a book called *Gestalt Therapy Verbatim* (1969b). In this work, we looked for topics that had been covered in *Ego, Hunger and Aggression* to see whether or how Perls had changed over the years. We must keep in mind that now Perls is sometimes speaking with an audience, whereas before he was writing in solitary or perhaps with his wife, Laura Perls.

The three topics we looked at in *Ego, Hunger and Aggression* and that we try to trace in these later books to see if or how Perls changed deal with (1) organismic reorganization, (2) emotional resistances, and (3) self-consciousness. And we will look for the confused and emotionally silent internal silence.

The Gestalt Approach was written in the last years of Perls's life when he was in residence at the very supportive institute called Esalen on the coast of California. He was a central figure at Esalen, sometimes at the forefront of controversy, but more often the revered guru. He even took to wearing a robe in the fashion of Bly's "wild man," looking much like a Socrates of ancient Greece. Perls accommodated or adapted his manner of dress as well as his ideals and language to the culture of the American 1960s. As much as the earlier book reflected a European academic tradition, the later books reflect a populist American scene.

Perls felt that his earlier books including *Ego, Hunger and Aggression* were too full of jargon. He wished to speak to the layman in these last years. It seems to us, however, that he changed from psychoanalytic jargon to the 1960s American counseling jargon. This switch complicates our task. We searched for concepts that seem the same without the aid of the terms. This change in format and language was something expected of Perls by colleagues. "That was the way he did things, changing all the time. As soon as he saw that we were getting our feet anchored in any situation, he'd pull the rug out by switching the situation" (Barry Stevens in Gaines, 1979, p. 360).

Across the decades in his writing, Perls seemed to change, as his colleagues expected. Perls, more than Ellis or Rogers, seemed to move into new situations without finishing old ones, but might then make himself into a brilliant representative of the miniculture. He accommodated himself to the new situations. When he met Laura Perls and she was studying with the Wertheimer Gestalt school, Fritz Perls fit himself into this environment and then used this to build a clinical theory around the experimental school. Perls used the terminology and some of the concepts of the Gestalt school rather loosely for his own purposes. Now a Californian and part of the mid-century sociopolitical movements, Perls again accommodated his expression to the new words and some of the democratic and even socialistic ideas. It is a strong accommodation pattern. Perls moved toward light sources in his universe like a moth. In his search for such sources, we find his continuity, not necessarily in the adaptations he made once he found such a source. He was unlikely to commit entirely or to adapt himself in essential ways to the attraction.

As in *Ego, Hunger and Aggression*, there are three sections in *The Gestalt Approach*. They are the chapters "Gestalt Psychology" and "Neurotic Mechanisms" and then a set of chapters on therapeutic techniques such as "Here and Now Therapy," "Peeling the Onion," and "Shuttling,

Psychodrama and Confusion." Within each chapter, there are once again short sections. These chapters and sections are remarkably parallel to the three sections of the first more European and academic book. The overall form is the same. We also find within these chapters many similar topics. The pattern laid down two or more decades earlier is still prevalent, but there are changes.

Organismic Organization to Holistic Doctrine

What Perls previously called organismic organization seems closely akin to what is called the holistic doctrine in *The Gestalt Approach*. Once again, Perls presented the issue of the separation of the mind and body as the introduction to the holistic doctrine, just as he did in presenting the earlier concept in the organismic chapter. Now Perls suggested that if the mind and body were separate entities, we would need to treat them differently in therapy. However, he asserted that all the tasks performed by the mind – from dreaming to being aware to solving problems – are only a low-energy version of what the body could do. Mind and body are, psychologically, different forms of the same whole. He asserted that thought or linguistic symbol use are only more efficient than action, but not really different.

Although the holistic doctrine seemed fundamentally simple in form, Perls used the doctrine to make an interesting and important point for therapy: neither the patient nor the therapist is limited to spoken material. The body and the actions of the body are as informative about the patient's psychological state as what the patient might say, think, or fantasize. In other words, Perls made the body as much of an intelligible expresser as the mind-crafted words of the patient. In some other versions of this theory, he asserted that the body was less deceptive and, therefore, a better clue to psychological process. Here, though, he went one step further and ended the chapter with "Psychotherapy then becomes not an excavation of the past, in terms of repressions, Oedipal conflicts, and primal scenes, but experience in living in the present. In this living situation, the patient learns for himself how to integrate his thoughts, feelings, and actions not only while he is in the consulting room, but during the course of his everyday life" (1973, p. 15).

Perls picked up his early thoughts once again to state that the therapist does not need to go digging into the past to find significant events for analysis. All the early significant events are integrated into present action and thought. He was not agreeing with Ellis's claim that the past has no bearing on the present. His argument was almost the opposite. The past is so active in the present that concentrating on the present behavior and thought is sufficient and more important than old material. This philosophy, of course, while broadly demonstrable and not untrue, also allowed him to move away from any analysis of early relationships and away from constructing any meaningful long-term or continuous narrative of identity. Everything will be contained in the present, the "here and now."

As students of body language and emotional expression, we are already persuaded that the expressive body reveals much about a person, but there is a certain defensiveness in Perls's dismissive and, ultimately, contemptuous claim that therapists do not need to do any "excavation." Perls overstated the case for minute expressions to carry complex messages. This exaggeration suggests that there are aspects of the continuous, historical material that he wished to avoid and connections that he did not want to address.

One can surmise that pathology is the "tearing to shreds" of the whole person when the voice and body do not tell the same story. The cure is the sense of wholeness that arises from sameness. Perls never considered systems in any growing or developing dynamic sense. One part could be a check on another, could elaborate it or balance it. There is more than one way that different parts of a system might work together, but Perls saw only that they must be the same.

Perls came to a single solution to his organismic body–mind dilemma. His solution had a number of qualities unique to Perls. He stood nearly alone in his time having awareness of the narrative that body language told. He also was aware that the body's expression creates and maintains psychological identity at a subconscious level, as well as at the conscious level. This in itself was a major step and was often ignored in the history of psychology and psychotherapy.

Brilliant though the Holistic Doctrine is, in many ways it remained largely known only in the small field of Gestalt therapists because Perls proclaimed his prinicples in such a dramatic and personal manner that members of other schools were excluded. The ideas were locked in Perls and only shared by those who agreed with his premises. Especially at this later point in his life, his thoughts were assertions, not arguments or explanations. They could be very compelling and compellingly demonstrated by him but were nothing more than confusing and contemptuous statements when seen from a distance.

Like most doctrines, the holistic doctrine as written late in Perls's life is rather simple in logical terms. It is largely descriptive with a good deal of absolute assertion, as one might expect, since Perls was an expert on this topic now and appeared to have little to ponder. Recall, however, that a similar section in *Ego, Hunger and Aggression* involved quite complex argument.

As we have learned to expect from absolute logic and description, there was very little emotional elaboration. There was no statement of any feelings that Perls as the writer might have about his thoughts or his doctrine. He expected his audience or reader to find his ideas marvelous. He expected his clients to be aggressive and angry. This topic had lost both its original motivational edge and thoughtfulness in the newer popular doctrinaire version.

The style of writing, the logic, and the emotional context reflect a modified set of emotions in comparison with the earlier work. Forms of heightened interest – "eerie" or "marvelous"– were dominant. "We recognize that the ability to perform certain physical and physiological activities is built into man, and we have lost our *sense of wonder* at our *marvelous* efficiency [italics added]" (Perls, 1979, p. 9). The negative emotion he dealt with is anger, which, as with Rogers, came from examples of his clients, not referring to himself – "When he feels anger, and thinks about attacking an enemy, he still shows some overt physical signs" (Perls, 1979, p. 7). We went from an organismic tripartite system to holistic polarities; we went from emotionally elaborated to emotionally simple and from diverse cognitive systems to an assertive doctrine.

Emotional Resistance to Lack of Self-Expression

Perls did not use the term "emotional resistance" very often in the later work. However, there were many examples of patients who still seemed to have emotional resistances. Consider the example of the patient who had "no power of self-expression." Perls described a "fairly successful middle-aged man." This man complained about everyone and everything in his life from his wife and children to his work. Without telling us why he thought this is the best approach, Perls began with this patient by having him express his resentments to each of the offending people, addressing them in the therapy session as if they were really there. Perls directed the man's attention away from his internal feelings and onto fantasized objects. Perls claimed that they have "to shuttle" (of course, this is the introduction of new jargon in spite of his claimed wish to avoid it) between three objective positions: the complaining, the inadequate self-expression, and the self-interruptions. Perls explained that the client's complaining is a manipulation of the therapist meant to gain his sympathy. The inadequate self-expression is a lack of good contact and self-support, and the self-interruptions are inhibitions. Perhaps the self-interruptions are emotional resistances, or perhaps the package is emotional resistance; it is not clear.

Perls then gave us a possible dialogue with a patient that was annotated so that we know with each statement what Perls made of it. For example, the patient said, "My wife has no consideration for me." Perls commented, "This is a complaint, one of the techniques of manipulating the outside world to give him the support he cannot give himself" (1973, p. 90). At the end of the session, the patient was shouting "Shut up" at his imagined wife. So in a brief interaction with the therapist, the patient came to have less emotional resistance or inhibition or, perhaps, self-interruption from Perls's point of view. Perls immediately cautioned us that the patients should not act out neurotic tendencies outside of therapy but should use the meaning of their behavior, discovered in therapy, to find a creative solution to their communication problems.

The title "Self-expression" versus the title "Emotional Resistances" reflects a change in emphasis. When Perls first attempted to describe this problem, he was heavily invested in describing the part of the pattern that is resistant. The earlier chapter we examined had at least thirty-six references to shame and embarrassment – as ways to resist expression. In this later chapter, there are no references to shame and embarrassment. Earlier the second highest emotion category was the fear–worry category. In the later chapter fear was still important but was balanced by resentments and angers. The anger in the earlier chapter was infrequent but extreme – fury was mentioned rather than annoyance, for example.

In this later chapter, when the patient did not express his "resentments," Perls claimed it was because he "fears" to hurt his wife. The patient was no longer consumed with humiliation, but turned his anger or resentment outward and was aware of his hostile, fear-inducing feelings. Perls took away his awareness of the interruptions of shame and humiliation and blanketed it in projected fear. Perls no longer seemed aware of the interrupting shame.

The emotion and the cognitive style were simpler when Perls dealt with self-expression just as it was simpler with the Holistic Doctrine.

His description again was absolute and straightforwardly descriptive as if, once again, the answers or the techniques were simple and as if the awareness of anger is bringing forward absolute thinking.

In the early work, Perls presented many alternative approaches, sought emergent complex solutions. Before, when the questions were emotionally elaborated, he used a variety of intellectual styles. In this later expert or guru phase, he was less likely to reveal his thinking pattern and may not have been aware of the interruptions to his own thinking.

The development of simpler answers over time and experience, rather than increasingly complex answers with increasing knowledge, is reminiscent of an abortive study of our own. We asked parents to solve simple child-caring dilemmas such as "What do you do if your child puts on two different shoes?" The fathers gave complex and exploratory answers. They wanted to know the child's mind set and the context before stating their solutions. The mothers usually just gave a direct command. "Go and put the right shoes on." We had thought, incorrectly, that mothers, being more involved in child care and more experienced, would have the more complex answers. However, when we turned the dilemma to how to change a tire in a difficult situation, the mothers had the complex and exploratory answers, not the fathers. We realized, belatedly, that when people have well-practiced and workable procedures for an apparent problem, they may efficiently apply the solution. When they have to solve a relatively unfamiliar problem, they tend to show a longer reasoning process and often tell how they felt about the different turning points in the process. This is the problem with asking "experts" about their answers to problems. They are unlikely to explain the path to the problem solution accurately, if at all.

Apparently Perls no longer saw his client's emotional resistance as a puzzle, nor was it embedded clearly in his awareness of his own personal issues. At this point, it probably seemed to him that the answers were detached from his own feelings, that they had some objective reality that anyone could perceive just by looking. The lack of complexity in thought and the emergence of assertion, doctrine, or values represent the creation of efficient process or habit. The paradox is that this result is not the outcome that Perls would consciously have intended. His emphasis on change and not getting "in a rut" was intended to prevent such doctrinaire habits, but he was obviously not particularly successful here. Perls's habits stand in contrast to someone like Rogers who seemed to actually see new complexity in old problems. Ellis did not see new complexity, but he kept adding to his repertoire of approaches. Perls does not show either strategy in *The Gestalt Approach*, but rather a consolidation and simplification.

From Shame to Underdog

Though Perls was flooded with descriptions of shame, guilt, self-consciousness, and humiliation in *Ego, Hunger and Aggression*, these descriptions were nearly gone in *The Gestalt Approach*. It is so difficult to find mention of self-conscious feelings in this work, that we started to scan more writings to make certain they were gone. In *Gestalt Therapy Verbatim* (1969b), a work composed of workshops that Perls gave at Esalen, with some editing and perhaps some added commentary, we find examples like this: "If you need encouragement, praise, pats on the back from everybody, then you make everybody your judge" (1969b, p. 36). Previously, the comment about judgment would have been aligned with shame, but not here. The example is reminiscent of the earlier one. This quote is the end of a description that Perls had given of a three-year-old girl who "controls her world." She either "butters up" the adults so that she will be praised or she acts dependent in order to manipulate the adults. In no case did Perls consider that there might be a shared admiration or a sharing of helplessness and helpfulness. He isolated the girl, he isolated her needs, but, most importantly, he took her weakness and made it her weapon. This evaluation was possibly deliberate in that he argued that finding the polarities led to a more complete person. Therefore, the weakness would contain a strength. However, logically, the strength would contain a weakness (to complete the polarity), and Perls seemed to ignore this point. The hiding behavior of the shamed person is now manipulation. Shame and humiliation no longer exist as genuine feelings.

One must contrast this manipulating toddler with the one described so poignantly in *Ego, Hunger and Aggression*, where the child was creating a wonderful game but her mother saw only dirt. Consequently, the mother humiliated and punished the child. Nowhere was there a sense that the mother admired the child's creations or reflected the child's joy in his play. There was a large hole in the mother–child relationship that the child had not created. Earlier Perls was more ambivalent about the manipulative abilities of powerless people, slightly more aware that the judgments of parents may produce shame and humiliation. But even at that point he was inclined to give power and objectivity to shame, calling it a quisling – the betrayer commander. Now he seemed to have lost his ambivalence and had made both the child and the mother powerful as well as detached from each other.

This same issue will come up when Perls demonstrates his approach in the Gloria films. Perls showed that Gloria manipulated people she was interested in by hiding in a corner and getting them to help her. Separately he found that Gloria believed that other people demand respect, usually in a hostile manner. It took Perls quite a bit of work to bring Gloria around to accepting her own need for respect. However, Perls did not seem to see the connection between needing respect, feeling humiliated by hostile others who are demanding respect, and engaging in the behavior or fantasy of hiding. Perls seemed to believe that one could deny the humiliation – be strong. Gloria objected mightily to this and wanted to be acknowledged as the humiliated, hiding person that she felt she was. Perls absolutely refused to acknowledge that her feelings on this issue might be genuine.

More to the point in considering the omission in Perls's orientation to shame or humiliation is the emergence of the concepts topdog and underdog. These concepts were obviously a transformation of the earlier feelings of humiliation and shame into a thing instead of a feeling. The humiliation and demand for respect are externalized; they are no longer feelings inside oneself. The topdog and underdog became frequent metaphors both in the dialogues of therapy that Perls conducted and in his own autobiography and self-description. In *Gestalt Therapy Verbatim* Perls gave this description:

> If there is a *superego*, there must also be an *infraego*...Freud...saw the topdog, the superego, but he left out the underdog which is just as much personality as the topdog.... The topdog usually is righteous and authoritarian; he knows best. He is sometimes right, but always righteous. The topdog is a bully, and works with "you should" and "you should not".... The underdog manipulates with begging, defensive, apologetic, wheedling, playing the cry-baby, and such.... So you see the underdog is cunning and usually gets the better of the topdog because the underdog is not as primitive as the topdog. So the topdog and the underdog strive for control.... The inner conflict, the struggle between the topdog and the underdog, is never complete, because topdog as well as underdog fight for their lives (1969b, pp. 18–19).

In his autobiography, *In and Out of the Garbage Pail* (1969a), Perls gave topdog and underdog scripts to comment on his writing of the autobiography. For example, topdog comments contemptuously, calling his creator, Perls, names: "Look! Your readers will see you as a senile, loquacious rambler." Underdog replies to topdog: "And you are wasting too much of my and the reader's time.... Let me be just as I am, and stop your chronic barking."

Self-Conscious to Self-Actualization

Going back to *Gestalt Therapy Verbatim* (1969b) to find Perls's new approach to self-consciousness, we see that he was speaking of the necessity for everything that exists to "actualize" itself. Not to do so is to "lose the possibility of existence" (1969b, p. 34). In light of the previous transformations, this is especially interesting. As the organismic organization became a doctrine, as humiliation became underdog, Perls now stated directly that things, even feelings and ideas actualize themselves, command their existence. In other words, we have come to an extremely important point. What appears to have happened here, though, is that fragments of Perls's identity have achieved personalization and a somewhat independent existence in spite of his attempts to achieve integrated wholeness. The interruptions have separate selves that must be "shuttled" between, that speak to each other as independent beings, as Perls "shuttles" between topdog and underdog. Perls spoke of actualization both as the whole person and as the fragment of the person.

Rather than developing this potentially profound but incomplete description of actualization and achieving existence, Perls jumped to the "tools" we use to falsify our existence. His jumping and self-interruption still exist in spite of his efforts to provide continuity. Even within the description of the tools, there is discontinuity. One of these tools has a *"catastrophic expectation"* (1969b, p. 34), which is apparently something like Ellis's irrational fear. The expectation is that taking some risk will cause a catastrophe, but Perls embedded the few sentences of explanation in a longer paragraph. We then jumped to another tool that Perls called "hypnosis." He tries to "slip his 'wisdom' into" the students' guts without having them digest it for it will only be "puked" up again. This metaphor was, apparently, his definition of hypnosis, though it is a short, albeit bizarre, definition. He jumped again and never explained these tools sufficiently for anyone to know quite what he was talking about. He spoke discontinuously just as he had done when he referred to shame. Reference to shamefulness used to lead to these jumps and incomplete thoughts. However, now there was very little emotional content, even though the topics seemed emotionally very hot. Perls spoke of our very existence, about death and catastrophes, about creating within ourselves some killer. The only emotions casually mentioned are the "interest" and the "puking" of the student who listened to Perls. He only expected an alternating uncritical interest in and a violent nauseated rejection of his basic ideas.

Not only was this chapter missing emotional content, but it was also missing logic, just like certain chapters in *Ego, Hunger and Aggression*. There were many descriptive assertions but little propositional or explanatory material. If one stretches it, there may be a sequential sort of absolute logic. For example, he seemed to be asserting that if one takes a risk, one believes one will die. That was an absolute prediction, but Perls disclaimed it immediately – without justification either for it or against it. Another assertion was that if one listened to Perls one would be hypnotized but then would reject him. How or why one would be hypnotized or rejecting was not explained. Again, the process is missing and is only vaguely absolute in its logical style.

Perls arrived at a point in his speaking where problems are segmented and answers are known. He was the topdog, righteous and correct, but he was not comfortable with that position. He was alternately the underdog, cunning and nagging, constantly deriding topdog and interrupting some of his most creative work. However, he no longer seemed to feel shame directly but experienced his underdog proudly if that is possible. He named his problem and let it speak. Recognizing a problem is not the same as not having a problem. Consider the man who claims his bad temper, externalizes it, and pushes it into a section of himself. When told he has acted badly, he says "Sorry, but a bad temper makes me do it." He implies that when he does not have a bad temper, he will act differently, be another side of himself, but he has given up integrating the sides of himself and he is making others adapt to his needs. Similarly, Perls seemed to have accepted and claimed his shamed side and the resentment that went with it. Underdog and topdog still interrupted each other and provided constant undermining of any projects and feelings that Perls had, but they do so now as objects, not as feelings.

From Internal Babble to Fertile Void

Perls had in his earlier writing urged that people should learn to silence the babbling of the internal voice of criticism. Once again, it would be difficult to find exactly the same metaphor in the older Perls. However, we do find an interesting turn-around that seems derivative (Perls, 1969b, pp. 96–101). "And yet a good part of the fight against neurosis is won merely by helping the patient to become aware of, to tolerate, and to stay with his confusion and its correlative, blanking out" (Perls, 1969b pp. 96–7). The "confusion" might well be related to the babbling internal voice that, in the turn-around, Perls no longer silences. Perls proceeded to describe several patients who interrupted their own confusion and how he aided them to tolerate it, as opposed to trying to interrupt and silence it. But the interesting part came when he revealed a new dimension. "The final step in dealing with the areas of confusion is an eerie experience, often approaching a miracle when it first occurs. Eventually, of course, it becomes routine and is taken for granted. We call it *withdrawal into the fertile void*" (Perls, 1969b, p. 99). The fertile void "is awareness without speculation about the things of which one is aware" (Perls, 1969b, p. 91). This awareness is apparently the sense of being integrated without evaluation or even speculation. So the chaotic center became the fertile source of existence. Perls omitted a need for a countering organization or process. The void is preferable and more creative than the fractionation that occurred when he did speculate, evaluate, and think in a process manner.

In *Ego, Hunger and Aggression*, Perls listened to the internal voices, interruptions, and hallucinations. He heard judgments and criticisms and wanted to silence them. As an older man, he claimed that he found, in the confusion and chaos of his inner self, a richness that he could draw upon. Here "he has much more available than he believed he had" (Perls, 1969b, p. 100). Although the first descriptions of the internal silence sounded as if it were an unpleasant experience, Perls had not elaborated the description with much negative affect. In the whole early chapter, he managed only one directly described negative emotional experience – embarrassed. For Perls, this chapter was emotionally impoverished. In *Gestalt Therapy Verbatim* (1969b), we find the usual display of Perls-like emotional expression with an important addition. He began by describing the experience with terms like "unpleasant," "anxious," "ashamed," and "disgust" – the usual group of Perls interruption functions. So the idea of confusion and interruption is integrated into his usual way of viewing them. However, he then uses both "eerie" and "surprise" as transforming emotion and comes to excitement, which we know he views positively as the expressive nature of humans. He has become interested in his own confusion. Perhaps he was not sympathetic to it, but he did not need to hide from it. It is still an experience with "eerie" qualities, so one could not say that Perls was comfortable with it, but a real transformation seems to have occurred in his ability to tolerate his internal critical voices. This may have been a result of his compartmentalizing the criticism in the underdog personae. While hardly integrated or assimilated, this strategy was useful for Perls.

In addition, the early chapter was largely descriptive in its logical approach, having little or no formal logic in it. Now there was the usual range of absolute to relativistic logic with a tendency toward a dialectical presentation. The solution to anxious confusion is to embrace the confusion and to find within it the rudiments of the knowledge needed to decrease the confusion. Perls did not follow through on the dialectical emergence of new solutions from the cohesion of confusion and knowledge. Rather, he stayed with the absolute and linear position that one sees the real world more clearly after clearing up confusion. Perls was a bit like Rogers when it came to the miracles of surprise leading to positive feelings leading to insights. Neither of them seemed prepared to explain such a phenomenon though obviously both observed it.

The final paragraph in this section may well be a comment on Perls himself. "Our patients' interruptions and dissociations will show up in their Rorschach tests, their handwriting and their behavior. They will manifest themselves in the smallest details of thinking and feeling. If we change the patient's attitude about the interrupting behavior he presents ... [it] will ... spread and finally engulf his style, his character, his mode of life (Perls, 1969b, p. 101). This comment is interesting because it indicates that interruptions, dissociations, and probably jumping shifts in habits are not genuine change. They are the behavior that remains neurotically constant. The cycles of changing are the constancy for Perls and people like him. It may, as it did for Perls, lead to many creative leaps, but continuous hard work and closure on the development of the material would be inhibited by the constant shifting.

The question might be, has Perls changed his beliefs about his interrupting behavior? On the one hand, he seemed to have changed his beliefs toward his inner confusion. But perhaps this occurred as a result of his splitting out the critical underdog or infraego as he variously called it. This aspect of himself, which earlier cut across much of his self-presentation and work, has been actualized or objectified. Perls claimed to have changed, but the interruptions have continued, and the process of thinking, and perhaps of relating to others had simplified, became doctrinaire in many ways. So Perls's personality change remains open to doubt.

Summary

In our review of Perls, we focused on just a few themes, especially the emotional themes that were quieter and that dealt with humiliation. We did not explore the obvious themes of anger and hostility but not because they are unimportant. It is not just the use of humiliation that defined Perls but the pattern of emotion. The anger and hostility that formed a well-expressed theme for Perls would have supported the fragmenting style that he developed. Separating, dividing, conquering, confounding, and confronting were issues of comfort for Perls. Even the title of Perls's early book, *Ego, Hunger and Aggression*, illustrates his comfort with hostility. His description of his therapuetic technique as "confrontational" is yet another indication that he was quite comfortable with hostile expression and able to play around with it. On the other hand, Perls was wary of sadness and considered it a more dangerous feeling; one might "melt" into another with sadness in one formulation he had made. The side that separated, the hostile side, was more comfortable than the side that melted, the sad side. Still shame and humiliation primarily supported his self-interruption behavior. The development of that feeling into an actualized persona illustrates one of our main points about the relationship between emotions and personal identity, values, and work.

From his first to his later books, the description of Gestalt therapy seems to be largely the same over the decades. The general philosophy of Gestalt psychology was set down rather early by Perls and his colleagues. Some of the definitions of neurotic mechanisms shifted as they probably did for everyone working in the field at the time, but Perls was still basically concerned with the same neurotic mechanisms and not with some new phenomenon. Then we come to therapeutic practice. In *Ego, Hunger and Aggression*, Perls's Gestalt contribution was to (a) bring the body messages back into therapeutic consideration, (b) argue that behavior in the present is the target and topic of therapy rather than past history, and (c) focus the client on awareness of behavior and thought together through confrontation.

In the later books, Perls presented the very same points as accepted doctrine – not as insights that needed support or explanation. His earlier emotional concern with humiliation and shame disappeared as an emotional concern in the later, doctrinaire speeches and writings. The feeling has been transformed into a part of the self; it had a little personality and a name of its own – underdog.

A repeating theme for Perls was self-interruption, yet it was simply another way of talking about the swings between rising involvement, melting (to use his term) sadly into another, and turning away and becoming independent. There did not seem to be a happy middle ground, although there was a preference for the independent self. The therapeutic medium gave Perls an opportunity to act as an artist with other people, as he said himself. He had command of the materials, was the person in control, and went in and out of contact with the client at will.

Perls wanted us to be aware at all times of all moments in time, all forms of self in each moment, as if this were possible. He claimed that training in concentration and self-monitoring were possible. Perls was not aware of his particular obsession and how it colored his emotions, his thoughts, his relationships, and his work. This hyperawareness, of course, creates its own confusion because of the mass of information without organization that it implies. It also creates a sense of being in control through knowledge of "everything"– all moments, all movements, all words, all thoughts. The process that Gestalt implies of foreground and background being perceptual connotes an ongoing evaluation and selection that Perls ignored. The formation of perceived wholes where there is partial information was also ignored. The interruptions that plagued him led to the holes in continuity of experience that a whole Gestalt pattern implies.

Of the three psychologists, Perls has probably had a strong momentary influence on psychology in the United States but less of a lasting influence. His concerns and orientation to emotional and dynamic psychological process do not resonate particularly well with American themes. The cognitive and behavioral schools find more ready acceptance in their "can-do" attitude and their insistence – on the surface at least – in having procedures and choices that can be made freely by the client. Perls examined the aspects of the person that he or she is hiding even from the self. He, at his best, examined multiple and complex interactions of signals that require an expert degree of training but he did not promise results as one might expect from the expert surgeon but rather the results that one might obtain from the expert trainer after long devotion to the practice. It requires a degree of work and commitment and humility that is difficult to integrate with North American ethos.

On the other hand, Perls's role in the "wildness" and revolution of the 1960s was in tune with a broad cohort reaction to the intrusive and controlling child rearing that followed the anxiety of the Depression and World War II. Many people struggling with that constellation resonated to Perls's fundamental vitality. Perls embodied the 1960s generation with its concern over "phoniness" – hiding the feeling self under conventional insulation. Perls spoke for the release of a free and equal self, free "to be." Perls responded to complex themes across a challenging historical period, and from one perspective, he encouraged the liberation of anger from shame in the search for truth.

PART IV

Emotion as the Link in Therapeutic Behavior

10 Postures and Climate in Dyadic Interaction

Everyone's affective posture actually emerges in his or her behavior. There is probably no better way to demonstrate this observation than to examine the affective posture of our three therapists – Rogers, Perls, and Ellis – all with the same client, performing the same tasks. Of course, we will also want to know something about the affective posture of the client. Surely her unique characteristics will call out specific reactions from each therapist. The Shostrom film of Perls, Ellis, and Rogers with Gloria, a client, though not intended to be examined for affective interactions, is actually quite perfect for this task. We can compare the behavior of the therapist with his goals in therapy – his philosophy or theory of therapy, if you will, as well as compare how each therapist gets along with this particular client.

In this chapter we try to bring Gloria as a client more to life in the written text both as a figure in her own right and as an integral part of our discussion of the affective postures of each therapist. Even though we continue to focus primarily on Rogers, Perls, and Ellis, and do not have enough material to do justice to Gloria as a whole person, the unique ways that she expressed her thoughts and emotions reveals a depth to hidden aspects of the emotion system that cannot be sensed except in the dynamic interaction of people. Gloria allows us to see how the different approaches of each therapist are acted out in the emotional exchange. Because a dynamic interaction is an emergent product of the exchange that takes place during any dyadic exchange, we learn far more about Gloria as she interacts with all three therapists than if we had seen her with but one, just as we learn much more about each therapist when we see him interacting with Gloria and compare him with the other therapists. As we will see, Gloria's affective posture changes across the three interviews but also reveals some constant features. Her posture demonstrates how we are all flexible when we interact with different people but how we retain some aspects of our emotional signature even as we shift across situations or companions.

Affective Postures

In our terms, a person's affective or emotional posture is the "embodiment," or the physical representation, of the affective structure of personality. But this definition is too passive. Not only is posture a representation, but it also actively supports the structure of personality. The emotional gestures give information to everyone about the motivational value of each experience and create a shared understanding of the significance of events. If our partner reacts with gestures indicative of skepticism, doubt, and mild contempt, we will change the nature of our communication and our regard for our partner to show our understanding of this nonverbal message. If our partner reacts instead with puzzlement or open surprise, our response will be quite different, and the conclusions we draw about our partner's personality will also be different.

Affective postures are revealed in the multidimensional space of self-presentation, hand and head gestures, vocal tone and pacing, and facial expressions. Analyzing such fragments of behavior is part of the training for many fields from anthropology to medicine. The ways that such behaviors are analyzed varies somewhat, but a systematic analysis of such behaviors moves us from the intuitive suspicion of regularities in expression to a systematic knowledge of them (Ekman, 1984; Magai & McFadden, 1995; Tomkins, 1962, 1963).

Affective Fractals

As parts of the structure of personality, the affective postures are fractals – the small versions of elements with similar forms making up the larger form. Each person has his or her distinctive affective posture. In this chapter, we illustrate how an individual's affective posture reveals, and is congruent with, his or her goals, intentions, and wishes. We show just how and why such movements are fractals of personality. Because previous chapters introduced our therapists, let us begin this chapter with an introduction of Gloria.

Unlike the therapists, there are no published autobiographical accounts of Gloria's life from which we could easily abstract her intentions, though she apparently kept journals and was working on an autobiography before her death from cancer fifteen years after the film (Dolliver et al., 1980; Weinrach, 1986). There is no accumulated body of theoretical work written by her that we can use to divine her goals or probe her ideoaffectology. There are no biographies about her by admiring former students or theoretical acolytes. And yet we come to know and respect her from her interviews as she tried to fulfill her obligations to be the demonstration client to three therapists who will enter the history books of psychology.

Only the barest of circumstances of Gloria's life before or after the film are known. There are some sporadic biographical notes in the literature of the therapeutic community in the context of the pursuit of broader issues and a limited commentary by Gloria thirteen years after the session (Dolliver et al., 1980). In the latter, she revealed that she left waitressing and became a registered nurse; remarried; and bore two more children, one of whom she later lost to leukemia. We know from comments she made in an interview at the end of the demonstration film that she originally thought Rogers had little to offer her in terms of continued therapy. However, she changed her mind over time, sought him out in person on at least one occasion, and corresponded with him the rest of her life (Rogers, 1984). We know that she originally was so surprised and shaken by her encounter with Perls that she thought he might have the most to offer her, and that she might like to continue with him in therapy. These initial thoughts also went through a cycle of change, and she later concluded that he had treated her in a way that she found offensive (Rogers, 1984). Ellis seemed unable to make much impression on her. Finally, her beliefs about the value of her participation also changed. She was originally intrigued and challenged by the idea of participating in a unique videotaped session with three famous psychologists but later realized that she may have been exploited.

Despite the brevity of the sessions, we can gather some important information about Gloria's expressive behavior and the themes that preoccupied her at this young stage in her life. We can also discern certain features of her personality and ideoaffectology. Vocal, facial, postural, and content analysis of the transcribed sessions clearly revealed her own individuality and a certain continuity of presence across the three sessions but also showed that she was very much affected by the emotional climate created by each of the therapists. This speaks clearly to the emotional power of the therapists and perhaps of therapy in general. The amount of information that is gleaned from even such a short view of Gloria is itself a testament to the importance of careful analysis of emotion for the understanding of personality, as well as for therapeutic process. From the fractals of her behavior, we can see the larger outline of her life at that moment in time projected onto a bigger screen.

Analyses of Gloria's Roles in Therapy

Though there are several dozen research articles based on the Shostrom film, most have concerned themselves with comparisons of therapeutic modalities or personal aspects of the therapists. Must less attention has been devoted to the client in her own right. One exception is a Q-sort study of viewers' perceptions of Gloria (Miller, Prior & Springer, 1987), which focused on global views of her personality features. The viewers were all counseling students at the undergraduate or graduate level, not people necessarily well-trained in modes of analysis such as the ones we used here. With Rogers, the students concluded that Gloria felt guilty, was indecisive and overprotective of her daughter, was very worrisome, emotional, and desirous of close relationships with others. With Ellis, the students judged that not only was she interested in the opposite sex, but she was also talkative, introspective, unrelaxed, acceptant of blame, and aware of the impression she had on others. Finally, with Perls, the students saw her as anxious, talkative, facially expressive, defensive, and honest. Thus, in terms of global perceptions, Gloria seems to have projected somewhat different roles in each session so that observers believe that they see different emotional expressions. With Rogers she appears to be more concerned with guilt; with Ellis, she seems more tense; and with Perls, more anxious.

The topics Gloria discussed with each therapist varied. This fact, in itself, suggests that different people elicit varied forms of conversation about problems, that not all therapists will be presented with the same problem at first, although the underlying problems may all be the same, as we will see. With Rogers, Gloria focused on family, particularly parent–child relationships. With Ellis, the focus was on intimacy and adult sexual relationships. With Perls, there was a more traditional therapeutic focus on intrapsychic aspects of herself. Clearly, each therapist drew out from Gloria the areas in which *he* had the most interest and experience. It is not surprising that Gloria has well developed family roles, sexual relationships, or intrapsychic needs, but it may be somewhat surprising that each therapist focused so exclusively and probably unconsciously on his own interests. The exact content that each therapist learns about Gloria in the first session emerges from the goals of that therapist. Whether the actual roles or themes discussed are the most important part of the therapeutic process is debatable. Perhaps we all act out continuous aspects of our personality across our many roles, making the choice of roles irrelevant. In other words, the seeming differences in the three sessions may not matter much if each therapist arrives eventually at a similar core dilemma through his own pathway of analysis. However, this film is a dramatic example of how the discourse about oneself and one's psychological concerns is *constructed* during a therapeutic encounter. Such dialogue does not exist as something that is simply brought to therapy by a client and laid on the blank slate of the therapist no matter what type of therapist or therapeutic outlook is involved.

Coding Gloria's Affect

We also conducted a study with preprofessional psychology students in which we elicited global ratings of Gloria's dominant affect, using Izard's (1972) Differential Emotions Scale: here, guilt and shame were the most highly ranked negative affects for her across the different sessions. Their global coding missed what our own objective coding of her facial and postural expressions found. Though we limited ourselves to interval sampling of the overall tape, we found that Gloria repetitively displayed fleeting facial, gestural, and postural signals of contempt – at persons in her life and toward the therapists on occasion, but also toward herself and her values or feelings. That this is not just situation- or therapist-specific is revealed by the fact that contemptuous expression is prominent in all three sessions – vocally, verbally, posturally, and gesturally. The contempt is repeated again and again, despite the different roles the three therapists elicited from her and despite the fact that their own ideoaffective postures were so very different from one another.

Anxiety is also repetitively prominent in Gloria's defended body posture, a posture that is in evidence in each session. Some anxiety is, of course, understandable, given the unfamiliar setting, the film exposure, and the occasion of meeting "famous" psychologists. But the defensive posture persisted quite far into the sessions. Shame, as noted by most observers, was also prominent as detected by shame markers in speech and body language. These facial and postural/gestural codings of shame, anxiety, and contempt are congruent with Gloria's self-descriptions, including her many references to her lack of self-acceptance and her acknowledgments that she is defensive and "flip" with men. They are fractals, miniature signals of her doubts about herself and the way she defends herself. These expressive movements are but one more reflection of her whole self, a self that can be read from movement as well as, or even better than, from words.

Anyone who worked with Gloria would face the power and singularity of her strong ideoaffective structure pivoting on contempt and shame, but especially contempt, and the resulting dialogue that puts almost any relationship in the authority – subordinate domain. Not everyone would recognize this combination, though. Our graduate students missed it. Missing some emotional displays is very common, partly because the display may not match the culturally accepted emotional feeling for a particular situation. Our students found it hard to expect contemptuously defensive behavior in the therapeutic encounter.

Once we recognized that Gloria showed a good deal of contempt, many facets of her personality and her problems with people in her life fell into place. Just as many people have trouble with the "terrible twos" and "terrible teens," when both age groups are trying to assert their autonomy, so one might have had trouble with Gloria, who was also attempting to assert her independence. In passing one should note that this time and place in history were particularly difficult for women in Gloria's position. Women broke out of the dependent and subordinate roles with great difficulty. Sexual relationships were dominated especially in the United States by a stern Protestant ethic that was only beginning to be undermined by a backlash that would lead to the open sexuality of the 1960s. Gloria was on the cusp of the mid-century changes. Her conflicts were internal and psychodynamic, but they also reflected external cultural conflict. The therapists, too, are to a great extent embedded in the cultural conflict. They are not easily perceiving the broad social as well as personal conflict in their sessions and how it exacerbates Gloria's life dilemmas. In meeting with the therapists, Gloria reached out for this change, but they were all somewhat blinded by their time in history. It is only in retrospect that this internal–external conflict shines so brightly.

Because contempt is not an easily accepted emotion, there is a prejudice that a person who expresses contempt is not a "nice" person, not someone we would want to know or cherish. If we are "accused" of looking contemptuous, we know that we are socially unacceptable. From this common point of view, Gloria's likeableness quotient would seriously suffer. But as people who study emotion, we have a different bias. From a research position, emotions are somewhat like colors for an artist. We cannot imagine working without them all, and we want as many mixtures as we can imagine. All we ask is that the color expresses the artist's intent well. When it does, it does not matter if the color is pink or green. There are no "bad" colors.

If we think of Gloria as the artist, using her expressions to give us the picture of her feelings and attitudes, what is she creating with this contemptuous look? Is it a picture that is genuine, to use Rogers's terms? With the information in her interview, along with other information about the uses and functions of contempt, we can infer that she is bringing a complex emotional posture to the therapy session for which contempt may be the perfect signature.

The information on contempt that we look toward comes from adolescents. In early to mid-adolescence, children begin to show an enormous amount of nonverbal contempt to their parents (Kahlbaugh & Haviland, 1994; Malatesta-Magai & Dorval, 1992). They do this along with a fair amount of loving, affiliative behavior. The behaviors are not mutually exclusive, just as they are not mutually exclusive for Gloria. She, too, can show caring and interest along with her contempt. The contemptuous and disgust signals in adolescents appear to be nonverbal indicators of emerging autonomy linked to identity issues. It is possible that in Gloria's case – with the recent divorce, the beginnings of a new lifestyle, changes in mid-twentieth century American society, uncertainty about sexuality and long-term problems with self-esteem – such core issues about identity were also paramount for her.

Gloria's contemptuous nonverbal behavior goes appropriately with the general issues she brought to the session. She expressed a need for respect and the lack of it. She was concerned about resentment, enviousness, and so forth. The "Pammy" (her daughter) problem that emerged with Rogers was one manifestation of the position, as was her concern with respect from men in the session with Ellis, and respect from therapists with Perls. The adolescent's need for a secure emotional base in order to explore a distant emotional universe also applies to Gloria. She wanted to have some autonomy and showed, nonverbally, disrespect for authority as well as for her own authoritarian self, hence the conflict, but she also wanted to return to the secure base where she would be accepted whether she was rejecting the base and out exploring or was safely in the emotional home. Like the adolescent, she formed autonomous, contemptuous, and skeptical attitudes toward her authorities and used this to help support her autonomy.

Gloria's Use of Verbal Emotion

We counted the affective words, as well as the affective movements, used by each of the therapists and by Gloria in the three sessions. These emotional words are also fractals of her personality. They are miniature signals of her doubts about herself and the way she defends herself, among other things. To quantify the affective words and movements, we used the same typological framework as described earlier in this volume when we coded written works. We made a few additions to accommodate the live, interactional nature of the material. For the category of contempt, we not only counted words that denoted contempt, such as "looked down upon," but also expressions that conveyed contempt – derogatory statements such as "You are a phony, a flip little girl, and you are a show-off." We also noted nonverbal paralinguistic cues of shame such as speech dysfluencies, but these were bracketed and treated as a separate category. The coding approach and data on intercoder reliability are found in the appendix.

Using Gloria's verbal indicators of affect alone, summed across all three sessions, we found that the three largest categories of affect were joy, fear, and contempt; however, she also expressed paralinguistic indicators of shame at about half the rate of all the other affect expressions combined – a very high rate. On this basis, we might infer that fear, contempt, and shame were prominent among her negative feelings.

The salience of fear in this analysis (word content alone) was consistent with the global impressions people have of worry and anxiety as being characteristic of Gloria. The contempt seemed to relate to a global perception of defensiveness, but it was less clear that naive observers were as aware of this contempt display. Shame, an affect that individuals, especially males, in Western cultures find difficult to acknowledge and even perceive (Scheff, 1984), received a moderate level of acknowledgment by Gloria in the sessions, and the presence of a high rate of paralinquistic indicators of shame would seem to confirm that shame was an important dynamic in her personality. In this light, and given the dynamic that exists between shame, rage, and contempt, as discussed earlier, the prominence of contempt can be interpreted as an anti-shame defense. Gloria was ashamed of being the underdog, in Perls's terms, and so she angrily defended against this feeling by going to the opposite extreme and being a "show-off," a role that embodied her contempt for herself and for her intimates. As a show-off, she had the upper hand and looked down on other people. Obviously, this construction of Gloria is fragile and results in circular behavior patterns. She even was ashamed of her "flip" self, ashamed of being a show-off. Such fears were also part and parcel of being a woman in the mid-twentieth century. Putting oneself first or in front or crowing about oneself were all unfeminine and, hence, usually shameful. We have already a setting for ambivalence and a repetition of fractal behaviors that Gloria might have wanted to change.

Changes in Gloria Across Sessions

What is more interesting is the ebb and flow of these emotional expressions across the sessions as she interacted with the different therapists. In the session with Rogers, the most frequently used expression was that of joy, followed by guilt, contempt, and fear; paralinguistic shame was produced at a rate of 58 percent of all discrete affect expressions. The leading affects that Rogers expressed were joy, contempt, and guilt, and he emitted 2.5 times the rate of paralinguistic shame as total affect words, the highest of the three therapists. Thus, in comparing Gloria's and Rogers's profiles, we saw a fairly close correspondence between the emotional content of client and therapist. This is, in part, ascribable to the Rogerian technique of reflection, although the reflection rate was not outstanding since Rogers's rate of discrete affect words was only about 20 percent of Gloria's, and, as we have seen, the prominence of joy and shame was also characterologic in Rogers.

When we compared Gloria's affective behavior with Ellis, however, we saw a mixed pattern. There was good concordance for contempt. It was the second highest ranking affect for Ellis and the second highest ranking negative affect for Gloria. However, there was a mismatch for the next most dominant negative emotion in this session. For Ellis it was shame, whereas for Gloria it was fear. Paralinguistic shame was particularly low in both. For Ellis, this was largely because shame was masked by rapid speech; however, fast propulsive speech is seen by Helen Block Lewis (1971) and others as an index of "bypassed" or unconscious shame.

In the session with Perls, Gloria was more verbally emotionally expressive than with either of the other two therapists, and Perls was the most verbally emotionally expressive of the three therapists. Gloria's highest ranking emotions in this session were anger, fear, and contempt; there was a moderate level of paralinguistic shame. For Perls, the discrete emotion expression that dominated was contempt, accounting for

55 percent of his productions; fear and shame were the next most common terms and paralinguistic shame was low. Gloria matched Perls on the prominence of contempt and fear, and we know from sequences in the film that her anger was in direct response to Perls's derogatory and shaming comments. He calls her a "phony," and she reacted strongly and angrily to this statement.

One way of interpreting these patterns is to say that affect matching is a common pattern across the patient–therapist sessions. Rogers brought out Gloria's underlying shame; Ellis, her contempt; and Perls, her anger. A close examination of the filmed material also allowed us to track the interplay between client and therapist ideoaffectologies, the turbulence and eddies that were created as these ideoaffectologies came into contact with one another, and the assimilation and accommodation that took place over time. Thus, it was possible to track how Gloria came to show different sides of herself as well as how she asserted her core when we examined each session closely.

We now turn away from Gloria to a detailed examination of the emotional climates set by each of the three therapists. We will argue that the affective climate set by therapists via their affective postures acts as an induction for eliciting similar affective patterns in any reasonably cooperative client, and, in effect, recreates a powerful emotional climate in which the therapist may easily attain his particular goals. Indeed, the display of affective postures is probably essential to the attainment of the therapeutic goals. At the same time, characterologic aspects of the client's emotional organization compete with the therapist's organization to hold sway in the interchange. This concrete way of looking at transference and countertransference in therapy lets us grasp the phenomenon and track it in a way that has previously not been this transparent.

Setting the Emotional Climate

Previously we described the central organizing affects for each of the three therapists, distilled both from biographical or autobiographical materials, as well as from written theoretical works from each man. In the film, we have unique opportunities to observe how Ellis, Rogers, and Perls brought their mature scripts derived from emotional as well as cognitive structures to bear on the therapeutic process. These ideoaffective scripts are revealed not only in the therapists' introductory remarks but also in the emotional climates they set using bodily posture and gestures.

In fact, one could say that their nonverbal postures reveal another arena in which the working of emotional fractals can be observed, in which ideoaffective scripts are enacted in all their cross-channel splendor, and in which the therapist's self-similarity is induced in the client.

In the following discussion, we describe each therapist's emotional posture, illustrating how the posture establishes a particular kind of emotional climate and in large part sets the boundary conditions for the client's exploration of issues. We could say that the postures of Rogers, Ellis, and Perls are not only congruent with the therapeutic ideologies of Rogerian, Rational Emotive, and Gestalt therapy, respectively, but that they are actually part and parcel of them. It is highly unlikely that the three therapists were aware of their own postures or how they exemplified their theoretical positions. They would not have considered such postures as ideographic of their particular therapies and, therefore, worthy of deliberate instruction. Thus, although these postures are not explicitly taught in therapist training and are, in fact, ignored, we will argue that the study of the personal emotional environments created by therapists are of great importance. After we have circumscribed the postures and detailed their meanings, we will have made it possible for professionals with training in emotional expression to recognize such emotional climates.

At first we will limit our analysis of the emotional posture of each therapist to the introductory sections of the film. We used the opening or introductory material only as a matter of convenience; we readily could have sampled from the middle, toward the end, or from any randomly chosen section, since these postures are emblematic of each therapist's particular ideoaffectology and are found repetitively throughout the session.

The Film

Before we examine the individual sessions in turn, we take note of the beginning frames of the film when the therapist is alone. The opening scene of each film is of an academic-looking office bathed in subdued lighting and the walls are lined with rows of bookshelves and books. There is a secretary – an all-business sort of secretary – typing the names of the therapist and the client onto file cards, as if a new logbook on the client were being opened in the doctor's office. There is a brief note of thanks and introduction by the organizer of the series, Ed Shostrom. We note that he introduced each therapist formally by his family name and title, and Gloria, the client, informally with only her given name and that she is accorded praise for her courage in participating. From our vantage point several decades later, we note status and gender strains that were unconsciously introduced at the time that the film was prepared but that, although unconscious, nevertheless will have some effect on the therapeutic process.

Rogers: Therapeutic Intentions and Outcomes

The Genius of Emotional Environment and Posture

We will note the genius of Rogers's emotional posture in setting the environment almost instantly. It is highly unlikely that Rogers was aware of his emotional posture in the sense that he considered it part of Rogerian therapy. Even today therapists are not usually given instruction about their emotional posture and how it creates a therapeutic environment. Though Rogers's emotional posture is not consciously assumed, we will show that Rogers is able to begin his therapeutic process in the first seconds of the interview through masterful use and control of this nonverbal procedure.

Therapeutic Intentions and Outcomes

The postural setting that Rogers will create is congruent with his therapeutic intentions. Before meeting Gloria, Rogers spoke to the film audience about his intentions in therapy. He mentioned the necessity for the therapist to create the proper *environment* for therapeutic "movement" and "constructive change" and noted three necessary elements for this environment.

1. First, he asks of himself that he be *clear and open,* nothing hidden from the client.
2. Second, he asks of himself that he *prize* or care for the person.
3. Third, he asks that he be able to enter her inner world or feelings in a meaningful way, that he *move around in her feelings.*

Rogers, again in the introductory speech, told the viewers that if the proper environment could be established, they would be able to see several changes. The client would explore her feelings more deeply and discover hidden aspects of her feelings. Through the contagion from the therapist (this is Rogers's interpretation) of prizing she would prize herself more and listen more carefully to herself and catch new meanings. She would sense Rogers's "realness" and become more real herself. She would change from a focus on remote experiences to the experience of the immediate present – also the focus of the therapist, of course. The client would move from speaking of feelings and events that are in her past or future to speaking of feelings and events that occur in the present setting. She would be more accepting of herself and have less fear of acceptance in the relationship with the therapist. Her mode of evaluating and judging herself would be less reliant on external sources, more reliant on inner ones, and the evaluation itself would be less "black and white," more "tentative."

In this film introduction, Rogers suggested that understanding the client's inner world might require more than reflecting the client's feelings. The outcomes that Rogers predicted for the short therapy session also suggested a dynamic interpretation, but there is little in Rogers's own writings about nondirective therapy that offers much insight into the type of meanings for which he might be sensitive. In this case, his behavior offered more information than his professional writing.

In summary, Rogers expected Gloria to shift in her processing of information within even one short therapy session. Her focus and mode of evaluation will change, and although he avoided saying it, her changes will approximate his own way of processing information during therapy. Is this expectation possible or reasonable? Will he and Gloria manage to show that much shift in a single session? What steps does a Rogerian take and in what sense is it a spontaneous outcome of any therapeutic encounter? Even at the outset it is clear that Rogers is modeling the behavior that he expects the client to adopt. He expects her to adopt or learn more nondirective therapeutic methods – to *prize*, to *listen*, to be *tentative*, to *find hidden meanings*.

Environment and Static Posture

The picture of Rogers that emerges from the film is distinctive. Rogers is bald, quite shiny in fact. He is thin, not cadaverous, but the ridges of bone in his forehead are visible and the cartilage in his neck, for example, is slightly visible as it usually is in men past middle age who are quite thin. He is of about medium height. He is dressed for the office in a severely dark suit, perhaps it is black, a sharply pressed white shirt, and a very dark tie. There is no visible jewelry, nothing to break the ascetic and almost formal nature of his appearance. In fact, his dress could allow him to pass for a preacher or an old-fashioned business man. It is not rich or formal enough to suggest wealth or any of the professions that deal with wealth such as personal lawyers or private medical doctors. But it is very far from the daily costume of the working class or the farmers of America. As an academic or practicing psychologist, he appears to be restrained and on the formal side of that profession. Nothing in his dress or appearance could offend, but it definitely says, "I am a professional in my office" rather than "I am your casual friend or neighbor."

In spite of the office-like opening and Rogers's business attire, the scene or backdrop of the therapy session is more like a home than an office. There is an informal rattan two-seater couch for Gloria and a matching armchair for her therapist. They face each other across a coffee table. On the table are a plant, a box of tissues, which Gloria will use, and an ashtray, which Gloria will also use, but only with Perls after he lights a cigarette. There is an entrance area separated from the living room area by a room divider with plants. The back wall appears to have books on it. The overall effect is subdued and pleasant.

When the film opens, Rogers is seated in the rattan arm chair with his back to us. Gloria comes in the entrance and around the room divider. Gloria is much younger than any of the therapists. She is dressed in light colors, a sleeveless, high-necked fitted blouse and a matching pleated skirt. She carries a large white purse which she has to shift to shake hands with Rogers. She is wearing matching high heels as well. Her dark hair is short and curly, neat but not severe, and her make-up is similar. She is wearing lipstick and probably matching nail polish, a large necklace of white beads, and a conspicuous glittery watchband. She looks very much like a 1950s or 1960s office worker on her way to work or a young housewife on her way to a bridge game. Her dress, age, and gender lead us to suspect that she does not have the educational or professional advantages of the therapists; her position is clearly subordinate.

When Gloria enters, Rogers stands up. As she comes around the room divider he waits until she is quite close and then introduces himself and shakes her hand. Gloria was not quite prepared for this formality since she had her purse in her right hand and had to shift it awkwardly to shake hands. Rogers invites her to take a seat and seats himself. Even in their meeting and sitting, one grasps the nature of the opening encounter. Rogers has taken the lead and established his superior position with his professional garb, formal introduction – including a hand shaking ceremonial – and he took precedence with his prior place in the room.

Gloria, having been greeted and having been shown to be somewhat awkward even in that, wedges herself in the corner of the couch when she sits down. She crosses her legs and has her skirt initially covering her knees. Her arms are draped over the back and the arm of the couch and her head is up or up and back. She gives several messages with this posture. Her crossed and covered legs directly in front of Rogers indicate a closed position. Her backing up into the corner indicates a wariness, but her open arms indicate a willingness to proceed. We will notice at first that her hands even from the widespread positions on the back and side of the couch are used with the palms pushing toward Rogers or fluttered in front of him, another sign of her understandable ambivalence. One wonders what inducements were offered her to participate or how thoroughly the consequences were explained.

Clear and Open Posture

In great contrast to Gloria's ambivalent position, both open and closed – which is bound to be related to her inferior position as well as her personality – Rogers assumes a clear and open posture, a Western lotus position. He is seated in the armchair, of course, not on the floor, and does not cross his ankles, but the rest of his posture is lotus-like. He has made a cup of his lap by leaning over toward his knees. His legs are separated to make a wide lap and his arms also surround his lap. Sometimes at the sides of his lap and sometimes in the middle, his hands, which he uses expressively and frequently, are either palms up in a receptive position or resting caressingly on each other. The whole posture is one of reception and meditation or concentration. This open but contained or holding posture combined with his formal, ascetic appearance, his cupping hands, his nodding head, and his slight smile with the slightly furrowed brow create the environment for Rogers that he seeks to establish even before he speaks. He is the very image of the client-centered therapist.

The posture that Rogers uses announces his first two goals in the first moments of meeting and implies the third, which must of necessity be developed over time and through interaction. His posture prepares both himself and the client for receptivity and for caring. For better or for worse, his posture tells the client that he is the caretaker and the orchestrator of this encounter, the person who welcomes her into the inner sanctum. Whether Rogers wishes it or not, he also implies that the client will be a dependent or supplicant. There is no challenge in his emotional posture that would indicate that he expects mature opposition and autonomy and that he intends to "stand his ground" for example. Neither is there any questioning or ambivalence in his posture as there might be if some dialogue were needed to establish his stance. He is certain of his position before he has even met the client.

More than Clear – Focused

The "nothing hidden" aspect of Rogers is conveyed in his open posture. However, importantly, he acts out quite a bit more than he tells. Not only is the posture open, but it is also contained or professionally focused, as the clothing and bodily appearance are contained and professional. Rogers's instruction to have "nothing hidden" might imply to some beginning therapists that they are to reveal their rawest reactions; there is little in what Rogers *says* abstractly to contradict that suspicion. However, in his emotional posture, Rogers is clearly opposed to exposing the client to anything unpracticed or raw. It may be "real," but it is a sophisticated and finely honed reality. It is more the realness of the black belt karate expert in a demonstration, one who has practiced his concentration and meditation strategies until they are a well disciplined part of his deepest self as well as his physical movement. The posture that Rogers has prepared is, in fact, quite a difficult one to master as anyone who has tried to teach Rogerian "listening techniques" to students can affirm.

The unfortunate choice of words by Rogers and many others in the therapeutic profession has encouraged some counselors and psychologists to interpret being "real," "genuine," or "transparent," or "expressing what is felt on the inside" as an invitation to bring their personal life or spontaneous reactions into the counseling situation. But no one watching Rogers could be persuaded that he would do this. His "genuine" self in the therapeutic setting is the therapist self. There is nothing "false" about this posture but it is clearly also one side of Rogers. It is the same sort of concentration that the experienced surgeon brings to the surgery, that the talented engineer brings to the design of computers, or that the exceptional kindergarten teacher brings to the classroom. It is a focusing of all aspects of oneself on the task at hand to demonstrate mastery. Rogers in his Western lotus position is completely focused on being receptive to the client, on hearing everything she says, on seeing her every movement. He is prepared to "reflect" or mimic in miniature her behaviors to get a personal inner sense of her feeling state.

Rogers's "transparency" is the clearness of the focus and the clearness of the receptivity. What the client and the therapist see, hear, and feel is that Rogers is completely focused on the present issue and the present relationship in a particular way. If he brought his thoughts about his book contracts, or even his image of a good lunch to the therapy session, he would not be concentrating on the client, and he would not be himself-in-therapy. Rogers is somewhat deceptive in using terms like transparency or "real". His practice requires knowledge and training. It is not for the naive or the inexperienced. It is true that Rogers is transparent and genuine, but this reality is a product of many years of training.

It is quite difficult to concentrate for thirty or fifty minutes entirely on a particular problem without having interfering or intrusive thoughts. One of the better examples of the total immersion that Rogers projects might best be thought of as a highly learned physical activity. A mountain climber would show the same degree of focus and concentration and would use overlearned and graceful responses to the feel and shape of the mountain to shift her body and attention and planning second by second. Everything else falls out of consciousness in this process, but it is not an activity that occurs just because the climber is open to the experience. It requires hours and years of training and practice. It is the full body and mind practice that moves out of awareness when it is attained so that the person on the mountain is often not conscious of the decisions being made second by second. Neither is Rogers aware of his moment-to-moment decisions, nor can he immediately recall, by his own admission, at the end of the session more than a "few phrases" from the session. It is this well-honed concentration and totally controlled emotional set that Rogers brings and projects so transparently. That he is processing what he receives from the client in a particular way that also reflects years of training is apparent from the pattern of reaction, his adaptation to feeling his way along the mountain that is the client.

Prizing

The valuing or prizing–caring aspect of Rogers's posture lies also partly in its openness and in the holding-lap posture. He is ready to receive and anticipates nothing repulsive or hostile. Even when he looks down to break the eye contact, he is clearly still listening and concentrating. The way he focuses totally on the client indicates his type of caring.

Beyond the holding-lap posture, Rogers uses his arms and hands to embrace. The caressing nature in the movements of his hands also indicates a distinct pleasure in his focus. His nodding and smiling continue the presentation of caring and prizing. At critical points Rogers will also stroke his cheek in a thoughtful and loving manner broadening the slight caressive nature of his posture. Thus, Rogers has conveyed prizing in the encircling posture of both arms and legs and in self-caressing movements of hands, cheek, and even lip-licking.

Summary of the Rogerian Environment

Rogers established his environment before either he or the client even speak – in the first seconds of the encounter. The power of affective posture is greater than most people suppose in this vein. It is much faster than language when it is well handled, and it is very persuasive. It is not always "genuine." Most of us will have seen a talented actor or politician, sometimes even a conflicted therapist, move into a similar prizing posture to greet one person and then move back into a more aloof posture the next second. Any posture is difficult to maintain if it is not congruent with one's intentions, but it is certainly possible to create it even when it is superficial or momentary. If one is to do Rogerian therapy, adopting a Rogerian posture would be important and being able to maintain it and integrate it with other personal behaviors would be critical. Learning to adopt the posture could be difficult for some people, but even when it suits the person's ordinary posture, it could still require years of practice to acquire the consistency and complete congruence that Rogers has mastered and gives in his opening emotional posture. Everything fits together for Rogers's intent or philosophy: the dress, the polite speech, the receptive mode of sitting, the expressive hand gestures, the smile and concentrated brow, and the nodding. All the reflective pieces or fractals of his affective behavior show us the larger whole of his intention and goals.

Gloria is not captured entirely by Rogers's emotional posture. For about half of the session she stays outside the invisible circle of his lotus body and does not come forward into his implicit embrace. She leans away and stays in her corner with her legs crossed, and, as we shall soon see, this posture is emphasized even more when she begins to speak, although her posture lacks Rogers's consistency. In the language of psychologists, she displays resistance to his emotional climate and its implicit requests. In the language of emotional posture, she uses her position to maintain her distance and autonomy, but she is ambivalent and shifts frequently. This resistance and ambiguity is also genuine.

Moving Around in Feelings

Perhaps the question is, how will Rogers make progress in this short filming of an introductory session? How will he work with Gloria's distance and ambivalence and what form will the content of it take? From everything that Rogers has written, we know that he will avoid conflict and will attempt to avoid frustrating her further. But how will he create movement without frustration and conflict? The original psychotherapists emphasized the importance of the frustration and the intrinsic conflict of the therapeutic encounter, within a supportive context to be certain, but still there is a great deal of aggression in the original focus of therapists in the early part of the twentieth century, and much of it remains in some circles. As we will see later, Perls is a master of the school that fosters frustration to provide momentum.

What about the third requirement of therapeutic change? How is Rogers intending to understand the client's inner world, be sensitive, "move around in her feelings," or catch the "meanings beneath the surface" and how will he do this with his expressive behavior? This third requirement begins to sound quite psychodynamic, almost interpretive. In his writings, Rogers emphasized the work that the client would do with insight, not the therapist, and he strongly emphasized the spontaneous nature of insight simply emerging from the expression of feelings. We note, of course, that he has a talented and experienced hand laid on the feelings that will emerge in this setting and from our work would, therefore, predict that the particular insights that emerge will not be random but will be congruent with the emotional setting.

Moving Around in Feelings – Synchrony

The first thing that Rogers does after setting the seductively receptive, caring scene with his posture and dress is to introduce positive affect. Of course, this is also part of prizing and then the movement he intends. The first emotion word he uses is "glad." "I'd be glad to know what concerns you." He also provides partial synchrony in movement with Gloria. She is slightly tossing her head to the side to emphasize her speech, and Rogers follows this movement with head bobs. His direction is more affirmative, and hers borders on a negative head shake, but there is a reflection of movement that Rogers is beginning.

Gloria opens her remarks (remember her "cornered" posture in the couch) by stating her "nervousness" at which she laughs. Rogers smiles reflectively and notes verbally the "tremor" in her voice. So again there is a reflective synchrony being set by Rogers. Gloria sets up fears in her verbal statements, which Rogers acknowledges verbally, and she sets up a laugh nonverbally, which Rogers acknowledges nonverbally with his own supportive smile. Gloria then gives a slight grin and nod to Rogers, which he gives back quickly.

In a few seconds, Rogers has already begun to establish a rapport of intimacy and starts the movement he intends. Unlike Perls, who from the beginning frustrates Gloria by remarking on the lack of internal synchrony in her verbal and nonverbal behavior, Rogers uses Gloria's lack of synchrony to create a matching feeling for himself. He reflects her ambiguous statement at two levels, creating a slight ambiguity in himself as well. This is only a partial match. He does not match Gloria's cornered, partly open, partly closed posture. So he has his own solid base, but he does follow Gloria's lead in the pacing.

While Rogers set a positive emotional tone and will keep that fairly stable, he follows her micro movements with a matching tone but seldom with an identical emotional match. For example, when Gloria flashes a contempt attitude, Rogers will respond instantly with a mixture of sadness, interest, and shame, but not with contempt. When Gloria is ambiguous in her emotional expression, covering her contempt with a partial smile or laugh, Rogers will also be somewhat ambiguous. He is not taken in by the laugh, but will often nod and grin while mixing his response with a perplexed brow indicating a doubt in the positive gesture.

After the opening positivity and partial synchrony Gloria begins to tell Rogers that she is divorced and has been in therapy before. She was "comfortable" before with the divorce, but she wants to discuss a big change that is "sudden." In this introductory speech, Gloria is even less synchronous or congruent than before. Just when she says "the main thing I want to talk to you about is," she turns her head onto her shoulder almost away from Rogers, suggesting that she really wants to turn away in spite of her words. In her speech she sounds prepared to share her feelings, but in her nonverbal behavior she is much less certain. Her head seems to need the momentary support of her shoulder, but there is a contemptuous, shrugging aspect to the movement that suggests rejection at the same time. She mixes a distressed facial expression with a more contemptuous one throughout most of the session, and it is quite conspicuous here. When she finally gets to saying the words "newly divorced," she is fully contemptuous in her expression. We cannot see Rogers's face, but he most likely is expressing the distress part of her display and not the contempt. He is nodding and "uh hm-ing" at intervals.

Moving from Distant to Present

In the next instance, Gloria moves to telling about her daughter who "at one time had a lot of emotional problems." Already they have moved from the old history of divorce to present problems with a daughter. Gloria interrupts herself here to remark again on her nervousness, and both she and Rogers chuckle. Rogers has probably already caught at some level that she speaks seriously of someone else's distant emotional problem and then suggests her own present emotional problem is laughable. So far we have heard that Gloria was in therapy and that her daughter also had emotional problems. Rogers has said nothing beyond his "uh hmms." Gloria continues to say that she does not want to upset or shock the daughter. Statements especially at this juncture might alert the therapist to the fact that the client is, at one level, talking about the dilemma just as she states it but, at another level, talking about how she construes mother or parent–daughter relationships and at another level how she construes her present relationship with an authority figure of another kind – the therapist. Her daughter, as well as her own daughter self, and perhaps her client self, are the subject of emotional problems and need protection from shock and upset. Gloria says, "I want so bad for her [the daughter] to accept me." This implies deep sensitivity on Gloria's part to self-acceptance. Her daughter, her own daughter self, and her client self might find her parent and implicitly her therapist upsetting and shocking. In fact, this very sensitivity leads to the most distressing parts of her session with Perls and may have a great deal to do with why she did not connect to Ellis. Her own adult parent self might be unacceptable and shocking, while her child and client self needs support and protection, even respect and admiration. Of the three therapists, only Rogers takes this construction seriously and responds to Gloria's stated need for support.

It will be about half way through the session before Rogers or Gloria comment on Gloria's presentation of her divorce dilemma at any interpretative level, but this becomes the focus of the session. At this point, Rogers just continues to listen. In any case, by this point in the session, Rogers has firmly established his emotional setting. About half-way through the session Gloria begins to move into Rogers's emotional setting. She adopts more of Rogers's emotional gestures and postures and also, not surprisingly, begins to meet some of his goals for being "less black and white" in her thinking, for prizing herself a bit, and so forth. Rogers is fairly successful in meeting the goals that he intended. It is a good deal less surprising and spontaneous than he had implied when we analyze it in detail. We contend that the emotional setting is crucial as well as the dynamic emotional interplay for the emergence of these goals.

Ellis: Therapeutic Intentions and Outcomes

Stated Intentions

The postural setting that Ellis will create is just as congruent with his therapeutic goals as Rogers's was. Again, it is unlikely that Ellis realized exactly what he did. Before meeting Gloria in the film, Ellis also spoke to the film audience. In that introductory portion of the film, Ellis described the fundamentals of Rational Emotive Therapy and his plans for the session. He made direct eye contact with the camera with only occasional reference to his notes, displayed almost no facial affective movement, and delivered his introductory remarks with a distinct nasality, emphasizing words every so often in a somewhat sing-song fashion. The voice, moreover, had no resonance to it, as though he was unable to put his full being into his voice. His posture in front of the camera was extremely controlled but also restrained, perhaps avoidant. He proceeded to tell us that RET has several assumptions:

1. That what happened to the individual in the past is, per se, not important; rather it is the beliefs and ideas that the person "imbibed" or taught himself. This is the reason he will not delve into the client's history. In other words, his first concern is to tell us what he will not do or what he will avoid. Ellis *dismisses the past*.
2. That all behavior has ideological antecedents. For this reason, he will focus on logical, philosophical assumptions. His second concern is to emphasize the logical and philosophical nature of behavior, even irrational behavior. He stresses, that everything has an antecedent or

a cause. The second intention is to examine the logic behind emotional and irrational behavior. He intends to be rational, *use his head.*

3. That "negative emotions, self-defeating behavior, inefficiencies" all accrue from the fact that the individual is constantly reindoctrinating himself with faulty assumptions and erroneous ideas, including defeatist thoughts and negative emotions. His third concern is to affirm that the roots of bad feelings, defeats, and behavioral inefficiency lie in bad logic. He intends to identify and separate or *eliminate bad feelings.*

4. Finally, that treatment proceeds from helping the person reevaluate his philosophical assumptions: "only by work and practice, by continually reassessing and revaluing his own philosophic assumptions, will he ever get better." Ellis equated his work with that of science, and the scientific mind is extolled; he made several references to classic scholars, not to psychological traditions. He also introduced a strong work ethic in this statement about "*work and practice.*"

The goals of therapy therefore are clearly rational and work-oriented. From his introductory comments, we learn that Ellis sees the therapeutic relationships as one of teacher and student. He expects the client, as student, to have illogical, faulty, maladaptive, and inefficient ideas with negative feelings as a consequence. He, the therapist, as teacher, has logical processes to impart that, when learned, practiced, and used, will solve the client's problems including the negative emotional consequences. He will not deal directly with emotional feelings or a particular human dilemma. Because of the emphasis on expert teaching, we can expect that the session will be didactic. As a scientist, Ellis will "examine" and dissect the patient's ideas, and will "aggressively" challenge the patient's belief systems, to use his phrase. The last statement is worth noting because the aggressiveness of the challenge implies hostility. Hostility implies some sort of anger or contempt, even if it is a carefully controlled and focused hostility. It is the therapist who will use the aggressive approach as he battles against poor logic.

Ellis goes on to stress the necessity of action. "Just talking about things, thinking about things is nice but not necessary. Ah- [shakes his head] or I should say it's not a necessary condition for a psychotherapeutic can-change change." Thus, there will not be much of an interpersonal exchange, nor any unnecessary conversation. We might even expect that Ellis intends to lecture rather than listen, giving instruction on logical thought and behavior, and that he will dominate the "dialogue." He will work hard, efficiently, and aggressively; he probably expects the same from a good client. The session is task-oriented, and the goal is to change thoughts and get the patient to try new, more logical behaviors.

Toward the end of the introduction, almost in passing, Ellis just mentions the client's emotions. His thought about emotions is to minimize negative affect, in particular fear and hostility. Though the goal relates to the emotions, it is not to reflect or liberate emotion, not to examine it, or explore nuance. Ellis's goal with respect to emotion comes in his last, emphatic comment. The goal of the session is to "minimize, though never entirely to eliminate, the *terrible* anxiety and the- the atrocious hostility which unfortunately affects most of us in this existence." Ellis expects extreme fear and hostility to characterize human life rather generally. He seeks to reduce a nearly universal problem generally afflicting everyone, not a particular emotional problem that a particular client might have in particular circumstances. We presume that he would use his emotional environment to minimize anxiety and hostility, to express his orientation to logic, and to promote a solid work ethic. Let us examine the film to find out how he will do this.

Environment and Static Posture

The opening and setting of the filmed session are the same as they had been for Rogers. The same business-like office at first, the same more home-like setting for the session. Once again Ellis as the therapist precedes the client in the room. As Gloria enters the room, Ellis stands up and walks forward to meet her and shake her hand. He quickly and abruptly gestures for her to take a seat. Already he demonstrates his efficiency and directiveness. He wants Gloria to move quickly to her place and he takes his place. He takes no time to see how she might feel or to respond to her gestures. Already he minimizes her feelings by not attending to them.

Ellis is attired in a plain white open-necked, short-sleeved shirt and plain dark trousers. The clothes are casual but still neat. Eillis is not as formal as Rogers in his dress but is prepared for "roll-up-your-sleeves" work. Ellis appears to be in his late forties or early fifties and about medium height; he has a slight, stooping build, and his appearance is altogether unprepossessing, almost retiring. He wears outsized horn-rimmed glasses that give him a somewhat owlish look and, because the frames are thick, make it impossible to see his eyebrows. His hair, which has a slight wave and which is receding, is combed straight back and held in place by a heavy gel. Closeups of his face during the introduction and interview reveal a mostly immobile face. Ellis would fit most people's stereotypes of the lonely scientist unconcerned with appearances, not very attractive or particularly masculine in build, but prepared to focus and persist and be very logical about particular problems, while not being distracted by the human emotions around him. In spite of the immobility of his face, there are noticeable anger furrows between the brows. Again, the modern scientist comes to mind with his aggressive attack on problems, his jockeying to be first with his discoveries, and his desire to rid the world of superstition and "soft" or faulty thinking. On the other side of the coin, Ellis's eyes tend to dart about, giving him a skittish and guarded appearance, a vulnerable look. Even though he has an aggressive side, he appears constitutionally fearful. This more vulnerable region of the face creates contradictory tension with the lower half of his face. Though the mouth is also generally devoid of emotional expression, when he talks there is an intermittent lip raise on the right which exposes the incisor, giving an aggressive and contemptuous look to his countenance, even though his bodily posture suggests more fearfulness. While the image is a little fanciful, Ellis resembles a hatchling bird of prey, an unfeathered eaglet, perhaps. When approached, he exhibits both vulnerability and courage.

In contrast to the thin, unsubstantial body, the voice is strong in character, not soft, even booming at times; it is staccato in rhythm and somewhat propulsive, but largely neutral in tone throughout. He takes care to enunciate his words. Again he gives his message about his intentions in the opening seconds with his tone as well as his movements. His speech is confident, authoritative, even aggressive in its staccato pace and loudness, and yet it is strictly controlled – sometimes overcontrolled so it is not fluid. Nevertheless, his speech and choice of words all communicate the didactic, no-nonsense purpose of this session. His hand and head gestures add to the authoritative, aggressive style. He intersperses his didactic remarks with strong choppy movement of the whole hand, not just a finger wag, to hammer home certain points. At other times he uses vigorous thrusting of his head to emphasize his points. He also uses a number of dismissive head and hand gestures – head tossing and hand flipping – showing contempt where he is not aggressive. If he were a debating opponent, he would be formidable indeed. One does not need to *hear* Ellis's intentions to know what he intends. His nonverbal movements of face and body and the tone and style of his vocal expression give the message in just a few seconds. Ellis dismisses, shows contempt for faulty ideas, minimizes his own expression, and works hard with his thrusting gestures to get his points across repeatedly. Ellis is clearly master of the efficient art of moving toward logical argument with a workmanlike approach and no inquiries about feelings.

Head First

Ellis's first statement to Gloria is "Be seated please." Although he is polite, he is already telling Gloria what to do. His next statement is a question, getting right to the task at hand: "Well, would you like to tell me what's bothering you *most*?" Ellis circumvents any unnecessary social chatter or background and goes directly to Gloria's most troublesome problem. Since Gloria chooses a different important problem for each therapist, this question of whether a client can choose the most troublesome problem or whether the problems reside entirely in the client or whether they are a mutual choice of sorts is worth considering. When faced with the demand for an important problem with no preamble, no warming-up to the therapist, the client would be likely to choose a problem that appears to be rather public. Knowing about "hidden" matters, as Rogers or Perls might have put it, would not be likely with Ellis's direction.

Ellis sits leaning away from Gloria, with his back resting against the rattan chair. Leaning away from a person with whom you are having an intimate discussion is usually an indication of separation and sometimes of contemptuous or hostile feelings. Ellis's right leg rests upon the left one at a cross angle such that his leg forms a barrier between the client and himself, emphasizing the distance even further. Even though his lap is open, it is not open to Gloria. Ellis's hands are folded in his lap right in front of his belly, again signaling a closed and, in this instance, also a contained and held body structure. Ellis's head, on the other hand, is tilted forward, in a posture of interest, and there are also nodding head movements of encouragement.

Ellis's postural communications are thus fully and dramatically congruent with his therapeutic ideology. He is leading and welcoming with his head, thus inviting the client to present intellectual work. His guts or his body are shielded behind the gate of his folded hands and crossed legs and placed as far away as the situation allows. If there is to be any movement, it must come from the client who would move toward him – his position is pulled well away from her. We will see that Gloria does not move toward him but becomes ever more distant herself. Ellis will be lecturing and teaching Gloria in a directive rather than Socratic style. He does not intend to create an exchange. Gloria has nothing to offer him except her interest in his ideas. Ellis will not respond to Gloria in an empathic manner either at the level of content or on an emotional-expressive level, nor will he encourage her to be expressive.

Gloria is smiling broadly as she takes a seat though she almost immediately sighs. She holds on to the seat to the right of her on the couch and another armrest at the left. The full smile on her face is disqualified to a certain extent as she tilts her head, as if in question and uncertainty. Here and elsewhere we will see that Gloria brings her ambivalence with her across the sessions. Her legs are crossed at the knee, suggesting closedness, yet her arms are open at both sides, suggesting a willingness to take in and accept. As she sits, she arranges her skirt, at first pushing it forward, as if to cover, and then pulling it back. Almost every gesture shows an approach–avoidance conflict. But Ellis does not respond verbally or nonverbally.

As directed by Ellis, Gloria is able to identify a problem for him. In fact it will come out that she has prepared for this, like a good student. What bothers her most she claims, for Ellis, is "mostly men." Ellis was well known for his books on dating and sexual behavior by this time, and Gloria knows something of this. As she presents her problem, her legs are crossed in the seductive rather than demure mode, and she lowers her eyes and turns her head aside in an almost flirtatious fashion, smiling. She is going to mention one of his books, revealing her seriousness of purpose and perhaps looking for appreciation or approval, but then she questions whether it is appropriate for her to bring this up – another approach, then avoidance display. She is smiling and spreads her hand in a supplicating gesture, asking for help, reward, response – it does not matter, since Ellis does not respond. Next she says she is impressed with the work, *The Intelligent Woman's Guide to Manhunting*. She has shown herself to be knowledgeable, but quickly undermines her own authority by admitting that she is "not much of a reader," and that she "tried to follow it" apparently without success. Still, she says that it was "fun" reading the book and that she "sort of believes the same way you do." Gloria attempts to verbally align herself with Ellis but goes on to indicate that the message really did not take with her, for she quickly lapses into a distress face.

Gloria starts to describe the men she is attracted to, but when she says "men" she gives a disgusted face, and when she mentions the men she would like to become involved with, also expresses disgust as she mentions the word "men," and shakes her head. She says she gets too "shy" with them and it "just doesn't click." She mentions that she does not respect the men she is currently dating and emphasizes this with a look of contempt. In a somewhat plaintive voice, she says that she doesn't know why she attracts these men, if it is something about her, because "I really do want to meet this [other] kind of [attractive] men" (small, childlike voice), though she shakes her head. Gloria presents her feelings as well as the "problem" both in her description and in her gestures.

Practicing–Repeating

Ellis has set a climate of "work" rather than empathy at the outset and demonstrated with his emotional environment that he wants to work with the head, not with feelings. However, Ellis picks up on her only reference to "shyness" in the entire session – in this case shyness around the men she likes. He asks her what she is telling herself when she feels shy. He is searching for the logic or illogic, of course. Gloria does not answer him directly, but tells him that she typically acts "flip"; that is, she knows that her emotional default during situations of shy uncertainty and insecurity is contempt. Her voice, as well, is contemptuous when she speaks of herself. Ellis does not respond to the underlying anxiety that prompts this defense or the defensive contempt itself (in spite of the fact that Gloria will make multiple references to anxiety –33 percent of her negative affect words/phrases – which is exceeded only by contempt –52 percent). Instead, Ellis continues to pursue "shy" (which she mentions only once in the session) and even amplifies it with emotions from the same family – embarrassment and shame. He asks her again what she tells herself during these "shy" interactions. It is as if he casts off her continued emotional exploration, going back to the logic of the shyness.

At this juncture, Gloria looks down, gazes askance in a posture of shame rather than contempt. Either Ellis was correct that this shyness is most important or, more probably, he actually has induced shame in her with intrusive questioning. She admits that she knows what she says to herself. Once again punctuating her remarks with facial expressions of contempt, Gloria says of the kind of man she desires that she does not "stand up to his expectations. . . . He's superior to me. . . . I'm afraid I won't have enough to attract him." So Gloria follows her shamed gestures with shamed remarks. She is apparently "telling herself" that she is shy because the men she likes are quite superior to her. With just a little redirection, she and Ellis are on the same wavelength. Ellis has already established his method.

Now Ellis attacks Gloria's assumptions about her feelings – this is one of his goals. Ellis tells her that even though a man might indeed be superior to her, or wouldn't be attracted to her, *that* "would never upset you if you were only saying that . . . you're adding a second sentence to that, which is, if this is so, that would be awful."

Gloria is clearly disdainful of Ellis's interpretation or explanation. She looks at him skeptically, her lips parted in disgust, and tilts her head to the side, as her face slides into a smirk. She corrects him and tells him that it is not this extreme. As she elaborates, her face takes on a look of distress with deeply furrowed brows, and she once again punctuates her narration with sneers and head tosses; this time the contempt seems reserved for herself. She describes her attempts to be at her best, fails, and shows all her "bad qualities" such as her flippantness and defensiveness.

Teaching

Ellis concedes that he might be exaggerating, but counters with the fact that she must be "telling" herself other things, and that she's making things worse than they are. Again he does not appear to respond to her nonverbal message. Gloria seems to join him on this, by admitting that she fears that she is trapped in a pattern and will never get to have the kind of men she wants. She adds that she dislikes this idea intensely because "I don't like thinking of myself in that way. I want to put myself on a higher standard . . . [I don't want to be] just an average Jane Doe." She says this is a sing-song manner, mimicking Ellis's cadence, in a way mocking it, and at the end, flips her head and hand dismissively. Her voice has a frustrated ring to it. Again, Gloria follows Ellis's emotional lead, rather than the therapist following the client's lead. This is an intended difference between Rogers's style and Ellis's style, of course, but it is still amazing to see how it is accomplished in a minute or two.

Ellis does not answer Gloria's frustration, of course, or respond to her subtle mocking imitation. Instead, he cuts into her display and states that if in fact she were a Jane Doe, that it would not be terrible. He is contradicting her directly, dismissing her old fears. Ellis tells her it would be inconvenient and unpleasant, but that it would not cause shyness, embarrassment, and shame. In one conversational turn, Gloria has been contradicted and then instructed to downgrade, deny, and transform her emotional response and beliefs. Any of her nonverbal protests have been ignored. Ellis asks for her verbal agreement with his logic. Gloria conveys uncertainty in a plaintive, little girl voice, which is, ironically, quite appropriate to the subordinate position she has in this session. She knows she is wrong and is beginning to lose ground. Ellis continues to try to convince her that what she is telling herself is creating the problem, nothing else.

Gloria tosses her head, negating Ellis's demands, and verbalizes further frustration with the situation and having to accept "icky men," intoned with a disgust voice accompanied by a contempt face. Gloria tries to insist that icky men are a problem that is worth being upset about. At this point, Ellis introduces the word "catastrophizing" – again arguing that she is making the situation worse than it is. Gloria brings him back to her emotion: "Yes, but it feels like that to me at the time, it seems like forever." Ellis returns again to his position that Gloria's reaction is too extreme and flips his hand dismissively, negating her argument with his gesture as well as with his statements. He asks again for her verbal agreement that she does as he describes. Gloria finally replies, "yes," in a small voice with a furrowed brow, hand to heart protectively. She has begun to give ground and is thoroughly shamed and distressed. Even her contempt begins to desert her. Her gesture to cover her heart is not too subtle an expression of her position.

Work

Ellis moves into constructing new behaviors for Gloria now that she is firmly in the dependent-student position. He tells her to assume the worst – that she will never get the kind of a man she wants: "Look at all the other things you could do in life to be happy." He has taken her most pressing problem and told her that she could ignore it and do something else with her life. At this, Gloria tosses her head and breaks eye contact with Ellis. She turns to her purse to get a cigarette. Her more receptive position is closed off and she shakes her head as if to say, "I cannot accept this." And she makes yet another effort to assert her position. "Well, I don't like the whole process. . . . Even if it wasn't a catastrophe, even if I didn't look at it as a catastrophe, I don't like the way I'm living right now." She repeats this again, bringing her disgusted look back into the conversation. Gloria is actually a tough client for Ellis.

Ellis continues to minimize Gloria's interpretation of her feelings, just as he minimizes and dismisses her emotional expressions in the session. With his next conversational turn he simultaneously amplifies her affect and dismisses it. "But you're not, you're not merely concerned, you're *overconcerned*, you're anxious." He has returned to his theme that people get too emotional because they have the wrong thoughts.

Ellis and Gloria have been struggling for the lead for some time now. She has tried to assert herself, but he dominates and repeats with various aggressive head and hand movements that his agenda will prevail. They will have a few more turns like this, but she will concede. As Ellis increases his attack on her, he uses increasingly vigorous, intrusive, and assertive head and hand movements. These movements have a sharp instrumental feeling to them; they are firm and authoritative rather than fluidly expressive. At one juncture, his fingers are crossed except for the index fingers and thumbs which are pointed up and forward in a gunlike shape. Throughout, it is clear that Ellis is congruent in expressing his theoretical position through his nonverbal style as well as in his dialogue. He is aggressive, dismissive, interested, and persistent.

By about half-way through the session, Gloria gives up struggling to make Ellis take her position. She keeps a polite, semi-interested look on her face, nods from time to time, and murmurs agreement noises. She is no longer fighting – she is doing more listening and her arms are more open. She appears to be trying to absorb what he is saying; in part, the speed at which he talks forces concentration. The rest of the session is basically one long speech on the part of Ellis as he runs through the tenets of his theory as they apply to Gloria's stated problem.

Toward the close, Ellis tells Gloria how she can go about meeting men and trying new approaches with them. As the camera settles on her, we see that Gloria is smiling, she has one arm crossed across her body, resting her elbow on her other hand, supporting herself, and extending her hand into the air as if trying to grasp something above herself. She has a deeply lowered brow and her head is held a little in askance. She is suspending some disbelief, trying positively to reach something that Ellis is trying to give her, but holding herself in at the same time. She has adopted an Ellis sort of posture with this holding-in behavior.

Ellis suggests that Gloria take risks by striking up conversations with men. "What have you got to lose? The worst he can do is reject you. And you don't have to reject you if you were thinking along the lines that we've been talking about today. Does that make sense? Now, can you try to do that?" Gloria replies, "I think. I think so. It sort of gives me a spur to go out and see. And you're right, that's all I can do is be rejected." There is a lip raise on the right, suggesting some contempt for this idea, but she is smiling and nodding her head. There is no resolution of Gloria's ambivalence. She expresses just as much approach-avoidance conflict at the end of the session as she did in the beginning.

Rejection, frustration, lack of satisfaction with her own behavior – these feelings have been the themes of Gloria's most pressing problem. Can she do what Ellis tells her to do? She "thinks" she can. This is a cognitive evaluation, and yet it is marked by uncertainty both verbally and nonverbally. During the session, she has moved further away from her feelings and made more use of her head. She now has downgraded the significance of the feelings that will be associated with rejection – after all, *all* that can happen is that she will be rejected – she thinks.

Ellis and Gloria conclude on a harmonious note that does not sound genuine. He suggests that she try what she has already read. "And I'll be very interested in finding out what happened." She tilts her head and smiles. "Oh" (the voice is ambivalent), but then finishes with "I'm excited about it." Ellis concludes with, "Well, it was certainly nice meeting you, Gloria."

Throughout the session, Ellis has been mindful of the time, glancing at his watch. Finally, he signals that their time is over and proceeds to get up and end the session with the same directness that he began with: Gloria is not quite prepared for the speed with which the session has been concluded and must gather up her things while Ellis is standing before her. Their gestures remain out of synchrony from beginning to end.

Ellis stated in conclusion that he had accomplished what he intended. He worked with efficiency and determination. He remained focused on the goals of the session and guided the client to his agenda for her. Gloria's own agenda, on the face of it, was to deal with struggles related to her adjustment to single life after divorce. She articulated her anxious, self-conscious feelings when dating new men and her awareness of the role that she plays in her poor outcomes – her defensive behavior in the face of anxiety and lack of self-acceptance. She alludes to considerable frustration.

True to Ellis's opening remarks and goals for the session, this session has been didactic rather than emotive; it has been about cognition, not emotion; and it involved "challenging" Gloria's ideas. In fact, there was a dense section of "arguments" between the two before Gloria withdrew into a more passive posture.

Was the session a failure in some sense, as might be inferred from our description? It is true that Ellis was not able to create a sense of movement in the session. Gloria reported after the sessions that her interaction with Ellis was the least satisfying of the three. "I couldn't keep up with [him]. I had to think more with him, and I couldn't – I didn't feel as sharp with him. It took me a while to sink in what he was saying." And, "I'll almost say I felt more cold toward Dr. Ellis. I didn't have enough feeling." It is worth remarking that Gloria's dissatisfaction was not expressed as a dissatisfaction with the emotional connection primarily – the coldness perhaps sums that up – but she emphasizes her inability to think and to grasp his instructions. Given Ellis's goals, that is the least encouraging aspect of their session. Ellis also admitted that this session did not constitute his finest hour, which he largely ascribed to the brevity of the session. We, however, suspect that the difficulty arises from an overly fine match between two people with ambivalent avoidance. If Gloria could stay with Ellis long enough, a bond would likely form, but their ability to work together on attachment would be compromised. Gloria seems quite immune to Ellis's reinforcement strategy. This is also probably related to the severe approach-avoidance problems in her relationships. A "superior" person such as Ellis, who rewards Gloria, tends to remind her of troublesome dependencies in her life. These rewards increase her need for avoidance rather than drawing her into Ellis's therapeutic plans. It is not too surprising that her need for autonomy kept her from taking in what Ellis so forcefully tried to argue.

On the other hand, we must acknowledge that Ellis was sensitized to Gloria's shame. Though Gloria used but one shy/shame word, and her affective posture was one of contempt rather than shame, except on a few fleeting occasions, Ellis was able to attend to the shame implicit in the anti-contempt gestures and her lack of self esteem – possibly because he understands shame and antishame antidotes. This would be the in-road for RET in this case. Interestingly, Tomkins (1963) identified several antishame facial defenses as strategies to regulate shame, including the "frozen face" (i.e., tightly controlled facial expression), which contains the affect that would otherwise risk exposure; the "head-back look" or "snobby" look with nose and chin in the air, which provides a correction for a shamefully lowered head and gaze askance; and the "look of contempt" (i.e., upper lip raised in a sneer), which is an interpersonal repeller designed to remove the potentially shaming person.

Gloria gravitates to the head-back look and the look of contempt rather than the frozen face. But Ellis uses all strategies, including the frozen face, to defend against his vulnerabilities. As already discussed, his face was relatively immobile in terms of affective expression in both the introduction and the session with Gloria, except for some crystallized contempt. A photograph of Ellis at the age of eighteen (DiMattia & Lega, 1990) already indicates evidence of the crystallization of defensive shyness. In the photograph, an otherwise wan and shy-looking young man looks back over his shoulder at the camera: there is a unilateral lip raise and brow lift in the classic expression of facial contempt, although the teeth are not exposed. In the film, he intermittently exposes the right lateral and incisor teeth on the left, giving the expression an even more repelling quality. Additionally, anti-shame contempt gestures are in evidence in the film. In the session with Gloria, his face is rarely on camera, so virtually all we see is the head tosses and the chopping and dismissing hand movements. However, in the wrap-up, the relationship between contempt toward weak persons and contempt toward shameful feelings and ideas is quite visible:

> I enjoyed (contempt lip raise) talking with this interesting (lip raise) [patient].... [I was able to] show her that the reason (lip raise) she is feeling shy and (head toss) ashamed, and afraid ... we skip going back into the history, as some of the (head back) psychoanalysts do ... we skip some of the nonverbal expression (head toss) ... [If Gloria] stuck to [her] philosophy, she *had* to get negative and self-defeating results from it (head back, lip raise).

Although Ellis responded to and thereby validated Gloria's underlying shame – what he called her "shyness" and embarrassment – his approach was "rational" or at the verbal level only in accordance with his stated goals. However, it was not "unemotional," as the term is generally understood. Rationality was used within a context of reinforcing certain emotions and either punishing or ignoring others. This is an ideoaffective strategy for contemptuously minimizing and dismissing negative affect while attempting to increase interest in Ellis's problem solutions. In the session, Ellis was attempting to teach Gloria the techniques he himself has successfully mastered for routing negative affect from awareness – that is, denial, cognitive reframing, and transformation. And he has tried to encourage her to try new behaviors, but she appeared skeptical, shamed, and only slightly interested – her typical approach/avoidance stance.

The affect that receives attention from Ellis in the present session is shame/shyness as we noted previously. Ellis ignored most of the other affective vocabulary offered by Gloria to pick an affect of some familiarity to himself, having suffered from, and "successfully" treated, the shyness and social anxiety that afflicted his adolescent and young adult years. Though he claims in various written works to have defeated these inconvenient and self-defeating affects in himself, the fast propulsive speech, which is an index of bypassed or unconscious shame, belies that this dread has been permanently arrested. It is also open to question whether Ellis is specifically sensitive to Gloria's problem with shyness, shame, and self-esteem or whether Ellis works with this emotion regardless of how prominent it might be for the client. He could be so sensitive to it that he responds to it at very low levels.

We noted that despite the low frequency of shame references and low paralinguistic shame in Gloria's verbal and nonverbal output, Ellis is able to detect what is there and home in on it. We agree with him that she has a substantial shame dynamic; however, the interesting aspect is that he not only detects it but also has some success in avoiding its escalation. It is as though he is aware that contempt directed at the client from himself or others might escalate her defenses. Instead, his ideoaffective contempt is reserved for contemptible ideas, not persons.

In his session with Gloria, Ellis attempts to be not an adversary (though he struggles with her for the correct way of seeing things) but an ally, helping her dislodge her contemptible ideas and unnecessary and contemptible self-defeating behaviors. Moreover, he bears gifts; he directs her to tools she can use to battle the thoughts that give rise to her self-defeating behaviors. Unfortunately for Ellis's approach, Gloria does not have straightforward acceptance strategies for gifts from authority figures, nor is she willing to separate her thoughts from her feelings so readily.

From this session, we also learn something about how Ellis manages to relate to his clients. He appears to make his initial connection with clients by reflecting their own language for their emotions – within certain boundaries. He possesses an adroit ability to remember locutions that the client uses and to incorporate them in his own responses; he quickly picks up Gloria's use of "icky," "stinky," and "superior." Moreover, in using the client's own words, Ellis is able to demonstrate that he is not entirely arbitrary in using what may appear to be the formulaic approaches of RET; there is some customization. He does use the client's own words, albeit very selectively. But he reflects her words, not her nonverbal emotional feelings as they might be idiosyncratically associated with the words. This rather subtle separation of affect and cognition is also very congruent with his therapeutic aims, but it is also a reflective technique that he uses more than the other therapists and quite successfully with many clients.

Boundaries

Thus, despite the fact that Ellis did not connect with Gloria on an emotional level, and despite the fact that he argued her into submission, she left smiling, if somewhat puzzled, and thanking him rather than leaving in turmoil and with a sense of emotional unfinished business, as she had with Perls and in part with Rogers. In general, Ellis's avoidances and management strategies can be interpreted as reassuring boundaries. Many of our undergraduate students who watch Ellis on the film prefer him over the other therapists, sensing that he would not push them into territory that they might wish to avoid. Many of the young adults also prefer the seemingly unsubtle use of logic and reinforcement. It appears to make problems seem practical, solvable, and manageable, not somehow mysteriously hidden in an uncontrollable subconscious space. Furthermore, he has a rather unusual ability to be very interested in his partner in dialogue with his head attention, while giving clear clues that there are boundaries on his emotional or bodily involvement. To people with serious shame and self-acceptance problems, the clarity of the boundary along with the intense intellectual interest would be very supportive.

Ellis's themes of shame/shyness and concerns about acceptance are common, if not universal, human concerns. This makes for a particularly effective avenue of connection for Ellis. That is, he will almost never be entirely wrong with clients who come to him in distress because outside of certain kinds of clinically circumscribed narcissists, few people feel entirely self-confident and self-assured. Certainly among our undergraduate students who viewed the film and who preferred Ellis over the other therapists, concerns about self-acceptance and logical self-definition were paramount.

We note a strong distinction, however, between how Ellis works with shame and how the other two therapists work with it. Ellis masters shame essentially by bypassing it or reframing it. In this respect, the frequency and redundancy with which he mentions terms like shyness and allied emotions – embarrassment, shame – is a red herring. He is not dealing with these emotions qua emotions. Instead, he is trying to convert them into anti-shame thoughts and anti-shame activities. In contrast, Rogers accepts shame in himself and others and supports the client's exploration of these feelings. Perls induces or magnifies shame to prompt anger and defensive self-assertion. Ellis's claim that he is working with the client's "head," not her emotions, is not quite true from our point of view, but it is more subtle than it first appears.

In summary, Ellis's ideoaffectology and his affective organization are embedded in and support his prepared "philosophical" or "theoretical" statements. There is no real separation of emotion and theory. His ideoaffective posture sets the nature of the emotional climate or, in this case, the work climate for the session even more clearly. How he behaves as well as how he thinks is supported and given wholeness by the emotional components. The thrust of his logic and the emotional posture are all self-consistent and redundant – they are anti-anxiety, including anti-social anxiety or shame. His own anti-anxiety weapons – rationality (of which he is abundantly aware), contempt, and aggressive gestures (which he is much less aware of) – are very much in evidence throughout the session with Gloria.

Ellis marshals his resources, both words and behavior, in a directive, "therapeutic" way, as an assault on self-defeating ideas while providing a secure set of boundaries for therapy and for his engagement with the client. His fundamental assumption is that the client has faulty ideas that must be rooted out. Throughout the session Ellis urged Gloria to become more like himself, to take responsibility for herself, to work and practice at getting better, and to be more like a parent rather than a dependent child. By his behavior, he is also modeling for her a strategy of putting distance between the feelings that plague her and the rational goals that she wishes to attain.

Unfortunately, perhaps, Gloria is much like Ellis in that she is dominated by shame and anxiety and responds to her own shyness and anxiety with a contemptuous or dismissive, interruptive pattern. For Gloria, this strategy, while already adopted, has not been sufficient or balanced with other emotions. She has not found an interesting arena in which she can be capable – use her head – without reservation as Ellis has. She seems to want her interesting and capable arena to be the dating arena, but this definition of her problem is a bit presumptuous and ignores other serious problems. Ellis offers her a stronger defense of the sort she already has, but in the time allowed here, it is not sufficient.

If the client had been a person with a very different expressive style, one a little more different from Ellis's and one that was less shamed and defensively contemptuous, it is more likely that Ellis would have made more progress with that client even within the short period of time. The novelty of the approach offered by Ellis might have seemed like very new territory to such a person, and practicing it would offer surprising feelings of efficacy.

Perls: The Safe Emergency

Perls's Intentions and Goals

In the introduction Perls sets his goals just as the previous therapists had done, although, typical of Perls, some of his goals are difficult to identify or interpret: "Awareness equals present time equals reality," he states, leaving us to decode this cryptic message. He does not explain this mysterious sentence, but from other writing and speeches, we know that he means that one of the goals of therapy is to become more real or genuine in the moment or present time. The client should focus more on what is actually happening rather than what she imagines might happen or might have already happened. According to Perls, one knows reality – even past and future realities – by developing an awareness in the present time. This reminds us that Perls will focus on "being aware" as a goal of therapy rather than on solving cognitive problems, establishing relationships, or even expressing feelings. We anticipate that Perls's first goal is that he intends to help Gloria become aware of herself in the interaction with him.

The second focus within the therapeutic interaction comes out in his cryptic phrase that he will develop the Gestalt or the sense of the whole picture of "I and thou." We interpret this goal to be an extension of the previous one, that he will extend her awareness to the whole interaction between herself and Perls. We anticipate that Perls will steer Gloria away from reflections on her relationship with her daughter or with her father, both of which were explored with Rogers and away from her romantic relationships with men, which were explored with Ellis. If Perls meets his goal, all that Gloria should focus on is her relationship with Perls. Perls states that the problem patients present is that they cannot cope with the "here and now" and therefore are not using their entire potential in the therapy and presumably not elsewhere, either.

Extending further his goal of bringing the client into working completely on the present moment, Perls implies that his third goal for the patient is that she should recover her lost potential. He elaborates, saying that she will "integrate conflicting polarities" and come to understand the difference between game playing and genuine behavior. Perls has packed a dense set of intentions in this thought. Will he tell us how the client will recover lost potential or what that potential is? He states that there is a "civil war" of inner conflicts that weakens patients. Will he tell us how conflicting polarities are integrated to provide the strength needed by the client? Will he tell how he knows the difference between game playing and genuine behavior or why one is more desirable than the other? He says nothing in the introduction, but perhaps in his behavior during the session we will learn what he means.

Perls goes on to state why therapy is a special situation. Unlike Ellis, who sees therapy as a teaching opportunity and presumably not much different from ordinary discourse, Perls sees therapy as a "safe emergency," apparently a dangerous encounter. This idea of danger is magnified by his saying that the client will have to rely on her inner strength, not relying on the setting or the "environment" for support. To rely on personal inner strength would be Perls's definition of "maturity." To encourage the client to rely on her inner strength, Perls says that he will not explain things to the patient but that he will provide opportunities for her to understand and discover herself. Again, one can see a clear difference between Ellis and Perls. Ellis did intend to explain whatever he could to the client. But Perls says, "I manipulate and frustrate so that he confronts himself."

Of the three therapists, Perls seems to have the clearest idea about the power of his role as therapist. He intends not only to manipulate the client so that she can be aware of herself and "confront" her conflicted sides but also to manipulate, challenge, and frustrate her so that she will discover her own strength. Rogers and Ellis both deny that they are manipulating the client or frustrating her. Yet our analysis shows that they both powerfully persuade Gloria to follow their dictates and are somewhat frustrating. These are forms of manipulation. One might argue that as long as Rogers and Ellis are unaware of or even denying the power of their position, they are not in a good position to provide the client with an opportunity to achieve any kind of equality. This may seem paradoxical, but when a person recognizes that he is using his strength or power, he can make others aware of this, too.

Finally, Perls states that he will concentrate on the nonverbal level because it is less susceptible to self-deception. Why he believes nonverbal expression is less self-deceiving than verbal expression is not clear. Our analyses indicate that much of verbal display is also susceptible to self-deception at the level of emotion. Perhaps people are more aware that they are unaware of their nonverbal behavior and believe that they are aware and controlling of their verbal behavior. The level of belief may influence this process.

Perls on Tape: Establishing the Emotional Climate

Hiding. The videotape of the interaction is twenty-four minutes long. The first interesting detail to emerge is that Perls is never visible with his full face to the camera for more than a few seconds. In the introduction and ending evaluation, when he is alone with the camera, he keeps his face lowered with only glances upward to the camera. When he is with Gloria, he either maneuvers so that the camera is on her or he faces partly away from it. In the opening speech, Perls reads from notes low on his lap. He is hiding in his notes. Given that the lengthiest theme to emerge in the interaction with Gloria will be about her hiding in a fantasized corner, Perls ironically appears to need his own corner. Perhaps it is a bit of a stretch, but one might also say that the oblique and cryptic way that he has of presenting his goals for therapy is also a form of hiding. Perls is seldom direct and clear, although his incisive comments more often than not seem perfect for the clinical situation. However, it is as if he is behind cover, darts out with a cutting observation, and then disappears before he has to expose himself to attack.

We do not see Perls and Gloria greet each other – even that is hidden from the viewers. They are already seating themselves at the beginning of the film. Gloria appears much as she has for other sessions. Perls manages to look bohemian even though he is conventionally dressed in a black suit with a white shirt. The trim neatness of the other therapists is a distinct contrast to Perls's casual wrinkles. One can easily imagine that Perls has been wearing the same suit without pressing for days or weeks. Perls himself has a chubby face with hanging jowls. His belly rather clearly precedes him. In terms of dress codes among therapists, he is wearing the required black suit, but he wears it as if it were an old robe he had just thrown on. He does not appear to wish to give any regard to the conventions.

Manipulating–Frustrating. Perls opens by stating that "We are going to have an interview for a half hour." We cannot see his face when he makes this statement, but we can see his body from the rear. He is perched on the seat. He bounces once and shifts around holding his fingers pointing at each other and touching for a moment but then searching for and fingering a cigarette. We can tell from the side that he is smiling, even chuckling, at Gloria. At other times in the session, when Gloria smiles defensively, he will also laugh even while calling her a "phony," which makes Gloria furious. But here and now in the beginning of the interview Perls is searching for his smoking equipment, in his pockets, on the table. Perls's starting is about as ambivalent as Gloria's. He says they will have a session as if he is ready to begin it. But he is not beginning, he is searching for smoking things, he fidgets in the seat as if trying to find a comfortable spot. He will unsettle Gloria, perhaps keeping her on the edge of her seat. He leans forward as if to concentrate on Gloria, but then he shifts and glances away, apparently for the smoking things. Right at the outset, Perls informs Gloria with his posturing as well as his dress that there is little comfort or politeness in this interaction, that he will be disruptive and unsettling – manipulative and frustrating. Already his emotional posture has started to establish the therapeutic intention in the first moments of the session.

Crystallized Affect. Looking at the crystallized affect of Perls and Gloria, we might have suspected from the outset that they had considerable emotional overlap. Perls, although presumably not interacting expressively while delivering his prepared notes on Gestalt therapy to the camera audience (or to his lap), has visible lines on his brow that permanently mark two emotions – first, interest or excitement leading to surprise with the raised brow lines and, second, anger with the drawn together indentations between his brows. A third emotion, disgust, is crystallized in Perls's lower face. Perls has heavy jowls that hang in a distinctive way. If one makes a disgusted looking face and examines the way that the cheeks pouch one could see some of the jowl appearance that Perls has permanently or that is *crystallized*, as we define it.

Gloria is much younger and has fewer permanent lines and muscle cues. However, the smoothness between her nose and mouth and the beginnings of pouched jowls are faintly visible on Gloria, too. The indentation between her brows is also becoming fixed. On the other hand, Gloria does not share Perls's excitement or surprise, his fascination with novelty and discovery. What Perls can provide that would be different is the ability to be surprised, to notice change and novelty. As we will see, this ability is, in fact, intriguing to Gloria but not always welcome.

Danger, Conflict, and Polarities. Gloria is silent at first. Perls does not help her start. Actually Perls starts out leaning forward in his seat, appearing eager but also intruding somewhat on Gloria's space. Again, we note an important contrast with the other therapists. Where Rogers made a comforting space with his body and encouraged Gloria to come into this comfortable zone and Ellis established boundaries so that each person had a safe space, Perls intrudes upon Gloria's emotional space. He does not make a place for Gloria to enter but is pushing himself – with his hands, with his wagging finger, with his bounces and reaches – into Gloria's space. When they begin to talk, he sits up and then back when Gloria challenges him persistently; he defends himself and uses his pointer finger and wags it at Gloria almost accusingly, almost in her face. Of course, waiting for the silent Gloria to begin (without his help) as well as the intrusiveness is part of the contrary emotional environment "conflicting polarities" that he intended to establish. He demonstrates polarities in his nonverbal behavior as well as frustrating and "dangerous" maneuvers.

Finally Gloria says," Right away I'm scared." She is most likely responding to Perls's emotional environment, which is indeed intimidating. Perls responds immediately with his awareness of her nonverbal expression and his awareness of the conflicting polarity presented: "You say you're sacred but you are smiling. I don't understand how you could be scared and smiling at the same time." In the first seconds of the session Perls, a master of his own technique, just as Rogers and Ellis were, presents several of his goals nonverbally and now he begins to do so verbally. Some of this, like the unsettled sitting, he has probably done unconsciously. Some, like the intrusive confronting behavior, he may be using more consciously. The expression of polarities is done nonverbally and verbally.

After Perls claims not to understand, Gloria retorts that she thinks that Perls understands very well. Perls's technique for getting clients to rely on themselves is working fairly well. Gloria is already defending herself, not accepting Perls's remarks. Of course, Perls probably does understand what Gloria was doing, but this is his way of presenting a nonsupportive, challenging style – a safe emergency. Gloria is suspicious of Perls – perhaps more than she is afraid of him. Claiming not to know, when one does know, can make the client suspicious and untrusting. Perls ignores the trust aspect except that he claims that he will be "safe."

Awareness. Perls continues to draw attention to Gloria's verbal–nonverbal conflict, trying to make her more self-aware. Perls asks if she has stage fright. She has another silent gap and attends to her smoking, staring contemptuously into space for a second. Then she looks back and says she is mostly afraid of Perls and his direct attack that will get her in a corner. Perls returns to the nonverbal again. He interrupts Gloria (interruption is another of his confrontational and intrusive methods) and points out that she has put a protective hand on her chest just as she speaks of her corner. He is making her aware of her nonverbal behavior. Perls asks if this gesture represents her corner. He asks her to describe the corner she would like to go to, what she would do in her safe corner. Gloria begins to speak of going to a corner as a little girl. Perls interrupts again and demands, "Are you a little girl? Are you a little girl? How old are you?" He is being confrontational once again, going after the client nonverbally and verbally. Perls's goals of making the client aware of the nonverbal and of confronting the patient come into play both in his posture and in his speech.

When Gloria asks Perls to be more on her side, that is, to be less confrontational, he ignores this request and goes back to pick up on the corner issue once again. Gloria, who is definitely feeling frustrated by Perls's lack of response to her requests for support and attacked by his intrusive comments on her smiling, says that Perls could make her be dumb and stupid. Perls continues to focus on making her aware of the polarities and conflicts within herself. He asks what it would *do* for her to be dumb. He asks this a couple of times, but she just sits. Finally, Perls switches tactics and asks what it would do *to him* if she is dumb and stupid. He has been trying to make Gloria aware that being weak or stupid is a way of interacting with and perhaps manipulating other people. Perls is sitting forward pushing into Gloria's space and concentrating on Gloria, although he shifts back away now and again, usually as Gloria shifts.

Gloria again asks for help. Once again, Perls ignores the request and focuses on her nonverbal behavior and becomes even more frustrating. Perls smiles and asks if she is aware of *her* smile and says she is a phony. He imitates her squirming in her seat in a derisive way, repeats that she is phony and giving a performance. In terms of Perls's goals for the session, he now is showing how the client might be mixing up "game playing" with genuine behavior, but he is also demonstrating this confusion in his own behavior, which is also exaggerated game playing. Gloria gets quite angry at this taunting and is very direct and fluid in her retort. Perls does not comment on the content or the truthfulness of what Gloria is saying but on her way of responding. He says, "Wonderful," and puts his hand and arm out in the manner of acting out the presentation of an award.

Finally, he gives Gloria a gesture of approval and recognition, but his gesture is exaggerated, a game.

Perls begins more and more to get Gloria to develop awareness of her nonverbal movements, to take her hand movement and dance, for example. Gloria interrupts herself with laughing and embarrassment and asks to start the session over again. Perls allows this. He does not address the embarrassment or challenge it. Gloria wants to address the phoniness issue, however. She says that it is hard for her to show embarrassment. She hates to be embarrassed and smiles to cover this up, but the covering is not phony. Obviously she is asking for help again but in a different way, more directly. Perls stops his fidgeting, holds still and is focused on her entirely. Gloria ends saying she is mad at him. Neither of them comment on the close and intimate – I and thou – contact established by the anger and by Gloria's direct request. For a change, Perls is completely concentrating and combining interest and a little distress – a more sympathetic side.

I and Thou. Perls now has Gloria working completely in the "here and now" on her "I and thou" relationship with him, not on her daughter or her romances. Her entire focus is on the Perls–Gloria encounter. In that regard, Perls has accomplished one of his major goals. He has gotten there by frustrating Gloria and making her mad at him, which he also told us was his method. Gloria is not thinking of herself in any past or future relationship, but only of her feelings, mainly anger, about Perls. Perls seems quite comfortable with the anger, even welcoming it, which only frustrates Gloria more.

In the next phase of the session, Gloria continues to be angry at Perls, demonstrating her closeness – that she cares deeply about his views of her – to him even further. She comes very close to insulting Perls. She says that he demands so much respect, thinks he is so smart, and knows so much about psychology. Perls responds by turning this around, asking Gloria to act out being the person who demands respect. Here we see Perls dealing with the polarities within the person again. It would be his intention to effect some integration by having Gloria experience both sides. Gloria has said that she is easily embarrassed, but Perls wants her to act out the side of herself that is demanding respect, as Gloria puts it. Gloria at first denies that she might want respect. Finally, Gloria brings it into the "here and now" and she emphatically says that she would demand respect *from Perls* if she could. Perls tells her to do it. She says she cannot because Perls would leave her in the corner. She is claiming that when she stands up for herself she will be deserted and alone. Perls does not enter into this side of her explanation. He goes back to taunting and frustrating her. Perls says, "You need to have some one pull out little mam'sell in distress out of the corner. "His voice is dripping with contempt, Perls says that is the phony part – to crawl into a corner only to have someone come and pull you out instead of coming out by herself. Gloria says she is just as real in the corner as she would be being brave. Perls says, "But you are not sitting in a corner" bringing her back into the here and now of the session. Perls has his head up contemptuously, a tiny furrow on his brow. He is out of *his* hiding corner, too, and is showing contempt for Gloria as he calls her a phony. She retorts that Perls is passing judgment. Perls has made no progress trying to have Gloria be aware of demanding respect, but he has manipulated her into maintaining a strong confrontational position.

Perls shifts his direction as he does so often and asks what he should do when Gloria is in the corner. He gets no response, but it was probably another attempt on his part to get Gloria to experience both sides of herself – the person in the corner as well as the person who rescues her. Elis, in giving his assignments, did not try to have Gloria act out the assignment. We can see that when Perls asks Gloria to act out a direct assertive behavior where she would not usually do so, this is nearly impossible for her. Nevertheless, he can frustrate her into behaving more assertively. Although Perls says nothing about practice and assignments in contrast to Ellis, he is actually giving the client more direct experience with trying on new roles.

Gloria goes back to the judgment issue, that Perls is judging her. Perls asks her to pass judgment on him, once again working on the polarity. She will not do it but says, "I do not feel close to you at all." She is glaring at Perls but also sitting openly and doing some head tossing contemptuously with a lot of contempt in her face and voice when she speaks, but she sits very quietly and still when she is listening. When she says she does not feel close, we looked at the tape in slow motion. In the space of a second or two she has a full-face exaggerated contempt expression, she looks away and down in humiliation, looks back with a little distress, looks down to examine her hand (a hiding or embarrassed behavior), turns back to speak, raises her arm into a striking position, but then brings her arm to the back of the couch. She alternates the contempt and the embarrassment with touches of distress and anger. Perls says, reflectively, that he has hurt her, as indeed he has. Perls is not apologetic. Quite the contrary, he expands proudly and says he has hit a bull's eye as he wags his finger at her – once again intruding into her space. His hurting her is his surety that he has discerned her vulnerability.

To summarize, Perls has repeatedly worked on Gloria's "awareness." For example, he attempts to have Gloria see her gestures as corner (hiding) behavior. Or he asks, "What are you doing with your feet now?" Or he has her exaggerate gestures as in having her develop hand waving when she does not answer one of his challenges. This is all in the service of making Gloria more aware of her nonverbal messages and of how she affects people as she talks with them. What Perls does not say about this is that the very task of making people aware of their nonverbal behavior is manipulative and intrusive and therefore confrontational. He lets people know that he is in a privileged position, seeing things about them that they are not themselves aware of. He tells them to be aware, but this necessarily makes people self-conscious and often leads to anger in and of itself.

One could contrast Perls's frustration approach with Rogers's prizing approach. Both aim at having the client become more aware of her emotional and cognitive process. The novel information about herself that Perls intrudes upon Gloria certainly has her involved, but it is not as clear that she is coming to understand Perls's direction as well as she seemed to comprehend Rogers's.

There are many examples of Perls demonstrating his intrusive "confrontation" technique. Not only does he begin and continue to use intrusive and contemptuous or angry nonverbal behavior, but he also uses very consistent verbal dialogue. Perls challenges Gloria's feeling of being a little girl. "Are you a little girl?" He challenges her emotion display: "Are you aware of your smile?" He challenges her statements: "You do not believe what you say." He challenges her sense that she is genuine: "You are a phony. You put on a performance." Perls softens his confrontations with smiles and laughter also, but he shifts into a kind of contempt gesture including puffing on his cigarette and literally blowing and waving away her objections. This confrontation is effective in making Gloria angry, which Perls says is wonderful, presumably in the quick way that it gets her focused on the session with Perls, on the here and now. Gloria only gets more angry at the implied objective superiority.

Gloria is extraordinarily sensitive to the issue of superiority. As we noted earlier, the social inequities of the situation only exaggerate her personal vulnerability. Gloria is at a serious disadvantage with these famous men in almost every way, and asking her to ignore that publicly, on film, is asking quite a lot. None of the three therapists acknowledges the difficulty of Gloria's task in this larger sense. If any of them might have been aware of the subtleties it might have been Perls. But he is clearly not reflecting the underlying reality that Gloria experiences on top of her personal vulnerability.

Integrating Polarities. In several instances, Perls works on "polarities" needing "integration." Perls has Gloria play at "getting respect" herself rather than complaining that Perls demands respect. He has her play at scolding him for being dumb when she claims he makes her feel dumb. When she asks for comfort he has her play that she can hold Perls and comfort him.

The little exchange about caring and being cared for once again reveals the polarities in Gloria's demands as well as in her ambivalent nonverbal behavior. She wants to be cared for, but when she is cared for, she starts to act as if she has no respect for herself. Perls is the only one of the therapists who avoided getting trapped by this particular polarity, though he did not make any progress in its integration. Rogers played the part of Gloria's father being comforting and admiring for a moment and found Gloria rejecting him rather strongly. Ellis led Gloria to be dependent upon his advice and found that she was unable to take much, if any, of it in. Perls avoids this pitfall, and he intrigues Gloria with his recognition of these polarities. Nevertheless, as Perls said later, he could make little progress with Gloria's polarities.

Gloria repeatedly asks Perls for support. Perls turns this into a playing of the opposite role, again trying to integrate the polarity. He says, "Scold me like I was younger." Even here, Gloria is angry and contemptuous, but she is especially contemptuous that Perls is laughing and is not affected by her anger. Perls says, "We had a good fight," but Gloria disagrees, angrily, saying that we are not fighting. "You are so detached." Perls leans forward. Here again, Perls is more straightforward about the therapeutic process, but perhaps he is too extreme for Gloria. He says his caring is the caring of an artist bringing out the hidden. Their contact is too brief for anything else. Perls has his hands in his lap. He is biting his lip, very focused, interested, and concentrated, holding in his own distress. When Gloria then starts on the contact issue, Perls is nodding supportively. He asks very gently, "How should I be? How could I show you my concern?" Gloria shows even more distress. Perls is nodding, and Gloria is nodding. They are finally in empathic congruence.

When Perls and Gloria are finally in a brief empathic congruence, Perls remarks that Gloria is wonderfully genuine. However, Gloria does not like being the object of Perls's detached therapeutic commentary; she wants him to share her feelings. Perls, unlike Rogers, does not claim to share this wish. He pushes Gloria away with his hands and makes squawking noises to taunt her. Gloria becomes angry again and says that Perls would not accept her crying. Perls is looking at her quizzically, hands draped over the arms of his chair. He looks a little angry, concentrating but mixed with distress, again the gentle voice. Perls asks what Gloria would like him to do if she cries. Gloria is able to see herself as both comforted and comforting and she is able to recognize the conflicted feelings she has about both roles. Now Gloria is smiling again, and Perls remarks on it again, but this time Gloria accepts his awareness. Perls has Gloria's complete attention now. She leans forward and glances at him, leans farther forward using her hands caressingly on her shoulders. Perls is upright, a little smile, intense gaze, hands forward as if he were pulling her rather than his previous pushing movements.

As much as Perls claimed that his confrontation would make the greater change in Gloria, it is his empathy, his matching and accepting her distress, that is more significant here. Gloria then goes into stating that Perls is like her, would not show hurt feelings, would turn it back on her. Perls keeps reflecting her statements, but Gloria is confused and gets angry again. She goes on to say that if Perls would cry she would comfort him as a baby.

Perls ends it here, rather abruptly. Perls later commented that Gloria was blocking the real encounter of melting through crying, which was the emotional meaning of this meeting. Perls believed that he had assisted her in understanding her projections here and showed her the inconsistency of verbal and nonverbal. He felt that he failed in working with her embarrassment, which he said was protected by anger and brazenness. He reminded us that her brazenness is a pseudo-adaptation for coping with life as a vulnerable person.

Perls's Nonverbal Climate and Commentary

In terms of the analysis, we agree with Perls's assessment of Gloria and the efficacy of the session. What is missing, however, is Perls's assessment of *his own* nonverbal and verbal messages. He does not address his conflicting messages or the ambivalence in the emotional environment that he was presenting to Gloria. Possibly he was not aware of them.

Perls seemed to have the best understanding of the dynamics of Gloria's personality among the three therapists and the greatest flexibility in shifting strategies when she was blocked. This is partly reflected in Gloria's choice of Perls as a therapist when she is asked to choose among the three. However, in comparison with Rogers, Perls made less progress in getting Gloria to reexamine herself and see hidden connections, although his interaction on the polarity of comforting is extremely well balanced. Gloria spends a good deal of time being angry and rejecting Perls's comments whereas she gradually came to understand several of Rogers's points and elaborated on them. Perls also demonstrated an empathic matching in his posture. Rogers matched the timing, moving when Gloria moved, and the general affective tone, positive to positive and negative to negative. Ellis did not match in tempo or tone but did use some of Gloria's affective words. But Perls is quite different. He often matches Gloria's emotional expression as well as the timing of her moves. For example, Perls pointed out to Gloria that her statements and expressions are inconsistent: she claimed in the opening to be afraid of Perls, but she giggled and smiled while saying this. And even though Perls is commenting on this serious ambivalence, he also is smiling. He will cover his feelings with a smile just about as often as Gloria does. This matching may be what prompts Gloria to challenge Perls later in the session with the observation that he is much like her.

Perls is exciting and challenging but also frustrating in that he defends his own postures while intruding upon Gloria's. This intrusion encourages Gloria to examine her postures, but not necessarily to accept the way that they are revealed. Perls is also frustrating in the abrupt way he terminated the session. Gloria's initial statement that she might choose Perls to return to could almost be a reaction to the incompleteness of the session with him. Various studies have shown that people are more likely to remember and to return to incomplete problems. Perhaps Perls thought he had used the available time or he may have been sensitive to the overall scene, aware of her potential for "melting" through crying. This point at which Perls ended the session – and which might have not been appropriate in the public place of this filming – was perhaps something he could not handle in that setting.

Summary

The therapy sessions demonstrate that the affect ideologies we have been detailing are not "purely" ideas or internal personal beliefs. The emotional ideologies are deeply rooted and important across all aspects of each man's life, as much a part of his behavior as of his thought. We expected, and found, that ideas were linked to affects and to strategies designed to manage affects – to express or inhibit emotion and to express or inhibit particular kinds of emotion as well as the ideas being linked to emotions reciprocally. That is, we found that each man's emotional posture was congruent with his therapeutic intentions, even more clearly than we expected. We found that the behavior of each therapist was a fractal representation of his therapeutic intention and his personal emotional life. Here, in the behavior, we have found the key to the old mystery of Silvan Tomkins. By watching and listening to a person, Tomkins would be able to make surprising statements about the person's history. Even though he had a particular genius for this type of understanding, the underlying process is becoming clearer. Our behavior and words mirror and condense our personal history; the emotional posture may be the key we were missing.

This analysis of the three therapists with Gloria has brought many of the pieces of the ideoaffective process into the open, sometimes in a startlingly clear way and sometimes very subtly. We have seen how the emotional climate established by each therapist is a powerful medium in which to establish their ideas about therapy and goals for treatment. Notably, none of the therapists said anything about his emotional climate, setting, or environment when presenting their therapeutic goals and process. Not only do Rogers, Ellis, and Perls enter the interaction with Gloria demonstrating their emotional biases, which are completely appropriate and supportive of their therapeutic goals, but they are differently sensitive to Gloria's biases, as she is differently sensitive to theirs. The dynamic qualities of each interaction rely heavily on the emotional setting and its pervasive interweaving with knowledge, intention, and ethics.

The beauty and grace with which each duo brings out the advantages and disadvantages of each therapeutic approach also on a broader plane reveal the advantages and disadvantages of different emotional processes in general – even outside of therapy, at work or at play. Such processes are only more focused and controlled in therapy.

The previous chapters argued that ideoaffective biases and preferences hold together personality and cognitive process, and here in the therapy sessions we have seen this in action. In the action and movement, we not only appreciate the history of each person's emotional expectations but also see how these expectations lead to a constant recreation of the factors that support such expectations. The attempt to disrupt or change the circularity is made again and again – each therapist attempts with some success to influence the emotional climate of the client and she, in turn, attempts to influence theirs.

To the extent that each therapist is successful in creating an emotional climate in which his own dynamics can be employed, there is a truth in the expectations and theories of each therapist. *The circular part of this truth is that it is constantly being recreated and that there is more than one version of it.* All three therapists reach their goals at least in part. To a great extent, all three accomplish the process they intended. The vision each has of therapy is largely reified. This would not be restricted to Rogers, Ellis, and Perls. Any therapist, whether ostensibly cognitive or behavioral or dynamic in intentions, brings his and her ideoaffective dynamics to the enactment of therapy as well as to a unique interpretation of the accepted theory. This is not say that all are quite as adept as Rogers, Ellis, and Perls in enacting their intentions. The congruency of action, belief, and knowledge for these three therapists was remarkable, a credit to their genius.

Emotional Climate in Therapy

As one looks ever more closely at the emotional environment, it becomes clear that a great deal of therapy – and of communication in general – is accomplished by rapid nonverbal expression. The therapists' nonverbal emotion opens the encounter to set the therapeutic environment that each one wants. The matching, the reflection of movement or gesture, and the lack of movement or reflection all lead the dialogue, set the scene, and reinforce or model the expected responses. Each therapist controls some aspects of the emotional environment, manipulating some and ignoring others. Each therapeutic interaction is distinctly different from the others in almost any way that they are assessed from themes to dialogue to emotional environment and back again to goals. Each therapist is unique in his beliefs and his matching behavior. It seems that it would make a great difference which therapist Gloria saw with clear advantages and disadvantages to each one; the differences are not trivial even in the first seconds. Each man behaves very differently, has different goals, and brings out different sides of Gloria. Whether they would converge over time is still an open question.

Goals and Posture

Rogers intended to "create the proper environment for therapeutic movement" by modeling the behavior he expected Gloria to learn – to prize, to listen, to be tentative, to find hidden meaning. In Rogers everything was of a piece – the politeness, the tentative speech, the receptive mode of sitting, the caressing hand gestures, the smile, the sympathetic brow, and the nodding. During the session he was able to induct Gloria into his more tentative, exploratory, and shame – and sad – acceptant circle. However, the change was temporary. Gloria spoke of her feelings of hopelessness about getting her father to be more accepting and loving, and Rogers reflected this. She was then able to elaborate on her distressed, hopeless feelings and her sense of having been cheated; she was also very congruent as she spoke, very sad, teary, and shamed. She expressed a wish for a father like Rogers, and he responded warmly. Here, she rejected Rogers's affirmations of care. Her deep conflict and shame about being open with an authority figure would be brought out more clearly by Perls.

Rogers's therapeutic goals were also consistent with his own goal of finding "communion" with his valuing of connection. In fact, his affective posture set the emotional climate in which the client would be inducted into communion, where the focus would not be the past or the future but the moment at hand and the relationship at hand. There were more "close" moments of positive communion here for Gloria (and for Rogers) than there were for Gloria in the other two sessions. In that, too, Rogers was successful in achieving his goal. We also saw how Rogers began to work toward this from the first instant of the session.

Ellis's therapeutic intentions were also quite transparent and congruent with his affective posture but remarkably different from Rogers's. He intended to teach the client, to get her to give up selected ideas, to reduce the amount of negative affect, and to remain in a self-reliant, nonemotionally involved posture. In other words, Ellis intended to maintain boundaries between emotion and thought as well as between himself and the client. Everything about his posture fit the intention. He set up boundaries between thoughts and feelings and between himself and the client. He blocked her with his leg, sat well away from her, and yet inclined his head and his gaze to her. He led with his head and blocked his guts. Ellis's attire also signaled that practical work was to be done. His speech was didactic, he was forceful, his head and hand movements drove home points he made. Ellis did not respond to most of

Gloria's statements about her feelings – only the shy feelings related to self-confidence. When he did acknowledge them, he exaggerated them, invalidating her perception of her feelings, partly by escalating her feelings into the fearful, anxious domain and then showing her that she was quite safe.

Ellis had a modicum of success with Gloria in terms of inducting her into his belief system. She gave up asserting her feelings, shifted to a more receptive, though skeptical, mode, and accepted an assignment. In the session with Perls when she was asked to act out a role in which she had self-respect – or was self-confident, to use Ellis's terms – it became clearer what an impossible assignment this might have been. In a way, Ellis had urged Gloria to become more like himself; he urged her repeatedly to take responsibility for herself, to give herself assignments, and to "work and practice, work and practice," to the point where she would not be "overconcerned" with rejection and could be self-confident and un-shy. Would she stay very long in this kind of therapy? Though she wants "direction," and even asks for it from both Rogers and Ellis, acceding to her wishes places her in a dependent posture, one that she has rebelled against in the past and continues to rebel against. Ellis's therapeutic goals for Gloria were also consistent with what he himself values and his own goals for self-reliance and reduction of negative affect. Though he did try to relate to Gloria and demonstrate his willingness to work with her toward some objective goals, he did not attempt to establish an emotional bond; rather he deliberately set boundaries on such a bond, creating a very different kind of emotional climate. Although Ellis met his own goals for conducting therapy, he was not successful in persuading Gloria to accept them.

Perls's emotional posture is also completely self-consistent with his ideoaffectology and his therapeutic goals and intentions. Once again, from mode of dress to body movement to intruding, wagging finger, Perls sets the emotional climate to support his therapeutic goals. At the outset, Perls frustrates and unsettles the client by his own unsettled movements and intrusive behavior, pushing himself and his fingers and arms into her space. Perls rather quickly brings Gloria into concentrating totally on the here and now with this frustration. Naturally it leads to anger from Gloria, which is a very focusing emotion. She does focus on the anger in her relationship with Perls, the anger she has for intrusive authority figures. This anger gets Gloria involved more quickly than she did with the other two therapists. However, Gloria reacted defensively to Perls's derisive, taunting, and objective style and often would not act out his directives. Only when they shifted from respect and humiliation to caring and being cared for was Gloria able to take a step toward creating her polarities and possibly integrating them. In support of this reversal, Perls supported her with his distressed sympathy, not unlike Rogers in a similar interlude. Then Perls moved back into his interested, amused, aggressive, contempt postures. The changes in affective posture that Perls uses are very flexible so that he can maintain the excitement and unsettle or frustrate the client. He is inclined toward hostile affects, which are usually intrusive and directive, but they are also excellent for directed problem solutions. The quick change, the surprises, and the unfinished quality of this interview as well as the feeling that Gloria had in the distress interlude where she briefly felt that she and Perls shared similar feelings about hiding and covering with brazenness, about which she is probably quite correct, all led Gloria to initially prefer Perls as a therapist.

To the extent that Gloria has simultaneously strong wishes for acceptance, direction, and respect, she is in a place of deep existential conflict. In her conflict, to be accepted is to be close, but also humbled and dependent, even shamed, but to be respected is to be distant. With Rogers she mentioned her wish for acceptance ten times – from her daughter, from her father, and from authority figures. With Ellis, she expressed the wish for acceptance from the men she dates, and with Perls, acceptance by Perls himself in the here and now of the therapy session. She repeatedly asks for guidance. Every time that she is given direction, guidance, and acceptance, she rejects it. These conflicting goals are embodied in her emotional posture – alternately closed and open, alternately, and sometimes simultaneously, contemptuous and shy. Once again, she even shows her emotional history before she speaks in all three sessions. She always opens with a partly blocked and partly opened posture, with a smile and sneer, with a nod and a head shake.

Therapist Compatibility

The question we have raised is the question of the match in intersubjectivity. The nature of the fit between client and therapist has long been of interest to practicing clinicians as well as to many clients. However, it has proven difficult to cast these issues within a theoretical framework that lends itself to a test of claims. In Chapter 4 we introduced the concept of complementarity as it has evolved from the interpersonal school of psychology and as applied to social or interpersonal dimensions, and, more recently, as applied to expressive behaviors by Krause and colleagues (Anstadt et al., 1997; Krause et al., 1992; Merten et al., 1996; Villenave-Cremer et al., 1989). Krause proposed that successful therapy is predicated by responses from the therapist that *compensate* for, rather than match, a client's social and affective processes. If we make the assumption that complementarity is important, how do our three therapists align themselves with Gloria?

In the realm of emotional expression, both verbal and nonverbal, a complementarity thesis would argue that therapist and client should be paired on the basis of a complementary or compensatory emotional style. On the other hand, the similarity thesis says they should be matched so that they are concordant with one another – on the same emotional wavelength. In the realm of attachments, a complementarity thesis would expect attraction between avoidant individuals and more preoccupied or ambivalent individuals, whereas a similarity thesis would expect attraction between those with similar attachment styles.

Attachment Styles

Gloria conforms most closely to the fearful-avoidant style. She expresses approach-avoidance conflicts toward the therapists, her father, potential mates, her daughter, and her friends. She says that she would like to have Rogers as a father but ends telling him that he does not know her or understand her and that their contact is limited. She wants her father to understand and accept her, but she feels hopeless and behaves rebelliously. She wants to attract and keep "superior" men, but she acts flippant with them and drives them away. She wants her daughter's trust and confidence, to be close with her, but she also wants "respect," which is earned by distance and concealment of her actual behavior. She wants friends, but she doesn't want them to get "too close" to her.

As a potential attachment object, Rogers offers the most complementarity. Over time, Gloria does gravitate toward him. She maintained a special self-disclosing relationship with him, through letters, over the rest of her life. However, initially Gloria was attracted to Perls. We have characterized his attachment style as most closely resembling that of the disorganized pattern; it contains avoidance but also some of the emotional "heat" often found in the preoccupied pattern, that is, the tendency to galvanize affect. Perls has some complementarity and some similarity. Ellis, whose style is a mixed dismissive/fearful style and who, therefore, comes closest to Gloria's, leaves her cold. Thus, in terms of initial and longer term potential for a working alliance based on attachment, complementarity appears to rule.

Emotional Expression

The emotions that govern Gloria's interaction are the approach–avoidance ones of interest, shame, and contempt. Rogers had some affinity for shame related to his own achievement and as a method of regulating attachment, rather than as a balance against contempt and affiliation. He had little affinity for contempt, neither responding much to it nor modeling it. In this sense, Rogers is the most complementary and least similar to Gloria. Both Perls and Ellis use contempt or disgust to regulate distance and boundaries in much the same way as Gloria does. Although they differ from her on other dimensions, the distance regulation is similar. Gloria used contempt to regulate her interactions within parts of herself, between herself and others, and to modulate her ideas. We can see how this plays out in her session with Rogers. As in the other sessions, Gloria expressed contempt/disgust at a high rate. Whereas with all the other emotions, Gloria's nonverbal expression was strongly influenced by and reflected by Rogers, contempt/disgust was the exception. Rogers never reflected her disgust or contempt. He did not respond to her "crystallized posture" or background affect. Both Perls and Ellis seemed to respond to the defensiveness implied by the contempt, and both reflected this in their own responses.

Could Rogers's lack of fluency with contempt ever be a problem? Is it possible that similarity might be helpful? Many parents of adolescents reflect the contempt of their children rather skillfully. Kahlbaugh and Haviland (1994) reported that elevated contempt and disgust expressions in most adolescents are matched by an elevated contempt level in their parents, particularly their fathers. The adolescents' use of contemptuous expression was not subtle. The adolescents would snort and shrug, roll their eyes, and toss their heads. The parents', particularly the fathers', use of contempt was much more subtle, consisting of just a raised eyebrow or lip or a distancing indicated by a shift in posture to one with a greater barrier such as crossing arms across the chest. This subtle dialogue with contempt establishes distancing affects among adults and promotes adult behavior among the adolescents. It is just this sort of subtle and organized experience that Gloria lacked in her emotional displays. Her use of contempt and disgust was extreme, almost adolescent. It is unlikely that Rogers would modulate this directly. His method would be to work through other affective systems. In that regard, Ellis is the most secure in his use of contempt, but he did not appear to use it responsively with Gloria. Over time, however, she might have come to model Ellis's more subtle use of autonomous cues. It could be, though, that none of these three therapists is actually an ideal match for Gloria in the emotional domain.

Rogers is not alone in this inability to respond to contempt directly. Many therapists are drawn to the practice because it allows them to exercise their "soft" side as Gloria put it. They seduce the client with pleasant emotions and use of sad empathy and occasional shame signals to maintain a "caring" relationship. For clients who greatly fear relationships in general this may be the most important component of therapy, but for people such as Gloria, the emphasis on attachment without a reasonable emphasis on distancing may not be as helpful and could even be threatening.

Perls, as a therapist, was not discomfited by contempt – either his own or the client's – as long as he remained in control. And since Perls often remained emotionally "out of reach," as Gloria put it, he mostly did remain in control. Perls was not only comfortable with contempt, he also offered more modulated use of this distancing affect. In provoking Gloria's anger, he also gave her an opportunity to assert herself forcefully, to experience her own empowerment. This said, we must also acknowledge that he frustrated the part of her that valued connection. Gloria wanted to be able to assert herself, to make forays into the world as an autonomous human being, but she also needed to do so in the context of an environment where she felt cared for. Perls's limitations in this domain made him a less than ideal therapist for Gloria.

Rogers provided the kind of holding environment that Gloria needed. And there was some evidence that he might be able to work with her undeveloped emotions as a means of rounding the sharper corners of her ideoaffective contours. Rogers's greater affective power lay with sadness in alignment with shame and with happiness. He had a great desire for the happiness that comes with attachment, with acceptance in Gloria's terms. The two of them could have and already had used this in the touching moment when Rogers affirmed Gloria's feelings of utopia and did not deride them as she believed other people had (with "grins and giggles"). Rogers's ability to find a point of communion and happiness in addition to Gloria's desire to seek attachment would have given them a repeatedly rewarding component of the therapy. This connection as well might have been used to establish for Gloria a broader base of acceptance and the sense that other people, even authority figures, can be accepting and not overly derisive and critical, and consequently lead to acceptance of herself. Rogers had already used the sadness and shame components in his repertoire to bring Gloria into his working lotus circle. He managed to create in Gloria a depth of feeling about her "hopelessness" in her relationships that was neither contemptuous nor shameful, but extremely sad. This aspect of the session was probably what Gloria meant later on in the wrap-up session when she said that Rogers had brought out her softer side. It was also apparent in the summary that she did not at the time value this side of herself. In further pursuit of therapy with Rogers, it is likely that this would have been developed and perhaps merged with her utopian feelings of balance. Thus, we are suggesting that Rogers would probably not work much with Gloria's more powerful ideoaffective structure of contempt and ambivalence but would rely on undeveloped affects of sadness and joy and align them with the content of utopian wholeness.

This discussion helps to round out our discussion of the relative merits of complementarity and similarity. Earlier we had framed the issue as one of complementarity versus similarity. At this juncture, it should become clear that the situation is more complex. Complementarity *or* similarity can be useful if deployed skillfully and in consideration of the type of emotion at the heart of the client's ideoaffectology, and with respect to its relation to the goals of the client – both intrapersonal and interpersonal. Perls's similarity on contempt, given its more well-modulated aspect, could have been of some therapeutic benefit to Gloria; however, his avoidant characteristics would ultimately have proven dissatisfying to her. Rogers's ideoaffective posture was noncomplementary on contempt, shame, and sadness with respect to Gloria. Ellis was overly similar to Gloria in attachment style and emotional expression and, clearly, the least effective.

Gloria's sense in her summary statement that she understood that Rogers brought out her softer side was particularly perceptive. Rogers did bring out just one side of her ideoaffective structure, and she was wise to recognize this. She also recognized that Ellis and Perls had only worked with "sides" of her. Perls brought out the "fighting" side of her and Ellis, the "thinking" side. Gloria herself suggested some combination of the two. Thus, perhaps the "which one" question is the wrong question. Gloria might have needed and gotten different things from the different therapists at different points in time, or she might have needed to continue to search for a therapist. However, it seems clear that a particular therapist, no matter how talented and well trained, cannot be right for every client.

Do all therapists tend to have a particular talent or set of talents just like Rogers, Ellis, and Perls? Or are these three therapists unique in some way, with other therapists being more well-rounded? Do therapists with particularly one-sided ideoaffectologies and a drive toward recognition propel themselves to the top of their professions and thus not constitute a representative sample? Did recognition come to Rogers, Ellis, and Perls because they had the talents/limitations they had and because they packaged their particular talents in such a way that their limitations were transmuted into assets? From what we have observed of a range of very senior and seasoned therapists, some well known, others not at all famous, most have sides that are particularly well developed and other sides that are not quite as well elaborated. It seems to be more a rule of thumb that personalities are unique, that affective talents are unique, and that both are used uniquely. There are as many paths in good therapy as there are in any varied ecosystem.

Concluding with Gloria

Having begun our chapter with the life of Gloria herself, we conclude by returning our focus to her. Gloria had a brief encounter with each of three seasoned therapists. How much did these encounters affect her life? Who touched her most? While it is well known that she corresponded with Rogers for some fifteen years after the session and dubbed Rogers and his wife her surrogate parents, there is evidence that she continued to dwell on the lessons learned from all three. A conversation between Weinrach and Gloria's daughter, after her death, indicated that Gloria had kept "countless journals, papers, letters, and incomplete manuscripts chock full of her feelings and reflections" about the three men (Weinrach, 1986, p. 642). While we think that Rogers may have touched her most deeply and Perls may have disturbed her the most, at least temporarily, it is also entirely possible, given the chaotic ways of the world and of affects, in which small perturbations can stimulate systemwide changes, that Ellis may have had an immediately slight, but ramifying impact on her life – perhaps structurally as well as emotionally. It is certainly within the realm of possibility that Gloria followed Ellis's homework suggestion and began to strike up conversations with eligible men, perhaps even the doctor she fantasized about. Perhaps if papers from Gloria's estate are ever released, we will have a better answer to these and other tantalizing questions. In the meantime, for a fuller discussion of the issue of continuity and change, as well as others, we turn to the next chapter and a more in-depth analysis of what we have learned from this excursion into lives and ideoaffectologies.

PART V

Presenting a New View

11 Summarizing the Emotional Links

The wealth of material available to us from the three cases of practicing clinicians – through the various ideographic venues – afforded an excavation of a depth seldom available to the developmental researcher, although it is more common in clinical practice. To the clinician's rich access, we add insights from affect theory and attachment theory, quantitative and qualitative analysis of emotional and intellectual process over time, and contextualization within a dynamic systems framework. In so doing, we have arrived at deeper understandings about developmental process and several interesting discoveries involving attachment relationships, affects as dynamic systems, the transformation of affects into values, and continuity and change. Those new understandings are summarized and elaborated upon in this chapter as we bring the observations of the three lives together and consider what we have learned about different spheres of development.

In Chapter 2, we introduced several concepts from dynamic systems. One concept was that personality works as a system that originally arises from chaos and becomes self-organizing. Such dynamic systems are thought to be characteristic both of nonliving systems such as tornadoes and of living systems with concepts of "self" and identity. In human life, we have proposed, emotions are the energy forces and the primary organizers of experience. Emotion saturates experience with vitality or dread, hope or despair, feelings of omnipotence or weakness – which are powerful motivational forces. Emotion provides direction and force.

As the strange attractors of affective organizations (defined in earlier chapters) emerge in affective organization, they increasingly sweep up and bring together or else separate thoughts, perceptions, states of mind, theories of the world, values, attitudes, and all the stuff and meaning of human life. Emotions have a pervasive influence in the way we filter the world around us and the way we observe ourselves and others. This property is vividly in evidence in the three lives we have examined in the present work. We see these organizing forces at work in the small fractals of habits and gestures and in the fragments of facial expressions as well as in the larger fractals of theories and values. There are powerful connections across the whole organism.

Reviewing the Particulars of Small Expressive Behaviors

We found from our analysis of "word habits" – the kinds of emotion terms habitually used by the therapists in their written works and in their conversations with clients – that these small word gestures revealed a larger picture. These fragments of behavior were of a piece with each therapist's own beliefs about emotion and about relating to others or his style of attachment, as well as each man's scientific theory. Similarly, the small gestures of hand, face, and body were a supporting part of their respective emotion organizations. Facial expressions were particularly emblematic of the larger structure. Tomkins, of course, had already noted that small, fleeting facial gestures can sometimes reveal a whole dynamic history. It was that enigmatic penchant of his for canny insight based on facial expression that fascinated us from the very beginning. Now the puzzle pieces begin to fall into place.

When we put together the pieces from all three men, we found interesting regularities that were unique to each one. For example, we observed two instances of atypical and micro momentary facial expression fragments that carried information about larger structures. In the case of Rogers, the historical remnant of the repression of excitement was observed in a momentary interest brow that collapsed into distress. In Perls, we observed a brief flicker of fear in the context of an otherwise armored self-presentation. In Ellis, the facial facade is so rigid that no such pattern was observed, which is in itself a telling mark. The involuntary ticks that manage to break through in the case of Rogers and Perls, but are quickly banished, and the facial rigidity of Ellis are indicators of emotional repellor regions on the personality landscape. They provide information about parts of emotional life that each man avoids.

To expand our observations about information provided from facial expression, one of the present authors had graduate students in a seminar pose and hold ten facial expressions for three seconds. These poses were videotaped for later analysis. Almost all the students in the class were well known to the instructor, having served in the instructor's lab as research assistants for several years. When the students' facial productions were coded, it became clear that the facial behaviors revealed personality structure in miniature, that is, they revealed personality features such as dismissiveness and timidity.

The idiosyncratic patterns found in the laboratory study showed three patterns: (a) *rigidity*, or the absolute inability to make a particular facial expression; (b) *fleetingness*, seen in facial trembling or an inability to hold an expression; and (c) *slippages*, slipping from one emotion to another. The first two – rigidity and fleetingness – appeared to index repellor regions on the personality landscape. These emotions were discomfiting for the individual; therefore, encoding them was rendered difficult or impossible. To express the repellor emotion would be to have the experience of "not me" or even "the me I dread." The third – slippage, as in the slipping of a requested emotion expression, such as sadness, into another emotion, such as contempt – appears to index powerful attractor regions. In this case, the potential experience of sadness might be quickly transferred into disdain. Instead of an empathic approach to distressing experiences, one student who showed this pattern moved quickly to an analytic distancing. Ellis's expressive behavior, noted earlier, is an example of the first kind, and Rogers' is of the second kind. In Gloria's expressive behavior, we see the third facial signature in operation. While Gloria was capable of a wide expressive repertoire, her default was contempt, and we see repeated instances of slippage, where an emotion other than contempt is tentatively expressed, but then rapidly elides into a lip raise or is banished by a dismissive gesture.

We noted that the sequencing of affective expressions can give clues to personality. Tomkins had already suggested that when one emotion is followed rapidly by a shame expression that it indexes an "emotion bind." The preceding emotion is the forbidden emotion, which has been linked to punitive (shaming) socialization in the past. The forbidden emotion re-evokes shame, which then operates to bring the preceding emotion to task and curtail it. In our present analysis, we made the additional discovery that an emotion expression followed by contempt reflects much the same process; however, in this instance, Ellis and sometimes Perls identified with the shaming, contemptuous parent and also acted to provoke this emotion pattern in other people. To give an example, this process can be seen building in the often heard parental remark, "What are you crying over that thing for, what a baby you are." The emergence of contempt acts as an affect nullification process; it says the individual disqualifies the antecedent emotion, just as the parent would have disqualified the child's distress with her contempt. It may not be necessary that the covering emotion is shame or contempt. There may be scenarios for any emotion to become a cover. Fear could become a cover for distress if the comment heard went in the direction of threat, "If you do not stop that crying, I will give you something to cry about." Such scenarios and minute expressions tell in miniature what expectations or attractors have been established by previous experiences.

Affect also becomes crystallized in the face over time (Darwin, 1872), so that it can be seen even under static conditions of the face at rest (Malatesta et al., 1987). This may be especially true of persons who have a relatively restricted expressive repertoire, as in the case of Ellis. Before crystallization is complete, however, other patterns may be visible on the face. The 1931 photograph of Ellis at the age of eighteen, referred to earlier, shows the young man posed for a serious portrait (DiMattia & Lega, 1990). Contempt is visible in the mouth region as a slight unilateral lift of the lip. The brow, however, is at variance with the mouth. It does not parallel the contempt in the mouth, expressing more vulnerable affect. Moreover, it is a very odd and idiosyncratic mixture of fear and distress – that is, the inner corner of the brow is drawn slightly up as in the classic sad expression, but it is also raised as in fear, and appears frozen in mid air. This expression precedes Ellis's analytic thoughts about distress in which his (cognitive-analytic) distance protects him from the toxic experience. In the Shostrom film some thirty-five years later, the contempt in the mouth region has become magnified and crystallized. The lip raise is more pronounced, exposing left lateral and incisor teeth, giving him a somewhat menacing look, but the fear and distress have vanished. The rest of the face is immobile, except for mild tension in the brows and slight anger furrows. The masklike quality of the face throughout the session, in combination with the crystallized overlays, suggests an interior emotional landscape with attractors at anger and contempt and repellors for all other negative emotions. We see in this fractal of facial expression that fear and distress are effectively defended against. Other versions of this scenario appear across psychological spaces.

Together, the fleeting defaults of facial expressive behaviors in action and crystallized physiognomic characteristics constitute distinctive and idiosyncratic facial markers. From this analysis, it becomes ever more clear that they are signatures of deeper underlying emotion organizations. It is also true that affect blockages and parts of the repertoire that have "vanished" also provide rich diagnostic information. We will return to where "vanished" emotions go in a later section.

The underlying organizing influences on Rogers's adult life were interest (but *not* excitement) and joy, shame/shyness, and anger and allied hostile affects. Interest, joy, and shame were attractor states; they organized his fascination with communion and engaged him in his world of work and therapeutic goals. Hostile affects represented repellor regions on his personality landscape; these threatened a cutoff from those about whom he cared most and thus were unexpressed. True to the facial signature thesis, his brows avoided excitement and anger, preferring an empathic distress display, the mouth region rounded out with joy.

The organizing affects in Perls's adult life were shame, contempt, and fear. Fear constituted a repellor region on his personality landscape, a repellor of particular intensity; toxic fear signaled the threat of annihilation. Shame and contempt were attractor regions, almost in equal measure. In dynamic systems terms, they constituted a saddle attractor pattern. At times of contempt, he was boastful and arrogant, a preening self-congratulatory boor but also, paradoxically, self-derisive; at times of shame he felt on the edge of suicide but also, paradoxically, a powerful manipulator. These two coresident emotions could be simultaneously detected in his emotional posture at times or they might seem to appear singly. In the Shostrom film, his shameful body (i.e., his head bowed before the camera reading his notes, his stooped seating posture, his speech dysfluency) expressed shame. At variance with this picture is the hands akimbo, the dismissive hand gestures, and the derogatory comments, all of which express contempt. Contempt is the anti-toxic solution for shame, and the even more deeply buried fear. It is a strong emotion that helps Perls feel empowered, not vulnerable and not on the brink of annihilation, but it is not invariably successful. Shame, while perhaps more painful, also brings up a constellation of Machiavellian plots to make others care for him. This is why he can continue to swing back and forth between emotions that might appear at first glance to be contradictory.

For Ellis, the organizing affects are fear, distress, anger, and contempt. Fear and distress constitute formidable repellor regions, and much of his waking life is organized to ensure that these affects are not experienced. This watchfulness exerts an energy toll, since he must be ever vigilant. Anger and contempt are attractor regions; he gravitates to these states by default, which is not to say that he does not have some modulatory control over these emotions. He is able to reign in his predisposition for anger and maintain it at the level of a mere irritable edge. He carefully shields his clients from the harmful effects of interpersonal contempt by skillfully aligning himself with the client and reserving his contempt for contemptible ideas that need to be eradicated so as to bring more interest, joy, and pleasure into the client's life.

What is interesting about the preceding affective organizations is that they are not only deeply connected expressive behaviors but also replicated in form in theoretical positions, attachment styles, and even rational thinking patterns. As we bring together the three cases we will see these forms again and again.

Affective Organization, Theories, Values, and Goals

Earlier we alluded to the disappearance of certain affects from Ellis's expressive repertoire, most notably fear and distress. Where do problematic emotions go? They do not go away certainly. In the case of the three therapists, we found that they made their way into the therapists' theoretical positions and therapeutic postures. Here the problematic emotions are attacked repeatedly, though they are never fully defeated. Because they continue to be defended against they are present. We will also find the dreaded emotions defended against in theories of the nature of human beings and the goals of therapy – in other words, embedded in rational day-to-day work for these men.

The issue of where problematic emotions go is a broad issue that may have different answers for people in different walks of life. Since we are contending with therapists, the pattern we observe may be unique to this profession. It may even be unique to these three therapists and not others, but the fact that it is a common theme across three very different men suggests that we may have detected a more generalizable principle. Rogers's, Ellis's, and Perls's problematic affects have a special affinity for incorporation into theories about human nature and the conditions of healing and growth. It is here that we see the way that unexpressed emotions still help to form patterns that provide added meaning and information to each man about the largest issues. Indeed, each of the three theories behind client-centered, rational emotive, and Gestalt therapy contains within them an emotional "value" or an emotional goal for psychotherapy.

The content of the highly theoretical thoughts is not the only thing affected by emotions. Just as the emotions create a climate for therapy with the needed postures, matches and mismatches with the partner, pacing and timing, so emotions are related loosely to what we might call cognitive style. Ellis predominantly uses an absolute logical approach. He uses linear logic, breaks problems into independent pieces, and expects single correct answers if he can only set the problem up clearly enough. Ellis has little tolerance for cognitive styles that allow for uncertainty or multiple possibilities, much less evolving possibilities. Both the content and style of Ellis's most elaborate theoretical statements are given their unique character by their affinity with his emotional system. They are not independent, separate, purely "cognitive" facets of his being.

Once again with Perls we found that the style of his thought is also aligned with his emotions. Of the three men, Perls is the most likely to use all the modes of cognitive style that we considered. When shamed and aware of humiliation, he is quite likely to abort what he is thinking about or he may just drop the more complex dialectical and systemic analyses and switch abruptly to a concrete, perceptual style. He can swing from complex philosophy to absurd platitudes in the space of a few sentences. His most consistently dialectical work appears to be supported by close associates, his wife or intimate colleagues, or even an appreciative audience. This support probably reduces the shame he constantly defends against. When writing alone – as in writing his auto-biography *In and Out of the Garbage Pail* (1969a) – his self-contempt and shame give rise to grandiosity. Careful analysis largely disappears although his swift perceptual insights are often thought provoking. This is his contemptuous, topdog defending his positions, often by deriding the opposition or by exposing the short-sightedness of clients.

With Rogers, his personal avoidance of hostile emotion is reflected in the content of his theory where the therapist's chief concern is hostile emotion contained in the client. After the therapist acknowledges the hostility, it can be transformed into happiness and creative solutions. The defense against hostility also shows up in the cognitive style of Rogers's writing. Where a linear argument in an angry or even contemptuous absolute style might be useful, Rogers will not follow through, but will mysteriously change course. However, of the three men, Rogers is the most expressive of interest and happiness and actually had an increasingly wider range of emotional expressiveness as he grew older. This was paralleled by continued development of sophisticated cognitive style. Rogers is the most tolerant of relativism and of multiple possibilities and is the only one of the three men who changes his predominant style over the years.

To return to how the content of theory reveals emotional attractors and repellors, consider Ellis first. The value inherent in Rational Emotive Therapy, as practiced by Ellis, is the elimination of fear and distress, emotions that terrorized him as a young child. For Ellis, these terrors come back as phenomena tagged "terrible," "awful," and "catastrophic"; they are then systematically derided as exaggerations and illogical fabrications and ultimately banished from scrutiny. But note that they are never fully eradicated. If Ellis had truly defeated these furies, if he were actually convinced that they were forever laid to rest, we submit that he would retire from his particular branch of therapy and pursue other passions. If these emotions no longer held dread for him, they would become boring to him and would lose their motivational "oomph." Instead, he renews his attack on them time and time again. With each new client, Ellis has the opportunity to joust with his problematic affects anew.

Similar connections arise for Perls, though the emotions are different; therefore, the systems are quite different. The problematic emotions for Perls were shame/humiliation and rage/contempt. Shame made him angry, contempt helped protect him from shame. But like Ellis, Perls never defeated the shame and humiliation that pursued him all his life. This dynamic was so important for him that he eventually imported it into his Gestalt therapy as the topdog/underdog polarity. Once again, the emotional dynamic is not immediately visible; it has undergone transformation. The battle is no longer ostensibly about feelings, but about topdogs and underdogs, bullies and victims, power mongers and supplicants. And the goal is to see these two sides as part of the same gestalt, as providing wholeness to the person.

The values contained within the theoretical foundations of Perls's school of therapy also contain theories about the value of human attachment and relatedness. The Gestalt Prayer is a particularly well-parsed example of this. "I do my thing and you do your thing. I am not in this world to live up to your expectations and you are not in this world to live up to mine" (Perls, 1969b, p. 24). Part of Perls's theoretical stance on people in need of counseling is that they tend not to use their own resources but instead feel that they are in trouble because other people will not help them. This part of the Gestalt Prayer encapsulates the theory. Earlier we deconstructed this as an anti-toxic script for Perls's dual dreads of isolation and merger, which he also hopes to pull into the same gestalt or pattern to provide a wholeness without having any one side overwhelm the other.

Rogers is clearly not very comfortable with the more hostile emotions. As we showed in Chapter 6, although hostile emotions figure prominently in the language Rogers used to describe most of his clients and drive his stepwise program for therapeutic growth or the release of negative emotion through positive acceptance of them, he referenced these emotions only in the service of highlighting his own successful strategies for countering them with positive feelings. Rogers argued in his humanistic psychology that negative emotion should be fully expressed and accepted, but this effort was clearly the route out of pathology, not a goal in itself. The therapeutic outcome of the expression of hostile emotion would be the full expression of positive emotion. Negative, blocked emotions presented an extreme obstacle to personal growth. But Rogers's blocked emotions were actually a driving force in his theory. Of course, his attraction to the positive emotions was also a force in the construction of his theory.

Emotional Behavior and Scholarly Work

Part of the dualism in Western philosophy that leads even psychologists to separate thought and emotion also has led us to separate ideas and theories, especially scholarly and scientific theories from emotion, feeling, and motivation and thus from the personality of the person who proposed them. But emotion is as embedded in scholarly work as it is in relationships or any other part of human efforts to connect and to provide meaning to life. The relationships between emotions and thoughtful work are not colinear, simple, direct, or independent. Even though previous study has shown that happiness is conducive to creative and flexible thought or that sadness is related to slowed productivity but possibly also to detailed analysis and a desire to find a system in relativistic problems, these relationships do not predict much about a tendency to use the emotional systems to understand the problems that have meaning for us as unique individuals. There is no evidence that Freud was wildly happy when writing his innovative works on dreams, for example, or that Loevinger was sad when writing her theories of relativistic change in human development. Yet when people are taken individually, as we have done here, the unique connections are informative and repetitive and quite clear.

Attachment Relationships

Another way that emotion is embedded in personality is revealed in the way people relate to each other, their attachment styles. We touched upon emotional patterns that seemed emblematic of the different styles in earlier chapters. However, another discovery that became clear during the course of this work is that while there are relations between attachment styles and affective processes, they are no more colinear, independent, or "averaged" than any other part of this process.

In earlier stages of our thinking, when we were looking for idealized categories and linear relations, attachment typologies appeared to index particular styles of emotion organization. For example, in infancy, the ambivalent attachment classification seemed to capture the child whose emotions vacillate between anger and sadness, whereas the avoidant classification seemed to denote the child for whom hostility was a central organization (Adickman, 1993; Malatesta, 1990). Still other studies suggest that differences in attachment style are a matter of suppressed or expressed emotion, with avoidant children suppressing anger – and therefore expressing too little – and ambivalent children expressing anger to an extreme degree – thus expressing too much (Magai, 1995). One might, therefore, expect that individuals who have expressive deficits or surfeits (Malatesta & Wilson, 1988) for a particular emotion would show distinctive attachment profiles and that there would be linear relationships between emotion and relationship style.

Hunziker (1995) first challenged the proposal that emotion and relationship style were linearly related in a study of Type A behavior pattern. One of the classic hallmarks of the Type A person is hostility. People classified as Type A tend to suppress the expression of anger (Malatesta-Magai et al., 1992). Although several measures were used, no relationship was found between attachment and hostile behavior. The "hostile" Type A people were just as likely to be fearful-avoidant, preoccupied, or dismissing in their attachments as the non-Type A people. Hostility could be organized in several ways, and different people clearly used anger in different patterns.

We have had to conclude that attachment patterns are more varied and intermixed than we previously thought they were – they and the types may vary over time and contexts. But this does not mean that regularities between particular patterns of relating and particular affective styles do not exist. Our conceptualization of attachment styles is unnecessarily constrained by the narrowness of the typological approach, the limited forms of attachment being studied, and the application of nomothetic analyses.

With each case, the first thing we observed about the three attachment styles is that three categories are not sufficient to describe the real-life attachment development of the three adults under consideration here.

The examination of individuals makes this even clearer than the controlled studies of groups of people. That is, although there was some correspondence between the typological models and the style of becoming attached to people that each of the three men developed, there was also significant departure from the models. Each man had a unique pattern, one that was internally quite consistent, often consistent over decades, but not easily slotted to one of three types. For the attachment gloves to fit the behavioral hands, they had to be quite elastic and forgiving of anomalies. Even though Rogers was found to fit the pattern of the secure attachment profile more than either the preoccupied or dismissive, there were elements of distance that leavened the security and added a modicum of the tension of separation to his makeup. With Perls, we had the opportunity to observe what the grown-up version of the disorganized pattern of childhood may look like. In Perls's case, with his terrible war experiences and the nomadic life that followed, we see that factors beyond childhood also forge relationship styles. With Ellis, we found that clear signs of dismissiveness were mixed with concern for self and others, and while this caring was not overtly displayed in interpersonal warmth and gestures of affection, it was given expression in his choice of profession, the dedication he showed to his work, and aspects of his personal relationship with his partner. Let us review the attachment profile of each man in light of our view that more possibilities exist for attachment profiles.

Our previous overview of Rogers's early childhood suggested that, at least in rough outline, Rogers initially established a "secure" attachment to his mother, his primary caregiver. There is less evidence that this attachment lasted into adulthood. Rogers wrote of his parents with respect but gave no indication in his writings of a deep attachment later in life. His own biographical statements support this, and the subsequent patterns of relatedness verify a mixed history of intimacy.

Although the construct of secure attachment illuminated some important aspects of Rogers's personality, it did not enlarge our understanding of some of the more complex aspects of his life, and it did not throw light on certain inconsistencies. For example, there were some avoidant elements in Rogers's personality. Attachment theory suggests that if a person has a secure attachment with his primary caregiver, he will show a disposition to respond in a trusting, noncontentious way with other social partners. Rogers did not quite fit this ideal portrait. He was often distant with professional colleagues, sometimes argumentative and occasionally enraged, to his own chagrin. Ideologically he was a loner, cleaving to his own singular visions and dismissing other positions as reductionistic or simply unenlightened.

Rogers also had great difficulty in establishing intimacy with other men, as he himself admitted, even into late life. In addition, the intimacy that had characterized his earlier married life was disrupted when his wife began to reevaluate the wisdom of having subordinated her career to his. Another curiosity was the strange silence concerning the lives of Rogers's parents after he left home for college. There were no references in his autobiography about later contacts with his family, and the biography also had little to say about this. Had Rogers's break with his family's religious fundamentalism been severe enough to sever the bonds of affection? If so, the distance was not the kind that led to overt antipathy toward and disparagement of his parents – of the kind seen in the case of Perls and Ellis. Instead, Rogers appeared to take special pains to refer to them respectfully on the few occasions in which they were mentioned.

Another anomaly is encountered with respect to Rogers's restrained sociability. We do not tend to associate the term "security" in intimacy with traits of timidity and shyness, both of which suggest interpersonal anxiety and insecurity. And yet Rogers was clearly socially reticent at times in his life, and his nonverbal behavior, even in mature adulthood (as seen in the film), was punctuated with markers of shame and hesitation.

Part of the confusion may derive from attachment theory's choice of the term "security" to denote a style of social bondedness. The primary features of security, according to the attachment literature, are a trust in the availability of care from others and a general lack of fearfulness. Although this profile may have characterized Rogers's early life and possibly even his lifelong feelings about close intimates, it did not extend easily to other individuals or the wider social world. Apparently this is because, in Rogers's case, the split between family and nonfamily was one of the most salient markers in his emotion socialization. The family refrained from mixing with others, and this particular family value was reinforced through the strategic recruitment of disgust. As suggested in earlier chapters, this disjunction between family and nonfamily may have created a strong but unconscious sensitivity to intimacy, a longing for connection with others beyond the family, and an ambivalence about the goodness of separation among different types of people. This became part of Rogers's humanistic psychology and was realized in the conditions he created in psychotherapy.

In terms of affect regulation, Rogers displayed somewhat of a mixed picture, at least according to the longitudinal studies of attachment. While there are indications of a less than secure attachment style, Rogers's persistence in the face of professional hostility to his ideas would seem to put him in the secure category. He also showed great boldness and autonomy in breaking with the traditions of the past in his written work and psychotherapeutic approach. The dominance of positive affect in his persona and in the emphasis on releasing positive affect in psychotherapy also seem in accord.

The place, however, where the attachment glove does not quite fit Rogers is found in the regulation of negative affect. By theory, the securely attached child (or adult) is able to regulate distress in adaptive ways, neither avoiding the experience of negative affect nor becoming unduly incapacitated by it (Cassidy & Berlin, 1994). In contrast, avoidant individuals tend to modulate negative affect by restricting the acknowledgment of distress. In quite a different fashion, ambivalent individuals constantly galvanize negative feelings by attending to distress and potential distress in a hypervigilant fashion. Rogers is clearly not very comfortable with the more hostile emotions. Negative, blocked emotion presented an extreme obstacle to personal growth. As observed in practice, Rogers enacted this aversion to negative affect by his own muted emotional expression. Even in the context of empathizing with client distress, the most he appeared able to muster was an intense look of sympathetic concern. He was even less comfortable with hostile affect – his attempts to reflect anger were noteworthy for their lack of depth and resonance. In one film, the client (Cathy) reacted ever more angrily to his insincere appearance of reflected anger. Since Rogers's timing and emphasis were not in synchrony with Cathy's, it almost appeared as if he mocked her angry feelings.

From the preceding details, we are left with the impression of both secure and avoidant elements in Rogers, as well as elements that do not ordinarily enter into the theory of attachment at all. This is difficult to reconcile with the very large body of attachment literature that frames attachment patterns as prototype styles. The attachment literature does not admit an attachment style that is both secure and insecure (avoidant), although it must be noted that in their original formulations, Ainsworth and colleagues (1978) clearly warned against understanding the classificatory system of attachment styles as absolutes; rather they were viewed as representing "a first step toward grasping the organization of complex behavioral data" (pp. 55–6). Is it possible that even in early childhood Rogers had different sorts of attachment relationship with different people – his mother and father may have been different, and his teachers and neighborhood peers may have required a variety of new relationships. Why would we want to predict such a degree of continuity, such a resistance to adaptation, so little import to new and spontaneous likes and loves and friendships and partnerships?

When it comes to Ellis, we find greater conformity to one of the attachment prototypes than is the case with the other two therapists, but even here there are significant departures from the model. Ellis fits the model in that he shows classic signs of the dismissing attachment pattern in his relatively low valuation of intimacy and his emphasis on self-reliance, emotional control, and achievement. But Ellis also shows signs of the fearful-avoidant individual in his masked but semitransparent longing for acceptance, his history of abject shyness as a child and adolescent, and the fact that there is a certain something about him that conveys a sense of vulnerability that is at variance with his assertive, self-confident professional persona.

Another way that Ellis does not quite fit the dismissive prototype is in his regulation of negative affect, as our close analysis showed. Avoidant individuals are said to route negative affect from consciousness, and to a large extent Ellis does just that. However, in his personal life, the routing of negative affect does not include anger, an emotion with which he is quite comfortable. With respect to his work with clients, we have seen that he does seek to deflect his clients from focusing on their experience of negative affect, but it seems that he is particularly tuned to the avoidance of fear and sadness.

Turning to Perls, we encounter more enigmas. Like Rogers, Perls presents us with a complex attachment profile that defies easy classification. Across time he shows elements of each of the attachment styles. In the terminology of Bartholomew and Horowitz (1991), he is sometimes secure – self-confident, thoughtful, and capable of feeling – but at other times he is fearful-avoidant – he shows signs of feeling fundamentally unloved and of having low-self esteem. At times he shows features of the preoccupied individual – he is very emotional and overly sensitive to others' opinions – but at other times he is dismissing – aloof, emotionally detached, and arrogant. In Ainsworth's terms, he sometimes shows the detachment and coolness of the avoidant child and sometimes the heat and enmeshment of the ambivalent child.

In terms of emotion regulation, Perls sometimes is hypervigilant for signs of distress – he can detect the slightest emotional signal in others – but at other times he seems to have a tin ear and turns a cold shoulder to distress. He can turn on emotional warmth and then turn it off in an instant, though these abrupt transitions do not appear to be readily under his direct control. As such, Perls's relatedness behaviors are quite mixed, especially across time and contexts. For this reason, as well as for reasons articulated in Chapter 5, Perls's attachment pattern seems best conceptualized as the adult analogue of the disorganized pattern of childhood.

Once again, it is clear that assigning a single attachment style, claiming that Perls *has* a disorganized style, does great disservice to comprehending Perls's attachment style. Perls certainly is discontinuous in many more ways than the other two men. This gives him the advantage of being more sensitive in some ways to context – more likely to respond differently in different contexts and to different people. He may have been inclined to seek out different contexts. To say that Perls is disorganized is to suggest a severe dysfunction that is difficult to support. Although Perls was difficult in his family intimacies, unloved by his children, a mixer of sexual and therapeutic loves in ways that are considered unethical, he was also loved and closely attended to by some colleagues and by many people who met him only briefly. He could be charismatic; he would annoy and offend and attract at the same time. Why would a person so "disorganized" be charismatic? Might we be missing something essential in these categories, might we miss the ingredients that make every sort of style adaptive and valuable in certain contexts?

From our summary point, we can see that adult values and emotional expressive patterns when viewed as unique patterns can tell a great deal about the development of attachment. True to the principles of dynamic systems, attachment predictions do not work very well in making predictions about where a person's path will go, but they are good ways to summarize the pattern of certain types of paths. In other words, they are rather good for a backward analysis.

On the basis of Perls's contempt (an interpersonal repellor) and his valuation of separation ("You do your thing, I do my thing"), we can hypothesize that merger and control were central developmental issues for him. Even in the Gestalt Prayer, the merger threat was found not only in the phrases concerning interpersonal expectations and demands but also in the mirroring of self/other in the couplets. It is as though he were refuting that he and the "other" were mirror images of one another and indistinguishable ("You do your thing, I want to be separate; you want me to conform, I want to control you").

Despite the sketchy history we obtain from his obfuscating autobiography and the skimpy biographical material on his early life, it is very likely that young Fritz was exposed to a mother who was over-controlling and manipulative of emotional expression and a distant, punitive and powerful father. In Jay Belsky's work on mother–infant interaction patterns (Belsky et al., 1984) and some of our own work (Malatesta & Haviland, 1982; Malatesta et al., 1989), caregivers who were overstimulating and intrusive when their infants were young unwittingly trained up aversion behaviors in their infants. Young infants exposed to such noxious conditions learned cutoff behaviors, namely head aversion and crying. Later in development, they often showed an avoidant attachment pattern, another kind of cutoff with deeper ramifications. Potentially, there might be other avoidance sequella in even later development.

An aversion (contempt or shame) response to attentive parents is an indication of needs for separation and independence at almost any age. Work with adolescents, mentioned earlier, indicates that even previously secure and warmly expressive adolescents come to use contempt to separate from their families and blaze a path to identity development. At first, the adolescent's use of this emotional expression is quite unmodulated and not very skillful, but it usually becomes miniaturized and embedded in larger patterns of expression for most individuals. In Ellis, we saw a sophisticated expressive pattern with contempt that mixed with interest and allowed him to maintain identity boundaries during the therapeutic encounter. In the individual for whom contempt becomes an attractor region, it may or may not be an obstacle to the establishment of intimacy, although contempt is indeed a quintessential cutoff emotion. As indicated earlier, contempt sets firm boundaries between people and communicates that the owner's self is not to be intruded upon. As people grow and become more complex, the categories of attachment as well as emotional patterns probably become more unique, identifying the individual, carrying information, and being replicated in order to stabilize the identity of the individual.

Attachment and Therapy

We have already noted that emotion organizes the theories and behavior of Ellis, Rogers, and Perls relative to the way they conduct therapy. We are calling this the replication of fractal patterns throughout the person, but it can be extended to the attachment and relationship styles as well.

Emotional patterns also reflect each other within the therapeutic scene. Each of the three men was observed to reproduce aspects of his own adult attachment pattern (already noted to be organized with emotional attractors and repellors).

In the filmed dyadic interaction with Gloria, Rogers produced the nurturing and supportive environment of the secure caregiver, one that allowed Gloria to examine her more vulnerable side. Ellis produced an environment with clear emotional boundaries, one more conducive to task-oriented mental and behavioral work. Perls kept his clients in the hot seat of unpredictability. Like the mothers of ambivalent babies, he was inconsistent in his affective posture toward clients, being alternatively distant and seductive, and mixing affective signals within any given instant. At times, he could even seem emotionally abusive. Of course, as a skilled therapist, he could integrate this into a designed frustration of the client's complacency and lack of awareness. He managed to create confusion, heat, and tension, which accounts for some of the galvanizing effect of his personality and can help explain why people were drawn to him in spite of themselves.

The tendency for a therapist to reproduce his or own attachment dynamic with clients has not been made explicit in the literature of therapy, though of course the constructs of transference and countertransference hover around some of the relational material. Even though some approaches claim to be more free of the therapist's input than others, we doubt that any of the schools or approaches could actually be divorced from the dynamics of the individual therapist. Our earlier analyses show how the three therapists masterfully set the emotional climate for their sessions within a few seconds. Even Ellis, whose cognitive behaviorist school more often makes the claim that they emphasize technical expertise over interpersonal dynamics, clearly sets the session up with his own personal emotional dynamics and continues to direct it throughout. His personal emotional dynamics are so well integrated into the technique that it is easy to miss the strong emotional undercurrents. Psychotherapy practice is quintessentially relational. Thus, it cannot help but tap into attachment representations and activate well-established patterns of relatedness. The emotional dynamics of the therapist must be central to therapy and should be analyzed.

One primary aim of training analysis and supervision in psychotherapy practice is to equip the supervisee with the ability to detect potential client–therapist entrapments and the skills to *avoid* falling into the client's enactments of conflicts. Much less attention is given to an analysis of the therapist's emotional, attachment, and cognitive style and, correspondingly, what kind of relational climate and context will be reproduced in the therapists' office or how it might interface with – for good or ill – the internal working models of particular kinds of clients.

In the Shostrom film of Gloria with each of the three therapists, Gloria's more avoidant style was maximally engaged by the more pre-occupied and enmeshing style of Perls; was maximally disengaged by the complementary, avoidant style of Ellis; and was rendered most ambivalent under the seductive, low-pressure nurturing environment that Rogers offered. Thus it appeared that complementarity was more powerful early on in the therapeutic alliance, at least in this instance. However, it is an open question as to whether complementarity or similarity or even something in between constitute the most "therapeutic" kind of involvement over time. Perhaps it is the case that all troubled clients ultimately need an environment that offers safety and promotes the formation of new, secure, relational capabilities. However, in the beginning, the disequilibrium created by contrasting attachment systems may be the requisite turbulence necessary to interrupt old patterns so that new perceptions and models can be developed and internalized. In other words, Gloria might have done well to begin with someone more like Perls and end with someone more like Rogers. With new views of emotion and the dynamics of personality come new questions and new ways of formalizing old questions.

Our analysis also brought into bold relief the fact that emotionally avoidant and insecure individuals may be attracted to the practice of psychotherapy, and that it might even be quite common. At first blush, and on a naive psychology level, one might think it would be unlikely for a relatively dismissive or fearful-avoidant individual to be attracted to clinical psychology, given its relational nature, but this is contradicted by everyday observation. All kinds of persons are drawn to the profession of psychotherapy, and, since so many different "schools" have sprung up since Freud's time, psychotherapy can be practiced in any number of different ways. Though the therapeutic practice is dyadic and relational, it can sustain varying degrees of intimacy. Some psychotherapies require the capacity to form more emotional connectedness with clients than others. This raises an interesting and provocative question – whether more relationally avoidant individuals are drawn to more relationally distant psychotherapies. Different therapies have different premises and goals. Those therapists who prefer a less intense interpersonal involvement or who satisfy their attachment needs outside of therapy may be more comfortable with, and also more skilled at cognitive-behavioral interventions than those who are drawn to more intense emotional involvements with clients and who may gravitate toward more psychodynamic styles, as did Perls and Rogers. Once again we remind ourselves that though the categories of "types" comes into play, within the types are multitudes of unique variations.

Be that as it may, the range of psychotherapeutic eclecticism that is possible in the twenty-first century was not the fashion of the times in mid-twentieth century North America. On the contrary, client-centered, Gestalt, and Rational Emotive therapy were created de novo by their originators, much against the grain of the times, and all roughly at the same time. This would suggest that the historical period is not a factor differentiating the therapies, though it may be critical in generating diversity, but the content and style of each therapy is idiosyncratic and personal, or as we would say, more socioemotionally grounded. As such, it should not be all that surprising that each of the three therapeutic ideologies would reflect each man's idiosyncratic feelings about attachment scenes, or that they would tend to reproduce these scenes in their work with clients.

Emotions Set Boundary Conditions for Growth and Change

Consideration of the therapeutic changes that were the goals of each therapist as well as the changes that developed in each man's life brings us to emotions as the conditions for change or stability. Some emotional patterns seem, themselves, to set the boundary conditions for change, determining whether the self system is more of an open system or a closed system in terms of intersubjectivity. That is, the type(s) of emotion(s) in which an individual's personality is grounded comprises a set of parameters governing whether the system operates in a feedback or feedforward fashion. Particular emotions influence boundaries in certain ways. Considered at least metaphorically as energies, each emotion contains a rate or speed of process as apart of its definition – very fast for *surprise*, for example. Emotions also contain a direction – approaching and uplifting in the case of *happiness*. The example of Ellis as defended against fast-changing processes such as *fear* demonstrates the potential power of this metaphor. Ellis was defended not only against particular emotional experiences but also against the sequence of processes that would usually be entrained with them.

Different emotions are more or less intra- and intersystemically open. Emotions such as anger, contempt, and disgust are more refractory to change and inimical to creativity, especially, perhaps, contempt and disgust. Others may be more conducive to change, such as surprise (Magai & Nusbaum, 1996). The qualities of joy and interest and the capacity for surprise made for a particular receptivity to new ideas in Rogers and to the cultivation of persons and relationships that could in themselves affect him and introduce change into his life. Shame, with its permeable self boundaries, meant that he too was vulnerable to the absorption of others' emotions, and emotions themselves are forces for change. All three therapists emphasized and displayed intense interest and occasional bouts of joy or excitement. Their interest in therapy and their client was in marked contrast to the expressed interest or excitement of the client. That may be one reason why they all tried to move her in the direction of curiosity, testing, and ambivalence. It may also be a feature of therapists in general that they are capable of intense and prolonged interest.

In the life of Ellis, we have a good illustration of how anger and contempt, as organizational structures of personality, set boundary conditions in which change is less likely. Unlike Rogers, whose personality became more emotionally elaborated over time and his writing, more creative, Ellis's ideas remained organized around the same principles even though his theory incorporated more and more material and became a little more eclectic over time. The structure of Ellis's personality constituted a kind of negative feedback loop with cascading constraints over time. His system became more stable, moving more and more to equilibrium.

Contempt played a role in Gloria's resistance to change as well. In the film, one can observe how difficult it was for Rogers, who was very skilled in his approach to Gloria, to shift her ideoaffective posture away from contempt to a more receptive mode of knowing and relating; however, she was still relatively young, actively seeking newer ways of being, and Rogers could reach those places of vulnerability inside of her, even if only fleetingly.

Perls also had a significant contempt component to his personality, but here it was conjoined with system instability and swings back and forth with shame. Perls's personality system can be characterized as a less stable and more of a "far from equilibrium" system than Ellis's. As such, he was not only more variable but also more responsive to external perturbations; this meant that he was vulnerable to being swept up in all kinds of new relationships. However, he was also vulnerable to inconstancy in personal affections. As we saw, few of the relationships he formed were of any great duration, for he could not make or sustain commitments without external support. His wife, Laura Perls, also a therapist and founder of the Gestalt school, moved in and out of his life and his work and even came to him as he was dying, but they could not sustain a compatible long-term living arrangement. However, with Gloria, Perls was able to create the unsettling of her overly stable system. This challenge to Gloria's equilibrium gave us a glimpse of the utility of Perls's personality in therapeutic interaction.

Perls's humiliation/contempt saddle made for unstable mood states, which in turn made for an unstable identity status. It will seem ironic to some, but the great California guru of Esalen fame never really knew, on any deep and abiding level, who Fritz Perls actually was. In writing his autobiography, the Perls identity is elusive. He seemed to recapture historical moments and remember himself only by reference to one of the many of his short-lived and tempestuous affairs. People, especially those who emitted the heat of passion or fury, had the ability to affect him in ways that made him feel alive and capable of remembering himself. At the same time, they threatened engulfment and loss of self.

The condition of a saddle attractor pattern and unstable sense of self made for a unique combination of therapeutic talents and shortcomings. On the one hand, Perls was exquisitely attuned to what others wanted and needed. By observing the fractals of emotional signals a person unconsciously emitted and using them as the runes of personality, he could discern just who each individual was at his or her most fundamental level. He gave up his own boundaries and entered their skin, just long enough to absorb who they were, but not so long as to be engulfed in them and trapped in merger. Because of his own unstable sense of identity and his ability to mirror and become the persona of anyone with whom he spent even a brief period of time, he struck people as possessing an uncanny access to their innermost feelings. In this context, client "insights" sprouted like fast-blooming hothouse flowers and earned Perls a reputation of having almost magical abilities. On the other hand, because of this very same system instability, he had to guard against an influx of too much emotion, which would be destabilizing to an extreme degree, or at least this is what he intuitively feared. As such, Perls could be amazingly accommodative in the moment without being caring in the long run. He could take on the identity and feelings of any one else, he could mirror them to an exquisite degree, but he equally needed to resist the contagion of empathic distress and the risk of being out of control.

Emotions as Agents of Developmental Divergence

Older models of developmental change are undergoing reevaluation in the context of newer, more dynamic conceptualizations across many domains of science. In the next chapter, we examine this new look and its implications. Before we turn to that, we want to return to the concepts and terms introduced in Chapter 2.

Jung originally introduced the idea of nonnormative, qualitative change in the adult life course, a bold stroke at the time. He suggested that crises propelled individuals into a state of reassessment, with the potential for positive ontogenetic change in patterns of behavior, personality, and affect. This line of thinking has been pursued more recently by Gould (1978) and Levinson and colleagues (1978), among others. Even though the concept of developmental change and transition in the lifecourse has provided a valuable heuristic for the life sciences, the idea that crises are necessary for change, or the corresponding notion that developmental divergence is governed by signal gifts or talents or abrupt events, ignores or underplays other occasions of change and other dynamics. Today there is increasing evidence that singular developmental changes do not always take place in the context of large or peak events of an individual's life. We used Virginia Woolf's description of a fictitious female Shakespeare to make this point earlier. The girl had the gift of poetic talent to equal William Shakespeare. It took her out of her home to London and the theater but there she was forbidden the stage and her natural exploration of love led to pregnancy. As Woolf noted, there was no single talent that could produce a female Shakespear. Woolf argued that many a gifted Shakespeare has never lifted her poetic voice. Thus, we note that developmental divergence may, on occasion, appear to be caused by a single peak event or special gift, but there may be just as well underlying and historically aggregative dynamics that are not immediately visible.

Dynamic systems theory distinguishes between two types of change (Prigogine & Stengers, 1984). First-order change involves gradual shifts or adjustments. Living systems need to avoid entropic depletion, and thus they must import energy to keep self-organizing tendencies propagating. They are thus energy hungry and responsive to mild transitory fluctuations in energy flow. In our terms, living systems seek out emotional energy and flux. Tomkins, ahead of his time, claimed that the goal of a complex living system was not equilibrium, but emotional variation. As the energy flow subsides or waxes, the system shifts along with it in an accommodative, mutually adaptive fashion. These kinds of changes are mild, gradual, and relatively smooth. The other kind of change, second-order change, is more precipitous. When the turbulence created by energy flow reaches a certain threshold, system instability occurs, and elements in the systems are thrust into new patterns of interaction, which may or may not settle into a new, dramatically different form of organization.

In personality functioning, emotions constitute the energy flow within and outside of the system that can provoke change. First-order changes in personality are modeled by the slow, gradual adjustments accruing from everyday experiences over a long developmental period, as in the crystallization of basic temperament styles over time or improved emotional functioning over the course of a year of psychotherapy. Second-order change is modeled by the more dramatic life changes that are seen in religious conversions, post-traumatic stress disorder, and other great enchantments, disenchantments, and terrors (Magai & McFadden, 1995). What are some of the elements of second-order personality change? In the developmental literature, the notion of "crisis" has been used as an explanatory dynamic behind change. But there are no theoretical accounts of why "crisis" should lead to growth. It could just as easily lead to disorganization and entropic depletion.

Earlier we suggested that the nature of particular emotions, as embedded in ideoaffective organizations, set the boundary conditions for growth and change. They also set the conditions for stability, and even for chaos and entropy. Here we reiterate our view that an individual's unique emotional organization is recruited during moments of crisis and transition to assist coping by providing well-worn information patterns to accommodate the information in the crisis situation. This organization may magnify pretransition personality differences. For example, a person with a personality landscape organized to defend against anxiety – having a high mountain of defense against anxiety – can become more rigid and defended over the course of events that cause turbulence. The added experiences only strengthen the repellor region. The need for defense actually leads to greater defenses being developed. On the other hand, where strong emotions are introduced by persons, events, or psychopharmacological agents, they may introduce identity confusion, overwhelm the individual and precipitate crisis. The defenses may not hold but, like a clay bank beside a stream, may crumble.

An individual's personal identity, which is mediated by a particular pattern of ideoaffective organization, plays a fundamental role in guiding behavior and, in the context of normative and nonnormative developmental crises, determines the interpretation and integration of these events. Identities are normally well grounded and stable, and provide the sense of continuity of self that is so vital to psychological well-being.

Identities that are not grounded in stable, reliable moods would seem to be more open to change (as well as identities with attractors for emotion like surprise that attract change events). The saddle emotion pattern shown by Perls and described earlier gave rise to an unstable identity. This kind of instability, although given to intrapsychic and interpersonal turmoil, does not necessarily result in productive life change in the sense of growing more in emotional depth, or creatively, or even achieving greater interpersonal harmony. This is because the instability has an entrenched pattern of its own, with deep attractor regions vying for dominance. For some people though, there is a possibility for growth.

Conditions do exist where traumatic events can cause significant emotional upheavals and introduce destabilization. Once experienced, strong emotions, previously unexperienced due to psychological defense, may cause such a fundamental sense of disorientation that old patterns of thinking and relating are disrupted. In the wake of these novel experiences, the edge of chaos has been reached, providing the opportunity for significant life change. Whether it is used creatively and adaptively for personality growth or provokes disintegration is a matter that persons resolve uniquely. But it is the occasions of intense mood changes that challenges personal identity and introduces system instability.

When Prozac, the powerful selective serotonin reuptake inhibitor used to combat depression, first came on the market it was hailed as a miracle drug. Then there emerged scattered reports that it led to personality disturbances. This finding now appears to be more common than previously estimated. In many cases, as the person emerges from years of depression, he enters a period of turbulence and identity crisis. The relief from depression, rather than being experienced joyously, is experienced over time as disorienting and even as a strange sort of "uplift anxiety" (Fox, 1998; Slater, 1998). Old ways of thinking and behaving, largely organized by depressive affect, no longer seem "right." The newly undepressed person finds that he must navigate the world in unaccustomed ways that can feel very disorganizing. Why does a change in affect cause such disorientation and disruption of behavioral patterns? It is because affect contours the world for us; it determines the kinds of thoughts we have, the perceptions we have of ourselves and others, the interpretations and judgments we make, and the emotional climate we create around us. When affect changes, the lens through which the world was previously perceived is radically altered. This identity disequilibrium also has a counterpart in interpersonal turbulence. People in whom mood disturbances remit often find that as they begin to relate to the world in different ways, their social environment is thrown into disarray. People emerging from depression often end up divorcing or separating or, on the other hand, falling in love or finding a new type of work.

Emotion attractors and repellors are typically stable regions on the personality landscape, with repellors in some fashion resembling areas of psychological defense (Lewis & Junyk, 1997); defenses in part act to ensure stability of identity. In Rogers's case, we encountered a prime example of how an alien emotion, even if experienced in a secondhand contagious fashion, can have a destabilizing influence and invoke a state of disorder. After his personal crisis, it was two years before Rogers regained his sense of himself as healed and his sense of personal identity restored. By then, however, change had been set into play, and it continued to exert an influence on his identity and ideoaffective patterns. Recall that, in the analysis of Rogers's written works, we observed that his reference to hostile affect in clients declined over time, especially in his later work following this crisis. Another change that occurred after this point in his life was a shift in his writings to a greater emphasis on the self and the self's perspectives. This is the point in his life that Rogers became more self-accepting and receptive to his own affect. Thus, although the crisis precipitated a period of intense personal distress, it initiated another protracted period of introspection and transformation. He was less vigilant for anger and more self-accepting and demonstrated a broader, more fluent affective vocabulary and a more fluent and complex cognitive style.

Change: Crisis Versus Small Effects

We return, finally, to an idea that we introduced earlier in this chapter. The view that a single event or idea is the sole cause of developmental change may occasionally be true, but it is more likely that such events only symbolize, in a particularly vivid way, the smaller events.

One often sees news accounts of tragic suicides described as the result of love gone awry or heavy money dobts, as if one great crisis accounted for suicide. As all the background research tells us, there were repeated, escalating losses in the person's life. The depressed state attracted more and more support, becoming more stable. These small events do not require any large precipitous change. Neither do they eliminate the alternate attractors that might confuse us. A depressed person may have bits of his life that are ecstatic. The shifting of context can then obscure the regularities that do exist and confuse us if we expect linear simplicity. We can also be confused if we think that a large crisis is always necessary. Small effects can also precipitate sudden, precipitous change or "quantum change" (Miller & C'deBaca, 1994).

Baumeister (1994) described sudden change following very small events in his studies of accounts of individuals who left relationships or defected from religious groups, as the "crystallization of discontent." Baumeister discerned a pattern in a phenomenon that may be more common than previously thought. A seemingly minor event ("a small change") is assimilated to a whole pattern with sudden insight; this new perception then provokes an upsurge of negative emotion. Associative links are formed among many unpleasant, unsatisfactory, negative features of a situation. Although all these features may have been present prior to the crystallization of discontent, the person previously experienced them as unconnected.

The crystallization or attraction process gathers negative features into a critical mass. Suddenly, they take on a whole new meaning that undermines and changes the nature of the role or relationship, as well as the commitment one has made to them. A new attractor has formed on the personality landscape. Baumeister makes it clear that focal events are not the source of change but rather triggers that bring into focus dissatisfactions that previously had only been subliminal – or in our view disassociated features. In the same fashion, we surmise that Rogers's pivotal encounter with the prepsychotic client and the turmoil that her rage precipitated was itself not the source of change but instead the trigger for inner turbulence that permitted undeveloped and latent elements to reorganize within Rogers.

12 Lives and Change

Emotional Repetition and Uniqueness in Linear, Complex, and Chaotic Personality Systems

In undertaking this work, we have immersed ourselves in the splendid, unfolding, and confounding detail of three men's lives. Each man's life, his loves, his ambitions, his accomplishments, and his defeats have become not only a part of our work, of how we view emotion, but also of ourselves. The paths of their lives have altered the paths of our lives. Of course, in a mundane sense, it is always true that what you work on becomes you, means become ends, as we have said before. Because of that, we are even more thankful that these three lives are easy to respect, that the men are easy to be charmed by and attracted to, and that the ideas they leave behind are so compelling and still sometimes refreshing.

At the beginning of this psychological examination of three individuals' personal and work lives, we were fixed largely on adding information about emotion to the major developmental theories of our time – we were fixed on filling in the emotion gap. We began our project thinking about emotion almost as a distinct part of the human being. To be a genius at emotion, we thought, was to have mastered that compartment of life. One would detect emotion, understand emotion, manage emotion, and manipulate one's own and other's emotions efficiently. However, the emotional data from just three lives speaks of and tells us far more than we expected. The management of emotion, while still interesting, is almost incidental. The real genius of emotion lies not in the management of emotion but in its role in the creation of an individual, unique personality. Emotion is the dynamic energy of the force field of every personality. To know even a little of the dynamics of a person's emotional system is to know also about his or her ways of thinking, deep values, and even pattern of social exchange or attachment. By relegating emotion to the underground, as we have done for many decades, psychologists missed seeing the threads that hold the many sides of a person in one field. The dynamic force field is the genius of emotion.

Now at the end of our work we find that we present a very different sense about the ecology of personality and the place of emotion. Two major points have arisen repeatedly in the analyses that push us to present a new view. These two "problems" are *connection/replication* and *uniqueness/information.*

First, let us look at *connection/replication.* Every part of the person that we studied was connected to or replicated in every other part that we studied in some way. It turned out that emotion was the missing piece that allowed us to see that modes of intelligence, relationships or attachments, and life goals or ambitions are not separable but instead form a larger pattern that makes up the whole person. Viewing the whole and then taking one piece out at a time allows us to see that the pieces tend to be small versions of the wholes or fractals in different contexts. People are oddly consistent in their own self-organized patterns.

Second, let us consider *uniqueness/information.* The patterned coherence within a complex person is not simply repeated across people, not even across people similar in age, history, gender, occupation, or fame. Even though Perls, Ellis, and Rogers are each adaptive, developing, and consistently self-organized adults living in approximately the same historical time and with the same occupation, the pattern and the pace of adaptive change within the pattern that identifies each man is unique. The fact that each man is unique in a particular way means that the uniqueness also carries the identifying information about that person. That which we share does not identify us; that which is unique does identify us. Personalities are necessarily unique. It is a bit like a DNA fingerprint. The individual elements may be quite common, but the pattern of activated elements is unique to the individual. People are much more different from each other in their complex patterns and identifying features than we ever suspected.

Old Psychology

Reflecting on the importance of these connections/replications and on uniqueness/information has brought us back around to rethink Tomkins and his ability to understand and explain people's idiosyncracies. At first we thought his extraordinary ability was due solely to the knowledge and theories he had of emotion. Now we think that it was that his knowledge of emotion put other aspects of the person in the emotional context. He knew about aptitude and intelligence testing backward and forward; he knew personality traits and themes and the theories that pertained to them. Perhaps just as critical he did his graduate work in philosophy, attaining that certain sense of philosophers that knowing in oneself is proof enough. This experience relieved him from the quantitative search for the shared commonalities. The knowledge of emotion was the bit of knowledge that put him in a different category from his fellows, but that knowledge without the other would not have been powerful enough for him to see individual patterns in people. Now we see that he put together the patterns from a wide array of puzzle pieces – emotion certainly, but also language, thought complexity, and so on.

Most psychologists are trained to doubt the personal wise insight and the "logical" proof – quite rightly usually. They continue to use the rules, now varied in other scientific disciplines, requiring that any strong effect be repeatable – across people, across time, across controlled situations. Of course, one cannot discover unique information patterns because they will not repeat across people; thus, one cannot discover that such patterns replicate within the person. In other words, we miss the inner connections and the unique information that identifies a person. Only through the thorough examination of individuals have we found these basic elements of the patterns that underlie personality. Perhaps it is not too presumptuous to claim once again that psychology ultimately is the study of the whole, individual person, all the parts of pattern of the person and its flowing through time.

New Views

We had been trained in traditional psychology to believe that the key to understanding human development would come from fitting in the missing pieces. But we were wrong. Developmental psychologists, like people in general, have been expecting that one general law of human development would emerge if only we could all start with the same abilities and have maximal access to support for those equal abilities. The major developmental theories of the past century have tended toward fairly linear descriptions of development. The basic models have been stage or accretion models, which have framed development in mutually exclusive terms, forcing us to accept the condition that "one size fits all," an assumption, it turns out, that may not be justified. Both stage and growth models purport to be universal models that describe development over the lifecourse. In stage models, such as those proposed by Freud and Erikson, people are seen as evolving through developmental epochs. Each stage has a qualitatively different nature and occurs in a predictable pattern, though there is some interindividual variation based on how stages are resolved. In the contrasting accretion models, including certain behavioral and temperament theories, and even cognitive theories, personal qualities become ever more well formed and structuralized over time. As individuals develop, they become more well articulated and more fully evolved versions of their younger selves.

These old models do not help us understand individual difference or developmental divergence. The old models do not answer the questions we posed in the opening chapters. Why did Rogers, Ellis, and Perls, as individuals, become the kinds of men and psychologists that they were? When did they learn to express their emotions as they did, to think as they did, to relate to others as they did, to engage others in the particular therapeutic dance that they led? In particular, when did they become Client-centered or Rational Emotive or Gestaltist? We noted before that very few differences would emerge in the broad sociological descriptions. They were all middle-class and well educated. They shared the same discipline of clinical psychology and practiced it in the same historical time and in the same part of the world. Although Perls was European and had lived in South Africa, all three would gain their fame and establish themselves in to United States. Gender did not defferentiate them. They would differ somewhat in the stability of their marriages, their relationships with their children. Likewise they would differ in the stability of their work lives. Only Rogers remained in the academic world for a lengthy period. Although all three would establish or associate with institutes, their relationships with the institutions would vary. They differed somewhat in religious background. Rogers grew up a conservative Protestant Christian while both Perls and Ellis were raised in Jewish families. None of the three would continue religious practices as adults. However, even these few differences hardly seem to explain the enormous differences in emotional style, values, motivations, ways of managing clinical practice, modes of thinking and particularly not personality. Nor do either the similarities nor the differences allow us to predict the modes of development and change that are most likely for each man in his adult years.

It is obvious that the answers to questions about the process of individual development do not lie on the surface of major sociological events or, for the most part, in the social demographics of individual circumstances, though these provide important boundaries on development and are woven into the available events of everyone's life. Additionally, when we examine the structure and changes in personality, work, and interpersonal relations of these three men over the lifecourse, we discern that they do not all follow the same stages or accretional growth, a point to which we return later. In fact, we will find that *there is a person for almost any theory, but there is not a theory for all people.*

Western science, as so many philosophers and historians have pointed out (e.g., Harre, 1983), presents a cultural view of the person that we all have in the background of ourselves. This Western omniperson, or identity, is felt to be rational at its very core; that is, the true person will test possibilities and make choices. The omniperson is self-determined and is also responsible for these rational, self-made choices. Goodness or malevolence is based on commitment to rational choices. Our science of the person, psychology, has also rested on the assumption that people are rational and self-determined and responsible, that we have in common a shared understanding of rationality and a shared ability to perceive choices. Driven by rational abilities and real choices, people in the same situations should, science argues, come to share the same motivations and values and goals, to be similar on various, independent aspects of themselves. When their situations differ, they become "types" of people, a straight line being drawn between the particular condition and the particular result, a line that is assumed to exist for everyone of the type.

Perhaps the presumptions of Western culture are limited and perhaps even our belief in them does not make them real. But we now have an entire science of psychology built on the premise of logically separable modules within the person. We expect each module such as intelligence or empathy or language or depressiveness to be stable, and we expect people with matched modules to be similar. Within very limited boundaries, these expectations can be met. But we have started to push the boundaries. Why does IQ predict so little about adult life? Why does early attachment not necessarily predict the relationships of later life? These are reasonable questions. The old myths of stability – continuity and early experience – are very limited in their ability to explain human development.

We cannot explain the information we have gleaned on three lives if we rely on the old representations and hypotheses. When we compare the relationships of Perls, Rogers, and Ellis, they are all different and do not fall easily into types. There is no one intellectual lifespan change and no simple accretion of intelligence that they all reach. Even in therapeutic posture and emotional climates created for therapy, there is not much in common, even though they all practice the same profession. Each man has a personally coherent and consistent pattern, and when we know that pattern, we have enough information to make many predictions, but when we look closely, there is too little interperson similarity to make sense of the patterns within the old theories. These men have features in common, but those common features in no way explain the dynamic progress of their adult development. Even those features that may look so similar when isolated become different when embedded in the context of the whole person.

Uniqueness of the person is actually something we have always known; we have just not been prepared to approach it in scholarly work. Think how amazed you would be if your mother or best friend changed her unique manner of speech, of smiling, of being nervous, of solving some problems. What our study shows is how connected and self-supporting and self-organizing each person's identifying pattern becomes. We are all identifiable because the elements of ourselves are *not* the identifying aspects of humanity. Because it is an organized pattern, we can be identified from many different perspectives without causing much overload on those who would identify us since there is replication of information across the perspectives. Five people of the same height, color, occupation, or anything else are not confused because they have common features. In each case, the common features become background. Even if they are nearly identical from the point of comparing them on isolated variables, the way these variables interact will still distinguish them. Even if one had two photographs that contained identical amounts of black and white, one would not be likely to confuse them as long as the patterns of black and white were different. So it is with people. Having identical amounts of some trait does not mean that people are similar. *It is the pattern, not the quantity, that provides information.*

Means Become Ends

There are often changes in nature that are like human development – a forest may mature to old growth or a beaver pond may become a meadow. Ecologists know that the forces contributing to change do not operate on a strict time course and may apparently stabilize for long periods or even reverse in response to crisis or chaos. The elimination or addition of any part of the ecological system may lead to cascading changes of the entire system, may absorb the change without much perturbation, or may eradicate the change, restabilizing itself. There are as many ways of developing any set of personality characteristics as there are ways of developing any other piece of nature. Many paths can lead to similar goals – of being a therapist for example. Even though Rogers, Ellis, and Perls had many things in common including many of their ambitions, their paths to those goals were not common. The differences in their work incorporated the unique developmental path taken by each man just as changes in any ecology incorporate the mode of change. The means becomes the ends in interesting ways. The reason for this we believe now is that patterns and connections are established and maintained across changes in the elements of life. *Personality is a pattern, not a selection of attributes.*

Personality emerges from people's abilities and opportunities to gather information about themselves and their world, their time in history. It emerges from their abilities and opportunities to organize this information, interpret it, and make predictions from it at the time it might be pertinent. Personality emerges from the ways that people value and are motivated by the world they live in and love in and work in and from the other people who enter their lives. In other words, personalities are like ecological adaptations. Unless history requires very narrow definitions of people at a certain time, requirements that would probably be self-limiting (i.e., would die out), we would not expect tendencies toward an entropy of personality in which all types of diverse peoples tend toward simple adaptive categories or additive skills.

Although we gravitate toward using language that implies that people actively construct their personality or their self-identity, that they consciously choose it, this language is itself a mark of our own embeddedness in modern Western culture. Our account of Rogers, Ellis, and Perls challenges the assumption that people simply are accretions of rational and self-determined decisions. We point to the rational inconsistencies even in their most rational works, their scholarly works. We also point, as have many others, to the lack of continuity across a lifespan in what constitutes rationality. The way a young Rogers is rational is very different from an older Rogers; nevertheless, he tells his autobiography as if there is one rationality, as do we all, most of the time. Second, our analyses point to how limited our self-determinism might be. Taking our identities to be dynamic systems means we then take for granted that we cannot produce for ourselves the cascading effects of change when we make decisions. The use of computer models for dynamic systems has made this quite clear. We cannot predict, as Gleick (1987) so eloquently explained, how the flight of a butterfly in the Midwest will influence the wind on the east coast of America, but it may, on occasion, have a profound effect. No more can we predict how a decision to take a day off in the country will affect our lives. We can, however, develop computer models that give us the probability and limits on such effects even if we cannot ourselves make the prediction without the aid of large calculators. Even so, we are now thinking only of probabilities and boundaries, not of absolute prediction. *There is considerable randomness in the personality system, a kind of built-in opportunity for creativity.*

Many authors (Harre, 1983; Janz, 1995; Shweder & Bourne, 2000) have called the underlying assumptions about identity, the "public conception" of personality or identity. Much of modern religion and government is based on these beliefs. This public conception of the features of personality is extremely important to us as social beings, as members of a larger group. When individuals become distinct from the group, as we all also strive to be, while still maintaining membership, a certain tension inevitably results. Inevitably this tension between older and new, potentially conflictual views of identity, self, personhood, and personality emerge in science in general and specifically here in our work. There is an inevitable tension between the history and culture in which identity can be conceived and between the individual identity and its place in the concept of the person (see Haviland & Kahlbaugh, 2000). When we present a new view of the person, we present new possibilities for large changes in many social institutions.

Dynamic Systems: A New View

Having moved away from our intention of adding a new particle to developmental psychology, turning away from simply studying emotion and adding it to the study of cognition or pathology, turning away from only reflecting that human beings are rational, self-determined, and so forth, we arrive back at complex systems – ecologies, if you will – and the possibility that people are not continuously predictable. As have scientists, mathematicians, and scholars in so many other disciplines, we, too, have found ourselves needing to use concepts from dynamic systems theory, complexity, and self-organizing systems. Dynamic systems theories, complexity theories, and self-organizing theories evolved within the mathematical and physical sciences in response to the need of scientists to better describe and comprehend systems that could not otherwise be understood using familiar but limited linear systems approaches. It should come as no surprise that many psychological problems that have not been understood using the same familiar linear systems have been awaiting the discoveries in mathematics to lead to new ways of understanding and setting up problems and solutions.

In fact, though it is metaphorical, we have even described the overall pattern of personality development for each of the therapists studied using names from these new views. We have described Perls as having characteristics of more chaotic patterns, Rogers as having more characteristics of the complex pattern, and Ellis as having more characteristics of the ordered patterns. Of course, these are only meant to illustrate tendencies that have implications for individual change. Ellis with his ordered personality is very stable for long periods. Rogers is more likely to evolve, always adding complexity to his own patterns. Perls is likely to be so adaptive to changing conditions that he becomes chameleon-like. It is not specifically the particles that make up these personal patterns, but the energy forces and channels within the patterns themselves that emerge as the most significant. The closer one gets to the individual, as opposed to the average of the group, the clearer it becomes that adaptive processes are too responsive to individual and ecological needs to be governed by rigid general rules, the sorts of rules we have been looking for in linear scientific approaches.

After reviewing the interweaving trajectories and development of three individuals, we also claim that the different forms of development, even oversimplified as stable, chaotic, and complex, are linked to emotions. Emotions as dynamic forces in the equations set boundary conditions on how easily lives may be touched by the many perturbations of personal and historical forces. When the emotional current is strong and swift, it will gather up events and sweep them into one dimension. Where the emotional current is broad and meandering, many little changes in the landscape can influence its course. But even the swiftest and strongest of currents can be altered by infinitesimally small events as well as large and dramatic ones. As it should now be obvious, our basic premise is that ideoaffective organizations and emotional turbulence are the key to understanding both continuity and discontinuity, consolidation and transformation. *Ideoaffective forces work through replication of patterns and are sustained by the amount of adaptive information that they provide about identity in its context.* (See Haviland, Boulifard & Magai, 2001.)

We are not alone in coming to these conclusions about the importance of dynamic systems. For example, theorists in residence at the Santa Fe

Institute, a multidisciplinary think-tank in New Mexico, have come to understand that living creatures are complex adaptive systems that operate in a far-from-equilibrium dimension. Because they have qualities of both openness and boundedness, they are responsive to a certain degree of flux and perturbation in the environment while maintaining some cohesiveness. Rather than succumb to the pull of entropic dissipation, they use replication and information storage to self-organize in creative and adaptive ways. This model of living systems works well with human beings, as it should.

Many years ago, Silvan Tomkins (1962) noted that two of the most interesting and adaptive qualities of the emotion system were what he called its redundancy – what we call its replication feature – and its flexibility, which is part of the openness. Unlike drives, with which emotions are often confused, emotions are not necessarily linked to any particular person, context, event, time, or periodicity. One could become interested, angered, or disgusted by anything under the sun and beyond. This is the reason that they are considered energy forces as well as structures or features – something like the relative way that light can be particles or waves in physics.

In terms of emotion within personality structure, Tomkins (1963) identified four basic types of emotion organization or pattern. In what he called the "monopolistic" structure, a single emotion tends to dominate the affective life of the individual – as in the seriously depressed or hostile person. In the intrusion type, a minor element in the general structure of personality occasionally intrudes and displaces a dominant emotion under specific conditions. But when it intrudes, it can dominate. Perhaps phobias would be an example of this. In the competition type, one emotion-based structural aspect of personality perpetually competes with others in the interpretation of information. Perls's shame/contempt competition is an example of this model. Whenever he views the world through the eyes of shame, he will almost inevitably put on glasses of contempt and see it differently. In Tomkins's (1963) integration model, no single affect bias dominates personality, which is to say that there is an adaptive balance and that the individual retains the flexibility to negotiate the vicissitudes of life.

In our work, we have taken Tomkins's notion of emotion patterns in categories and directed it more toward the process and system of patterns. We tried to move away from categorical types, which will always be influenced by cultural context. We suggested that such organizational processes could be viewed as types of attractor patterns.

Ellis's organization conforms more to the point attractor or limit cycle described in Chapter 2. He hovers closely around an anger/contempt attractor region and is repelled by a fear region. This attractor pattern seems closest to Tomkins's monopolistic configuration. It has the added advantage (over Tomkins's) of pointing to repellors, which help to sustain the boundaries on the attractor region, and as the word "attractor" implies, it tends to be a system of accretion, a system that continuously adds to itself. Perls's system is best characterized as having a saddle attractor pattern; he periodically slips from one side of the saddle – contempt (topdog) – to the other side – shame (underdog). This attractor pattern seems to conform most closely to Tomkins's competitive type of organization. Even though it is a system in constant flux, it is still fairly predictable and fairly stable. One might think of Perls on a race track. While you might not be able to predict where he would be on the track, he would still be found somewhere on that track. Rogers's system does not conform to either of these patterns because his personality landscape is populated with more varied attractor regions and fewer repellor regions. His system is more open and more likely to evolve. Rogers's pattern comes closest to Tomkins's integrative organization and interestingly is the only one that shows clear signs of adult growth in stages.

Our view is that any single individual's life may conform to a stage-like trajectory, a straight-line trajectory, some combination of the two, or even something else (e.g., regressive or chaotic trajectories). It is possible for a person to change the organization across decades or to not change in any noticeable way across the decades. Now that our society is changing rapidly, we can probably expect more people to change than might have in past centuries. When social forces combine to produce stability, this would be reflected in the probability of patterns that form in that historical period. When social forces combine to produce rapid change, this also should be reflected in individual patterns. *This is our commonality – that we create ourselves, a fractal view of our society – not that we share some common element.*

In the past, our theories of development seem to have exaggerated the commonalities of early development (Lewis, 1997; Van Geert, 1994). The fact that people begin at one place and end at another does not tell us that the path between is common to us all. Neither does it mean that there is no predictability; it just takes more complex forms. Actual computer models have been developed to show the probability of developmental change in terms of stages of complex understanding of meaning within personality. Using just a few variables (e.g., conflict, changes in thought process, and available resources) in a dynamic systems model, Kunnen and Bosma (2000) show systematic variation in probable patterns. With optimal resources and periodic conflict, there is stagelike growth in understanding of self. Some people have a high probability of becoming more complex. As the resources are restricted in the model and the relationship between conflict and level of understanding varied (high conflict at a point of lower comprehension versus at a point of higher comprehension – a type of coping), the probability of change lessens. There is always, by chance, some variation that shows change, but there is more stability in a sense. Their model is more complicated than can be presented here, but the point is that there are systematic predictions that can be made, though they refer only to the probability of development in a particular direction. The amount of randomness in a system, its openness to change, and the degree of interference or conflict, among other variables, enter into creating this picture. They will run 1,000 repetitions or iterations of their model to find the probabilities. Even Kunnen and Bosma (2000) "simply cannot imagine the effect of one change after two or three iterations. To grasp such effects of changes, for instance, to predict the development of a specific individual, we need . . . . a computer model." Gone are the days of simple, general models of observing and making theories from simple logic.

When we try to apply our descriptions of patterns to our three lives, we find some interesting relations. In terms of general developmental patterns, Rogers's trajectory was more stagelike than that of either of the other two men with respect to the successive evolution of his theory and of his personality. His mode of thought evolved through a stage in which his thinking was largely absolutistic to one that was more relativistic to one that was gradually more dialectic. In his emotional life, he became more emotionally elaborated and, toward the end, was more fluent and comfortable with anger. Perls's trajectory was saltatory but did not really seem to evolve toward a more sophisticated or advanced form. Rather, he seemed to alternate between the throes of two different emotional weather fronts, sometimes riding high on inflated opinions of himself and sometimes dragged down into the canyon of shame and self-loathing. Similarly, his theories varied from complexly dialectical, inclusive of historical reference and hypotheses that one might humbly present, to simple concrete assertions of egocentric observation. Finally, Albert Ellis's path was essentially one of accretion and consolidation. Once he had started down the path of short-circuiting fear and rerouting distress, he continued to repeat and perfect the strategies that allowed him to avoid the confrontation with these vulnerable feelings. Like Rogers, his early modes of thought were primarily absolutistic; however, unlike Rogers, he did not evolve appreciably toward relativistic or dialectical patterns.

Despite the power of ideoaffective structures to organize experience in certain defined ways once they have acquired some degree of consolidation, the emotion system, as a unique type of complex adaptive system within the complex adaptive system of personality, can evolve and change as well. Like Tomkins, we suggest that emotional events are the driving forces behind structural change. However, we go beyond this formulation to maintain that it is the particular pattern or form of emotional organization that influences the trajectory of individual development in the sense of its permeability to change.

Emotions as Change Agents in a Contextual Environment

Dynamic systems are those systems whose component parts are capable of interacting in a nearly infinite number of actions or states. Though the component parts of complex systems tend to gravitate toward certain probable patterns, it is also the case that they can develop independently of one another and that new forms of behavior can arise from small changes in any one of the system's components. Biological systems, as complex adaptive systems, evolve and self-organize over time because they are open systems rather than systems that are centrally controlled and closed. As such, they occupy a space between order and disorder, or what has been described as the "edge of chaos" (Kauffman, 1995) where growth and adaptative potential are maximized. This is especially true of social species such as ants and humans. Social insects represent only 2 percent of all insect species, but they constitute more than 50 percent of the insect biomass (Lewin, 1992). Thus, they have been prodigiously successful, and it appears that it is their social organization that confers such considerable fitness advantage. The human organism is also quintessentially social – the offspring of this altricial species require protracted years of nurturing – and its well-developed limbic brain is oriented toward forging and sustaining social connection. Human life is thus also situated at the edge of chaos, with the attendant potential for creative interaction with the natural and social environment, and one that affords continued evolution and development. However, the edge of chaos is a double-edged sword, as the waxing and waning and, at times, total extinction of tribes, cultures, and whole nations testifies.

Because we are social creatures the expression of emotion figures prominently in the regulation of interpersonal relationships, the evolution and practice of culture, and the transaction of intercultural commerce, even learning and psychotherapy. On a more molecular level, they play a vital role in our personalities and our personal identities, our self-concepts, and our concepts of self-in-relation. Indeed, self-concepts are increasingly conceptualized by developmental and personality psychologists as intersubjective selves (e.g., Masterpasqua, 1997).

Emotion organizations, like views of self, in contextualist and intersubjectivity frameworks are quintessentially responsive to all social processes from the individual to the historical. This feature of intersubjectivity and social interactivity constitutes one of the major sources of dynamic perturbation and, at least potentially, personal change and development (Magai & Nusbaum, 1996). For example, in a recently completed longitudinal investigation of personality change (Magai, 1999b), study participants reported moderate changes in perspectives, personality, feelings, and ways of relating over the course of eight years, as did outside informants recruited for purposes of verification. Interestingly, personality change was associated with positive and negative interpersonal life events of an intimate nature such as marriage, divorce, and death of loved ones, but not with other, less interpersonal, high and low points in peoples' lives involving careers, changes in residence, and more distant social relationships.

Two branches of dynamic systems theory have evolved during the latter half of the twentieth century, and more will surely follow. We have had the Brussels school, which is closely associated with the name of Pirgogine (1980) and his work on self-organizing systems, and the American school, which is known for chaos theory. The first popular views of this were demonstrated with physical systems such as weather and water patterns, Gleicks' (1987) book *Chaos* is an excellent example. Dynamic systems theory is also sometimes called complexity theory. It is increasingly used in the social sciences including economics. Waldrop's (1992) popular book *Complexity* gives an interesting history of changing theoretical and mathematical approaches to economics away from linear, particle models that require stability, equilibrium, and so forth.

Linear systems, as we noted previously, are those in which input is proportional to output. More effort results in more products, more product results in more rewards, and so on. However, many examples from life and science depart from these simple models. One does not just get more and more of the same thing with more effort, nor even just less and less. More and more water in your tomato does not just make a bigger tomato; however, it influences the tomato's texture and taste and the viability of the skin. But we have been influenced by this type of linear thinking. We made the linear prediction that more emotion expression would mean more understanding of the values and motivations attached to events and would lead to more elegant cognitive processing. Clearer emotion expression led to clearer thoughtfulness. Although this prediction is true in limited cases, we found a much more complicated system than we had predicted. Within the emotion system, both very little and very much expression are limiting, and the connector pattern of different emotion expressions can have major effects on the influence of any one emotional process.

One example of the systems that are built out of emotions but not determined by them comes from Ellis. Ellis's more hostile emotional expression forms a particular empathic boundary pattern edged with his strong interest emotions. One does not usually expect empathy to be supported by any kind of hostility, and it would probably not emerge if the interest were not present with the hostility. The combination is intense and creates empathic safety boundaries that Ellis uses for his cognitive-behavior approach. This pattern repeats itself continuously for Ellis and supports his personality and theories, but neither hostility nor interest separately or out of context would predict the "hot boundary" that is uniquely Ellis.

Dynamic systems tend to be governed by nonlinearity as well as other properties that were first modeled in mathematics. In nonlinear systems, input is not proportional to output, as in the well known dose–response curve in pharmaceutics – increasing doses of medicine do not result in a corresponding increase in effect. Likewise, increasing crying is not likely to result in corresponding increase in sympathy, but as with medicine it can have a poisonous effect, even though the moderate or correct dose may be curative. Additionally, in dynamic systems, small inputs (effects) can elicit large outputs, as in isochronic iterative equations. Think here of the very small nonverbal expressions that Perls, Rogers, and Ellis make at the beginning of their therapeutic sessions and the increasingly large effects that these have on Gloria. We have no reason to believe that larger expressions would have larger effects of the same sort.

A linear systems perspective and notions of equilibrium have dominated the physical and social sciences for most of their histories.

This historical fact helps explain why models of human development – including the ones we began with involving the romances of early experience and continuity – have been dominated by causal models of development, a preoccupation with issues of stability, and the utilization of inferential statistics based on linear models. These models include major theories that we have leaned upon such as attachment theory and Piagetian cognitive stage theories. These approaches do not lend themselves very well to the articulation of change processes that are not stable or that show continuous increases. In our analyses, these old models, while often useful in establishing boundaries, are quite limited in accuracy.

Order, Complexity, and Chaos

Self-organization theory and related notions from chaos theory provide exciting possibilities for discovery in psychology. These ideas enable us to examine and model both stability and change in human development. *Chaos* allows us to understand the mechanics of stability and change away from stability in physical terms. *Self-organization* provides the important additional element of energy flow and its tendency to replicate form and have those forms become information carriers or meaningful. To incorporate these notions into a developmental psychology of personality, we must consider the human being as an adaptive system. Systems – whether they are physical systems like tornados or whirlpools or living systems with cycling elements of cognition and emotion and social attachment and work output – emerge originally from chaos. Over time, patterns evolve as the system self-organizes in real time in response to both internal flux and flow and the perturbations and turbulence of surrounding systems. At phase transitions, further chaos is created, leading to new self-organization and new emergent forms. There is no need for an ideal form, pattern, or module to exist or to be the goal toward which all development might gravitate. Any adaptive system that can emerge may well do so.

The notions of order, complexity, and chaos in living systems are giving us new views not only of development and personality but also of health and mental health. Although the layman's sense of chaos is of dysadaptive disorganization, the science of complexity indicates that the edge of order and chaos – complexity – may be at the heart of successful adaptation in complex systems. This suggests that both chaos and order are essential to adaptation. If we assume that the goal is continuous change and adaptation rather than a possible finished product in equi-librium, we will be moving toward complexity. The old notion that all motivation was destined to return us to a point of quiesence and of not needing anything probably does not occur often. Instead, the function of motivation is to keep us on the edge – not too risky or frightening, but not too boring and settled either. What can keep us on that edge may change also (Csikszentmihalyi, 1991).

In terms of mental health models, the old science model based on equilibrium theory suggested that when a person is disordered, the therapist must act to restore order, to bring the person back to a state of stability. This model fits in with our concept of mental health pharma-ceuticals as making a person still and regular, even compliant, but not agitated, anxious, depressed, or unfocused and active, and especially not highly variable. The new views suggest the opposite may be just as likely or more likely. Dysfunctional psychological patterns may be too stable and resistant to change. The person cannot adapt to differ-ent contexts; he cannot mature; in meeting new people he behaves as if they must intend to repeat his old expectations, and so forth. Therefore, therapy would consist of producing measured doses of chaos as well as order. We would intentionally assist the person in moving closer to chaos and complexity to "tentativeness" or uncertainty as Rogers would have put it.

In education, we often search for the edge of chaos. When students have achieved the ability to solve an easy problem, we add new contra-dictory elements to the problem situation so that the old method will no longer work. Thus we create a kind of regression in their ability to solve problems that is somewhat chaotic as they attempt a variety of new ap-proaches – some that will not work at all, some that will work some of the time, and, hopefully, eventually, some that will work all the time. And then we add new elements and start again, but we are starting at a new place. In education, there is actually evidence that when children are changing their strategies, they do regress even in their ability to do the problems that used to seem easy to them. This is likely to be true for many systems of change.

Complexity and chaos theories offer enormous heuristic potential for the study of lives and human development. After sporadic attempts by individual psychologists to grasp the grand principles of human devel-opment by studying the whole individual – notable attempts include Freud's case analyses, Block's *Lives Through Time*, Erikson's Gandhi and Martin Luther – the field essentially abandoned such efforts as offering little in the way of generality. Lives seemed hopelessly complex, and this approach often was called unscientific. The chaos and complex change within one person's life could not be grasped, much less the variation across many lives. However, the recent lessons from chaos theory and self-organization theory suggest that this was not the *problem* but was, in fact, the *answer*. It was not the study and observation that were flawed but the scientific approach. The search for regularity, for equilibrium, for additive predictive relationships within limited domains was mistaken with respect to individual lives.

The new scientific approach in psychology requires the study of individuals rather than agglomerated groups. After many years of studying emotional behavior with traditional methods, we have learned from the close study of changes and connections in just three lives many things that never arose in previous research, that could not arise. Not just in personality but in many other aspects of human development, the individual process is important. For example, Esther Thelen (Thelen & Smith, 1994), while studying motor behavior such as crawling and walking, found that it was only by studying individuals that the change processes could be seen. Thelen's thesis goes beyond the recognition that everything in nature is unique; her conceptualization of the individual emerges from her new views. Given that human growth and development is a quintessentially dynamic system – responsive to its own internal variability as well as environmental perturbations – group analyses obscure the dynamics of self-organizing processes. The study of individuals, formerly dismissed as too narrow and nongeneralizable, is seen as the proper and most legitimate way of closing in on essential developmental principles.

Though human life trajectories may resemble a "random walk" generated by conditional probabilities with no foreordained or predictable stops along the way, the phenomena under inspection are completely deterministic in the sense that each output along the trajectory or the random walk of the individual human life is a function of conditions established by each preceding input. Seldom does one leap away from the path one is on, but which direction it will turn is not easy to predict. This does not mean that we cannot learn about developmental principles or about types of outcomes by studying the individual. Thelen argued that understanding individual outcomes can be apprehended only by studying individual trajectories. After individual developmental paths are identified, we may find patterns or forms. In this emerging tradition, of course, we have proposed personality systems that verge toward chaos like Perls or toward order like Ellis or that are more complex like Rogers. These patterns can predict the probable susceptibility to change, attraction to various emotions and cognitive processes, and even attachment styles. Chaos theory understands patterning to be intrinsic to chaotic systems or complex adaptive systems.

Singular Events and Personality

One advantage of dynamic systems is that they allowed us to consider singular events as significant. Most systems of analysis require that one be able to repeat events, always producing the same result. This requirement is limiting even to common sense. We have all observed that most little life events, repeated or not, seem to add up to almost nothing, whereas some little things turn the path one is on. Events may happen that affect personality either immediately or slowly, over time. We suggest that when encounters and events have emotional significance, sometimes a particular kind of emotional significance, perhaps fitting the fractal pattern already in operation, they are likely to have effects producing certain types of personality. We think that the process of feedback that dynamic systems uses in other areas of study may pertain in psychology as well. When there is feedback, aspects of a system can become coupled or entrained. This implies even that singular or repeated events of the past can acquire emotional significance in the future, making both the prior (previously insignificant) events significant and providing a path for future development. For example, it is one of the hallmarks of therapeutic change that old events take on new emotional meanings and that the existing personal landscape leading to future change is thereby rearranged.

Other theories claim that associationism or operant conditioning might account for the coupling. Some habits and even social biases or personality traits may be described by simple learning chains, but this explanation does nothing to describe why some connections appear and others are very unlikely or why singular events can be important. If the energy force that holds behavior together over time, that supplies significance and value is emotional meaning, that would not be explained in associationism or operant conditioning. For example, in operant conditioning, things are tied together by "reinforcers." However, a reinforcer is defined as that which increases the likelihood of establishing the chain of associations, a circular explanation. Some dynamic systems explanations attempt to rely on associationist chance to explain coupling. In Lewis's (1997) theory of personality, for example, two things become coupled due to first one chance couplings and then repetitive chance couplings. This may happen of course, but it accounts neither for the many repeated chance events that never result in stable patterns nor in the probability that emerges in paths of change after just one event. However, when emotions enter into the equations, they provide organizational systems in and of themselves. As Tomkins (1962, 1963) argued, they amplify, rather than simply reward, other processes. The amplification is, as noted previously, the result of replication of pattern (not of event) and of information or meaning supplied. This amplification provides an organizational pattern, complex no doubt, but not completely random.

In our studies of these three individuals, there are many instances of important singular events. For example, Ellis, already interested in sexual behavior, met, by chance, a person who started him on his publishing career on a train coming back from a conference. Perls met and married a woman who happened to be working in the Gestalt psychology arena. Rogers headed off to China on a college trip and found his religious convictions and career intentions challenged and changed. Each of these events occurred only once, was not a predictable part of everyone's life, and yet was quite significant in changing the lives of our three therapists. One should note that there appear to be limits. Would Perls, Rogers, or Ellis be likely candidates for each other's pivotal events? Would it have mattered if Perls had met a publisher interested in sexual behavior or if Ellis had met a woman with a professional interest in Gestalt psychology?

It is not only in early childhood that singular events may have strong effects. They may happen at any point in the lifecourse. Early experiences are important in that they may put one on particular emotional paths. But they do not predict the large story of life very well, partly because emotional tendencies or cognitive skills, or preferences for particular relationships are in themselves usually very adaptive to wide varieties of later experience. We have all noticed that two children who have grown up in the the same family may have widely differing interests and personalities. In dynamic systems terms, this happens because we each have a tendency for unique self-organization and reorganization, we all enter into unpredictable intersystemic perturbation (meaning that a chance event may interact unpredictably with previous patterns), and later events may be sensitive to small differences in initial contexts. Even people who begin rather similarly will not necessarily follow similar life paths.

Initial Conditions

Small differences in initial conditions, combined with unpredictable perturbations, can produce quite divergent courses. If one thinks of two people starting off in life near each other, in the same environment, but having their lives stirred by gifts and punishments and so on with just little differences in the timing of the stirring or the breadth of the spoon or the severity of the punishment, and so on, the points that they begin at may provide very little predictive validity for the pattern that results. The points of origin should provide some information, but will not determine the pattern or the similarity among patterns. If two brothers begin life in a slum during war time and suffer from starvation, these boundaries will always carry some information. Nevertheless, one person may devote his life to avoiding privation and amass a fortune, whereas the other may devote his life to preventing wars. Those are only two extremely different possibilities from a wide variety of possible lives. In both cases, the war experience is part of the means toward the ends achieved by each brother, but it is certainly not predictive of life development. Ellis claimed in his autobiography that his early experience led him to extreme rationality and control where his sister's early experience in the same family led her to neurotic and dependent behavior. Whether he was correct or not, such family differences are common. This is precisely why simple linear and categorical descriptions of life patterns, of any sort, are so limited in their predictability and always will be.

Patterns and Attractors

Dynamic systems theory leads one to expect that although we may not be able to predict individual lives, we may be able to discover "patterns" that repeat themselves. In the physical and biological sciences, activity that on the surface appears to be random or erratic is often disclosed to have underlying order and pattern, to be drawn in by what are now called "strange attractors." These are events or behaviors or forces around which other events, behaviors, or forces organize themselves. In our work, we found that replicated emotion/cognition complexes can be attractors organizing large amounts of information, behavior, and events in people's lives. Much of Rogers's behavior and work is organized around anger and the control or avoidance of anger, for example, whereas much of Ellis's behavior is organized around fearfulness and the control or avoidance of anxiety. A great deal of Perls's life is organized around shame and the control or avoidance of shame. None of these men is defined by one repellor entirely; they are much too complex for such simplicity, but a great deal can be learned about them from locating such repellors. Note also that they have different attractors. It makes little sense to compare them on anxiety, anger, or shame. The comparison of one emotion to another is not particularly relevant since one person may use one emotion as an organizer and another person may not. The meaningfulness of each emotion is different for each person depending upon how it is embedded in a pattern. Red lights in a "red light district" direct one to prostitution; red lights in the traffic stop light have an entirely different meaning. The 'redness" is important, but it does not carry the information without the pattern or context. This means that the emotional patterns might be comparable in their form without being comparable in their content, as well as that different emotions might be aligned with different patterns.

Development

The science of development in the twenty-first century is not going to be a field for people who like sharply defined problems and solutions. It is not likely that we will find a general law in pattern formation in nonequilibrium systems. That is one of the last things one would expect. Growth and development may be seen as continuously emerging products of complex and chaotic systems. The order that emerges in an initially chaotic condition is holistic in nature and derives from mutual effects across emotion, cognition, behavior, and context. Within a system or between systems, an interdependence of variables with push and pull vectors coeffecting components drive the components to settle into a coherent pattern over time. With respect to the replication of patterns, the support for this is ample in the films of the three individuals presented in this volume. Each therapist replicated his pattern across dimensions and repeatedly within a short period of time. With respect to information carried by the pattern, each unique pattern identifies the person and allows prediction of behavioral tendencies because they tell how the individual perceives and organizes new information. As mathematicians and statisticians working in the area of complexity can demonstrate with their models, when elements tend toward complex organization, they are viable because they tend also to be able to replicate themselves and because the patterns carry recognizable and meaningful information. *Patterns do not seem to need much else other than replicability and information, so the possibilities for individual uniqueness and diversity are nearly infinite.*

State Changes

One of the features of nonlinear systems is that they demonstrate qualitative changes in state. The changes or phase shifts in a system occur spontaneously in far-from-equilibrium conditions; they do not occur under conditions of equilibrium. Energy flow plays a crucial role in the creation of such order. Energy flow occurs in the physical world as in weather system in living systems such as colonies of ants, and in supra living systems such as urban cities. Even in the lives of our therapists, there is a fairly clear example of energy flow. Rogers makes a phase shift in his emotional organization during a period where he has little equilibrium. He became the more complex Rogers most people remember only after a period of retreat and therapy in his forties.

As emotions and thoughts co-occur, they become coupled and through mechanisms of positive and negative feedback become entrained to one another such that activation of one of the co-assembled elements leads to the activation of the other element with which it has become coupled. Normally, the emotion of anger will provoke attention to possible barriers and obstacles and will be coupled with thoughts of needing to overcome and prevail. However, the emotion of anger may become coupled with something else, say interest. To use a cross-cultural example, Japanese mothers do not react to their toddler's anger directly but tend to divert the infant's attention to the interesting features of something else in the environment. In contrast, American mothers engage in behaviors that, at least initially, amplify the anger as they respond with anger to anger. If the parent prevails, the child will acquire an anger/humiliation bind such that when anger is aroused, shame is experienced, which in turn subdues the expression of anger. If the child consistently prevails in the battle of wills, then an anger/pride link will be forged, promoting the elaboration of anger within the personality. Thus, there are naturally occurring couplings as well as idiosyncratic couplings. Since the system is far from equilibrium in early development, and since the emotion system may take on many different patterns, it has many degrees of freedom, as does the cognitive system and many other systems. Thus, chance associations, especially if repeated over time, will create individuality in the personality landscape even within stable cultures.

There is duality and multiplicity in various parts of the developing system. In the larger social context of relationships, people, each of them sets of systems, also become coupled. They come from a chaotic interaction system into a complementary and reciprocal response system. In considering lifespan development, we must keep in mind both the individual system and joint or interdependent system and the relationships among systems and also systems of systems. Unique change occurs in part because several systems are interacting. The multiplicity of systems leads to interesting psychological problems, however. For example, many theorists suspect that consciousness emerges from the complexity of the diverse systems – that it is not to be found in particles of matter but in the dynamic interactions. If so, reality will prove stranger than fiction as complex systems not presently considered by human beings to be animate may have the potential for consciousness.

Strange Attractors

Another kind of duality is encountered in the description of the "strange attractor." Physicists working with chaotic systems found that random and chaotic systems tended toward patterns or forms. One way of thinking about this is to consider that the chaos permits adaptive order to emerge and that chaos is the main source of adaptive possibilities allowing us to be innovative, original enough to survive under changing conditions in the long run. Systems that appear to be very stable sometimes break apart suddenly, or they may grow and shrink for long periods and then dissolve into chaotic states. If these patterns are seen in other parts of nature, why not expect them in human growth and development as well?

Determinism and Nondeterminism

Self-organizing systems are both deterministic and nondeterministic. Certain constraints are imposed on the system due to its inherent properties. For example, gender presents certain boundaries on reproduction. So the reproductive qualities of humans are strictly bounded, though this is not so for all living creatures. Then there are open areas within the boundaries. In personality development, innate temperament traits and physiognomic characteristics set the initial stage for a particular course of development; sometimes they set boundaries for development. Within the boundaries there are an infinite array of developmental possibilities, depending on the dynamics of self-organization and upon environmental contingencies. Certain preferences for solving problems, for valuing motivations, for people and for events will develop over time. In dynamic systems terms, these preferences might be called attractors. Similarly, a person will develop certain aversions to solving certain problems, for certain motivational phases, for people and for events. These could be called repellors. As preferences and aversions develop, they appear to follow a trajectory, to have a direction as well as a rate of movement. One might as well say that they create a direction, but the path remains sensitive to changing conditions, and the direction may change.

State Spaces of Personality

In dynamic systems terms, a system has a state space, which is a bound-aried mapping of a system. In terms of topographic metaphors, it has elevations and depressions but in more than three dimensions. Each of these "spots" has a pattern for catching the event, for assimilating it, for being changed by it, and so forth. If Rogers is repelled by awareness of his own anger, for example, it would take considerable force to get him into a phase that rose to his repellor state. It is not that Rogers would never be angry – when angry he might be extremely angry – just that the force required and the precipitousness of the rise would be a distinctive quality in his personality landscape or ecology. We argue that the existence of emotion attractors and repellors is what gives the personality system its impression of stability.

Recognizing an Organized Pattern

One of the difficulties for us all in using the new view of systems is to move to a more concrete description. We run the risk of looking at personality as we used to look at the stars before there were telescopes. Without a guide, we would end up with mythological personality "constellations." We need to know the equivalent in personality of star systems with planets, moons, comets, or galaxies with spirals and movement across time. We predict that, as a place to start, it will be sufficient to define a patterned "space" in the landscape of personality as meaningful when we can detect its ability to carry information and to replicate itself. One might argue that a constellation carries information in that the image or story and the visual pattern allow one to navigate, to place oneself in a meaningful universe. The catch is that constellations do not replicate themselves – even in fractals. They are not descriptions of living and changing systems. A living pattern replicates itself in smaller subsystems of the larger one and it continuously reorganizes and searches for information that allows for replication, even though in some instances there is an evolution in the replication, an adaptive change.

Summary and Concluding Thoughts

For us as authors, this excursion into the lives of three individuals over time has been an absorbing and compelling experience that has rewarded us with many insights and discoveries about lives, affect, and transformation. In our intersubjective mode, we hope that the reader has been just as fascinated. In this work, we studied the lives of three men in great depth and detail through biographical material, personal documents, and behavior captured in film. We attended to the idiosyncratic biographical details of each man's life as any trained psychologist or biographer would do. And we examined each man's written output with intense scrutiny. However, unlike most psychobiographers, we brought multiple theories and modes of analysis to bear on our examination – attachment theory, cognitive development theory, dynamic systems theory, and complementarity theory. And like modern literary critics, we applied lessons from postmodernism, taking the texts produced by Rogers, Ellis, and Perls as objects of analysis. However, perhaps what distinguishes this work from more traditional approaches most is the fact that we brought a set of fundamental premises about emotion and the role of emotion in the organization and development of personality to bear in this critical analysis. Two premises in particular guided the present work.

First, we took emotions to be the primary agents or energic movers of human personality development. We viewed them as comprising a dynamic, self-organizing, and self-defining system, a system that would be manifest in any element of behavior, thought, or action one wished to examine. Given this premise, we attended to the minutest gesture and facial expression on up to the clusters of word patterns, and yet further to the overarching theories. The data supported the legitimacy of the premise. Ideoaffective patterns replicate themselves across systems. They search for supporting information but can adapt to changing conditions. However, we ourselves were at times stunned by the consistency and the extent to which ideoaffective patterns played themselves out in fractal-like replications across wide domains of behavior and thought.

Second, we assumed that emotional organizations not only defined individual differences in personality but also served as explanatory factors in observed continuities in lives as well as deviations in the lifecourse. We looked for both short-term and long-term deviations over the lifespan. Once again, even with the premise that emotions were pivotal, either setting boundary conditions on personal growth and constraining the course of development or permitting, even precipitating, change, we were surprised at the various and individual ways that this could play out.

Finally, we assumed that there are differing motivational properties inherent in all the dimensions of emotions from the changes aligned with happiness and interest to those aligned to fear and anger, never neglecting sadness or shame or even contempt. The emotional dimensions combine in diverse and multivariate ways, creating new emotional combinations and forces as they unfold in unique developmental contexts and become structuralized in overarching adaptive and creative organizations of personalities.

Using these assumptions, we found that some basic principles of personality organization emerged. Even though emotional elements seem to swirl in unpredictable life events and personal relationships that challenge people's lives in novel ways, neverthless, the individual patterns will not be random or unpredictable. The dimension of emotion evoked and the person's previous organization lend predictability and stability to personality systems. The stability and replication of pattern across subsystems of the person provide a meaningful and stable identity and modes of change to the individual. No wonder the world at large is endlessly fascinated by the progress and transformation of lives. We look to the stories of other lives to understand and to transform our own, recognizing that change is inherent to the human condition and the wide sweep of history. Each life tells us ever more about the affect dynamics of life itself. Ultimately, we have learned from the lives studied at this scientific juncture to follow the principles of dynamic change and development in every life.

Appendix
Coding Schemes

Autobiographies

Affect

Each of the three autobiographies was coded for affective content in terms of discrete emotions and more undifferentiated or ambiguous terms. The coding scheme for the discrete affect terms was based on the theoretical framework of Izard's (1971, 1977) differential emotions theory. According to the theory, there are ten basic or primary emotions, designated as discrete emotions. Each of the ten basic emotions can vary in intensity or magnitude. The ten emotions, which are listed here, are expressed as continua from the weaker to the stronger form of emotion. The coding of these terms included, but was not limited to, the examples listed here; cognates and synonyms were also included. Additionally, affect was coded even when it was being denied or minimized (e.g., "I was disinterested" or "not mad"). The more global, undifferentiated, nondiscrete emotional terms were also coded.

Discrete Emotions
Interest–Excitement: interested, stimulated, curious, excited, fascinated, eager
Anger–Rage: anger, irritated, mad, annoyed, frustrated, hostile, hate, rage, enraged.
Contempt–Scorn: contempt, put-down, disapprove, belittle, scorn.
Fear–Terror: fear, tense, tension, anxiety, afraid, scared, terror, horror, terrified, panic.
Distress–Anguish: sadness, blue, feeling low, sorrow, unhappy, anguish, suffering, depressed, distressed, hopeless feeling, agony.

Surprise–Startle: surprise, startled, astonished, incredulous, shocked.

Enjoyment–Joy: enjoy, joyful, pleased, pleasure, happy, rewarding, like, delighted, ecstatic.

Shame, shyness–Humiliation: shame, shy, ashamed, embarrassed, feel small, mortified, humiliated.

Disgust–Revulsion: disgusted, appalled, repelled, loathe, revulsion, nauseated, horrible, repulsed.

Guilt: guilt, remorse, regret, guilty, sorry.

Global Emotional Terms

Positive Feelings: Feeling words that have a positive valence but that do not fall readily into any of the positive discrete emotion categories of interest, joy, or surprise. Examples are "feel comfortable," "admiration," and "deeply awed."

Negative Feelings: Feeling words that have a negative valence but that do not fall readily into any of the negative discrete emotion categories of anger, distress (sadness), guilt, shame, fear, contempt or disgust. Examples are "uncomfortable," "gloom-casting," and "great disappointment."

Unspecified Feelings: Feeling words that have an uncertain emotional valence – not obviously negative or obviously positive. Examples are "I was moved," "feel like sorting myself out," "feeling," "emotion," and "yearning."

Inter-Coder Reliability. Two coders, one a skilled affect coder with many years of experience and one a predoctoral student in psychology who trained with the first coder for well over 20 hours on practice material, served as coders for the autobiographical material, for both emotions and themes. (They also coded the therapist/client interview.) In the first stage, each coder independently recorded all references to affect that appeared in the material. Over the three autobiographies, there was an 85 percent overlap in material recorded – the remainder were omissions by one or the other coders. Next, the two lists from the two coders for each autobiography were merged into one file to make a comprehensive list of affective references for each therapist. The two coders then coded the material independently for type of affect. The inter-coder reliabilities (agreement) were .94, .93, and .90 for Rogers, Ellis, and Perls, respectively. Discrepancies were resolved by consensus.

Themes

How one identifies themes in narrative material is a matter of choice (Krippendorff, 1981). A first decision involves choosing the coding unit (i.e., the size of the unit that will be searched for instances of the theme). The coding unit may be a word, a sentence, a phrase, a paragraph, or perhaps an entire document. In terms of enumeration, coders may count every instance of the theme within the designated unit (i.e., its absolute frequency) or simply indicate the presence (1) or absence (0) of the theme.

In the case of the autobiographies, the material was coded thematically; that is, the coders flagged each theme as it emerged in the narrative. Themes could be one sentence in length or span several paragraphs. Coders recorded all themes that were detected and specified the whole autobiography as the coding unit. A frequency count approach to enumeration was taken, with the following condition: only the first occasion of successive repetitions of a theme was counted. A particular theme could be coded once again if a different theme intervened between the two instances of the theme.

Inter-Coder Reliability. As a first step, each coder coded the material independently to cull the themes for subsequent coding. The two lists of themes were then reviewed for discrepancies, and a new "merged" list was compiled that was inclusive without being redundant. In the case of Rogers, twenty-two themes were detected; for Ellis, it was twenty-six; and for Perls, twenty-five. All category reliabilities were at .79 or better for Rogers .81 or better for Ellis, and .77 or better for Perls.

Therapist/Client Interview

Affect Words

In the filmed sessions, we coded only discrete emotion terms, using the same coding scheme as used with the narrative material of the autobiographies. Because the nature of the dialogic on-line material differed from the written word, we coded certain linguistic indicators of affect.

> **Shame**: Speech dysfluencies such as um, uh, I–I, and false starts
> **Contempt**: Sounds such as "tsk (See Malatesta-Magai & Dorval, 1992, for a complete set of shame and contempt indicators.)

Anger: Anger-inflected nonword utterances (e.g., "oooh!") and indirect expression of anger (i.e., use of swear word)

Additionally, in the case of contempt, we coded derogatory statements as examples of contempt (i.e., utterances connoting disdain, derision, or scoffing).

Inter-Coder Reliability. The inter-coder reliabilities (agreement) of affect words for Rogers, Ellis, and Perls were .91, .94, and .96, respectively.

Facial Expressions

Procedure for Coding. The facial expressions of Rogers, Ellis, Perls, and the client Gloria in the Shostrom film were coded by a class of undergraduate university students who were trained on MAX facial coding (Izard, 1979). Only students who could achieve a reliability of at least .75 on each region (mouth, brows, eyes) on the MAX training tape within two weeks coded the films. Three students were assigned to code each film. There were nine coders in all. The students worked independently. They coded each of the two interactants on separate days. The person not being coded and the part of the body not being coded were usually covered. This was not always possible due to movement of the person being coded.

Selecting Minutes of Interaction. Some of the facial expression is obscured on the tape (particularly for Perls). To obtain similar amounts of material, the students began by finding the first three minutes of observable material and the last three minutes of observable material in each film. Then they decided together on one three-minute segment near the middle of the film in which both participants were observable and there was some variety of expression. In this way, each person was coded for part of the beginning, middle, and end of the session. Gloria was coded for all three sessions, of course. The coding was done second by second. Therefore, each person had about of 540 codes for each region – brow, eye, and mouth. The inter-rater reliabilities of the coders ranged from .68 (on some mouth segments) to .99 (on some brow segments). We recoded segments that contained discrepancies and resolved them. Using the MAX system, we collapsed the MAX codes for regions of the face into affects – happy, sad, anger, shame, fear, etc. – for each second coded. We transcribed the tapes and made additional observations. (We are both expertly trained in the MAX coding systems, which are included in the chapter descriptions.)

Theoretical Works

Each of the therapists – Rogers, Ellis, and Perls – wrote extensively across their lifespans. In each case, an early, middle, and late exemplar of their books was chosen. When possible, we looked for the same topics so that changes in ideas across the lifespan could easily be compared. For example, all the books chosen for Ellis concerned his clinical work focusing on neurosis rather than his work on sexual functioning or other topics. Within books, chapters were selected again to match on topics. For Rogers, for example, we compared topics related to the dichotomy of "qualitative" versus "quantitative" analysis in the later two books. For the sake of continuity, these chapters were always chosen for comparison.

In summary, we chose the following books for each author:

Rogers: *The Clinical Treatment of the Problem Child* (1939)
 Counseling and Psychotherapy (1942)
 On Becoming a Person (1961)
Ellis: *How to Live with a Neurotic* (1957)
 Humanistic Psychotherapy (1973)
 Overcoming Resistance (1985)
Perls: *Ego, Hunger and Aggression* (1947)
 Gestalt Theory Verbatim (1969)
 The Gestalt Approach and Eye Witness to Therapy (1973)

Affects

The affect coding scheme for the theoretical work was nearly the same as the coding scheme for the autobiographies; however, it was more conservatively based on Izard's (1971) list of emotion words. Although we may have missed affective words that were idiosyncratic for the writers, we had so much material available that we reasoned that there would be sufficient evidence of affective word usage from this modest approach. In addition, we coded unspecified affect words (e.g., "feelings," "emotional," "moods") in the unspecified category. However, since so much material was available for this coding, we did not code general positive feelings or general negative feelings separately (e.g., "feel comfortable" or feel uncomfortable"). In these unspecified instances, only the "feel" part was coded as an unspecified emotion.

This method relied upon previous research (Haviland, 1984; Haviland & Kramer, 1991) in which a similar simple coding schema was used to demonstrate individual differences. Assuming that the use of emotion terms reflects individual sensitivity to cultural gestures and personal style, as well as immediate emotional crisis, both conscious and subconscious, we focused on simple emotion words. Such a direct approach leads to summations of types of emotion that are predominant at particular times or in relation to other items coded. Such terms can be dense or sparse in a variety of emotions. One can be highly variable, be relatively nonspecific, or demonstrate use of particular types of affect words such as Ellis's preference for words in the fear category.

After we agreed upon a coding list, we made no judgment, only a careful scan. In this case, we did not take reliability measures. In some instances, we had the material scanned into a computer file, and then the computer searched for the words. We compared the computer coding with the manual coding. The only misses occurred when the computer search missed a tense or case change in the words. Any errors were errors of omission and were clearly rare.

Intellectual Style

To assess cognitive development, we used an adaptation of the Haviland and Kramer (1991) approach. There is evidence that when the thinking of people is coded in this way, cognitive structures, which may initially indicate developmental change but may also in adults be interpreted as intellectual style, appear. The coding model used here follows the writer through three styles: absolute, relativistic, and patterned.

Absolute thinking is derived from Pepper's 1942 analytic scientific and world views of formism and mechanism. It posits a belief in a fixed, stable world, to which consciousness has direct access, either through reflective abstraction or scientific experiments (Kramer, 1983). The absolute thinker is prone to categorize using criteria that are inherent and fixed and to think in terms of absolute principles and ideals. *Relativistic thinking* came from the assumptions of Pepper's contextual scientific or world views, which posit a changing, unknowable world. Consequently, all knowledge is subjective and constantly changes within fluctuating contexts. Contradiction is accepted as inherent and irreconcilable;

thus, it is difficult to make decisions and commitments. Finally, *patterned* (sometimes called *dialectical) thinking* developed from an attempt to integrate absolute and relativistic concepts, in order to find continuity within change, and to make commitments within plurality. Like relativity, it construes all phenomena as changing and contradictory. However, it provides order and direction to the change and treats contradictions as apparent, rather than real, and as the impetus for growth through resolution. Knowledge through resolution of contradiction is seen as evolving through increasingly integrated structures characterized by emergence (novel features) and reciprocity (systemic characteristics). In the coding schema we used, we emphasized the importance of the integrative feature.

Previous use of the intellectual style codings instructed the coder to code each sentence independently. As a result of the large amount of coding here we changed the frequency to each page of published text rather than each sentence. Coders read the entire page (with appropriate beginnings and endings of sentences from the previous and subsequent pages) and made a decision about the occurrence of each style. Since the integrative style is less frequent than the relativistic style, which is less frequent than the absolute style, we decided to give the page code to the least frequent of the possible styles available. Therefore, if there were some evidence of both absolute and relativistic styles on a page, the code would go to the relativistic. A second trained coder independently coded fifty pages from each author. Percentage agreement on the main categories of absolute, relativist, and integrative thought was .78. Only .04 of the cases consisted of disagreements between the absolute and patterned categories. These values are in the same range as those obtained in other work using the same or similar scoring system as well as those obtained by investigators using other qualitative scoring systems (Labouvie-Vief et al., 1989; Loevinger & Wessler, 1970).

References

Adickman, J. D. (1993). Children's emotion biases: Their relation to internal representations of attachment security and to patterns of perceived maternal discipline. Unpublished doctoral dissertation. Long Island University.

Ainsworth, M. D. S. (1967). *Infancy in Uganda: Child care and the growth of love.* Baltimore: Johns Hopkins University Press.

    (1989). Attachments beyond infancy. *American Psychologist, 44,* 709–16.

Ainsworth, M. D. S., Blehar, M. C., Waters, E., & Wall, S. (1978). *Patterns of attachment: A psychological study of the strange situation.* Hillsdale, NJ: Erlbaum.

Alexander, I. E. (1988). Personality, psychological assessment, and psychobiography. *Journal of Personality, 56,* 265–93.

Allport, G. W. (1942). *The use of personal documents in psychological science.* Vol. 49. New York: Social Science Research Council.

Anderson, J. W. (1988). Henry A. Murray's early career: A psychobiographical exploration. *Journal of Personality, 56,* 139–71.

Anstadt, T., Ullrich, B., Merten, J., Buchheim, P., & Krause, R. (1997). Affective dyadic behavior, core conflictual relationship themes, and treatment outcome. *Psychotherapy Research, 7,* 397–417.

Arnheim, R. (1974). 'Gestalt" misapplied [Letter to the Editor]. *Contemporary Psychology, 19,* 570.

Atwood, G. E., & Tomkins, S. S. (1976). On the subjectivity of personality theory. *Journal of the History of the Behavioral Sciences, 12,* 166–77.

Baltes, P. B., & Smith, J. (1990). Toward a psychology of wisdom and its ontogenesis. In R. J. Sternberg (Ed.), *Wisdom: Its nature, origins, and development,* pp. 87–120. New York: Cambridge University Press.

Baltes, P. B., & Staudinger, U. M. (1993). The search for a psychology of wisdom. *Current Directions in Psychological Science, 2,* 75–80.

Bandura, A. (1982). The psychology of chance encounters and life paths. *American Psychologist, 37,* 747–55.

Bartholomew, K., & Horowitz, L. M. (1991). Attachment styles among young adults: A test of a four-category model. *Journal of Personality and Social Psychology, 61,* 226–44.

Basseches, M. (1980). Dialectical schemata: A framework for the empirical study of the development of dialectical thinking. *Human Development, 23,* 400–21.

Baumeister, R. F. (1994). Personality stability, personality change, and the question of process. In T. F. Heatherton & J. L.Weinberger (Eds.), *Can personality change?*, pp. 253–80.Washington, DC: American Psychological Association.

Beck, A. T. (1967). *Depression: Causes and treatment*. Philadelphia: University of Pennsylvania Press.

Belsky, J., & Isabella, R. (1988). Maternal, infant and social-contextual determinants of attachment security. In J. Belsky & T. Nezworski (Eds.), *Clinical implications of attachment*. Hillsdale, NJ: Erlbaum.

Belsky, J., Rovine, M. J., & Taylor, D. G. (1984). The Pennsylvania Infant and Family Development Project: III. The origins of individual differences in infant-mother attachments: Maternal and infant contributions. *Child Development, 55*, 718–28.

Bertalanffy, L. Von. (1968). *General system theory*. New York: Braziller.

Blanchard-Fields, F. (1986). Reasoning on social dilemmas varying in emotional saliency: An adult developmental perspective. *Psychology and Aging, 1*, 325–33.

Block, J. (in collaboration with Haan, N.). (1971). *Lives through time*. Berkeley, CA: Bancroft Books.

Bly, R. (1992). *Iron John*. New York: Vintage Books.

Bohr, N. (1950). Complementarity. *Science, 3*, 51–4.

Bowlby, J. (1969). *Attachment and loss: Vol. 1. Attachment*. New York: Basic Books.
(1973). *Attachment and loss: Vol. 2. Separation*. New York: Basic Books.
(1980). *Attachment and loss: Vol. 3. Loss, sadness and depression*. New York: Basic Books.

Bradshaw, S. L., Ohlde, C. D., & Horne, J. B. (1993). Combat and personality change. *Bulletin of the Menninger Clinic, 57*, 466–78.

Broughton, J. (1978). Development of concepts of self, mind, reality, and knowledge. *New Directions for Child Development, 1*, 75–100.

Bruner, J. S. (1986). *Actual minds, possible worlds*. Cambridge, Mass: Harvard University Press.
(1990). Culture and human development: A new look. *Human Development, 33*, 344–55.

Bühler, C. (1933). The social behavior of children. In C. Murchison (Ed.), *A handbook of child psychology*, pp. 374–416. New York: Russell & Russell.
(1934). *Drei Generationen im Jugendtagebuch*. Jena: Verlag von Gustav Fischer.
(1935). The curve of life as studies in biographies. *Journal of Applied Psychology, 19*, 405–9.

Cadwallader, E. H. (1984). Values in Fritz Perls's Gestalt therapy: On the dangers of half–truths. *Counseling and Values, 28*, 192–211.

Carlson, L., & Brincka, J. (1987). Studies in Script theory III: Ideological and political imagination. *Political Psychology 8*, 563–74.

Carlson, L., & Carlson, R. (1984). Affect and psychological magnification: Derivations from Tomkins' script theory. *Journal of Personality 52*, 36–45.

Caspi, A., Bem, D. J., & Elder, G. H., Jr. (1988). Moving away from the world: Life-course patterns of shy children. *Developmental Psychology, 24*, 824–31.

Caspi, A., Elder, G. H., and Bem, D. J. (1987). Moving against the world: Life-course patterns of explosive children. *Developmental Psychology, 23,* 308–13.

Cassidy, J. (1994). Emotion regulation: Influences of attachment relationships. In N. A. Fox (Ed.) *The development of emotion regulation. Monographs of the Society for Research in Child Development,* Vol. 59, Nos. 2–3, pp. 228–49. Chicago: University of Chicago Press.

Cassidy, J., & Berlin, L. J. (1994). The insecure/ambivalent pattern of attachment: Theory and research. *Child Development, 65,* 971–91.

Chandler, M. (1987). The Othello effect: Essay on the emergence and eclipse of skeptical doubt. *Human Development, 30,* 137–59.

Costa, P. T., Jr., McCrae, R. R. (1994). "Set like plaster"? Evidence for the stability of adult personality. In T. Heatherton & J. Weinberger (Eds.), *Can personality change?* Washington, DC: American Psychological Association.

(1996). Mood and personality in adulthood. In C. Magai & S. H. McFadden (Eds.), *Handbook of emotion, adult development, and aging,* pp. 369–83. San Diego: Academic Press.

Costa, P. T., Jr., McCrae, R. R., & Arenberg, D. (1980). Enduring dispositions in adult males. *Journal of Personality and Social Psychology, 38,* 793–800.

Csikszentmihalyi, M. (1991). *FLOW: The psychology of ultimate experience, steps toward enhancing the quality of life.* New York: Harper Perennial.

Cushman, P. (1992). Psychotherapy to 1992: A historically situated interpretation. In D. K. Freedheim (Ed.). *History of Psychotherapy,* pp. 21–64. Washington, DC: APA Press.

Darwin, C. E. (1872). *The expression of emotion in man and animals.* London: J. Murray. Reprinted in 1965, Chicago: University of Chicago Press.

Datan, N., Rodeheaver, D., & Hughes, F. (1987). Adult development and aging. *Annual Review of Psychology, 38,* 153–80.

DiMattia, D., & Lega, L. (1990). *Will the real Albert Ellis please stand up?* New York: Institute for Rational-Emotive Therapy.

Dolliver, R. H., Williams, E. L., & Gold, D. C. (1980). The art of Gestalt therapy or: What are you doing with your feet now? *Psychotherapy: Theory, Research and Practice, 17,* 136–42.

Dossey, L. (1989). Commentary on Stephenson's *"quantum theory of subjectivity,"* *Integrative Psychiatry, 6,* 180–95.

Ekman, P. (1984). Expression and the nature of emotion. In K. Scherer & P. Ekman (Eds.), *Approaches to emotion,* pp. 329–43. Hillsdale, NJ; Erlbaum.

Elkind, D. (1969). Conservation and concept formation. In D. Elkind & J. H. Flavell (Eds.) *Studies in cognitive development,* pp. 171–89. New York: Oxford University Press.

Ellis, A. (1950). An introduction to the principles of scientific psychoanalysis, *Genetic Psychology Monographs, 41,* 147–212.

(1951). *The folklore of sex.* New York: Charles Boni.

(1957). *How to live with a neurotic – at home and at work.* New York: Crown.

(1960). *The art and science of love.* New York: Lyle Stuart.

(1971). *Growth through reason.* North Hollywood, CA: Wilshire Book Company.

(1972a). *The civilized couple's guide to extramarital adventure.* New York: Peter H. Wyden.

(1972b). Psychotherapy without tears. In A. Burton and Associates (Eds.) *Twelve therapists.* San Francisco: Jossey-Bass.

(1973). *Humanistic psychotherapy.* New York: McGraw-Hill.

(1982). Intimacy in rational-emotive therapy. In M. Fisher & G. Stricker (Eds.), Intimacy. New York: Plenum.

(1985). *Overcoming resistance: Rational-emotive therapy with difficult clients.* New York: Springer.

(1996). How I learned to help clients feel better and get better. *Psychotherapy, 33,* 149–51.

Elshtain, J. B. (1981). *Public man, private woman.* Princeton, NJ: Princeton University Press.

Emde, R. N. (1980). Toward a psychoanalytic theory of affect: II. Emerging models of emotional development in infancy. In S. I. Greenspan & G. H. Pollock (Eds.), *The course of life: Psychoanalytic contributions toward understanding personality development. Vol. I: Infancy and early child-hood,* pp. 85–112. Washington, DC: National Institutes on Mental Health.

Erikson, E. H. (1950). *Childhood and society.* New York: W. W. Norton.

(1958). *Young man Luther: A study in psychoanalysis and history.* New York: Norton.

(1963). *Childhood and society* (rev. ed.). New York: W. W. Norton.

(1969). *Gandhi's truth: On the origins of militant nonviolence.* New York: Norton.

Eysenck, H. J. (1953). *The structure of human personality.* New York: Methuen.

Fischer, A. H., & Janz, J. (1995). Reconciling emotions with western personhood. *Journal for the Theory of Social Behavior, 25,* 59–79.

Foa, E. B., & Riggs, D. S. (1995). Posttraumatic stress disorder following assault: Theoretical considerations and empirical findings. *Current Directions in Psychological Science, 4,* 61–5.

Fogel, A. (1992a). Movement and communication in human infancy: The social dynamics of development. *Human Movement Science, 11,* 387–423.

(1992b). Co-regulation, perception and action. *Human Movement Science, 11,* 505–23.

Forgas, J. I. P. (1982). Episode cognition: Internal representations of interaction routines. In *Advances in Experimental Social Psychology, Vol. 15.* New York: Academic Press.

Foucault, M. (1973). *The order of things: An archaeology of human sciences.* New York: Vintage Books.

(1988). The political technologies of individuals. In L. Martin, H. Gutman, & P. Huttons (Eds.), *Technologies of the self: A seminar with Michael Foulcault,* pp. 145–61. Amherst: University of Massachusetts Press.

Fox, M. (October 4, 1998). With Prozac, the rose garden with hidden thorns. *New York Magazine,* Vol. 148, Section 4, p. 3.

Frank, A. (1953). *Anne Frank: The diary of a young girl.* New York: Simon and Schuster.

French, M. (1985). *Beyond power: On women, men, and morals*. New York: Summit Books.

Gaines, J. (1979). *Fritz Perls: Here and now*. Millbrae, CA: Celestial Arts.

Gardner, H. (1983). *Frames of mind*. New York: Basic Books.

Gell-Mann, M. (1994). *The quark and the jaguar: Adventures in the simple and the complex*. New York: W. H. Freeman.

George, C., Kaplan, N., & Main, M. (1984). Attachment interviews for adults. Unpublished manuscript. University of California, Berkeley.

Getz, I., & Lubart, T. I. (1998). Le rôle de l'emotion dans la transformation de soi. In J.-M. Barbier & O. Galatanu (Eds.). *Action, affects et transformation de soi*, pp. 98–114. Paris: Presses Universitaires de France.

Gleick, J. (1987). Chaos: Making a new science. New York: Penguin Viking Press.

Goldberger, A. L. (1991). Is the normal heartbeat chaotic or homeostatic? *News in Physiological Science, 6*, 87–91.

Goleman, D. (1995). Emotional Intelligence. New York: Bantam Books.

Gottschalk, L. A., & Gleser, G. C. (1969). *The measurement of psychological states through the content analysis of verbal behavior*. Berkeley: University of California Press.

Gould, R. L. (1978). *Transformations: Growth and change in adult life*. New York: Simon & Schuster.

Greenberg, L. S. (1993). Emotion and change processes in psychotherapy. In M. Lewis & J. Haviland (Eds.), *Handbook of emotions*, pp. 499–508. New York: Guilford.

Grossmann, K. E. (1996). Ethological perspectives on human development and aging. In C. Magai and S. McFadden (Eds.) *Handbook of emotion, adult development, and aging*, pp. 43–66. San Diego: Academic Press.

Gunmar, M. R., & Maratsos, M. (Eds.) (1992). *Modularity and constraints in language and cognition: Vol. 25. The Minnesota Symposia on Child Psychology*. Hillsdale, NJ: Earlbaum.

Harre, R. (1983). *Personal being: A theory for individual psychology*. Oxford: Blackwell.

Hatfield, E., Cacioppo, J. T., & Rapson, R. L. (1994). *Emotional contagion*. UK: Cambridge University Press.

Haviland, J. M. (1984). Thinking and feeling in Woolf's writing: From childhood to adulthood. In C. E. Izard, J. Kagan, & R. B. Zajonc (Eds.), *Emotions, cognition, and behavior*, pp. 515–46. Cambridge, England: Cambridge University Press.

   (1991). Fears and phobias in adolescence. In R. M. Lerner, A. C. Peterson & J. Brooks-Gunn (Eds.), *Encyclopedia of adolescence*, pp. 365–8. New York: Garland.

Haviland, J. M., & Goldston, R. B. (1992). Emotion and narrative: The agony and the ecstacy. *International Review of Studies on Emotion, 2*, 219–47.

Haviland, J. M., & Kahlbaugh, P. (2000). Emotion and identity. In M. Lewis & J. M. Haviland, (Eds.), *Handbook of emotions*. New York: Guilford Press.

Haviland, J. M., & Kramer, D. A. (1991). Affect-cognition relationships in adolescent diaries: The case of Anne Frank. *Human Development, 34*, 143–59. New York: Karger & Basel.

Haviland-Jones, J., Boulifard, D., & Magai, C. (2001). Old-new answers and new-old questions of personality and emotion: A matter of complexity. In S. Kunnen & H, Bosma (Eds.), *Identity and emotions: A self-organisational perspective*. London: Cambridge University Press.

Hazen, C., & Shaver, P. (1987). Romantic love conceptualized as an attachment process. *Journal of Personality and Social Psychology, 52*, 511–24.

Henley, M. (1978). Gestalt psychology and Gestalt therapy. *Journal of the History of the Behavioral Sciences, 14*, 23–32.

Horney, K. (1950). Neurosis and human growth. New York: Norton.

Hsee, C. K., Hatfield, E., & Chemtob, C. (1991). Assessment of the emotional states of others: Conscious judgements versus emotional contagion. *Journal of Social and Clinical Psychology, 17*, 113–19.

Hudson, J. A., Gebelt, J., Haviland, J., & Bentivegna, C. (1992). Emotion and narrative structure in young children's personal accounts. *Journal of Narrative and Life History, 2*, 129–50.

Hunziker, J. E. (1995). The influence of early emotional experience on the development of adult Type A behavior pattern. Unpublished doctoral dissertation. Long Island University.

Isen, A. M. (1990). The influence of positive and negative affect on cognitive organization: Some implications for development. In N. Stein, B. Leventhal & J. Trabasso (Eds.), *Psychological and biological approaches to emotion*, pp. 75–94. Hillsdale, NJ: Erlbaum.

Izard, C. E. (1971). *The face of emotion*. New York: Appleton-Century-Crofts.

    (1972). *Patterns of emotions: A new analysis of anxiety and depression*. New York: Academic Press.

    (1979). *The maximally discriminative facial movement coding system (MAX)*. Newark: Office of Instructional Technology, University of Delaware.

    (1977). *Human emotions*. New York: Plenum Press.

James, W. (1890). *The principles of psychology*. New York: Norton. (New York: Dover, 1950).

Jersild, A. T. (1946). Emotional development. In L. Carmichael (Ed.), *Manual of child psychology*, pp. 833–917. New York: John Wiley & Sons.

Jung, C. G. (1921). Psychological types. *Collected Works 6*. Princeton, NJ: Princeton University Press, 1977.

Kagan, J. (1979). Overview: Perspectives on human infancy. In J. Osofsky (Ed.), *Handbook of infant development*, pp. 1–28. New York: Wiley.

Kagan, J., & Snidman, N. (1991). Infant predictors of inhibited and uninhibited profiles. *Psychological Science, 2*, 40–4.

Kagan, J., Snidman, N., & Arcus, D. M. (1992). Initial reactions to unfamiliarity. *Current Directions in Psychological Science, 1*, 171–4.

Kahlbaugh, P. E., & Haviland, J. M. (1994). Nonverbal communication between parents and adolescents: A study of approach and avoidance behaviors. *Journal of Nonverbal Behavior, 18*, 91–113.

Kahn, E. (1996). The intersubjective perspective and the client centered approach: Are they one at their core? *Psychotherapy, 33*, 30–42.

Kaufman, G. (1989). *The psychology of shame: Theory and treatment of shame-based syndromes*. New York: Springer.

Kaufman, S. (1995). *At home in the universe: The search for laws of self-organization and complexity*. New York: Oxford.

Keating, D. P. (1990). Developmental processes in the socialization of cognitive structures. In *Development and learning: Proceedings of a symposium in honour of Wolfgang Edelstein on his 60ᵗʰ birthday*. Berlin: Max Planck Institute.

Keller, E. F. (1983). *A feeling for the organism: The life and work of Barbara McClintock*. New York: W. H. Freeman and Company.

Keltner, D. (1996). Facial expressions of emotion and personality. In C. Magai & S. H. McFadden (Eds.), *Handbook of emotion, adult development, and aging*, pp. 385–402. San Diego: Academic Press.

Kiesler, D. J., & Goldston, C. S. (1988). Client-therapist complementarity: An analysis of the Gloria films. *Journal of Counseling Psychology, 35*, 127–33.

Kirkpartick, L. A., & Davis, K. E. (1994). Attachment style and relationship stability: A longitudinal analysis. *Journal of Personality and Social Psychology, 66*, (3), 502–12.

Kirschenbaum, H. (1979). *On becoming Carl Rogers*. New York: Delacorte Press.

Koch, S. (Ed.). (1959–63). *Psychology: A study of a science*. New York: McGraw-Hill.

Kohlberb, L. (1964). Development of moral character and moral ideology. In M. L. Hoffman & L. W. Hoffman (Eds.), *Review of child development research*, vol. 1, 283–332. New York: Sage.

Kohut, H. (1971). *The analysis of the self*. New York: International Universities Press.

Kovel, J. (1980). The American mental health industry. In D. Inglesby (Eds.), *Critical psychiatry: The politics of mental health*, pp. 72–101. New York: Random House.

Kramer, D. A. (1983). Post-formal operations? A need for further conceptualization. *Human Development, 26*, 91–105.

  (1989). Development of an awareness of contradiction across the lifespan and the question of post-formal operations. In M. L. Commons, J. D. Sinnott, F. A. Richards, & C. Armon (Eds.), *Beyond formal operations II: Comparisons and applications of adolescent and adult developmental models*, pp. 133–59. New York: Praeger.

Kramer, D. A., & Woodruff, D. S. (1986). Relativistic and dialectical thought in three adult age groups. *Human Development*, 29, 280–90.

Krause, R., Steimer-Krause, E., & Ullrich, B. (1992). The use of affect research in dynamic psychotherapy. In M. Leuzinger-Bohleber, H. Schneider, & R. Pfeifer (Eds.), *Two butterflies on my head. Psychoanalysis in the scientific dialogue*, pp. 227–91. Heidelberg: Springer.

Krause, R., Steimer-Krause, E., Merten, J., & Ullrich B. (In press). Dyadic interaction regulation, emotion and psychopathology. In William F. Flack & James Laird (Eds.), *Emotions and psychopathology: Theory and Research*. New York: Oxford University Press.

Krippendorff, K. (1981). *Content analysis: An introduction to its methodology*. Beverly Hills, CA: Sage.

Kunnen, E. S., & Bosma, H. A. (2000). Development of meaning making. A dynamic systems conceptualization. *New Ideas in Psychology, 18*, 57–82.

  (Eds.) (2001). *Identity and emotion: Development through self-organization*. Cambridge, England: Cambridge University Press.

Labouvie-Vief, G. (1994). *Psyche & eros.* New York: Cambridge University Press.

Labouvie-Vief, G., Hakim-Larson, I., DeVoe, M., & Schoeberlein, S. (1989). Emotion and self-regulation: A life span view. *Human Development, 32,* 279–99.

Lang, P. J., Kozak, M. J., Miller, G. A., Levin, P. N., & McLean, A. E. (1980). Emotional imagery: Conceptual structure and pattern of somato-visceral response. *Psychophysiology, 17,* 179–92.

Lazarus, A. (1996). The role of coping in the emotions and how coping changes over the lifecourse. In C. Magai & S. H. McFadden (Eds.). Handbook of emotion, adult development, and aging, pp. 289–306. San Diego: Academic Press.

Leibowitz, H. (1989). *Fabricating lives.* New York: Knopf.

Leventhal, H. (1984). A perceptual-motor theory of emotion. In L. Berkowitz (Ed.), *Advances in social psychology, Vol. 17,* pp. 117–82. New York: Academic.

Levinson, D. J., Darrow, C. M., Klein, E. B., Levinson, M. H., & McKee, B. (1978). *The seasons of a man's life.* New York: Knopf.

Lewin, R. (1992). *Complexity: Life at the edge of chaos.* New York: Macmillan.

Lewis, H. B. (1971). *Shame and guilt in neurosis.* New York: International University Press.

Lewis, H. B. (1981). *Freud and modern psychology. Volume I: The emotional basis of mental illness.* New York: Plenum.

Lewis, M. (1997). *Altering fate: Why the past does not affect the future.* New York: Guilford.

Lewis, M. D. (1995). Cognition-emotion feedback and the self-organization of developmental paths. *Human Development, 38,* 71–102.

(1996). Self-organising cognitive appraisals. *Cognition and Emotion, 10,* 1–25.

(1997). Personality self-organization: Cascading constraints on cognition-emotion interaction. In A. Fogel, M. C. Lyra, & J. Valsiner (Eds.), *Dynamics and indeterminism in developmental and social processes.* Mahwah, NJ: Erlbaum.

Lewis, M. D., & Douglas, L. (1997). A dynamic systems approach to cognition-emotion interactions in development. In M. F. Mascolo & S. Griffen (Eds.), *What develops in emotional development?*, pp. 59–188. New York: Plenum.

Lewis, M. D., & Junyk, N. (1997). The self-organization of psychological defenses. In F. Masterpasqua & P. Perna (Eds.), *The psychological meaning of chaos: Self-organization in human development and psychotherapy,* pp. 41–73. Washington, DC: American Psychological Association.

Lewis, M., & Saarni, C. (Eds.). (1985). *The socialization of emotion.* New York: Plenum.

Lillienfield, S. O., Wood, J. M., & Garb, H. N. (2000). The scientific status of projective techniques. *Psychological Science in the Public Interest, 1,* 27–66.

Loevinger, J., & Wessler, R. (1970). *Measuring ego development. I. Construction and use of a sentence completion test.* San Francisco: Jossey-Bass.

Magai, C. (1995). Personality theory: Birth, death, and transfiguration. In R. D. Kavanaugh, B. Zimmerberg, & S. Fein (Eds.), *Emotion: Interdisciplinary perspectives,* pp. 171–202. Mahwah, NJ: Erlbaum.

Magai, C. (1999a). Affect, imagery, attachment: Working models of interpersonal affect and the socialization of emotion. In J. Cassidy & P. Shaver (Eds.) *Handbook of attachment theory and research,* pp. 787–802. New York: Guilford.

(1999b). Personality change in adulthood: Loci of change and the role of inter-personal process. *International Journal of Aging and Human Development, 49,* 339–52.

Magai, C., & Hunziker, J. (1993). Tolstoy and the riddle of developmental transformation: A lifespan analysis of the role of emotions in personality development. In M. Lewis & J. Haviland (Eds.), *Handbook of emotions,* pp. 247–59. New York: Wiley.

(1998). To Bedlam and part way back: Discrete emotions theory examines borderline symptoms. In W. F. Flack, Jr., & J. D. Laird (Eds.), *Emotions in psychopathology: Theory and research.* New York: Oxford University Press.

Magai, C., & McFadden, S. H. (1995). *The role of emotions in social and personality development.* New York: Plenum.

Magai, C., & McFadden, S. H. (Eds.). (1995). *Handbook of emotion, adult development, and aging,* pp. 289–306. San Diego: Academic Press.

Magai, C., & Nusbaum, B. (1996). Personality change in adulthood: Dynamic systems, emotions, and the transformed self. In C. Magai & S. H. McFadden (Eds.), *Handbook of emotion, adult development, and aging,* pp. 403–20. San Diego: Academic Press.

Magai, C., & Papouchis, N. (1997). Subjectivity and complementarity in the therapeutic process. Unpublished manuscript. Long Island University.

Magai, C., Hunziker, J., Messias, W., & Culver, C. (2000). Adult attachment styles and emotional biases. *International Journal of Behavioral Development, 24,* 301–309.

Mahoney, M. J., & Norcross, J. C. (1993). The relationship styles and therapeutic choices: A commentary on the preceding four articles. *Psychotherapy, 30,* 423–6.

Main, M. (1986). Discovery of an insecure-disorganized/disoriented attachment pattern. In B. T. Brazelton & M. Yogman (Eds.). *Affective development in infancy,* pp. 95–124. Norwood, NJ: Ablex.

Main, M. & Goldwyn, F. (1984). *Adult attachment scoring and classification system.* Unpublished manuscript, University of California at Berkeley.

Main, M., & Morgan, H. (1996). Disorganization and disorientation in infant strange situation behavior: Phenotypic resemblance to dissociative states. In L. K. Michelson & W. J. Ray (Eds.) *Handbook of dissociation: Theoretical, empirical, and clinical perspectives,* pp. 107–38. New York: Plenum.

Main, M., Kaplan, N., & Cassidy, J. (1985). Security in infancy, childhood, and adulthood: A move to the level of representation. In I. Bretherton & E. Waters (Eds.), *Growing points of attachment theory and research. Monographs of the Society for Research in Child Development, 50,* pp. 66–106. Chicago: University of Chicago Press.

Malatesta, C. Z. (1990). The role of emotion in the development and organization of personality. In R. Thompson (Ed.), *Socioemotional development* (Nebraska Symposium on Motivation), pp. 1–56. Lincoln: University of Nebraska Press.

Malatesta, C., & Haviland, J. M. (1982). Learning display rules: The socialization of emotion expression in infancy. *Child Development, 53,* 991–1003.

Malatesta, C., & Wilson, A. (1988). Emotion/cognition interaction in personality development: A discrete emotions, functionalist analysis. *British Journal of Social Psychology* (Special issue on emotions), *27*, 91–112.

Malatesta, C., Culver, C., Tesman, J., & Shepard, B. (1989). The development of emotion expression during the first two years of life. *Monographs of the Society for Research in Child Development*, *54*, (1–2), 1–103.

Malatesta, C., Fiore, M. J., & Messina, J. (1987). Affect, personality, and facial expressive characteristics of older individuals. *Psychology and Aging*, *1*, 64–9.

Malatesta-Magai, C. (1991). Development of emotion expression during infancy: General course and patterns of individual difference. In J. Garber & K. A. Dodge (Eds.), *The development of emotion regulation and dysregulation*, pp. 49–68. New York: Cambridge University Press.

Malatesta-Magai, C., & Dorval, B. (1992). Language, affect, and social order. In M. Gunnar & M. Maratos (Eds.). *Modularity and constraints in language and cognition, 25th Minnesota Symposium on Child Psychology*. Hillsdale, NJ: Erlbaum.

Malatesta-Magai, C., Jonas, R., Shepard, B., & Culver, C. (1992). Type A personality and emotional expressivity in younger and older adults. *Psychology and Aging*, *7*, 551–61.

Masterpasqua, F. (1997). Toward a dynamical developmental understanding of disorder. In F. Masterpasqua & P. A. Perna (Eds.), *The psychological meaning of chaos*. Washington, DC: American Psychological Association.

McAdams, D. (1992). Introduction. *Journal of Personality, Special Issue, 60*, 1.

McCrae, R. R., & Costa, P. T., Jr. (1990). *Personality in adulthood*. New York: Guilford.

McWilliams, N. (1994). *Psychoanalytic diagnosis: Understanding personality structure in the clinical process*. New York: Guilford.

Merten, J., Ullrich, B., Anstadt, T., Buchheim, P., & Krause, R. (1996). Experiencing of affects and facial behavior in the psychotherapeutic process and its relation to success. A pilot study. *Psychotherapy Research, 7*, 198–212.

Meyer, M. F. (1933). That whale among the fishes – The theory of emotions. *Psychological Review, 40*, 292–300.

Miller, A. (1981). *The drama of the gifted child*. New York: Basic Books.

(1982). *For your own good*. New York: Farrar, Straus and Giroux.

Miller, M. J., Prior, D., & Springer, T. (1987). Q-sorting Gloria. *Counselor Education and Supervision*, September, 61–8.

Miller, W. R., & C'deBaca, R. (1994). Quantum change: Toward a psychology of transformation. In T. F. Heatherton & J. L.Weinberger (Eds.), *Can personality change?*, pp. 253–80.Washington, DC: American Psychological Association.

Mueller-Brettel, M., Schmitz, B., & Schoepflin, J. (July 1993). Bibliometric analysis of trends in psychology. Paper presented at 3rd European Congress of Psychology, Tampere, Finland.

Ogilvie, D. M. (1987). The undesired self: A neglected variable in personality research. *Journal of Personality and Social Psychology, 52*, 379–85.

Ohman, A. (1999). Fear and anxiety: Evolutionary, cognitive, and clinical perspectives. In M. Lewis & J. M. Haviland-Jones (Eds.), *Handbook of emotions*, (2nd ed) pp. 573–93. New York: Guilford Press.

Orange, D. M., Atwood, G. E., & Stolorow, R. D. (1997). *Working intersubjectivity: Contextualism in psychoanalytic practices.* Hillsdale, NJ: Analytic Press.

Orlinsky, D. E., Grawe, K., & Parks, B. K. (1994). Process and outcome in psychotherapy – Noch einmal. In A. E. Bergin & S. L. Garfield (Eds.), *Handbook of psychotherapy and behavior change,* pp. 270–339. New York: John Wiley & Sons.

Panksepp, J. (1992). A critical role for "affective neuroscience" in resolving what is basic about basic emotions. *Psychological Review, 99,* 554–60.

Pepper, S. C. (1942). *World hypotheses.* Berkeley: University of California Press.

Perls, F. (1947/1969). *Ego, hunger and aggression.* New York: Random House.

(1969a). *In and out of the garbage pail.* Moab, UT: Real People Press.

(1969b). *Gestalt therapy verbatim.* Moab, UT: Real People Press.

(1973). *The Gestalt approach and eye witness to therapy.* New York: Behavior Books.

Perls, F. S., & Clements, C. C. (1975). Acting out vs. acting through. In J. O. Stevens (Ed.). *Gestalt is.* Moab, UT: Real People Press.

Perls, F. S., Goodman, P., & Hefferline, R. F. (1951). *Gestalt therapy: Excitement and growth in the human personality.* New York: Julian Press.

Perry, W. C. (1970). *Forms of intellectual and ethical development in the college years.* New York: Holt, Rinehart, & Winston.

Piaget, J. (1951). *Play, dreams and imitation in childhood.* London: Routledge & Kegan Paul.

Piechowski, M. M. (1991). Emotional development and emotional giftedness. In N. Calangelo & G. A. Davis (Eds.), *Handbook of gifted education,* pp. 285–306. Boston: Allyn and Bacon.

Poincare, H. (1952). *Science and method.* New York: Dover.

Polkinghorne, D. E. (1991). Narrative and self-concept. *Journal of Narrative and Life History, 1,* 135–53.

Porges, S. W., Doussard-Roosevelt, J. A., & Maiti, A. K. (1994). Vagal tone and the physiological regulation of emotion. In N. A. Fox (Ed.), *The development of emotion regulation. Monographs of the Society for Research in Child Development,* Serial No. 240, Vol. 59, pp. 167–88. Chicago: University of Chicago Press.

Prigogine, I. (1980). *From being to becoming.* New York: W. H. Freeman.

Prigogine, I., & Stengers, I. (1984). *Order out of chaos: Man's new dialogue with nature.* New York: Bantam Books.

Retzinger, S. M. (1991). *Violent emotions: Shame and rage in marital quarrels.* Newbury Park, CA: Sage Publications.

Ricoeur, P. (1981). *Hermeneutics and the human sciences.* Edited and trans. by J. B. Thompson, Cambridge, England: Cambridge University Press.

Rogers, C. R. (1951). *Client-centered therapy: Its current practice, implications and theory.* Boston: Houghton-Mifflin.

(1961). *On becoming a person.* Boston: Houghton Mifflin.

(1972). My personal growth. In A. Burton and Associates (Eds.), *Twelve therapists.* San Francisco: Jossey-Bass.

(1980). *A way of being.* Boston: Houghton Mifflin.

(1984). Gloria – A historical note. In R. F. Levant & J. M. Shlien (Eds.), *Client-centered therapy and the person-centered approach: New directions in theory, research, and practice,* pp. 423–5. New York: Praeger.

Rogers, C. R. (1939). *The clinical treatment of the problem child*. New York: Houghton Mifflin.

(1942). *Counseling and psychotherapy*. Cambridge, MA: Riverside Press.

Rogers, H. E. (1965). A wife's-eye view of Carl Rogers. *Voices, 1*, 93–8.

Rozin, P., Markwith, M., & Stoess, C. (1997). Moralization: Becoming a vegitarian, the conversion of preferences into values and the recruitment of disgust. *Psychological Science, 8*, 67–73.

Ruth, J. E., & Kenyon, G. (1996). Biography in adult development and aging. In J. E. Birren, G. Kenyon, J. E. Ruth, J. J. F. Schroots, & T. Svensson (Eds.), *Aging and biography: Explorations in adult development*, pp. 1–20. New York: Springer.

Sabelli, H. C., Carlson-Sabelli, L., Patel, M., Levy, A., & Diez-Martin, J. (1995). Anger, fear, depression, and crime: Physiological and psychological studies using the process method. In R. Robertson & A. Combs (Eds.), *Chaos theory in psychology and the life sciences*, pp. 65–88. Mahwah, NJ: Erlbaum.

Salovey, P., & Mayer, J. D. (1990). Emotional intelligence. *Imagination, Cognition and Personality, 9*, 185–211.

Schafer, R. (1981). *Narrative actions in psychoanalysis*. Worcester, MA: Clark University Press.

Scheff, T. J. (1984). The taboo on coarse emotions. *Review of Personality and Social Psychology, 5*, 146–70.

(1987). The shame-rage spiral: A case study of an interminable quarrel. In H. B. Lewis (Ed.), *The role of shame in symptom formation*. Hillsdale, NJ: Erlbaum.

Schwartz, G. E. (1990). Psychobiology of repression and health: A systems approach. In J. L. Singer (Ed.), *Repression and dissociation*, pp. 405–34. Chicago: The University of Chicago Press.

Schwartz, G. E., & Weinberger, D. A. (1980). Patterns of emotional responses to affective situations: Relations among happiness, sadness, anger, fear, depression, and anxiety. *Motivation and Emotion, 4*, (2), 175–91.

Selye, H. (1956). *The stress of life*. New York: McGraw-Hill.

Sexton, V. S. (1983). Humanistic psychology in the United States. In G. Bittner (Ed.), *Personale psychologie: Festschrift fuer Ludwig J. Pongratz*. Goettingen: Hogrefe.

Shepard, M. (1975). *Fritz*. New York: Dutton.

Shostrom, E. L. (Producer), (1966). *Three Approaches to Psychotherapy* [Film]. Santa Ana, CA: Psychological Films.

Shweder, R. A. (2000). The cultural psychology of emotions: Ancient and new. In M. Lewis and J. M. Haviland (Eds.), *Handbook of emotions: Vol. 2*, pp. 397–414. New York: Guilford Press.

Simpson, J. A. (1990). Influence of attachment styles on romantic relationships. *Journal of Personality and Social Psychology, 59*, 971–80.

Sinnott, J. D. (1984). Postformal reasoning: The relativitistic stage. In M. L. Commons, F. A. Richards, & C. Armon (Eds.), *Beyond formal operations: Late adolescent and adult cognitive development*, pp. 298–325. New York: Praeger.

Skolnick, A. (1986). Early attachment and personal relationships across the life course. *Life Span Development and Behavior, 7*, 173–206.

Slater, L. (1998). *Prozac diary*. New York: Random House.

Solomon, R. C. (1999). The philosophy of emotions. In M. Lewis & J. M. Haviland-Jones (Eds.), *Handbook of Emotions*, 2nd ed., pp. 3–15. New York: Guilford Press.

Spence, D. (1982). *Narrative truth and historical truth: Meaning and interpretation in psychoanalysis*. New York: Norton.

Spitz, R. A. (1965). *The first year of life*. New York: International Universities Press.

Stearns, C. Z. (1988). "Lord help me walk humbly": Anger and sadness in England and America, 1570–1790. In C. Z. Stearns & P. N. Stearns (Eds.), *Emotion and social change: Toward a new psychohistory*. New York: Holmes & Meier.

Stein, N. L., & Liwag, M. D. (1997). A goal-appraisal process approach to understanding and remembering emotional events. In P. Vanden Broek, P. Bauer, & T. Bourg (Eds.), *Developmental spans in event comprehension and representation*, pp. 199–236. Hillsdale, NJ: Erlbaum.

Stern, D. (1985). *The interpersonal world of the infant*. New York: Basic Books.

Sternberg, R. J. (1977). *Intelligence, information processing, and analogical reasoning: The componential analysis of human abilities*. Hillsdale, NJ: Erlbaum.

Stewart, A. J., Franz, C., & Layton, L. (1989). The changing self: Using personal documents to study lives. *Journal of Personality, 56*, 41–74.

Stoehr, T. (1994). *Here now next: Paul Goodman and the origins of Gestalt therapy*. San Francisco: Jossey-Bass.

Stolorow, R. D., & Atwood, G. E. (1992). *Contexts of being: The intersubjective foundations of psychological life*. Hillsdale, NJ: Analytic Press.

Strupp, H. H. (1993). The Vanderbilt psychotherapy studies: Synopsis. *Journal of Consulting and Clinical Psychology, 61*, 431–33.

Tansey, M. J. (1989). *Understanding countertransference: From projective identification to empathy*. Hillsdale, NJ: Analytic Press.

Teasdale, J. D., & Banard, P. (1993). *Affect, cognition, and change*. Hillsdale, NJ: Erlbaum.

Thelen, E. (1987). Self–organization in developmental processes: Can systems approaches work? In M. Gunnar & E. Thelen (Eds.), *Systems and development: The Minnesota Symposium on Child Psychology: Vol. 22*, pp. 77–117. Hillsdale, NJ: Erlbaum.

(1990). Dynamical systems and the generation of individual differences. In J. Colombo & J. Fagen (Eds.), *Individual differences in infancy: Reliability, stability, prediction*, pp. 19–43. Hillsdale, NJ: Erlbaum.

Thelen, E., & Smith L. B. (1994). *A dynamic systems approach to the development of cognition and action*. Cambridge, MA: The MIT Press.

Thompson, W. R., & Grusec, J. (1970). Studies of early experience. In P. H. Mussen (Ed.), *Manual of child psychology*, pp. 565–654. New York: Wiley.

Tomkins, S. S. (1962). *Affect, imagery, consciousness. Vol. 1: The positive affects*. New York: Springer.

(1963). *Affect, imagery, consciousness. Vol. 2: The negative affects*. New York: Springer.

(1965). The psychology of knowledge. In S. S. Tomkins and C. Izard (Eds.), *Affect, cognition and personality*. New York: Springer.

(1966). Psychological model for smoking behavior. *American Journal of Public Health, 56*, 17–18.

(1975). The phantasy behind the face. *Journal of Personality Assessment, 39*, 550–62.

(1987). Script theory. In J. Aronoff, A. I. Rabin, & R. A. Zucker (Eds.), *The emergence of personality*, pp. 147–216. New York: Springer. Company.

(1991). *Affect, imagery, consciousness. Vol. 3: Anger and fear.* New York: Springer.

(1993). *Affect, imagery, consciousness. Vol. 4: Cognition – Duplication and transformation of information.* New York: Springer.

Tosca, G. A., & McMullen, L. M. (1992). Interpersonal complementarity and antitheses within a stage model of psychotherapy. *Psychotherapy, 29*, 515–23.

Tracey, T. J. (1994). An examination of the complementarity of interpersonal behavior. *Journal of Personality and Social Psychology, 67*, 864–78.

Tracey, T. J., & Hays, K. (1989). Therapist complementarity as a function of experience and client stimuli. *Psychotherapy, 26*, 462–8.

Traue, H. C., & Pennebaker, J. W. (Eds.). (1993). *Emotion inhibition and health.* Seattle: Hogrefe & Huber.

Troll, L. (1975). *Early and middle adulthood.* Belmont, CA: Wadsworth.

Van Geert, P. (1994). *Dynamic systems of development: Change between complexity and chaos.* New York: Harvester Wheatsheaf.

Vidal, F. (1994). *Piaget before Piaget.* Cambridge, MA: Harvard University Press.

Villenave-Cremer, S., Kettner, M., & Krause, R. (1989). Verbale Interaktion von Schizophrenen und ihren Gespraechspartnern. *Zeitschrift fuer Klinische Psychologie und Psychotherapie, 37*, 401–21.

Wachtel, P. (1989). *The poverty of affluence: A psychological portrait of the American way of life.* Philadelphia: New Society.

Waldrop, M. M. (1992). *Complexity: The emerging science at the edge of order and chaos.* New York: Touchstone.

Weiner, D. N. (1988). *Albert Ellis: Passionate skeptic.* New York: Praeger.

(1986). Ellis and Gloria: Positive or negative model. *Psychotherapy, 23*, 642–8.

Whitbourne, S. K., Zuschlag, M. K., Elliot, L. B., & Waterman, A. S. (1992). Psychosocial development in adulthood: A 22–year sequential study. *Journal of Personality and Social Psychology, 63*, 260–71.

White, R. W. (1952). *Lives in progress: A study of the natural growth of personality.* New York: Holt, Rinehart & Winston.

(1982). Circumplex models of interpersonal behavior in clinical psychology. In P. C. Kendall & J. N. Butcher (Eds.), *Handbook of research methods in clinical psychology*, pp. 183–221. New York: Wiley.

Wiggins, J. S., & Pincus, A. L. (1992). Personality: Structure and assessment. *Annual Review of Psychology, 43*, 473–504.

Winnicott, D. W. (1964). *The child, the family, and the outside world.* New York: Penguin.

Woolf, L. (1963). *Beginning again.* New York: Harcourt Brace Jovanovich.

Woolf, V. (1929). *A room of one's own.* New York: Harcourt Brace Jovanovich.

Subject Index

absolute thinking (see logic systems)

accommodation, 340, 367, 394

adaptation, 35, 119, 140, 488–9

addictive script, 50

affect biases, 11

affect hunger, 117, 128, 144

affect theory, 14–15, 20, 26, 32, 38, 62, 76, 84, 92, 96, 100, 147, 184, 229, 447

affective posture (see nonverbal behavior)

anger, 6, 10–11, 48–9, 58, 60, 70, 78–9, 81, 83, 85–6, 96, 98–100, 105, 120, 182–3, 189–93, 207, 230, 232–40, 244–7, 256–8, 262–5, 275–6, 282, 292–3, 306, 370–2, 379–81, 393, 407, 409, 428–32, 437, 450–1, 453, 456, 459–62, 466, 487

anti-anxiety, 421

anti-distress, 121

anti-shame, 392, 417–18, 420

anxiety, 113–14, 119, 140, 142, 183, 189, 191, 194–5, 219, 222, 256, 289, 304–5, 326, 331, 334, 335–8, 344–6, 350, 381, 392, 408, 421, 469–70, 494

assimilation, 394

attachment theory, 20, 27, 32–3, 108–9, 143, 498

   dismissive, 49, 110–12, 139

   disorganized, 50, 178–82, 187, 461

   preoccupied, 49, 144

   secure, 20, 58–64, 72, 84, 108–9, 170, 457–9

attractors (also see dynamic systems), 35, 44–5, 48–9, 118–20, 168–9, 453–4, 467, 471, 482–3, 493–4, 496–7

   point attractors, 35, 45, 139, 483

autobiography (see biography)

autonomy, 32, 87, 109, 391, 417

backed up affect, 117, 144

behaviorism, 23–4, 127

bifurcation, 46, 111

biography, 16–17, 31–2, 84, 104–6, 150–4, 166–9, 206–7, 303, 323, 453

bypassed shame, 87, 185

Cartesian, 4, 7, 149, 285

chaos theory, 27, 33–7, 203, 226, 447, 469–70, 485–6, 488–91, 496

client-centered therapy, 25, 55, 73, 77, 82, 87, 90, 95, 97, 125, 240, 277, 282, 399, 452, 465

cognition, 9, 38, 119, 204, 269, 287, 309, 329, 419, 480, 488, 493

complementarity, 42, 46, 136–7, 140–1, 438–40, 442, 464, 498

complexity theory, 480–1, 486, 488–9, 494, 496

   uniqueness in, 474, 478, 495

   replication in, 462, 474, 478, 481–2, 492, 494, 498

521

Author Index